NATIONAL REGISTER OF PSYCHOTHERAPISTS 1999

NATIONAL REGISTER OF PSYCHOTHERAPISTS

1999

United Kingdom Council for Psychotherapy

ROUTLEDGE

UKCP
UK COUNCIL FOR PSYCHOTHERAPY

First published 1999
by Routledge
11 New Fetter Lane, London EC4P 4EE

Simultaneously published in the USA and Canada
by Routledge
29 West 35th Street, New York, NY 10001

Typeset in Gill Sans by Routledge

Printed and bound in Great Britain by
Unwin Brothers Ltd, Old Woking, Surrey

British Library Cataloguing in Publication Data
A catalogue record for this book is available from the British Library

Library of Congress Cataloguing in Publication Data
A catalogue record for this book has been requested

ISBN 0-415-20405-4

ISSN 1461-0175

TABLE OF CONTENTS

FOREWORD

It is now 28 years since the Foster Report proposed that psychotherapy should become a regulated registrable profession. The lengthy and difficult task of bringing together all the major differing modalities of psychotherapy practised in the United Kingdom into one organisation was finally completed with the formal establishment in 1993 of the UKCP, and the launch of the first official National Register of Psychotherapists.

The UKCP's prime objective is that of protection of the public. It has had charitable status from its inception. It has now developed, by reason of its growth, into an Incorporated Charitable Company. This requires that the UKCP shall be open and accountable both to the Charity Commissioners and to Companies House in the way that it is run.

The UCKP also demands accountability of its Member Organisations, of its eight Sections which represent the different modalities of psychotherapy, and of its registered practitioners themselves. No organisation may become part of the UKCP unless it conforms to substantial criteria, and no individual may be registered unless they are ethically accountable to the Member Organisation. Thus the UKCP's 78 Member Organisations which cover over 4,300 psychotherapists are expected to adhere to and apply guidelines for standards of training and ethical practice that are intended to protect the vast numbers of the public who use these services. Any registered psychotherapist who is found guilty of serious misconduct, or otherwise acts in contravention of the Member Organisation's own Code of Ethics, is at risk of penalty or in the final instance of being struck off the Register. This degree of accountability is reflected in the National Register of qualified psychotherapists.

The UKCP was established with the goal of creating a broadly based profession of psychotherapy that would be as well regulated as are other traditional professions. This is still its goal. Until statutory registration is a reality, and no longer an ideal towards which we are working, the UKCP is committed to ensuring that as high standards of self regulation as possible are adopted by UKCP Member Organisations and their practitioners, in the public interest.

The UKCP is now nationally well known and respected. Its Register of qualified psychotherapists can be located in main libraries, medical centres, and other public health institutions throughout the country. The UKCP itself, and the Register in particular, enables the public to know about the different kinds of psychotherapy available in the United Kingdom, where to contact the relevant organisations, and helps members of the public to find an appropriately qualified psychotherapist for the particular modality being sought.

The UKCP is active not only in this country but also plays a leading part in helping to forge the boundaries of the profession throughout western and eastern European countries through the European Association of Psychotherapy and beyond. There is now a World Council of Psychotherapy. In both of these overseas arenas the UKCP carries influence and prestige for that which it has already achieved in Great Britain. Its Register of British UKCP registered psychotherapists is, in part, the public expression of that effort and achievement.

Helen Tarsh

Helen Tarsh
Chair of Registration Board

USING THE REGISTER

The *National Register of Psychotherapists* is designed to make it easy to find and contact a psychotherapist in your area. The names, addresses and telephone numbers of registered psychotherapists are listed alphabetically within geographical areas.* Each entry includes a brief description of the type of psychotherapy offered and a code denoting the organisation(s) to which the psychotherapist belongs. A list of these codes and the organisations they relate to appears on page xx. The register also lists practitioners under the organisation(s) to which they belong.

Each of the eight sections of UKCP has a **Flag Statement** outlining its purpose and distinguishing it from the other sections. The **Flag Statements** and a list of organisations belonging to each section appear on pages xvii.

We hope that you will find this register easy to use and that you will write with your comments to:

United Kingdom Council for Psychotherapy
167-69 Great Portland Street, London W1N 5FB
Tel: 0171 436 3002
Fax: 0171 436 3013
email: UKCP@psychotherapy.org.uk
http://www.psychotherapy.org.uk

The information contained in the Register was accurate at the time of going to print. Additions and deletions to the Register are published biannually in the UKCP newsletter, *The Psychotherapist*. The UKCP database of the *National Register of Psychotherapists* is continually updated.

*County boundary changes affecting Avon and Somerset will be shown in next year's publication.

GOVERNING BOARD

REGISTRATION BOARD

Helen Tarsh
Chair

David Winter
Vice Chair

Experiential Constructivist Therapies Section

Judy Ryde
Honorary Secretary

Humanistic and Integrative Psychotherapy Section

John Burnham
Family, Couple, Sexual and Systemic Therapy Section

Petruska Clarkson
Universities Psychotherapy Association

Adrian Dickinson
Psychoanalytic and Psychodynamic Psychotherapy Section

Peter Haworth
Humanistic and Integrative Psychotherapy Section

Pearl Hettiaratchy
Royal College of Psychiatrists

Ray Keedy-Lilley
Hypno-psychotherapy Section

Georgia Lepper
Analytical Psychology Section

Deena Marcus
Humanistic and Integrative Psychotherapy Section

Eileen Orford
Psychoanalytically-based Therapy with Children Section

Lesley Parkinson
British Psychological Society

Tom Ryan
Psychoanalytic and Psychodynamic Psychotherapy Section

Tom Sensky
Institutional Member

Ruth Williams
Behavioural and Cognitive Psychotherapy Section

Tim Woolmer
Psychoanalytic and Psychodynamic Psychotherapy Section

ETHICAL GUIDELINES

of the United Kingdom Council for Psychotherapy

1. Introduction

1.1 The purpose of a Code of Ethics is to define general principles and to establish standards of professional conduct for psychotherapists in their work and to inform and protect those members of the public who seek their services. Each organisation will include and elaborate upon the following principles in its Code of Ethics.

1.2 All psychotherapists are expected to approach their work with the aim of alleviating suffering and promoting the well-being of their clients. Psychotherapists should endeavour to use their abilities and skills to their client's best advantage without prejudice and with due recognition of the value and dignity of every human being.

1.3 **All psychotherapists on the UKCP Register are required to adhere to the Codes of Ethics and Practice of their own organisations which will be consistent with the following statements and which will have been approved by the appropriate UKCP Section.**

2. Codes of Ethics

Each Member Organisation of UKCP must have published a Code of Ethics approved by the appropriate UKCP Section and appropriate for the practitioners of that particular organisation and their clients. The Code of Ethics will include and elaborate upon the following ten points to which attention is drawn here. All psychotherapists on the UKCP Register are required to adhere to the Codes of Ethics of their own organisations.

2.1 **Qualifications:** Psychotherapists are required to disclose their qualifications when requested and not claim, or imply, qualifications that they do not have.

2.2 **Terms, Conditions and Methods of Practice:** Psychotherapists are required to disclose on request their terms, conditions and, where appropriate, methods of practice at the outset of psychotherapy.

2.3 **Confidentiality:** Psychotherapists are required to preserve confidentiality and to disclose, if requested, the limits of confidentiality and circumstances under which it might be broken to specific third parties.

2.4 **Professional Relationship:** Psychotherapists should consider the client's best interest when making appropriate contact with the client's GP, relevant psychiatric services, or other relevant professionals with the client's knowledge. Psychotherapists should be aware of their own limitations.

2.5 **Relationship with Clients:** Psychotherapists are required to maintain appropriate boundaries with their clients. They must take care not to exploit their clients, current or past, in any way, financially, sexually or emotionally.

2.6 **Research:** Psychotherapists are required to clarify with clients the nature, purpose and conditions of any research in which the clients are to be involved and to ensure that informed and verifiable consent is given before commencement.

2.7 **Publication:** Psychotherapists are required to safeguard the welfare and anonymity of clients when any form of publication of clinical material is being considered and to obtain their consent whenever possible.

2.8 **Practitioner Competence:** Psychotherapists are required to maintain their ability to perform competently and to take necessary steps to do so.

2.9 **Indemnity Insurance:** Psychotherapists are required to ensure that their professional work is adequately covered by appropriate indemnity insurance.

2.10 Detrimental Behaviour:

(i) Psychotherapists are required to refrain from any behaviour that may be detrimental to the profession, to colleagues or to trainees.

(ii) Psychotherapists are required to take appropriate action in accordance with Clause 5.7 with regard to the behaviour of a colleague which may be detrimental to the profession, to colleagues or to trainees.

3. Advertising

Member organisations of UKCP and individual psychotherapists are required to restrict promotion of their work to a description of the type of psychotherapy they provide. Psychotherapists are required to distinguish carefully between self-descriptions, as in a list, and advertising seeking enquiries.

4. Code of Practice

Each Member Organisation of UKCP will have published a Code of Practice approved by the appropriate UKCP Section and appropriate for the practitioners of that particular organisation and their clients. The purpose of Codes of Practice is to clarify and expand upon the general principles established in the Code of Ethics of the organisation and the practical application of those principles. All psychotherapists on the UKCP Register will be required to adhere to the Codes of Practice of their own organisations.

5. Complaints Procedure

Each Member Organisation of UKCP must have published a Complaints Procedure, including information about the acceptability or otherwise of a complaint made by a third party against a practitioner, approved by the appropriate UKCP Section and appropriate for the practitioners of that particular organisation and their clients. The purpose of a Complaints Procedure is to ensure that practitioners and their clients have clear information about the procedure and processes involved in dealing with complaints. All psychotherapists on the UKCP Register are required to adhere to the Complaints Procedure of their own organisations.

5.1 **Making a complaint:** A client wishing to complain shall be advised to contact the Member Organisation.

5.2 **Receiving a complaint:** A Member Organisation receiving a complaint against one of its psychotherapists shall ensure that the therapist is informed immediately and that both complainant and therapist are aware of the Complaints Procedure.

5.3 Appeals:

(i) After the completion of the Complaints Procedure within an organisation, provision must be made for an appeal, stating time limits, grounds and procedures.

(ii) After the completion of all procedures in an organisation, an appeal may be made to the Section on grounds of improper procedure.

(iii) **Reference to UKCP Governing Board:** Appeals not resolved by the Section or those where the Section cannot appropriately hear the appeal shall be referred to the Governing Board of UKCP.

5.4 **Reports to UKCP Section:** Where a complaint is upheld the Section shall be informed by the organisation.

5.5 **Report to the UKCP Registration Board:** Member Organisations are required to report to the UKCP Registration Board the names of members who have been suspended or expelled.

5.6 **Complaints upheld and convictions:** Psychotherapists are required to inform their Member Organisations if any complaint is upheld against them in another Member Organisation, if they are convicted of any notifiable criminal offence or if successful civil proceedings are brought against them in relation to their work as psychotherapists.

5.7 **Conduct of colleagues:** Psychotherapists concerned that a colleague's conduct may be unprofessional should initiate the Complaints Procedure of the relevant Member Organisation.

5.8 The resignation of a member of an organisation shall not be allowed to impede the process of any investigation as long as the alleged offence took place during that person's membership.

6. Sanctions

Psychotherapists who are suspended by, or expelled from, a Member Organisation are automatically deleted from the UKCP Register.

7. Monitoring Complaints

7.1 Member Organisations shall report to the Registration Board annually concerning the number of complaints received, the nature of the complaints and their disposition.

7.2 The Registration Board shall report annually to the Governing Board on the adequacy of Member Organisations' disciplinary procedures.

SECTIONS AND FLAG STATEMENTS

1 Analytical Psychology Section

This stems from the work of C G Jung. The central idea is that what we do and feel, how we think of ourselves and other people, depend on forces and processes we are not aware of - the 'unconscious'. These may be part of our common human nature or particular to the individual.

The analytical psychologist (also known as a Jungian analyst) tries to understand these unconscious elements in what the patient says and the dreams they report. Particular attention is given to how the patient regards the analyst and vice versa. It can be beneficial for a patient to understand how this 'transference' mirrors the early family situation, enabling them to take conscious control. Jungian analysts believe that we are all highly capable of healing ourselves and taking charge of our lives.

Analytical psychologists treat people suffering from emotional disorders or problems with relationships, but can also help 'normal' people who are discontented with themselves or have lost a sense of direction in their lives. So it is not necessary to be 'ill' to benefit from Jungian analysis, since self-discovery and the exploration of the inner world are valuable in themselves.

Analytical psychology also has much to say about society and culture, showing how unconscious processes affect the groups and institutions we belong to.

Organisations

Association of Jungian Analysts
The Independent Group of Analytical Psychologists
Society of Analytical Psychology

2 Behavioural and Cognitive Psychotherapy Section

The Behavioural and Cognitive Psychotherapies are used to treat a wide range of emotional disorders, using a problem-solving approach. There is a large body of research evidence which demonstrates the effectiveness of these psychotherapies in treating problems such as: depression, panic attacks, agoraphobia, obsessive-compulsive disorder, post-traumatic stress disorder, eating disorders, chronic pain, irritable bowel syndrome.

Therapist and client work as a team to identify problems and examine these in terms of the relationship between thoughts, feelings, behaviour and the individual's environment.

The main focus in treatment is on the here and now (as opposed to the past) and how current problems interfere with the client's daily life. The aim of therapy is to help the client understand their problems and develop practical ways of dealing with them. There is an emphasis on self-help and the therapist will ask the client to deliberately practise applying their new knowledge and skills to their problems in between therapy sessions.

Typically treatment consists of 12-30 weekly sessions of an hour. This may be in health centres, specialist departments or hospital out-patient clinics. The behavioural cognitive psychotherapies are widely available in the NHS, as well as the private sector. Many healthcare professionals are trained in these therapies, including clinical psychologists, psychiatric nurses and social workers.

Organisations

British Association for Behavioural and Cognitive Psychotherapies

3 Experiential Constructivist Therapies Section

These therapies are based on the assumption that our world is not just given to us complete, but that we construct our individual picture of it from our own personal experiences. Then, what we do, what we believe, what we feel, is largely dictated by this picture, or model. For a person badly treated, the world may be seen as cruel or unreliable, whereas, for one well treated, it may appear a good place. We are constantly modifying our models in the light of experience.

The first task in therapy is to help the client clarify the models they use, consciously or not, to represent the world to themselves. They will need to explore and try out different ways of constructing their model and living within it, with no suggestion that any particular model is the 'correct' one. Changes may come in a small way in different behaviour or more extensively in revision of values, beliefs and identity.

These therapies often have a specific focus and expect to effect positive change in the short term, as well as dealing with the underlying issues which may require longer term therapy. The setting may be one-to-one or in a group. A wide range of methods is used, imaginatively tailored to the individual, who is involved at every stage. The process, depending on mutual respect between therapist and client, is designed to enable the client to take better charge of their life.

Organisations

Association for Neuro-Linguistic Programming
Centre for Personal Construct Psychology

4 Family, Couple, Sexual and Systemic Therapy Section

This group of organisations are based on the assumption that the problems and difficulties of any of us cannot be understood without considering the families and groups that we belong to. When things go wrong with an individual, we need to look at what is happening between the members of the family or group, who is filling which role and for what purpose. It is useful to look at the group as a 'system' with its own rules and goals, made up of roles or functions which can be filled by different people without changing the system itself. The aim of therapy is to uncover these patterns and suggest alternative ways of using them. Within this general purpose, the therapist may work with individuals, couples, families or parts of them, or with other networks which matter to people.

Organisations

Association for Family Therapy
British Association for Sexual and Marital Therapy
The Family Institute, Cardiff
Institute of Family Therapy
Kensington Consultation Centre

5 Humanistic and Integrative Psychotherapy Section

This Section includes different psychotherapies which approach the individual as a whole person including body, feelings, mind and spirit. Members welcome interdisciplinary dialogue and an exploration of different psychological processes with particular emphasis on integration within the Section. Organisations in this Section practice approaches compatible with the following:

Humanistic Psychotherapy is an approach which tries to do justice to the whole person including body, mind and spirit. It represents a broad range of therapeutic methods. Each method recognises the self-healing capacities of the client and believes that the greatest expert on the client is the client. The humanistic psychotherapist works towards an authentic meeting of equals in the therapy relationship.

Existential Psychotherapy aims at enabling clients to find constructive ways of coming to terms with the challenges of everyday living. The focus is on clients' concrete individual experience of anxiety and distress leading to an exploration of their personal beliefs and value system, in order to clarify and understand these in relation to the specific physical, psychological and socio-cultural context. The experience and influences of the past, present and future are given equal emphasis. The questioning of assumptions and facing up to the possibilities and limitations of living is an important part of this interactive, dynamic and direct approach.

Transpersonal / Psychospiritual Psychotherapy can be defined by its orientation which includes the spiritual dimension rather than the content of therapy. It views the human psyche as having a central core Self or Soul as the centre of identity as well as a personal ego. Psychotherapists draw on a wide range of therapeutic methods towards the uncovering of past psychological material within a context of the individual's potential based on spiritual insight and experience. Within this perspective there is both a movement of the personal centre to the Self and a movement of the Self to manifest its nature through and in the personal centre. Thus therapy includes both repair and individuation.

Integrative Psychotherapy can be distinguished from eclecticism by its determination to show there are significant connections between different therapies, which may be unrecognised by their exclusive proponents. While remaining respectful to each approach, integrative psychotherapy draws from many sources in the belief that no one approach has all the truth. The therapeutic relationship is the vehicle for experience, growth and change. It aims to hold together the dual forces of disintegration and integration, as presented by the psychologically distressed and disabled. The integrative therapeutic experience leads towards a greater toleration of life's experiences and an increase of creativity and service.

Organisations

Association of Accredited Psychospiritual Psychotherapists
Association of Cognitive Analytic Therapists
Association of Humanistic Psychology Practitioners
Bath Centre for Psychotherapy and Counselling
British Psychodrama Association
Centre for Counselling and Psychotherapy Education
Centre for Transpersonal Psychology
Chiron Centre for Body Psychotherapy
The Gerda Boyesen Centre
The Gestalt Centre, London
Gestalt Psychotherapy Training Institute
The Institute of Psychosynthesis
Institute of Transactional Analysis
Institute for Arts in Therapy and Education
Karuna Institute
London Association of Primal Psychotherapists
Metanoia Institute
The Minster Centre
North Staffs. Association for Psychotherapy
Psychosynthesis and Education Trust
Regent's College School of Psychotherapy and Counselling
Re.Vision
The Sherwood Psychotherapy Training Institute
Spectrum
Stockton Centre for Psychotherapy and Counselling

6 Hypno-Psychotherapy Section

Hypno-psychotherapy is the branch of psychotherapy which uses hypnosis. It rests on an extensive body of work and publications over the last three hundred years, leading to that of Milton Erickson and those influenced by him. It understands that we have a learned model of the world which can restrict the way we feel, what we understand, our attitudes and behaviour. Hypnosis is a state of relaxation which people enter voluntarily, during which there occurs an altered state of conscious awareness. The therapist can intervene to draw the individual's attention to new possibilities, to alternative patterns of thought, emotion and behaviour. The methods and strategies used in therapy are designed to make use of the resources and capabilities that reside within all people, and do not require the individual to fit into a standardised pattern. Hypnotherapy may be valuable for anyone seeking to resolve specific problems, or for personal development.

Organisations

British Association for Autogenic Training and Therapy
Centre Training School of Hypnotherapy and Psychotherapy
The National College of Hypnosis and Psychotherapy
The National Register of Hypnotherapists and Psychotherapists
National School of Hypnosis and Psychotherapy

7 Psychoanalytic and Psychodynamic Psychotherapy Section

These therapies are based on psychoanalytic theory and practice. They may take place one-to-one or in a group. They may be of long or short duration. The central principle is that much distress has been caused by events in early life which we are no longer aware of. The therapy offers a reliable setting for the patient to explore free associations, memories, phantasies, feelings and dreams, to do with past and present. Particular attention is given to the interaction with the therapist, through which the patient may relive situations from their early life, the 'transference'. In these ways, the patient may achieve a new and better resolution of longstanding conflicts.

Organisations

Arbours Association
Association for Group and Individual Psychotherapy
The Association of Independent Psychotherapists
British Association of Psychotherapists
Cambridge Society for Psychotherapy
Centre for Attachment-Based Psychoanalytic Psychotherapy
Centre for Freudian Analysis and Research
Centre for Psychoanalytical Psychotherapy
Centre for the Study of Psychotherapy (University of Kent) and the Canterbury Consortium of Psychoanalytic and Psychodynamic Psychotherapists
The Forum for Independent Psychotherapists
The Guild of Psychotherapists
The Guildford Centre for Psychotherapy
The Hallam Institute of Psychotherapy
Institute of Group Analysis
Institute of Psychotherapy and Counselling (WPF)
Institute of Psychotherapy and Social Studies
Liverpool Psychotherapy Diploma Organisation (University of Liverpool)
London Centre for Psychotherapy
Nafisiyat
Northern Association for Analytical Psychotherapy
North West Institute of Dynamic Psychotherapy
Philadelphia Association
Severnside Institute for Psychotherapy
South Trent Training in Dynamic Psychotherapy
Tavistock Marital Studies Institute
University of Leicester Diploma in Psychodynamic Studies
West Midlands Institute of Psychotherapy
Westminster Pastoral Foundation
The Women's Therapy Centre
Yorkshire Association for Psychodynamic Psychotherapy

8 Psychoanalytically-based Therapy with Children Section

Therapists in this Section work with children who have problems beyond the resources of parent or school. Psychoanalytic theory is used to understand what the children have to say, consciously or unconsciously, in conversation, play, drawings and educational tasks. The aim is to restore the child to the stage of development appropriate to their age. This is done by observing the child within a reliable setting and interpreting their behaviour, including how they relate to the therapist and how they use materials supplied. As children depend on adults and the environment they provide, the work often includes contact with parents and families and treatment of them.

Organisations

Association of Child Psychotherapists
Forum for the Advancement of Educational Therapy and Therapeutic Teaching

Institutional Members

A category of full membership of UKCP open to those psychotherapy organisations whose large size and complexity make it inappropriate for their membership to be confined to any individual Section. Institutional members have two seats on the Governing Board.

Organisations

Association of University Teachers of Psychiatry
Tavistock Clinic
Universities Psychotherapy Association

Special Members

Two organisations, of unique importance to the profession of psychotherapy and encompassing other related disciplines, have retained this special category of full membership. Each has a seat on the Governing Board. (This is not an open category of membership and cannot be applied for.)

Organisations

British Psychological Society
Royal College of Psychiatrists

Friends of the Council

A non-voting category for organisations closely associated with UKCP but not seeking full membership.

Organisations

British Association for Counselling

ORGANISATION CODES

Code	Organisation
AAPP	Association of Accredited Psychospiritual Psychotherapists
AIP	Association of Independent Psychotherapists
ARBS	Arbours Association
ACAT	Association of Cognitive Analytic Therapists
ACP	Association of Child Psychotherapists
AFT	Association for Family Therapy and Systemic Practice in the UK
AGIP	Association for Group and Individual Psychotherapy
AHPP	Association of Humanistic Psychology Practitioners
AJA	Association of Jungian Analysts
ANLP	Association for Neuro-Linguistic Programming
AUTP	Association of Univeristy Teachers of Psychiatry
BABCP	British Association for Behavioural and Cognitive Psychotherapy
BAC	British Association for Counselling
BAFATT	British Association for Autogenic Training and Therapy
BAP	British Association of Psychotherapists
BASMT	British Association for Sexual and Marital Therapy
BCPC	Bath Centre for Psychotherapy and Counselling
BPA	British Psychodrama Association
BPS	British Psychological Society
BTC	The Gerda Boyesen Centre
CAPP	Centre for Attachment-Based Psychoanalytic Psychotherapy
CCBP	Chiron Centre for Body Psychotherapy
CCPE	Centre for Counselling & Psychotherapy Education
CFAR	Centre for Freudian Analysis and Research
CPCP	Centre for Personal Construct Psychology
CPP	Centre for Psychoanalytical Psychotherapy
CSP	Cambridge Society for Psychotherapy
CSPK	Centre for the Study of Psychotherapy (University of Kent)
CTP	Centre for Transpersonal Psychology
CTS	Centre Training School for Hypnotherapy and Psychotherapy
FAETT	Forum for Advancement of Educational Therapy & Therapeutic Teaching
FIC	The Family Institute, Cardiff
FIP	Forum for Independent Psychotherapists
GCL	The Gestalt Centre, London
GCSP	Guildford Centre and Society for Psychotherapy
GPTI	Gestalt Psychotherapy Training Institute
GUILD	Guild of Psychotherapists
HIP	Hallam Institute of Psychotherapy
IATE	Institute for Arts in Therapy and Education
IFT	Institute of Family Therapy
IGA	Institute of Group Analysis
IGAP	The Independent Group of Analytical Psychologists
IPC (WPF)	Institute of Psychotherapy and Counselling (WPF)
IPS	Institute of Psychosynthesis
IPSS	Institute of Psychotherapy and Social Studies
ITA	Institute of Transactional Analysis
KCC	Kensington Consultation Centre
KI	Karuna Institute
LAPP	London Association of Primal Psychotherapists
LCP	London Centre for Psychotherapy
LPDO	Liverpool Psychotherapy Diploma Organisation (University of Liverpool)
MC	Minster Centre
MET	The Metanoia Institute
NAAP	Northern Association for Analytical Psychotherapy
NAFSI	NAFSIYAT
NCHP	National College of Hypnotherapists and Psychotherapists
NRHP	The National Register of Hypnotherapists and Psychotherapists
NSAP	North Staffs. Association for Psychotherapy
NSHAP	National School of Hypnosis and Psychotherapy
NWIDP	North West Institute for Dynamic Psychotherapy
PA	Philadelphia Association
PET	Psychosynthesis & Education Trust
RCSPC	Regent's College School of Psychotherapy and Counselling
RCPsych	Royal College of Psychiatrists
RE.V	Re.Vision
SAP	Society of Analytical Psychology
SCPC	Stockton Centre for Psychotherapy and Counselling
SIP	Severnside Institute for Psychotherapy
SPEC	Spectrum
SPTI	The Sherwood Psychotherapy Training Institute
STTDP	South Trent Training in Dynamic Psychotherapy
TAVI	Tavistock Clinic
TMSI	Tavistock Marital Studies Institute
ULDPS	University of Leicester Diploma in Psychodynamic Studies
UPA	Universities Psychotherapy Association
WMIP	West Midlands Institute of Psychotherapy
WPF	Westminster Pastoral Foundation
WTC	The Women's Therapy Centre
YAPP	Yorkshire Association for Psychodynamic Psychotherapy

GEOGRAPHICAL LISTING

AVON

ASH, Robert
Psychoanalytic Psychotherapist
Top Flat, 54 Cotham Road, Cotham, Bristol BS6 6DW
01275 341314/0117 942 7079
SIP

AYLARD, Paul
Psychodynamic Psychotherapist
Heath House Priory Hospital, Heath House Lane, Off Bell Hill, Bristol BS16 1EQ
0117 952 5255
YAPP

BARNES, Hugh
Family Therapist
Child & Adolescent Service, Bristol Royal Hosp. Sick Children, St. Michael's Hill, Bristol BS2 8BJ
0117 929 4530
AFT

BARRETT, Julie Patricia Ann
Humanistic and Integrative Psychotherapist
Lower Brook Cottage, Woollard, Pensford, Bristol BS39 4HU
BCPC

BARROWS, Paul
Child Psychotherapist
Knowle Clinic Child & Adolescent Service, Broadfield Road, Knowle, Bristol BS4 2UH
0117 972 4227/0117 973 4989
ACP

BARWELL, Peter
Psychoanalytic Psychotherapist
51 Woodstock Road, Redland, Bristol BS6 7EW
0117 9247 580
GUILD

BAZELEY-WHITE, Diana
Family Therapist
33 Upper Cranbrook Road, Westbury Park, Bristol BS6 7UR
AFT

BOX, Sally
Psychoanalytic Psychotherapist
22 Clifton Wood Road, Clifton, Bristol BS8 4TW
0117 926 2902
SIP

BROWN, Ray
Psychoanalytic Psychotherapist
15 Nottingham Road, Bishopston, Bristol BS7 9DH
0117 942 6105
SIP

BROWN, Robin Gordon
Psychoanalytic Psychotherapist
14 Ambra Vale West, Clifton Wood, Bristol BS8 4RD
0117 914 7669(f)/0117 926 2886
SIP, BAP

CARDER, Misha
Hypno-Psychotherapist
76 Lower Oldfield Park, Bath BA2 3HP
01225 313531
NSHAP

CHALKLEY, A.J.
Cognitive Psychotherapist
Psychology Department, St. Martin's Hospital, Midford Road, Bath BA2 5RP
01225 832255
BABCP

CHAMPS, Thomas
Psychoanalytic Psychotherapist
8 Duchess Road, Bristol BS8 2LA
WMIP

CLAPHAM, Miles
Psychoanalytic Psychotherapist
5 Belgrave Place, Camden Road, Bath BA1 5JL
23 Rautangi Road, Mt Eden, Auckland, New Zealand
01225 428 964
PA

CLYNE, Rachel
Psychosynthesis Psychotherapist
2 Mendip View, Highbury Street, Coleford BA3 5NT
01373 813 349
AAPP

COLLENS, Louise
Psychoanalytic Psychotherapist
120 Chesterfield Road, St. Andrews, Bristol BS6 5DU
0117 924 7118
SIP

COLLIS, Whiz
Humanistic Psychotherapist
74 York Road, Montpelier, Bristol BS6 5QF
0117 955 9600
AHPP, BCPC

COTTMAN, Barbara
Psychoanalytic Psychotherapist
Church Cottage, Corston, Bath BA2 GAY
01225 874237
SIP

CRISPIN, Jean
Humanistic and Integrative Psychotherapist
22 Westerleigh Road, Pucklechurch, Bristol BS17 3RD
0117 9373191
BCPC

CUBIE, Paul
Systemic Psychotherapist
8 Wrenbert Road, Staple Hill, Bristol BS16 5JQ
0117 957 0096
AFT

CUTLER, Jane
Psychosynthesis Psychotherapist
66 Dunkerry Road, Windmill Hill, Bristol BS3 4LA
0117 9632 505
AAPP

DAVIES, Sheila
Psychoanalytic Psychotherapist
35 Bath Hill, Keynsham, Bristol BS18 1HJ
0117 986 1020
SIP

AVON

DEWEY, George
Humanistic and Integrative Psychotherapist
21 Nutgrove Avenue, Bedminster, Bristol BS3 4QE
0117 966 1100
BCPC

DOUGLAS, Dana
Psychosynthesis Psychotherapist
Wellspring, Faukland BA3 5UX
01373 834 338
AAPP

DRESSER, Iain
Psychoanalytic Psychotherapist
23 Highbury Villas, Kingsdown, Bristol BS2 8BY
0117 923 9038
SIP

DUNCAN, Fraser
54 Charlton Road, Kingswood, Bristol BS15 1HB
0117 907 3102
NSHAP

ELMAN, Anthony
Humanistic and Integrative Psychotherapist
143 North Road, Bristol BS6 5AH
0117 9247668
BCPC

ESSEX, Suzanne
Family Therapist
Garden Flat, 13 Windsor Road, St. Andrews, Bristol BS6 5BW
0117 9664283/0117 9422016
AFT

FEILDEN, Tish
Humanistic and Integrative Psychotherapist
The Barn, Sheephouse Farm, Warleigh, Bathford BA1 8EE
01225 858301
BCPC

FISHER, Anstice
Integrative Psychosynthesis Psychotherapist
9 Eastville, Claremont Road, Bath BA1 6QN
01225 445 653
RE.V

FORTUNE, Rosalind
Cognitive Behavioural Psychotherapist
1 Halsbury Road, Westbury Park, Bristol BS6 7SS
Cabot CMHT, 12 Grove Road, Redland, Bristol BS6 6UJ
0117 973 5142
BABCP

GABRIEL, Jill
Humanistic and Integrative Psychotherapist
Langridge House, Langridge, Bath BA1 9BX
01225 318834
SPEC

GARDNER, Fiona
Psychoanalytic Psychotherapist
Suite 3,4/ 5 Bridge Street, Bath BA2 4AP
01225 332693/01225 463054
SIP

GARDNER, Peter
Integrative Psychotherapist
Harpers Batch, Winford, Bristol, BS40 8AF
01275 472598
RCSPC

GASKELL, Christine
Family Therapist
28 Claremont Avenue, Bristol BS7 8JE
Riverside Adolescent Unit, Blackberry Hill Hospital, Bristol BS16 2EN
0117 9240808
AFT

GELL, Eva
Psychoanalytic Psychotherapist
116 Redland Road, Bristol BS6 6QT
0117 909 5730
LCP, SIP, WTC

GOSLING, Pat
Psychoanalytic Psychotherapist
White Hart Cottage, 38 High Street, Rode, Bath BA3 6PA
25 High Street, Rode, Bath BA3 6PA
01373 830901/01373 830172 (f)
GUILD, SIP

GRAHAM, Margaret
Humanistic and Integrative Psychotherapist
18 The Tyning, Widcombe, Bath BA2 6AL
01225 425181
BCPC

GREEN, Sylvia
Psychoanalytic Psychotherapist
29 Calton Gardens, Bath BA2 4QG
01225 421746/01225 482326
SIP

GREGORY, Judith
Gestalt Psychotherapist
'Fernlea', Yate Road, Iron Acton, Bristol BS17 1XY
01454 228418
GPTI

GRESTY, Julie
Core Process Psychotherapist
71 Mendip Road, Bedminster, Bristol BS3 4BP
0117 9637 285
AAPP

HAHN, Herbert
Psychoanalytic Psychotherapist
Suite 4, The Old Chapel, Fairview Drive, Bristol BS6 6PW
0117 942 5078/0117 924 4623 (f)
SIP

HAMBLIN, David
Psychosynthesis Psychotherapist, Humanistic and Integrative Psychotherapist
11 Kensington Gardens, Bath BA1 6LH
01225 317 272
AAPP, BCPC

HANLEY, Marie
Psychoanalytic Psychotherapist
3 Exeter Buildings, Redland, Bristol BS6 6TH
0117 946 6910
LCP, SIP

HARWOOD, Matthew
Analytical Psychologist-Jungian Analyst
1 Battlefields House, Lansdown, Bath BA1 9DD
0117 932 9204
IGAP

HASTINGS, Jon
Humanistic and Integrative Psychotherapist
29 Cobourg Road, Montpelier, Bristol BS6 5HT
0117 935 0915
BCPC

HASTINGS, Kim
Humanistic and Integrative Psychotherapist
42A Upper Cheltenham Place, Montpelier, Bristol BS6 5HR
0117 954 0649
BCPC

HAWDON, Sheila
Psychoanalytic Psychotherapist
Ashlands, Belmont Road, Combe Down, Bath BA2 5JR
01225 840420
SIP

HAWKINS, Peter
Humanistic and Integrative Psychotherapist
285 Bloomfield Road, Bath BA2 2NU
01225 836191
BCPC, AHPP

HAYWOOD, Carol
Transpersonal Psychotherapist
Flat 8, 21 Victoria Square, Bristol BS8 4ES
01179 743 717 (t/f)
CTP

HIGGINS, Judith
Gestalt Psychotherapist
5 Fairfield Road, Montpelier, Bristol BS6 5JN
0117 985 0391
GPTI

HOLLOWAY, Max
Integrative Psychotherapist
33 Honeysuckle Cane, Stapleton, Bristol BS16
0117 952 2126
MC

HORWOOD, Tone
Psychoanalytic Psychotherapist
14 Strathmore Road, Horfield, Bristol BS7 9QJ
0117 952 0112
IPSS

HUGHES, Hatty
Attachment-based Psychoanalytic Psychotherapist
11 Orchard Street, Bristol BS1 5EH
0117 954 1843
CAPP

HUTCHINSON, Gary
Integrative Psychosynthesis Psychotherapist
33 Apsley Road, Bath BA1 3LP
01225 421735
RE.V

JAMES, Glenys
Psychoanalytic Psychotherapist
Flat 1, 20 The Belmont, Lansdown, Bath BA1 5DZ
01225 463324/01380 871818
SIP

JAMES, Pat
Psychoanalytic Psychotherapist
2 The Dymboro, Midsomer Norton, Bath BA3 2QU
01761 415538
WMIP, SIP

JEFFRIES, Rosie
Integrative Psychotherapist
129 Mina Road, St. Werburgh's, Bristol BS2 9YF
01179 763818/01179 551471
MET

JEZARD-CLARK, P.H.
Cognitive Behavioural Psychotherapist
Petherton, 3 Petherton Road, Hengrove, Bristol BS14 2BP
01275 834048
BABCP

JOHNSON, Pat
Integrative Psychotherapist
9b Alpha Road, Southville, Bristol BS3 1DH
0117 9631610
MC

JONES, Rhiannon Marie
Cognitive Behavioural Psychotherapist
55 Waverley Road, Redland, Bristol BS6 6ET
0117 974 2002
BABCP

KEVLIN, Kunderke
Psychosynthesis Psychotherapist
12 Avon Vale, Stoke Bishop, Bristol BS9 1TB
0117 968 7748
AAPP

KUHN, Sue
Cognitive Analytic Therapist
13 Belgrave Crescent, Bath BA1 5JU
01225 465846
ACAT

LAPWORTH, Phil
Integrative Psychotherapist, Transactional Analysis Psychotherapist
Lilac Cottage, 65 Murhill, Limpley Stoke, Bath BA3 6HQ
01225 722348
ITA, MET

LEIGHTON, Tim
Cognitive Analytic Therapist
35 Belvedere, Bath BA1 5HR
01225 447706
ACAT

MACKEWN, Jennifer
Integrative Psychotherapist
Southstoke House, Packhorse Lane, Southstoke, Bath BA2 7DJ
01225 836 090(t/f)
GPTI, MET

MARKHAM, Angela
Family Therapist
23 Highbury Villas, Kingsdown, Bristol BS2 8BY
0117 923 9038
AFT

MATTHEWS, Shane
Family Therapist
14 Malmesbury Close, Bristol BS6 7TR
0117 924 5600
FIC

MCGOWAN, Fran
Humanistic and Integrative Psychotherapist
1 Abermarle Terrace, Joy Hill, Hotwells, Bristol BS8 4NA
01179 260632
BCPC

MCLOUGHLIN, Brendan
Psychoanalytic Psychotherapist
Open House Centre, Manvers Street, Bath BA1 1JW
01225 481297
IPC

MCNAMARA, Barbara
Psychoanalytic Psychotherapist
31 Sommerville Road, St. Andrews, Bristol BS7 9AD
0117 944 4206
SIP

MILTON, Thelma
Humanistic and Integrative Psychotherapist
26 Salisbury Road, Redland, Bristol BS6 7AP
0117 9427 518
BCPC

MITCHESON BROWN, Muriel
Psychoanalytic Psychotherapist
16 Woodstock Road, Redland, Bristol BS6 7EJ
0117 9241 676
SIP, GUILD

NAYDLER, Nick
Humanistic and Integrative Psychotherapist
4 Seddon Road, St. Werburghs, Bristol BS2 9YA
0117 9550752
BCPC

NEWMAN, Alexander
Psychoanalytic Psychotherapist
2 Evans Road, Redland, Bristol BS6 6TQ
0117 904 7829
SIP

NYE, Georgiana
Psychosynthesis Psychotherapist
45 Canynge Road, Clifton, Bristol BS8 3LH
0117 973 3769
AAPP

PADGETT, Louise
Core Process Psychotherapist
6 Fenton Road, Bishopston, Bristol BS7 8ND
01179 426 332
AAPP

PARLETT, Malcolm
Gestalt Psychotherapist
51 Fernbank Road, Redland, Bristol BS6 6PX
0117 924 0126
GPTI

PATTERSON, Linda
Psychoanalytic Psychotherapist
10 Brookleaze Buildings, Larkhall, Bath BA1 6RA
01225 463054/01225 311163
SIP

PIECZORA, Marek
Systemic Psychotherapist
124 Somerset Road, Upper Knowle, Bristol BS4 2JB
FIC

PIRANI, Alix
Individual and Group Humanistic Psychotherapist
1 Avondale Court, Goodeve Road, Bristol BS9 1NU
BCPC, AHPP

POPE, Sian
NLP Psychotherapist
4 Henbury Road, Westbury-on-Trym, Bristol BS9 3HJ
01179 504869
ANLP

PREECE, Rob
Transpersonal Psychotherapist
56 Dunkery Road, Windmill Hill, Bristol
16 Nattadon Road, Chagford, Devon TQ13 8BE
0164 743 2363/0117 924 0832
CTP

PURKISS, Jane
Humanistic and Integrative Psychotherapist
93 Stackpool Road, Southville, Bristol BS3 1NX
0117 966 2957
BCPC

RICHARDS, Christopher
Psychoanalytic Psychotherapist
4 St. Ronan's Avenue, Redland, Bristol BS6 6EP
0117 909 3474 (t/f)
GUILD, SIP

RICHARDSON, Gillian
Sexual and Marital Psychotherapist
Maycroft Cottage, Highbury Villas, Kingsdown, Bristol BS2 8BY
0117 925 0115
BASMT

ROSE, Alivia
Gestalt Psychotherapist
21 Nutgrove Avenue, Victoria Park, Bedminster, Bristol BS3 4QE
0117 966 1100
GCL

ROWE, Jill
Psychoanalytic Psychotherapist
8 Somerset Street, Kingsdown, Bristol BS2 8NB
0117 942 1016
SIP

ROYS, Clare
Systemic Psychotherapist
35 Calcott Road, Knowle, Bristol BS4 2HB
FIC

RYALL, Sue
Integrative Psychosynthesis Psychotherapist
34 Cornwall's Crescent, Clifton, Bristol BS8
0117 973 8880
RE.V

RYDE, Judy
Humanistic and Integrative Psychotherapist
285 Bloomfield Road, Bath BA2 2NU
01225 836191(f)
BCPC, AHPP

SAWERS, Martin
Humanistic and Integrative Psychotherapist
24 Ambrose Road, Clifton Wood, Bristol BS8 4RJ
109 Stafford Avenue, Slough, Berks SL2 1AP
01735 673765/0117 909 8196
BCPC

SAYERS, Jacqui
Family Psychotherapist
36 Devonshire Buildings, Bath BA2 4SU
01225 313542/01225 319192 (f)
FIC

SCHREIBER-KOUNINE, Christa
Cognitive Behavioural Psychotherapist
2 Upper Camden Place, Bath BA1 5HX
Psychology Department, Woodside, Barrow Hospital, Barrow Gurney BS19 3SG
0117 928 6551/4/01225 330731
BABCP

SELBY, Anne
Humanistic and Integrative Psychotherapist
Prospect House, 4 Prospect Place, Beechen Cliff, Bath BA2 4QP
01225 428826
BCPC

SHEEHAN, Nuala
Family Psychotherapist
6 Thomas Street, Bath BA1 5NW
01225 334957 (t/f)
IFT

SIMMONS, Alison
Psychodrama Psychotherapist
Lower Hounsley Farm, Pool Lane, Ridgehill, Nr. Winford, Bristol BS40 8BP
01275 472264/01179 730225
BPA

SINCLAIR, Ilse
Sexual and Marital Psychotherapist
19 Whately Court, Whately Road, Bristol BS8 2PS
0117 973 3384
BASMT

SLATTERY, David
Humanistic and Integrative Psychotherapist
37 Stafford Road, St. Werburghs, Bristol BS2 9UR
52 George Street, Nailsworth, Glos. GL6 0AG
0117 985 9210/0145 383 2215
BCPC

SMITH, Donna
Family Therapist
The Old Rectory, Bradford Road, Rode, Nr. Bath BA3 6PR
01373 830710
AFT

SMITH, Gill
Integrative Psychotherapist
Centre for Whole Health, 12 Victoria Place, Bristol BS3 3PB
0117 923 1138/01225 334624
MC

SPROSTON, Suzanne
Psychoanalytic Psychotherapist
7 Hampton Park, Redland, Bristol BS6 6LG
0117 909 4366
SIP, LCP

STALLARD, Paul
Cognitive Behavioural Psychotherapist
Dept. Child & Family Psychiatry, Royal United Hospital, Coombe Park, Bath BA1 3NG
01225 825075
BABCP

STONES, Christine
Psychoanalytic Psychotherapist
31 Barley Croft, Westbury-on-Trym, Bristol BS9 3TG
0117 9682397
SIP

STRATFORD, Jacqueline
Family Therapist
8 Owen Grove, Henleaze, Bristol BS9 4EF
0117 956 6025/0117 962 8627
AFT

SUTTON-SMITH, Deirdre
Group Analyst, Psychoanalytic Psychotherapist
12 Sydenham Road, Bristol BS6 5SH
0117 942 4510/01453 757981
IGA, WTC

TUTE, Iris
Psychoanalytic Psychotherapist
46 Eastfield, Bristol BS9 4BE
40a Eastfield, Bristol BS9 4BE
0117 962 1460/0117 962 4631
SIP

VALENTINE, Christine
Humanistic and Integrative Psychotherapist
42 Millmead Road, Oldfield Park, Bath BA2 3JP
01225 337372
BCPC

VINE, Francis
NLP Psychotherapist
11 Argyle Place, Cliftonwood, Bristol BS8 4RH
0117 927 3205
ANLP

WALKER, George
Family Therapist
Gloucester House, Southmead Hospital, Westbury on Trym, Bristol BS10 5NB
0117 9595807
AFT

WARNER, Kerri
Transactional Analysis Psychotherapist
4 Laburnum Road, Hanham, Bristol BS15 3DU
01753 820303/0117 9090784
ITA, MET

WEBB, Deborah
Biodynamic Psychotherapist
17 Rockcliffe Road, Bath BA2 6QN
01225 461361
BTC

WELLS, Martin
Transactional Analysis Psychotherapist
11 Clare Road, Cotham, Bristol BS6 5TB
Psychotherapy Unit,Cedar House, Manor Road, Fishponds, Blackberry Hill Hospital, Bristol BS16 2EW
0117 9656061 ext 4641/0117 9247457
ITA

WHEWAY, John Kirti
Humanistic and Integrative Psychotherapist
5 Fairfield Road, Montpelier, Bristol BS6 5JN
0117 985 0391
BCPC

WHITE, Jan
Family Therapist
Rosebank, Silver Street, Congresbury, Bristol BS19 5EY
01179 289000
AFT

WILLIAMS, Chris
Analytical Psychologist-Jungian Analyst
8 Stuart Place, Bath BA2 3RQ
01225 463054/01225 427705
AJA

WILLS, Frank
Cognitive Psychotherapist
7 St. Matthews Road, Cotham, Bristol BS6 5TS
0117 924 3574
BABCP

WILSON, Alexandra
Psychoanalytic Psychotherapist
Flat 7, Abbey House, Abbey Green, Bath BA1 1NR
01225 336591
SIP

WITT, John
Humanistic and Integrative Psychotherapist
2 Fircliff Park, Portishead, Bristol BS20 7HQ
Spectrum, 7 Endymion Road, London N4 1EE
01275 818580/0181 347 8735
SPEC

YARIV, Gaila
Psychoanalytic Psychotherapist
121 York Road, Montpelier, Bristol
BS6 5QG
0117 955 1827
IPC, SIP

BEDFORDSHIRE

ADLER, Eve
Sexual and Marital Psychotherapist
301 Sharpenhoe Road, Streatley, Nr.
Luton, Bedfordshire LU3 3PP
01582 881927
BASMT

BUDGELL, Rosemary
Integrative Psychotherapist
7 Blaydon Road, Luton, Bedfordshire
LU2 0RP
01582 488808
RCSPC

CLACKSON, Suzanne
Psychoanalytic Psychotherapist
21 Bradgate Road, Bedford MK40 3DE
01234 268876/01234 356996
GUILD

CLARE, Louise
Psychoanalytic Psychotherapist
11 Warden Abbey, Bedford
MK41 0SW
01234 267405
GUILD

CODD, Anne Marie
Psychoanalytic Psychotherapist
The Old School House, High Street,
Lidlington, Bedfordshire MK43 0RN
01525 406300
AGIP

COX, Keith
Family Therapist
5 Britannia Avenue, Limbury, Luton
LU3 1XD
01582 708 101/01582 652290
AFT

DUTTON, Andrew
Psychoanalytic Psychotherapist
Flat 4, Priory Terrace, Roise Street,
Bedford MK40 1JE
01234 267903
GUILD

GILKES, Pauline
Hypno-Psychotherapist
1 Mill Cottage, 101 Mill Road,
Sharnbrook, Bedford MK44 1NP
01234 781533
NRHP

HANNAH, Chris
Systemic Psychotherapist
39 Summer Street, Slip End, Luton,
Beds LU1 4BL
01582 422578
KCC

HANNAH, Clare
Systemic Psychotherapist
39 Summer Street, Slip End, Luton,
Bedfordshire LU1 4BL
01582 422578
KCC

HEATH, C.A.
Family Therapist
95 High Street, Langford, Bedfordshire
SG18 9RY
AFT

HEATH, Christine
Child Psychotherapist
Luton Child & Family Psychiatric Clinic,
Liverpool Rd Health Centre, 9 Mersey
Place, Liverpool Road, Luton, Beds
LU1 1HH
01582 708 140/01462 700 021
ACP

HICKMAN, Sue
Systemic Psychotherapist
Barford Avenue Centre, 29 Barford
Avenue, Bedford
11 Colchester Way, Bedford
MK41 8BG
01234 215610/01234 343506
KCC

HUSZCZA, Anna K.
Cognitive Behavioural Psychotherapist
Watton Place Clinic, 60 High Street,
Watton-At - Stone, Herts. LU1 1HJ
25 Baker Street, Luton, Bedfordshire
LU1 3PX
01582 757765
BABCP

KING, Madeleine
Systemic Psychotherapist
41 Leighton Road, Toddington,
Dunstable, Bedfordshire LU5 6AL
01525 872298
KCC

KRAUSE, Inga-Britt
Family Therapist
4 The Coach House, Bromham
Hall,Bromham, Bedford MK43 8HH
0171 624 8605/01234 823880
AFT

MCGUINNESS, Maureen
Psychosynthesis Psychotherapist
38 Woodgreen Road, Luton,
Bedfordshire LU2 8BU
01582 455681
AAPP

MCKAY, Barbara
Systemic Psychotherapist
Quince Cottage, 54 Wood End Road,
Wood End, Kempston,Beds MK43 9BD
KCC

MOORE, Rosemary
Psychoanalytic Psychotherapist
147 Dudley Street, Bedford MK40 3SY
01234 344736
GUILD

MORRIS, Peter A.
Cognitive Behavioural Psychotherapist
Beacon House, 5 Regent Street,
Dunstable, Bedfordshire LU6 1LR
01582 478850
BABCP

PARAMOUR, Annabelle
Psychoanalytic Psychotherapist
30 Bushmead Avenue, Bedford
MK40 3QN
01234 345553
CSP

PEART, Mary
Psychosynthesis Psychotherapist
3 School House Mews, High Street,
Silsoe, Bedfordshire MK45 4DY
01525 862139
AAPP

PHILPS, Janet
Child Psychotherapist
Bedford Child & Family Consultation
Clinic, Union Street Clinic, Union
Street, Bedford MK40 2SH
01234 881365/01234 342437
ACP

ROGERS, Anne
Psychoanalytic Psychotherapist
32a Church End, Renhold, Bedfordshire
MK41 0LU
01234 771595
AGIP, FIP

SIMS, Lyn
Family Psychotherapist
162a High Street, Cranfield,
Bedfordshire MK43 0EN
01234 750871
AFT

TRUSTAM, Gillian
Psychoanalytic Psychotherapist
86 High Street, Oakley, Beds
MK43 7RH
01234 822985
AGIP

VAN DER EIJK, Mike
Systemic Psychotherapist
2 Laburnham Cottage, Soulbury, Nr.
Leighton Buzzard, Bedfordshire
LU7 0DA
01525 270922
KCC

WARBURTON, Kitty
Integrative Psychotherapist
18 The Warren, Clapham, Bedfordshire
MK41 6DW
01234 793362/01234 271938
RCSPC

WILSON, Maureen
Psychoanalytic Psychotherapist
21a Bradgate Road, Bedford
MK40 3DE
01234 360677(t/f)
AGIP, FIP

BERKSHIRE

ADAMS, Janet
Attachment-based Psychoanalytic
Psychotherapist
24 Stone Street, Reading, Berkshire
RG30 1HU
01189 676500
CAPP

ALLISON, Virginia
Psychoanalytic Psychotherapist
Hollycopse House, Tothill Burghclere,
Newbury, Berkshire RG20 9ED
01638 278390
IPC

ASMUS, Elke
Psychoanalytic Psychotherapist
27 Addington Road, Reading, Berkshire
RG1 5PZ
0118 966 5557
LCP

BURNET-SMITH, Tamara
Humanistic Psychotherapist, Autogenic
Psychotherapist
71 Westfield Road, Caversham,
Reading, Berkshire RG4 8HL
01189 479957
AHPP, BAFAT

CLAXTON, Patricia
Psychoanalytic Psychotherapist
8 St. Stephen's Close, Caversham,
Reading, Berkshire RG4 8BX
0181 947 0763
AGIP

COLLINS, Jane
Sexual and Marital Psychotherapist
Magnolia House Surgery, Sunningdale,
Ascot, Berkshire SL5 0QJ
01344 637800
BASMT

COOPER, Jan
Family Therapist
5 Buckhurst Way, Earley, Reading
RG6 7RL
0118 962 6095/0118 966 1543
AFT

COXWELL-WHITE, Jenny
Integrative Psychotherapist
113 New Road, North Ascot,
Berkshire SL5 8PZ
01344 884142
CCBP

DONALD, Philippa
Transpersonal Psychotherapist
Reading, Berkshire
0118 961 1150
CCPE

EATON, John
Hypno-Psychotherapist, NLP
Psychotherapist
Waterloo House, 158 London Road,
Newbury, Berkshire RG14 2AX
462 Roman Road, London E3
01635 569285(f)/01635 44444
ANLP, NSHAP

ENGLAND, David
Psychosynthesis Psychotherapist
48 Trenchard Road, Holyport,
Maidenhead, Berkshire SL6 2LR
01628 639313
AAPP

GRIFFITHS, Thelma
Transpersonal Psychotherapist
40 The Crescent, Reading, Berks
RG6 7NN
01189 668092
CCPE

HUGHES, Patrick
Group Analyst
12 Instow Road, Earley, Reading
RG6 2QJ
01734 873049
IGA

JOHNSON-SMITH, Camilla
Group Analytic Psychotherapist
Rainbow's End, Cock Lane, Southend
Bradfield, Nr. Reading RG7 6HN
0973 110029/0118 974 4650
LCP, AHPP

KANAKAM, Jonathan
Hypno-Psychotherapist
50 Farnham Road, Slough, Berks
SL1 3TA
01753 524038
NSHAP

KLEIN, Wendy
Family Therapist
12 St. James Close, Pangbourne,
Reading RG8 7AP
01734 842856
AFT

KNOWLES, Jane
Group Analyst
7 Albert Road, Caversham, Reading,
Berks RG4 7AN
01734 561250/01734 478872
IGA

MCGREGOR, Tony
Hypno-Psychotherapist
127 Kingsley Close, Shaw, Newbury,
Berkshire RG14 2EB
01635 34231
NRHP

MELTON, Jane
Cognitive Analytic Therapist
46 Clifton Road, Wokingham,
Berkshire, RG41 1NB
01734 771409
ACAT

PARR, John
Transactional Analysis Psychotherapist
Norcot House, 131 Norcot Road,
Tilehurst, Reading RG30 6BS
01189 454477/01189 453388
ITA

PECKITT, R.G.
Cognitive Behavioural Psychotherapist
Broodmore Special Hospital, Crowthorne, Berkshire RG4 7EG
01344 773 111
BABCP

POOL, Nicky
Transpersonal Psychotherapist
Purton House, Purton Lane, Farnham Royal, Bucks SL2 3LY
01753 646625
CTP

PRESTON, Janet
Child Psychotherapist
14 Thames Avenue, Pangbourne, Berkshire RG8 7BU
01753 869755/01189 844193
ACP

QUOILIN-LEBRUN, Michelle
Biodynamic Psychotherapist
4 Mornington Avenue, Finchamstead, Wokingham RG11 4UE
01734 730870
BTC

RICHARDS, Janet
Psychoanalytic Psychotherapist
35 Bulmershe Road, Reading, Berks RG1 5RH
0118 9269545
GUILD

SCOVELL, Janet
Integrative Psychotherapist
25 The Grove, Reading, Berks RG1 4RB
0118 956 1976
MC

SELBY, Gina
Personal Construct Psychotherapist
Ships Cottage, Ashford Hill, Newbury, Berks RG20 8BD
0118 9811793
CPCP

SHORT, Pat
Systemic Psychotherapist
Broadmoor Hospital, Psychology Department, Crowthorne, Berkshire RG45 7EL
KCC

TYTEL, Laurie
Psychoanalytic Psychotherapist
24 Russet Glade, Caversham, Reading, Berkshire RG4 8UJ
0118 947 0625
LCP

VETERE, Arlene
Family Therapist
Reading Safer Families, 11 Headley Road, Reading RG5 4JB
0118 962 2299
AFT

VON BÜHLER, José
Sexual and Marital Psychotherapist
The Cardinal Clinic, Bishop's Lodge, Oakley Green, Windsor SL4 5UL
0973 442146
BASMT

WAGSTAFF, Susan
Family Therapist
7 Melrose Avenue, Reading, Berkshire RG6 2BN
0118 9666018
AFT

WARD, Hilary
Transpersonal Psychotherapist
Blair Villa, Wokefield Row, Mortimer, Berkshire RG7 3AL
CCPE

WHITE, Ruth
Transpersonal Psychotherapist
Dragon Den, 3 Manor Farm Mews, Manor Farm Lane, Tidmarsh, Nr. Reading, Berks RG8 8EY
0118 984 5480/01734 845480
CTP

BUCKINGHAMSHIRE

ADAMS, Ghislaine
Hypno-Psychotherapist
41 London Road, Stony Stratford, Milton Keynes MK11 1JQ
01908 654160/01908 566362
NSHAP

ALDER, Helena
Integrative Psychotherapist
Woodside Corner, 11 Baring Crescent, Beaconsfield, Bucks HP9 2NG
01494 673557
MC

ALDER, Roger
Integrative Psychotherapist
Woodside Corner, 11 Baring Crescent, Beaconsfield, Bucks HP9 2NG
01494 673557
MC

ANTAO, Ivor
Group Analyst
45 Grenville Green, Aylesbury, Bucks HP21 8HB
01296 393363/01296 27197
IGA

AXSON, Barbara Astrid
Educational Therapist
'Westways' Milton Avenue, Gerrards Cross Bucks SL9 8QW
01753 886928 (t/f)
FAETT

BOLLINGHAUS, Elaine
Psychoanalytic Marital Psychotherapist
'Loudhams', Burtons Lane, Little Chalfont, Buckinghamshire HP8 4BS
01494 765947
TMSI

BURNS, Elizabeth
Family Therapist
11 Green End Street, Astow Clinton, Aylesbury, Bucks HP22 5JE
01296 630048
IFT

BUTCHER, Barbara
Hypno-Psychotherapist
35 Lowfield Way, Hazlemere, Buckinghamshire HP15 7RR
01494 814306
NSHAP

DALE, Anne M.
Hypno-Psychotherapist
Little Grove, Grove Lane, Chesham, Buckinghamshire HP5 3QQ
01494 776066/01494 778610
NSHAP

DE GROOT, Marianne
Sexual and Marital Psychotherapist
Antlers, 52 Longfield Drive, Amersham, Buckinghamshire HP6 5HE
BASMT

GALLOWAY, Jan
Sexual and Marital Psychotherapist
Gyldernscroft, 1 Henley Road, Marlow, Bucks SL7 2BZ
BASMT

GILBOY, Carol A.
Cognitive Behavioural Psychotherapist
Clinical Psychology Services, The Campbell Centre, The Hospital Campus, Eaglestone, Milton Keynes MK6 5NG
01908 243982/01908 231948(f)
BABCP

GOLDING, Pauline
Hypno-Psychotherapist
Kingsgate Therapy Centre, 32 The Rowans, Gerrards Cross, Bucks SL9 8SE
01753 883062
NRHP

GORDON, John Fredrick
Psychoanalytic Psychotherapist
Medical Officer & Psychotherapist, HM Prison Grendon, Grendon Underwood, Aylesbury HP18 0TL
PA

HARRISON, Susan
Sexual and Marital Psychotherapist
Briar Patch, Little London Green, Oakley, Aylesbury, Bucks HP18 9QL
01844 238313
BASMT

JACKSON, Jo
Systemic Psychotherapist
Acorn Cottage, Bigmore Lane, Cadmore End, Bucks HP14 3UR
01494 882692
KCC

JEFFERIES, Alison
Integrative Psychotherapist
116 Mansion Lane, Iver, Bucks SL0 9RF
01753 650893
MC

KEMPS, Charmaine
Family Therapist
Eaglestone Health Centre AFT, The Hospital Campus, Standing Way, Eaglestone,Milton Keynes MK6 5AZ
AFT

LEON, Barbara D.
Psychoanalytic Psychotherapist
10 Darlington Close, Amersham-on-the-Hill, Buckinghamshire HP6 5AD
01494 729903/01494 729327
IPC

LEVITSKY, Patricia D.
Integrative Psychotherapist
Sportsman's Cottage, Beacon Hill, Penn, Bucks HP10 8NJ
01494 812219
GPTI

MARATOS, Jason
Group Analyst
Briarwood Cottage, 4 Mitchell Walk, Amersham, Bucks HP6 6NN
01494 535727/01494 728203
IGA

MASON, Letizia
Transpersonal Psychotherapist
96 New Road, Marlow, Buckinghamshire SL7 3NW
CCPE

MCGRATH, Patrick
Group Analyst
71 Eaton Avenue, Bletchley, Milton Keynes, Bucks. MK2 2HN
01908 372 868/01908 835 810
IGA

MCNAB, Sue
Family Therapist
Dell House, Wash Hill, Wooburn Green, Bucks. HP10 0JA
01628 526275
AFT

MEAD, Janet
Cognitive Analytic Therapist
Campbell Centre, Milton Keynes CMHT, Milton Keynes, Bucks MK6 5NG
01908 660033
ACAT

NEWSON, Mary
Psychosynthesis Psychotherapist
The Dower Cottage, 5 Little Shardeloes, Amersham, Buckinghamshire HP7 0EF
01494 727 141
AAPP

PALMER, Lisa Elaine
Cognitive Behavioural Psychotherapist
Psychotherapy Dept, Tindal Centre, Bierton Road, Aylesbury, Bucks HP20 1HU
01296 393363 ext 364
BABCP

PANCHKOWRY, Marion
Group Analyst
Bramble Cottage, Dunton, Nr. Buckingham MK18 3LW
01296 393 363 x 525/01525 240 083
IGA

POLLARD, Cynthia
Cognitive Analytic Therapist
Mill End, Mill Lane, Gerrards Cross, Bucks SL9 8AZ
01753 885526(f)/01753 885164
ACAT

RAND, Judith Ann
Psychosynthesis Psychotherapist
310 Berkhamsted Road, Chesham, Bucks HP5 3EZ
0171 403 7814/01494 773719
AAPP

REDDY, Michael
Transactional Analysis Psychotherapist
90 Church Road, Woburn Sands, Bucks MK17 8TR
01908 281271/01908 285200
ITA

REIDY, Rachel
Cognitive Analytic Therapist
Woodbine Cottage, 81 Totteridge Lane, High Wycombe, Bucks HP13 7QA
The Surgery, 65 Desborough Avenue, High Wycombe, Bucks HP11 2SD
01494 526006/01494 527597
ACAT

ROBERTS, Alison
Systemic Psychotherapist
Dormers, Buckland Village, Nr Aylesbury, Buckinghamshire HP22 5HY
01296 630256
KCC

ROBERTS, Jeff
Group Analyst
Hazel Cottage, 42 Stubbs Wood, Chesham Bois, Bucks. HP6 6EX
0171 935 3103/01494 726317
IGA

ROSSETER, Bill
Psychoanalytic Psychotherapist
14 Lower Way, Great Brickhill, Milton Keynes MK17 9AG
01525 261493
IPC

ROY, Jane
Sexual and Marital Psychotherapist
10 Faraday Drive, Shenley Lodge, Milton Keynes MK5 7DA
01908 674118
BASMT

STEINER, Monika
Psychoanalytic Psychotherapist
13 Lansdown Road, Chalfont St. Peter, Buckinghamshire SL9 9SP
01753 882112
IPSS

WORTH, Piers
NLP Psychotherapist
4 Hollow Rise, High Wycombe, Bucks
HP13 5NU
01494 464297
ANLP

YOUNG, Diana
Transpersonal Psychotherapist
Damien House, 23 High Street, Great Missenden, Buckinghamshire
HP16 9AA
01494 866 440
CCPE

CAMBRIDGESHIRE

ARRIENS, Pamela
Psychoanalytic Psychotherapist
3 Middlemoor Road, Whittlesford, Cambridge CB2 4PB
01223 832877/01223 834665 (f)
CSP

BACON, Roger
Psychoanalytic Psychotherapist
112 Canterbury Street, Cambridge
CB4 3QE
Cambridge Psychotherapy Practice, 26 Newnham Road, Cambridge CB3 9EY
01223 369894/01223 560262
GUILD

BELL, Lydia J.
Cognitive Behavioural Psychotherapist
The Phoenix Centre, Adolescent Eating Disorders, Ida Darwin , Fulbourn, Cambridge CB1 5EE
01223 886501
BABCP

BRIANT, Michael
Psychoanalytic Psychotherapist
Kingfisher Cottage, 1 Church Rate Walk, Cambridge CB3 9HJ
01223 332865/01223 464611
GUILD

BRIANT, Steve
Psychoanalytic Psychotherapist
57 Victoria Road, Cambridge
CB4 3BW
01223 327165
CSP

BRIEGER, Johanna
Analytical Psychologist-Jungian Analyst
29 Ventress Farm Court, Cherry Hinton Road, Cambridge CB1 4HD
0171 328 9430/01223 213639
SAP, BAP

BROSAN, Lee
Cognitive Behavioural Psychotherapist
Dept of Cognitive Behavioural Therapy, Box 190, Addenbrooke's Hospital, Cambridge CB2 2QQ
01223 217944
BABCP

BYFORD, Sally
Biodynamic Psychotherapist
The Little Orchard, Long Lane, Linton
CB1 6NS
BTC

CAMERON, Angela
Integrative Psychotherapist
18 Clare Street, Cambridge CB4 3BY
01223 361043
RCSPC

CARR, Samantha
Systemic Psychotherapist
27 Meadow Way, Great Paxton, Huntingdon, Cambridgeshire PE19 4RR
01480 474552 (t/f)
KCC

CHURCHILL-MOSS, Duncan
Cognitive Behavioural Psychotherapist
18 Hinton Road, Fulbourne, Cambridge
CB1 5DZ
01223 723020/01223 514861
BABCP

CONROY, Jennifer J.
Cognitive Behavioural Psychotherapist
22 Green End, Fen Ditton, Cambridge
CB5 8SX
Dept of Cognitive Behavioural Psy., Psychological Treatment Service, Box 190/ Portacabins, Addenbrookes Hospital Cambridge CB2 2QQ
01223 292124/01223 217944
BABCP

CORRIGALL, Jenny
Psychoanalytic Psychotherapist
10 Willow Walk, Cambridge CB1 1LA
01223 361703/01223 566643 (f)
CSP

DASGUPTA, Carol
Psychoanalytic Psychotherapist
1 Dean Drive, Holbrook Road, Cambridge CB1 4SW
01223 212179
CSP

DAVIES, Alison
Psychoanalytic Psychotherapist
27 Priory Road, Cambridge CB5 8HT
01223 510171
PA

DAVIES, Judy
Psychoanalytic Psychotherapist
12 Barton Road, Cambridge CB3 9JZ
01223 515526/01223 515527 (f)
CSP

DENMAN, Francesca
Cognitive Analytic Therapist
Department of Psychotherapy, Box 190, Addenbrookes Hospital, Cambridge CB3
019323 226477
ACAT

DIGGLE, Sedwell
Analytical Psychologist-Jungian Analyst
92 Canterbury Street, Cambridge
CB4 3QE
01223 351310
SAP

DYSON, Margaret
Integrative Psychotherapist, Body Psychotherapist
4 Kimberley Road, Cambridge
CB4 1HH
01223 367311
MC

FARRELL, Margaret
Psychoanalytic Psychotherapist
The Old Stores, 5 High Street, Grantchester, Cambridge CB3 9NF
01223 369894
GUILD, CSP

FITZGERALD-KLEIN, Marianne
Transpersonal Psychotherapist
17 Cambridge Road, Madingley, Cambridge CB3 8AH
01954 211 350(t/f)
CCPE

GAGNERE, Maryline
Biodynamic Psychotherapist
6 Chalky Road, Great Abington, Cambridgeshire CB1 6HT
BTC

GENTRY, Valerie
Psychoanalytic Psychotherapist
30 Hinton Avenue, Cambridge
CB1 4AS
01223 212821
CSP

GORDON, Leila
Psychoanalytic Psychotherapist
37 Herbert Street, Cambridge
CB4 1AQ
01223 367912
CSP

GREAVES, Sarah
Psychoanalytic Psychotherapist
33 Eltisley Avenue, Cambridge
CB3 9JQ
01223 354526
CSP, GUILD

GUEST, Hazel
Humanistic Psychotherapist,
Transpersonal Psychotherapist
44 Beaufort Place, Thompson's Lane,
Cambridge CB5 8AG
01223 369148
CTP, AHPP

GUILD, Liz
Psychoanalytic Psychotherapist
198 Sturton Street, Cambridge
CB1 2QF
01223 311042
PA

HALL, David
Psychoanalytic Psychotherapist
47 Cavendish Avenue, Cambridge
CB1 4UR
01223 249 732
GUILD

HARDY, Liz
Psychoanalytic Psychotherapist
90 Tenison Road, Cambridge
CB1 2DW
01223 367850
PA

HARRSON, Gillian
Family Therapist, Systemic
Psychotherapist
21 Dillington Road, Cambridge
CB3 9HW
01480 415300/01223 357778
IFT

HARVEY, Paul
Personal Construct Psychotherapist
21 Gurney Way, Cambridge CB4 2ED
01223 301 387
CPCP

HAYNES, Eric
Hypno-Psychotherapist
33A Bridewell Road, Cherry Hinton,
Cambridge CB1 4EN
01223 214281
NSHAP

HOLLAND, Louise
Child Psychotherapist
21 Richmond Road, Cambridge
CB4 3PP
01223 353029
ACP

HUTCHISON, Eric
Analytical Psychologist-Jungian Analyst
77 Long Road, Cambridge CB2 2HE
01223 840381
BAP

KILGOUR, Mimi
NLP Psychotherapist
332 Eastfield Road, Peterborough,
Cambridgeshire PE1 4RA
01733 312900/01733 762599 (f)
ANLP

KING, Lucy
Psychoanalytic Psychotherapist
7 Water Street, Chesterton,
Cambridge CB4 1NZ
Cambridge University Counselling
Service, 14 Trumpington Street,
Cambridge CB2 1QA
01223 367742
PA, CSP

KLUG, Liebe
Psychoanalytic Psychotherapist
70 Cavendish Avenue, Cambridge
CB1 4UT
01223 248959/01223 242774 (f)
CSP

LEW, Clara
Psychoanalytic Psychotherapist
20 Owlstone Road, Cambridge
CB3 9JH
Addenbrookes Hospital, Cambridge
CB2 2QQ
01223 217958/01223 356744
CSP

LEWINGTON, Paul
Family Therapist, Systemic
Psychotherapist
Brookside Family Consultation Clinic,
Douglas House, 18d Trumpington
Road, Cambridge CB2 2AH
01223 746001
IFT

LINTOTT, Bill
Group Analyst
7 Haverhill Road, Stapleford,
Cambridge CB2 5BX
01223 69894/01223 842008
IGA

MARTIN, Angela
Sexual and Marital Psychotherapist
Woodfield, 53 Church Street,
Warmington, Peterborough PE8 6TE
01832 280212
BASMT

MCDOUALL, Veronica
Psychoanalytic Psychotherapist
119 Thornton Road, Cambridge
CB3 0NE
71 Bridge Street, Cambridge CB2 1UR
01223 576648/01223 313515
IPC

MILLER, Michael
Psychoanalytic Psychotherapist
11 Bishops Road, Trumpington, Cambs
CB2 2NQ
Cambridge Psychotherapy Practice, 26
Newnham Road, Newnham,
Cambridge CB3 9EX
01223 69894/01223 845030
GUILD

MORGAN, Sian
Psychoanalytic Psychotherapist
The Cambridge Psychotherapy
Practice, 26 Newnham Road,
Cambridge CB3 9EY
12 Lower End, Swaffham Prior,
Cambridge CB5 0HT
01638 741390/01223 369894
GUILD, CSP

MURDIN, Lesley
Psychoanalytic Psychotherapist
32 Belvoir Road, Cambridge CB4 1JJ
01223 312848/01223 328390(f)
IPC

MURPHY, Derry
Personal Construct Psychotherapist
18 Mallets Road, Cherry Hinton,
Cambridge CB1 4HA
01223 245 210
CPCP

PAIN, Jean
Hypno-Psychotherapist, NLP
Psychotherapist
7 Way Lane, Waterbeach,
Cambridgeshire CB5 9NQ
01223 860 356
ANLP, NRHP

PARKINSON, Dorn
Psychoanalytic Psychotherapist
Archway House, Town Street, Upwell, Wisbech PE14 9AD
The Health Centre, Townley Close, Upwell, Wisbech PE14 9BT
01945 773941
CSP

PEGLAR, Graham
Psychodynamic Psychotherapist
26 Malta Road, Cambridge CB1 3PZ
01223 411514
ULDPS

POLLARD, James
Attachment-based Psychoanalytic Psychotherapist
60 Montague Road, Cambridge CB4 1BX
01223 314398
CAPP

RANDALL, Rosemary
Psychoanalytic Psychotherapist
113 Gwydir Street, Cambridge CB1 2LG
01223 313539
CSP

REYNOLDS, Alun
Humanistic Psychotherapist
12 Orchard Avenue, Cambridge CB4 2AH
01223 461744
AHPP

ROBINSON, Carole
Psychoanalytic Psychotherapist
University of Cambridge Counselling Service, 14 Trumpington Street, Cambridge CB2 1QA
01223 332865
CSP

SCOTT, Glenys
Psychoanalytic Psychotherapist
Hill Farm, 128 Green End, Comberton, Cambs CB3 7DY
01223 332865/01223 262925
GUILD

SERPELL, Vivienne
Sexual and Marital Psychotherapist
Scotts, High Street, Whittlesford, Cambridge CB2 4LT
01223 833218
BASMT

SINCLAIR, Alison
Psychoanalytic Psychotherapist
99 Windsor Road, Cambridge CB4 3JL
01223 565985/01223 369894
GUILD

SINCLAIR, Fiona
Psychoanalytic Psychotherapist
14 Brookside, Cambridge CB2 1JE
01223 364834
FIP

SMITH, Gillian
Psychoanalytic Psychotherapist
5 Alpha Terrace, Trumpington, Cambridge CB2 2HS
01223 842073
CSP

STRATTON-WOODWARD, Sally
Integrative Psychotherapist
15 East Street, Bluntisham, Huntingdon, Cambs PE17 3LS
01487 841659
SPTI

STYLES, Heather
Gestalt Psychotherapist
109 Vinery Road, Cambridge CB1 3DW
01223 414595
GCL

TAUSSIG, Hanna
Psychoanalytic Psychotherapist
296 Hills Road, Cambridge CB2 2QG
01223 246643
GUILD

TODD, Gillian
Cognitive Psychotherapist
6 Hauxton Road, Trumpington, Cambridge CB2 2LT
Barton House, Box 220, Addenbrookes Hospital, Cambridge CB2 2LT
01223 257153/01223 841151
BABCP

TOUTON-VICTOR, Patricia
Psychoanalytic Psychotherapist
18 Bateman Street, Cambridge CB2 1NB
01223 573865/01223 364793
PA

TREGEAR, Barbara
Psychodrama Psychotherapist
79 Gough Way, Cambridge CB3 9LN
St. Columba Group Therapy Centre, 3 Downing Place, Cambridge CB2 3EL
01223 365963/01223 357221
BPA

VOIKHANSKAYA, Marina
Psychoanalytic Psychotherapist
20 Garden Walk, Cambridge CB4 3EN
01223 67747
GUILD

WARWICK, Heather
Sexual and Marital Psychotherapist
31 Sedley Taylor Road, Cambridge CB2 2PN
01223 245380
BASMT

WATERSTON, John
Humanistic Psychotherapist
20 Waverley Park, Orchard Road, Great Shelford, Cambridge CB2 5BA
01223 843894
AHPP

WESTLAND, Gill
Body Psychotherapist, Humanistic Psychotherapist, Integrative Psychotherapist
8 Wetenhall Road, Cambridge CB1 3AG
01223 573345 (f)/01223 214658
AHPP, CCBP

WHITTLE, Lorna
Psychoanalytic Psychotherapist
28 Missleton Court, Cambridge CB1 4BL
01223 213969
ARBS

WILDE, Deborah
Psychoanalytic Psychotherapist
45 Riverside, Cambridge CB5 8HN
01223 562519
CSP

WOODCOCK, Therese M-Y.
Child Psychotherapist
Brookside Family Consultation Clinic, Douglas House, 18b Trumpington Road, Cambridge CB2 2AH
4 Earlham Grove, Wood Green, London N22 5HJ
0181 889 3353/01223 746001
ACP

WOOLLISCROFT, Jenny
Humanistic Psychotherapist, Gestalt Psychotherapist
80 Andrew Road, Eynesbury, St. Neots, Huntingdon PE19 2QL
01480 470804
AHPP

CHANNEL ISLANDS

BOWEN, Barry
Family Therapist
Flat 6,23 Havre des Pas, S. Helier, Jersey JE2 4UQ
e-mail Barann@super.net.uk/01534 874 855
AFT

DYER, Ian P.
Cognitive Behavioural Psychotherapist
Queens House, St Saviours Hospital, La Route de la Hougue Bie, St Saviour JE2 7UW
5 Marina Cottages, La Route de la Hougue Bie, St Saviour, Jersey JE2 7UW
01534 857992/01534 623223
BABCP

FARMER, Christopher
Psychodrama Psychotherapist
La Couture, Belval Road, Vale, Guernsey, Channel Islands GY3 5LW
01481 45334/01481 58406 (f)
BPA

LUCAS, Rosemarie
Cognitive Behavioural Psychotherapist
Villa Angia, Les Ruisseaux, St. Brelade, Jersey JE3 8DD
01534 43326/01534 498241 (f)
BABCP

NELSON, Maureen
Sexual and Marital Psychotherapist
Relate, 2 St Mark's Lane, St. Helier, Jersey
BASMT

SINGLETON, Kryin
Transpersonal Psychotherapist
La Neurve Charterie, Frie au Four, St Saviour's, Guernsey GY7 9TG
044 81108541/01481 67187
CCPE

CHESHIRE

ALDERTON, Chris
Cognitive Behavioural Psychotherapist
70 Tarvin Road, Littleton, Chester CH3 7DF
01244 335417
BABCP

BANNISTER, Anne
Psychodrama Psychotherapist
Glebe Cottage, Church Road, Mellor, Stockport SK6 5LX
0161 427 3307
BPA

BENBOW, Susan
Systemic Psychotherapist
24 Arthog Road, Hale, Altrincham, Cheshire WA15 0LY
Carisbrooke Resource Centre, Wenlock Way, Gorton, Manchester M12 5LF
0161 273 4383/0161 980 5719
FIC

BERMAN, Paul
Group Analyst
The Moorings, Mereside Road, Knutsford, Cheshire WA16 6QR
IGA

BERRY, Mary
Sexual and Marital Psychotherapist
24 Leafield Road, Disley, Stockport, Cheshire SK12 2JF
BASMT

BIRD, John
Psychoanalytic Psychotherapist
17 Macclesfield Road, Wilmslow, Cheshire SK9 2AA
01625 523292
NWIDP

BORONAT, Dascha
Group Analyst
South Trafford Community Mental Health, St. Anne's Hospital, Woodville Road, Bowden, Altrincham WA14 2AN
5 Victoria Avenue, Cheadle, Hulme, Cheshire SK8 5DJ
0161 928 9626/0161 488 4504
IGA

BRERETON, June
Transactional Analysis Psychotherapist
'Pendene', 116 Stocks Lane, Stalybridge, Cheshire SK15 2TQ
0161 862 9456/0161 303 7925
ITA

BURROWS, Joanna
Family Therapist
3 Mount Pleasant, Rainow, Nr. Macclesfield, Cheshire SK10 5TJ
0161 495 4902/01625 434352
AFT

BUTCHER, Josie
Family Psychotherapist
Nantwich Health Centre, Beam Street, Nantwich, Cheshire CW5 5NX
BASMT

CLARKE, Elaine
Psychoanalytic Psychotherapist
8 Windmill Lane, Preston-on-the-Hill, Warrington, Cheshire WA4 4AZ
01928 713811
LPDO

COLLINS, Gloria
Psychoanalytic Psychotherapist
Halton Psychotherapy and Family Services, Thorn Road Clinic, Thorn Road, Runcorn, Cheshire WA7 5HQ
01928 575073
LPDO

COOPER, Graham
Psychoanalytic Psychotherapist
Denton House, Denton Drive, Northwich, Cheshire CW9 7LU
01606 353800
LPDO

DEARSLEY, Sandra
Hypno-Psychotherapist
17 Lumley Road, Chester CH2 2AQ
01244 390490
NRHP

DOOGAN, Kevin
Sexual and Marital Psychotherapist
17 Willan Road, Blacon, Chester CH1 5PU
BASMT

DORNDORF, Rhoda
Psychoanalytic Psychotherapist
Flat 12, Brocklehurst Manor, Brocklehurst Avenue, Macclesfield, Cheshire SK10 2RX
01625 425193
LPDO

FARQUHARSON, Kay
Sexual and Marital Psychotherapist
Oak Lodge, Windmill Lane, Appleton, Warrington, Cheshire WA4 5JN
01925 262767
BASMT

FERNANDEZ, Nigel R.
Cognitive Behavioural Psychotherapist
Dept. of Clinical Psychology, Stepping Hill Hospital, Poplar Grove, Stockport SK2 7JE
0161 419 4678/0161 612 8653
BABCP

FITTON, Freda
Gestalt Psychotherapist
15 The Beeches, Upton, Chester
CH2 1PE
01244 348843
GPTI

GELDEARD, Bryan W.J.
Psychoanalytic Psychotherapist
Halton General Hospital, East Lane,
Runcorn, Cheshire WA7 2DA
01928 714567 ext 3175
LPDO

GLYNN, Julie
Psychoanalytic Psychotherapist
Garven Place Clinic, Sankey Street ,
Warrington, Cheshire WA4 6PY
LPDO

GONSALKORALE, Wendy
Hypno-Psychotherapist
Westward, Brooklands Crescent, Sale,
Cheshire M33 3NB
0161 976 1248
CTS

GREEN, Barbara A.
Psychoanalytic Psychotherapist
Stockport Psychology Services,
Stepping Hill Hospital, Poplar Grove,
Stockport SK2 7JE
0161 419 5793
LPDO

GREENFIELD, Terence
Cognitive Behavioural Psychotherapist,
Hypno-Psychotherapist
First Floor, 157 Ashley Road, Hale,
Altrincham, Cheshire WA14 3UW
0161 928 3898/0161 929 0361
BABCP, NRHP

HANNAH, Francesca
Transactional Analysis Psychotherapist
16 Norman Road, Heaton Moor,
Stockport SK4 4HJ
0161 431 5968
ITA

HAWORTH, Ann
Psychoanalytic Psychotherapist
Gifford Mount, East Downs Road,
Bowden, Nr. Altrincham, Cheshire
WA14 2LG
0161 928 7101
LPDO

HOBBES, Robin
Transactional Analysis Psychotherapist
Elan Training, 217 Ashley Road, Hale,
Altrincham, Cheshire WA15 9SZ
0161 928 9997/0161 929 6916 (f)
ITA

HOLYOAK, Patricia
Cognitive Behavioural Psychotherapist
8 Wicker Lane, Guilden Sutton,
Chester CH3 7EL
01244 300513
BABCP

HUMPHREYS, A-L.
Cognitive Behavioural Psychotherapist
Elmwood, Wirral & W.Cheshire
Comm. NHS Trust, Liverpool Road,
Chester CH2 1UL
Lifespan Therapy Consultants, The
Cottage, Little Lane, Parkgate, Wirral,
Cheshire L64 6DS
01244 364893/0410 414814
BABCP

HUNT, Patricia
Psychoanalytic Psychotherapist, Sexual
and Marital Psychotherapist
Rose Cottage, Foxwist Green,
Whitegate, nr. Northwich, Cheshire
CW8 2BJ
01606 882170
NWIDP, BASMT

ISAAC, Toni-Lee
Hypno-Psychotherapist
3 Victoria Dr, Sale Moor, Cheshire
M33 3HZ
0161 973 6357
CTS

JONES, Janet D.
Cognitive Behavioural Psychotherapist
Directorate of Clinical Psychology,
West Cheshire (NHS) Trust, Liverpool
Road, Chester CH2 1UL
01244 364046
BABCP

KILGOUR, Joyce
Systemic Psychotherapist, Family
Therapist
8 Moss Lane, Bramhall, Stockport
SK7 1EH
0161 440 0886/0161 439 7982
AFT

KIRK, Kate
Psychodrama Psychotherapist
222a Chester Road, Helsby, Frodsham,
Warrington WA6 0AW
01928 722918
BPA

LAWRENCE, E.
Sexual and Marital Psychotherapist
Hillcroft, Park Lane, Little Bollington,
Altrincham, Cheshire WA14 4TH
BASMT

LEE, Denis
Family Psychotherapist
CAMHS F Block, Macclesfield
DGH,East Cheshire, NHS Trust,
Victoria Road, Macclesfield SK10 3BL
01625 663770/01625 663772
AFT

LEWIS, Ken
Cognitive Behavioural Psychotherapist
7 Brown Heath Road, Waverton,
Chester CH3 7PP
Working Psychology, 91 Parkgate Road,
Chester CH1 4AQ
01244 336774
BABCP

LILLEY, Diana
Group Analyst
Thorn Lea House, 32 Grappenhall
Lane, Stockton Heath, Warrington
WA4 2AG
01925 268322
IGA

LITTLEWOOD, Ann
Psychodynamic Psychotherapist
69 Oldfield Road, Altrincham, Cheshire
WA14 4BH
0161 928 2792
HIP

LOVELL, Karina
Cognitive Behavioural Psychotherapist
22 Grangeway, Handforth, Cheshire
SK9 3HZ
01625 5408438
BABCP

MAHON, David
Hypno-Psychotherapist
7 Grammar School Road, Warrington,
Cheshire WA4 1JN
01925 635662
NRHP

MCBURNIE, Dolores
Psychosynthesis Psychotherapist
Moor House, Dig Lane, Frodsham,
Cheshire WA6 6VN
01928 731 406
AAPP

MCCORMICK, Helen
Psychoanalytic Psychotherapist
13 Lyceum Way, Coppenhall, Crewe, Cheshire CW1 3YF
01270 256397
WMIP

MCINTEE, Jeannie
Psychoanalytic Psychotherapist
Chester Therapy Centre, 20 Walpole Street, Chester CH1 4HE
01244 390121
LPDO

MCKAY, Molly
Cognitive Behavioural Psychotherapist
Dept. of Psychological Therapies, Warrington Community Health Care, Garven Place Clinic, Sankey St., Warrington WA1 1RH
01925 653295/01925 655221 x 3838
BABCP

NEILL, Denis E.
Family Therapist
17 Sunnybank, Holly Road South, Wilmslow, Cheshire SK9 1ND
01625 539707
AFT

NEVIN, Jaqui
Psychoanalytic Psychotherapist
Denton House, Denton Drive, Northwich, Cheshire CW9 7TU
01606 353800
LPDO

O'CARROLL, Pierce J.
Cognitive Behavioural Psychotherapist
University College Chester, Parkgate Road, Chester CH1 4BJ
0151 231 4233
BABCP

OATES, Stephanie
Transactional Analysis Psychotherapist
Swallowfield, Slade Lane, Mobberley WA16 7QN
ITA

PANTALL, Marlis
Integrative Psychotherapist
7 Balmoral Avenue, Cheadle Hulme, Cheadle, Cheshire SK8 5EG
0161 4855274
NSAP

POLLET, Sheena
Psychoanalytic Psychotherapist
Cherry Tree Farm, Kingswood, Nr. Frodsham, Cheshire WA6 6HX
01928 740296
LPDO

POLLITT, Mo
Cognitive Behavioural Psychotherapist
Lane End, 1 Lache Lane, Chester CH4 7LP
01244 681130
BABCP

READING, Clive
Cognitive Behavioural Psychotherapist
Dept of Clinical Psychology, Stepping Hill Hospital, Stockport, Cheshire SK2 7JE
0161 419 5755
BABCP

REDGRAVE, Kenneth
Hypno-Psychotherapist
11 Parker Avenue, Hartford, Northwich, Cheshire CW8 3AH
01606 74874
NRHP

ROFF, Hermione
Family Therapist
St George's Vicarage, 28 Buxton Road, Stockport SK2 6NU
0161 480 2453
AFT

SEXTON, Janette G.
Psychoanalytic Psychotherapist
West Cheshire N.H.S. Trust, West Cheshire Hospital, Liverpool Road, Chester
01244 365000
LPDO

SZABO, Heather
Psychoanalytic Psychotherapist
7 Water Tower Street, Chester CH1 2AE
01244 348183
LCP

THOBURN, Marjorie
Sexual and Marital Psychotherapist
White Gables, Vicarage Hill, Helsby, Cheshire WA6 9AD
01928 722304
BASMT

THOMAS, Sandra V.M.
Psychodynamic Psychotherapist
27 Heath Road, Stockport, Cheshire SK2 6JJ
Brookfield House, 193 Wellington, Road South, Stockport, Cheshire SK2 6NG
0161 429 6100/0161 419 9001
HIP

TUNWELL, Ann
Sexual and Marital Psychotherapist
Waulkmill Cottage, Ingersley Vale, Bollington, Macclesfield SK10 5BP
BASMT

WEBSTER, Lynne
Sexual and Marital Psychotherapist
77 Woodford Road, Bramhall, Stockport, Cheshire SK7 1JR
BASMT

WELLS, Peter G.
Psychodynamic Psychotherapist
High Trees, Dark Lane, Henbury, Macclesfield SK11 9PE
01625 420872
LPDO

WESTERN, Simon
Family Therapist
Field House, Shed Lane, Chester CH3 5NG
01244 342703
AFT

WHITTAM, Enid
Integrative Psychotherapist
1 Dorfold Way, Upton-on-Chester, Chester CH2 1QS
01244 380737
NSAP

WILDE, Verina
Cognitive Behavioural Psychotherapist
40 Little Aston Close, Macclesfield, Cheshire SK10 2UE
Psychology Department, District General Hospital, Victoria Road, Macclesfield SK10 3BL
01625 431 483
BABCP

WILSON, Mary
Cognitive Behavioural Psychotherapist
3 Back Jodrell Street, New Mills, Stockport, Cheshire SK12 3HL
01663 745219/0850 297276
BABCP

CLEVELAND

ANDREWS, Carol
Transactional Analysis Psychotherapist, Integrative Psychotherapist
100a The Grove, Marton, Middlesbrough, Cleveland TS1 8AN
SCPC

FIRTH, Sue
Psychoanalytic Psychotherapist
86 High Street, Great Broughton, Middlesbrough, Cleveland TS1 3BL
01642 247311
NAAP

HAVEMAN, Jolien
Cognitive Psychotherapist
Centre for Health & Medical Research, School of Health, University of Teesside, Borough Road TS1 3BA
01642 384124
BABCP

HELLER, Mary B.
Psychoanalytic Psychotherapist
Woodlands Road Clinic, Middlesbrough, Cleveland TS1 3BL
01642 247311
NAAP

HOMER, Marjorie
Transactional Analysis Psychotherapist, Integrative Psychotherapist
2 Hebron Road, Middlesbrough, Cleveland TS5 6RD
01642 814270
SCPC, ITA

LISTER-FORD, Christine
Transactional Analysis Psychotherapist, Integrative Psychotherapist
Stockton Centre for Psychotherapy and Counselling, 77 Acklam Road, Thornaby-on-Tees, Cleveland TS17 7BD
01642 649004/01642 649005 (f)
ITA, MET, SCPC

MCNAMARA, Jennifer
Integrative Psychotherapist, Transactional Analysis Psychotherapist
Stockton Centre for Psychotherapy and Counselling, 77 Acklam Road, Thornaby-on-Tees, Cleveland TS17 7BD
01642 649004/01642 649005 (f)
ITA, SCPC

MIDGLEY, David
Transactional Analysis Psychotherapist
13 Barker Road, Linthorpe, Middlesbrough, Cleveland TS5 5EW
01642 821254
ITA

RICHARDSON, Sue
Attachment-based Psychoanalytic Psychotherapist
22 Queens Road, Middlesbrough, Cleveland TS5 6EE
01642 817658
CAPP

STRANG, Susi
NLP Psychotherapist
Sun Dial House, 29 High Street, Skelton, Saltburn by the Sea, Cleveland TS12 2EF
01287 654175/0831 224901
ANLP

SZARY, Gerard
NLP Psychotherapist
98 Oxbridge Lane, Stockton on Tees, Cleveland TS18 4HW
01642 678 653
ANLP

THACKER, Rose
Transactional Analysis Psychotherapist, Integrative Psychotherapist
13 Ruskin Avenue, Saltburn, Cleveland TS12 1QB
01287 622947
SCPC, ITA

WILLIAMS, Steve
Cognitive Psychotherapist
The Spinney, Hutton Village, Guisborough, Cleveland TS14 8EP
The Garth Surgery, Westgate, Guisborough, North Yorkshire TS14 6AT
01287 637416/01287 632206
BABCP

CORNWALL

BURROWS, Brian
Transpersonal Psychotherapist
Penzance, Cornwall
01736 788454
CCPE

COOMBS, Suzanne
Psychoanalytic Psychotherapist
'Garth', Steeple Lane, Trelyon Downs, Cornwall TR26 2AP
01736 7950
GUILD

CRAMER, William
Psychodrama Psychotherapist
Trevillick Cottage, Trevillick, Tintagel, Cornwall PL34 0DN
01840 770691
BPA

DUHIG, Mary
Psychoanalytic Psychotherapist
1 Tregarland Close, Beacon, Camborne, Cornwall TR14 7BJ
01209 714012
PA

EDWARDS, Michael P
Analytical Psychologist-Jungian Analyst
93 Marlborough Road, Falmouth, Cornwall TR11 3LR
0374 761 973/01326 211536
IGAP

FOWLES, Anne
Transpersonal Psychotherapist
Rainbow's End, 22 York Street, Penzance, Cornwall TR18 2PW
01736 363114
CTP

FRANSELLA, Fay
Personal Construct Psychotherapist
The Sail Loft, Mulberry Quay, Market Strand, Falmouth, Cornwall TR11 3HD
01326 314 871/01326 212 085
CPCP

FRENCH, Jean
Transactional Analysis Psychotherapist
The 12 Steps, Trenance, Mawgan Porth, Nr. Newquay, Cornwall TR8 4BX
ITA

GIMBLETT, Jeanne
Cognitive Behavioural Psychotherapist
Highland Cottage, St. Breward, Bodmin, Cornwall PL30 4NU
01208 850597
BABCP

GREEN, Marion
Gestalt Psychotherapist
2 Gibbons Field, Mullion, Helston, Conwall TR13 3EA
SPTI

GRIGG, Roz
Core Process Psychotherapist
10 North Hill Park, St. Austell, Cornwall PL25 4BJ
01726 61675
AAPP

HAYWARD, Mark
Family Therapist
Little Clicker, Hornington Tops,
Liskeard, Cornwall PL14 3QA
0172 272360/0175 272328
AFT

HODD, Amanda
Family Therapist
Child & Family Centre, Royal Cornwall
Hospital, Treliske, Penventinnie,
Cornwall TR2 4DH
01872 354377/01872 354350
AFT

HUDSON, Peter
Family Therapist
1 Lanhydrock Villas, Kenwyn Road,
Truro, Cornwall TR1 3LQ
01872 354 379/01872 354 350
AFT

KEMP, Paul David
Cognitive Behavioural Psychotherapist
Trevillis House, Lodge Hill, Liskeard,
Cornwall PL14 4EN
01579 343097
BABCP

KING, Michael
Family Therapist
8 Amble Road, Callington, Cornwall
PL17 7QE
01579 382216
AFT

MORRIS, David
Cognitive Behavioural Psychotherapist
The Old Parsonage, 58 Church Street,
Mevagissey, St Austell PL26 6SR
07771 983159/01726 844818(t/f)
BABCP

PAYNE, John
Psychoanalytic Psychotherapist
Greenscombe House, Luckett,
Callington, Cornwall PL17 8LF
01579 370149
GUILD

RETALLICK, Malcolm
Gestalt Psychotherapist
48 Molesworth Street, Wadebridge,
Cornwall PL27 7DP
01208 812048
GPTI, MET

SEVER, Michael
Hypno-Psychotherapist
'Veritas', 25 Polwithen Drive, Carbis
Bay, St. Ives, Cornwall TR26 2SP
01736 798399
NRHP

SIMPSON, Kevin J.
Psychoanalytic Psychotherapist
2 Broad Park, St Keyne, Liskeard,
Cornwall PL14 4RH
01579 345285
LPDO

THORNTON, Andy S.
Cognitive Behavioural Psychotherapist
Trengweath, Penryn Street, Redruth,
Cornwall TR15 2SP
01209 219232
BABCP

TREWHELLA, John
Hypno-Psychotherapist
Castle Gayer, Leys Lane, Marazion,
Cornwall TR17 0AQ
01736 711548/01736 711110 (f)
NRHP

WILSON, Gillian
Child Psychotherapist
Elderbush Cottage, Longstone, St.
Mabyn, Bodmin, Cornwall PL30 3BY
01208 841439
ACP

COUNTY DURHAM

ALLINSON, Mary A.
Cognitive Behavioural Psychotherapist
Teesdale Community Health Services,
Victoria Road, Barnard Castle, Co.
Durham DL12 8HT
6 Cardinal Gardens, Darlington,
Co.Durham DL3 8SD
01833 637795
BABCP

BIRCHMORE, Terry
Group Analyst
3 Moor end, Belmont, Durham
DH1 1BJ
0191 333 3866
IGA

CATERSBY, Cynthia
Integrative Psychotherapist
Badgers Green, West End, Sedgefield,
Co Durham TS21 2BS
01740 620440
SPTI

CLARKE, Stephen Lawrence
Cognitive Behavioural Psychotherapist
The Derwent Clinics, Bede House,
Shotley Bridge Hospital, Consett, Co.
Durham DH8 0NB
01207 583583 x 4660/4069
BABCP

COOPER, Margaret
Psychoanalytic Psychotherapist
2 Manor Close, Shincliffe Village,
County Durham DH1 2NS
0191 386 5818
NAAP

DRAPER, Pim
Cognitive Behavioural Psychotherapist
Department of Psychology, Darlington
Memorial Hospital, Hollyhurst Road,
Darlington DL3 6HX
01325 352515
BABCP

GILBERT, Barbara
Psychoanalytic Psychotherapist
68 Gurney Valley, Bishop Auckland, Co.
Durham DL14 8RW
01388 604418
NAAP

HURREN, Karolyn
Psychoanalytic Psychotherapist
Bede House, Shotley Bridge General
Hosptial, Consett DH8 0NB
01207 503456 x 651
NAAP

JOHNSON, Janette
Transactional Analysis Psychotherapist,
Integrative Psychotherapist
3 Bluecoat Buildings, Claypath, Durham
DH1 1RF
18 Church Street, Durham DH1 3DQ
0191 386 6144/0191 386 2540
SCPC, ITA

LEMON, Marcia
Psychosynthesis Psychotherapist
47 Hawthorn Terrace, Durham
DH1 4EL
0191 384 5526/0191 477 1011
AAPP

LOISEAU, Kate
Integrative Psychotherapist
Cholet Cottage, Killerby, Darlington
DL2 2UQ
01325 374606
SPTI

LOUDON, Julia
Sexual and Marital Psychotherapist
Department of Clinical Psychology, The Memorial Hospital, Hollyhurst Road, Darlington, Co Durham DL3 6HX
BASMT

MILES, Carolyn
Psychoanalytic Psychotherapist
University Health Services, 42 Old Elvet, Durham DH1 3JF
NAAP

STANBURY, Christine
Psychoanalytic Psychotherapist
Derwent Clinic, Shortley Bridge
Consett, Durham DH8 0NB
01207 586 049
NAAP

WATSON, Pauline
Psychoanalytic Psychotherapist
Shotley Bridge Hospital, Shotley Bridge, Consett, Co.Durham
NAAP

CUMBRIA

APPLEGARTH, Janet
Psychoanalytic Psychotherapist
2 Tallows Whins, Lazonby, Penrith
CA10 1AR
01768 898390
LPDO

BAYNES, Monica
Psychoanalytic Psychotherapist
5 Stainbank Green, Brigsteer Road, Kendal, Cumbria LA9 5RP
01539 740605
LPDO

BURGESS, Alison
Family Therapist
Child & Fam.Con. Unit, Workington Infirmary, Infirmary Road, Workington,Cumbria CA14 2UN
01900 6022440
AFT

COLE, Shanti
Hypno-Psychotherapist
'Four Winds', Church Hill, Arnside, Cumbria LA5 0DQ
01524 762524
NSHAP

CONROY, Beth
Psychosynthesis Psychotherapist
Fern Cottage, 7 Causeway End, Levens, Nr. Kendal, Cumbria LA8 8PW
01539 60188
IPS

COOK, Jane
Integrative Psychotherapist
Castle Gate Barn, Castle Carrock, Near Carlisle, Cumbria CA4 9LT
01228 70646
MC

COX, Mary
Transactional Analysis Psychotherapist
Cambrai House, Calderbridge, Seascale, Cumbria CA20 1DH
01946 841110 (f)/01946 841239
ITA

FORSYTH, Angus
Cognitive Behavioural Psychotherapist
104 Greenacres, Wetheral, Carlisle, Cumbria CA4 8LD
01228 561786
BABCP

HEATH, John
Transactional Analysis Psychotherapist
76 Captain French Lane, Kendal, Cumbria LA9 4HX
01539 723356
ITA

KELLY, Gillian
Gestalt Psychotherapist, Body Psychotherapist
Dillygarth, Loughrigg, Ambleside, Cumbria LA22 9HF
01539 433903
CCBP

KENNY, Peter
Psychoanalytic Psychotherapist
26 Spital Park, Kendal, Cumbria LA9 6HG
WMIP

LONGFORD, Joan
Psychoanalytic Psychotherapist
6 High Bank Close, Carlisle, Cumbria
NAAP

MACDONALD, Alasdair
Family Therapist
8 Wellgate Close, Scotby, Carlisle CA4 8BA
01228 602468/01228 513005
AFT

MCQUILLIN, Jane
Transactional Analysis Psychotherapist
31 Prince's Street, Ulverston, Cumbria LA12 7NQ
01229 588404 (t/f)
ITA

NEWSON, John
Analytical Psychologist-Jungian Analyst
Hebblethwaite Hall, Cautley, Sedbergh, Cumbria LA10 5LX
01539 621307
AJA

TOD, Ian
Psychoanalytic Psychotherapist
The Brough Medical Centre, Brough, Nr. Kirby Stephen, Cumbria CA17 4AY
NAAP

WHITLEY, Liz
Transactional Analysis Psychotherapist
38 Brunswick Square, Penrith, Cumbria CA11 7LS
76 Captain French Lane, Kendal, Cumbria LA9 4HX
01539 723356/01768 899941
ITA

DERBYSHIRE

BENNISON, Judy
Psychodynamic Psychotherapist
Moorland View Farm, Commonside Road, Barlow, Derbyshire S18 5SJ
Psychotherapy Centre, 13 Rustlings Road, Sheffield S11 7AA
0114 266 3910/0114 289 0898
HIP

BERRY, Juliet
Psychodynamic Psychotherapist
Cobb Barn, Smalldale, Bradwell, Derbyshire S30 2JQ
001433 620618
HIP

DANIELS, Frank
NLP Psychotherapist
103 Hands Road, Heanor, Derbyshire, DE75 7HB
01773 532195
ANLP

DENNESS, Brian
Psychoanalytic Psychotherapist
Department of Psychotherapy (NHS), Temple House, Mill Hill Lane, Derby DE3 6SA
01332 364512
STTDP

EVANS, G.E.
Sexual and Marital Psychotherapist
34 Hockley Lane, Wingerworth, Chesterfield S42 6QG
BASMT

FITZGERALD, Patricia
Integrative Psychotherapist
61 Hollywood Avenue, Littleover, Derby DE23 6JD
SPTI

FOX, Hugh
Family Therapist
15 Quarry Lane, Matlock, Derbyshire DE4 5LG
01629 56431
AFT

HORTON, Barbara
Sexual and Marital Psychotherapist
Everglades, Willington Road, Findon, Derby DE65 6AS
01283 702298
BASMT

HOWELL, Hilary
Systemic Psychotherapist
Psychology Department, Kingsway Hospital, Kingsway, Derby DE22 3LZ
01332 624592/01332 624594(f)
FIC

JOHNSON, Michael
NLP Psychotherapist
5 Glenthorne Close, Chesterfield, Derbyshire S40 3AR
01246 273002
ANLP

JONES, Sue
Integrative Psychotherapist
9 Hob Hill Meadows, Hague Street, Glossop, Derbyshire SK13 8LW
01457 858045
MET

JORDAN, Karen
Gestalt Psychotherapist
17 Vernon Street, Derby DE1 1FT
SPTI

LEAKEY, Peter
NLP Psychotherapist
Clinical Psychology Department, Walton Hospital, 82 Whitecoates Lane, Chesterfield S40 3HW
01246 277 100(f)/01246 552871
ANLP

MANSALL, Cordelia
Integrative Psychotherapist
30 Toadmoor Lane, Ambergate, Derbyshire DE55 2GN
01773 8539168
RCSPC

MUSCHAMP, Maureen
Transpersonal Psychotherapist
Hillcroft, 37 Summer Lane, Wirksworth, Derby DE4 4EB
01629 823146
CTP

OVERS, Nicola
Personal Construct Psychotherapist
The Cottage, Longnor Nr Buxton, Derbyshire SK17 0LA
01298 83806
CPCP

PARKINSON, Jillian
Transactional Analysis Psychotherapist
19 Chapel Street, Measham, Derbyshire DE12 7JD
01530 272772
ITA

PROCTER, Sue
Cognitive Psychotherapist
Shirley Centre, 16A South Street, Derby DE1 1DS
34 Coronation Avenue, Alvaston, Derby DE24 0LQ
01332 292160/01332 571765
BABCP

ROBINSON, Gary
Systemic Psychotherapist
2 Foxcroft, Sunny Bank, Tibshelf, Derbyshire DE55 5QR
01332 365221
FIC

SCHRÖDER, Thomas
Psychoanalytic Psychotherapist
Derby Dept. of Psychotherapy (NHS), Temple House, Mill Hill Lane, Derby DE23 6SA
01332 364 512
STTDP

SERIEYS, Nicholas Michael
Cognitive Behavioural Psychotherapist
14 Balmoral Close, Littleover, Derby DE23 6DY
01332 606808/0973 520550
BABCP

SHAW, Robert
Integrative Psychotherapist
41 St. John Street, Ashbourne, Derby DE6 1GP
Derven House, 32 Friar Gate, Derby DE1 1BZ
01335 300440/01332 371184
SPTI

SMITH, David
Psychoanalytic Psychotherapist
Derby Dept. of Psychotherapy (NHS), Temple House, Mill Hill Lane, Derby DE23 6SA
01332 364512
STTDP

SMITH, Janet M.
Psychoanalytic Psychotherapist
Dept. of Psychotherapy, Temple House, Mill Hill Lane, Derby DE23 6SA
01332 364512
NWIDP

TAYLOR, Jon
Cognitive Behavioural Psychotherapist
55 Church Street, Littleover, Derby, DE23 6GF
01332 272434/01283 505330
BABCP

VIPAN, Sheila
Psychodynamic Psychotherapist
Echo Gate, Foolow Road, Eyam, Hope Valley, S32 5QS
01433 630 940
HIP

WALSH, Belinda
Cognitive Behavioural Psychotherapist
Clinical Psychology Department, Walton Hospital, Whitecotes Lane, Chesterfield S40 3HN
01246 277271 x 5520
BABCP

WATSON, Clare
Psychoanalytic Psychotherapist
Derby Department of Psychotherapy (NHS), Temple House, Mill Hill Lane, Derby DE3 6SA
01332 364512
STTDP

DEVON

ADEY, John
Integrative Psychotherapist
Woodlands, Christow, Exeter, Devon EX6 7PJ
01647 252684/01392 403446
RCSPC

DEVON

ANJALI, Yon
Core Process Psychotherapist
53 Penys Road, Totnes, S Devon
TQ9 5TL
01803 862 543
AAPP

ARMBRUSTER, P.K.
Child Psychotherapist
Young Peoples' Centre, Mount Gould
Hospital, Plymouth, Devon PL4 7QD
01752 272320/01822 840162
ACP

BADENOCH, Marion
Psychosynthesis Psychotherapist
Flat 2, 1 Dart Villas, Totnes, Devon
TQ9 5ET
01803 864 509
AAPP

BENNUN, Ian
Family Therapist
Department of Psychology, Newton
Abbot Hospital, East Street, Newton
Abbot, Devon TQ12 4PT
01626 54321/01626 332105
AFT

BIRCH, Cathy
Transpersonal Psychotherapist
Higher Trickeys Cottage, Morebath,
Tiverton, Devon EX16 9AL
01398 331023
CTP

BOOTH, Nick
Family Therapist
Exeter & District Community Health
Service, Dept. of Psychology, Church
Lane, Heavitree, Exeter EX2 5SH
01392 403170
AFT

BOSTON, Mary
Child Psychotherapist
Marina, Golf Links Road, Westward
Ho, Bideford, Devon EX39 1HH
01237 470424
ACP

BROUGH, Julie
Family Therapist
77 Mill Street, Torrington, Devon
EX38 8AN
01805 624048
AFT

BUCKLAND, Richard
Child Psychotherapist
Burraton House, Ermington, Ivybridge,
South Devon PL21 9LA
01752 272360/01752 881260
ACP

CALLAWAY, Hazel
Attachment-based Psychoanalytic
Psychotherapist
8 Victoria Avenue, Millbridge, Plymouth
PL1 5NH
01752 509535
CAPP, WTC

CAMPBELL, Margaret
Core Process Psychotherapist
1 Kiln Cottages, Broadhempston,
Totnes, Devon TQ9 6BT
01803 813144
AAPP

CAMPBELL-BEATTIE, John
Hypno-Psychotherapist
Rosemary Hill, 64A Underlane,
Plymstock, Plymouth PL9 9JZ
01752 484265
NRHP

CASSIDY, Anita
Psychoanalytic Psychotherapist
5 Putsborough Close, Braunton, Devon
EX32 1JX
01271 890 615
NAFSI

DAVID, Ann
Integrative Psychotherapist,
Transactional Analysis Psychotherapist
Maryknowle, Malborough, Kingsbridge,
Devon TQ7 3DB
01548 842159 (t/f)
ITA, MET

DAVID, Julian
Analytical Psychologist-Jungian Analyst
Luscombe Farm, Buckfast Leigh, Devon
TQ11 0LP
01364 642373
IGAP

DAWSON, Jenny
Gestalt Psychotherapist
36 Raleigh Road, Exmouth, Devon
EX8 2SB
01395 269076/01395 223231 (f)
GPTI

DYEHOUSE, Pat
Psychoanalytic Psychotherapist
Hazel Tor Barn, Lower Soar, Soar Mill
Cove, Malborough, Kingsbridge, Devon
TQ7 3DS
01548 561450
ARBS

DYMOND, Christina
Core Process Psychotherapist
Maybelle Cottage, Sandford, Crediton,
Devon EX17 4LR
01363 775138
AAPP

ETHERINGTON, Mary
Transactional Analysis Psychotherapist
42 Oak Drive, Oak Park, Cullompton,
Devon EX15 1NW
ITA

FERRIS, Mary
Core Process Psychotherapist
27 Lawn Vista, Sidmouth, Devon
EX10 9BY
01395 577588
AAPP

FISH, Sue
Integrative Psychotherapist,
Transactional Analysis Psychotherapist
'Maryknowle', Malborough, Nr.
Kingsbridge, Devon TQ7 3DB
01548 842159
GPTI, MET, ITA

GEDDES, Heather
Educational Therapist
Alfington House, Church Lane,
Alfington, East Devon EX11 1PE
01404 850329
FAETT

GOLZ, Angelika
Humanistic Psychotherapist
Flat 1, 19 Bridgetown, Totnes, Devon
TQ9 5BA
01803 867413
AHPP

HACKETT, Jenny
Humanistic and Integrative
Psychotherapist
Hillcross, Stockland, Honiton, Devon
EX14 9DA
01404 881565
BCPC

HALLEN, Gervaise
Core Process Psychotherapist
11 Butterdon Walk, Ivybridge, Devon
PL21 0HS
01752 896154
AAPP

HENSHAW, Judith
Transactional Analysis Psychotherapist
'Ollivers', Halsfordwood Lane,
Nadderwater, Nr. Exeter EX4 2LD
ITA

HEWSON, Julie Ann
Transactional Analysis Psychotherapist
Iron Mill, Oakford, Tiverton, Devon
EX16 9EN
01398 351379
ITA

HOARE, Ian
Humanistic and Integrative
Psychotherapist
36 Raleigh Road, Exmouth, Devon
EX8 2SB
01395 269076
BCPC

HODGES, Barbara
Psychodrama Psychotherapist
Seymour House, 62 Lipson Road,
Plymouth, Devon PL4 8RH
Student Services, 40 Portland Square,
University of Plymouth, Drake Circus,
Plymouth
01752 232254/01752 661730
BPA

HOLMES, Jeremy
Psychoanalytic Psychotherapist
The Old Rectory, Stoke Rivers,
Barnstaple EX32 7LB
01271 322666/01598 710291
SIP

HORTON, Annie
Transactional Analysis Psychotherapist
28 Halyards, Ferry Road, Topsham,
Exeter, Devon EX3 0JU
ITA

JENKINS, Dinah
Cognitive Behavioural Psychotherapist
Occupational Health & Safety Unit,
Derriford Hospital, Plymouth, Devon
PL6 8DH
01503 262067/01752 763586
BABCP

JONES, Nicole
Psychoanalytic Psychotherapist
57 Thornton Hill, Exeter, Devon
01392 254408
SIP

KALISCH, David
Core Process Psychotherapist,
Humanistic Psychotherapist
'Warrencroft' 56 East Budleigh Road,
Budleigh Salterton, Devon EX9 6EJ
01395 446307
AAPP, AHPP

KARP, Marcia
Psychodrama Psychotherapist
Holwell International Centre for
Psychodrama, North Walk, Lyton,
N.Devon EX35 6HJ
01271 850267/01271 850863 (f)
BPA

KERRIDGE, Petra
Psychosynthesis Psychotherapist
Riverside Barn, Woodcourt Road,
Harbertonford, Totnes, Devon
TQ9 7TY
01803 732604
AAPP

KIRBY, Alan
Humanistic Psychotherapist
Little Pomeroy, Somerset Place,
Bridgetown, Totnes, Devon TQ9 5AX
01803 866922
AHPP

LANGLEY, Dorothy
Psychodrama Psychotherapist
Hanningfields, Warborough Hill,
Kenton, Exeter, Devon EX6 8LR
01626 890433
BPA

LEWIS, Philip J.
NLP Psychotherapist
33 Northfield Road, Okehampton,
Devon EX20 1BB
01837 54061
ANLP

LINNELL, Maxine
Core Process Psychotherapist
6 Pengilly Way, Hartland, Nr. Bideford,
Devon EX39 6HR
01237 441691
AAPP

LLEWELLYN, Alice
NLP Psychotherapist
Bay Villa, Plymouth Road, Totnes,
Devon TQ9 5PQ
01803 866706
ANLP

LOXTERKAMP, Lorne
Child Psychotherapist
Family Consultancy, Health Centre,
Vicarage Street, Barnstaple, North
Devon EX32 7BT
01271 71761/01271 814901
ACP

LUCE, Peter James
Hypno-Psychotherapist
13 Littleton Place, Stoke, Plymouth,
Devon PL2 1DY
01752 563703
NRHP

MALONEY, Sean
Core Process Psychotherapist
1 Orchard Terrace, Tuckenham, Totnes,
Devon TQ9 7EJ
01803 732 264
AAPP

MCCONVILLE, Lily
Psychoanalytic Psychotherapist
9 Woodside, Greenbank, Plymouth
PL4 8QE
01752 664222
LCP

MCGOURAN, Gill
Transpersonal Psychotherapist
South West Counselling Centre, 45
New Street, The Barbican, Plymouth
PL1 2ND
01752 250621
CTP

MERRIOT, Peter
Transpersonal Psychotherapist
58 Church Road, Wembury, Devon
PL9 0JG
01752 862224
CTP

MILLS, Judith
NLP Psychotherapist
Higher Thatch, Ebford Lane, Ebford,
Exeter, Devon EX3 0QX
01392 873984
ANLP

MOORE, Jill
Sexual and Marital Psychotherapist
3 Marlow Close, Shiphay, Torquay, Devon TQ2 6DQ
01803 614644
BASMT

NICHOLSON, Elizabeth
Psychoanalytic Psychotherapist
White Oaks, 18 St. Brannocks Park Road, Ilfracombe, Devon EX34 8HX
01271 864003
GUILD

NIGHTINGALE, Eileen
Psychosynthesis Psychotherapist
Blackmore House, May Terrace, Sidmouth, Devon EX10 8EN
01395 513923
AAPP

NOACK, Miké
Individual and Group Humanistic Psychotherapist
The Maisonette, 50A Fore Street, Totnes, Devon TQ9 5RP
01803 862805
AHPP

NORTH, Joanna
Core Process Psychotherapist
16 Granary Lane, Budleigh Salterton, Devon EX9 6JD
01395 225 315
AAPP

O'REILLY, Paul
Family Therapist
Dept. of Clinical and Community Psychology, Church Lane, Heavitree, Exeter EX2 5SH
01392 403186/01392 403189
AFT

OLDFIELD, Nina
Integrative Psychotherapist
3 Bolberry Court, Malborough, Kingsbridge TQ7 3DY
07050 043081/01548 561013 (t/f)
RCSPC

OPENSHAW, Sally
Sexual and Marital Psychotherapist
North Down House, North Down Road, Bideford, North Devon EX39 3LT
01237 476757
BASMT

PEHRSSON-TATHAM, Lena
Psychoanalytic Psychotherapist
Maynards, Cornworthy, Totnes, South Devon TQ9 7HB
01803 864466/01803 732733
SIP

ROBERTSON, Zuleika
Psychoanalytic Psychotherapist
6 Prospect Park, off Old Tiverton Road, Exeter, Devon EX4 6NA
013924 30162
GUILD

RODDICK, Mary
Family Therapist
Coombe Farm, Christow, Exeter EX6 7NR
01647 252553
AFT

ROTAS, Joanna
Core Process Psychotherapist
3 Western Villas, Collins Road, Totnes, Devon TQ9 5PW
01803 864990
AAPP

SARRA, Nicholas
Group Analyst
Nibbscott, Washfield, Tiverton Devon EX16 9QY
0131 447 6038/01884 256 349
IGA

SCHNEIDER, Caroline
Family Therapist
Dept. of Child and Adolescent Mental Health, Erme House, Mount Gould Hospital, Mount Gould Rd., Plymouth
01752 272316
AFT

SCOTT HAYWARD, Anna
NLP Psychotherapist
16 Brunswick Terrace, Torquay, Devon TQ1 4AE
01803 323885
ANLP

SEYMOUR CLARK, Vivienne
Psychoanalytic Psychotherapist
25 Brooklands, Bridgetown, Totnes, Devon TQ9 5AR
01803 864976
CSP

SHELDON, Brian
Cognitive Behavioural Psychotherapist
Centre for Evidence Based Soc Serv, Amory Building, University of Exeter, Exeter EX4 4RJ
01392 263323/01392 263229
BABCP

SIERODA, Helen
Psychosynthesis Psychotherapist
Eaglehurst, Mill Street, Chagford, Devon TQ13 8AR
AAPP

SILLS, Franklyn
Core Process Psychotherapist
Natsworthy Manor, Widecombe-in-the-Moor, Newton Abbot, Devon TQ13 7TR
01647 221 457
AAPP

SILLS, Maura
Core Process Psychotherapist
Natsworthy Manor, Widecombe-in-the-Moor, Newton Abbot, Devon TQ13 7TR
01647 221 457
AAPP

SKEET, Maggie
Gestalt Psychotherapist
6 Matford Mews, Matford, Exeter EX2 8XP
01392 218783
GPTI

SPRAGUE, Ken
Psychodrama Psychotherapist
Hoelwell Centre, North Walk, Lynton, North Devon EX35 6HJ
01271 850267/01271 850863 (f)
BPA

SPURGEON, Richard
Psychosynthesis Psychotherapist
Flat 2, 1 Dart Villas, Totnes, Devon TQ9 5ET
01803 864 509
AAPP

STEWART, Lindsey
Humanistic Psychotherapist
Burnside, Avonwick, South Brent, Devon TQ10 9EZ
01364 73201
AHPP

SWALLOW, Joan
Transpersonal Psychotherapist,
Integrative Psychotherapist
Bridge House, Culmstock, Collumpton,
Devon EX15 3JJ
01884 840513/01884 840862 (f)
CTP

SWALLOW, Reynold
Transpersonal Psychotherapist
Bridge House, Culmstock, Collumpton,
Devon EX15 3JJ
01884 840513/01884 840862 (f)
CTP

TATHAM, Peter
Psychoanalytic Psychotherapist,
Analytical Psychologist-Jungian Analyst
Maynards, Cornworthy, Totnes, South
Devon TQ9 7HB
01803 732733
IGAP, SIP

TAYLOR, Crispin
Family Therapist
23 South Avenue, Heavitree, Exeter
EX1 2DZ
01392 276348/01392 219894
AFT

TAYLOR, Helen
Personal Construct Psychotherapist
56 Camperdown Terrace, Exmouth,
Devon EX8 1EQ
01395 267615
CPCP

THOMAS, Alyss
Core Process Psychotherapist
River Cottage, Bow Road,
Harbertonford, Totnes, Devon
TQ9 7TJ
01803 732 751
AAPP

THOMPSON, Joy
Group Analyst
The Palace, Exeter, Devon EX1 1HY
01392 72362
IGA

TILLEY, Alison
Gestalt Psychotherapist
1 Railway Cotts, Lapford, Nr Crediton,
Devon EX17 6QU
SPTI

URRY, Amy
Family Therapist
30 Normandy Road, Exeter, Devon
EX1 2SR
01392 210456
AFT

WARD, Barbara
Psychosynthesis Psychotherapist
3 Wheelwright Court, Walkhampton,
Yelverton, Devon PL20 6LA
01822 855 619
AAPP

WARIN, Judy
Cognitive Analytic Therapist
Psychotherapy Department, Wonford
House Hospital, Dryden Road, Exeter
EX2 5AF
01392 403446/01392 403422
ACAT

WATSON, Gay
Core Process Psychotherapist
Coombery, Tuckenhay, Totnes, Devon
TQ9 7EP
01803 732 272
AAPP

WEBBER, Wendy
Core Process Psychotherapist
Cutteridge Farm, Whitestone, Exeter,
Devon EX4 2HE
01392 811203
AAPP

WEIR, Felicity
Child Psychotherapist
The Day Unit, Child & Family
Consultation Service, 187 Newton
Road, Torquay, Devon TQ2 7AJ
01803 615980 (t/f)
ACP

WHEADON, Sylvia
Psychodrama Psychotherapist
Littlecroft, 16 Clampitt Road, Ipplepen,
Newton Abbot, Devon TQ12 5TE
01803 813443
BPA

WILLOW, Angela
Core Process Psychotherapist
1 Orchard Terrace, Tuckenhay, Totnes,
South Devon TQ9 7EJ
01803 732264
AAPP

WILSON, Jancis
Core Process Psychotherapist
Church Close, Throwleigh EX20 2HX
01647 231 264
AAPP

WILSON, Michael
Psychoanalytic Psychotherapist
Church Cottage, Hawkchurch
Axminster, Devon EX13 5XD
01297 6783755
GUILD

WOODING, Sandra
Psychodrama Psychotherapist
Lower Cator Farmhouse, Lower Cator,
Widecombe-in-the-Moor, Devon
TQ13 7TX
01364 621239
BPA

WRIGHT, Maureen
Psychodrama Psychotherapist
Thornlea, Town Lane, Woodbury, Nr.
Exeter, Devon EX4 1NB
01395 232001
BPA

YELDHAM, Denise
Psychoanalytic Psychotherapist
Liesse, Grange Road, Buckfast, South
Devon TQ11 0EH
01364 642189
BAP

DORSET

BENNETT, Gerald A.
Cognitive Behavioural Psychotherapist
Community Drug Team, Park Lodge,
Gloucester Road, Bournemouth,
Dorset BH7 6JF
01202 397003
BABCP

BOTTERILL, Willie
Personal Construct Psychotherapist
Northleigh House, Northleigh Lane,
Colehill, Wimbourne, Dorset
0171 278 59045
CPCP

BRAY, Stephen
NLP Psychotherapist
Roughwood, Letton Park, Blandford
Forum, Dorset DT11 7EG
01258 458889 (t/f)
ANLP

DORSET

CLARKE, Susan Elizabeth
Cognitive Psychotherapist, Cognitive Analytic Therapist
DOPTAC, St Ann's Court, St Ann's Hospital, Canford Cliffs, BH13 7LN
01202 706562 (f)/01202 492129
BABCP, ACAT

DENNIS, Stephen
Transactional Analysis Psychotherapist
Flat 6,Kings Court, Quarr Drive, Sherbourne, Dorset DT9 4HZ
ITA

FINCH, Auberon
Core Process Psychotherapist
29 South Walks Road, Fordington, Dorchester, Dorset DT1 1ED
01305 267428/01305 761100
AAPP

GESSERT, Astrid
Psychoanalytic Psychotherapist
c/o Winterbourne Hospital, Herringston Road, Dorchester, Dorset DT1 2DR
3 Hall View Cottages, Lower Sea Lane, Charmouth, Dorset DT6 6LJ
01305 263252/01297 560397
CFAR

HARRIS, Neil
Gestalt Psychotherapist
Roundhay, Chapel Lane, Bransgore, Dorset BH23 8BN
01425 673395
GPTI

JELFS, Martin
Humanistic and Integrative Psychotherapist
65 North Street, Wareham, Dorset BH20 4AD
14 Chesterton Road, London E13 8BA
0973 504121/01929 556563
AHPP

KELLY, Philip
Cognitive Behavioural Psychotherapist
25 Granville Road, Weymouth, Dorset DT4 0BQ
01305 786905/01305 779027
BABCP

LACY-SMITH, Jo
Humanistic and Integrative Psychotherapist
2 Ackerman Road, Dorchester, Dorset DT1 1NZ
01305 266721
BCPC

LILLITOS, Aleathea G.
Child Psychotherapist
60 Dorchester Road, Maiden Newton, Dorset DT2 0BE
01300 321 349
ACP

LOGUE, Nancy
Sexual and Marital Psychotherapist
Halves House, 132 East Street, Corfe Castle, Dorset BH20 5EH
01929 481163
BASMT

LONG, Jennifer
Cognitive Behavioural Psychotherapist
Dept. of Psychological Therapies, 16-18 Tower Road, Boscombe, Bournemouth, Dorset BH1 4LB
01202 304634
BABCP

MARCH-SMITH, Rosie
Humanistic and Integrative Psychotherapist
Ellerslie, Cattistock, Dorchester, Dorset DT2 0JL
01300 321355
AHPP, BCPC

NEWBERY, Christopher
Humanistic and Integrative Psychotherapist
12 St. George's Avenue, Weymouth, Dorset DT4 7TU
01305 786172
BCPC, AHPP

OSTLER, Dorothy
Systemic Psychotherapist
White Lodge, 255 Sandbanks Road, Lilliput, Poole, Dorset BH14 8EY
FIC

PHILLIPS, Laurie
Psychoanalytic Psychotherapist
11 Viking Way, Mudeford, Christchurch, Dorset BH23 4AQ
01425 276417/01425 276278 (f)
AGIP

RICKETTS, Susan
Child Psychotherapist
Child, Adolescent & Family Mental Health Service, Poole General Hospital, Longfleet Road, Poole, Dorset BH15 2JB
01703 284 352/01202 442 741
ACP

ROBINSON, Martin
Analytical Psychologist-Jungian Analyst, Psychoanalytic Psychotherapist
White Hill Farmhouse, Stoke Wake, Nr. Blandford Forum, Dorset DT11 0HF
Studio E, 49 The Avenue, London NW6
0181 459 5442/01258 817301
AJA, SIP

ROSE, Stuart
Cognitive Behavioural Psychotherapist
Highfield, Lee Lane, Bridport, Dorset DT6 4AJ
31 Community Road, Greenford, Middlesex UB6 8XF
01308 458600
BABCP

RUBIE, Val
Attachment-based Psychoanalytic Psychotherapist
5 Partway Lane, Hazelbury Bryan, Sturminster Newton, Dorset DT10 2DP
01258 817496
CAPP

SEPPING, Paul
Group Analyst
4 Seacombe Road, Sandbanks, Poole, Dorset BH13 7RJ
01202 442 029
IGA

SONES, Joanne
Child Psychotherapist
West Dorset Childrens' Centre, Damers Road, Dorchester, Dorset DT1 2LB
01305 254737(f)/01305 254712
ACP

SONES, Michael
Child Psychotherapist
Child, Adolescent & Family Mental Health Service, Poole General Hospital, Longfleet Road, Poole, Dorset BH15 2JB
01202 442741/01202 661671 (f)
ACP

TOMLINSON, Andy
Hypno-Psychotherapist
71 Wareham Road, Corfe Mullen, Wimborne, Dorset BH21 3JX
01202 659883
NSHAP

TRACY, Colin
Humanistic and Integrative Psychotherapist
2 Ackerman Road, Dorchester, Dorset DT1 1NZ
01305 266721
BCPC

VENKI, Malathi
Cognitive Behavioural Psychotherapist
11 William Road, Queens Park, Bournemouth, Dorset BH7 7BB
01202 246719
BABCP

WALLACE-SMITH, Nigel
Sexual and Marital Psychotherapist
Canford Cottage, 27 Pottery Road, Poole, Dorset BH14 8RA
01202 738052
BASMT

WATERFIELD, Julia
Integrative Arts Psychotherapist
1 Old Bakery Cottages, Charlton Marshall, Blandford Forum, Dorset DT11 9NH
01258 480691
IATE

WILDASH, Sheila
Psychoanalytic Psychotherapist
10 Fairway Drive, Northmoor Park, Wareham, Dorset BH20 4SG
01929 553097
AGIP

WILTSHIRE, Gill
Cognitive Behavioural Psychotherapist
61 Lowther Road, Bournemouth, Dorset BH8 8NW
01202 398233
BABCP

WITHERS, Jacqueline
Cognitive Behavioural Psychotherapist
Addiction Service, 16-18 Tower Road, Boscombe, Bournemouth BH1 4LB
01202 443200
BABCP

WOTTON, Annette
Psychoanalytic Psychotherapist
Bure Homage Lodge, Bure Lane, Christchurch, Dorset BH23 4DP
01425 272 204
AGIP

ESSEX

ANDERSON, Janet
Child Psychotherapist
North Essex Child & Family Consultation Service, Whitehills Road, Loughton, Essex IG10 1TS
0181 508 4660/0181 530 2378
ACP

ARUNDELL, Jane
Group Analytic Psychotherapist
Dukes Priory Hospital, Springfield, Chelmsford, Essex CM1 7SJ
01245 346177(f)/01245 345345
IPC

BEIGHTON, Chris
Sexual and Marital Psychotherapist
Marital Counselling Service, 150 The Maples, Harlow, Essex CM19 4RD
BASMT

BINGHAM, Jane
Psychoanalytic Psychotherapist
20 Marine Close, Leigh-On-Sea, Essex SS9 2RD
01702 558969
IPC

BOSWOOD, Bryan
Group Analyst
Burnside, Ingatestone Road, Blackmore, Ingatestone, Essex CM4 0NZ
0171 935 3103/01277 821309
IGA

BRANKIN, Irene
Psychosynthesis Psychotherapist
14 Lynton Road, Hadleigh, Essex SS7 2QQ
01702 555420
AAPP

BRIGGS, Andrew
Child Psychotherapist
North Essex Child & Fam.Consult.Serv, Whitehills Road, Loughton, Essex IG10 1TS
0181 478 3393/0181 508 4660
ACP

BRIGGS, Margarete
Psychoanalytic Psychotherapist
11 Home Close, Harlow, Essex CM20 3PD
01279 423093
CSP

BRITTEN, Stewart
Jungian Child Analyst, Child Psychotherapist
The Rows, Layer de la Haye, Colchester, Essex CO2 0EU
01206 738299
ACP

BURTON, Jean
Family Therapist
Child & Family Consultation Service, Wych Elm House, Wych Elm, Harlow, Essex CM20 1QR
01279 417793/01279 417815
AFT

CAIN, Dennis
Transpersonal Psychotherapist
55 Rokeby Gardens, Woodford Green, Essex IG8 9HS
c/o CCPE, Beauchamp Lodge, 2 Warwick Crescent, London W2
CCPE

CAMERON, Katherine
Psychoanalytic Psychotherapist
57 Castle Street, Saffron Walden, Essex CB10 1BD
01799 527449
IPSS, FIP

CHAMPION, Lynn
Child Psychotherapist
Child & Family Consultation Service, Queensway Health Centre, Essex Street, Southend-on-Sea SS2 5TD
01702 616322
ACP

CHAPMAN, Maureen
Psychoanalytic Psychotherapist, Analytical Psychologist-Jungian Analyst
The Rectory, Theydon Mount, Epping, Essex CM16 7PW
01992 578723
IPC

CLARK, Margaret
Psychoanalytic Psychotherapist
Linscott House, Flat D, Russell Road, Buckhurst Hill, Essex IG9 5QE
0181 669 8772/0181 504 6128
LCP

CLEMENTS, Sue
Family Therapist
The Acorns, 220 Stamford Road, Dagenham, Essex RM9 4EL
0181 270 6572
AFT

ESSEX

CLEMENTS-JEWERY, Sue
Sexual and Marital Psychotherapist
Bodey House, Stock Road, Stock, Essex
CM4 9DH
01277 840668
BASMT

CONYERS, Marie
Psychoanalytic Psychotherapist
Crushes Manor House, 247 Rayleigh Road, Hutton, Nr. Brentwood, Essex
CM13 1PJ
01277 232585
LCP

COUSSENS, Kay
Integrative Psychotherapist
42 Glenwood Drive, Gidea Park, Romford, Essex RM2 5AS
01708 755384
MC

CROUCH, Carol
Integrative Psychotherapist
Woodside, 61 Russell Road, Buckhurst Hill, Essex IG9 5QF
0181 504 0059
RCSPC

D'AGUILAR, Yvonne
Systemic Psychotherapist
2 Link Way, Hornchurch, Essex
RM11 3RW
KCC

DEEBLE, Elizabeth A.
Cognitive Behavioural Psychotherapist
Psychology Dept., Goodmayes Hospital, Barley Lane, Goodmayes, Essex IG3 8XJ
0181 970 8434
BABCP

EL-HADI, Ali
Psychoanalytic Psychotherapist
Brookside Young People's Unit, 117A Barley Lane, Goodmayes, Ilford, Essex
IG3 8BY
18 Colworth Road, Leytonstone, London E11 1HY
0181 970 8130/0181 539 5496
BAP

ELLIS, Sian
Psychoanalytic Psychotherapist
171 Theydon Grove, Epping, Essex
CM16 4QA
c/o AGIP, 1 Fairbridge Road, London
N19 3EW
0171 272 7013/01992 574018
AGIP, FIP

FOX, Almuth-Maria
Integrative Psychotherapist
101 Hadleigh Road, Leigh-on-Sea, Essex
SS9 2LY
01277 840668/01702 472634
RCSPC

GALE, Derek
Humanistic Psychotherapist
The Gale Centre, Stable Cottage, Whitakers Way, Loughton, Essex
IG10 1SQ
0181 508 9344/0181 508 1240 (f)
AHPP

GILBERT, Sharon
Psychosynthesis Psychotherapist
128 Meads Lane, Seven Kings, Ilford, Essex IG3 8PE
0181 590 3850
AAPP

GOODCHILD, Margaret
Child Psychotherapist
Basildon Child & Family Consultation Services, Great Oaks, Basildon, Essex
SS14 1EH
01268 523355
ACP

GRAINGER, Eve
Child Psychotherapist
Barking & Dagenham Child & Family Consult. Service, 31 Woodward Road, Dagenham, Essex RM9 4SJ
0181 270 6427/8/0181 348 5457
ACP

GRAVELLE, John
Integrative Psychotherapist
8 Gordon Road, Chelmsford, Essex
CM2 9LL
01245 491795
MC

GREAVES, Thomas
Core Process Psychotherapist
4 Tylers Close, Loughton, Essex
IG10 3BD
0181 502 1708
AAPP

GREENWOOD, Angela
Educational Therapist
34 Sea View Road, Leigh on Sea, Essex
SS9 1AT
01702473540
FAETT

HACKER HUGHES, Jamie G.H.
Cognitive Behavioural Psychotherapist
7 Rainsford Avenue, Chelmsford, Essex
CM1 2PJ
Brentwood CMH Team, Lime Grove House, Highwood Hospital, Geary Drive, Brentwood Essex CM15 9DY
01621 850211
BABCP

HARVEY, Linda Mary
Cognitive Analytic Therapist
Norbrook, Eastwick, Nr. Harlow, Essex
CM20 2QX
01279 410 435
ACAT

HARVEY, Pam
Systemic Psychotherapist
Department of Psychology, Goodmayes Hospital, Barley Lane, Goodmayes Essex IG3 8XJ
42 Barleycroft Road, Welwyn Garden City, Hertford AL8 6JU
0181 970 8430/01707 322339
KCC

HENDRY, Devam
Psychosynthesis Psychotherapist
14 Home Close, Harlow, Essex
CM20 3PD
01279 414470
AAPP

HOLLINGWORTH, Amanda
Sexual and Marital Psychotherapist
Old Fairfields, Hatfield Peverel, Chelmsford, Essex CM3 2NT
01245 381480
BASMT

HORMASJI, Faridoon
Hypno-Psychotherapist
2A Cross Road, Romford, Essex
RM7 8AT
7 Park Crescent, London W1N 3HE
01708 724847/01708 764740
NRHP

HOWARD, Trevor
Systemic Psychotherapist
10 Southsea Avenue, Leigh on Sea, Essex SS9 2AX
01702 474351
KCC

HOWTONE, Christina
Hypno-Psychotherapist
139 Sevenoaks Close, Harold Hill, Essex RM3 7EF
01708 373175
NSHAP

HUDSON, Rachel
Psychoanalytic Psychotherapist
30 Gordon Road, Ilford, Essex IG1 1SP
0181 553 3089
IPC

HURST, Margaret
Child Psychotherapist
North Essex Child & Family Consultation Service, Rannoch Lodge, 146 Broomfield Road, Chelmsford, Essex CM1 1RN
01245 354188/01245 493463 (f)
ACP

JACOBSON, Rosemary
Integrative Psychotherapist
Dept. of Clinical Psychology, Mental Health Unit, Princess Alexandra Hospital, Harlow, Essex CM20 1QX
0181 444 8009/01279 827276
RCSPC

JOHNSTONE, Janice
Hypno-Psychotherapist
40 Saffron Court, Saffron Walden, Essex CB11 4HB
01799 500540
NRHP

JONES, Amanda
Systemic Psychotherapist
King George Hospital, Paediatric Department, Barley Lane, Goodmayes, Essex IG3 8YB
Charing Cross Hospital, Dept. of Psychiatry, 3rd Floor-North Wing, Fulham Palace Rd., London W6 8RF
0181 846 1340/0181 970 8098
KCC

JULIEN, Michael
Integrative Psychotherapist
497 Aldborough Road North, Newbury Park, Ilford, Essex IG2 7SY
0181 599 0625
RCSPC

KENDRICK, Margaret
Hypno-Psychotherapist
3 Seaview Parade, Maylandsea, Essex CM3 6EL
01621 742745
NSHAP

KWEI, Daniel
Gestalt Psychotherapist
6 Brentwood Place, Sawyers Hall Lane, Brentwood, Essex CM15 9DN
01277 226834
GPTI

LAU, Annie
Family Psychotherapist
Child Guidance Clinic, Loxford Hall, Loxford Lane, Ilford, Essex IG1 2PL
0171 478 7211/0181 478 3101 (f)
IFT

LEITE DA COSTA, Mariza
Child Psychotherapist
14 Marshalls Road, Braintree, Essex CM7 2LL
01376 327372(f)/01376 550886
ACP

LEWIS, Jo-Ann
Psychoanalytic Psychotherapist
6 Fairview Gardens, Woodford Green, Essex IG8 1BJ
0181 559 1318
AGIP, FIP

MANNING, Tony
Family Therapist
12 The Drive, Loughton, Essex IG10 1HB
0181 478 3101/0181 281 7093
AFT

MATHEWS, Trevor J.
Cognitive Behavioural Psychotherapist
1 Moat Edge Gardens, Billericay, Essex CM12 0NJ
11 Arundel Mews, Billericay, Essex CM12 0FW
01277 631554/01245 351441
BABCP

MILLAR, David
Child Psychotherapist
North Essex Child & Family Consultation Service, Stanwell House, Stanwell Street, Colchester, Essex CO2 7DL
01206 579190/01206 768211
ACP

NEENAN, Michael
Cognitive Behavioural Psychotherapist
36 Shearers Way, Boreham, Essex CM3 3AE
Community Drug Team, 92 Broomfield Road, Chelmsford, Essex CM1 1SS
01245 468262/01245 351441
BABCP

PARKER, Michael
Group Analyst
18 Mildmay Court, Mildmay Road, Chelmsford, Essex CM2 0DY
01245 346 759/01277 840 263
IGA

PARMLEY, Alison
Gestalt Psychotherapist
8 Orchard Close, Great Baddow, Chelmsford, Essex CM2 9SL
01245 600159
GPTI

PENN, Joyce
Hypno-Psychotherapist
213 York Road, Southend-on-Sea, Essex SS1 2RU
01702 462191
NRHP

RAICAR, Maeja
Attachment-based Psychoanalytic Psychotherapist
8 Feering Road, Billericay, Essex CM11 2DR
Merewood Therapy Centre, Rayleigh, Essex
01268 770990/01277 654351
CAPP

REYNOLDS, Michelle
Psychoanalytic Psychotherapist
The Long House, 6 Church Street, Saffron Walden, Essex CB10 1JW
01799 522677/01799 524082
LCP

RICE, Paul
Behavioural Psychotherapist
Blackwater House, 81 Riverside Way, Kelvedon, Colchester, Essex CO5 9LX
CMHT 8 Lime Grove House, Highwood Hospital, Geary Drive, Brentwood Essex CM15 9DY
01376 571515/01708 464238
BABCP

RIX, Sandra
Sexual and Marital Psychotherapist
Coopers, Coopers Hill, Ongar, Essex CM5 9EG
01277 362912
BASMT

ROBINSON, Mardi
Group Analyst
The Cottage, Mill Street, Polestead, Colchester, Essex CO6 5AD
01206 263104
IGA

SABAYINDA, Michael
Integrative Psychotherapist
287 Prittlewell Chase, Westcliffe-on-Sea, Southend, Essex SS0 0PL
01702 393680
RCSPC

SALMON, Cindy
Transpersonal Psychotherapist
Friars Cottages, 68 Castle Road, Colchester, Essex CO1 1UN
01206 573721
CTP

SAWYER, Noel F.
Cognitive Behavioural Psychotherapist
Chelmsford & Essex Centre, New London Road, Chelmsford, Essex CM2 0QH
Dukes Priory Hospital, Stump Lane, Springfield Green, Chelmsford CM1 5SJ
01245 287440
BABCP

SCHREIBER, Kaye
Systemic Psychotherapist
Child & Family Consultation Service, 8 Kenneth Road, Hadleigh, Essex
18 Brunswick Road, Southend-on-Sea, Essex SS1 2UH
01268 366 800/01702 611 973
KCC

SCOTT, Michael
Group Analyst
20 Thornwood, Colchester, Essex CO4 5LR
01255 220226/01206 854965
IGA

SHOOTER, Lesley
Psychoanalytic Psychotherapist
38 Links Avenue, Gidea Park, Romford Essex RM2 6ND
01708 727002(f)/01708 760286
AIP

SHRIMPTON, David
Psychodynamic Psychotherapist
Oakleigh, Church Road, Wickham St Paul, Essex CO9 2PN
WMIP

SMITH, Richard
Transpersonal Psychotherapist
15 Squirrel's Field, Myland Gate, Mill Road, Colchester, Essex
01206 844 032
CCPE

STABLEFORD, Joyce
Hypno-Psychotherapist
18 Alma Close, Benfleet SS7 2EG
01702 557 649
CTS

STACEY-ONG, Lesley
Systemic Psychotherapist
9 The Copse, Bannister Green, Felsted, nr Dunmow, Essex CM6 3NP
01371 821428
KCC

STEEL, Patricia
Hypno-Psychotherapist
Apple Bee, 56 Burnway, Emerson Park, Hornchurch, Essex RM11 3SG
01708 472573
NRHP

SUCHER, Ingerborg
Psychoanalytic Psychotherapist
The Priest's House, 2 Walden Road, Littlebury, nr Saffron Walden, Essex CB11 4TA
01799 526437
IPSS

TEMPEST, Jeanette
Psychosynthesis Psychotherapist
21 St. Andrews Road, Shoeburyness, Essex SS3 9JA
01702 294 754
AAPP

TENG, Christina
Systemic Psychotherapist
33 Furrowfelde, Kingswood, Basildon, Essex SS16 5HA
01268 533769
KCC

THOMPSON, Joan
NLP Psychotherapist
31 Priory Crescent, Prittlewell, Southend-on-Sea, Essex SS2 6JY
01702 613828
ANLP, CPCP

TROSH, Joanna
Cognitive Behavioural Psychotherapist
Behavioural Psychotherapy Dept., Chelmsford and Essex Centre, New London Road, Chelmsford CM2 0QH
01245 287440
BABCP

TUNE, David
Body Psychotherapist, Integrative Psychotherapist
23 Rectory Road, Wivenhoe, Essex CO7 9EP
01206 827863
CCBP, AHPP

TURNER, Diana
Psychoanalytic Psychotherapist
2 Parsonage Terrace, Vicarage Road, Finchingfield, Essex CM7 4LD
01245 493622/01371 810727
ARBS, FIP

WALKER, Steven
Family Psychotherapist
Naze Crest, 4 Sunny Point, Walton on the Naze, Essex CO14 8LD
01255 677830
AFT

WELSH, Anne
Psychosynthesis Psychotherapist
Blacksmith's Cottage, Clavering, Nr. Saffron Walden, Essex CB11 4QL
01799 550 024/0181 202 4525
AAPP

WESTCOTT, Bernard
Group Analyst
67 Somerset Road, Laindon, Basildon, Essex SS15 6PP
01268 450402/01268 450403
IGA

WHATLEY, Ann
Family Therapist
Ansden, 9 Colehills Close, Clavering, Saffron Walden, Essex CB11 4QY
01799 550807
AFT

WHEELEY, Eleanor
Sexual and Marital Psychotherapist
Cromwell House, 7 Cromwell Avenue, Billericay, Essex CM12 0AE
BASMT

WOODCRAFT, Paul
Cognitive Behavioural Psychotherapist
Chelmsford and Essex Centre, New London Road, Chelmsford, Essex CM2 0QH
01245 287440
BABCP

YUSEF, Dori Fatima
Transpersonal Psychotherapist
Dickens Lodge, High Road, Chigwell, Essex IG7 6QB
0181 502 7095
CCPE

GLOUCESTERSHIRE

ADAMS, Eve
Integrative Psychosynthesis Psychotherapist
Lantern Cottage, Stockend, Edge, Stroud GL6 6PN
01452 813355
RE.V

AGAR, James
Transactional Analysis Psychotherapist
Spring Cottage, High Street, South Woodchester, Stroud, Glos. GL5 5EL
ITA, MET

ALLAN, Kay
Psychoanalytic Psychotherapist
111 Promenade, Cheltenham, Gloucestershire GL50 1NW
01242 224779/01242 252902
IPC, SIP

ARREDONDO, Beverly
Transactional Analysis Psychotherapist
7 Mountpellier House, Suffolk Square, Cheltenham, Glos. GL50 2DY
0958 945 496
ITA

ATKINS, Coral
Psychoanalytic Psychotherapist
Spinners, South Woodchester, Gloucestershire GL5 5EL
Coral Atkins Childrens Homes, Gyde House, Painswick, Glos.
01453 872291
GUILD

BATTEN, Cecilia
Psychoanalytic Psychotherapist
58 Leckhampton Road, Cheltenham, Gloucestershire GL53 OBG
01242 521768
SIP, BAP

BURRITT, William
Analytical Psychologist-Jungian Analyst
1 Merestones Drive, The Park, Cheltenham GL50 2SU
IGAP

CARTER, Paula
Sexual and Marital Psychotherapist
Seeps Barn, Calcot Farm, Calcot, Cheltenham GL54 3JZ
01285 720996
BASMT

CROSS, John
Psychoanalytic Psychotherapist
The Old Coach House, Lye Lane, Cleeve Hill, Cheltenham, Glos. GL54 5DQ
P.E.T.T. Archive & Study Centre, Church Lane, Toddington, Cheltenham GL54 5DQ
01242 678895/01242 620125
AGIP

DAVIES, Miranda
Child Psychotherapist, Jungian Child Analyst
Hillslie House, Lower Littleworth, Amberley, Stroud, Gloucestershire GL5 5AN
Room F5, Bucknall Suite, The Old Convent Centre, Beeches Green, Stroud GL5 4AD
01453 763536/01453 873 552
SIP

DE HOOGH-ROWNTREE, Patricia
Analytical Psychologist-Jungian Analyst
Ivy Cottage, Church Lane, Sapperton, near Cirencester, Gloucestershire GL7 6LQ
01285 760209
BAP, SIP

DIEPEVEEN, Johanna Maria
Psychosynthesis Psychotherapist
Highfield Cottage, Ocker Hill, Randwick, Stroud, Gloucestershire GL6 6HY
01453 764215
AAPP

ELLIOTT, Lea K.
Psychoanalytic Psychotherapist
18 Eldorado Road, Cheltenham, Glos. GL50 2PT
01242 518642/01242 221271 (f)
WMIP, SIP

EMELEUS, Frances
Sexual and Marital Psychotherapist
1 Church Cottages, Notgrove, Cheltenham, Glos. GL54 3BT
01451 850397
BASMT

FRYE, Helen
Psychoanalytic Psychotherapist
52 Gratton Road, Cheltenham, Gloucestershire GL50 2BY
01242 518113
SIP

GOODRICH, Anne
Psychoanalytic Psychotherapist
6 Wychbury Close, Leckhampton, Cheltenham, Glos GL53 0HT
01242 262526
IPC

GOWLING, David
Transactional Analysis Psychotherapist
Red House Farm, Foxmoor Lane, Westrip, Stroud, Gloucestershire GL5 4PL
01453 750716
ITA, MET

GRACIE, Jane
Psychoanalytic Psychotherapist
10 Somerford Road, Cirencester, Gloucestershire GL7 1TN
01285 650143
SIP

GROCOTT, Annie
Psychoanalytic Psychotherapist
20 Moorend Crescent, Leckhampton, Cheltenham, Gloucestershire GL53 0EL
01242 572290
GUILD, SIP

HALL, Kelvin
Humanistic and Integrative Psychotherapist
Cherry Tree Cottage, Shortwood, Nailsworth, Glos. GL6 0SB
01453 833 861
BCPC

HEDLEY, Karen
Psychosynthesis Psychotherapist
Half Moon Cottage, Wick Street, Stroud GL6 7QR
01452 813 288
AAPP

HEDLEY, Nick
Psychosynthesis Psychotherapist
Highfield Cottage, Ocker Hill, Randwick, Stroud, Gloucestershire GL6 6HY
01453 750131
AAPP

HUMPHRIES, Harold
Psychoanalytic Psychotherapist
Praha, 11 Heazle Place, Stroud, Gloucestershire GL5 1UW
c/o AGIP, 1 Fairbridge Road, London N19 3EW
01453 757900/0171 272 7013
AGIP

LESTER, Clare
Integrative Psychotherapist
24 Acre Street, Stroud, Glos GL5 1DR
01453 755241
MC

LUTHY, Barbara
Humanistic and Integrative Psychotherapist
College Farm, Beacon Lane, Haresfield, Glos. GL10 3ES
01452 720934
BCPC, AHPP

MASLEN, Gill
Humanistic and Integrative Psychotherapist
195 Gloucester Street, Cirencester, Glos. GL7 2DP
01285 656280
BCPC

MCOSTRICH, June
Psychosynthesis Psychotherapist
Forge House, Kemble, Gloucestershire GL7 6AD
01285 770 538/01285 770 013 (f)
AAPP

MOGGRIDGE, Cass
Psychodrama Psychotherapist
Priory Mill, Kelmscott Road, Lechlade, Glos. GL7 3HB
01367 253334
BPA

MORRIS, Elizabeth
Humanistic and Integrative Psychotherapist
Buckholdt House, The Street, Frampton on Severn, Gloucestershire GL7 7ED
01452 741106/01452 741520 (f)
AHPP

MORRIS, Stephen
Psychoanalytic Psychotherapist
53 Slad Road, Stroud, Glos GL5 1QT
01453 750765
SIP

O'HARA, Karen
Integrative Psychotherapist, Body Psychotherapist
2 Mount Pleasant, Rack Hill, Chalford, Stroud, Glos. GL6 8LA
01453 885037
CCBP

PETERS, Maggie
Transpersonal Psychotherapist
27 Landsdown, Stroud, Gloucestershire GL5 1BG
CTP

PORTER, Ruth
Psychoanalytic Psychotherapist
Pittville Lodge Cottage, Malden Road, Cheltenham GL52 2BU
GUILD

SACKETT, Kate
Cognitive Analytic Therapist
Clinton Cottage, Silver Street, Chalford Hill, Stroud, Glos. GL6 8EL
01453 882765
ACAT

SEIGAL, Elizabeth
Psychoanalytic Psychotherapist
Westbourne, 43 Middle Street, Stroud, Glos GL5 1DZ
01453 751114
SIP, BAP

SILMON, Mary
NLP Psychotherapist
114 London Road, Gloucester GL2 0RR
01452 414976
ANLP

SKAILES, Claire
Analytical Psychotherapist
5 Fairview Terrace, Wallsquarry, Brimscombe, Stroud GL5 2PB
01453 885229
WMIP, SIP

STEPHENS, Lyn
Psychoanalytic Psychotherapist
9 Montpellier Grove, Cheltenham, Gloucestershire GL50 2XB
01242 576497/01242 521945
AGIP, FIP

THOMAS, Penny
Humanistic and Integrative Psychotherapist
6 Wallow Green, Horsley, Nailsworth, Stroud GL6 0PB
01453 833752
BCPC

WARD, Shona
Transactional Analysis Psychotherapist
Spring Cottage, High Street, South Woodchester, Stroud, Glos. GL5 5EL
01453 873023 (f)/01453 872703
ITA

WATKINS, Judy
Psychoanalytic Psychotherapist
Broadwell, Church Road, Leckhampton, Cheltenham GL51 5XX
01242 580214
GUILD, SIP

ZINKIN, Hindle
Analytical Psychologist-Jungian Analyst
The Coach House, Paradise, Painswick, Glos. GL6 6TN
9d Maresfield Gardens, London NW3 6SJ
0171 435 9219/01452 812272
FIP

HAMPSHIRE

AMEZ, Susana
Child Psychotherapist
Child & Fam. Therapy Services, Battenburg Avenue Clinic, Battenburg Avenue,Northend, Portsmouth PO2 0TA
01705 428804(f)/01705 653433
ACP

ANTHIAS, Louise
Family Therapist
Old School House, Knapp Lane, Ampfield, Romsey, Hants SO51 9BT
Psychological Therapies Services, Dept of Psychiatry, RSH Hospital, Brintons Terrace SO14 0YG
01703 825392/01794 368102
IFT

ASHCROFT, Dinah
Gestalt Psychotherapist, Integrative Psychotherapist
6 - 8 The Soke,, Alresford, Hants SO24 9DB
01962 733 219
GPTI

ATTRIDGE, Brian
Core Process Psychotherapist
Flat 1, 16 Victoria Grove, Southsea, Hampshire PO5 1NE
01705 863266 (t/f)
AAPP

BARDEN, Nicola
Analytical Psychotherapist
9b Worsley Road, Southsea, Portsmouth, Hants PO5 3DY
01705 297585
WMIP

BARING, Anne
Analytical Psychologist-Jungian Analyst
White Lodge, Grange Park, Alresford, Hants SO24 9TG
01962 732744
AJA

BEACH, Jan D.
Cognitive Behavioural Psychotherapist
G Block, Royal Hospital Haslar, Gosport, Hants PO12 2AA
01705 584255 x 2173
BABCP

BENNETT, Ross
Humanistic and Integrative Psychotherapist
Kwanti, Jermyns Lane, Ampfield, Romsey, Hampshire SO51 0QA
Portsmouth Natural Health & Psychotherapy Centre, 20 Landport Terrace, Portsmouth PO1 2RG
01794 368012
SPEC

BERRY, Eileen
Group Analyst
4 Eastgate Street, Winchester, Hants SO23 8EB
01962 854439
IGA

BLACK, Nicholas J.
Cognitive Behavioural Psychotherapist
Clinical Psychology Service, Royal Hampshire County Hospital, Romsey Road, Winchester SO22 5DG
Brook House, 15 Burley Close, Chandlers Ford, Eastleigh SO53 4NS
01962 824351/01962 824418
BABCP

BORGHGRAEF, Guy
Sexual and Marital Psychotherapist
Myrtle Cottage, Hastards Lane, Selborne, Hampshire GU34 3LB
01420 511440
BASMT

BOULD, Jane
Psychodrama Psychotherapist
17 Tudor Avenue, Emsworth, Hampshire PO10 7UG
01243 431637
BPA

BRANDWOOD, Pat
Psychodrama Psychotherapist
59 Bassett Green Road, Southampton, Hampshire SO16 3DW
BPA

BROCK, Sue
NLP Psychotherapist
4 Paddockfields, Old Basing, Basingstoke, Hampshire RG24 7DB
01256 462293(f)/01256 326176/354688
ANLP

BUCKLEY, Judy
Psychoanalytic Psychotherapist
Beech Lodge, Sleepers Hill, Winchester, Hants SO22 4ND
01962 852763
IPSS, FIP

CARRUTHERS, Dianna
Humanistic and Integrative Psychotherapist
Portsmouth Natural Health & Psychotherapy Centre, 20 Landport Terrace, Portsmouth, Hampshire PO1 2RG
01705 830558
SPEC

CHARLEY, Geoff
Transpersonal Psychotherapist
2 Northend Farm Cottages, Milland, Near Liphook, Hampshire GU30 7LT
01428 741533
CCPE

CHILDS-CLARKE, Adrian
Cognitive Behavioural Psychotherapist
Psychological Therapies Service, Department of Psychiatry, Royal South Hants Hospital, Graham Road, Southampton SO14 0YG
01703 634288 x 2536
BABCP

CLANCY, J Patricia
Cognitive Behavioural Psychotherapist
Ravenswood House, Knowles Hospital, Fareham, Hants PO17 5NA
01329 834780(f)/01329 836023
BABCP

CLARKE, Isabel
Cognitive Behavioural Psychotherapist
Psychological Therapies Service, Department of Psychiatry, Royal South Hants Hospital, Southampton, SO14 0YG
01703 825531
BABCP

CLIFFORD-POSTON, Andrea
Educational Therapist
Osborne House, Kingsley, Hampshire GU35 9LW
01420 476042
FAETT

CLIFTON, S.
Sexual and Marital Psychotherapist
3 Hermitage Gardens, Waterlooville, Hampshire PO7 7PR
BASMT

COLES, Peter J.
Cognitive Behavioural Psychotherapist
100B London Road, Cowplain, Waterlooville, Hants. PO8 8EW
01705 471661
BABCP

COPLEY, Brian
Cognitive Behavioural Psychotherapist
Marchwood Priory Hospital, Hythe Road, Marchwood, Southampton, Hants SO4 4WU
01703 840044
BABCP

DAHLE, Josephine
Humanistic and Integrative Psychotherapist
Grove Natural Therapy Centre, 22 Grosvenor Road, Highfield, Southampton SO13 1RT
01703 571 888(f)/01703 582245
SPEC

DANIELS, Mo
Psychodrama Psychotherapist
14 Sir Georges Road, Southampton, Hampshire SO15 3AT
01703 227778
BPA

DE JONG, Corrie
Group Analytic Psychotherapist
47 Telegraph Lane, Four Marks, Hants GU34 5AX
01420 561802
IPC

DRAPER, Ros
Family Therapist, Systemic Psychotherapist
37 Lower Wardown, Herne Farm, Petersfield, Hampshire GU31 4PA
The Family Institute, 105 Cathedral Road, Cardiff CF1 9PH
01730 260023
IFT

DUPONT-JOSHUA, Aisha
Psychoanalytic Psychotherapist
32 Lark Rise, Liphook, Hants GU30 7QT
01428 727 694
NAFSI

DYER, Paula
Sexual and Marital Psychotherapist
11 Basingbourne Close, Fleet, Hants
GU13 9TF
01252 628744
BASMT

ELLIOTT, John
NLP Psychotherapist
Woolston Lodge Surgery, 66
Portsmouth Road, Southampton
SO19 9AL
01703 363568(f)/01703 363566
ANLP

ELLIOTT, Peter
Cognitive Behavioural Psychotherapist
Dept. of Psychology, Building 44,
University of Southampton, Highfield,
Southampton SO17 1BJ
01703 595322
BABCP

EVANS, Peter L.
Child Psychotherapist
24 Chequers Road, Basingstoke,
Hampshire RG21 7PU
01256 422771
ACP

EVERINGTON, Madeleine
Psychoanalytic Psychotherapist
Hamesford House, East Harting,
Petersfield, Hants. GU31 5LY
01730 825383
LCP

FAGAN, Anthony F.
Transpersonal Psychotherapist
1 Grange Road, Alresford, Hants
SO24 9HD
01962 733896(f)/01962 732262
CCPE

FINCHAM, Felicity
Cognitive Behavioural Psychotherapist
1 Hope Cottage, Little Shore Lane,
Bishops Waltham, Southampton, SO32
1ED
01489 893753/01703 475247
BABCP

FRY, Julie
Gestalt Psychotherapist
28 Church Road, Bishopstoke, Hants
SO50 6BJ
59 Eastwood Road, Bramley, Guildford
GU5 0DX
01483 892599/01703 618582
MET, GPTI

GLASSPOOL, Patricia
Hypno-Psychotherapist
12 Hocombe Drive, Chandlers Ford,
Eastleigh, Hants SO53 5QE
Southgate Natural Therapy Clinic, 13
Southgate Street, Winchester, Hants
SO23 9DZ
01962 866903/01703 255678
NRHP

GOOLD, Peter
Personal Construct Psychotherapist
Coudray House, Herriard, Nr
Basingstoke, Hants RG25 2PN
01256 381787
CPCP

GORDON, P. Kenneth
Cognitive Behavioural Psychotherapist
59 Romsey Road, Winchester, Hants
SO22 5DE
01962 825600/01962 825601 (f)
BABCP

GOTTESMAN, Robert
Psychoanalytic Psychotherapist
St James Hospital, Locksway Road,
Portsmouth, Hants PO4 8LD
01705 822444 ext4201
FIP

GRAY, Sally
Cognitive Analytic Therapist
110 Oakwood Drive, Lordswood,
Southampton SO16 8EN
Psychotherapy Department, Royal
South Hants Hospital, Brintons
Terrace, Southampton SO14 0YG
01703 321771
ACAT

GREAVES, Margaret
Humanistic and Integrative
Psychotherapist
Portsmouth Natural Health &
Psychotherapy Centre, 20 Landport
Terrace, Portsmouth, Hampshire
PO1 2RG
01705 830558
SPEC

GREGORY, Peter
Sexual and Marital Psychotherapist
19 Chatsworth Road, Boyatt Wood,
Eastleigh, Hampshire SO5 4PE
01703 617990
BASMT

GURR, Rosalie
Sexual and Marital Psychotherapist
The Old Village Stores, Braishfield,
Romsey, Hampshire SO51 0PQ
01794 368315
BASMT

HALL, Linda
Transpersonal Psychotherapist
The Maples, Lingmala Grove, Church
Crookham, Fleet, Hants GU13 0JW
01252 628506 (t/f)
CCPE

HANNIGAN, David J.
Cognitive Behavioural Psychotherapist
Totton and Waterside L.M.H.T., 67-69
Ringwood Road, Totton, Hampshire
SO40 8DX
01703 868886/01703 666981 (f)
BABCP

HATSWELL, Valerie
Psychoanalytic Psychotherapist
Stillions, 3 Windmill Hill, Alton,
Hampshire GU34 2RY
01420 82385
GCP, FIP

HENDRA, Theresa
Family Therapist
Portsmouth Healthcare NHS, The
Merlin Centre, 19 Villiers Road,
Southsea PO5 2NR
01705 293669/01705 821912
AFT

HOOK, Beatrice
Group Analyst
31 Southview Road, Shirley,
Southampton SO15 5JD
01703 496488
IGA

HOOK, John
Group Analyst
31 Southview Road, Shirley,
Southampton SO15 5JD
01703 496488
IGA

HOOPER, Christine M.
Family Therapist
'Ellesmere', The Crescent, Romsey,
Hampshire SO51 7NG
01794 512102
IFT

HOPKINS, Vera M.
Psychodynamic Psychotherapist
'Oakwood', 4 The Grange, Everton, Lymington, Hants SO41 0ZR
01590 643335
HIP

HURST, Hannah
Attachment-based Psychoanalytic Psychotherapist
Corner House, Ridge Common Lane, Steep Hants GU32 1AW
95 Leighton Road, Kentish Town, London NW5 2QL
0171 482 4450/01730 231557
CAPP

ISAACS HEMMINGS, Gillian
Psychoanalytic Psychotherapist
The Consulting Room, Levers, North Lane, South Harting, Petersfield, Hants. GU31 5NW
01730 825 947
LCP

JACKSON, Paul
Sexual and Marital Psychotherapist
66 Middle Brook Street, Winchester, Hampshire SO23 8DQ
01962 851333/817026
BASMT

KIRKLAND-HANDLEY, Nick V.
Psychoanalytic Psychotherapist
c/o 89 Springvale Road, Kingsworthy, Winchester, Hampshire SO23 7RB
01962 880603
LPDO

LANG, Christine
Sexual and Marital Psychotherapist
15 Douro Close, Baughurst, Tadley, Hants RG26 5PG
0118 981 2748
BASMT

LETHBRIDGE, Sue
Psychoanalytic Psychotherapist
41 Laburnam Grove, North End, Portsmouth, Hants PO2 0HQ
23 Strand Hill, Dawlish, S Devon EX7 9JJ
01626 867210/01705 662715
AGIP, GCP, FIP

LEVER, Maureen
Integrative Psychotherapist
Nelson House, 15 High Street, Old Portsmouth, Hants PO1 2LP
01705 838625
RCSPC

LIPPITT, Gwenda
Psychoanalytic Psychotherapist
Loyal Cottage, 3 The Street, Old Basing, Nr. Basingstoke, Hants RG24 0BH
01256 21178
CPP

LUNT, Aidan
Psychoanalytic Psychotherapist
The Firs, 1 Barrs Wood Road, New Milton, Hampshire BH25 5HS
01425 610398
NWIDP

LYON, Heather
Group Analyst
2a Hillborough Crescent, Southsea, Hants PO4 2AN
01705 827 681
IGA

MALONE, Sue
Systemic Psychotherapist
Tresco, Forest Road, Liss Forest, Hampshire GU33 7BL
01730 893034
BASMT

MARSHALL, Cherrith A.
Systemic Psychotherapist
'Sunnyside', Blissford Cross, Blissford, Fordingbridge, Hants SP6 2JG
01452 655218
FIC

MASSARA, Catharine
Integrative Psychotherapist
c/o 40 Archer's Road, Eastleigh, Hants SO50 9AY
01703 320641
RCSPC

MATTHEWS, Helen P.
Cognitive Behavioural Psychotherapist
Western Community Hospital, Walnut Grove, Millbrook, Southampton, SO16 4XE
01703 475400
BABCP

MCANDREW, Brigitte
Psychoanalytic Psychotherapist
46 Cleveland Road, Southsea, Hants PO5 1SG
01705 861090
ARBS

MELDRUM, Ron
Rational Emotive Behaviour Therapist
12 Atherley Road, Upper Shirley, Southampton SO15 5DQ
07970 336647I/01703 631308
BABCP

MEREDITH, Judith
Transpersonal Psychotherapist
1 Green Leys, Church Crookham Fleet, Hants GU13 0PN
01252 624 388(f)/01252 628428
CCPE

MOORE, Terry
NLP Psychotherapist
58 Northern Parade, Portsmouth, Hampshire PO2 8NE
01705 645774
ANLP

MULVEY, Josephine
Sexual and Marital Psychotherapist
3 Combe Down, Shawford, Nr. Winchester, Hampshire SO21 2AA
01962 715130
BASMT

O'CONNOR, Michael
Systemic Psychotherapist
136 Alexandra Road, Farnborough, Hampshire GU14 6RN
01252 515053
KCC

PARRACK, Norma
Rational Emotive Behaviour Therapist
Central Hall, St Marys Street, Southampton SO16 7DL
01703 237230
BABCP

PERCY, David
Psychoanalytic Psychotherapist
10 Nightingale Close, Winchester, Hants SO22 5QA
01962 877962
GUILD

PIDGEON, Patricia
Systemic Psychotherapist
Family Consultancy, Charlton Road Health Centre, Andover, Hants
01264 324597
KCC

PLANT, Barbara
Sexual and Marital Psychotherapist
Theydon, Sarum Road, Winchester, Hants SO22 5QT
BASMT

PLATTS, June Elizabeth
Cognitive Behavioural Psychotherapist
24 Telegraph Lane, Four Marks, Alton, Hampshire GU34 5AX
01420 561797
BABCP

PORTER, David
Psychoanalytic Psychotherapist
161 Hursley Road, Chandlers Ford, Eastleigh, Hants SO53 1JH
01703 269603
IPC

QUIN, Barbara
Psychodrama Psychotherapist, Family Therapist
9 Campbell Road, Southsea, Hampshire PO5 1RH
01705 294818/01705 359431 (f)
BPA, AFT

REAY, Ruth
Family Therapist
Greensleeves, Thorns Lane, Whiteleaf, HP27 0LT
01844 275052
AFT

ROBINSON, Margaret
Systemic Psychotherapist, Family Therapist
Merryways, Owslebury, Winchester, Hants SO21 1LP
01962 777368
IFT

ROSE-SMITH, Gillian
Humanistic and Integrative Psychotherapist
Portsmouth Natural Health & Psychotherapy Centre, 20 Landport Terrace, Portsmouth PO1 2RG
Spectrum, 7 Endymion Road, London N4 1EE
01705 830558/0181 341 3413
SPEC

ROSS, Susan M.
Cognitive Behavioural Psychotherapist
Clinical Psychology Department, Department of Psychiatry, Royal South Hants Hospital, Southampton SO14 6HW
01702 825531
BABCP

SALTER, Gill
Humanistic and Integrative Psychotherapist
The Grove Centre, 22 Grosvenor Road, Southampton SO17 1RT
01703 582245/01489 893105
SPEC

SAUNDERS, Sally
Psychoanalytic Psychotherapist
Coles Farm Cottage, Awbridge Hill, Romsey, Hampshire SO51 OHE
01794 511219
LCP

SCHEMBRI, Veronica
Humanistic Psychotherapist
5 Solent Drive, Hatch Warren, Basingstoke, Hampshire RG22 4XS
01256 334123 (f)/01256 465853
AHPP

SCOTT, Brigitte
Biodynamic Psychotherapist
6 Alden Drive, Aldenholt, Fordingbridge, Hants SP6 3EP
01425 652577
BTC

SEYMOUR, E. John
Psychoanalytic Psychotherapist
Racton, 36 Breach Avenue, Emsworth, Hants PO10 8NB
01243 373608
GCP

SHELLEY, Trevor
Sexual and Marital Psychotherapist
Fernside, Crookhill, Braishfield, Hampshire SO51 0QB
01794 368169
BASMT

SMITH, Peter
Psychoanalytic Psychotherapist
53 North Street, Pennington, Lymington, Hants SO41 8GB
01590 688064
ARBS

STANWOOD, Frederick
Psychoanalytic Psychotherapist
34 St. David's Road, Southsea, Portsmouth, Hampshire PO5 1QN
01705 421 742(f)/01705 793983
AGIP, GCP, FIP

STIMPSON, Quentin
Transpersonal Psychotherapist
2 Derlyn Road, Fareham, Hampshire PO16 7TJ
01329 826 621
CCPE

STOLTE, Eva
Psychoanalytic Psychotherapist
34 St. David's Road, Southsea, Portsmouth, Hants PO5 1QN
01705 421742(f)/01705 793983
AGIP, GCP, FIP

STONE, Barry L
Systemic Psychotherapist
The Baring Centre, 35 Sarum Hill, Basingstoke, Hampshire GU13 8PT
70 London Road, Southampton, Hampshire
01256 516 006/01703 635 011
KCC

SYMES, Jan
Systemic Psychotherapist
Butts Cottage, The Butts, Alton, Hampshire GU34 1RD
BASMT

WILLIAMS, Ann
Hypno-Psychotherapist
Centre for Personal & Professional Development, The Mill at Shawford, Nr Winchester, Hants SO21 2BP
01962 714621(f)/01962 715838
NRHP

HEREFORDSHIRE

ANDERSON, Christine
Cognitive Behavioural Psychotherapist
Old House, Yarpole, Near Leominster HR6 0BE
01568 780621
BABCP

ASTON, John
Integrative Psychotherapist
Community Mental Health, Rose Cottage, Belle Orchard, Ledbury, Herefordshire HR8 1DD
01531 633872
RCSPC, WMIP

BRUNT, Mervyn
Transactional Analysis Psychotherapist
Willow Glen, 19 Clive Street, Hereford HR1 2SB
01432 342789
ITA

BYRNE, Deidre
Psychoanalytic Psychotherapist
Aricon, Bromsash, Ross-on-Wye
HR9 9PJ
01989 7504267
IPSS

DAVIES, Stephen
Cognitive Behavioural Psychotherapist
Alcohol Service Herefordshire,
Stonebow Unit, County Hospital,
Union Walk HR1 2ER
0468 750591/01432 355 444
BABCP

ELLIS, June
Psychoanalytic Psychotherapist
Shinns Croft, Bosbury Ledbury,
Herefordshire HR8 1QD
01531 640 552
WMIP

FENTON, Christopher
Psychoanalytic Psychotherapist
The Leys, Aston, Kingsland,
Leominster, Herefordshire HR6 9PU
01568 708632
IPC

FORRYAN, Barbara
Psychoanalytic Psychotherapist
5 Dormington Drive, Tupsley, Hereford
HR1 1SA
01432 268937
SIP

JACOBS, Paula
Transpersonal Psychotherapist
The Wren's Nest, Brampton Road,
Madley, Hereford HR2 9LU
Russel Square WC1
01981 25157(f)/01981 250597
CCPE

OLIVER, Jenny
Psychosynthesis Psychotherapist
The Willows, Yarkhill, Hereford
HR1 3TE
01531 670 477/01989 564 082
AAPP

PALMER BARNES, Fiona
Analytical Psychologist-Jungian Analyst,
Psychoanalytic Psychotherapist
Rock Cottage, St. Margaret's,
Herefordshire HR2 0QW
01981 510613
AJA, IPC, SIP

STERN, Michele
Child Psychotherapist
Hereford Child & Family Guidance
Centre, Gaol Street, Hereford
HR1 2HU
01432 357351
ACP

TURNER, Philip
Psychoanalytic Psychotherapist
Roundway House, 48 Southbank Road,
Hereford HR1 2TL
01432 355746
SIP

HERTFORDSHIRE

ADCOCK, Margaret
Family Psychotherapist
1 Cunningham Hill Road, St. Albans,
Hertfordshire AL1 5BX
01727 858276
IFT

ALDRED, Sue
Transpersonal Psychotherapist
18 Baldock Road, Letchworth,
Hertfordshire SG6 3JX
01462 480 336
CCPE

ALLPORT, Maggie
Gestalt Psychotherapist
65 Mymms Drive, Brookmans Park,
Hatfield, Hertfordshire AL9 7AE
14 Mount Pleasant Road, Tunbridge
Wells TN1 1QU
01707 656250/01707 661301 (f)
GCL

ANDERSON, Eleanor
Systemic Psychotherapist
9 Money Hill Road, Rickmansworth,
Hertfordshire WD3 2EE
0181 962 4362
KCC

BACTAWAR, Charles D.
Cognitive Behavioural Psychotherapist
5 Aubrey Avenue, London Colney, St.
Albans, Herts AL2 1NE
01727 824870
BABCP

BALLANCE, Gillian
Analytical Psychologist-Jungian Analyst
30 Westminster Court, St. Albans,
Hertfordshire AL1 2DX
01727 858361
SAP, BAP

BARRATT, Sara
Systemic Psychotherapist
26 Bushey Grove Road, Bushey,
Hertfordshire WD2 2JQ
Tavistock Clinic, 120 Belsize Lane,
London NW3 5BA
0171 435 7111/01923 817247
IFT

BERGER, Iris
Sexual and Marital Psychotherapist
18 Chalk Lane, Cockfosters, Barnet,
Hertfordshire EN4 9HJ
BASMT

BERRY, Peter
Psychoanalytic Psychotherapist
9 Sandridgebury Lane, St. Albans,
Hertfordshire AL3 6DD
01727 761789
GUILD

BEVAN, Judith Lesley
Systemic Psychotherapist
14 Cranfield Crescent, Cuffley, nr.
Potters Bar, Hertfordshire EN6 4EA
01707 878874
KCC

BIRD, Jane
Autogenic Psychotherapist
18 Holtsmere Close, Garston,
Watford, Hertfordshire WD2 6NG
01923 675501
BAFAT

BLACKER, Sandra R
Systemic Psychotherapist
12 Parker Close, Letchworth, Herts
SG6 3RT
KCC

BUCKROYD, Julia
Psychoanalytic Psychotherapist
15 Heath Road, St. Albans,
Hertfordshire AL1 4DS
01727 841007
GUILD

BUSOLINI, Don
Hypno-Psychotherapist
45 Valley Road, Welwyn Garden City,
Hertfordshire AL8 7DH
01707 330557
NSHAP

CHARTER, Anne
Attachment-based Psychoanalytic Psychotherapist
2 The Brambles, Prospect Road, St. Albans, Hertfordshire AL1 2DP
01727 846244
CAPP

CLENDON, David
Psychoanalytic Psychotherapist
1 Docklands, Pirton, Hitchin, Hertfordshire SG5 3QF
01462 712741
GUILD

CLOVER, Gillian
Psychosynthesis Psychotherapist
19 Chapel Street, Tring, Hertfordshire HP23 6BL
01442 825706
AAPP

COHEN, Barbara
Family Therapist
57 Valley Road, Chorleywood, Hertfordshire WD3 4DT
0171 288 5530/01923 773 984
AFT

COLLINS, Leila
Integrative Psychotherapist
2 King Edward Road, Barnet, Hertfordshire EN5 5AP
0181 362 6734/0181 440 9776
RCSPC

COLMAN, Warren
Psychoanalytic Marital Psychotherapist, Analytical Psychologist-Jungian Analyst
2nd Floor, 16 Chequer Street, St. Albans, Herts AL1 3YD
01727 810337
SAP

CROFT, Janet
Core Process Psychotherapist
24 Long View, Berkhamsted, Hertfordshire HP4 1BY
01442 872 822
AAPP

DANIELL, Dorothy
Psychoanalytic Psychotherapist
17 Crossfell Road, Leverstock Green, Hemel Hempstead, Hertfordshire HP3 8RF
0171 359 4943/01442 254766
LCP

DARCY, Gillian
Psychoanalytic Psychotherapist
32 Ripon Way, Borehamwood, Hertfordshire WD6 2HS
14 North Brink, Wisbech, Cambridgeshire PE13 1JR
0181 207 1314/01945 475212
CFAR

DAVIS, Valerie
Biodynamic Psychotherapist
39 Vesta Avenue, St. Albans, Herts AL1 2PE
01727 853823
BTC

DEERING, Christine
Psychoanalytic Psychotherapist
18 Coldharbour Lane, Bushey, Hertfordshire WD2 3NS
0181 950 5151
LCP

DOREY, Mary
Psychodynamic Psychotherapist
6 Victoria Crescent, Royston, Hertfordshire SG8 7AX
01763 242157
AIP

EGAN, Jude
Systemic Psychotherapist
33 North Road, Berkhamstead, Hertfordshire HP4 3DU
KCC

ELDON, Martin
NLP Psychotherapist
Broomfield Cottage, The Heath, Hatfield Heath, Herts CM22 7DZ
01279 731699/01279 731649
ANLP

EVANS, Michael
Psychoanalytic Psychotherapist
Old White Horse, Francis Road, Ware, Herts SG12 9EZ
01920 462101
CSP

EVEREST, Pauline
Psychoanalytic Psychotherapist
79 Whitney Drive, Stevenage, Herts SG1 4BL
01438 357151
AIP

FALKOWSKA, Merlyn
Biodynamic Psychotherapist
Dovedale Cottage, 28 Chipperfield Road, Apsley, Hemel Hampstead HP3 0AS
01442 264203
BTC

FAUSSET, Ann
Systemic Psychotherapist
21 Royal Oak Lane, Pirton, Hitchin, Herts SG5 3QT
01462 712343
KCC

FEENEY, Michael
Group Analyst
34 Money Hill Road, Rickmansworth, Herts WD3 2EQ
01923 775 875
IGA

FITZSIMMONS, Janet
Psychoanalytic Psychotherapist
29 Calvert Road, Barnet, Hertfordshire EN5 4HH
0181 449 3868
LCP

FOX, Annie
Transpersonal Psychotherapist
41 Bendysh Road, Bushey, Hertfordshire WD2 2HZ
CCPE

FREE-PEARCE, Carolyn
Autogenic Psychotherapist
13 Northaw Park, off Coopers Lane Road, Northaw, Nr. Potters Bar, Herts EN6 4BY
01707 664224
BAFAT

GERRARD, Jackie
Psychoanalytic Psychotherapist
'Julay', 39 Lodge Avenue, Elstree, Herts WD6 3NA
0181 207 5019
LCP

GOURNAY, Kevin
Behavioural Psychotherapist
14 Cassandra Gate, Cheshunt, Herts EN8 0XE
01992 446817/0181 882 8191
BABCP

GRAY, Anne
Psychoanalytic Psychotherapist
55 Watford Road, St. Albans, Herts
AL1 2AE
01727 852669
GUILD

GREY, David
Psychoanalytic Psychotherapist
59 Queens Road, Royston, Herts
SG8 7AN
93 Alleyn Park, London SE21 8AA
0181 299 9918/01763 249775
IPSS

GRUBER, Angela
Transpersonal Psychotherapist
204 Nevells Road, Letchworth, Herts
SG6 4TZ
01462 635027
CCPE

GUNTON, Gaye
Integrative Psychotherapist
106 Oaklands Avenue, Oxhey,
Watford, Hertfordshire WD1 4LW
01923 828948/01923 241626
RCSPC

HADDON, Jarmaine
Systemic Psychotherapist
Greenacres, Staines Green, Nr
Hertford, Hertfordshire SG14 2LN
01992 583965
KCC

HALE, John
Systemic Psychotherapist
9 Park Avenue, Watford, Hertfordshire
WD1 7HR
01923 461553
AFT

HAMILTON, Kim
Psychoanalytic Psychotherapist
224 Hagden Lane, Watford,
Hertfordshire WD1 8LS
01923 212230
AGIP

HARRIS, Dianne
Analytical Psychologist-Jungian Analyst
6 Whitelands Avenue, Chorleywood,
Rickmansworth, Herts WD3 5RD
01923 283600
BAP

HARRISON-MAYOR, Susan
Integrative Psychotherapist, Analytical
Psychologist-Jungian Analyst
86 Handside Lane, Welwyn Garden
City, Herts AL8 6SJ
01707 320782
MC, AJA

HOLTROP, Anna
Integrative Psychotherapist
36 Cedar Road, Berkhamsted,
Hertfordshire HP4 2LB
01441 864708
MC

HONIG, Peter
Family Therapist
Hope Cottage, 77 Orchard Road,
Melbourn, Hertfordshire SG8 6BB
01763 261696
AFT

HUISH, Margot
Sexual and Marital Psychotherapist
96 Hadley Road, New Barnet, Herts
EN5 5QR
0181 440 4092
BASMT

HUMPHREYS, David
Family Therapist
12 Pinelands, Bishops Stortford, Herts
CM23 2TE
Family Works, Thorley Health Centre,
Villiers Sur Marne Ave., Bishops
Stortford, Herts CM23 4EG
0850 193501/01279 757571
IFT

JAMIESON, Eileen
Family Therapist
4a Hubbards Road, Chorleywood,
Herts WD3 5JJ
01494 452673/01923 282965
AFT

KANJI, Nasim
Autogenic Psychotherapist
147 Hampermill Lane, Oxhey,
Hertfordshire WD1 4PH
01923 225402
BAFAT

KAUR-LOVE, Jasminder
Psychoanalytic Psychotherapist
2 Abrams Lane, Chrishall,
Hertfordshire SG8 8QD
01763 838 522
NAFSI

KELL, Midge
Psychoanalytic Psychotherapist
6 Hall Grove, Welwyn Garden City,
Herts AL7 4PN
01707 34552(t/f)
IPC

KILICH-WALPOLE, Suna
Psychoanalytic Psychotherapist
9 Nascot Street, Watford, Herts
WD1 3RB
01923 447587
LCP

LAW, Heather
Psychoanalytic Psychotherapist
344 Whippendell Road, Watford, Herts
WD1 7PD
01923 231174
IPSS

LEARY-JOYCE, John
Gestalt Psychotherapist
64 Warwick Road, St. Albans, Herts
AL1 4DL
01727 864806/01727 838891 (f)
GCL

LEARY-TANNER, Judith
Gestalt Psychotherapist
64 Warwick Road, St Albans, Herts
AL1 4DL
01727 765521 (t/f)
GCL

MARKS-PINFOLD, Shirley
Sexual and Marital Psychotherapist
'Rhondda', Barnet Lane, Elstree, Herts
WD6 3RH
0181 953 3992
BASMT

MAUDLING, Caroline
Gestalt Psychotherapist
7 Holwell Court, Hertford Road,
Essendon, Nr. Hatfield, Hertfordshire
AL9 5RE
01582 462601
SPTI

MCCANN, Anita
Child Psychotherapist
Barnet Child & Family Consultation
Service, Vale Drive Child Guidance
Clinic, Vale Drive, Barnet EN5 2ED
0181 440 8668/0171 538 3698
ACP

MCCANN, Damian
Family Therapist, Sexual and Marital Psychotherapist
35 Hart Road, St. Albans, Herts
AL1 1NF
Dept. of Child & Family Psychiatry, Edgware General Hospital, Edgware, Middlesex
0181 905 6679/93/01727 856690
IFT

MCCARTNEY, Meryl
Child Psychotherapist
Marlowes Health Centre, Marlowes, Hemel Hempstead, Herts HP1 1HE
01442 259132/01442 218310 (f)
ACP

MCCONNACH, Judith
Psychoanalytic Psychotherapist
Priory Cottage, 174 High Road, Bushey Heath, Herts WD2 1NP
0181 950 5121
LCP

MILANI, Belinda
Systemic Psychotherapist
Westfield Gardener's Cottage, Grubb's Lane, Nr. Hatfield, Herts AL9 6EF
01707 659326
KCC

MITCHELL, Richard
Individual and Group Humanistic Psychotherapist
31 Chiswell Green Lane, St. Albans, Herts AL2 3AJ
01727 851251
AHPP

MORGAN, Barbara
Gestalt Psychotherapist
32 Church Road, Stotford, Hitchin SG5 4NB
Dunton Centre for Counselling and Psychotherapy, St Dunton, Biggleswade, Beds
01767 601259/01462 733267
GCL

MORGAN-WILLIAMS, Sue
Existential Psychotherapist
16 Kingsland Way, Ashwell, Herts SG7 5PZ
01462 743296
RCSPC

MORRISON, Barbara
Integrative Psychotherapist
35 Drury Road, Hadley Green, Barnet EN5 5PU
0181 440 4585/0181 440 8735
MC

NAYLOR-SMITH, Alan
Psychoanalytic Psychotherapist
2 Fishery Passage, Horsecroft Road, Hemel Hempstead, Hertfordshire HP1 1RF
01442 247230
GUILD

NGONE, Mary
Integrative Psychotherapist
19 On-the-hill, Carpenders Park, Watford, Hertfordshire WD1 5DS
0181 421 2419/0181 950 9090
RCSPC

PALLENBERG, Sue
Sexual and Marital Psychotherapist
101 St. Albans Road, Sandridge, St. Albans, Hertfordshire AL4 9LH
01727 832403
BASMT

PARR, Meriel A
Integrative Psychotherapist
'Derwood', Todds Green, Stevenage, Herts SG1 2JE
01438 748478/01438 361491
RCSPC

PATCHETT, Angela
Transpersonal Psychotherapist
Mimosa Cottage, 9 Springhead, Ashwell, Hertfordshire SG7 5LL
01462 743109
CCPE

PAWSON, Sheila
Biodynamic Psychotherapist
10 Hunters Park, Berkhamstead, Herts HP4 2PT
01442 862029
BTC

PAYNE, Helen
Humanistic Psychotherapist
1 The Wick, High Street, Kimpton, Herts SG4 8SA
01438 833440/01707 285861
AHPP

PIKE, Margery
Family Therapist
19d Hill Street, St. Albans, Herts AL3 4QS
01727 830059
IFT

PINCH, Christine
Autogenic Psychotherapist
37 Ramsbury Road, St. Albans, Hertfordshire AL1 1SN
01727 851574
BAFAT

POPPLE, Gillian
Integrative Psychotherapist
27 St. John's Road, Watford, Hertfordshire WD1 1PY
01753 793169/01923 247567
RCSPC

POZZI, Maria E.
Child Psychotherapist
North Herts Consultation Clinic, Southgate Health Centre, Stevenage, Herts SG1 1HB
01438 781406/7 (t/f)/0181 340 6167
ACP

RENWICK, John
Transactional Analysis Psychotherapist
101 St. Albans Road, Sandridge, St. Albans, Herts AL4 9LM
MET, ITA

RICHARDSON, Elizabeth
Psychoanalytic Psychotherapist
43 Barleycroft Road, Welwyn Garden City, Hertfordshire AL8 6JX
01707 336696
FIP

RICHTER, Nicola
Transpersonal Psychotherapist
63 Doggetts Way, St Albans, Herts AL1 2NF
01727 750088
CCPE

RICKETT, Marion
Psychoanalytic Psychotherapist
15 George Street, Old Town, Hemel Hampstead, Herts HP2 5HJ
40 High Street, Old Town, Hemel Hempstead HP1 3AE
01442 250294/01442 61712
GUILD

ROSSOTTI, Nicole
Personal Construct Psychotherapist
22 Church End, Redbourn, Nr. St Albans, Herts AL3 7DU
01582 792 970
CPCP

SADOWSKI, Joseph
Child Psychotherapist
20 The Ridings, Thorley Park, Bishop's Stortford, Hertfordshire CM23 4EH
01279 507864
ACP

SHERNO, Peggy
Gestalt Psychotherapist
22 Garden Row, Hitchin, Herts SG5 1QD
01462 432439 (t/f)
GCL

SLADDEN, Anna
Analytical Psychologist-Jungian Analyst
45 Kings Road, Berkhamsted, Herts HP4 3BJ
01442 862072/01442 384406 (f)
BAP

SPROUL-BOLTON, Robin
Group Analyst
c/o Shrodell's Unit, Watford General Hospital, Vicarage Road, Watford, Herts WD1 8HD
01923 244366 x 447 or x 250
IGA

SPYROPOULOS, Nick
Child Psychotherapist
74 Normandy Road, St. Albans, Herts AL3 5PW
01727 54402
ACP

STACEY, Linda
Psychosynthesis Psychotherapist
218 Stanstead Road, Bishops Stortford, Herts CM23 2AR
01279 504048
AAPP

STEEL, Sandra
Integrative Psychotherapist
10 Abbotts Park, London Road, St Albans, Herts AL1 1TW
01727 830378
MC

STOVELL, Joy
Psychoanalytic Psychotherapist
46 Oakroyd Avenue, Potters Bar, Herts EN6 2EL
01707 655464
IPSS

THIEL, Geoffrey
Transpersonal Psychotherapist
17 Browning Road, Harpenden, Herts AL5 4TS
01582 764579
CCPE

THORMAN, Chris
Personal Construct Psychotherapist
115 Pickford Hill, Harpenden, Herts AL5 5HJ
01582 712454
CPCP

TIDY, Deirdre
NLP Psychotherapist
8 Herkomer Road, Bushey, Hertfordshire WD2 3NL
01923 249210(f)/0181 950 1825
ANLP

TIMMANN, S.
Cognitive Behavioural Psychotherapist, Hypno-Psychotherapist
16 Brackendene, Bricket Wood, St. Albans, Hertfordshire AL2 3SX
01923 672880
NRHP, CCPE, BABCP

TOMPKINS, Susan
Psychoanalytic Psychotherapist
43 Ridge Lea, Hemel Hempstead, Herts HP1 2AZ
01442 249919
IPC

WALKER, Jillian
Integrative Psychotherapist
209 Chambersbury Lane, Hemel Hempstead, Hertfordshire HP3 8BQ
01442 256738/01442 221651
RCSPC

WANLESS, Peter
Integrative Psychotherapist
36 Cedar Road, Berkhamsted, Hertfordshire HP4 2LB
31 Helmsdale House, 43 Carlton Vale, London NW6 5EN
01442 864708/0171 328 7641
MC

WANTMAN, Linda
Psychoanalytic Psychotherapist
27 Shenley Hill, Radlett, Herts WD7 7AU
01923 853895
LCP

WEBB, Ann
Systemic Psychotherapist
Mulberry Bush Unit, North Herts NHS Trust, Lister Hospital, Stevenage, Herts
01438 781010
KCC

WHAN, Michael
Analytical Psychologist-Jungian Analyst
39 Common Lane, Batford, Harpenden, Hertfordshire AL5 5BT
IGAP

WIGGLESWORTH, Julia K
Systemic Psychotherapist
10 Stanhope Road, St. Albans, Herts AL1 5BL
KCC

WINTER, David
Personal Construct Psychotherapist
Psychology Department, Barnet Healthcare NHS Trust, Napsbury Hospital, Nr. St. Albans AL2 1AA
01727 823333
CPCP

WISEMAN, Anna
Integrative Psychotherapist
Kettle Barn, Kettle Green, Much Hadham, Herts SG10 6AE
01279 842739
MC

WOODER, Bernard
Core Process Psychotherapist
17 Farrant Way, Borehamwood, Hertfordshire WD6 4TE
0181 207 3457
AAPP

WOOLF, Ralph
Psychoanalytic Psychotherapist
3 Burywick, Beeson End, Harpenden, Hertfordshire AL5 2AD
01582 761472
LCP

HUMBERSIDE

BLACKBURN, Paul
Systemic Psychotherapist
Station House, Station Road, Gt. Hatfield, Hull, East Yorkshire HU11 4UY
01964 536327
IFT

BLAKE, Nancy
NLP Psychotherapist
102 Park Avenue, Kingston upon Hull, North Humberside HU5 3ET
01482 447765 (t/f)
ANLP

BOLSOVER, G.N.
Psychoanalytic Psychotherapist
6A Station Road, Brough, Nr. Hull, East Yorkshire HU15 1DX
01482 665412
HIP, YAPP

DERRICK, Stephen
Gestalt Psychotherapist
7 Highfield, Sutton, Hull HU7 4TW
SPTI

EMM, Susan
Transpersonal Psychotherapist
The Rectory, Church Lane, North Thoresby, Lincs DN36 5QG
01472 840029
CCPE

HOSTICK, Kathie
Transactional Analysis Psychotherapist
'Belcarres', 735 Holderness Road, Hull HU8 9AR
01482 701268
ITA

LITTLEDALE, Nadine
Psychodrama Psychotherapist
33 Barrow Lane, Hessle HU13 0PJ
01482 444463
BPA

PARKER, Jonathan
Cognitive Behavioural Psychotherapist
Family Assessment & Support Unit, School Community & Health Studies, University of Hull, Hull HU6 7RX
01482 465011
BABCP

WANG, Michael
Cognitive Behavioural Psychotherapist
Deptartment of Psychology, University of Hull, Cottingham Road, Hull HU6 7RX
BABCP

ISLE OF WIGHT

JACQUES, Roma
Transpersonal Psychotherapist
5 Dower House, 80 Mitchell Avenue, Ventnor, Isle of Wight PO38 1DS
01983 856 365
CCPE

KENNEDY, Fiona
Cognitive Behavioural Psychotherapist
The Gables, Halberry Lane, Newport, Isle of Wight PO30 2ER
01983 525326
BABCP

PASSEY, Miranda
Child Psychotherapist
Department of Child & Family Psychiatry, 7 Pyle Street, Newport, Isle of Wight
01983 523602/01983 531312
ACP

SIMON, Dave
Family Therapist
Ashton House, 4 West Street, Ryde, Isle of Wight PO33 2NN
01983 614795
AFT

VINE, Mike
Family Therapist
37 College Road, Newport, Isle of Wight PO30 1HD
01983 521290
AFT

WHITE, Eve
Psychodrama Psychotherapist
Little Shate, Mill Lane, Brighstone, Newport, Isle of Wight PO30 4BU
01983 740429
BPA

KENT

ALNUAIMI, Christine
Family Therapist
Child, Family & Adolescent Service, Glendinning House, 11 Bromley Common, Bromley, Kent BR2 9LS
23 Welton Road, London SE18 2JE
0181 460 9278/0181 460 5593
AFT

ASH, Jonathan
Cognitive Behavioural Psychotherapist
Behavioural Psychotherapy Unit, Bethlem Royal Hospital, Monks Orchard Road, Beckenham BR3 3BX
0181 776 4051(f)/0181 776 4146
BABCP

AVERBECK, Marcus
Family Therapist
Orchard House, Family Mental Health Centre, 17 Church Street, St. Peters, Broadstairs CT10 2TT
AFT

BAMBER, Nicola
Psychoanalytic Psychotherapist
Monckton Manor Mountain Street, Chilham, Canterbury CT4 8DQ
East Kent Community NHS Trust Psychotherapy Dept., 2 Cossington Road, Canterbury
01227 597100/01227 730767
FIP

BEARD, Dorrie
Psychoanalytic Psychotherapist, Analytical Psychologist-Jungian Analyst
4 Groveland Road, Beckenham, Kent BR3 3QA
0181 650 9057
IPC, BAP

BHUNNOO, Z.
Behavioural Psychotherapist
305 Maidstone Road, Bridgewood, Chatham, Kent ME5 9SE
01233 643407/01634 861440
BABCP

BLAKE, Adrian
Hypno-Psychotherapist
42 East Street, Bromley, Kent BR1 1QW
93 Birkbeck Road, Sidcup, Kent DA14 4DJ
0181 402 5421/0181 300 5465
NRHP

BLENCH, Graeme
Integrative Arts Psychotherapist
Kenfield Cottage, Kenfield Hall, Petham, Nr. Canterbury, Kent
01227 700775
IATE

BLOWS, Derek
Analytical Psychologist-Jungian Analyst
2 Blackmoor House, Roodlands Lane, Four Elms, Edenbridge, Kent TN8 6PG
01732 700 770
SAP

BOSANQUET, Camilla
Analytical Psychologist-Jungian Analyst
Wyndside, Church Road, Ryarsh, West Malling, Kent ME19 5LB
34E Upper Montagu Street, London W1H 1RP
01732 842351
GUILD, SAP

BOTHA, Marie
Group Analytic Psychotherapist
70 Bradbourne Road, Sevenoaks, Kent TN13 3QA
01732 455903
IPC

BOUSFIELD, Anne
Systemic Psychotherapist
NCH Action for Children, 479 Margate Road, Broadstairs, Kent CT10 2QA
01843 864636 (f)/01843 601101
IFT

BOYD, Suzanne
Transactional Analysis Psychotherapist
The Old Farm House, Biddenden Road, Frittenden, Cranbrook, Kent TN17 2BE
01580 852414/01580 852595 (f)
ITA

BRINDLE, Elisabeth
Sexual and Marital Psychotherapist
Milestones, Packhorse Road, Sevenoaks, Kent TN13 2QP
BASMT

BUCKNALL, Valerie
Attachment-based Psychoanalytic Psychotherapist
26 Burnt Ash Lane, Bromley, Kent BR1 4DH
0181 290 6817
CAPP

BUNKER, Carol
Psychoanalytic Psychotherapist
Ivy Cottage, The Lees, Boughton Aluph, Ashford, Kent TN25 4JB
01233 620000
CSPK

BUNKER, Nigel
Psychoanalytic Psychotherapist
Ivy Cottage, The Lees, Boughton Aluph, Ashford, Kent TN25 4JB
01233 620000
CSPK

CAIRNS, Mary
Psychoanalytic Psychotherapist
39 Chapel Lane, Blean, Canterbury, Kent CT2 9HE
01227 472439
CSPK

CANT, Diana
Child Psychotherapist
Breeches Field Oast, Egerton, Kent TN27 9HA
01233 756552
ACP

CAREY, Jean
Psychoanalytic Psychotherapist
1 The Close, Bridge, Canterbury, Kent CT4 5NJ
01227 831405
CSPK

CARSLEY, Carol
Integrative Psychotherapist
Boulders, Beckenham Place Park, Beckenham, Kent BR3 5BP
0181 650 7264
RCSPC

CARTWRIGHT, Alan
Psychoanalytic Psychotherapist
Little Yockletts, Duckpit Lane, Waltham, Canterbury, Kent CT4 5PZ
01227 700849
CSPK

CARTWRIGHT, Kate
Psychoanalytic Psychotherapist
Little Yockletts, Duckpit Lane, Waltham, Canterbury, Kent CT4 5PZ
01227 700849
CSPK

CHALLENDER, David
Family Therapist
Flat 2, Lardergate, 29a The Precincts, Canterbury, Kent CT1 2EP
01227 595548/01227 700067
AFT

CLARK, Christine
Group Analytic Psychotherapist
Lydens, 28 Pembury Road, Tonbridge, Kent TN9 2HX
01732 352637
IPC

COLEBY, Gillian
NLP Psychotherapist
c/o The Albany Clinic, 11 Station Road, Sidcup, Kent DA15 7EN
0181 300 4361
ANLP

COOPER, Heather
Cognitive Behavioural Psychotherapist
40 Stone Road, Broadstairs, Kent CT10 1DZ
01843 863643
BABCP

COOPER, Ian
Psychoanalytic Psychotherapist
2 Ashwood Court, 16 Albemarle Road, Beckenham, Kent BR3 5XN
0181 658 6967
IPC

COUTTS, Linda
Hypno-Psychotherapist
4 Ashleigh Gardens, Headcorn, Kent TN27 9TW
Grovehurst Surgery, Bramble Field Clinic, Kemsley, Sittingbourne, Kent
01622 890720
NSHAP

CRONIN, Jeremiah
Psychoanalytic Psychotherapist
St. Augustine's, Deanwood Drive, Rainham, Kent ME8 9PG
The Canterbury Clinic, 47 Castle Street, Canterbury, Kent CT1 2YP
01634 377396/01303 267946
GUILD, CSPK

CUNNINGHAM, Diane
Psychoanalytic Psychotherapist
Willow Farmhouse, Upper Harbeldown, Nr. Canterbury, Kent CT2 9AL
01227 768131
AGIP, CSPK

CUNNINGHAM, Valerie
Integrative Psychotherapist, Transactional Analysis Psychotherapist
19 Birling Road, Tunbridge Wells, Kent TN2 5LX
ITA, MET

CURWEN, Bernadette
Cognitive Behavioural Psychotherapist
Gravesend C.M.H.T., 6 High Street, Gravesend, Kent DA11 0BQ
01474 534200
BABCP

DANIELS, Deborah
Integrative Psychotherapist
6 Tinbridge Oast, Canterbury Road, Faversham, Kent ME13 9LJ
01795 533311
RCSPC

DANIELS, Kate
Family Therapist
15 Ashburnham Road, Tonbridge, Kent TN10 3DU
01732 359 120
AFT

DARNLEY, Hazel
Psychoanalytic Psychotherapist
Dove Cot, Anvil Green, Waltham, Canterbury, Kent CT4 7EU
01227 700752
CSPK

KENT

DAVIES, Peggy
Transactional Analysis Psychotherapist
11 Oakhurst Close, Walderslade, Kent
ME5 9AN
01634 861262 (t/f)
MET, ITA

DAWSON, Joyce
Psychoanalytic Psychotherapist
23 Mapledene, Kemnal Road,
Chislehurst, Kent BR7 6LX
0181 295 0286
IPC

DUCK, Dorothy M.
Hypno-Psychotherapist
Fairhaven, Station Road, Pluckley,
Ashford, Kent TN27 0Q2
01233 840263
NSHAP

DUGUID, Kathleen
Child Psychotherapist
Child & Family Adolescent Service,
Ravensbourne Trust, Glendinning
House, 11 Bromley Common, Kent
BR2 9LS
0181 672 6049
ACP

FRASER, Daphne
Transpersonal Psychotherapist
Herne Bay, Kent
01227 740 580
CCPE

FREEMAN, David
Analytical Psychologist-Jungian Analyst
222 Mackenzie Road, Beckenham, Kent
BR3 4SJ
0181 659 0108(t/f)
AJA

GAUSDEN, Christopher
Hypno-Psychotherapist
Alsirat, 1 Village Green Way, Biggin Hill,
Kent TN16 3NB
01959 540601
NRHP

GREEN, Eliott
Transactional Analysis Psychotherapist
St. Mary's Health Centre, Vicarage
Road, Strood, Rochester, Kent
ME2 4DG
01634 868809
ITA

HARMAN, Josephine
Integrative Psychotherapist
96 Springhead Road, Northfleet, Kent
DA11 9QY
01474 574022/01474 535335
RCSPC

HEADON, Christopher
Sexual and Marital Psychotherapist
79 Goodhart Way, West Wickham,
Kent BR4 0ET
0181 777 6422
BASMT

HEIMANN, Michael
Group Analyst
44 Queen's Road, Beckenham, Kent
BR3 4JL
0181 725 5055/0181 650 7567
IGA

HEINITZ, Karin
Biodynamic Psychotherapist
Flat 2, 12 Tankerton Road, Whitstable,
Kent CT5 2AB
01227 273580
BTC

HEWITT, Philip J.
Psychoanalytic Psychotherapist
27 Barnmead Road, Beckenham, Kent
BR3 1JF
Westminster School, 7 Dean's Yard,
London SW1 3PB
0171 963 1099/0181 402 2984
BAP

HIESTAND, Rene
Cognitive Behavioural Psychotherapist
Deal Mental Health Centre, Bowling
Green Lane, Deal, Kent CT14 9HF
01304 381321
BABCP

HILLS, John
Family Therapist
47 St Augustines Road, Canterbury,
Kent CT1 1XR
01227 786322/01227 452155
AFT

HIRON, Ruth
Psychoanalytic Psychotherapist
1 Lavender Bank, Beesfield Lane,
Farningham, Kent DA4 0DA
01322 862629
CSPK

HUGHES, Carol
Child Psychotherapist
Department of Child and Family
Psychiatry, George Trule House, 53
London Road, Canterbury CT2 8LF
01795 531 605/01227 462733
ACP

HUGHES, Jennifer
Psychoanalytic Psychotherapist
2 The Cheynes, Broad Street, Sutton
Valence, Maidstone Kent ME17 3AJ
01622 844937
IPC, CSPK

ISSA, Soraya
Cognitive Behavioural Psychotherapist
Psychology Service, Sevenoaks
Hospital, Hospital Road, Sevenoaks
TN13 3PG
c/o 6 The Green, High Street, Brasted,
Kent TN16 1JL
01732 740538
BABCP

JAKES, Simon
Cognitive Behavioural Psychotherapist
Psychological Services, Gablestones,
Stone House Hospital, Dartford
DA2 6AU
01322 6220661
BABCP

JONES, Margaret
Psychoanalytic Psychotherapist
Mill Cottage, 120 Heathfield Road,
Keston, Kent BR2 6BA
01689 853881
GUILD

JONES, Pamela
Hypno-Psychotherapist
25 Harrow Way, Weavering,
Maidstone, Kent ME14 5TU
Bramblefield Clinic, Grovehurst
Surgery, Sittingbourne, Kent ME10 2ST
01622 739266
NSHAP

KELLY, Bridget
Psychoanalytic Psychotherapist
54 Beacon Drive, Bean, Dartford, Kent
DA2 8BG
01474 705171
ARBS

LANCZI, Katalin
Psychoanalytic Psychotherapist
37 Preston Lane, Faversham, Kent
ME13 8LG
01795 590653
ARBS

LEE, John
Group Analyst
The Rectory, Chiddingstone,
Edenbridge, Kent TN8 7AH
01892 870478
IGA

LEIPER, Rob
Psychoanalytic Psychotherapist
Huntley Cottage, 122 Wateringbury
Road, East Malling, Kent ME19 6JD
Psychotherapy Service, The Courtyard,
Pudding Lane, Maidstone, Kent
ME14 1PA
01622 776355/01732 842349
CSPK

LENNOX, Graham
NLP Psychotherapist
72 Queens Road, Tankerton,
Whistable, Kent CT5 2JQ
01732 843830
ANLP

LETTINGTON, Lisa
Cognitive Analytic Therapist
9 Waldegrave Road, Bickley, Bromley,
Kent BR1 2JP
The Campshill Surgery, Campshill
Road, London SE13 6QU
0181 852 1384/0181 467 5513
ACAT

MARLOWE, Martin
Cognitive Analytic Therapist
Folkstone CMHT, 2 - 4 Radnor Park
Avenue, Folkstone CT19 5HN
01303 222444/01303 222422
ACAT

MCCOY, Sean
Cognitive Behavioural Psychotherapist
1 Sussex Road, West Wickham, Kent
BR4 0JX
0181 777 9837/01622 686123
BABCP

MENDELSSOHN, Penny
Family Therapist
The Coach House, Uckfield Lane,
Hever, Nr. Edenbridge, Kent TN8 7LQ
01732 862865
AFT

MORGAN, Ruth
Integrative Psychotherapist
206 Croydon Road, Beckenham, Kent
BR3 4DE
0181 658 3791
MC

MORRISH, Susan
Transactional Analysis Psychotherapist
Savannah, Sheerwater Road, Elmstone,
Canterbury, Kent CT3 1HJ
01227 721 783(t/f)
ITA

NELSON, Denise
Sexual and Marital Psychotherapist
4 St Anne's Court, off Buckland Road,
Maidstone, Kent ME16 0UQ
0585 427 659
BASMT

NELSON, Margaret
Existential Psychotherapist
39 Winchelsea Street, Dover, Kent
CT17 9ST
01304 213508
RCSPC

O'SULLIVAN, Renee
Integrative Psychotherapist
3 Town Road, Petham, Canterbury,
Kent CT2 8JY
01227 459700/01227 700898
RCSPC

OWENS-WARD, Lyn
Integrative Psychotherapist
58 Hayes Road, Bromley, Kent
BR2 9AA
0181 466 8802
RCSPC

PAE, Linda L S
Integrative Psychotherapist
93 Elwill Way, Park Langley,
Beckenham, Kent BR3 6RX
0171 955 4582/0181 658 5735
RCSPC

PALGRAVE, Lesley
Cognitive Analytic Therapist
2 Gainsborough Square, Bexleyheath,
Kent DA6 8BU
0181 301 2793
ACAT

PARKER, Niki
Child Psychotherapist
Child and Adolescent Mental Health
Service, 18 Crook Log, Bexleyheath,
Kent BR6
0181 303 4786/0181 693 3805
ACP

PENWARDEN, Mary M.
Child Psychotherapist
Lenworth Clinic, Dept. of Child &
Family Psychiatry, 329 Hythe Road,
Ashford, Kent TN24 0QE
0171 351 9429/01233 629875
ACP

PLUNKETT, Eileen
Integrative Arts Psychotherapist
Institute of St Anselm, Edgar Road,
Cliftonville, Margate, Kent CT9 2EU
01843 221865
IATE

QUINN, John J
Systemic Psychotherapist
41 Highfield Road, Chislehurst, Kent
BR7 6QY
0973 254385
KCC

RAE, Frances
Systemic Psychotherapist
21 Court Road, Tunbridge Wells, Kent
TN4 8EB
01892 543025
KCC

READING, Bill
Psychoanalytic Psychotherapist
1 Denstead Oast, Chartham Hatch,
Canterbury, Kent CT4 7SH
01227 730808
CSPK

REILLY, Anne
Psychoanalytic Psychotherapist
20 Beverly Road, Canterbury, Kent
CT2 7EN
01227 462295
CSPK

RICHARDS, Maureen
Sexual and Marital Psychotherapist
5 Lapins Lane, Kings Hill, West Malling,
Kent ME19 4LA
01732 875096
BASMT

RIDGEWAY, Nicola Louise
Cognitive Psychotherapist
9B Hatherley Road, Sidcup, Kent
DA14 4BH
0181 309 7369
BABCP

RIDING, Ann
Psychoanalytic Psychotherapist
32 Cromwell Road, Canterbury, Kent
CT1 3LE
01227 462511
CSPK

RIDING, Nick
Psychoanalytic Psychotherapist
Kent Institute of Medicine and Health Science, The University, Canterbury, Kent CT2 7PD
01227 823380/01227 462511
CSPK, UPA

RING, Brendan
Transactional Analysis Psychotherapist
10 St. James' Road, Gravesend, Kent
DA11 0HE
01474 359126
ITA

ROBERTS, Jane
Psychoanalytic Psychotherapist
5 Meadowbrook, Sandgate, Kent
CT20 3NY
01303 248538
CSPK

ROBERTS, Pauline
Psychoanalytic Psychotherapist
2 Knoll Road, Bexley, Kent DA5 1AZ
01322 553807
IPC

ROGERS, Lesley A.
Cognitive Behavioural Psychotherapist
202 Lower Higham Road, Gravesend, Kent DA12 2NN
Day Hospital, Orchard House, Joyce Green Hospital, Temple Hill, Dartford
01474 534200/01474 363584
BABCP

ROWLAND, Gail
NLP Psychotherapist
7 Lower Green Road, Pembury, Tunbridge Wells, Kent TN2 4DZ
01892 825667(f)/01892 825640
ANLP

ROYSTON, Robin
Analytical Psychologist-Jungian Analyst
The Red House, Stonewall Park Road, Langton Green, Tunbridge Wells, Kent
01892 863858
AJA

SCHAEDEL, Maggie
Psychoanalytic Psychotherapist
The Spinney Cottage, Knockholt Road, Halstead, Sevenoaks, Kent TN14 7EX
01959 532510
ARBS

SHAW, Maureen
Psychoanalytic Psychotherapist
20 Westbere Lane, Westbere, Canterbury, Kent CT2 0HH
01227 710505
CSPK

SMITH, Susan Diane
Hypno-Psychotherapist
The Bromley Stress Management Centre, 42 East Street, Bromley, Kent
BR1 1QW
0181 402 5421
NRHP

SPALDING, John
Psychoanalytic Psychotherapist
32 Aldermary Road, Bromley, Kent
BR1 3PH
Therapies Team, Stepping Stones, Oxleas Trust, 38 Masons Hill, Bromley
BR2 9JG
0181 466 2500/0181 464 8292
AGIP

SPARKS, Rebecca
Sexual and Marital Psychotherapist
Summerlea, Warren Avenue, Orpington, Kent BR6 6HX
BASMT

STEVENSON, Alice
Transactional Analysis Psychotherapist
Upper Green, Sandhurst, Hawkhurst, Kent TN18 5JX
01580 850361
ITA

STEVERSON, Jill
Psychosynthesis Psychotherapist
27 Baywell, Leybourne, Kent
ME19 5QQ
01732 872 290/01732 873 658
AAPP

THOMASON, June
Psychoanalytic Psychotherapist
South Cottage, High Street, Staplehurst, Kent TN12 0BH
01580 891402
CSPK

TOTMAN, Maria
Psychosynthesis Psychotherapist
61 Avenue Road, Erith, Kent DA8 3AT
01322 334139
AAPP

TOYNE, Joy K.
Hypno-Psychotherapist
Oast Meadow, Burns Hill, Brenchley, Tonbridge, Kent TN12 7AT
01892 723799
NRHP

TRAYLING, Laurie
Psychoanalytic Psychotherapist
14 Poyntell Road, Staplehurst, Kent
TN12 0SA
176 Holland Park, London W14 8AH
0171 602 4655/01580 892 939
IPC

TRUSCOTT, Frances
Child Psychotherapist
9 Sandown Close, Sandown Park, Tunbridge Wells, Kent TN2 4RL
01892 822093
ACP

TSE, Claude
Behavioural Psychotherapist
Dillywood Corner, Dillywood Lane, Higham, Rochester ME3 7NT
01634 717601
BABCP

TUBBS, I.A.
Cognitive Behavioural Psychotherapist
Englewood, Farningham Hill Road, Farningham, Kent DA4 0JR
01322 862158
BABCP

TULLY, Daphne
Sexual and Marital Psychotherapist
6 Monkton Gardens, Cliftonville, Margate, Kent CT9 3HN
BASMT

TWELVETREES, Heidy
Gestalt Psychotherapist, Humanistic Psychotherapist
Park Lodge, 38 Longlands Road, Sidcup, Kent DA15 7LT
0181 302 3800
AHPP

VAN-LOO, Douglas
Family Psychotherapist
5 Foxdown Close, Cangerbury, Kent
CT2 7RR
01227 781045
IFT

VINCENT, Christopher
Systemic Psychotherapist
Adolescent Resource Team, Dept. of Social Services & Housing, J. Lancaster Hall, Civic Ctr., Rafford Way, Bromley BR1 3UH
0181 464 3333 x 5213
KCC

VIRGO, Leslie
Integrative Psychotherapist
The Rectory, Skibbs Lane, Chelsfield, Kent BR6 7RH
01689 825749
MC

WALKER, David
Group Analyst
Dairy Cottage, 17 Dower House Crescent, Southborough, Kent TN4 0TT
01892 520239
IGA

WARREN, Yvonne
Integrative Psychotherapist
The Archdeaconry, Rochester, Kent ME1 1SX
01634 842527
RCSPC

WATERS, Anne
Transactional Analysis Psychotherapist
Benton Cottage, Dingleden, Benenden, Kent TN17 4JX
ITA

WATTERS, Tamara
Integrative Psychotherapist
26 Glen Iris Avenue, Canterbury, Kent CT2 8HP
01227 463342
MET

WESTCOTT, Rosemary
Psychoanalytic Psychotherapist
235 Southlands Road, Bromley BR1 2EG
0181 464 3136
GUILD

WHITMORE, Diana
Psychosynthesis Psychotherapist
Southfield, Leigh, Nr. Tonbridge, Kent TN11 8PJ
0171 403 2100
AAPP

WILLIS, James
Cognitive Behavioural Psychotherapist
25 Shelley Road, Maidstone, Kent ME16 8NS
28 Marsham Street, Maidstone, Kent ME14 1HG
BABCP

WILSON, Veronica
Integrative Arts Psychotherapist, Humanistic Psychotherapist
1 Hunts Hill, Moons Green, Wittersham, Kent TN30 7PR
01797 270621
IATE, AHPP

WOODROFFE, Roe
Integrative Psychosynthesis Psychotherapist
38 Prospect Road, Tunbridge Wells, Kent TN2 4SH
01892 543 596
RE.V

LANCASHIRE

ALEXANDER-GRAHAM, Cassy
Psychodrama Psychotherapist
Lane End Cottage, Cockerham Road, Bay House, Lancaster LA2 0HG
01524 792076/01772 204999 (f)
BPA

ARKWRIGHT, Lynda
Psychoanalytic Psychotherapist
Hazeldene, 48 Lytham Road, Fulwood, Preston, Lancs
01254 822121 x 2850/01172 719 942
NWIDP

ASHWORTH, Freda
Hypno-Psychotherapist
Mulsanne, 16 Harefield Drive, Heywood nr. Rochdale, Lancashire OL10 1RN
01706 368193
NRHP

BARTON, Alan
Psychodrama Psychotherapist
18 Jubilee Street, Read, Burnley, Lancashire BB12 7PR
01282 774136
BPA

BENTLEY, Ros
Gestalt Psychotherapist
Preston Therapy Centre, 57 Garstang Road, Preston PR1 1LB
42 Primrose Street, Lancaster LA1 3BN
01524 841993/01772 886994
GPTI

BLACK, Margaret
Hypno-Psychotherapist
3/6 Westcliffe House, Braddocks Close, Hurstead, Rochdale, Lancashire OL12 9UZ
01706 6310990
NSHAP

BONNEBAIGHT, Andre
Hypno-Psychotherapist
17 Fifield Close, Fitton Hill, Oldham, Lancs. OL8 2LE
0161 626 3275
CTS

BROWN, Philip
Psychoanalytic Psychotherapist
Department of Psychotherapy, 1 Albert Road, Fulwood, Preston PR2 8PS
01772 787197
NWIDP

CALLAGHAN, Joan
Psychoanalytic Psychotherapist
7 Aldford Close, Breightmet Drive, Bolton BL2 6NR
01204 387065
LPDO

CARTWRIGHT, Tony
Family Psychotherapist
37 Wolseley Road, Preston PR1 8EU
01772 882871
FIC

CASSON, John
Psychodrama Psychotherapist
62 Shaw Hall Bank Road, Greenfield, Saddleworth, Lanc OL3 7LE
01457 877659/01457 877161
BPA

CORNELL, Maria
Psychoanalytic Psychotherapist
Clinical Psychology Dept., Lancaster Moor Hospital, Quernmore Road, Lancaster LA1 3JR
01524 586400/01524 586564 (f)
NWIDP

CROSSLING, Paddy
Systemic Psychotherapist
22 The Square, Dobcross,
Saddleworth, Oldham OL3 5AA
FIC

CURTIS, Marjorie
Hypno-Psychotherapist
Mahogany, 38 Merefield, Astley Village,
Chorley, Lancashire PR7 1UR
01257 233089
CTS

CUTNER, Adrienne
Hypno-Psychotherapist
28 Tithebarn Hill, Glasson Dock,
Lancaster LA2 0DQ
01524 752080
CTS

DOYLE, Alan
Hypno-Psychotherapist
2 Westview, Ormskirk, Lancashire
L39 2DJ
01695 575001
CTS

FAGBADEGUN, Rufus
Group Analyst
Elton Grange Farm, Elton Vale Road,
Bury, Lancs BL8 2RZ
01282 773321/0161 763 3833
IGA

FERGUSON, Mary
Psychoanalytic Psychotherapist
Psychiatric Outpatient Department,
Royal Oldham Hospital, Rochdale
Road, Oldham OL1 2JH
0161 627 8330
LPDO

FLANAGAN, June
Cognitive Behavioural Psychotherapist
Palmers Greave, Lovely Hall Lane,
Salesbury, Lancashire BB1 9EQ
01524 389504/01254 246653
BABCP

FOWLER, Barry
Cognitive Behavioural Psychotherapist
Clinical Psychology Department, Birch
Hill Hospital, Union Road, Rochdale,
Lancs. OL12 9QB
01706 755 744
BABCP

FOXEN, Tom
Cognitive Behavioural Psychotherapist
4 Blenheim Street, Tyldesley, Lancashire
M29 8JL
01942 799015
BABCP

JARRETT, Betty
Psychodynamic Psychotherapist
449 Padham Road, Burnley, Lancashire
BB12 6TE
01282 412291
ULDPS

JUDKINS, Malcolm
Psychoanalytic Psychotherapist
Adelphi House Psychotherapy Unit, 12
Queen Street, Blackpool, Lancs.
FY1 1PD
01253 628653/01253 291336
NWIDP

KIEMLE, Gundi
Psychoanalytic Psychotherapist
NACTU (North)/Bolton Centre for
Sexual Health, Bolton General
Hospital, Minerva Road, Farnworth,
Bolton BL4 0JR
01204 390988/01204 390 775
LPDO

LAMB, Kirsten
Psychoanalytic Psychotherapist
Department of Clinical Psychology,
Bolton General Hospital, Minerva
Road, Farnworth, Bolton BL4 0JR
01204 390680
LPDO

LEGGATT, Claire
Psychoanalytic Psychotherapist
2 Lindow Square, Lancaster LA1 1SE
Psychotherapy Clinic, Lancaster Moor
Hosp., Quernmore Road, Lancaster
LA1 3JR
01524 586400/01524 383822
AGIP

LIDDLE, Helen
Psychoanalytic Psychotherapist
Adelphi House Psychotherapy Service,
12 Queen Street, Blackpool FY1 1PD
01253 628653
NWIDP

MACALISTER, Eileen
Group Analyst
14 Oulder Hill Drive, Rochdale,
Greater Manchester OL11 5LB
01706 45883
IGA

MAGUIRE, Claire
Psychoanalytic Psychotherapist
Dept. of Clinical Psychology, Fairfield
General Hospital, Rochdale Old Road,
Bury BL9 7TD
0161 705 3538
LPDO

MAKIN, Anne
Gestalt Psychotherapist
27 Beeston Close, Bolton BL1 7RT
01204 594000
GPTI

MARKLOW, Christine
Cognitive Behavioural Psychotherapist
Highfield Hospital, Manchester Road,
Rochdale, Lanc OL11 4LZ
Dept of Clinical Psychology,
Northowarm Hospital, Halifax
HX3 7SW
01422 201101/01706 655121
BABCP

MARKOVIC, Olivera
Family Therapist
Clinical Psychology Department,
Whitegate Drive, Blackpool FY3 9HG
01253 763740/01253 763232
AFT

MAY, Kath
Sexual and Marital Psychotherapist
29 Albert Street, Padiham, Burnley,
Lancs. BD12 8HE
BASMT

MCALLISTER, Susan
Psychoanalytic Psychotherapist
Specialist Psychological Therapy
Services, 1 Albert Road, Fulwood,
Preston, Lancs. PR2 8PJ
01772 787197
NWIDP

MOON, Barbara
Hypno-Psychotherapist
90 Watkin Road, Clayton-le-Woods,
Chorley, Lancashire PR6 7PX
01257 275169
CTS

MORRIS, Ann
Psychoanalytic Psychotherapist
Gable End, 44 Lyndeth Road, Silverdale,
Cannorth, Lancashire LA5 0TX
01524 702080
NAAP

PAMPHLETT, Nicholas
Transactional Analysis Psychotherapist
The Corner House, 97 Woone Lane,
Clitheroe, Lancs BB7 1BJ
01200 429450
ITA

RENWICK, Fran
Hypno-Psychotherapist
89 Ferndale Oak Meadows,
Skelmersdale, Lancashire WN8 6QY
01695 556323
CTS

ROSS, Julie
Psychoanalytic Psychotherapist
Psychology Department, 314 - 316
Oldham Road, Royton, Oldham
OL2 5AS
0161 624 0420 x 5350
LPDO

SAVAGE, Peter J.D.
Hypno-Psychotherapist
National College of Hypnosis &
Psychotherapy, 12 Cross Street,
Nelson, Lancs BB9 7EN
01282 699378/01282 698633 (f)
NRHP

SHELDON, Helen
Psychoanalytic Psychotherapist
Department of Clinical Psychology,
Bolton General Hospital, Minerva
Road, Farnworth, Bolton, Lancashire
BL4 0JR
01204 390675/01204 390669 (f)
NWIDP

SPRATT, Graham S.
Cognitive Behavioural Psychotherapist
Dept. of Clinical Psychology, Billinge
Hospital, Billinge, Wigan WN5 7ET
01695 626181
BABCP

STOKES, Fergus
Hypno-Psychotherapist
6 Kensington Road, Lytham St. Annes,
Lancashire FY8 4ET
01253 730588
CTS

SUDBURY, John
Psychodynamic Psychotherapist
139 Calderbrook Road, Littleborough,
Lancs OL15 9JW
01706 377577
HIP

SUMMERS, Graeme
Transactional Analysis Psychotherapist
1 Hollins Lane, Arnside, Cumbria
LA5 0EG
Manchester Gestalt Centre,
Manchester, 7 Norman Road M14 5LF
0161 225 2202/01524 762 607
MET, ITA

TAYLOR, Elizabeth
Hypno-Psychotherapist
5 Stonefold, Rising Bridge, Accrington
BB5 2DP
01706 210404
CTS

TURTON, Mike
Gestalt Psychotherapist
Preston Therapy Centre, 57 Garstang
Road, Preston, Lancs PR1 1LB
01772 886994
GPTI

VORA, Valerie
Sexual and Marital Psychotherapist
196 Manchester Road, Westhoughton,
Bolton BL5 3LA
01942 813647
BASMT

WALLACE, Daphne
Psychoanalytic Psychotherapist
The Vicarage, Skipton Road, Earby
Colne, Lancs BB8 6JL
01282 841608
LPDO

WALSH, Stuart
Psychodrama Psychotherapist, Family
Therapist
4 Woodlea, Church Road, Todmorden,
West Yorkshire OL14 8EZ
Rawnsley Building, York Place, MRI
Oxford Road, Manchester
01706 819873/0161 276 5370
AFT, BPA

WASHINGTON, Sue
Hypno-Psychotherapist
145 Chapel Lane, Longton, Preston
PR4 5NA
01772 614 211(f)/01772 617663
CTS

WELLER, Celia
Gestalt Psychotherapist
11 Park Avenue, Lancaster LA1 3DX
01524 63812
GPTI

WESSON, Peter M.J.
Hypno-Psychotherapist
Bury Complementary Health Centre,
12 Tenterden Street, Bury, Lancashire
BL9 0EG
Darlington Street Practice, Premier
House, Darlington Street,
Wolverhampton, West Midlands
0161 763 1660 (t/f)
NRHP

WILKIN, Peter
Psychoanalytic Psychotherapist
198 Railway Street, Summerseat, Bury
BL9 5QB
01204 882040
LPDO

WILLIAMS, Jane
Group Analyst
107 Clay Lane, Rochdale, Lancs.
OL11 8TD
IGA

LEICESTERSHIRE

BAILEY, James
Psychoanalytic Psychotherapist
Leicester Psychotherapy Dept. (NHS),
Humberstone Grange Clinic,
Thurmaston Lane, Leicester LE5 0TA
0116 225 6430
STTDP

BALL, Derek
Sexual and Marital Psychotherapist
Baker Vaughan Counselling Services,
Victoria House, 172-174 London Road,
Leicester LE2 1ND
BASMT

BARKER, John F.
Psychoanalytic Psychotherapist
Highways, Main Street, Cold Newton,
Leicestershire LE7 9DA
0116 259 5205
WMIP

BRADLEY, Marie
Psychoanalytic Psychotherapist
Leicester Psychotherapy Department
(NHS), Humberstone Grange Clinic,
Thurmaston Lane, Leicester LE5 0TA
0116 225 6430
STTDP

BUTTON, Eric
Personal Construct Psychotherapist
Dept. of Clinical Psychology, Psychiatric Dept., Leicester General Hospital, Gwendolen Road, Leicester LE5 4PW
0116 258 4770/0116 258 4745 (f)
CPCP

CHALLIS, Raymond T.
Hypno-Psychotherapist
2c HollyTree Close, Hoton, Loughborough LE12 5SE
85-91 Derby Road, Sandieacre, Nottingham NG10 5HZ
01509 881536
NRHP

CURRY, Naomi
Psychoanalytic Psychotherapist
Leicester Psychotherapy Dept. (NHS), Humberstone Grange Clinic, Thurmaston Lane, Leicester LE5 OTA
0116 225 6430
STTDP

DAVIES, Dilys
Cognitive Analytic Therapist
8 Church Lane, Quorn, Loughborough, Leicestershire LE12 8DP
01203 350111/01509 413866
ACAT

DAVIES, Rae
Gestalt Psychotherapist
171 Main Street, Willoughby-on-the-Wolds, Nr. Loughborough, Leicestershire LE12 6SY
01509 880850
SPTI

DENT, Peter
Psychodynamic Psychotherapist
40 Leicester Road, Hinckley, Leicestershire LE10 1LS
01455 63340
ULDPS

GOULD, Geraldine
Hypno-Psychotherapist
8 Moat Close, Thurlaston, Leicester LE9 7TM
01455 888276
NSHAP

HILLS, Janet
Integrative Psychotherapist, Body Psychotherapist
4 Storer Road, Loughborough, Leicestershire LE11 5EQ
01509 235948
CCBP

HIRST, Hazel
Transactional Analysis Psychotherapist
Holly Cottage, 26 Church Street, Billesdon, Leicestershire LE7 9AE
0116 259 6851
ITA

HURWOOD, Judith
Psychodynamic Psychotherapist
21 Park Road, Blaby, Leicester LE8 4ED
0116 277 0778
ULDPS

JACOBS, Michael
Psychodynamic Psychotherapist
22 Brookside Drive, Oadby, Leicester LE2 4PD
0116 271 8469
ULDPS

JEWSON, Sue
Psychodynamic Psychotherapist
42 Laureston Drive, Leicester LE2 2AQ
0116 270 0354
ULDPS

JONES, Richard
Psychoanalytic Psychotherapist
Leicester Psychotherapy Dept. (NHS), Humberstone Grange Clinic, Thurmaston Lane, Leicester LE5 0TA
0116 225 6430
STTDP

KING, Gail
Psychodynamic Psychotherapist
4 Hillcrest Avenue, Market Harborough, Leicestershire LE16 7AR
01858 461570
ULDPS

LEIPER, Elizabeth
Gestalt Psychotherapist
Fir Tree House, 6 Sandy Lane, Scalford, Nr. Melton Mowbray LE14 4DS
01664 444266
GPTI, MET

MACKENZIE, Liz
Gestalt Psychotherapist
69 Dulverton Road, Leicester LE3 0SE
0116 233 4726
GPTI

MADDEN, Felicity W.
Psychoanalytic Psychotherapist
Linden House, Great Easton, Market, Harborough LE16 7AR
01536 770 320
WMIP, ULDPS

MARSHALL, Hazel
Transpersonal Psychotherapist
52 Station Road, Leicester LE7 7HD
01162 364256
CTP

MARSHALL, Pam
Psychoanalytic Psychotherapist
Leister Psychotherapy Dept (NHS), Humberstone Grange Clinic, Thurmaston Lane, Leicester LE5 0TA
0116 225 6430
STTDP

MCFARLAND, Alf
Psychoanalytic Psychotherapist (Jungian)
29 Gimson Road, Western Park, Leicester LE3 6DZ
0116 255 3549
WMIP

MONK-STEEL, John
Transactional Analysis Psychotherapist
43 Stoneygate Road, Leicester LE2 2BP
0116 2700 290
ITA

MOUNTAIN, Anita
Transactional Analysis Psychotherapist
Beechwood, 56 Main Street, Desford, Leicester LE9 9GR
01455 824475 (t/f)
ITA

PERRY, Janet
Sexual and Marital Psychotherapist
78 Holmfield Road, Leicester LE2 1SB
0116 273 9912
BASMT

PORTER, Jim
Hypno-Psychotherapist
3 Ashmead Crescent, Birstall, Leicester LE4 4GS
0116 2672612
NSHAP

RATIGAN, Bernard
Psychoanalytic Psychotherapist, Psychodynamic Psychotherapist
36 Arthur Street, Leicestershire LE11 3AY
Nottingham Psychotherapy Dept (NHS), St.Ann's House, 114 Thorneywood Mount, Nottingham NG3 2PZ
0115 952 9454/01509 213 7709
STTDP, ULDPS, UPA

RAYSON, Joan
Sexual and Marital Psychotherapist
9 Mountbatten Road, Oakham, Rutland
LE15 6LS
01572 2573
BASMT

RICHARDSON, Sacha
Transpersonal Psychotherapist
Market Harborough, Leicestershire
01858 463211
CCPE

RUSSELL, Gillean
Psychoanalytic Psychotherapist
10 Renishaw Drive, Leicester LE5 5TY
0116 274 5424
IPC

SCHAVERIEN, Joy
Analytical Psychologist-Jungian Analyst
1 The Square, South Luffenham,
Oakham, Leicestershire LE15 8NS
01780 720117 (t/f)
WMIP

STRANG, Jenny
Psychodynamic Psychotherapist
University of Leicester Counselling
Service, 161 Welford Road, Leicester
LE2 6BF
0116 255 2550
ULDPS

TWIST, Graham
Cognitive Analytic Therapist
9 Wellesbourne Drive, Glenfield,
Leicester LE3 8ER
0116 233 1939
ACAT

WALKER, Moira
Psychodynamic Psychotherapist
22 Brookside Drive, Oadby, Leicester
LE2 4PD
0116 271 8469
ULDPS

WHITWORTH, Patricia
Integrative Psychotherapist
93 Melton Road, Barrow -on-Soar,
Leicester LE12 8NT
01509 413327
SPTI

WHYTE, Chris
Psychoanalytic Psychotherapist
Leicester Psychotherapy Dept. (NHS),
Humberstone Grange Clinic,
Thurmaston Lane, Leicester LE5 0TA
0116 225 6430
STTDP

WILLIAMS, Sherly
Psychoanalytic Psychotherapist
31 Kingsway Road, Evington, Leicester,
Leics. LE5 5TN
0116 273 7713
IPC, WMIP, ULDPS

LINCOLNSHIRE

BUCKLEY, Nicky
Psychoanalytic Psychotherapist
Lincoln Department of Psychotherapy,
1 St. Anns Road, Lincoln LN2 5RA
01522 512000
ARBS, WTC, STTDP

CLEGG, Ian
Hypno-Psychotherapist
5 Richards Avenue, Lincoln,
Lincolnshire LN6 8SJ
01522 688142
NSHAP

DIXON, Linda
Psychoanalytic Psychotherapist
44 High Street, Nettleham, Lincoln
LN2 2PL
01522 752226
UPA

EAST, Patricia
Psychodynamic Psychotherapist
Frogs Leap, 615 Newark Road, Lincoln
LN6 8SA
01522 681510
ULDPS

FISK, Geoff
Psychoanalytic Psychotherapist
Lincoln Dept. of Psychotherapy (NHS),
1 St Anne's Road, Lincoln LN1 5RA
01522 512000
STTDP

FLANNERY, Jean
Psychoanalytic Psychotherapist
8 Church Drive, Lincoln LN6 7AX
01522 526777/01522 514453
AGIP

HASSALL, Alan
Integrative Psychotherapist
'Cobblers', 34 High Street, Navenby,
Lincoln LN5 0DZ
01522 810940
NSAP

HEADWORTH, Jean
Psychoanalytic Psychotherapist
Glenbrooke, 5 Morden Close,
Metheringham, Lincoln LN4 3DU
01526 320 743
STTDP, HIP

JANICKYJ, John
Psychodynamic Psychotherapist
22 Main Street, Ewerby, Sleaford,
Lincolnshire NG34
01529 460546
ULDPS

MILLER, Lynda
Psychoanalytic Psychotherapist
8 Meynell Avenue, Lincoln LN6 7UT
Portsmouth Point, 82 Victoria Street,
Stromness, Orkney KW16 3BS
01522 530267
AGIP

PARIS, Jan
Integrative Psychotherapist
20 Drury Lane, Lincoln LN1 3BN
01522 533169
SPTI

SCOTT COMBES, Jacqueline
Gestalt Psychotherapist
11 Main Street, Wilsford, Grantham
NG32 3NS
01400 230224
SPTI

SUTHERLAND, Janet
Biodynamic Psychotherapist
Celandine House, 4 St Andrews Street,
Heckington, Sleaford, Lincs NG34 9RE
01529 461571
BTC

THOMSON, Alan
Personal Construct Psychotherapist
Highfield House, Glentham, Lincoln
LN8 2EU
01673 878508/01673 878774 (f)
CPCP

WALLIS, V.A.
Sexual and Marital Psychotherapist
9 Chestnut Close, Sudbrooke, Lincoln
LN2 2RD
01522 751211
BASMT

WARD, Ruth
Psychoanalytic Psychotherapist
The Old Rectory, Church Lane, East
Keal, Spilsby, Lincolnshire PE23 4AT
01790 752477
HIP

LONDON CENTRAL

ALTMAN, Michelle
Cognitive Behavioural Psychotherapist
262 Shakespeare Tower, Barbican, London EC2Y 8DR
Dept Psychological Medicine, St Bartholomew's Hospital, London EC2Y 8DR
0171 628 9719
BABCP

ARMSTRONG-PERLMAN, Eleanore
Psychoanalytic Psychotherapist
1 Endsleigh Place, London WC1H 0PL
Flat 1, 13 Endsleigh Street, London WC1
0171 387 8914
GUILD

ASHWIN, Mary
Integrative Psychotherapist
9 Nottingham Mansions, Nottingham Street, London W1M 3FJ
0171 486 3567
RCSPC

BEECHER-MOORE, Naona
Psychosynthesis Psychotherapist, Humanistic Psychotherapist
3 Temple Gardens, Middle Temple Lane, London EC4 9AU
0171 353 2101/0171 936 3449 (f)
AAPP, AHPP

BENTOVIM, Arnon
Family Psychotherapist
Child & Family Consultation Service, 234 Great Portland Street, London W1N 5PH
The Paddock, Harriots Close, Nuthurst, Near Horsham, West Sussex RH13 6LJ
0171 390 8377/01403 891588
IFT

BOADELLA, David
Individual and Group Humanistic Psychotherapist
BCM Chesil, London WC1N 3XX
00411 342 04444
AHPP

BOLLINGER, Charmian
Sexual and Marital Psychotherapist
124 Montagu Mansions, London W1H 1LA
BASMT

BOR, Robert
Family Therapist
Psychology Department, City University, Northampton Square, London EC1V 0HB
0171 477 8523/0171 477 8590 (f)
IFT

CAMPHER, Rosemary
Integrative Psychotherapist
140 Harley Street, London W1N 1AH
0171 224 3387/0171 722 8992
RCSPC

CROSS, Malcolm C
Personal Construct Psychotherapist
Department of Psychology, City University, Northampton Square, London EC1V 0HB
0171 477 8590(f)/0171 477 8531
CPCP

CUTTERIDGE, Simon
Systemic Psychotherapist
Covent Garden Counselling, 23 Bedfordbury, London WC2N 4BL
0171 240 1911
KCC

DACHY, Vincent
Lacanian Analyst
Oxford Circus W1
0171 580 9708
CFAR

DALY, Kevin
Cognitive Behavioural Psychotherapist
49 Queen Victoria Street, London EC4N 4SA
0171 431 1794
BABCP

DAVIDSON, Brian
Autogenic Psychotherapist
86 Harley Street, London W1N 5AE
0171 580 4188
BAFAT

DEAHL, Kieron
NLP Psychotherapist
Ability, 29 Crawford Street, London W1H 1PL
0171 419 9657
ANLP

DRANEY, Sue
Psychoanalytic Psychotherapist
Flat 1, Clare Court, Judd Street, London WC1H 9QW
0171 833 4156
GUILD

DU RY, Marc
Lacanian Analyst
31 Wimpole Street, London W1M 7AE
0171 224 1259/0370 888116
CFAR

EHLERS, Hella
Psychoanalytic Psychotherapist
Flat 12, Byron Court, 26 Mecklenburgh Square, London WC1N 2AF
0171 278 2212
ARBS

FARLEY, Nancy M.
Cognitive Behavioural Psychotherapist
London Medical Centre, 144 Harley Street, London W1N 4AH
0171 9350023
BABCP

GANN, Sandra
Sexual and Marital Psychotherapist
Dept. of Social Work, St. Bartholomew's Hospital, West Smithfields, London EC1V 7BE
0171 601 8718
BASMT

GLADSTONE, Guy
Psychoanalytic Psychotherapist, Individual and Group Humanistic Psychotherapist
The Open Centre, 188 Old Street, London EC1V 9FR
0171 272 6672
IPSS, AHPP

GLEDHILL, Maureen
Psychoanalytic Psychotherapist
93 Harley Street, London W1 1DF
0171 935 1163/0181 455 7211
LCP, CPP

GREEN, Brian
Psychoanalytic Psychotherapist
91 Bedford Court Mansions, Bedford Avenue, London WC1B 2AE
11 Alwyne Road, Islington N1 2HH
0171 354 3119(t/f)
IPC

GREENE, Alice
Autogenic Psychotherapist
86 Harley Street, London W1N 5AE
0171 580 4188 (t/f)
BAFAT

GREW, Lesley
Hypno-Psychotherapist
11 Clare Court, Judd Street, London
WC1H 9QW
0171 837 9772
NRHP

HALLAM, Richard S
Cognitive Behavioural Psychotherapist
319 Endsleigh Court, Upper Woburn
Place, London WC1H 0HF
0171 387 0069
BABCP

HODGES, Jill
Child Psychotherapist
Dept. of Psychological Medicine, Great
Ormond Street Hospital, Great
Ormond Street, London WC1N 3JH
0171 829 8888 X 5578/0181 809 2834
ACP

HOLDEN, John
Psychoanalytic Psychotherapist
Priest's Court, 4 Foster Lane, London
EC2V 6HH
0171 606 1863
IPC

KALITOWSKI, Matthew
Hypno-Psychotherapist
27, Midhope House, Midhope Street,
London WC1H 8HH
0171 916 3681
NSHAP

KEE, Cynthia
Educational Therapist
35 Goodge Street, London W1P 1FD
0171 636 3243
FAETT

KORTE, Achim
Biodynamic Psychotherapist
Flat 8, 52 Langham Street, London
House W1N 5RF
0171 636 7514
BTC

LEADER, Darian
Lacanian Analyst
Flat 2, 5 Bulstrode Street, London W1
0171 487 5415
CFAR

LILLEY, Davina
Group Analyst
13a Chadwell Street, London EC1R
IGA

LILLIE, Francis
Cognitive Behavioural Psychotherapist
27a Harley Place, London W1N 1HB
0171 323 2370
BABCP

LLOYD, Patricia
Sexual and Marital Psychotherapist
3 De Walden Street, London W1M 7PJ
0171 224 6872
BASMT

LOOSE, Judith Green
Child Psychotherapist
6 Montagu Square, London W1H 1RA
0171 224 6028/0171 935 0802 (t/f)
ACP

MAGAGNA, Jeanne
Child Psychotherapist
Dept. of Psychological Medicine, Great
Ormond Street Hospital, Great
Ormond Street, London WC1N 3JH
0171 829 8679/0171 829 8657 (f)
ACP

MAGUIRE, Anne
Analytical Psychologist-Jungian Analyst
23 Harley Street, London W1N 1DA
17 Wellington Street, St John's,
Blackburn BB1 8AF
IGAP

MANGLANI, Dona
Psychoanalytic Psychotherapist
13 Riceyman House, Lloyd Baker
Street, London WC1X 9BH
Astis, 311a New Cross Road, London
SE14 6AS
0181 691 9771/0171 837 8924
IPSS

MARKOVIC, Desa
Systemic Psychotherapist
23 Bedfordbury, London WC2N 4BL
0171 2401911
KCC

MCKENNA, Clare
Integrative Psychotherapist
44 Harley Street, London W1N 1AD
0171 636 1192
RCSPC

MOSES, Susan
Psychoanalytic Psychotherapist
9 Amen Court, Warwick Lane, London
EC4M 7BU
0171 489 0779
IPC

MYCROFT, Jessica
Psychoanalytic Psychotherapist
26 Northampton Square, London
EC1V 0ES
0171 253 6963/0171 253 3765
IPSS, FIP

NIELSEN-CERNKOVICH, Rudy
Psychoanalytic Psychotherapist
AVPS, 127 City Road, London
EC1V 1JB
0171 490 3311
ARBS

PARISSIS, Maria
Integrative Psychotherapist
5a Nottingham Mansion, Nottingham
Street, London W1M 3FY
0171 935 9995
RCSPC

PERRING, Michael
Integrative Psychotherapist, Sexual and
Marital Psychotherapist
Optimal Health, 114 Harley Street,
London W1N 1AG
La Tuque, 33220 Ste. Foy La Grande,
SW France
0171 935 5651/0171 935 3858 (f)
MET, BASMT

SHERLOCK, Teresa
NLP Psychotherapist
46 Harley Street, London W1N 1AD
0171 580 9431
ANLP

SIMON, Gail
Systemic Psychotherapist
5 Tavistock Place, London WC1
01535 635 444
KCC

TAIT, Mike
Group Analyst
Counselling and Advice Service,
Medical Centre of City University, 20
Sebastian Street, Islington EC1V 0HB
202 Hoxton Street, London N1 5LH
0171 477 8000/0956 898450
IGA

VIBERT, Eva
Transpersonal Psychotherapist
22 Queen Anne Street, London
W1M 9LB
0171 631 1334
CTP

VICK, Philippa
Transpersonal Psychotherapist
44 Gloucester Place Mews, London
W1H 3PL
Well Cottage, Kingweston Road,
Charlton Mackrell, Somerton,
Somerset TA11 6AH
0171 935 2294/01458 822 3099
CTP

WATTS, Mary
Cognitive Behavioural Psychotherapist
Department of Psychology, City
University, Northampton Square,
London EC1V 0HB
0181 239 6947/0171 477 8528
BABCP

WELLINGS, Nigel
Psychoanalytic Psychotherapist
44 Gloucester Place Mews, London
W1H 3PL
0171 935 2294/01485 223099
AGIP, AIP, CTP

WHITFIELD, Gwyn
Systemic Psychotherapist
5 Tavistock Place, London WC1
01535 636 444
KCC

WILLIAMSON, Ian
Jungian Child Analyst, Child
Psychotherapist
17 Wimpole Street, London
W1M 7AD
53 Bouverie Road, London N16 0AH
0171 486 0044/0181 802 9189
SAP, ACP

WILSON, Peter
Child Psychotherapist, Psychoanalytic
Psychotherapist
Young Minds, 2nd Floor, 102-108
Clerkenwell Road, London EC1M 5SA
74 Dukes Avenue, London N10 2PU
0171 336 8445/0181 883 6370 (f)
ACP, BAP

WOLF, Darren
Integrative Psychotherapist
5c Peabody Building, Herbrand Street,
London WC1N 1JJ
0171 209 1285
RCSPC

WRIGHT, Laurie Jo
Attachment-based Psychoanalytic
Psychotherapist
16 Bingham Place, London W1M 3FH
Mousehole Farm, Willingham Lane,
Burwash Weald, East Sussex
TN19 7HR
01435 882756/0171 486 2608
CAPP

YAPP, Robin
Cognitive Behavioural Psychotherapist
25 Galway House, Radnor Street,
London EC1V 3SL
BABCP

LONDON EAST

ADAMS, Martin
Existential Psychotherapist
84 Middleton Road, London E8 4LN
0171 254 2707
RCSPC

AGGETT, Percy
Family Therapist, Systemic
Psychotherapist
Child and Family Consultation Service,
250 - 252 Katherine Road, London
E7 8PN
69 Glenarm Road, Hackney, London
E5 0LY
0181 533 0594/0181 218 7440
IFT

ANDREWS, Gill
Psychoanalytic Psychotherapist
67A Navarino Road, London E8 1AG
0171 249 2674
NAFSI

ANSON, Carol
Systemic Psychotherapist
7 Upper Walthamstow Road,
Walthamstow, London E17 3QG
0181 521 7932
KCC

ATKINSON, Paul
Psychoanalytic Psychotherapist
6A St. Mark's Rise, London E8 2NJ
0171 241 2506
GUILD

BANNISTER, Gill
Psychoanalytic Psychotherapist
78 Lichfield Road, Bow, London E3 5AL
0181 981 2244
IPC

BENDER, Helen
Child Psychotherapist
Child & Family Consultation Centre,
Royal London Hospital, London E1 1BB
0171 377 7390/0181 445 4798
ACP

BICKERTON, Tricia
Psychoanalytic Psychotherapist
86 Eleanor Road, Hackney, London
E8 1DN
0171 249 2770
GUILD

BOND, Lesley
Transpersonal Psychotherapist
59 Godwin Road, Forest Gate, London
E7 0LF
0181 555 8869
CCPE

BOULTON, John
Psychoanalytic Psychotherapist
10 Cardigan Road, Bow, London
E3 5HU
0181 980 0934
CPP

BRION, Marion
NLP Psychotherapist
59 Osborne Road, London E7 0PJ
0181 534 5494
ANLP

BURGESS, Shanti
Hypno-Psychotherapist
64 Queenswood Gardens, Wanstead,
London E11 3SF
0181 530 4413
NSHAP

BURLINGTON, Maggie
Psychosynthesis Psychotherapist
68 Devonshire Road, London E17 8QJ
0181 521 3269
AAPP

CHAPMAN, Sandy
Analytical Psychologist-Jungian Analyst
148 Millfields Road, London E5 0AD
0181 986 3792
BAP, FIP

CHESNER, Anna
Psychodrama Psychotherapist
64 Manchester Road, London E14 3BE
089 314 9250(f)/089 3143458
BPA

COLLINS, Natalie
Psychoanalytic Psychotherapist
133 Larkshall Road, North Chingford, London E4 6PE
0181 529 4986
GUILD

COLLOMS, Anita
Child Psychotherapist, Psychoanalytic Psychotherapist
Lower Clapton Child & Fam.Consultation Serv., 36 Lower Clapton Road, London E5 0PQ
6 Archibald Road, London N7 0AL
0171 607 1640/0181 986 7351
ACP, BAP

COOPER, Rebecca
Humanistic Psychotherapist
99 Eleanor Road, London E8 1DN
0171 254 7186
AHPP

CORBETT, Martyn
Group Analyst
73 Richmond Road, London E8 3AA
0171 923 4549
IGA

COX, Philip
Psychoanalytic Psychotherapist
63 Somerset Road, London E17 8QN
0181 520 9391
AGIP

CRAWFORD, Joan
Integrative Psychosynthesis Psychotherapist
56 Gordon Road, London E11 2RB
0181 518 8699
RE.V

CROMBIE, Clare
Gestalt Psychotherapist
103 Wellington Row, London E2 7BN
0171 729 3810
GCL

D'ARDENNE, Patricia
Sexual and Marital Psychotherapist
Dept of Clinical Psychology, City & Hackney Community Services, NHS Trust, 50-52 Clifden Road, London E5 0LJ
0181 510 8661
BASMT

DANIEL, Barbara
Psychoanalytic Psychotherapist, Family Therapist
78 Rushmore Road, Lower Clapton, London E5 0EX
0181 986 8377
GUILD, AFT, AFT

DANIEL, Catherine
Educational Therapist
11b Grosvenor Road, London E11 2EW
0181 530 4866
FAETT

DAVID, Anna
Integrative Psychotherapist
22B Montague Road, Hackney, London E8 2HW
0171 923 1019
RCSPC

DAWSON, Linda
Child Psychotherapist
Wellington Way Centre, 1A Wellington Way, Bow, London E3 4NE
0181 981 1441(f)/0181 980 3510
ACP

DELVE, Stuart
Family & Relationship Psychotherapist
33 Sherrard Road, London E7 8DN
0181 471 7498
AFT

DUFFY, Rosemary
Child Psychotherapist
Newham Child and Family Consultation Service, 84 West Ham Lane, London E15 4PT
0171 250 7347/0181 250 7355 (f)
ACP

EKDAWI, Isabelle
Systemic Psychotherapist
Community House, 430 Barking Road, Plaistow, London E13 8HJ
0171 445 7777
KCC

FARUKI, Shirley
Hypno-Psychotherapist
38 Pulteney Road, South Woodford, London E18 1PS
0181 989 6734
NRHP

FRANKS, Julia
Transpersonal Psychotherapist
61 Nightingale Road, London E5 8NB
0171 682 0090/0060
CCPE

FROSHAUG, Ann
Analytical Psychotherapist
196 Queensbridge Road, London E8 4QE
0171 254 4041
LCP, FIP

GAUCI, Kate
Cognitive Behavioural Psychotherapist
63 Reighton Road, Stoke Newington, London E5 8SQ
0181 442 6124/0171 502 1582
BABCP

GAWLER-WRIGHT, Pamela
Hypno-Psychotherapist, NLP Psychotherapist
Beeleaf House, 34 Grove Road, London E3 5AX
The Helios Centre
0181 983 9699
NSHAP, ANLP

GIBSON, Jenny
Transactional Analysis Psychotherapist
36 Morecambe Close, Beaumont Square, Stepney Green, London E1 4NH
MET, ITA

GOOD, Simon
Psychoanalytic Psychotherapist
38 Addison Road, London E11 2RG
0181 201 8525/0181 989 6529
GUILD

GOODES, Deborah
Psychoanalytic Psychotherapist
8 Oakdale Road, Leytonstone, London E11 4DL
0181 926 0797
ARBS

GRAVES, Jane
Psychoanalytic Psychotherapist
1a Albert Road, Silvertown, London E16 2DW
0171 511 8703
CPP

GRAY, Kati
Psychoanalytic Psychotherapist
30 Skelton Road, London E7 9NJ
0181 471 8016
GUILD

HARDING, Celia
Psychoanalytic Psychotherapist
36 Richmond Road, Leytonstone, London E11 4BU
0181 556 5089
IPC

HASLAM, Deidre
Humanistic Psychotherapist, Cognitive Analytic Therapist
85 Rushmore Road, London E5 0EX
0181 986 3051
AHPP, ACAT

HAWKES, Bernadette
Psychoanalytic Psychotherapist
32 Canning Road, Walthamstow, London E17 6LT
0181 509 1484
IPSS

HENDERSON, John
Child Psychotherapist
Newham Child & Family Consultation Service, 252 Katherine Road, London E7 8PW
0181 552 5171/0181 340 2275
ACP

HERINGTON, Steve
Family Psychotherapist
7 Upper Walthamstow Road, London E17 3QG
0181 521 7932
IFT

HOANG, Astrid
Group Analytic Psychotherapist
'Gratton Lodg', 40 Spruce Hills Road, Walthamstow, London E17 4LD
0181 527 7258/0181 503 3840 (f)
IPC

HUSON, Richard
Psychosynthesis Psychotherapist
Flat 7, Sugar Loaf Walk, London E2 0JQ
0181 981 2428
AAPP

JACQUES, Glenys
Gestalt Psychotherapist
15 Kemey's Street, Homerton, London E9 5RQ
0181 533 2948 (t/f)
GPTI, MET, AHPP

JONES, Dave
Humanistic Psychotherapist
8 Forest Glade, Leytonstone, London E11 1LU
0181 989 6565
AHPP

KANE, Ros
Psychoanalytic Psychotherapist
15 Matcham Road, London E11 3LE
0181 555 5248
GUILD

KEANE, Agnes
Transpersonal Psychotherapist
29 Dunton Road, Leyton, London E10 7AF
CCPE

KIRKLAND, Margot
Psychosynthesis Psychotherapist
Ashwin Street Practice, The Print House, 18 Ashwin Street, London E8 3DL
0171 254 9202
AAPP

LAMPRELL, Michael
Psychoanalytic Psychotherapist
36 Richmond Road, Leytonstone, London E11 4BU
0181 556 5089
IPC

LEVINE, Hanelle G
NLP Psychotherapist
148 Sewardstone Road, Bethnal Green, London E2 9HN
0181 983 0581
ANLP

MALKIN, Julius
Cognitive Behavioural Psychotherapist
Professional Development Foundation, 21 Limehouse Cut, 46 Morris Road, London E14 6NQ
0181 340 2692/0171 987 2805
BABCP

MAZARAKI, Angeliki
Psychoanalytic Psychotherapist
22 Idmiston Road, London E15 1RG
0181 519 5995
ARBS

MCCANN, Linda
Systemic Psychotherapist
67 Clapton Common, London E5 9AA
Department Child Psychiatry, Queen Elizabeth Hospital, Hackney Road E2 9AA
0171 608 6361/0181 806 9370
IFT

MCCARRON, Gerard
Cognitive Psychotherapist
92 Onslow Gardens, South Woodford, London E18 1NB
0181 442 6528/0181 491 7756
BABCP

MCGRATH, Rita
Family Therapist
17 Warwick Road, Wanstead, London E11 2DZ
0181 989 2834
IFT

MESSENT, Philip
Family Psychotherapist
Emanuel Miller Centre, Gill Street, London E14 8HQ
44 Glenwood Road, London N15 3JU
0181 245 4372/0171 515 6633
IFT

MOOREY, Stirling
Cognitive Behavioural Psychotherapist
City and Hackney Community Services, 50 - 52 Clifen Road, London E5 0LJ
0181 510 7842(f)/0181 510 8242
BABCP

NESBIT, Judith
Psychoanalytic Psychotherapist
32 Thornby Road, London E5 9QL
0181 986 5286
AGIP, FIP

O'BRIEN, Ann
Hypno-Psychotherapist
88b Antill Road, Bow. London E3 5BP
Bodywise, 119 Roman Road, Bethnal Green, London E2 0QN
0181 981 6938/0181 981 3082
NSHAP

O'KEEFFE, Tim
Psychoanalytic Psychotherapist
60 St Mary Road, Walthamstow, London E17 9RE
0181 309 3920 (f)/0181 520 3766
AGIP

O'LEARY, Carmen
Group Analyst
14 Queen's Grove Road, London E4 7PT
0181 919 5555 x 8630/0181 529 3536
IGA

PAPADOPOULOS, Renos
Analytical Psychologist-Jungian Analyst, Family Psychotherapist
20 Woodriffe Road, London E11 1AH
0181 556 3180/0181 532 8313 (f)
IGAP, AFT

PEARMAIN, Rosalind
Psychoanalytic Psychotherapist
69 Gordon Road, Wanstead, London
E11 2RA
0181 989 8891/0171 487 7553 (f)
GUILD, RCSPC

PHILBIN, Mairead
Psychosynthesis Psychotherapist
St. Joseph's Hospice, Mare Street,
Hackney, London E8 4SA
0181 986 2285/0181 985 0861
AAPP

PIXNER, Stefanie
Integrative Psychotherapist
94 Colvestone Crescent, Hackney,
London E8 2LJ
0171 254 6216
MC

PLEN, Rene
Systemic Psychotherapist
57 Mayola Road, London E5 0RE
BASMT

ROWAN, John
Individual and Group Humanistic
Psychotherapist
70 Kings Head Hill, North Chingford,
London E4 7LY
0181 524 7381/0181 523 7281 (f)
AHPP

SANDELSON, Jennifer
Sexual and Marital Psychotherapist
9 Meynell Crescent, London E9 7AS
0181 525 0772
BASMT

SCOTT, Tricia
Individual and Group Humanistic
Psychotherapist
8 Shrubland Road, London E8 4NN
0171 254 4490
AHPP

SHEARMAN, Christine
Integrative Psychotherapist,
Transactional Analysis Psychotherapist
Hawthorn, 24 Hollybush Hill, London
E11 1PP
ITA, MET, GPTI

SHETLAND, Llrich
Psychoanalytic Psychotherapist
76A Lauriston Road, London E9 7HA
0181 986 5889
IPSS

SHUTTLEWORTH, Alan
Child Psychotherapist
Walthamstow Child & Family
Consultation Service, Shernhall Street,
London E17 3EA
0181 509 2452/0181 883 7908
ACP

SLADE, John
Integrative Psychotherapist
86 Clifden Road, London E5 0LN
0181 533 0022 (t/f)
MC

SMART, Tanya
Systemic Psychotherapist
East Ham Day Centre, Shrewsbury
Road, Forest Gate, London E7 8QR
0181 586 5000
KCC

SMITH, Gerrilyn
Family Psychotherapist
Clinical Psychologist, PO Box 6568,
London E5 0XD
0171 391 9150/0181 985 8081
IFT

SOMERVILLE, Gwynnedd
Psychoanalytic Psychotherapist
23 Mornington Grove, London E3 4NS
0181 983 1085
IPC

SPENDELOW, Lyndsay
Integrative Psychotherapist
9 Mountague Place, Poplar, London
E14 0EX
0956 235995/0171 987 2275
RCSPC

STEDMAN, Maire Aine
Family Therapist
Child and Family Consultation Serv,
252 Katherine Road, Forest Gate,
London E7 8PN
0181 469 0975/0181 218 7449
IFT

STIASNY, Jennifer
Child Psychotherapist
Newham Child & Family Consultation
Service, 84 West Ham Lane, London
E15 4PT
0181 250 7347/0181 250 7355 (f)
ACP

SUTHERLAND, Elisabeth
Psychosynthesis Psychotherapist
50 Blondin Street, Bow, London
E3 2TR
0181 981 1553
AAPP

TAYLOR, Mary
Psychoanalytic Psychotherapist
118 Glenarm Road, Hackney E5 0NA
0181 986 1108
LCP

TAYLOR, Tracey
Cognitive Behavioural Psychotherapist
Psychotherapy Department, 50 - 52
Clifden Road, Hackney, London E5 0LJ
0181 510 7842(f)/0181 510 8287
BABCP

THOMAS, Mark
Gestalt Psychotherapist
209 Richmond Road, London E8 3NJ
0181 985 4386
GPTI

TOGHER, Margaret
Systemic Psychotherapist
Chingford Health Centre, 109 York
Road, Chingford, London E4 8LF
0181 523 8479/0468 132 381
KCC

TRISTRAM, Sue
Integrative Psychotherapist, Body
Psychotherapist
231 Glyn Road, London E5
0181 749 3155
CCBP

TUFNELL, Guinevere
Family Psychotherapist
Child & Family Consultation Service,
Shernhall Street, London E17 3EA
0181 509 0424/0181 509 2452 (f)
IFT

URWIN, Catherine
Child Psychotherapist
Emanuel Miller Centre, The Health
Centre, 11 Gill Street, London
E14 8HQ
0171 515 6633/0181 802 8593
ACP

VAS DIAS, Susan
Child Psychotherapist, Attachment-based Psychoanalytic Psychotherapist
69 Gordon Road, London E18 1DT
Diagnostic Unit, Queen Elizabeth Hosp. for Children, Hackney Road, London E2 8PS
0171 739 8422 x 6425/0181 559 1244
ACP, CAPP

VINCENT, David
Group Analyst
15 Draycot Road, Wanstead, London E11 2NX
0181 535 6899/0181 989 6028
IGA

VIRTANEN, Helena
Systemic Psychotherapist, Family Therapist
64 Goldsmith Road, Walthamstow, London E17 6AW
0181 527 5460
IFT

WARWICK, Kate
Child Psychotherapist
Lower Clapton Child & Family Consultation Service, 36 Lower Clapton Road, London E5 0PQ
0181 809 7791/0181 986 7351
ACP

WOOLLISCROFT, Jessica
Humanistic Psychotherapist, Gestalt Psychotherapist
28 Whitehall Gardens, London E4 6EH
0181 559 3568
AHPP

LONDON NORTH

ABELES, Margi
Systemic Psychotherapist
6 Beech Drive, London N2 9NY
0181 374 0634
KCC

ABLACK, Joanne
Integrative Psychotherapist, Gestalt Psychotherapist
71 Burghley Road, London N8 0QG
0181 888 6010
CCBP

ABRAHAMS, Elisabeth
Integrative Psychotherapist
57 Holdenhurst Avenue, Finchley, London N12 0JA
0181 346 7104
MC

ABRAM, Jan
Psychoanalytic Psychotherapist
18 Ridge Road, London N8 9LG
0181 292 0263 (f)/0181 292 8584
LCP

ABSE, Susanna
Psychoanalytic Marital Psychotherapist
17 Muswell Avenue, Muswell Hill, London N10 2EB
0181 883 5746/0181 883 3985 (f)
TMSI

AL JARRAH, Nadina
Psychoanalytic Psychotherapist
12 Regina Road, Islington, London N4 3PP
0171 272 3253
NAFSI

AL RUBAIE, Talal
Hypno-Psychotherapist
41 Denison Close, East End Road, East Finchley, London N2 0JU
0181 444 9567
NSHAP

ALBRECHT, Gisela
Psychoanalytic Psychotherapist
45 Ashley Road, London N19 3AG
0171 281 1265
IPC

ALEXANDER, Sandra
Sexual and Marital Psychotherapist
39 Outram Road, London N22 4AB
BASMT

ALFEROFF, Tamara
Transpersonal Psychotherapist
London N19 3BG
0171 272 3589
CCPE

ALLAN, Brenda
Family Psychotherapist
61 Woodland Rise, London N10 3UN
0181 883 0385/0181 444 0851
AFT

ALLSOP, Paul
Humanistic and Integrative Psychotherapist, Gestalt Psychotherapist
Spectrum, 7 Endymion Road, London N4 1EE
0181 883 3246
SPEC

AMIEL, Olivia
Psychoanalytic Psychotherapist
16 Elms Avenue, London N10 2JP
0181 442 0753 (t/f)
GUILD

ANDERSON, Elizabeth
Psychoanalytic Psychotherapist
140 Muswell Hill Road, London N10 3JD
c/o AGIP, 1 Fairbridge Road, London N19 3EW
0181 444 2507 (f)/0171 272 7013
AGIP, FIP

ANDRY, Robert
Psychoanalytic Psychotherapist, Group Analyst
44 Cholmley Crescent, London N6 5HA
0181 340 7293
LCP, BAP, IGA

ANKER, Ofra
Psychosynthesis Psychotherapist
13 Oldfield Mews, London N6 5XA
0181 341 1759 (t/f)
AAPP

ARIEL, Seema
Psychoanalytic Psychotherapist
22 Durham Road, London N2 9DN
0181 883 7386
AGIP

ARNOLD, Katherine
Child Psychotherapist
57 Cecile Park, Crouch End, London N8 9AX
0181 340 2922
ACP, CPP

ARNOLD, Rosemary
Psychoanalytic Psychotherapist
3 Stanmore Road, London N15 3PR
48 Freeman Street, Wells-Next-The-Sea, Norfolk NR23 1BA
0181 889 7335
GUILD

ASHERI, Shoshi
Integrative Psychotherapist, Body Psychotherapist
22b Uplands Road, Crouch End, London N8 9NL
0181 340 7168
CCBP

AZGAD, Racheli
Psychoanalytic Psychotherapist
67 Dollis Road, London N3 1RD
0181 346 1525
PA

BAKER, Adrienne
Integrative Psychotherapist
16 Sheldon Avenue, Highgate, London N6 4JT
0181 340 5970/0171 487 7644
RCSPC

BALOGH HENGHES, Tessa
Child Psychotherapist
92 Highgate Hill, London N6 5HE
0181 348 7731
ACP

BAR, Vivien
Psychoanalytic Psychotherapist, Lacanian Analyst
5 Stanmore Road, London N15 3PR
0181 889 5925
GUILD, CFAR, WTC

BARADON, Tessa
Child Psychotherapist
22 Edmund Walk, London N2 0HU
0181 455 6886/0181 883 9308
ACP

BARKER, Gina
Humanistic Psychotherapist
50 Burma Road, London N16 9BJ
0171 275 8002
CAPP

BARRATT, Gillian
Psychoanalytic Psychotherapist, Group Analyst
19 Clifton Road, London N8 8JA
0181 451 8424/0181 348 1735
IGA, BAP

BARRY, Anne
Integrative Psychotherapist
43 Dukes Avenue, Muswell Hill, London N10 2PX
0181 365 3261
NSAP

BARTLETT, Francesca
Child Psychotherapist
Child and Adolescent Mental Health, St. Ann's Hospital, St. Ann's Road, London N15 3TH
0181 442 6467/0171 226 9933
ACP

BEAUMONT, Mia
Psychoanalytic Psychotherapist, Educational Therapist
13 Highbury Terrace, London N5 1UP
0171 226 8103
GUILD, FAETT

BECKETT, Dale
NLP Psychotherapist
18 Ockenden Road, Islington, London N1 3NP
0171 354 5170(f)/0171 704 9999
ANLP

BEHR, Harold
Group Analyst
81 Gordon Road, London N3 1ER
0181 965 5733/0181 346 8323
IGA

BENSIMON, Marlene
Psychoanalytic Psychotherapist
31 Rookfield Avenue, London N10 3TG
0181 444 5878
IPSS

BENTLEY, Patrick Joseph
Systemic Psychotherapist
Hackney Child & Family Consultation Service, Woodberry Down Unit, John Scott Health Centre, Green Lanes, London N4 2NU
44 Sydney Road, London N10 2RL
0181 809 5577/0181 883 9943
KCC

BERESFORD, Marie
Psychosynthesis Psychotherapist
153c Brecknock Road, Tufnell Park, London N19
0171 267 7643
AAPP

BERKE, Joseph
Psychoanalytic Psychotherapist
5 Shepherd's Close, London N6 5AG
0181 348 4492/0181 348 4733 (f)
ARBS

BERRY, Sally
Psychoanalytic Psychotherapist
11 Cecile Park, London N8 9AX
0181 340 5161
ARBS, WTC

BHATT, Vibha
Psychoanalytic Psychotherapist
85 Sydney Road, London N8 0ET
0181 348 9313
GUILD

BIANCO, Vicky
Family Therapist
16 Willow Bridge Road, Canonbury, London N1 2LA
0171 226 1931
IFT

BIERSCHENK, John H.
Analytical Psychologist-Jungian Analyst
58 Queen's Avenue, London N10 3NU
0181 883 3567 (T/F)
AJA

BILDER, Tessa
Transpersonal Psychotherapist
61 Huntingdon Road, London N2 9DX
0181 444 5289
CCPE

BINNINGTON, Linda
Psychoanalytic Marital Psychotherapist
6 Tyndale Terrace, Canonbury Lane, London N1 2AT
0171 704 1444
TMSI

BLACK, Judith
Hypno-Psychotherapist
Clissold Park Natural Health Centre, 154 Stoke Newington Church Street, London N16 0JU
31 Merritt Road, Crofton Park, London SE4 1DT
0181 691 1168
NSHAP

BLACKWELL, Frances
Psychoanalytic Psychotherapist
2 Victoria Road, Finsbury Road, London N4 3SQ
0171 281 1552
IPSS

BOWMAN, Heather
Integrative Psychotherapist
9 Leadale Road, Stamford Hill, London N16 6BZ
0181 800 8476
MC

BOWNAS, Jo
Systemic Psychotherapist
4 Clyro Court, Tollington Park, London N4 3AQ
0171 263 1897
KCC

BOYDEN, Christina
Hypno-Psychotherapist
69 Goddard Place, off Monnery Road, London N19 5GT
0171 281 9650(f)/0171 281 9663
NSHAP

BRADLEY, Catrin
Child Psychotherapist
Hackney Child & Family Consultation Service, Woodbury Down Unit, John Scott Health Centre, Green Lanes, London N4 2NU
0181 809 5577/0181 444 4733
ACP

BRADLEY, Jonathan
Child Psychotherapist
54 Durham Road, London N2 9DT
Tavistock Clinic, 120 Belsize Lane, London NW3 5BA
0171 435 7111/0181 444 7433
ACP, CPP

BRADLEY, Rex
Humanistic and Integrative Psychotherapist
Spectrum, 7 Endymion Road, London N4 1EE
0181 341 2277/01705 649266 (f)
SPEC

BRATERMAN, Eleanor
Hypno-Psychotherapist
36E Portland Rise, London N4 2PP
0181 802 9206
NSHAP

BRAUNER, Rita
Transactional Analysis Psychotherapist
Upper Flat, 69 Rectory Road, London N16 7PP
0171 241 1477
NAFSI, ITA, MET

BRAVE-SMITH, Anna
Psychoanalytic Psychotherapist
59 Holmesdale Road, London N6 5TH
0181 340 9137
IPSS

BRENNAN, Damian
Personal Construct Psychotherapist
81 Sperling Road, London N17 6UJ
0181 808 7873
CPCP

BRENNAN, Stan
Humanistic and Integrative Psychotherapist
Spectrum, 7 Endymion Road, London N4 1EE
0181 340 9690
SPEC

BROADBENT, Keith
Cognitive Behavioural Psychotherapist
15 Linzee Road, Hornsey, London N8 7RG
0956 353041
BABCP

BROWN, Sara
Psychoanalytic Psychotherapist
6 Carlingford Road, Turnpike Lane, London N15 3EH
0181 889 3464
AGIP

BUNSTER, Jane
Analytical Psychologist-Jungian Analyst, Jungian Child Analyst
93 Tufnell Park Road, London N7 0PS
0171 221 4656/0171 607 8468
ACP

BURGOYNE, Bernard
Lacanian Analyst
5 Stanmore Road, London N15 3PR
0181 889 5925
CFAR

BURRIDGE, Ellora Polly
Educational Therapist
34 Mercers Road, London N19 4PJ
0171 272 2069
FAETT

BURROUGHES, Christopher
Family Therapist
143 Kyverdale Road, London N16 6PS
0181 806 3577/106614,2225@compuserve.com
AFT

BURY, Dennis R.
Personal Construct Psychotherapist, Cognitive Behavioural Psychotherapist
Minds Eye (I) Practice, 47 Mayfield Road, Hornsey, London N8 9LL
0181 348 9181/0181 341 7873 (f)
CPCP, BABCP

BUSS-TWACHTMANN, Christel
Psychoanalytic Marital Psychotherapist
Flat 1, 75 Cromwell Avenue, London N6
0181 341 1358
TMSI

BYGOTT, Catherine
Analytical Psychologist-Jungian Analyst
28 Cornwall Avenue, London N22 4DA
0181 881 0929
AJA

BYRING, Carola
Biodynamic Psychotherapist
32 Rosemary Avenue, London N3 2QN
0181 343 0255
BTC

CAMERON, Anna
Psychoanalytic Psychotherapist
37 Orpington Road, Winchmore Hill, London N21 3PD
0181 482 0787
ARBS

CAMERON, Michael John
Rational Emotive Behaviour Therapist
3A Thyra Grove, Finchley, London N12 8HD
0181 445 1369
BABCP

CAMERON, Roderick
Psychoanalytic Psychotherapist
37 Orpington Road, Winchmore Hill, London N21 3PD
0181 350 7164 (f)/0181 482 0787
ARBS

CAMPBELL NYE, Aileen
Analytical Psychologist-Jungian Analyst
The Garden Flat, 25a Penn Road, London N7 9RD
0171 609 4364
IGAP

CAMPBELL-THOMSON, Christina
Psychoanalytic Psychotherapist
21 Sussex Way, London N7 6RT
0171 686 4080
ARBS

CAROLAN, Nicholas
Psychoanalytic Psychotherapist
55 Horsham Avenue, North Finchley, London N12 9BG
0181 361 4512
LCP

CARROLL, Penny
Psychosynthesis Psychotherapist
38 Ridgeway Gardens, Hornsey Lane, Highgate, London N6 5XR
0171 281 2300
AAPP

CASHFORD, Jules
Analytical Psychologist-Jungian Analyst
136 Cloudesley Road, London N1 0EA
0171 278 2383(f)/0171 278 6468
AJA, AIP

CATHIE, Sean
Psychoanalytic Psychotherapist
23 Brookfield Mansions, Highgate West Hill, London N6 6AS
0181 347 7050
IPC

CAVISTON, Paul
Psychoanalytic Psychotherapist
54 Leswin Road, London N16 7NH
0181 970 8130/0171 254 7188
PA

CHAMLEE-COLE, Laurena
NLP Psychotherapist
38 Middle Lane, London N8 8PG
0181 340 8156
ANLP

CHANDLER, Philip
Psychoanalytic Psychotherapist
31 Huntingdon Road, London N2
0181 444 7690
GUILD

CHARALAMBOUS, Praxoulla
Psychoanalytic Psychotherapist
48 Old Park Road, Palmers Green, London N13 4RE
0181 886 8488
LCP, WTC

CHATFIELD, Anne
Group Analyst
88 Woodland Gardens, Muswell Hill, London N10 3UB
0181 883 4085
IGA

CHIN, John C L
Cognitive Behavioural Psychotherapist
169 firs Lane, Winchmore Hill, London N21 3HY
01708 386477/0181 7869
BABCP

CHINA, Jacques
Psychoanalytic Psychotherapist
54 Compton Road, London N1 1EJ
0171 354 1533
GUILD

CHRISTOPHER, Elphis
Analytical Psychologist-Jungian Analyst
35 Wood Vale, London N10 3DJ
0181 442 6810/0181 883 0085
FIP

CLIFFORD, Jennifer
Psychoanalytic Psychotherapist
10 Alwyne Place, London N1 2NL
0171 354 3930 (t/f)
IPC

CLIFFORD, Victoria
Attachment-based Psychoanalytic Psychotherapist
Pure Balance Mind & Body Centre, 1A Leicester Mews, Leicester Road, London N2 9DJ
0181 883 4316
CAPP

COHEN, David
Psychoanalytic Psychotherapist
43 Burma Road, Stoke Newington, London N16 9BH
0171 249 4917
LCP

COHEN, Maggie
Child Psychotherapist
Neonatal Intensive Care Unit, Whittington Hospital, Highgate, London N19 5NF
0171 288 5530/0171 485 7913(f)
ACP

COHEN, Sylvia
Psychoanalytic Psychotherapist
11 Clifton Avenue, London N3 1BN
0181 343 4097 (t/f)
GUILD

COHN, Nancy
Child Psychotherapist, Psychoanalytic Psychotherapist
108 Dartmouth Park Hill, London N19 5HT
0171 272 3529
ACP, GUILD

CONOLLY, J M P
Psychoanalytic Psychotherapist, Lacanian Analyst
48 Beresford Road, London N1 1DR
0181 340 6044
CFAR

COOKLIN, Alan
Family Therapist
89 Southwood Lane, London N6 5TB
0181 340 5895/0181 374 2577 (f)
IFT

COOPER, Howard
Psychoanalytic Psychotherapist
37 Lansdowne Road, London N3 1ET
0181 349 3891
AGIP

COOPER, Jillian
Existential Psychotherapist
24 Rocliffe Street, London N1 8DT
0171 253 1651
RCSPC

COOPER, Sara
Psychoanalytic Psychotherapist
37 Lansdowne Road, London N3 1ET
0181 349 3891
GUILD

COOPER, Terry
Humanistic and Integrative Psychotherapist, Body Psychotherapist
Spectrum, 7 Endymion Road, London N4 1EE
0181 341 2277/0181 340 0426 (f)
SPEC

COULSON, Susan
Child Psychotherapist
Hornsey Rise Child Guidance Unit, Beaumont Rise, London N19 3YU
0171 530 2444/0181 348 5726
ACP

COUZYN, Jeni
Psychoanalytic Psychotherapist
30 Chestnut Avenue, London N8 8NY
0181 340 5697
GUILD

COWAN-JENSSEN, Susan
Primal Psychotherapist
West Hill House, 6 Swains Lane, Highgate, London N6 6QU
0171 267 9616
LAPP

CRACE, Gay
Psychoanalytic Psychotherapist
125 Ashurst Road, London N12 9AD
0181 446 1251
AIP

CRAWFORD, Stephen
Psychoanalytic Psychotherapist
29 Cromwell Close, East Finchley, London N2 0LL
0181 444 8570
IPC

CRITCHLEY, Bill
Integrative Psychotherapist, Gestalt Psychotherapist
1 Northolme Road, London N5 2UZ
0171 354 0745/0171 354 8216
MET, GPTI

CROWLEY, Julia
Psychoanalytic Psychotherapist
61 East End Road, East Finchley, London N2 0SF
0181 346 1337
IPC

CROWTHER, Catherine
Analytical Psychologist-Jungian Analyst
50 Leconfield Road, London N5 2SN
0171 226 3112
SAP

CRYER, Valerie
Psychoanalytic Psychotherapist
40 Oakleigh Park South, London N20 9JN
0181 343 7659
AGIP

CURTI-GIALDINO, Francesca
Family Therapist
29 Parolles Road, London N19 3RE
0171 281 3861
AFT

DALAL, Farhad
Group Analyst
51 Evering Road, Stoke Newington, London N16 7PU
0171 249 5118
IGA

DANIELS, Orpa
Psychoanalytic Marital Psychotherapist
4 Shortgate, Woodside Park, London N12 7JP
0181 445 8117
TMSI

DANIELS, Susan
Psychoanalytic Psychotherapist
4 Finsbury Park Road, London N4 2JZ
0171 503 8154
IPSS

DANTHOIS, Didier
Biodynamic Psychotherapist
32 Rosemary Avenue, London N3 2QN
0181 343 0255
BTC

DARLING, Liv
Psychoanalytic Psychotherapist
318 Long Lane, East Finchley, London N2 8JP
0181 349 9792
AGIP

DAVENPORT, Marie-Laure
Psychoanalytic Psychotherapist
28 Onslow Gardens, London N10 3JU
0181 444 4695
PA, WTC

DIANIN, Gianni
Psychoanalytic Psychotherapist
24 Morley Avenue, Wood Green, London N22 6LY
0181 888 7338
ARBS, FIP

DOBBS, Wendy
Psychoanalytic Psychotherapist
2 Giesbach Road, London N19 3EH
0171 272 4207
AGIP, FIP

DOMB, Yair
Child Psychotherapist
1 Coleraine Cottages, Fortis Green, London N2 9HJ
0181 883 7694
ACP

DOUST, Gill
Humanistic and Integrative Psychotherapist
1 Duckett Road, London N4 1BJ
0181 341 9168
SPEC

DRIVER, Christine
Psychoanalytic Psychotherapist
71 Umfreville Road, London N4 1RZ
0181 340 3324
IPC

DUFFELL, Nick
Psychosynthesis Psychotherapist
128a Northview Road, Hornsey, London N8 7LP
0181 905 5937/0181 341 4885
AAPP

DUNN, Jenny
Psychoanalytic Psychotherapist
3 Monsell Road, London N4 2EF
0171 354 2100
GUILD

DUNN, Mark
Cognitive Analytic Therapist
49 Princes Avenue, Wood Green, London N22 4SB
Munro Clinic, Guy's Hospital, London SE1 9RT
0171 955 4822/0181 888 9629
ACAT, UPA

DUTTON, Jane
Systemic Psychotherapist
97 Foulden Road, London N16 7UH
Institute of Family Therapy, 24 - 32 Stephenson Way, London NW1 2HX
0171 249 3993/0171 391 3150
IFT

ECCLES, Barbara
Child Psychotherapist
Dept. of Clinical Psychology, St. Ann's Hospital, St. Ann's Road, London N15 3TH
0181 442 6467/0181 442 6737 (f)
ACP

EGERT, Susan
Psychoanalytic Psychotherapist
136 Winston Road, London N16 9LJ
0181 3621 5651/0171 254 0526
GUILD

EINHORN, Sue
Group Analyst
37 Stanhope Gardens, London N4 1HY
0181 800 7247/0171 607 2789
IGA, WTC

EINZIG, Hetty
Psychosynthesis Psychotherapist
42 Norcott Road, London N16 7EL
0171 843 6099/0181 806 3730
AAPP

EISEN, Susan
Psychoanalytic Psychotherapist
53 Benthal Road, London N16 7AR
0181 806 8313/0181 806 8703
GUILD

ELDER, Penny
Psychoanalytic Psychotherapist
24 Muswell Road, Muswell Hill, London N10 2BG
0181 883 3399
LCP

ELEFTHERIADOU, Zack
Integrative Psychotherapist
9 Woodside Avenue, London N6 4SP
0181 444 4042
RCSPC

ELLIOTT, Lois
Psychoanalytic Psychotherapist
112 Nelson Road, London N8 9RN
0181 348 8419
ARBS

ELLIS, Mary Lynne
Psychoanalytic Psychotherapist
78 Huddleston Road, London N7 0EG
0171 263 2410
PA

ELLIS, Michael
Gestalt Psychotherapist, Humanistic Psychotherapist
5a Cromartie Road, London N19 3SJ
0171 263 4778 (t/f)
GCL, AHPP

EMANUEL, Louise
Child Psychotherapist
52 Inderwick Road, London N8 9LD
0181 348 7032
ACP

EMERY, Pamela
Transpersonal Psychotherapist
66 Whitehall Park, London N19 3TN
0171 263 8689
CCPE

ENDER, Beckett
Psychosynthesis Psychotherapist
124b Northview Road, Hornsey, London N8 7LP
0191 281 8500/0191 276 3962
AAPP

ENDER, Dorry
Psychosynthesis Psychotherapist
36 Heysham Road, London N15 6HL
0181 809 6061/0171 380 0608
AAPP

EPSTEIN, Frances
Integrative Psychotherapist
156 Gladesmore Road, London N15 6TH
0181 802 0761
RCSPC

ERNST, Sheila
Group Analyst, Psychoanalytic Psychotherapist
53 Manor Road, London N16 5BH
0181 800 7371
IGA, WTC

ERSKINE, Ruth
Family Psychotherapist
12 Priory Avenue, London N8 7RN
Maudsley Hospital, Childrens Dept., Denmark Hill, London SE5
0171 919 2545/0181 340 4642
IFT

FAGAN, Margaret
Psychoanalytic Psychotherapist
76 Twyford Avenue, London N2 9NN
0181 883 9095
ARBS

FARRELL, Em
Integrative Psychotherapist
26 Freegrove Road, London N7 9RQ
0171 609 0507/0171 607 8306
RCSPC

FAWKES, Caroline
Psychoanalytic Psychotherapist
90 Woodland Gardens, London N10 3UB
0181 372 0728
ARBS

FELDBERG, Marilyn
Psychosynthesis Psychotherapist
21 Clifton Avenue, London N3 1BN
0181 349 9429
AAPP

FELDMAN, Wendy
Child Psychotherapist
5 Cholmeley Crescent, Highgate, London N6 5EZ
0171 340 0878/0181 340 0463 (f)
ACP

FERGUSON, Geoff
Psychoanalytic Psychotherapist
113 Wargrave Avenue, London N15 6TX
0181 802 4353
NAFSI

FERNANDEZ, Valentina
Cognitive Behavioural Psychotherapist
18C Beaconsfield Road, London N11 3AB
The Hillside Practice, 1 Hillside, Highgate Road, London NW5 1QT
0181 361 3108
BABCP

FIELD, Nathan
Analytical Psychologist-Jungian Analyst, Analytical Psychotherapist
14 Talbot Road, Highgate, London N6 4QR
0181 341 0904
LCP, BAP

FIGLIO, Karl
Psychoanalytic Psychotherapist
Flat 5, 5-7 Marlborough Road, London N19 4NA
24 Rosebery Avenue, Colchester CO1 2UJ
01206 866954/0171 281 1740
AGIP, LCP

FINLAY, Rosalind
Analytical Psychologist-Jungian Analyst
31 Hampstead Lane, London N6 4RT
0181 340 6211
AJA

FLINSPACH, Elisabeth
Integrative Psychotherapist
50c Albert Road, Finsbury Park, London N4 3RP
3 The Syke, Brigstock, Kettering, Northamptonshire NN14 3HR
01536 373 058/0171 263 2098
MC

FLOWER, Steven
Psychosynthesis Psychotherapist
47 Winton Avenue, London N11 2AS
0181 881 4155
AAPP

FOGELBERG, Don
Personal Construct Psychotherapist
16 Hewitt Road, London N8 0BL
0181 340 9612
CPCP

FORD, Susan
Psychoanalytic Psychotherapist
48 Crayford Road, London N7 0ND
0171 609 9019(f)/0171 609 4800
FIP

FORTI, Laura
Psychoanalytic Psychotherapist
38 Berkeley Road, London N8 8RU
0181 348 6933/0181 340 2936 (f)
ARBS

FOX, Loretta
Psychosynthesis Psychotherapist
1 Helen Court, Hendon Lane, Finchley, London N3 3SX
0181 349 0448
AAPP

FRAZER, Diane
Psychoanalytic Psychotherapist
c/o AGIP, 1 Fairbridge Road, London
N19 3EW
0171 272 7013
AGIP

FREEMAN, Catherine
Psychoanalytic Psychotherapist
c/o AGIP, 1 Fairbridge Road, London
N19 3EW
0181 442 6528/0171 272 7013
AGIP

FREEMAN, Sue
Psychoanalytic Psychotherapist
5a Winchester Road, London
N6 5HW
0181 348 8889
IPC

GALLAGHER, Teresa
Integrative Psychotherapist
16 Evershot Road, London N4 3BB
0171 272 7906/0171 686 9408
RCSPC

GEE, Irene
Family Therapist
41 Eastern Road, London N2 9LB
0181 444 9832
IFT

GILBERT, Gillie
Biodynamic Psychotherapist
27 Sandringham Gardens, North
Finchley, London N12 0NY
0181 445 8424
BTC

GILDEBRAND, Katarina
Transactional Analysis Psychotherapist,
Integrative Psychotherapist
25 Grove Avenue, London N3 1QS
0181 349 9827 (f)
ITA, MET

GODSIL, Geraldine
Analytical Psychologist-Jungian Analyst
60 Ealing Park Gardens, London
N5 4EU
0181 960 5744
FIP

GOLDBLATT, Phyllis
Psychoanalytic Psychotherapist
104 Southwood Lane, London N6 5SY
0181 348 4125
GUILD

GOODRICH, Diana
Psychoanalytic Psychotherapist
Open Door, 12 Middle Lane, London
N8
16 Clifton Road, London N8 8JA
0181 340 6397 (Tel & Fax)/0181 348
5947
GUILD

GORDON, Elizabeth
Analytical Psychologist-Jungian Analyst
68 Hornsey Lane, London N6 5LU
0171 263 3898/0171 263 3725
IGAP

GOSLETT, Kate
Psychoanalytic Psychotherapist
83 Axminster Road, London N7 6BS
0171 272 8322
IPSS

GOW, Marion
Psychoanalytic Psychotherapist
76b Inderwick Road, London N8 9JY
0181 347 8748
GUILD, WTC

GRAHAM, Judy
Humanistic Psychotherapist
12 Almeida Street, London N1 1TA
53 New Cavendish Street, London
W1M 7RF
0171 354 2240
AHPP

GRANOWSKI, Margaret
Integrative Psychotherapist
191 Brecknock Road, London
N19 5AB
0171 485 5274
MC

GRANT, Rosamund
Psychoanalytic Psychotherapist
84 Raleigh Road, London N8 0JA
0181 341 7339
GUILD, WTC, NAFSI

GREALLY, Brid
Psychoanalytic Psychotherapist
25 Clonmell Road, London N17 6JY
0181 885 1866
IPC

GREEN, Margaret
Psychoanalytic Psychotherapist
158a Stapleton Hall Road, London
N4 4QJ
0171 263 3775
ARBS, WTC

GREEN-THOMPSON, Cyril
Hypno-Psychotherapist
4 Alexandra National House, 330
Seven Sisters Road, London N4 2PF
0181 802 7103
NSHAP

GRIFFITHS, Sheila
Systemic Psychotherapist
22 Church Crescent, London
N10 3ND
0181 883 0289
KCC

GROSS, Grete
Autogenic Psychotherapist
21 Walfield Avenue, London N20 9PS
0181 445 8275
BAFAT

GROSS, Stephen
Analytical Psychologist-Jungian Analyst,
Psychoanalytic Psychotherapist
5 Barnard Hill, London N10 2HB
0181 444 0598
BAP, AIP

GROSS, Vivien
Systemic Psychotherapist, Family
Therapist
5 Barnard Hill, Muswell Hill, London
N10 2HB
Institute of Family Therapy, 24 - 32
Stephensons Way, London NW1 2HX
0171 391 9150/0181 444 0598
IFT

GURION, Michal
Child Psychotherapist
28 Princes Avenue, London N22 4SA
0181 881 0026
ACP

GÜNGÖR, Dilek
Psychoanalytic Psychotherapist
278 Seven Sisters Road, London
N4 2HY
0181 881 1921
NAFSI

HADARY, Gideon
Child Psychotherapist
Dept. of Clinical Psychology, St. Ann's
Hospital, St. Ann's Road, London
N15 3TH
0181 442 6467/0181 442 6737 (f)
ACP

HALL, Guy
Psychoanalytic Psychotherapist
13 Falkland Avenue, London N3 1QR
0181 343 0069
FIP

HALL, Kirsty
Psychoanalytic Psychotherapist
134 Dukes Avenue, London N10 2QB
0171 267 2848/0181 883 9681
ARBS, FIP

HALTON, William
Child Psychotherapist
10 Lincoln Road, London N2 9DL
0181 444 7497
ACP

HAMILTON, Dorothy
Psychoanalytic Psychotherapist
1 Fairbridge Road, London N19 3EW
0171 272 7013
AGIP

HAMILTON-DUCKETT, Paule
Psychoanalytic Psychotherapist
132 St. James Lane, Muswell Hill, London N10 3RH
0181 444 3577
IPC

HAMROGUE, Tom
Group Analyst
33 Victoria Road, London N22 4XA
01707 297 9000/7949/0181 888 6315
IGA

HANCOCK, Maureen
Gestalt Psychotherapist
233 Biddestone Road, London N7 9UE
0181 700 3298
GCL

HANNON, Sr. Mary Letizia
Educational Therapist
53 Bethune Road, London N16 5EE
0181 802 3430
FAETT

HARGREAVES, Judy
Humanistic and Integrative Psychotherapist
Spectrum, 7 Endymion Road, London N4 1EE
34 Bassein Park Road, London W12 9RZ
0181 341 2277/0181 749 1964
SPEC

HARLEY, Ki
Transactional Analysis Psychotherapist
25 Grove Avenue, Finchley Central, London N3 1QS
ITA, MET

HARPER, Anita
Transpersonal Psychotherapist
62 Highgate Hill, London N19 5NQ
0171 263 2005
CCPE

HARRIS, Tirril
Psychoanalytic Psychotherapist
6 Tufnell Park Road, London N7 0DP
0171 272 9235/0171 272 8570 (f)
LCP, BAP

HARRISON, Jane
Psychosynthesis Psychotherapist
60 Beaconsfield Road, London N15 4SJ
0181 800 3704/0181 802 2649
AAPP

HARTMAN, Wendy
Psychoanalytic Psychotherapist
19 Baalbec Road, Highbury Fields, London N5 1QN
0171 226 4775
IPC

HASKINS, Nicola
Transpersonal Psychotherapist
Highbury, London N5
0171 226 6680
CCPE

HAY, Jennifer
Integrative Psychotherapist
Flat 2, 5 Brendon Grove, London N2 8JE
0181 349 4035
RCSPC

HAZELTON, Sally
Integrative Psychotherapist
10 Glaserton Road, London N16 5QX
0171 502 8129/0181 802 9313
RCSPC

HEISMANN, Elisabeth
Systemic Psychotherapist
81 - 83b Arlington Avenue, London N1 7BA
0171 226 3946
KCC

HEMMING, Judith
Gestalt Psychotherapist
79 Ronalds Road, London N5 1XB
0171 359 3000/0171 359 6920(f)
GPTI, MET

HENDERSON, David
Analytical Psychotherapist
Basement Flat, 16 Marlborough Road, London N19 4NB
0171 281 6219
AIP

HENDERSON DALAL, Pauline
Integrative Psychotherapist
51 Evering Road, London N16 7PU
0171 249 5118
MC

HEWITT, Amanda
Family Therapist
Home Farm, Totteridge Green, London N20 8PH
0181 445 7882
AFT

HIGH, Helen
Educational Therapist, Child Psychotherapist
7 Hillside Gardens, London N6 5SU
0181 340 7037/0181 347 5997 (f)
FAETT, ACP, BAP

HILDER, Alison
Child Psychotherapist
7 Quick Street, London N1 8HL
0171 278 2088
ACP

HILLER, Ruth
Analytical Psychologist-Jungian Analyst
20 Canonbury Park North, London N1 2JT
0171 226 3723
IGAP

HOLENDER, Gisele
Psychoanalytic Psychotherapist
1 Coleraine Cottages, Fortis Green, London N2 9HJ
0181 883 7694
LCP

HOLLAND, Stevie
Attachment-based Psychoanalytic Psychotherapist
7 Cheverton Road, London N19 3BB
0171 263 4184/0171 281 3190
CAPP

HOLLINGS, Avril
Humanistic and Integrative Psychotherapist
Spectrum, 7 Endymion Road, London N4 1EE
0181 341 7214
SPEC

HOLLOWAY, Sheila
Educational Therapist
175 Albert Road, London N22 7AQ
0181 888 8851
FAETT

HOPE, Francis
Psychosynthesis Psychotherapist
4 Highbury Terrace Mews, London
N5 1UT
07050 196299/0171 241 2776
AAPP

HOSKING, John
Attachment-based Psychoanalytic Psychotherapist
58 Woodlands Gardens, London
N10 3UA
0181 444 3664
CAPP

HOWELL, Carolyn
Transpersonal Psychotherapist
21 Millington House, Stoke Newington Church Street, London N16 9JA
0171 241 2817
CCPE

HUDSON, Inge
Group Analyst, Psychoanalytic Psychotherapist
22 Scarborough Road, Stroud Green, London N4 4LT
0171 281 1710
IGA, WTC

HUDSON, Pauline
Systemic Psychotherapist
68 Tetherdown, Muswell Hill, London
N10 1NG
0411 533 819/0181 883 7662
KCC

HUGHES, Ann
Psychoanalytic Psychotherapist
92 Hemingford Road, London N1 1DD
0171 607 0803
GUILD

HUNT, Maggie
Psychosynthesis Psychotherapist
79 Grange Park Avenue, London
N21 2LN
0181 360 1024
AAPP

INLANDER, Antonia
Psychoanalytic Psychotherapist
Flat 7, Victoria Mansions, 135 Holloway Road, London N7 8LZ
0171 272 7013/0171 607 9805
AGIP

IVESON, Diana
Family Psychotherapist
77 Muswell Avenue, London N10 2EH
Brief Therapy Practice, 4d Shirlland Mews, London W9 3DY
0181 968 0070/0181 883 5731
IFT

JACKSON, Eve
Analytical Psychologist-Jungian Analyst
54 Eade Road, London N4 1DH
0181 800 1418 (t/f)
IGAP

JAMES, Jessica
Group Analyst, Psychoanalytic Psychotherapist
26 Kyverdale Road, Hackney, London
N16 7AH
0181 806 4820
IGA, WTC

JENNINGS, Lyn C.
Educational Therapist
25 Hoodcote Gardens, London
N21 2NG
0181 360 5423
FAETT

JENSSEN, Einar D.
Primal Psychotherapist
West Hill House, 6 Swains Lane, Highgate, London N6 6QU
0171 267 9616
LAPP

JOBBINS, Bryan
Psychoanalytic Psychotherapist
220 Stapleton Hall Road, London
N4 4QR
0181 341 3286
LCP

JORDAN, Ruth
Integrative Psychotherapist
10 Brighton Road, Stoke Newington, London N16 8EG
0171 249 0897
MC

JOYCE, Angela
Psychoanalytic Psychotherapist
25 Drylands Road, London N8 9HN
0181 341 9429/0181 348 6320
GUILD

KAVANAGH, Sister Catherine
Systemic Psychotherapist
9 Rosemont Road, North Acton, London
Mater Dei, 49 Hammersmith Grove, London W6 0NE
KCC

KEEDY-LILLEY, Ray
Hypno-Psychotherapist
28 Finsbury Park Road, London N4 2JX
0171 226 6963
NSHAP

KELLY, Michael
Psychoanalytic Psychotherapist
132 Stapleton Hall Road, London
N4 4QB
0181 340 9597
ARBS

KENNY, Angela
Psychoanalytic Psychotherapist
128 Nevill Road, London N16 OSX
0171 254 8558
AGIP

KENNY, Miranda
Analytical Psychologist-Jungian Analyst
63 Maury Road, Stoke Newington, London N16 7BJ
0181 806 9202
BAP

KERR, Libby
Integrative Psychotherapist
93B Shakespeare Walk, London
N16 8TB
0171 254 0384
RCSPC

KESHET-ORR, Judi
Individual and Group Humanistic Psychotherapist, Sexual and Marital Psychotherapist
28 Woodland Gardens, London
N10 3UA
0181 444 9217
BASMT, AHPP

KESSEL, Inge
Humanistic and Integrative Psychotherapist
1 Uplands Road, Crouch End, London
N8 9NN
0181 348 2315
BCPC

KIDD, Lee
Psychoanalytic Psychotherapist
13 Brambledown Mansions, Crough Hill, London N4 4SA
0171 281 3435
IPC

KINGSLEY, Mary
Transpersonal Psychotherapist
6 Avenue Lodge, 13 Avenue Road, Highgate, London N6 5DJ
0181 348 4487
CCPE

KITTO, Jane
Psychoanalytic Psychotherapist
2 The Park, London N6 4EU
0181 348 6506
LCP

KLEANTHOUS, Dina
Psychoanalytic Psychotherapist
41 Cheverton Road, London N19 3BA
0171 263 7270/0171 263 8084
ARBS

KNOWLES, Valerie
Psychoanalytic Psychotherapist
1 Florence Villas, Holmesdale Road, London N6 5TJ
0181 348 3251
IPC

KOSTIC, Jasna
Primal Psychotherapist
West Hill House, 6 Swains Lane, Highgate, London N6 6QU
0181 800 6952
LAPP

KREEGER, Angela
Psychoanalytic Psychotherapist
37c Cromwell Avenue, Highgate, London N6 5HN
0181 347 5337
PA

KRZOWSKI, Sue
Psychoanalytic Psychotherapist
39A Axminster Road, London N7 6BP
0171 272 6379
GUILD, WTC

LABWORTH, Yig
Core Process Psychotherapist, Humanistic and Integrative Psychotherapist
9 Eastwood Road, Muswell Hill, London N10 1NL
0181 444 8506
AAPP, BCPC

LAFARGUE, Martine
Primal Psychotherapist
West Hill House, 6 Swains Lane, Highgate, London N6 6QU
0171 267 9616
LAPP

LALLAH, Regine
Psychoanalytic Psychotherapist
2 Greville Lodge, 40 Avenue Road, London N6 5DP
0181 340 9943
IPC

LAND, Patricia
Psychoanalytic Psychotherapist
4 Schofield Road, Islington N19 3EX
0171 272 6077
WTC

LANDESMANN, Sonya
Psychoanalytic Psychotherapist
31 Clifton Road, London N8 8JA
0181 348 9221
NAFSI

LANG, Richard
Integrative Psychotherapist
87B Cazenove Avenue, London N16 6BB
0181 806 3710
MC

LAWLEY, James
NLP Psychotherapist
9 Southwood Lawn Road, Highgate, London N6 5SD
0181 341 1062 (t/f)
ANLP

LAZARUS, Myrna
Family Therapist
30 Jackson's Lane, Highgate, London N6 5SX
0181 340 6628
AFT

LEDERMAN, Tsafi
Biodynamic Psychotherapist
15 Harberton Road, London N19 3JS
0171 263 8551/0171 263 6912
BTC

LEE MESSNER, Heather
Primal Psychotherapist
142 Ferme Park Road, London N8 9SE
0181 348 8989
LAPP

LEGGATT, Jenny
Analytical Psychotherapist
67 Huddleston Road, London N7 0AE
University of Oxford Counselling Service, 11 Wellington Square, Oxford OX1 2HY
01865 270 300/0171 609 2069
AGIP

LEMMA, Alessandra
Integrative Psychotherapist
43 Tavistock Terrace, London N19 4BZ
0171 380 7777/0171 281 6719
RCSPC

LEPPER, Georgia
Analytical Psychologist-Jungian Analyst
99 Sotheby Road, London N5 2UT
0171 226 9353
SAP, CSPK

LETTS, Muriel
Psychoanalytic Psychotherapist
2 Queens Avenue, London N20 0JE
0181 445 2888
IPSS

LEVENS, Mary
Psychodrama Psychotherapist
12 Edmund Walk, East Finchley, London N2 0HU
0181 946 7711 ext 413
BPA

LEVITT, Olga
Systemic Psychotherapist
'Normandy', Northcliffe Drive, London N20 8JX
0181 446 1313/0181 445 3670 (f)
KCC

LEWIS, Jacqueline
Integrative Psychotherapist
92 Creighton Avenue, London N10 1NT
0181 444 4911/0181 444 9457
RCSPC

LEYGRAF, Bernd
Humanistic Psychotherapist, Sexual and Marital Psychotherapist
73 Gaskell Road, London N6 4DU
3 Highcroft, North Hill, London N6 4RD
0181 348 7167(f)/0181 342 9956
BASMT, AHPP

LIEBLING, Lauren
Biodynamic Psychotherapist
6 Crescent Street, Barnsbury, London
N1 1BT
0171 700 3995
BTC

LIMBARDET, Jean-Pierre
Sexual and Marital Psychotherapist
Flat 1, Bridge House, 79 Hornsey Lane, London N6 5LQ
BASMT

LIPKIN, Marion
Psychoanalytic Psychotherapist
Flat C, 3 Church Crescent, London
N10 3NA
0181 444 7922
LCP

LISTER, Patricia Anne
Cognitive Behavioural Psychotherapist
23 Wray Crescent, Islington, London
N4 3LN
0171 686 4048
BABCP

LODRICK, Michael
Psychoanalytic Psychotherapist
The Garden Flat, 20 Poets Road,
London N5 2SL
0171 226 6939 (t/f)
IPC

LORET DE MOLA, Maria
Child Psychotherapist
12 Herons Lea, Sheldon Avenue,
London N6 4JT
0181 340 7415
ACP

LOUSADA, Olivia
Psychodrama Psychotherapist
14 Allerton Road, London N16 5UJ
0181 802 5284/0171 503 6494
BPA

LOWN, Judy
Core Process Psychotherapist
8 Fortior Court, 100 Hornsey Lane,
London N6 5LD
0171 794 0575/0171 272 5738
AAPP

LUCA-STOLKIN, Maria
Integrative Psychotherapist
22 de Beauvoir Square, London N1 4LE
0171 249 9658/0171 477 3505
RCSPC

LUCKCOCK, Ronald Cosmo
Hypno-Psychotherapist
11 Laseron House, Tottenham Green
East, London N15 4UA
110A Alexandra Park Road, Muswell
Hill, London N10 2AE
0181 801 4137
NSHAP

MALLARDO, Renee
Hypno-Psychotherapist
Pure Balance Mind & Body Centre, 1A
Leicester Mews, Leicester Road, East
Finchley, London N2 9DJ
Old Forge Cottage,, 39 Ringmore
Road, Shaldon, Devon TQ14 0AG
01626 873881/0181 883 4316
NRHP

MARCUS, Deena
Psychosynthesis Psychotherapist
37 The Grove, Finchley, London
N3 1QT
0181 346 0282
AAPP

MARGOLIS, Susanne
Cognitive Behavioural Psychotherapist
16 Parkland, London N3 3HA
BABCP

MARK, Peter
Group Analyst
14 Montenotte Road, Shepherd's Hill,
London N8 8RL
0181 374 2416/0171 873 2613
IGA

MARSDEN, Lee
Educational Therapist
100 Seymour Road, London N8 0BG
0181 348 9471
FAETT

MARSHALL, Antoinette
Psychoanalytic Psychotherapist
73 Alexandra Park Road, London
N10 2DG
0181 444 9357
IPSS

MARSHALLSAY, Carol
Psychoanalytic Psychotherapist
32 Priory Avenue, Hornsey, London
N8 7RN
0181 340 0169
LCP

MARTIN, Stephen
Child Psychotherapist
22 Blythwood Road, London N4 4EU
0171 272 5090 (t/f)
ACP

MASON, Barry
Family Psychotherapist, Systemic
Psychotherapist
21 Manor Road, Stoke Newington,
London N16 5BQ
0181 802 9165
IFT, FIC

MAYER, Robert
Family Therapist
Highgate Group Practice, 44 North
Hill, London N6 4QA
36 Park Avenue South, London N8 8LT
0181 340 6628/0181 340 4712
IFT

MAYER-JOHNSON, Jessica
Group Analyst
26 St. Paul's Place, London N1 2QG
0171 359 4925
IGA

MCCAFFERTY, Stewart
Systemic Psychotherapist
PO Box 13936, London N21 2WA
0956 377685
KCC

MCCLURE, John
Cognitive Behavioural Psychotherapist
Grovelands Priory Hospital, The
Bourne, Southgate, London N14 6RA
0181 882 8191/0181 447 8138(f)
BABCP

MCGEE, Colin
Psychoanalytic Psychotherapist
24 Palace Road, Crouch End, London
N8 8QJ
0181 348 1848
IPSS

MCHUGH, Brenda
Family Psychotherapist
24a Compton Terrace, London
N1 2UN
0171 704 5112/0171 704 9620 (f)
IFT

MCKENZIE, Maggie
Humanistic and Integrative
Psychotherapist
Spectrum, 7 Endymion Road, London
N4 1EE
0181 341 2277/0181 340 0426 (f)
SPEC

MCKEON, Mary
Psychoanalytic Psychotherapist
219 Fox Lane, Palmers Green, London
N13 4BB
0181 886 0766
IPC

MCNAIR, Ann G
Systemic Psychotherapist
29 Halstead Road, Winchmore Hill,
London N21 3DY
0181 360 2942
KCC

MCNEIL, Delcia
Humanistic and Integrative
Psychotherapist
Flat 2, 56 Queens Avenue, London
N10 3NU
Laundry Cottage, Whitbarrow Lodge,
Witherslack, Grange-over-
sands,Cumbria LA11 6SL
0181 442 0391/015395 52047
SPEC

MEAD, Betty
Psychoanalytic Psychotherapist
13 St. Marks Mansions, 60 Tollington
Park, London N4 3QZ
0171 263 5822
AGIP

MELLOWS, David
Psychoanalytic Psychotherapist
34 Curzon Road, London N10 2RA
0956 370111/0181 883 6230
FIP

MELLOWS, Hilary
Psychoanalytic Psychotherapist
34 Curzon Road, London N10 2RA
0181 883 6230
FIP

MESSNER, Hans Jorg
Primal Psychotherapist
142 Ferme Park Road, London N8 9SE
0181 348 8989
LAPP

METHUEN, Oriel
Humanistic and Integrative
Psychotherapist, Gestalt
Psychotherapist
Spectrum, 7 Endymion Road, London
N4 1EE
0181 883 3246
SPEC

MEZA, Ann L.
Transpersonal Psychotherapist
25 Crane Grove, London N7 8LD
0171 607 6805
CCPE

MICHAEL, Jess
Attachment-based Psychoanalytic
Psychotherapist
40 Leadale Road, Stamford Hill, London
N16 6DE
0181 800 5533
CAPP

MILLER, Penny
Attachment-based Psychoanalytic
Psychotherapist
3 Carysfort Road, Stoke Newington,
London N16 9AA
0171 249 7846
CAPP

MILLER, Riva
Systemic Psychotherapist
24 Wood Lane, Highgate, London
N6 5UB
Haemophilia Centre, Royal Free
Hospital, Pond Street, London
NW3 2QG
0181 340 3548/0171 830 2807
IFT

MODEL, Elizabeth
Child Psychotherapist
11 Bevan Street, London N1 7DY
0171 226 8339
ACP

MONTERO, Isabel
Psychoanalytic Psychotherapist
55 Birley Road, London N20 0HB
0181 446 2581
ARBS, WTC

MORDECAI, Aslan
Psychoanalytic Psychotherapist
76 Grove Avenue, London N10 2AN
0181 883 3707(f)/0181 883 9996
NAFSI, BAP, FIP

MORDECAI, Kay
Psychoanalytic Psychotherapist
76 Grove Avenue, London N10 2AN
0181 883 3707 (f)/0181 883 9996
NAFSI, BAP, FIP

MORGAN, Anne
Group Analyst
Mountgrove Practice, 82 Mountgrove
Road, London N5 2LT
0171 354 0436
IGA

MORLEY, Elspeth
Psychoanalytic Psychotherapist,
Psychoanalytic Marital Psychotherapist
43 Highbury Place, London N5 1QL
0171 288 0265(f)/0171 359 2282
BAP, FIP

MORLEY, Robert
Psychoanalytic Psychotherapist,
Psychoanalytic Marital Psychotherapist
43 Highbury Place, London N5 1QL
0171 288 0265(f)/0171 359 2282
BAP, FIP

MORRIS, Allan
Family Therapist
127 Mount View Road, London N4 4JH
0181 292 4404/0181 341 9238
IFT

MORRIS, Shosh
Psychoanalytic Psychotherapist
23C Milner Square, London N1 1TL
0171 359 0258
GUILD

MORTON, Gillian
Educational Therapist
Flat 5, 17 Haslemere Road, London
N8 9QP
0181 340 5686
FAETT

MULHERN, Alan
Analytical Psychologist-Jungian Analyst
30 Danvers Road, London N8 7HH
0181 348 9809
AJA

MUSIC, Graham
Integrative Psychotherapist
90 Huddleston Road, London N7 0EG
0171 281 1989
MC

MYERS, Piers
Integrative Psychotherapist
94A Bethune Road, London N16 5BA
0181 802 9290
RCSPC

NAISH, Julia
Humanistic and Integrative
Psychotherapist
Spectrum, 7 Endymion Road, London
N4 1EE
0181 341 2277
SPEC

NAVARRO, Trinidad
Psychoanalytic Psychotherapist
Garden Flat, 13 Christchurch Road,
London N8 9QL
0181 348 9244
ARBS

NEIVA, Judith
Psychoanalytic Psychotherapist
Flat 2, 26 Lofting Road, London
N1 1ET
0171 609 7049
AGIP

NEVINS, Peter
Psychoanalytic Psychotherapist
45 Queen's Head Street, Islington,
London N1 8NQ
0171 354 9430
PA

NGAH, Zah
Child Psychotherapist
47 Pentoville Road, London N1 9LP
1 Halton House, London N1 2EJ
0181 442 6467/0171 359 8233
ACP

NIPPODA, Yuko
Psychoanalytic Psychotherapist
c/o Nafsiyat, 278 Seven Sisters Road,
London N4 2HY
0958 213 456
NAFSI

NOACK, Amelie
Analytical Psychologist-Jungian Analyst
The Garden Flat, 213 Tufnell Park
Road, London N7 OPX
0171 609 8380
AJA

NOBLE, Jane
Psychoanalytic Psychotherapist
54 Redston Road, London N8 7HE
0181 348 2801
GUILD

NODELMAN, Marsha
Primal Psychotherapist
West Hill House, 6 Swains Lane,
Highgate, London N6 6QU
0171 267 9616
LAPP

O'CARROLL, Madeline
Cognitive Behavioural Psychotherapist
174a St. Ann's Road, London N15 5RP
0181 802 0131
BABCP

O'CONNOR, Noreen
Psychoanalytic Psychotherapist
78 Huddleston Road, London N7 0EG
0171 263 2410
GUILD

OHENE, Margaret D.
Systemic Psychotherapist
16 Wilton Road, Muswell Hill, London
N10 1LS
0181 444 9662
KCC

OLIVER, Rosamund
Core Process Psychotherapist
29 Beversbrook Road, Islington,
London N19 4QQ
0171 272 3666/0171 272 9355
AAPP

PARKER, Rosie
Psychoanalytic Psychotherapist
17 Archibald Road, London N7 0AN
0171 700 2097/0171 609 5717 (f)
IPC

PARKS, Val
Psychoanalytic Psychotherapist
18 Rosemary Avenue, Finchley, London
N3 2QN
IPC, FIP

PATERSON, Stuart
Humanistic and Integrative
Psychotherapist, Body Psychotherapist
Spectrum, 7 Endymion Road, London
N4 1EE
0181 342 9594
SPEC

PATTERSON, Anna
Humanistic and Integrative
Psychotherapist
Spectrum, 7 Endymion Road, London
N4 1EE
0181 341 2277
SPEC

PEARCE, George
Psychoanalytic Psychotherapist
288 Park Road, London N8 8JY
0181 340 1233
ARBS

PENALOSA-CLARKE, Adriana
Systemic Psychotherapist
Flat 5, 75 Torrington Park, London
N12 9PN
0181 446 5683
KCC

PENGELLY, Paul
Psychoanalytic Marital Psychotherapist
103 Tottenham Court Road, London
N1 4EA
Abraham Cowley Unit (NHS),
Holloway Hill, Lyne, Chertsey Surrey
KT16 0AE
01932 872010/0171 254 3581
TMSI

PENNYCOOK-GREAVES, Wil
Group Analyst
Flat B, Malpas Cottage, Edison Road,
London N8 8AE
0181 341 3747
IGA

PEPELI, Hara
Lacanian Analyst
10 The Avenue, London N8 0JR
0181 888 7104
CFAR

PERRY, Ann
Psychoanalytic Psychotherapist
35 Huntingdon Street, London N1 1BP
0171 609 3378/0171 609 2300 (f)
AIP

PETRIE, Bill
Transpersonal Psychotherapist
123 Dukes Avenue, London N10 2QD
0181 372 9474
CCPE

PETTLE, Sharon
Systemic Psychotherapist
10 Priory Avenue, Crouch End, London
N8 7RN
Centre for Relationship Studies, 1-3
Wolverton Gardens, London W6 7DQ
0181 846 7806/0181 340 2539
IFT

PICKSTOCK, Keith
Psychosynthesis Psychotherapist
105 Clissold Crescent, Stoke
Newington, London N16 9AS
0171 254 4975
AAPP

PIERIDES, Stella
Psychoanalytic Psychotherapist
15 Victoria Road, London N4 3SH
0171 272 5957
ARBS

PIMENTEL, Edna
Humanistic Psychotherapist
41 Springcroft Avenue, London N2 9JH
0181 883 0511/0181 374 1756 (f)
AHPP

PIPER, Robin
Psychoanalytic Psychotherapist, Group Analytic Psychotherapist
148 Mercers Road, London N19 4PX
2 Well Place Farm Cottages, Well Place, Penshurst, Kent TN11 8BH
0171 272 4002/01892 870 387
LCP

POLLEDRI, Patricia
Psychoanalytic Psychotherapist
White Gables, 10 Oakleigh Road Nouth, London N20 9AR
0181 445 2861
CPP

POTKONJAK, Dusan
Psychodrama Psychotherapist
Doctor's Residence, St. Luke's Hospital, Woodside Avenue, London N10
0181 219 1832/0181 219 1833
BPA

PRESANT, Fern
Integrative Psychotherapist
22 Osbaldeston Road, London N16 7DP
0181 806 8119
MC

PRIEST, Caroline
Systemic Psychotherapist
Flat 8, 38 Mayfield Road, London N8 9LP
0181 341 6488
KCC

RADLETT, Marty
Existential Psychotherapist
46 Noel Road, London N1
0181 868 5836
RCSPC

RAWAT, Shenaz
Personal Construct Psychotherapist
2c Queen Elisabeth's Walk, Stoke Newington, London N16 0HX
0181 809 3336
CPCP

REA, Judith
Psychoanalytic Psychotherapist
11 Anson Road, London N7 0RB
0171 607 0546
GUILD

READ, Tim
Group Analyst
28 St. John's Villas, London N19 3EG
0171 636 8333 x 3306/7/0171 263 8965
IGA

REDDISH, Elisabeth
Psychoanalytic Psychotherapist
16 Chardmore Road, London N16 6JD
0181 806 9857
CPP

RÉGUIS, Marie-Christine
Psychoanalytic Psychotherapist
36 Warrender Road, London N19 5EF
0171 263 8105
ARBS

REID, Liz
Lacanian Analyst, Psychoanalytic Psychotherapist
376 Hornsey Road, Islington, London N19 4HT
St Michaels, Blanche Lane, South Mimms, Herts EN6 3PA
0171 272 6609/0860 250553
CFAR, FIP

RENOUX, Martine
Integrative Psychotherapist
4 Canning Crescent, London N22 5SR
0181 889 9980
MC

RENTOUL, Lynette
Psychoanalytic Psychotherapist
27 Pages Hill, Muswell Hill, London N10 1PX
0171 872 3021/0181 883 3687
BAP

RHIND, Sue
Psychosynthesis Psychotherapist
35 Long Lane, Church End, Finchley, London N3 2PS
0181 343 4325/0181 202 4525
AAPP

RICHARDS, Val
Psychoanalytic Psychotherapist
28 Ravensdale Avenue, London N12 9HT
0181 445 6120/0181 446 8449
GUILD, IPSS

RIDLEY, Wendy
Psychosynthesis Psychotherapist
15 Elmar Road, London N15 5DH
0181 802 7984
AAPP

RITCHIE, Sheila
Psychoanalytic Psychotherapist
Flat 2, 18 Alexandra Grove, London N4 2LF
0181 802 2908
WTC, AGIP

ROBERTS, Sylvia M
Systemic Psychotherapist
12 Redston Road, Haringey, London N8 7HJ
0181 340 6336
KCC

ROMISCH-CLAY, Liza
Integrative Psychotherapist
7 Rookfield Close, London N10 3TR
0181 883 6575
RCSPC

ROSEN, Maria
Psychoanalytic Psychotherapist
40 Priory Gardens, London N6
0181 348 0597
LCP

ROTENBERG, Claudio
Child Psychotherapist
10 Lime Avenue, London N12 8QN
0181 445 1322(t/f)
ACP

ROTH, Jenner
Humanistic and Integrative Psychotherapist
Spectrum, 7 Endymion Road, London N4 1EE
0181 340 0426(f)/0181 341 2277
SPEC

ROWAN, Alan
Lacanian Analyst, Psychoanalytic Psychotherapist
16 Claigmar Gardens, London N3 2HR
CFAR

ROWE, Dorothy
Personal Construct Psychotherapist
The Garden Flat, 40 Highbury Grove, London N5 2AG
0171 354 3498
CPCP

ROZENBERG, Rosette
Psychoanalytic Psychotherapist
26 Orchard Road, London N6 5TR
0181 348 5472
AGIP

RUND, Malcolm
Psychoanalytic Psychotherapist
42 Market Place, London N2 8BB
0181 444 6354
ARBS

RUSSELL, Marion
Humanistic and Integrative Psychotherapist
Spectrum, 7 Endymion Road, London N4 1EE
0181 341 3413/0171 704 6761
SPEC

RYAN, Joanna
Psychoanalytic Psychotherapist
26 Kyverdale Road, London N16 7AH
0181 802 1641
PA

RYAN, Tom
Psychoanalytic Psychotherapist
11 Cecile Park, London N8 9AX
0181 292 8908
ARBS

RYZ, Patsy
Child Psychotherapist
36 Essex Park, London N3 1NE
0181 349 2263
ACP

SABBADINI, Andrea
Psychoanalytic Psychotherapist
38 Berkeley Road, Crouch End, London N8 8RU
0181 340 2936
ARBS

SALLES, Miriam
Biodynamic Psychotherapist
38 Onslow Gardens, London N10 3JU
0181 883 9698
BTC

SALTIEL, Adam
Psychoanalytic Psychotherapist
35 Corbyn Street, London N4 3BY
0171 281 9875
ARBS, FIP

SAMUELS, Andrew
Analytical Psychologist-Jungian Analyst
148 Mercers Road, London N19 4PX
0171 272 2122 (f)/0171 272 1292
SAP, FIP

SAMUELS, Carole
Psychoanalytic Psychotherapist
14 Deansway, East Finchley N2 0JF
0181 883 7823
LCP

SAVILLE, Sue
Psychoanalytic Psychotherapist
9 Twyford Avenue, East Finchley, London N2 9NU
0181 444 4826/0181 444 1442(f)
IPC

SCHAFFER-FIELDING, Wendy
Child Psychotherapist
25 Wickliffe Avenue, London N3 3EL
0181 346 1483/0181 359 3801
ACP

SCHIMMELSCHMIDT, Michael
Transpersonal Psychotherapist
66 Whitehall Park, London N19 3TN
0171 263 8689(f)/0171 263 2718
CCPE

SCHLAPOBERSKY, John
Group Analyst, Psychoanalytic Psychotherapist
5 Southwood Lawn Road, Highgate, London N6 5SD
0181 348 6475
IGA

SCHONFIELD, Tamar
Psychoanalytic Psychotherapist
71 Woodland Rise, London N10 3UN
0181 352 1456(f)/0181 365 3226
ARBS

SEGLOW, Ruth M.
Child Psychotherapist
6 Redston Road, London N8 7HJ
0181 347 7097(f)/0181 592 4445
ACP

SELBY, Marilyn
Educational Therapist
34 Arden Road, London N3 3AN
0181 349 2507
FAETT

SERADI, Adriana
Psychoanalytic Psychotherapist
27 Hertford Road, London N2 9BX
0181 444 7885
AGIP

SERFATY, Marc A.
Cognitive Behavioural Psychotherapist
Senior Lecturer & Consultant, Grovelands Priory Hospital, The Bourne, Southgate N14 6RA
0181 882 8191
BABCP

SEYMOUR, Charlotte
Family Therapist
65 Muswell Road, London N10 2BS
0181 883 9367
AFT

SHABAN, Dervishe
Transpersonal Psychotherapist
Powys Lane, New Southgate, London N11
0181 881 5164
CCPE

SHAPIRO, Adella
Integrative Psychotherapist
41a Fairmead Road, London N19 4DG
0171 272 5868
MC

SHARP, Belinda
Psychoanalytic Psychotherapist
54 Park Drive, London N21 2LS
0181 360 6020 (t/f)
IPC

SHAW, Elizabeth
Cognitive Behavioural Psychotherapist
Psychology Service, St Ann's Hospital, St Ann's Road, London N15 3TH
0181 442 6458
BABCP

SHAWE-TAYLOR, Metka
Cognitive Behavioural Psychotherapist
Psychology Service, St Ann's Hospital, St Ann's Road, London N15 3TH
0181 442 6458
BABCP

SHINGLER, Christopher
Psychosynthesis Psychotherapist
36a Mildmay Road, London N1 4NG
Ash Cottage, 33/ 34 Snape Road, Sudbourne, Suffolk IP12 2BA
AAPP

SIMMONS, Gloria
Systemic Psychotherapist, Family Therapist
'Timbers', 64 Manor Drive, Whetstone, London N20 0DU
0181 361 3740
AFT

SIMMONS, Monty
Psychoanalytic Psychotherapist
64 Manor Drive, Whetstone N20 0DU
0181 361 3740
LCP

SINGH, Satwant
Cognitive Behavioural Psychotherapist
68 Sutherland Road, Edmonton,
London N9 7QG
0181 292 7719
BABCP

SMITH, Jonathan
Psychoanalytic Psychotherapist
59 Holmesdale Road, London N6 5TH
0181 340 9137
IPSS

SMITH, Margaret E.
Systemic Psychotherapist
40 Vallance Road, Wood Green,
London N22 7UB
0181 889 0358
KCC

SMITH, Ruthie
Psychoanalytic Psychotherapist
63 Lothair Road South, London
N4 1EN
0181 692 2969
WTC

SOLEMANI, Hannah
Psychoanalytic Psychotherapist
82 Cecile Park, London N8 9AU
0181 341 1612
ARBS

SOLOWAY, Clare
Integrative Psychotherapist
100 Sydney Road, Muswell Hill, London
N10 2RN
0181 442 0928
MC

SQUIRES, Brenda
Psychosynthesis Psychotherapist
7 Elm Grove, London N8 9AH
0181 341 1315/0181 292 4164 (f)
AAPP

STEIN, Yvonne
Family Therapist, Integrative
Psychotherapist
48 Finchley Park, North Finchley,
London N12 9JL
0181 905 6693/79/0181 446 4913
AFT, RCSPC

STEVENS, Ann
Family Therapist
54 Pulford Road, South Tottenham,
London N15 6SP
0181 809 1502
IFT

STEVENSON, Krystyna
Hypno-Psychotherapist
52 Windermere Avenue, London
N3 3RA
0181 346 8648
NRHP

STEWART, Angus
Psychoanalytic Psychotherapist
44 Etheldene Avenue, London
N10 3QH
0181 883 9247
LCP

STOGDON, Mark
Family Therapist
11 Oak Avenue, Crouch End, London
N8 8LJ
0181 341 4504
IFT

STUART, Gillian
Analytical Psychologist-Jungian Analyst
68 Tottenham Lane, Crouch End,
London N8 7EE
0181 341 6477
AJA

SUNDERLAND, Margot
Gestalt Psychotherapist, Integrative
Arts Psychotherapist
'Terpsichore', 70 Cranwich Road,
London N16 5JD
0181 809 5866/0171 704 2534
IATE, GPTI

SWYNNERTON, Richard
Integrative Psychotherapist
11 Links View, Dollis Road, Finchley
Central, London N3 1RN
0181 371 0443
RCSPC

SüNKEL, Sue
Psychoanalytic Psychotherapist
1 Foxham Road, London N19 4RR
0171 281 5193
IPSS

TAN, Richard
Psychoanalytic Psychotherapist
4 Ingram Road, East Finchley, London
N2 9QA
0181 883 2820
CPP

TAYLOR, Alan
Analytical Psychotherapist
8 Victoria Mansions, 135 Holloway
Road, London N7 8LZ
0171 607 0210
AIP

TAYLOR, Harvey
Psychoanalytic Psychotherapist
c/o AGIP, 1 Fairbridge Road, London
N19 3EW
0171 272 7013/0181 349 9792
AGIP, LCP

THISTLETHWAITE, Harriet
Psychoanalytic Psychotherapist
63 Mercers Road, London N19 4DS
0171 272 5984
LCP, FIP

THOMPSON, Paul
Psychoanalytic Psychotherapist
10 Huntingdon Road, London N2 9DU
0181 444 0795
LCP

TICKTIN, Steven
Existential Psychotherapist
29 Churchgarth, Pemberton Gardens,
London N19 5RN
0171 272 9214/0171 272 2474
RCSPC

TILLETT, Penny
Educational Therapist
2 The Drive, Fordington Road, London
N6 4TD
0181 883 7599(f)/0181 444 7073
FAETT

TOIBIN, Eileen
Psychoanalytic Psychotherapist
1 Aubrey Road (Top Flat), Crouch End
N8 9HH
0181 974 7045
LCP

TOMPKINS, Penny
NLP Psychotherapist
9 Southwood Lawn Road, Highgate,
London N6 5SD
0181 341 1062 (t/f)
ANLP

TREVATT, David
Child Psychotherapist
4 Stonenest Street, London N4 3BA
0171 224 6028/0171 272 3982
ACP

USISKIN, Judith
Child Psychotherapist
110 Chanctonbury Way, London
N12 7AB
0171 445 5671
ACP

UTTING, Julia
Psychoanalytic Psychotherapist
59 Albert Road, Wood Green, London
N22 4AA
0181 881 1775
IPSS

VALENTINE, Marguerite
Psychoanalytic Psychotherapist
56 Osbaldeston Road, London
N16 7DR
0181 806 3655
ARBS

VALENTINE, Victoria
Integrative Psychotherapist
21 Thorpedale Road, London N4 3BH
0171 263 2518
MET

VAN SCHOOR, Linda
Family Psychotherapist
3 Logan Road, Edmonton Green,
London N1 0LP
0181 884 2859
IFT

VASTARDIS, Gethsimani
Child Psychotherapist, Psychoanalytic
Psychotherapist
36 Dresden Road, London N19 3BD
Canonbury Child Guidance Unit, River
Place Heath Centre, River Place,
London N1 2DE
0171 530 2940/0171 272 3894
ACP, BAP

VEALE, Maurice
Gestalt Psychotherapist, Individual and
Group Humanistic Psychotherapist
148 Corbyn Street, Finsbury Park,
London N4 3DB
0171 263 4079
GCL

VELLACOTT, Julia
Psychoanalytic Psychotherapist
4 Compton Terrace, London N1 2UN
0171 359 2831
LCP

VERNON, Paul
Psychoanalytic Psychotherapist
46B Ferntower Road, London N5 2JH
0171 359 4943/0181 806 6046
BAP, FIP

WADDELL, Margot
Psychoanalytic Psychotherapist, Child
Psychotherapist
5 Cardozo Road, London N7 9RJ
Child & Family Department, Tavistock
Clinic, 120 Belsize Lane, London
NW3 5BA
0171 607 3492/0171 435 7111
ACP, WTC

WARD, Sharron
Transpersonal Psychotherapist
96A Hanley Road, London N4 3DW
0171 281 4086
CCPE

WATERFIELD, Hilary
Psychoanalytic Psychotherapist
160 Albion Road, London N16 9JS
0171 690 9048
ARBS

WATT, Ferelyth
Psychoanalytic Psychotherapist
23 Mercers Road, London N19 4PH
The Lancaster Centre, 26 Bennett's
Yard, off Lancaster Road, Uxbridge
UB8 9JH
0171 272 7421/01895 256521
BAP, ACP

WEAVER, Ziva
Integrative Psychotherapist, Body
Psychotherapist
226c Brecknock Road, London
N19 5BG
0171 681 8098
CCBP

WEERAMANTHRI, Tara
Family Therapist
12c Petherton Road, London N5 2RD
0171 701 7371/0171 701 8697
AFT

WHITBY, Susan
Psychoanalytic Psychotherapist
1A Windsor Road, Finchley, London
N3 3SZ
0181 349 2645
IPSS

WHITE, Jean
Psychoanalytic Psychotherapist
Flat 5, 77 Sunnyside Road, London
N19 3SL
0171 263 7417
GUILD

WHITE, Nuala
Gestalt Psychotherapist
10 Alexander Road, London N19 3PQ
0171 263 2076
GCL

WHITTLE, Sonia
Psychoanalytic Psychotherapist
6 Church Lane, Hornsey, London
N8 7BU
0181 348 8419
ARBS

WIELAND, Christina
Psychoanalytic Psychotherapist
50 Fernleigh Road, London N21 3AL
0171 272 7013/0181 882 9531
AGIP, FIP

WIESELBERG, Huguette
Family Therapist
8 Broughton Avenue, London N3 3ER
0181 349 9180
IFT

WILCE, Gillian
Psychoanalytic Psychotherapist
3 Farleigh House, 25/27 Halton Road,
London N1 2EL
0171 354 2942
GUILD

WILLIAMS, Kate
Humanistic and Integrative
Psychotherapist
126 Chase Way, Southgate, London
N14 5DH
0181 368 9868
SPEC

WILLIAMS, Susan
Analytical Psychologist-Jungian Analyst
64b Rokesly Avenue, Crouch End,
London N8 8NH
0181 340 6020
AJA

WILLMOTT, Susan
Humanistic and Integrative
Psychotherapist
Spectrum, 7 Endymion Road, London
N4 1EE
0181 341 3413/01494 758069
SPEC

WILSON, Carol
Integrative Psychotherapist
88 Talbot Road, London N6 4RA
0895 237071/0181 348 1988
RCSPC

WILSON, Jilian
Child Psychotherapist, Psychoanalytic Psychotherapist
74 Dukes Avenue, London N10 2PU
Department of Child and Adolescent Psy., North Middlesex Hospital, Sterling Way, London N18 1QX
0181 887 4231/0181 883 6370
ACP, BAP

WILSON, Shula
Integrative Psychotherapist
50 Mayfield Avenue, London N12 9JD
0181 359 5341/0181 445 7541
RCSPC

WOOD, Rob
Psychoanalytic Psychotherapist
19 Baalbec Road, London N5 1QN
0171 226 4775
IPC

WOODWARD, Nicola
Child Psychotherapist
17 Bryanstone Road, London N8 8TN
0181 347 6831
ACP

WORRALL, Chrysoula
Psychoanalytic Psychotherapist
15 Gresley Road, London N19 3LA
0171 272 4133
GUILD

WYNANT, Vivienne
Psychosynthesis Psychotherapist
1 Blythwood Road, Islington, London N4 4EU
0171 272 0780
AAPP

YATES, Tony
Group Analytic Psychotherapist
27 Toyne Way, London N6 4EG
0181 374 9788
IPC

YOUNG, Margot
Integrative Psychotherapist
132 Highbury Hill, London N5 1AT
0171 690 9326/0171 704 8876
MC

YOUNG, Robert M.
Psychoanalytic Psychotherapist
26 Freegrove Road, London N7 9RQ
0171 607 8306
IPSS

ZIMMERMAN, Frankie
Family Therapist
46 Denison Close, East Finchley, London N2 0JU
0181 4446388
AFT

LONDON NORTH WEST

ADAMS, Sue
Humanistic and Integrative Psychotherapist
4 Torriano Cottages, Kentish Town, London NW5 2TA
33 Jessop Court, Graham Street, Islington, London N1 8LG
0171 267 3631/0171 608 1093
BCPC

ADLER, Hella
Analytical Psychologist-Jungian Analyst
19 Burgess Hill, London NW2 2DD
0171 435 7424
AJA

ALBRIGHTON, Sylvia
Integrative Psychotherapist, Body Psychotherapist
28 Marley Walk, Lennon Road, London NW2 4PX
0181 452 2201
CCBP

ALLEN, Dorothy
Transpersonal Psychotherapist, Gestalt Psychotherapist
20 Fleetwood Road, Dollis Hill, London NW10 1ND
0181 830 6434
CTP

ALTSCHULER, Jenny
Family Therapist
Tavistock Clinic, 120 Belsize Lane, London NW3
0171 435 7111
AFT

ALVAREZ, Anne
Child Psychotherapist
Children & Families Department, Tavistock Clinic, 120 Belsize Lane, London NW3 5BA
O71 435 7111/0171 435 7075 (f)
ACP

ANDERSON, Linda
Group Analyst
60 All Soul Avenue, London NW10 3BG
0181 965 5872
IGA

ANDERTON, Michael
Analytical Psychologist-Jungian Analyst
100 Harvist Road, London NW6 6HL
0181 960 4780
IGAP

ARNOTT, Biddy
Group Analyst
21 Constantine Road, London NW3 2LN
0171 267 1732
IGA

AUSTIN, Lesley
Integrative Psychotherapist
48 Carlton Hill, London NW8 0ES
0976 238287/0171 624 6862
RCSPC

AUSTIN, Neil
Psychoanalytic Psychotherapist
23 College Crescent, London NW3 5LL
0171 431 1395
ARBS

BAILEY-SMITH, Yvonne A
Systemic Psychotherapist
110 Brondesbury Park, London NW2 5JR
0181 459 6579
KCC

BANDLER BELLMAN, Debbie
Child Psychotherapist
34 Solent Road, London NW6 1TU
0171 794 3519
ACP

BAR-YOSEPH, Talia Levine
Integrative Psychotherapist, Gestalt Psychotherapist
18a Heriot Road, London NW4 2DG
GPTI, MET

BARNETT, Ruth
Psychoanalytic Psychotherapist
73 Fortune Green Road, London NW6 1DR
0171 431 0837
LCP, FIP

BARRETT, Jean
Psychoanalytic Psychotherapist
31 Harvard Court, Honeybourne Road, London NW6 1HL
0171 435 3166
GUILD

BARTELS-ELLIS, Phillida
Psychoanalytic Psychotherapist
12 Blenheim Gardens, London NW2
0181 450 4048
NAFSI

BATHAI, Parizad
Integrative Psychotherapist
Flat C, 85 Melrose Avenue, London NW2 4LR
0181 208 1095
MC

BATTERSBY, Audrey
Psychoanalytic Psychotherapist
83 Belsize Lane, London NW3 5AU
0171 722 2784
GUILD

BAYNES, Gay
Psychoanalytic Psychotherapist
56 Aberdare Gardens, London NW6 3QD
0171 624 1728 (t/f)
IPC

BECKER, Amely
Gestalt Psychotherapist, Individual and Group Humanistic Psychotherapist
26A Gayton Road, London NW3 1TY
0171 794 2821
GCL, AHPP

BENJAMIN, Haydene
Child Psychotherapist
7 Turners Wood, London NW11 6TD
0181 455 2065
ACP

BENSON, Pauline
Cognitive Behavioural Psychotherapist
54 Hendon Hall Court, Parson Street, London NW4 1QY
0181 203 6060
BABCP

BISHOP, Bernardine
Psychoanalytic Psychotherapist
7 Patshull Road, London NW5 2JX
0171 485 4911
LCP

BLANDY, Evanthe
Child Psychotherapist, Psychoanalytic Psychotherapist
2 Montrose Avenue, Queens Park, London NW6 6LB
0181 964 3813/0181 960 3040 (f)
ACP, GUILD

BLUM, Anita
Sexual and Marital Psychotherapist
18 Foscote Road, London NW4 3SD
BASMT

BODGENER, Sue
Gestalt Psychotherapist
9 Brownlow Road, Harlesden, London NW10 9QN
0181 961 2763
GPTI

BONNEFIN, Valerie
Autogenic Psychotherapist
83 Nottingham Terrace, London NW1 4QE
0171 486 6367
BAFAT

BORSIG, Su
Integrative Psychotherapist
90 Harvist Road, London NW6 6HL
0181 964 2719
MET

BRUGGEN, Joan
Family Therapist
21 Makeson Road, London NW3 2LU
0171 530 3704/0171 485 6771
AFT

BUCKINGHAM, Linda
Child Psychotherapist, Psychoanalytic Psychotherapist
31 Harvard Court, Honeybourne Road, London NW6 1HL
0171 435 3166
ACP, GUILD

BURCH, Nigel
Psychoanalytic Psychotherapist
1a Laurier Road, London NW5 1SD
0171 267 2785
ARBS, FIP

BURCK, Charlotte
Family Therapist, Systemic Psychotherapist
Senior Clinical Lecturer in Social Work, Tavistock Clinic, 120 Belsize Lane, London NW3 5BA
Inst. of Family Therapy, 24-32 Stephenson Way, London NW1 2HX
0171 435 7111
IFT

BURNS, Alex
Psychoanalytic Psychotherapist
Flat 26, 119 Haverstock Hill, Belsize Park, London NW3 4RS
30 Langton Road, Rugby, Warwicks CV21 3UA
0171 586 7076/01788 536446
IPSS

BURTON, Mary V.
Psychoanalytic Psychotherapist
Flat 1, 40 Belsize Park, London NW3 4EE
0171 586 9708
WMIP

BURTT, Isobel Lucy
NLP Psychotherapist
147 Bathurst Gardens, London NW10 5JJ
0181 968 4894(f)/0181 964 4894
ANLP

BUTT, Diana
Family Psychotherapist, Family Therapist
19 Priory Road, London NW6 4NN
0171 624 0543
IFT

BYNG-HALL, Sue
Family Psychotherapist
24 Shirlock Road, London NW3 2HS
0171 485 6602
IFT

CAMPBELL, David
Systemic Psychotherapist
Child & Family Dept., Tavistock Clinic, 120 Belsize Lane, London NW3 5BA
0171 435 7111 ext 2287/0171 447 3733 (f)
IFT

CAMPBELL, Donald
Child Psychotherapist
Portman Clinic, 8 Fitzjohns Avenue, London NW3 5NA
0171 794 8262/0171 722 7573
ACP

CAMPBELL, Elizabeth
Psychoanalytic Psychotherapist
2 Provost Road, London NW3 4ST
0171 722 7573
GUILD

CANETE, Maria
Group Analyst
57 Hamlet Square, London NW2 1SR
0181 450 5167
IGA

CARLSON, Theresa
Transpersonal Psychotherapist
18 Chalcot Crescent, Primrose Hill, London NW1 8YD
0171 722 2317
CCPE

CARVALHO, Richard
Analytical Psychologist-Jungian Analyst
51 Woodsome Road, London NW5 1SA
0171 482 1187
SAP

CAVE, Prue
Psychoanalytic Psychotherapist
Top Flat, 41 Buckland Crescent, London NW3 5DJ
0171 284 1578
ARBS

CAZALET, Deborah
Psychoanalytic Psychotherapist
Flat 1, 12 Abercorn Place, London NW8 9XP
0171 286 6024
IPC

CHANDWANI, Lilian
Psychoanalytic Psychotherapist
18 Park Drive, London NW11 7SP
0181 458 8204/0181 455 3742(f)
IPSS

CHAPPELL, Claire
Educational Therapist
46 Princess Road, London NW1 8JL
0171 722 9716(t/f)
FAETT

CHARVET, Anne
Systemic Psychotherapist
60 Compayne Gardens, London NW6 3RY
0171 328 4174
KCC

CHINA, Giselle
Psychoanalytic Psychotherapist
24B South Hill Park Gardens, London NW3 2TG
0171 435 6361
IPSS

CHRISTMANN, Cornelia
NLP Psychotherapist
147 Bathurst Gardens, Kensal Green, London NW10 5JJ
0181 964 9843/0181 968 4894(f)
ANLP

CLULOW, Christopher
Psychoanalytic Marital Psychotherapist
T.M.S.I., Tavistock Centre, 120 Belsize Lane, London NW3 5BA
62 Clarence Road, St. Albans, Herts AL1 4NG
0171 435 7111/01727 868 108
TMSI

COCKBURN, Andrew
Analytical Psychotherapist
30 Southway, Hampstead Garden Suburb, London NW11 6RU
0181 731 7887
LCP

COHEN, Pauline
Child Psychotherapist
4 Kidderpore Gardens, London NW3 7SR
0171 794 6046
ACP

COLAHAN, Mireille
Family Therapist
9 Lyme Street, London NW1 0EH
0171 209 9149/0171 482 0303
AFT

COLLEDGE, Lorraine
Psychoanalytic Psychotherapist
7 Ash Tree Dell, London NW9 0AG
0181 200 7964
LCP

COLLIS, Jeffrey
Sexual and Marital Psychotherapist
Turning Point, The Junction Project, 27 Station Road, London NW10 4UP
BASMT

CONNOLLY, Christopher
Psychosynthesis Psychotherapist
28a Hampstead High Street, London NW3 1QA
0171 794 4066/0171 794 6700 (f)
AAPP

CONWELL, Jim
Integrative Psychotherapist
2 Kemplay Road, London NW3 1SY
0171 435 7477
MC, LCP

COOPER, Hilary
Psychoanalytic Psychotherapist
14 Dartmouth Road, London NW2 4EU
0181 208 3349
PA

COOPER, Robin
Psychoanalytic Psychotherapist, Group Analyst
14 Dartmouth Road, London NW2 4EU
0181 208 3349
IGA, PA, IGA

COPLEY, Beta
Child Psychotherapist
25 Pilgrims Lane, London NW3 1SX
0171 794 4780
ACP

CORBETT, Gemma
Integrative Psychotherapist
83 St. Gabriels Road, London NW2 4DU
0181 452 3844
RCSPC

CORNISH, Ursula
Systemic Psychotherapist
39 Chalcot Square, London NW1 8YP
0171 586 2582
IFT

COSTELLO, Marie
Psychoanalytic Psychotherapist
18 Maresfield Gardens, Hampstead, London NW3 5SX
0171 431 8159
IPC

COULTER, Theresa
Psychoanalytic Psychotherapist
Flat 30, 35-36 Belsize Square, London NW3 4HL
0171 794 7930
IPSS

COUSINS, Jan
Child Psychotherapist
102 Prince of Wales Road, London NW5 3NE
0171 482 4923
ACP

CRADDOCK, Jenny
Analytical Psychotherapist
3 Dunstan Road, London NW11 8AG
0410 492801/0181 381 4429
LCP

CRISP, Dave
NLP Psychotherapist
30A The Loning, Colindale, London NW9 6DR
0181 205 5989/0181 200 4944
ANLP

CUDMORE, Lynne
Psychoanalytic Marital Psychotherapist, Analytical Psychologist
T.M.S.I., Tavistock Centre, 120 Belsize Lane, London NW3 5BA
70 Mill Hill Road, London W3 8JJ
0171 435 7111/0181 993 1534
TMSI

DALE, Barbara
Systemic Psychotherapist
Child & Family Dept., Tavistock Clinic, 120 Belsize Lane, London NW3 5BA
0171 435 7111/0171 447 3785 (f)
IFT

DANIELL, Diana
Psychoanalytic Marital Psychotherapist
23 College Crescent, London NW3 5LL
0171 794 9782
TMSI

DAUM, Minna
Family Therapist
Malbrough Family Service, 38 Marlbrough Place, London NW6 6LP
0171 328 2085/0171 624 8605
AFT

DAVIDE, Adele
Analytical Psychologist-Jungian Analyst
49 Llanvanor Road, Child's Hill, London NW2 2AR
0181 922 0471
AJA

DAVIDS, Jennifer
Child Psychotherapist
Anna Freud Centre, 21 Maresfield Gardens, London NW3 5SH
0171 794 2313/0171 372 3403
ACP

DAVIS, Helen
Integrative Psychotherapist
73 Staverton Road, London NW2 5HA
0181 451 7802
MC

DAVIS, Wendy
Humanistic Psychotherapist
St. Mildreds, 35 Flower Lane, London NW7 2JG
0181 906 9204
AHPP

DAWS, Dilys
Psychoanalytic Psychotherapist, Child Psychotherapist
43 Heath Hurst Road, London NW3 2RU
Child and Family Department, Tavistock Clinic, 120 Belsize Lane, London NW3 5BA
0171 435 7111/0171 435 9248
ACP, BAP

DE MARE, Patrick
Group Analyst
5 Holly Place, London NW3 6QU
0171 794 3171
IGA

DELL, Judith
Humanistic Psychotherapist
45 Litchfield Way, London NW11 6NU
0181 458 7893
AHPP

DENTON, Marika
Group Analyst, Psychoanalytic Psychotherapist
11 Oakhill Avenue, London NW3 7RD
0171 435 2086
IGA, WTC

DICKINSON, Adrian
Analytical Psychotherapist
84a Hillfield Road, West Hampstead, London NW6 1QA
0171 435 9079
LCP, FIP

DIYALJEE, Angeli
Hypno-Psychotherapist
Flat 6, 346 Finchley Road, Hampstead, London NW3 7AJ
0171 431 4943
NRHP

DOGMETCHI, Geri
Psychoanalytic Psychotherapist
18 Spencer Rise, London NW5 1AP
0171 485 2883
IPSS

DOORLEY, Damien
Analytical Psychologist-Jungian Analyst
75 Goldhurst Terrace, London NW6 3HA
0171 624 6524
AJA

DOVER, Jennifer
Educational Therapist
11 Gainsborough Gardens, London NW3 1BJ
0171 794 6510/0171 431 2675 (f)
FAETT

DOWLING, Emilia
Family Psychotherapist
Child & Family Department, Tavistock Clinic, 120 Belsize Lane, London NW3 5BA
Child & Family Dept., 29 Lynmouth Road, London N2 9LR
0171 435 7111/0181 444 6795
IFT

DRYDEN, Windy
Rational Emotive Behaviour Therapist
14A Winchester Avenue, London NW6 7TU
0171 328 9687
BABCP

DU PLOCK, Simon
Existential Psychotherapist
School of Psychotherapy and Counselling, Regent College, Inner Circle, Regents Park, London NW1 4NS
0171 487 7680
RCSPC

DUBINSKY, Helene
Child Psychotherapist
Child and Family Department, Tavistock Clinic, 120 Belsize Lane, London NW3 5BA
0171 435 7111/0171 794 5047
ACP

DUCKWORTH, Moira
Analytical Psychologist-Jungian Analyst, Psychoanalytic Psychotherapist
24 Achilles Road, London NW6 1EA
0171 431 0811
AJA, IPC

DUDDINGTON, Alexander
Analytical Psychologist-Jungian Analyst
18 East Heath Road, London NW3 1AJ
0171 435 2301
AJA

DUNN, Nicola
Integrative Psychotherapist
53 Shirlock Road, Gospel Oak, London NW3 2HR
0171 267 4106
MC

EAGLES, Marjorie
Psychoanalytic Psychotherapist, Group Analyst
107 Frognal, Hampstead, London NW3 6SR
0181 954 6745/0171 431 1465
IGA

EASTER, Judith
Psychoanalytic Psychotherapist
77 Torbay Road, London NW6 7DU
0171 328 6250
GUILD

EDGCUMBE, Rose
Child Psychotherapist
5 Sandringham Road, London NW11 9DR
0181 455 9385
ACP

EDWARDS, Dagmar
Gestalt Psychotherapist, Integrative Psychotherapist
28 Blenheim Gardens, London NW2 4NS
0181 208 1235/0181 452 3134 (f)
GPTI, MET

EDWARDS, Judith
Child Psychotherapist
Bishop Harvey Family Service, St. Josephs Way, The Burroughs, London NW4 4TY
0171 727 8759/0181 202 5115
ACP

EISENHAUER, Gary
Integrative Psychotherapist
80 Ashburnham Road, Kensal Green, London NW10 5SE
0181 968 4568
RCSPC

ELKAN, Judith
Child Psychotherapist
31 Coleridge Walk, London NW11 6AT
0181 455 8845
ACP

ELLIOTT, Barbara
Group Analyst
36 Dennington Park Road, London NW6 1BD
0171 371 7555/0171 794 6014
IGA

EMANUEL, Ricky
Child Psychotherapist
Dept. of Child & Adolescent Psychiatry, Royal Free Hospital, Pond Street, London NW3 2QG
0171 830 2931/0181 348 7032
ACP

ERSKINE, Archibald
Psychoanalytic Psychotherapist, Analytical Psychotherapist
130 Walm Lane, London NW2 4RT
0181 452 9251
LCP, BAP, FIP

ESSENHIGH, Caroline
Child Psychotherapist
Flat 1, 47 Compayne Gardens, London NW6 3DB
0171 328 1114
ACP

EVANS, Joan
Psychosynthesis Psychotherapist
Institute of Psychosynthesis, 65A Watford Way, Hendon, London NW4 3AQ
0181 202 4525/0181 202 6166 (f)
AAPP

EVANS, Roger
Psychosynthesis Psychotherapist
Institute of Psychosynthesis, 65A Watford Way, Hendon, London NW4 3AQ
0181 202 4525/0181 202 6166 (f)
AAPP

EZQUERRO-ADAN, Arturo
Group Analyst
57 Hamlet Square, London NW2 1SR
0181 390 0102 x 5147/0181 450 5167
IGA

FANNING, Alexandra
Psychoanalytic Psychotherapist
46 Westbere Road, London NW2 3RU
0171 794 4010/0171 435 5712 (f)
FIP

FARHI, Nina
Psychoanalytic Psychotherapist
11 North Square, London NW11 7AB
0181 455 5329/0181 731 6109 (f)
GUILD

FARZIM, Pari
Family Therapist
52 Teignmouth Road, London NW2 4DX
0181 452 3585
IFT

FELDBERG, Tom
Psychoanalytic Psychotherapist
24 Brookfield Park, London NW5 1ER
0171 267 2577
IPSS

FENTIMAN, John
Transpersonal Psychotherapist
Flat 1, 62 Canfield Gardens, London NW6 3EB
0171 328 7083
CCPE

FERID, Heidi
Psychoanalytic Psychotherapist, Attachment-based Psychoanalytic Psychotherapist
20 South Hill Park, Hampstead, London NW3 2SB
0171 794 9130
IPSS, CAPP

FESTENSTEIN, Geraldine
Group Analyst
8 Briardale Gardens, London NW3 7PP
0171 435 2741
IGA

FIASCHE, Mara
Psychoanalytic Psychotherapist
29 Fordwych Court, Shoot-Up Hill, Kilburn, London NW2 3HP
0181 830 6955
IPSS

FICARRA, Berthe
Psychoanalytic Psychotherapist
7 Estelle Road, London NW3 2JX
0181 482 3399
GUILD

FIELDER, Michael
Psychoanalytic Psychotherapist
Top Flat, 41 Buckland Crescent, London NW3 5DJ
0171 722 2589
PA

FIELDHOUSE, Pauline
Transpersonal Psychotherapist
12 Goldhurst Terrace, London NW6 3HU
0171 624 2787
CTP

FOSTER, Angela
Psychoanalytic Psychotherapist
14 Hoveden Road, London NW2 3XD
0181 450 2713
LCP

FRANKLYN, Frank
Psychoanalytic Psychotherapist
26 Sydney Grove, Hendon, London
NW4 2EH
0181 202 7546
IPSS

FRIEDMAN, Debbie
Psychosynthesis Psychotherapist
1189a Finchley Road, London
NW11 0AA
0181 458 5760
AAPP

FRIEDMAN, Joe
Psychoanalytic Psychotherapist
Top Flat, 41 Buckland Crescent,
London NW3 5DJ
0171 722 5077
PA

FRY, Richard P.W.
Family Therapist
4 Plympton Avenue, Brondesbury,
London NW6 7TJ
0171 624 0923
AFT

FYVEL, Susan
Family Therapist
59 Broomleigh Street, London
NW6 1QQ
0171 624 8605
AFT

GAL, Oshrat
Psychoanalytic Psychotherapist
54a Woodstock Avenue, London
NW11 9RG
7 Artillery Lane, London E1
0171 377 8865/0181 455 5333
GUILD

GANS, Steve
Psychoanalytic Psychotherapist
c/o Diorama Arts, 34 Osnaburgh
Street, London NW1 3ND
0171 916 5433
PA

GAVSHON, Audrey
Child Psychotherapist
Anna Freud Centre, 21 Maresfield
Gardens, London NW3 5SH
0171 794 2313/0181 348 0276
ACP

GEEN, Sheryle
Integrative Psychotherapist
95b Leighton Road, London NW5 2QJ
0171 482 4537
MC

GEORGE, Dorothy
Integrative Psychotherapist
610 Jacqueline House, 52 Fitzroy Road,
London NW1 8UA
0171 586 8862
RCSPC

GEORGE, Pamela
Psychoanalytic Psychotherapist
Flat 1, 2 Inglewood Road, London
NW6 1QZ
0171 794 1588
LCP

GHIACI, Golshad
Psychoanalytic Psychotherapist
Flat B, 20 Lady Somerset Road, London
NW5 1UP
PA, FIP

GIBSON, Walter
Integrative Psychotherapist
12 Parkfield Road, Willesden, London
NW10 2BJ
0181 537 2302
MC

GILL, Douglas
Psychoanalytic Psychotherapist
Diorama Arts, 34 Osnaburgh Street,
London NW1 3ND
0171 916 5429/0171 916 5282
PA

GOLD, Bonnie
Group Analyst
18 Manor Hall Avenue, Hendon,
London NW4 1NX
0171 431 2949/0181 203 2279
IGA

GOLDEN, Ellen
Child Psychotherapist
Flat 3, 113 Dartmouth Road, London
NW2 4ES
0181 450 0624
ACP

GOMEZ, Lavinia
Integrative Psychotherapist
21 Mill Lane, London NW6 1NT
0171 794 5308
MC

GOOD, Liz
Psychoanalytic Psychotherapist
47a Golders Green Road, London
NW11 8EL
38 Addison Road, Wanstead, London
E11 2RG
0181 989 6529/0181 208 8526
AGIP

GORDON, Paul
Psychoanalytic Psychotherapist
74 Victoria Road, London NW6 6QA
0171 624 3053
IPSS, PA

GORMAN, Susan
Group Analyst
Flat 4, 9 Ambleside Road, London
NW10 3UH
0181 451 0070
IGA, WTC

GORNEY, Carry
Systemic Psychotherapist
43 Spencer Rise, London NW5 1AR
0171 267 6619
KCC

GRANT, Iona
Psychoanalytic Psychotherapist
75 Fleetwood Road, London
NW10 1NR
0181 452 4479
ARBS, WTC

GRAY, Elizabeth
Family Therapist
11 Well Road, London NW3 1LH
AFT

GREEN, Viviane
Child Psychotherapist
Anna Freud Centre, 21 Maresfield
Gardens, London NW3 5SH
0171 794 2313/0171 435 4960
ACP

GREENFIELD, Frances
Core Process Psychotherapist
Milton Cottage, Vale of Heath, London
NW3 1AX
0171 243 4020
AAPP

GRUNBERG, Sheena
Child Psychotherapist
Child & Family Dept., Tavistock Clinic,
120 Belsize Lane, London NW3 5BA
0171 435 7111/0171 267 1379
ACP, IGA

GUEST, Nicola
Child Psychotherapist
c/o ACP, 120 West Heath Road,
London NW3 7TU
ACP

GUILFOYLE, John F.
Sexual and Marital Psychotherapist
40 Brooksville Avenue, Queen's Park, London NW6 6TG
0181 969 7856
BASMT

GULCZ, Magdalena
Cognitive Behavioural Psychotherapist
13 Belsize Grove, Flat 1, London NW3 4UX
0171 586 0482
BABCP

HACKER, Roger
Psychoanalytic Psychotherapist
5 Chalcot Gardens, London NW3 4YB
0171 586 4144
ARBS

HADARY, Orna
Psychoanalytic Psychotherapist
5A Coverdale Road, London NW2 4DD
0181 459 3881
CPP

HAINE, Ann
Psychoanalytic Psychotherapist
Flat B, 96 Fortess Road, London NW5 2HJ
0171 267 8936
LCP, FIP

HAINE, Stephen
Psychoanalytic Psychotherapist
96C Fortress Road, London NW5 2HJ
0171 813 9069/ 0171 813 5573 (f)
AGIP

HANNA, Gilli
Transpersonal Psychotherapist
London, NW10
0181 960 4849/0171 436 2720
CCPE

HARDING, Michael
Existential Psychotherapist
24 Birchington Court, West End Lane, London NW6 4PB
0171 487 7694/0171 328 1823
RCSPC

HARLAP, Nahum
Integrative Psychotherapist
5a Northgate, Prince Albert Road, London NW8 7RD
0171 586 4228
RCSPC

HARRIS, Jonathan
Transpersonal Psychotherapist
65 Clifford Gardens, London NW10 5JE
0181 964 9599
CCPE

HARVARD-WATTS, Olivia
Psychoanalytic Psychotherapist
44 Woodsome Road, London NW5 1RZ
0171 424 0233/0171 485 6582
GUILD

HAUSSMAN, Rochelle
Educational Therapist
46 Lodore Gardens, Kingsbury, London NW9 0DR
0181 930 1876
FAETT

HAYNES, Jane
Analytical Psychologist-Jungian Analyst
32 Priory Terrace, London NW6 4DH
0171 624 2981
SAP

HENRY, John
Attachment-based Psychoanalytic Psychotherapist
27 Elm Grove, London NW2 3AE
0181 452 8865/0181 452 4956(f)
CAPP

HERST, Edward
Analytical Psychologist-Jungian Analyst
9 Fitzroy Road, London NW1 8TU
0171 722 1661/0171 586 0361 (f)
SAP, BAP

HERTZMANN, Leezah
Attachment-based Psychoanalytic Psychotherapist
The Child & Family Department, Tavistock Clinic, 120 Belsize Lane, London NW3 5BA
55 Dartmouth Park Road, London NW5
0956 670 410/0171 435 7111 x2513
CAPP

HILDEBRAND, Judy
Family Therapist, Systemic Psychotherapist
43 Oak Village, London NW5 4GL
0171 267 2910
IFT

HILL, Philip
Lacanian Analyst, Psychoanalytic Psychotherapist
1 Hillside, Highgate Road, London NW5
36 Stanhope Gardens, London N6 5TS
0181 340 9941
CFAR

HOLDEN, Maxine
Transpersonal Psychotherapist
8A Lymington Road, London NW6 1HY
0171 431 8757
CTP

HOLLAND, Ray
Integrative Psychotherapist
25 Greenhill Road, Harlesden, London NW10 8UD
0181 838 3423/0181 961 7874 (f)
CCBP

HOLM, Kirsti E.
Hypno-Psychotherapist
48 Shirehall Park, London NW4 2QX
0181 202 3654
NSHAP

HOLMES, Carol
Integrative Psychotherapist
School of Psychotherapy, Regent College, Inner Circle, London NW1 4NS
0171 487 7428
RCSPC

HOOPER, Anne
Sexual and Marital Psychotherapist
179c Haverstock Hill, London NW3
BASMT

HOPPER, Earl
Psychoanalytic Psychotherapist, Group Analyst
11 Heath Mansions, The Mount, Heath Street, London NW3 6SN
0171 435 2053/0171 435 4350
IGA, BAP

HORNE, Ann
Child Psychotherapist
Portman Clinic, 8 Fitzjohns Avenue, London NW3 5NA
0171 794 8262/0181 673 6486
ACP

HOUSTON, Gaie
Gestalt Psychotherapist
8 Rochester Terrace, London
NW1 9JN
0171 485 9265
GCL

HOWARD, Angela
Psychoanalytic Psychotherapist
1 Tower Close, Lyndhurst Road,
London NW3 5TB
0171 431 6410/0171 794 3314 (f)
GUILD

HURRY, Anne
Child Psychotherapist, Psychoanalytic
Psychotherapist
Anna Freud Centre, 21 Maresfield
Gardens, London NW3 5SH
Garden Flat, 15 Lambolle Road,
London NW3 4HS
0171 794 2313/0171 794 1762
ACP, BAP

HUSSAIN-SHACKLE, Shakrukh
Psychoanalytic Psychotherapist
20 Kingswood Avenue, London
NW6 6LG
0181 960 6794(f)/0181 964 8493
NAFSI

HUTCHINSON, Sylvia
Group Analyst
2 St. Gabriel's Road, London NW2 4RY
0171 431 2693/0181 450 2791
IGA

INGLEBRIGHT, Shanti
Family Psychotherapist
Marlborough Family Service, 38
Marlborough Place, London NW8 0PJ
0171 328 2135 (f)/0171 624 8605
IFT

ISAACSON, Zelda
Integrative Psychotherapist
19 Windermere Avenue, London
NW6 6LP
0181 960 5121
RCSPC

ISAKSSON-HURST, Gun I.E.
Transactional Analysis Psychotherapist
137B Goldhurst Terrace, London
NW6 3EU
0171 372 5537
MET, ITA

JACOBS, Joe
Child Psychotherapist
Flat 3, 50 Well Walk, London
NW3 1BT
0171 433 1927
ACP

JARVIS, Charlotte
Child Psychotherapist
The Brandon Centre, 26 Prince of
Wales Road, London NW5
0171 267 4792/0171 226 0623
ACP

JENSEN, Greta
Psychosynthesis Psychotherapist
6 Rockhall Road, London NW2 6DT
AAPP

JOFFE, Riva
Psychoanalytic Psychotherapist
6 Peploe Road, Queens Park, London
NW6 6EB
0181 969 0288
IPSS

JOHN-WILSON, Deb'bora
Gestalt Psychotherapist
Flat 6, Carlton House, 319 West End
Lane, London NW6 1RN
0171 431 9041
GCL

JOLLIFFE, John
Attachment-based Psychoanalytic
Psychotherapist
Flat 4, Laurier Court, Laurier Road,
London NW5 1SE
0171 284 4334
CAPP

JONES, Janet
Psychoanalytic Psychotherapist
1A Exeter Road, London NW2 4SJ
0181 452 5860
IPC

KADISH, Faigie
Psychoanalytic Psychotherapist
1b Alverstone Road, London NW2 5JS
0181 451 1559
LCP

KAHR, Brett
Integrative Psychotherapist
Suite 6, 4 Marty's Yard, 17 Hampstead
High Street, Hampstead, London
NW3 1QW
0171 435 2955
RCSPC

KAPLAN, Myron
Psychoanalytic Psychotherapist
1 Clarence Gate Gardens, Glentworth
Street, London NW1 6AY
0171 724 3062
AGIP

KARBAN, Barbara
Existential Psychotherapist
Flat 3, 15 Alma Square, London
NW8 9QA
0181 967 5096/0171 286 0019
RCSPC

KELLY, Caro
Gestalt Psychotherapist
CHOICE Psychotherapy Practice, 18a
Heriot Road, Hendon, London
NW4 2DG
6A West Avenue Road, London E17
0181 520 4595/0181 202 1023
GPTI, MET

KENRICK, Jennifer
Child Psychotherapist
Child and Family Department,
Tavistock Clinic, 120 Belsize Lane,
London NW3 5BA
0171 435 7111/0171 352 2525
ACP

KERBEKIAN, Rosalie
Child Psychotherapist
Garden Flat, 31 Willow Road, London
NW3 1TL
0171 431 1888
ACP

KERNOFF, Marilyn
Psychosynthesis Psychotherapist
Flat 3, 64 Aberdare Gardens, London
NW6 3QD
0171 624 0587
AAPP

KHALEELEE, Olya
Psychoanalytic Psychotherapist
10 Golders Rise, London NW4 2HR
0181 202 7097
LCP

KLEIN, Mavis
Transactional Analysis Psychotherapist
1 Estelle Road, London NW3 2JX
0171 267 0784 (t/f)
ITA

KLEINOT, Pamela
Psychoanalytic Psychotherapist
12 Sherriff Road, London NW6 2AU
0171 624 2936
ARBS

KNIGHT, Michael
Cognitive Analytic Therapist
Garden Flat, 66 Belsize Park, London
NW3 4EH
0171 722 9007
ACAT

KOHON, Valli
Child Psychotherapist
31 Beechcroft Avenue, London
NW11 8BJ
0181 455 4173
ACP

KOPPELMAN, Liora
Psychoanalytic Marital Psychotherapist
60 Corringham Road, London
NW11 7BX
0181 455 3092
TMSI

KRISTAL, Barbie
Integrative Psychotherapist
The Garden Flat, 27a Belsize Park
Gardens, London NW3 4JH
0171 586 8077
RCSPC

LA TOURELLE, Maggie
NLP Psychotherapist
70A Caversham Road, London
NW5 2DS
0171 485 4215(t/f)
ANLP

LAPORT-STEUERMAN, M.
Child Psychotherapist
34 Ornan Road, London NW3 4QB
0171 435 4376
ACP

LAWLOR, Virginia Katherine
Integrative Psychotherapist
c/o Dewey, 43 Shirlock Road, London
NW3 5HR
0973 353 702
RCSPC

LEDER, Catherine
Humanistic Psychotherapist,
Biodynamic Psychotherapist
12a Ravenshaw Street, London
NW6 1NN
0171 794 2995
AHPP

LEHRER, Pam
Psychoanalytic Psychotherapist
Heath Riding, 32 Wildwood Road,
London NW11 6XB
0181 458 0638(f)/0181 458 8750
IPSS

LEVITSKY, Jackie
Psychoanalytic Psychotherapist
95 Willifield Way, London NW11 6YH
0181 455 6413
LCP

LIKIERMAN, Meira
Child Psychotherapist, Psychoanalytic
Psychotherapist
5 Downshire Hill, London NW3 1NR
Child and Family Department,
Tavistock Clinic, 120 Belsize Lane,
London NW3 5BA
0171 435 7111/0171 435 9888
LCP, ACP

LINDEN, Roger
Psychoanalytic Psychotherapist, NLP
Psychotherapist
14 Boscastle Road, Dartmouth Park,
London NW5 1EG
The Old Covent, Beeches Green,
Stroud, Glos GL5 4AD
0171 485 2292
IPC, ANLP

LINDSEY, Caroline
Family Psychotherapist, Systemic
Psychotherapist
Child & Family Dept., Tavistock Clinic,
120 Belsize Lane, London NW3 5BA
23 Gresham Gardens, London
NW11 8NX
0181 455 2882/0171 447 3808
IFT

LÖVENDAL-SÖRENSEN, Helena
Psychosynthesis Psychotherapist
18b North End Road, London
NW11 7LP
0181 905 5937/0181 341 1849 (f)
AAPP

LOW, James
Cognitive Analytic Therapist, Sexual
and Marital Psychotherapist
78B Princess Road, London NW6 5QX
BASMT, PA, ACAT

LUNARDON, Francesco
Psychoanalytic Psychotherapist
69 Hamilton Road, London
NW10 1NH
0181 450 5332
ARBS, FIP

LYNDON, Barbara
Educational Therapist
8 Honiton Road, London NW6 6QE
0171 372 8009
FAETT

MACGREGOR, Catherine
Psychosynthesis Psychotherapist
24 Harley Road, Hampstead, London
NW3 3BN
0181 969 3587/0171 722 6067
AAPP

MACHADO, Danuza
Lacanian Analyst
14 Eton Hall, Eton College Road,
London NW3 2DW
0171 722 7383
CFAR

MAITRA, Begum
Analytical Psychologist-Jungian Analyst
38 Nant Road, London NW2 2AT
0171 221 4656/0181 458 2510
AJA

MALKIN, Marion
Integrative Psychotherapist
108C Priory Road, South Hampstead,
London NW6 3NH
0171 372 3979
RCSPC

MALTBY, Jane
Child Psychotherapist
Bishop Harvey Family Service, St.
Josephs Way, The Burroughs, London
NW4 4TY
0181 202 5115
ACP

MANDER, Gertrud
Psychoanalytic Psychotherapist
24 Chalcot Crescent, London
NW1 8YD
0171 722 0033
IPC

MANDIN, Philippe
Family Therapist, Systemic
Psychotherapist
Marlborough family Service, 38
Marlborough Place, London NW8
0171 624 8605
IFT

MANIFOLD, Claire
Integrative Psychotherapist
23 Lawn Road, London NW3 2XR
0181 853 2395/0171 586 3077
RCSPC

MARKS, Gaby
Psychoanalytic Psychotherapist
39 Goldhurst Terrace, London
NW6 3HB
0171 624 7185/0181 455 9783
LCP, FIP

MARRONE, Mario
Psychoanalytic Psychotherapist, Group Analyst
6 Oman Avenue, London NW2 6BG
0181 452 3088
LCP, IGA

MARTIN, Christine
Child Psychotherapist
Child & Family Unit, Park Royal Mental Health Unit, Acton Lane, London NW10 7NS
0171 453 2697 (f)/0181 453 2357
ACP

MARX, Philippa
Group Analytic Psychotherapist
88 Olive Road, Cricklewood, London NW2 6UP
0181 450 3385
IPC

MCDERMOTT, Paul
Transpersonal Psychotherapist
64 Fleet Road, Hampstead, London NW3 2QT
0171 482 4296
CCPE

MCEVOY, Patricia E
Systemic Psychotherapist
The American School in London, 2 - 8 Loudoun Road, London NW8 0NP
31 Chomley Gardens,, Aldred Road, Hampstead, London NW6 1AG
0171 435 6597/0171 813 3759(f)
KCC

MCKENZIE-SMITH, Bryce
Psychoanalytic Psychotherapist
34 Dudley Court, Finchley Road, London NW11 6AE
0181 731 6961
AGIP, AIP

MCKENZIE-SMITH, Savi
Child Psychotherapist, Psychoanalytic Psychotherapist
12 Springfield Court, 41 Eton Avenue, London NW3 3ER
0171 794 9026
ACP, AIP

MCKEOWN, Andy
Integrative Psychotherapist
Choice, 18A Heriot Road, London NW4 2DG
Fairleigh House, Leigh Street, Leigh upon Mendip, Somerset BA3 5QQ
0181 998 9390/01373 812237
MET

MCLEAN, Julienne
Analytical Psychologist-Jungian Analyst
Flat 21, Christchurch Court, 171 Willesden Lane, London NW6 7XF
0181 451 5255 (t/f)
AJA

MENDELSOHN, Annette
Child Psychotherapist
Department of Child & Adolescent Psychiatry, Royal Free Hospital, Pond Street, London NW3 2QG
0171 830 2931/0171 794 8708
ACP

MILLER, John Andrew
Psychoanalytic Psychotherapist
22 Fitzjohns Avenue, London NW3 5NB
0181 905 5937/0171 435 1079
AGIP

MILLER, Lisa
Child Psychotherapist
Child & Family Department, Tavistock Clinic, 120 Belsize Lane, London NW3 5BA
0171 435 7111/0171 435 7057 (f)
ACP

MILLINGTON, Malcolm
Psychoanalytic Marital Psychotherapist
T.M.S.I., The Tavistock Centre, 120 Belsize Lane, London NW3 5BA
0171 435 7111
TMSI

MITTWOCH, Adele
Psychoanalytic Psychotherapist, Group Analyst
1 Chestfield Gardens, London NW3 7DD
0171 935 1397(F)/0171 435 8589
LCP, IGA, BAP

MOJA-STRASSER, Lucia
Existential Psychotherapist
144A Abbey Road, London NW6 4SR
0171 487 7406/0171 372 6407
RCSPC

MONDADORI, Roberta
Child Psychotherapist
11 Melina Place, London NW8 9SA
0181 360 7391/0171 286 0422
ACP

MOORE, Julie
Integrative Psychotherapist
126 College Road, London NW10 3PE
0181 969 2726
MC

MORGAN, Mary
Psychoanalytic Marital Psychotherapist
T.M.S.I., Tavistock Centre, 120 Belsize Lane, London NW3 5BA
191 Mornington Road, Leytonstone, London E11 3DT
0171 435 7111/0181 558 8929
TMSI

MORRIS, Monique
Psychoanalytic Psychotherapist
35 Highcroft Gardens, London NW11
0181 440 5111/0181 455 4306
GUILD

MOSSE, Lucy
Psychoanalytic Psychotherapist
21 Parliament Hill, London NW3 2TA
0171 794 3441
LCP

MOURATOGLOU, Vassilis
Family Therapist
90 Grove End Gardens, Grove End Road, St John's Wood, London NW8 9LP
0171 286 3126
AFT

MURPHY, Alan
Transpersonal Psychotherapist
42 Georgiana Street, London NW1 0EB
0171 485 0358
CCPE

NABARRO, Elizabeth
Psychoanalytic Psychotherapist
58 Croftdown Road, London NW5 1EN
0171 485 3597
GUILD

NAGLE, Robin
Child Psychotherapist
13 Carlingford Road, London NW3 1RY
0171 435 6038
ACP

NANCARROW, Christine
Cognitive Behavioural Psychotherapist
19 Linacre Road, London NW2 5AY
0181 451 0647
BABCP

NATHAN, Gill
Group Analyst
31 Langland Gardens, London NW3 6QE
0171 794 7136
IGA

NEAL, Charles
Humanistic and Integrative Psychotherapist
23 Rossendale Way, Elm Village, Camden, London NW1 0XB
0171 387 6758
SPEC

NEWTON, Kathleen
Analytical Psychologist-Jungian Analyst
25C Fitzjohn's Avenue, London NW3 5JY
SAP

NORBURN, Veronica
Psychoanalytic Psychotherapist
18a Tanza Road, London NW3 2UB
0171 794 8697
IPSS

NORRINGTON, Susan
Psychoanalytic Psychotherapist
6a Lady Somerset Road, London NW5 1UT
0171 284 1818
LCP

NOYES, Elizabeth
Cognitive Behavioural Psychotherapist
33 Downside Crescent, London NW3 2AN
0171 794 8321/0171-794 8321
BABCP

O'CALLAGHAN, Lesley
Integrative Psychotherapist
53 Okehampton Road, London NW10 3EN
0181 830 1912
MC

O'CLEARY, Susan
Psychoanalytic Psychotherapist
23 College Crescent, London NW3 5LL
0171 431 1395
ARBS

O'CONNELL, Victoria
Psychoanalytic Psychotherapist
93 Chevening Road, London NW6 6DA
0181 960 1065
LCP, AGIP, FIP

O'GORMAN, Mary Pat
Integrative Psychotherapist
17 Lambolle Road, London NW3 4HS
0171 794 5468
MC

OAKLEY, Haya
Psychoanalytic Psychotherapist
62 Upper Park Road, London NW3 2UX
0171 722 1628
GUILD, AFT

OATEN, Gae
Integrative Psychotherapist
8 Holly Mount, London NW3 6SG
0171 435 4238
RCSPC

OCLANDER GOLDIE, Silvia
Child Psychotherapist
40 Parkhill Road, London NW3 2YP
0171 485 6558/0171 916 8203 (f)
ACP

ODGERS, Andrew
Attachment-based Psychoanalytic Psychotherapist
36b South Hill Park, London NW3 2SJ
0171 431 0687
CAPP

OLIVER-BELLASIS, Elizabeth
Child Psychotherapist
76 Burghley Road, London NW5 1UN
0171 485 6998
ACP

OLNEY, Felicia
Psychoanalytic Marital Psychotherapist
T.M.S.I., Tavistock Centre, 120 Belsize Lane, London NW3 5BA
10A Oakford Road, London NW5 1AH
0171 435 7111/0171 482 3172
TMSI

ORBACH, Susie
Psychoanalytic Psychotherapist
2 Lancaster Drive, London NW3 4HA
0181 794 8226
WTC, LCP

ORFORD, Eileen
Child Psychotherapist
30 Regents Park Road, London NW1 7TR
0171 485 4012
ACP

ORLANS, Vanja
Gestalt Psychotherapist, Integrative Psychotherapist
28 Blenheim Gardens, London NW2 4NS
0181 208 1235/0181 452 3134 (f)
GPTI, AHPP, MET

ORMAY, Tom
Psychoanalytic Psychotherapist, Group Analyst
113 Goldhurst Terrace, London NW6 3HA
0171 625 6576
IGA

PACEY, Susan
Sexual and Marital Psychotherapist
42 Bartholomew Villas, London NW5 2LL
0171 916 7055
BASMT

PARSONS, Marianne
Child Psychotherapist
60 Brondesbury Road, London NW6 6BS
0171 624 0600
ACP

PATALAN, Anna-Maria
Group Analyst
4 Somerton Road, London NW2 1SA
0181 450 1630
IGA

PAULSON, Diana
Family Therapist
34 Alma Street, London NW5 3DH
Canonbury Child & Family Consultation Service, River Place Health Centre, Essex Road, London N1 2TS
0171 530 2940/0171 267 4857
IFT

PAWSON, Chris
Biodynamic Psychotherapist
33 Croftdown Avenue, Highgate, London NW5
01442 862029
BTC

PETERS, Linda
Psychoanalytic Psychotherapist
6 Sandwell Crescent, West Hampstead, London NW6 1PB
0171 435 5414(t/f)
IPC

PETERSON, Corinna
Analytical Psychologist-Jungian Analyst
107A Hamilton Terrace, London NW8 9QY
0171 286 3995
SAP

PITCHON, Eduardo
Child Psychotherapist, Psychoanalytic Psychotherapist
110 Cholmley Gardens, Fortune Green Road, London NW6 1UP
0171 4350496
LCP, ACP

PLATT, Sue
Integrative Psychotherapist
6 Marion Road, Mill Hill, London NW7 4AN
0181 959 6560
MC

POKORNY, Michael
Psychoanalytic Psychotherapist, Group Analytic Psychotherapist
167 Sumatra Road, London NW6 1PN
0171 431 4693/0171 435 5712(f)
AGIP, FIP

POLLARD, Elena
Psychoanalytic Psychotherapist
82 Christchurch Avenue, London NW6 7PE
0181 459 1945
LCP

POWELL, Angela
Psychoanalytic Psychotherapist
167 Sumatra Road, London NW6 1PN
30 Deacon Road, London NW2 5QH
0171 794 1433/0181 830 3773
ARBS, WTC

POWER, Kevin
Group Analytic Psychotherapist
7 Coverdale Road, London NW2 4DB
0181 830 2791
FIP

PRALL, Werner
Integrative Psychotherapist
61 Riffel Road, Willesden Green, London NW2 4PG
0181 452 9438
CCBP

PREISINGER, Kristiane
Humanistic and Integrative Psychotherapist
14 Richborough Road, London NW2 3LU
0181 452 6703
MC, AHPP

PUDDY, Jane Kahan
Gestalt Psychotherapist
78 Tennyson Road, London NW6 7SB
0171 624 9109
GCL

PURPURA, Davide
Integrative Psychotherapist
47 Asmuns Place, London NW11 7XE
0181 731 8249
RCSPC

QUINN, Eilish
Psychoanalytic Psychotherapist
c/o LCP, 32 Leighton Road, London NW5 2QE
0171 482 7149
LCP

RABIN, Judith
Existential Psychotherapist
33 West Heath Drive, London NW11 7QG
0181 458 1007
RCSPC

RABIN, Norman
Psychoanalytic Psychotherapist
33 West Heath Drive, London NW11 7QG
0181 458 1007
IPSS

RADFORD, Patricia
Child Psychotherapist, Psychoanalytic Psychotherapist
Flat 2, 14 Ferncroft Avenue, London NW3 7PH
0171 435 4265
ACP, BAP

RAPHAEL, Francesca
Integrative Arts Psychotherapist
16 Aldershot Road, London NW6 7LG
0171 624 3146
IATE

RAPP, Hilde
Psychoanalytic Psychotherapist
21 Priory Terrace, London NW6 4DG
0171 625 4287/0171 813 4718 (f)
IPSS, UPA

RAVENSDALE, Verity
Psychoanalytic Psychotherapist
2 Gloucester Crescent, London NW1 7DS
0171 485 4514
ARBS

READ, Celia
Psychoanalytic Psychotherapist
31 St Albans Road, London NW5 1RG
0171 485 0256
LCP

REDFEARN, Joseph
Analytical Psychologist-Jungian Analyst
Garden Flat, 38 Frognal, London NW3 6AG
London House,, 90/92 High Street, Brithtlingsea CO7 0EG
0120 630 5374/0171 794 6116
SAP, GUILD

REDLER, Leon
Psychoanalytic Psychotherapist
c/o Diorama Arts, 34 Osnaburgh Street, London NW1 3ND
0171 916 5191
PA

REID, Susan
Child Psychotherapist
Child & Family Department, Tavistock Clinic, 120 Belsize Lane, London NW3 5BA
0171 435 7111/0171 435 0467
ACP

REIK, Herta
Group Analyst
7 Oakhill Park Mews, London NW3 7LH
0171 794 7517
IGA

RENTON, Mirjana
Child Psychotherapist
36 Silsoe House, 50 Park Village East, London NW1 7QH
0171 387 5689
ACP

RHODE, Maria
Child Psychotherapist
Child & Family Dept., Tavistock Clinic, 120 Belsize Lane, London NW3 5BA
0171 435 7111/0171 221 6263
ACP

RICHARDS, Diana M
Psychoanalytic Psychotherapist
71 The Avenue, London NW6 7NS
0181 459 3180
NAFSI

ROBERTS, Phil
Family Therapist
55 Torbay Road, Brondesbury, London NW6 7DU
0171 701 7371/0171 372 5510
AFT

ROBERTSON, Chris
Integrative Psychosynthesis Psychotherapist
97 Brondesbury Road, London NW6 6RY
0181 357 8881
RE.V

ROBERTSON, Ewa
Integrative Psychosynthesis Psychotherapist
Re.Vision, 97 Brondesbury Road, London NW6 6RY
0181 357 8881
RE.V

ROBINSON, Hazel
Psychoanalytic Psychotherapist
75A Hartland Road, London NW6 6BH
0171 624 0877
GUILD

ROEBER, Johanna
Psychoanalytic Psychotherapist
9 Laurier Road, London NW5 1SD
0171 209 5199
LCP

ROITH, Estelle
Psychoanalytic Psychotherapist
7 Hogarth Hill, London NW11 6AY
0181 455 1514
LCP

ROMM-BARTFELD, Goldie
Psychoanalytic Psychotherapist
28 Bentinck Close, Prince Albert Road, London NW8 7RY
0181 458 9611
CPP

ROSE, Kevin
Psychoanalytic Psychotherapist
37 Ashbourne Avenue, London NW11 ODT
0181 455 5936
IPSS

ROSENTHALL, Joanna
Psychoanalytic Marital Psychotherapist
T.M.S.I., Tavistock Centre, 120 Belsize Lane, London NW3 5BA
0171 435 7111
TMSI

ROSS, Ronald J
Psychoanalytic Psychotherapist
111 Royal College Street, Camden Town, London NW1
0171 388 4253
NAFSI

ROTH, Priscilla
Child Psychotherapist
12 Parkhill Road, London NW3 2YN
0171 485 4038/0171 284 3331
ACP

ROTH, Ruth
Humanistic and Integrative Psychotherapist
16 Oman Avenue, London NW2 6BG
0181 452 7376
MC, BCPC

ROYLE, Anthony
Integrative Psychotherapist
4 Denning Road, Hampstead, London NW3 1SU
0171 435 4798
RCSPC

RUSBRIDGER, Richard
Child Psychotherapist
27 Normanby Road, London NW10 1BU
0181 452 1880/0181 830 6743 (f)
ACP

RUSHTON, Malcolm
Analytical Psychologist-Jungian Analyst
Flat 3, 13 Belsize Grove, London NW3 4UX
0171 722 1989
SAP

RUSSELL, Julian
NLP Psychotherapist
86 South Hill Park, London NW3 2SN
0171 794 7366(f)/0171 435 0731
ANLP

RUSTIN, Margaret
Child Psychotherapist
3a Exeter Road, London NW2 4SJ
0181 452 9276 (t/f)
ACP

SAABOR, Geraldine
Transpersonal Psychotherapist
43 Abbey Road, London NW8 0AA
0171 624 8428
CTP

SACHS, Adah
Integrative Psychotherapist
23 College Crescent, London NW3 5LL
0171 722 4246
RCSPC

SAWYER, Alice
Family Therapist
The Marlborough Family Service, 38 Marlborough Place, St. John's Wood, London NW8 0PJ
AFT

SCARLETT, Jean
Psychoanalytic Psychotherapist
3 Byron Villas, Vale of Heath, London NW3 1AR
0171 435 2362
LCP, BAP, GCP

SCHATZMAN, Morton
Psychoanalytic Psychotherapist
35 Croftdown Road, London NW5 1EL
0171 267 0304/0171 267 3210 (f)
ARBS

SCHIEMANN, Margot
Integrative Psychotherapist
17b Frognal, London NW3 6AR
0171 431 1810
MC

SCHILD, Maureen
Psychosynthesis Psychotherapist
11 Christchurch Avenue, London NW6 7QP
0181 451 4772
AAPP

SCHNEIDER, Evelyne
Group Analyst
Garden Flat, 8 Belsize Park, London NW3 4ET
0171 794 8834
IGA

SCHNURMANN, Anneliese
Child Psychotherapist
Flat 5, 11 Netherall Gardens, London NW3 5RN
0171 435 9315
ACP

SCHOENFELD, Hilde
Attachment-based Psychoanalytic Psychotherapist
47 Hardinge Road, London NW10 3PN
0181 537 0314
CAPP

SCHWARTZ, Joe
Attachment-based Psychoanalytic Psychotherapist
2 Lancaster Drive, London NW3 4HA
0171 794 8226
CAPP

SEGAL, Barbara
Child Psychotherapist
Flat 4, 19 Wadham Gardens, London
NW3 3DN
0181 722 7844
ACP

SELIGMAN, Eva
Psychoanalytic Marital Psychotherapist
9 Hillcrest Avenue, London NW11 0EP
0181 458 4566
TMSI

SEU, Irene Bruna
Psychoanalytic Psychotherapist
40 King's Road, London NW10 2BP
0181 459 3423
ARBS, FIP

SHEARER, Ann
Analytical Psychologist-Jungian Analyst
26 Lambolle Place, London NW3 4PG
0171 794 4913
IGAP, AIP

SHERMAN, Arthur
Analytical Psychologist-Jungian Analyst
4 Springfield Court, 41 Eton Avenue,
London NW3 3ER
0171 431 1175
AIP

SHIVAKUMAR, H.
Analytical Psychotherapist
14B Portsdown Avenue, London
NW11
AIP, SAP

SHMUKLER, Diana
Integrative Psychotherapist,
Transactional Analysis Psychotherapist
23a Bracknell Gardens, Hampstead,
London NW3 7EE
0171 433 3648 (f)/0171 431 9031
SPTI, ITA

SILVERMAN, Carl M.
Analytical Psychologist-Jungian Analyst
34 Douglas Road, London NW6
0171 912 0803
AJA

SILVESTER, Keith
Psychosynthesis Psychotherapist
5 Kings College Court, Primrose Hill
Road, London NW3 3EA
0171 722 8183/0171 586 4594
AAPP

SIMMONDS, Tina
Integrative Psychotherapist
14 Park Avenue, London NW11 7SJ
0181 455 9102
MC

SINASON, Valerie
Child Psychotherapist
Children & Families Department,
Tavistock Clinic, 120 Belsize Lane,
London NW3 5BA
O71 435 7111/0171 794 1655
ACP

SINEY, Sky
Psychoanalytic Psychotherapist
43 Rudall Crescent, London NW3 1RR
0171 431 8498
AGIP

SINGER, Daniela
Integrative Psychotherapist
167 Sumatra Road, London NW6 1PN
0171 431 2883
RCSPC, AHPP

SKYNNER, Robin
Group Analyst
8 South Square, Hampstead Garden
Suburb, London NW11 7AL
0181 458 4085
IGA

SLESS, Deborah
Transactional Analysis Psychotherapist
23 Patshull Road, London NW5 2JX
0171 485 2664
ITA

SMITH, Alison
Personal Construct Psychotherapist
61b Cambridge Road, London
NW6 5AG
NWL Mental Health NHS Trust,
Solution Based Practice, Unit 5,1/13
Elkstone Road, London W10 5NT
0171 624 2597/0181 960 0880
CPCP

SMITH, Carol
Psychoanalytic Psychotherapist
86 Canfield Gardens, London
NW6 3EE
0171 624 8035 (f)/0171 624 5721
IPSS

SMITH, Judith
Psychoanalytic Psychotherapist
59 Greenside Road, London
NW12 9JZ
26 Prospect Place, Camden, Bath
BA1 SJD
0181 743 9096/01225 44789
LCP, SIP

SOOKDEB, S.
Cognitive Behavioural Psychotherapist
The Courtyard, 5 -6 Avenue Road,
Harlesden, London NW10 4UG
BABCP

SOUTHGATE, John
Attachment-based Psychoanalytic
Psychotherapist
12 Nassington Road, London
NW3 2UD
0171 433 1263
CAPP

SOVIN, Edna
Psychoanalytic Psychotherapist
74 Corringham Road, London
NW11 7EG
0181 455 0868
LCP

SPECTERMAN, Liz
Psychosynthesis Psychotherapist
26 Priory Terrace, West Hampstead,
London NW6 4DH
0171 624 8569
AAPP

SPEYER, Josefine
Humanistic Psychotherapist
20 Heber Road, London NW2 6AA
Neal's Yard Therapy Rooms, 2 Neal's
Yard, Covent Garden, London
WC2 9DP
0181 208 0670/0181 452 6434 (f)
AHPP

SPURLING, Lawrence
Psychoanalytic Psychotherapist
4 Marty's Yard, 17 Hampstead High
Street, London NW3 1PX
0171 431 5471
GUILD

SPYER, Natalie
Psychoanalytic Psychotherapist
38 Temple Fortune Lane, London
NW11 7UD
0181 455 3050
IPSS

STADLEN, Anthony
Psychoanalytic Psychotherapist, Existential Psychotherapist
64 Dartmouth Park Road, London NW5 1SN
0171 485 3896
LCP, RCSPC, AIP

STAFFORD, Barbara
Psychoanalytic Psychotherapist
14 Shirlock Road, London NW3 2HS
0171 485 9224
LCP

STEELE, Miriam
Child Psychotherapist
Anna Freud Centre, 21 Maresfield Gardens, London NW3 5SH
0171 794 2313/0171 794 6506 (f)
ACP

STEHLE, Peter
Existential Psychotherapist
2 The Clock Tower, Holly Hill, 49 Heath Street, London NW3 6UD
0171 431 6155
RCSPC

STERNBERG, Janine
Child Psychotherapist, Psychoanalytic Psychotherapist
9 Keats Grove, London NW1 2RR
Tavistock Mulberry Bush Day Unit, 33 Daleham Gardens, London NW3
0171 794 3394/0171 794 6505
ACP, BAP

STEVENSON, Bruce
Body Psychotherapist, Integrative Psychotherapist
20 Goodhall Street, London NW10 6TU
0181 961 7802
CCBP

STEWART, John A
Psychoanalytic Psychotherapist
51 Hendale Avenue, Hendon, London NW4 4LP
0181 203 9079
IPC

STEYN, Angela
Group Analytic Psychotherapist
5 Denman Drive, London NW11 6RE
0181 458 1214
IPC

STOBEZKI, Yael
Transpersonal Psychotherapist
Flat E, 46 Fairhazel Gardens, London NW6 3SJ
CCPE

STONE, Anthony
Humanistic and Integrative Psychotherapist
7 Westholm, London NW11 6LH
Spectrum, 7 Endymion Road, London N4 1EE
0181 455 0794
SPEC

STONE, Martin
Analytical Psychologist-Jungian Analyst
Flat 1, 62 Rosslyn Hill, London NW3 1ND
0171 794 8445 (t/f)/0171 435 6072
AJA

STONE, Miriam
Psychoanalytic Psychotherapist
39 Parliament Hill, London NW3 2TA
IPC, FIP

STONE, Sandra
Child Psychotherapist
31 Alma Square, London NW8 9PY
0171 286 3331
ACP

STRASSER, Freddie
Existential Psychotherapist
99 West Heath Road, Hampstead, London NW3 7TN
0181 455 0118/0181 458 0267(f)
RCSPC, UPA

SULLIVAN, Anita
Individual and Group Humanistic Psychotherapist
143 Melrose Avenue, London NW2 4LY
0181 450 2107
AHPP

SUTTERS, Amabel
Integrative Psychotherapist
140 Iverson Road, London NW6 2HH
0171 372 1329
MC

SYZ, Ann
Child Psychotherapist
Howard House, Garden Flat, 30 Belsize Park Gardens, London NW3 4AU
0171 431 4430/0171 722 2121
ACP

TAUBE, Idonea
Educational Therapist
15 Church Row, London NW3 6UP
0171 431 4543
FAETT

TAYLOR, Mary
Systemic Psychotherapist
39 Dartmouth Park Road, London NW5 1SU
0171 485 5719/0171 607 5092 (f)
KCC

TAYLOR-THOMAS, Caroline
Psychoanalytic Psychotherapist
9 Hayland Close, London NW9 0LH
0181 200 1609
IPC

TESTA, Rita
Child Psychotherapist
Department of Child & Adolescent Psychiatry, Royal Free Hospital, Pond Street, London NW3 2QG
01932 842633/0171 830 2931
ACP

THOMAS, Nigel
Cognitive Behavioural Psychotherapist
Charter Nightingale Hospital, 11-19 Lisson Grove, London NW1 6SH
0171 723 1987
BABCP

THOMSON, Jean
Analytical Psychologist-Jungian Analyst
1 Beatty Street, London NW1 7LN
0171 388 5508
SAP, FIP

TOUBKINS, Rita
Psychosynthesis Psychotherapist
77 Hampstead Way, London NW11 7LG
0181 455 4515
AAPP

TOWNLEY, Judy Rifkin
Child Psychotherapist
3 North Square, London NW11 7AA
0181 435 8934
ACP

TURKIE, Janine
Psychodrama Psychotherapist
32 Well Walk, Hampstead, London NW3 1BX
BPA

VAN HEEL, Carlien
Biodynamic Psychotherapist
Flat 4, 1a Laurier Road, London
NW5 1SD
0171 485 2922
BTC

VELLA, Norman
Group Analyst
45 Constantine Road, London
NW3 2LN
0171 837 6736/0171 267 2587
IGA

VINCENT, Christopher
Psychoanalytic Marital Psychotherapist, Psychoanalytic Psychotherapist
T.M.S.I., Tavistock Centre, 120 Belsize Lane, London NW3 5BA
0171 435 7111/01753 822 892
BAP, TMSI

WALBY, Jane
Systemic Psychotherapist
96 Savernake Road, London NW3 2JR
0171 267 3241
KCC

WALKER, Anne
Cognitive Behavioural Psychotherapist
Psychology Department, Northwick Park Hospital, Watford Road, Harrow Middlesex NW10 4RX
0411 571837/0181 965 8927
BABCP

WATSON, Lindsay
Lacanian Analyst, Psychoanalytic Psychotherapist
95 Parliament Hill Mansions, Lissenden Gardens, London NW5 1NB
0171 485 1274
CFAR

WEIDER, Bilha
Family Psychotherapist
4 Cranbourne Gardens, London
NW11 0HP
0181 732 4599/0181 455 6668
AFT

WEINRICH, Hildegard
Analytical Psychologist-Jungian Analyst
38 Cranhurst Road, London NW2 4LP
0181 450 0537
IGAP

WEISENSEL, Karin
Integrative Psychotherapist
18 Bartholomew Villas, London
NW5 2LL
0171 813 2145
RCSPC

WEIXEL-DIXON, Karen
Integrative Psychotherapist
36 Courthope Road, London
NW3 2LD
0171 485 1515
RCSPC

WELLS, Lindsay
Psychoanalytic Psychotherapist
19 Brondesbury Court, 235 Willesden Lane, London NW2 5RR
0181 830 3562
AGIP, AIP

WETHERELL, Jean
Analytical Psychologist-Jungian Analyst
31 Brondesbury Road, London
NW6 6BA
0171 328 1135
FIP

WHEELER, Meredith
Transpersonal Psychotherapist
51 Queens Crescent, London
NW5 3QG
0171 485 1619
CCPE

WHITE, Kate
Attachment-based Psychoanalytic Psychotherapist
12 Nassington Road, London
NW3 2UD
0171 794 4306
CAPP

WIDDICOMBE, Anastasia
Psychoanalytic Psychotherapist, Child Psychotherapist
75 Albert Street, London NW1 7LX
Barnet Child & Family Consultation Service, Edgware General Hospital, Edgware, Middx. HA8 0AD
0171 387 4288/0181 905 6679
ACP, BAP

WILKE, Gerhard
Group Analyst
75 St. Gabriels Road, London
NW2 4DU
0181 450 0469
IGA

WILLIAMS, Gianna
Child Psychotherapist
Child and Family Department, Tavistock Clinic, 120 Belsize Lane, London NW3 5BA
0171 435 7111/0181 455 5682
ACP

WISE, Penny
Psychoanalytic Psychotherapist
17 Lisburne Road, London NW3 2NS
0171 485 0005
IPSS

WITTENBERG, Isca
Child Psychotherapist
18 Helenslea Avenue, London
NW11 8ND
0181 455 4344 (t/f)
ACP

WOODS, John
Child Psychotherapist, Group Analyst
21 Hillfield Road, London NW6 1QD
0171 435 6276/0171 435 6274 (f)
ACP, IGA

WORRELL, Michael
Existential Psychotherapist
83 Riffel Road, London NW2 4PG
0181 450 8930/0181 453 2306
RCSPC

YASS, Marion
Psychoanalytic Marital Psychotherapist
5a Templewood Avenue, London
NW3 7UY
0171 794 2221
TMSI

ZAPHIRIOU WOODS, Marie
Child Psychotherapist
21 Hillfield Road, London NW6 1QD
0171 435 6274 (f)/0171 794 6276
ACP

LONDON SOUTH EAST

ADAMS, Tessa
Psychoanalytic Psychotherapist
122 Erlanger Road, London SE14
Goldsmith College, University of London, London SE14 6NW
0171 358 0018
GUILD

ALABASTER, Nigel
Family Psychotherapist
Greenwich Child Guidance Service, Plumstead Health Centre, Tewson Road, London SE18 1BH
0181 317 8319/0181 855 9254
AFT

ALEXANDER, Gina M V
Analytical Psychologist-Jungian Analyst
10 Shooters Hill Road, London SE3 7BD
0181 858 4758 (t/f)
FIP

ALLEYNE, Aileen
Psychoanalytic Psychotherapist
35 Pellatt Road, East Dulwich, London SE22 9JA
0181 693 4159
NAFSI

ANSARI, Shakir
Cognitive Analytic Therapist
10 Ivy Court, 109 Lee Road, Blackheath, London SE3 9EA
01322 525 919(f)/01322 526 282
ACAT

ANTHONY, Monica
Transpersonal Psychotherapist
43 Gomm Road, London SE16 2TY
Violet Hill Studios,, 6 Violet Hill, London NW8 9EB
0171 232 2562
CTP

APPLEBY, Sonia
Psychoanalytic Psychotherapist
12 Arran Road, Catford, London SE6 2NL
0181 698 6575
LCP

ATTIAS, Sandra
Transpersonal Psychotherapist
4 Sydcote, Rosendale Road, Dulwich, London SE21 8LH
0181 766 0101
CCPE

ATTWOOD, Peter
Family Therapist, Systemic Psychotherapist
317b Upland Road, East Dulwich, London SE22 0DL
NSPCC Parkside Project, Parkside Clinic, Lancaster Road, London W10 1QG
0171 243 4311/0181 299 3014
IFT

AYRES, Anthony
Psychoanalytic Psychotherapist
37 Donaldson Road, London SE18 3JZ
0181 856 1542
GUILD

BARTER, Ruth
Child Psychotherapist
29 Colte Road, London SE23 2ES
0181 291 1675
ACP

BASSAM, Bruce
Cognitive Behavioural Psychotherapist
Dept of Child and Fam.Psychiatry, Lambeth Healthcare NHS Trust, 35 Black Prince Road, Kennington SE11 6JJ
173 Shakespeare Road, Herne Hill, London SE24 0PY
0171 274 8336/0171 793 7113
BABCP

BEARD, Hilary
Cognitive Analytic Therapist, Psychoanalytic Psychotherapist
4 Grangewood Terrace, Grange Road, South Norwood, London SE25 6BA
Psychotherapy Unit, Dept. of Psychiatry, St Thomas Hospital, Lambeth Place Road, London SE1 7EH
0181 771 4475
ACAT, GUILD

BELL, Frances
Analytical Psychologist-Jungian Analyst
296 Commercial Way, Peckham, London SE15 1QN
0171 732 9709
AJA

BENNETT, Lesley
Psychoanalytic Psychotherapist
167 Brockley Rise, Forest Hill, London SE23 1NL
0181 690 7537
IPSS

BENVENUTO, Bice
Lacanian Analyst
60 Ivydale Road, London SE15 3BS
0171 639 8289
CFAR

BHAT, Radha
Group Analyst
186 Beulah Hill, Upper Norwood, London SE19 3UX
0181 240 7489/0181 460 5593
IGA

BISHOP, Patricia
Psychoanalytic Psychotherapist
156 Westcombe Hill, Blackheath, London SE3 7DH
0181 293 1995/0181 692 9260
IPSS

BLACK, Sandra
Psychoanalytic Psychotherapist
112 Friern Road, London SE22 OAX
0181 693 7524
IPSS

BLACKIE, Suzanne
Analytical Psychologist-Jungian Analyst
7 Balkaskie Road, Eltham, London SE9 1HQ
0181 333 2909/0181 850 0633
BAP

BLAND, John
Cognitive Behavioural Psychotherapist
92 Tuam Road, Plumstead Common, London SE18 2QU
Erith Centre, Park Crescent, Erith, Kent DA8 3EE
0181 856 4970/0181 473 5937
BABCP

BLOMFIELD, Valerie
Psychosynthesis Psychotherapist
12 Woodlands Park Road, Greenwich, London SE10 9XD
0181 853 0772
AAPP

BRIGHT, Jenifer A
Cognitive Behavioural Psychotherapist
Department of Clinical Psychology, Institute of Psychiatry, De Crespigny Park, Denmark Hill SE15 8AF
0171 919 3242
BABCP

BRITTAIN, Charlie
Transpersonal Psychotherapist
120 Sandyhill Road, London SE18 7BA
0181 316 4907
CCPE

BROOKS, Beverly
Cognitive Analytic Therapist
15 Cibber Road, Forest Hill, London SE23 2EF
0181 699 8836
ACAT

BRUCE, Ann
Analytical Psychologist-Jungian Analyst
54 Uffington Road, London SE27 0ND
0181 670 3783
SAP

CANTY, Josephine
Group Analyst
125 Taunton Road, Lee Green, London
SE12 9PA
0181 318 9023
IGA

CAREY, Faye
Psychoanalytic Psychotherapist
15 Holly Grove, London SE15 5DF
0171 639 1075
LCP

CARUANA, Charles Victor
Psychoanalytic Psychotherapist
Flat 6, 50 New Cross Road, London
SE14 5BD
46 Erlanger Road, London SE14 5TG
0171 277 7402(t/f)
AGIP

CHESSELL, Karen
Psychoanalytic Psychotherapist
329 Upland Road, East Dulwich,
London SE22 0DL
0181 299 2890
IPSS

CLEMINSON, Dorel
Integrative Psychotherapist
36 Seymour Gardens, Brockley,
London SE4 2DN
0171 635 6206/0171 639 5055
RCSPC

CLEMINSON, Richard
Biodynamic Psychotherapist
64 Sunderland Road, Forest Hill,
London SE23 2PY
01273 500 797
BTC

CLOUGH, Andrea
Psychosynthesis Psychotherapist
37 Harefield Road, Brockley, London
SE4 1LW
0181 692 7171 x 2248/0181 691 5303
AAPP

COMBES, Ann
Group Analytic Psychotherapist
53 South Norwood Hill, South
Norwood, London SE25 6BX
0181 771 2057
IPC

CORNECK, Susan
Psychoanalytic Psychotherapist
41 Creek Road, London SE8 3BU
0181 694 0221/0181 692 2749 (f)
AGIP, FIP

COWMEADOW, Pauline
Cognitive Analytic Therapist
45 Beauval Road, Dulwich, London
SE22 8UG
0171 955 4279/0181 693 1812
ACAT

CROWE, Michael
Sexual and Marital Psychotherapist
Maudsley Hospital, Denmark Hill,
London SE5 8AZ
0171 703 6333/0181 777 4823
BASMT

CURRAN, Annalee
Cognitive Analytic Therapist
108 Norwood Road, Herne Hill,
London SE24 9BB
0181 674 8702
ACAT

CZUBINSKA, Grazyna
Psychoanalytic Psychotherapist
2 Greenwich Park Street, Greenwich,
London SE10 9AA
0181 853 0156
IPC

DABOR, Thelma
Cognitive Behavioural Psychotherapist
19 Ridgeway, Central Hill, Upper
Norwood, London SE19 1EH
Greenwich Mind Networks, 37
Charlton Church Lane, Charlton,
London SE7 7AG
0181 305 2388/0181 766 6258
BABCP

DAWSON, Peter
Transpersonal Psychotherapist
8a Peabody Buildings, Camberwell
Green, London SE5 7BD
0171 708 5399
CCPE

DEALE, Alicia
Cognitive Behavioural Psychotherapist
Dept. of Psychological Medicine, Kings
College Hospital, Denmark Hill,
London SE5 9RS
0171 346 3181
BABCP

DEARNLEY, Barbara K.
Psychoanalytic Marital Psychotherapist
186 Court Lane, London SE21 7ED
0181 693 2603
TMSI

DENFORD, Lindsey D.
Cognitive Behavioural Psychotherapist
Section of Psychiatric Nursing, Institute
of Psychiatry, De Crespigny Park,
London SE5 8AZ
0171 919 3505
BABCP

DENIFLEE, Ursula
Biodynamic Psychotherapist
30 Styles House, The Cut, London
SE1 8DF
0171 401 3582
BTC

DILKS, Sarah L E
Cognitive Behavioural Psychotherapist
Community Rehabilitation Team,
Lewisham & Guys M. Health NHS
Trust, 8 Belmont Hill, Lewisham
SE13 5BD
0181 297 0021
BABCP

DODGE, Elizabeth
Family Therapist
Psychotherapy Section, Institute of
Psychiatry, De Crespigny Park,
Denmark Hill, London SE5 8AF
38 Rathcoole Gardens, London
N8 9NB
0171 919 3196/0171 919 3205 (f)
IFT

DOOLAN, Moira
Family Therapist
27 Barnmead Road, Beckenham, Kent,
BR3 2JF
0181 676 8495
AFT

DOWBER, Hilary
Psychoanalytic Psychotherapist
c/o Cassel Centre, 4 Walden Park
Road, Forest Hill, London SE23 2PN
0181 291 3436
IPSS

DUCKWORTH, Rosemary
Psychoanalytic Psychotherapist
14 Ashton Heights, 51 Horniman
Drive, Forest Hill, London SE23 3BS
0181 291 2916
IPSS

DUPUY, Alan
Personal Construct Psychotherapist
Flat 16, Dominic Court, 43 The
Gardens, Dulwich, London SE22 9QG
0181 693 4105 (f)/0181 693 5769
CPCP

EGERT, Stella
Family Psychotherapist
183 Rosendale Road, West Dulwich, London SE21 8LW
0181 670 3417
IFT

EILES, Clive
Psychoanalytic Psychotherapist
133 Ruskin Park House, Champion Hill, London SE5 8TL
0171 274 8142
ARBS, FIP

EISLER, Ivan
Family Therapist
Institute of Psychiatry, De Crespigny Park, Denmark Hill, London SE5 8AF
0171 919 3184/0171 919 3205 (f)
IFT

EISLER, Zizana
Sexual and Marital Psychotherapist
51 Thorpewood Avenue, London SE26 4BY
0181 699 6478
BASMT

ELLIOTT, Sandra A.
Cognitive Behavioural Psychotherapist
Community Clinical Psychology Service, Clinical Treatment Centre, Maudsley Hospital, Denmark Hill, London SE5 8AZ
0171 919 2194
BABCP

ELLIOTT, Victoria
Child Psychotherapist, Psychoanalytic Psychotherapist
Plumstead Child Guidance Unit, Plumstead Health Centre, Tewson Road, London SE18 1BH
43 Chalcroft Road, London SE13 5RE
0181 244 4732/0181 460 5593
ACP, BAP

ENNIS, Sally-Anne
Cognitive Analytic Therapist
25A Wincott Street, Kennington, London SE11 4NT
0171 587 5255
ACAT

ERSKINE, Judith
Attachment-based Psychoanalytic Psychotherapist
45a Tremaine Road, Anerley, London SE20 7UA
0171 919 2969 ext3576/0181 659 2465
CAPP

FARQUHAR, Kate
Psychoanalytic Psychotherapist, Lacanian Analyst
169 Peckham Rye, London SE15 3HZ
0171 358 1748(f)/0171 277 6890
CFAR, FIP

FINDLAY, David Alistair
Integrative Psychosynthesis Psychotherapist
207 Waller Road, Telegraph Hill, London SE14 5LX
0171 639 9732/0171 652 6467 (f)
RE.V

FIRMAN, Judith
Psychosynthesis Psychotherapist
Psychosynthesis & Education Trust, 92-94 Tooley Street, London SE1 2TH
0181 545 0873/0171 403 2100
AAPP

FISHER, Linda
Cognitive Behavioural Psychotherapist
C.F.S. Research Unit, The Rayne Institute, 123 Coldharbour Lane, London SE9 9NU
0171 737 4000 x 4096/0171 346 3363
BABCP

FLEMING, Robert W.K.
Child Psychotherapist, Psychoanalytic Psychotherapist
29 Croxted Road, West Dulwich, London SE21 8AZ
10 Shawbury Road, London SE22 9DH
0171 793 7113/0181 693 0019
ACP, BAP

FLETCHER, Joan
Humanistic and Integrative Psychotherapist
171 Algernon Road, Lewisham, London SE13 7AP
0181 690 8987
SPEC

FOSBURY, Jacqueline
Cognitive Analytic Therapist
Diabetes Centre, St Thomas' Hospital, London SE1 7EH
0171 928 9292 ext 3786
ACAT

FRENCH, Eileen
Analytical Psychologist-Jungian Analyst
London Practice, LF 1.9 The Leather Market Weston, Street, London SE1 4XE
14 Leverton Street, London NW5 2PJ
0171 357 0357/0171 485 1533
AJA

GARDINER, Margaret
Psychoanalytic Psychotherapist
44 Granville Park, London SE13 7DX
Student Counselling Service, Medical Centre, King's College, Strand, London WC2R 2LS
0171 837 2613/0181 318 3303
AGIP, FIP

GERAGHTY, Wendy
Family Therapist
82 Murillo Road, London SE13 5QQ
0181 463 9109
AFT

GOODFELLOW, Joanna
Gestalt Psychotherapist
27 Ansdell Road, London SE15 2DT
321 Portobello Road, London W10 5SY
0171 771 6323
GPTI

GORDON, Sheila
Psychoanalytic Psychotherapist
West Side Row, 222 South Norwood Hill, London SE25 6AS
0181 771 7074
LCP

GOTTSCHALK, Margaret S
Integrative Psychotherapist
9 Court Lane Gardens, London SE21 7DZ
0181 693 5112
MC

GRIFFIN, Mary
Sexual and Marital Psychotherapist
Out-Patient Department, Maudsley Hospital, Denmark Hill, London SE5 8AZ
BASMT

GRIFFITH, John
Psychoanalytic Psychotherapist
42 Elm Grove, Peckham, London SE15 5DE
c/o AGIP, 1 Fairbridge Road, London N19 3EW
0171 272 7013/0171 639 4963
AGIP

GURNEY, Paul
Psychoanalytic Psychotherapist
Flat 1, 13 Romola Road, London SE24 9BA
0181 244 4840
PA

HADDINGTON, Janet
Psychoanalytic Psychotherapist
2a Bromar Road, Camberwell, London
SE5 8DL
0171 725 1036/0171 326 1332
FIP

HANCHEN, Thomasz
NLP Psychotherapist
55 Cressingham Road, Lewisham,
London SE13 5AQ
0181 318 3102 (t/f)
ANLP

HANCOCK, Pauline
Psychosynthesis Psychotherapist
Flat 1, 194 Peckham Rye, East Dulwich,
London SE22 9QA
0181 299 1767
AAPP

HANNA, Dorothy
Psychosynthesis Psychotherapist
74 Auckland Hill, West Norwood,
London SE27 9QQ
0181 761 2855
AAPP

HARGADEN, Helena
Transactional Analysis Psychotherapist,
Integrative Psychotherapist
43 Brockley Park, London SE23 1PT
0181 690 3175 (t/f)
MET, ITA

HENDRY, Evelyn R.
Cognitive Behavioural Psychotherapist
York Clinic, Guy's Hospital, London
SE1 1NP
0171 955 4933
BABCP

HODGKISS, Andrew
Lacanian Analyst
Department of Liaison, Psychiatry,
Riddell House, St Thomas'Hospital,
London SE1 7EH
0171 928 9292 ext 2568
CFAR, CFAR

HOLDEN, Sarah
Group Analyst
15 Auckland Hill, West Norwood,
London SE27 9PF
0181 672 9911 x 42236/0181 473 3038
IGA

HORT, Daphne
Psychoanalytic Psychotherapist
36 Alanthus Close, Lee Green, London
SE12 8RE
0181 852 6914
GUILD, IPC

HOWARD, Heather
Psychoanalytic Psychotherapist
83 Blackheath Park, London SE3 0EU
0181 852 6564
IPSS

JACOBS, Brian
Family Therapist, Systemic
Psychotherapist
8 Mabenley Road, Upper Norwood,
London SE19 2JB
The Children's Dept., The Maudsley
Hospital, Denmark Hill, London
SE5 8AZ
0171 919 2556/0181 771 0342
IFT

JAMES, Christopher
Family Therapist
1 Gourock Road, Eltham, London
SE9 1JA
Greenwich Child Guidance Services,
Plumstead Health Centre, Tewson
Road, London SE18 1BH
0181 850 7561/0181 855 9254
IFT

JENKINS, Anne
Group Analyst
1 Clink Wharf, Clink Street, London
SE1 9DG
IGA

JENKINS, Hugh
Systemic Psychotherapist
83 Hurstbourne Road, Forest Hill,
London SE23 2AQ
0181 291 4791
IFT

JIAH, Hildah
Cognitive Behavioural Psychotherapist
Deptford Primary Care MHTeam, Lind
Clinic, James Lind House, Grove Street
SE8 3QF
Flat 3, 30 Gleneagle Road, Streatham,
London SW16 6AF
BABCP

JONES, Edgar
Psychoanalytic Psychotherapist
Dept of Psychological Medicine, Kings
College School of Medicine, 103
Denmark Hill, London SE5 SAZ
0171 734 4000 ext 4688
LCP

JONES, Merryn
Group Analytic Psychotherapist
8 Broadwall, London SE1 9QE
0171 401 2393
IPC

KERR, Anna
Psychoanalytic Psychotherapist
3 Talbot Place, London SE3 0TZ
0181 852 1751
GUILD

KERRIDGE, Jack
Psychoanalytic Psychotherapist
96 Langton Way, London SE3 7JU
0181 305 1287
GUILD

KING, Christine
Hypno-Psychotherapist
St Johns Park, Blackheath, London
SE3 7JB
P O Box 89, London SE3 7JN
0181 305 2317
NRHP

KLEIN, Josephine
Psychoanalytic Psychotherapist
58 Roupell Street, London SE1 8TB
0171 928 5747
LCP, FIP

KOEPPELMANN, Marianna
Psychosynthesis Psychotherapist
73 Lawnside, Blackheath, London
SE3 9HL
0181 318 0792/0171 318 0792
AAPP

KOWSZUN, Grazyna
Integrative Psychotherapist
127 Kinveachy Gardens, Charlton,
London SE7 8EQ
0181 854 0604
MET

LANG, Susan
Systemic Psychotherapist
40 Rosenthorpe Road, London
SE15 3EG
0171 639 0995
KCC

LANGDON, Monica
Psychoanalytic Psychotherapist
6 Upwood Road, London SE12 8AA
0181 318 0110
AGIP, CSPK

LANYADO, Monica
Child Psychotherapist
30 Brookway, Blackheath, London
SE3 9BJ
0181 852 1521/0181 297 0528 (f)
ACP

LASK, Judith
Family Therapist, Systemic
Psychotherapist
99 Underhill Road, London SE22 0QR
Inst. of Family Therapy, 24-32
Stephenson Way, London NW1 2HX
0171 391 9150/0181 693 6048
IFT

LEEMING, Gareth
Psychoanalytic Psychotherapist
Flat 8, 82 Wickham Road, Brockley,
London SE4 1LS
0181 469 0666
IPC

LESTER, Hilary
Humanistic Psychotherapist
235 Barry Road, East Dulwich, London
SE22 0JU
0181 299 4368
AHPP

LINESS, Sheena
Cognitive Behavioural Psychotherapist
Maudsley Hospital, 99 Denmark Hill,
London SE5 8AZ
0171 919 3458
BABCP

LONGLEY, Joan
Psychoanalytic Psychotherapist
Lavender Cottage, 9b Tudor Road,
London SE19 2UH
6 Owen Walk, Sycamore Grove,
Anerley, London SE20 8BY
0181 659 8486/0181 768 0224
AGIP

LOVE, Derek
Group Analyst
15 Thorncombe Road, London
SE22 8PX
0181 892 6584
IGA

LOVEL, Mary
Psychoanalytic Psychotherapist
59 Bungalow Road, South Norwood,
London SE25 6JY
0181 653 4178
IPSS

LOWE, Judith
NLP Psychotherapist
6 Denman Road, London SE15 5NP
0171 708 2358 (t/f)
ANLP

LYONS, Kathleen
Psychosynthesis Psychotherapist
Cenacle Sisters, 142a Rodney Road,
Walworth, London SE17 1RA
0171 708 3541
AAPP

MACDONALD, Laurie
NLP Psychotherapist
24 Robinscroft Mews, Greenwich,
London SE10 8DN
0181 691 6513 (t/f)
ANLP

MAKATINI, Zethu
Systemic Psychotherapist
31 Langford House, Evelyn Street,
Deptford, London SE8 5QJ
KCC

MANN, David
Psychoanalytic Psychotherapist
134 Westwood Park, London
SE23 3QH
0181 699 6498
LCP

MARSH, Jennifer
Psychoanalytic Psychotherapist
96 Elfindale Road, Herne Hill, London
SE24 9NW
0171 274 3467
GUILD

MARTIN, Edward
Analytical Psychologist-Jungian Analyst
17 Honor Oak Rise, London SE23 3QY
0181 699 2303
SAP

MAUNDER, Brian Lawrence
Psychoanalytic Psychotherapist
Badgers' Oak, 12 Chinbrook Road,
Grove Park, London SE12 9TH
0181 851 5702
IPC

MCCUTCHEON, Moira
Child Psychotherapist
Camberwell Child Guidance Centre,
Lister Health Centre, 1 Camden
Square, Peckham Road, London
SE15 5LA
0171 701 7371
ACP

MCKENZIE- MAVINGA, Isha
Psychoanalytic Psychotherapist
10 Wall Button Road, Brockley, London
SE4 2NX
NAFSI

MCLOUGHLIN, Brendan

Cognitive Behavioural Psychotherapist
Behavioural Psychotherapy Unit, 99
Denmark Hill, Maudsley Hospital,
London SE5 8AZ
0171 919 2101
BABCP

MCMAHON, Gladeana
Cognitive Behavioural Psychotherapist
11 Streetfield Mews, Blackheath Park,
London SE3 0ER
0181 852 4854
BABCP

MCMILLAN, Penny
Attachment-based Psychoanalytic
Psychotherapist
32 Congers House, Bronze Street,
London SE8 3DT
CAPP

MEARS, Sylvia
Psychoanalytic Psychotherapist
5 Quentin Road, Blackheath SE13 5DG
0181 852 0399
LCP, FIP

MILES, Fiona
Psychosynthesis Psychotherapist
104 Humber Road, Blackheath, London
SE3 7LX
0181 858 7338
AAPP

MILLAR, Gerry
Psychosynthesis Psychotherapist
1 Greenstreet Hill, Drakefell Road,
London SE14 5SR
Psychosynthesis & Education Trust, 92 -
94 Tooley Street, London SE11 2TH
0171 635 7754
AAPP

MONTICELLI, Wendy
Psychoanalytic Psychotherapist
19 Brunswick Quay, Rotherhithe,
London SE16 1PU
0171 231 4309
IPC

MORRIS, Brenda
Personal Construct Psychotherapist
31 Lewisham Park, London SE13 6QZ
CPCP

MUKUMA, Diana
Gestalt Psychotherapist
Flat 3, 194 Kennington Lane, London
SE11 5DL
0171 735 5442
GPTI

MURPHY, Susan
Integrative Psychotherapist
4 Egremont Road, London SE27 0BH
0171 323 6334/0181 670 6139
RCSPC

NATHAN, Jack
Psychoanalytic Psychotherapist,
Psychotherapist (Family & Relationship)
356 Upland Road, London SE22 0DP
0181 299 3779
LCP

NEWBIGIN, Alison
Integrative Psychotherapist
48 Surrey Square, London SE17 2JX
0171 703 9544
MC

NKUMANDA, Rachel
Psychoanalytic Psychotherapist
6 Kelso Court, 94 Anerley Park,
London SE20 8NZ
0181 459 3180
NAFSI

O'CALLAGHAN, Diane
Psychoanalytic Psychotherapist
16 Colwell Road, East Dulwich, London
SE22 8QP
AGIP, FIP

OAKLEY, Madeleine
Psychoanalytic Psychotherapist, Family
Therapist
Psychotherapy Department, Institute of
Psychiatry, De Crespigny
Park,Denmark Hill, London SE5 8AF
0171 919 3196
IPSS, AFT

PALANISAMY, Shan
Cognitive Behavioural Psychotherapist
55 Eastgate Close, Thamesmead,
London SE28 8PL
0181 311 5983/0181 855 8886
BABCP

PALMER, Stephen
Cognitive Behavioural Psychotherapist
Centre for Stress Management, 156
Westcombe Hill, Blackheath, London
SE3 7DH
0181 293 4114
BABCP

PARKINSON, Judy
Psychoanalytic Psychotherapist
Newlands Park Natural Health Care
Centre, 48 Newlands Park, Sydenham,
London SE26 5NE
0181 659 5001
IPC

PAWSEY, Jack
Psychoanalytic Psychotherapist
20 Addington Square, London SE5 7JZ
0171 701 8920
IPC

PEDDER, Jonathan
Psychoanalytic Psychotherapist
Maudsley Hospital, Denmark Hill,
London SE5 8AZ
AUTP

PETERS, Sheila
Hypno-Psychotherapist
102A Holmesdale Road, South
Norwood, London SE25 6JF
0181 653 4242
NRHP

PINTO, Eliano
Psychoanalytic Psychotherapist
16 Woolstone Road, Forest Hill,
London SE23 2SG
LCP

POMPE, Marie
Psychoanalytic Psychotherapist
102 Alleyn Road, London SE21 8AH
99 Herne Hill, London SE24 9LY
0181 670 6388
AGIP

PRICE, Annie
Psychoanalytic Psychotherapist
9 Pickwick Road, London SE21 7JN
0171 738 7565/0171 274 8794 (f)
AGIP

PRICE, Susan
Psychoanalytic Psychotherapist
15 Boyne Road, London SE13 5AL
0181 318 4410
GUILD

RANCE, Christopher
Group Analyst
43 Rosendale Road, Dulwich, London
SE21 8DY
0181 670 5023
IGA

RIMMER, Annie
Integrative Psychotherapist,
Transactional Analysis Psychotherapist
10 Mount Ash Road, London SE26 6LZ
0181 480 9119 (f)/0181 291 4091
MET, ITA

ROBINSON, Ferga
Cognitive Behavioural Psychotherapist
44 Brockwell Park Gardens, Herne Hill,
London SE24 9BJ
0181 674 2359
BABCP

ROGERS, Cynthia
Group Analyst
178 Turney Road, Dulwich, London
SE21 7JL
0171 274 4655
IGA

ROSS, Fiona
Analytical Psychologist-Jungian Analyst
17 Honor Oak Rise, London SE23 3QY
0181 699 2303
SAP

RUDDELL, Peter
Cognitive Behavioural Psychotherapist
Centre for Rational Emotive B.T., 156
Westcombe Hill, Blackheath, London
SE3 7DH
0181 293 4114
BABCP

RUMNEY, Boris
Psychoanalytic Psychotherapist
1 Foxes Dale, London SE3 9BD
0181 852 9015
GUILD

RYLEY, Brigitte
Humanistic Psychotherapist
Flat 1, 39a Glengarry Road, London
SE22 8QA
0181 693 6953
AHPP

SALMON, Gillian
Educational Therapist
46 Pepys Road, London SE14 5SB
0171 639 3062 (t/f)
FAETT

SARKIC, Julia
Hypno-Psychotherapist
5A Howard Road, London SE20 8HQ
0181 778 9524
NRHP

SCHAFFER, Tom
Core Process Psychotherapist
1 Faversham Road, Catford, London
SE6 4XE
0181 690 1769
AAPP

SEIGAL, Anthony
Sexual and Marital Psychotherapist
148 Woodwarde Road, London
SE22 8UR
0181 288 2383
BASMT

SHEPHERD, Eric
Cognitive Behavioural Psychotherapist
Division of Psychiatry and Psychology, UMDS Guy's & St. Thomas's, Guy's Hospital, London SE1 9RT
0171 955 4247
BABCP

SHERRIFF, Deanne
Cognitive Behavioural Psychotherapist
92 Tuam Road, Plumstead Common, London SE18 2QU
Meridian Locality Team, Memorial Hospital, Shooters Hill, London SE18
0181 473 5937/0181 855 8886
BABCP

SIEDERER, Carol
Gestalt Psychotherapist
76 Erlanger Road, London SE14 5TH
0171 732 1116
GCL

SMITH, David L.
Integrative Psychotherapist
New School of Psychotherapy and Counselling, Royal Waterloo House, 51 - 55 Waterloo Road, London SE1 8TX
0181 699 6687
UPA

SMITH, Juliet
Integrative Psychotherapist
11 Betsham House, Newcomen Street, London SE1 1YU
0171 403 5497
MET

SMITH, R.L
Cognitive Behavioural Psychotherapist
MHAC, 1 Southbrook Road, Lee, London SE12 8LH
0181 333 3030 x8117/0181 318 1339
BABCP

SMITH, Trevor E.L.
Cognitive Behavioural Psychotherapist
22 Pleydell Avenue, Upper Norwood, London SE19 2LP
Dept Behavioural/Cognitive Therapy, Avenue House CMHRC, 43 - 47 Avenue Road, Acton W3 8NJ
0956 810 585/0181 993 7892
BABCP

SPINELLI, Ernesto
Existential Psychotherapist
69 Oglander Road, East Dulwich
SE15 4DD
0171 487 7406/0181 693 9332
RCSPC

STANTON, Martin
Psychoanalytic Psychotherapist
169 Peckham Rye, London SE15 3HZ
0171 732 9431/0171 358 1748 (t/f)
LCP, FIP

STOPHER, Andy
Psychoanalytic Psychotherapist
5 Manwood Road, Crofton Park, London SE4 1AA
0181 690 0484
IPSS

STRICKLAND, Lynda
Cognitive Behavioural Psychotherapist
120 Sangley Road, Catford, London
SE6 2JR
13 Nelson Road, Greenwich, London
SE10 9JB
0181 858 8557/0181 461 2075
BABCP

STUART, Lilly H.
Transactional Analysis Psychotherapist
106 Heathwood Gardens, Charlton, London SE7 8ER
0181 854 3606
ITA

SULLIVAN, E. Mary
Integrative Psychotherapist
60 Humber Road, Blackheath, London
SE3 7LU
0171 487 7584/0181 305 9696
RCSPC

TANNER, Claire
Cognitive Analytic Therapist
26 Vancouver Road, Forest Hill, London SE23 2AF
ACAT

TOPLISS, Nick
Family Therapist
162 Kilmonie Road, Forest Hill, London
SE23 2SR
5 Baldwin Crescent, Camberwell, London SE15 9LQ
0171 733 6291/0181 244 0284
IFT

VAN HEESWYK, Paul
Child Psychotherapist
Bloomfield Clinic, Guys Hospital, St. Thomas Street, London SE1 9RT
0171 955 4581/0171 622 6493
ACP

WACH, Karin Marie
Psychoanalytic Psychotherapist
2 Pottery Street, Cherry Garden Pier, London SE16 4PH
0171 252 3947
ARBS

WALLER, Diane
Group Analytic Psychotherapist
Goldsmith College, University of London, Lewisham Way, London
SE14 6NW
01273 685 852
UPA

WARDLEY, Jean
Cognitive Behavioural Psychotherapist
58 Genesta Road, Shooters Hill, London SE18 3EU
0181 854 3014
BABCP

WATERS, Kathleen
Family Therapist
15a Colfe Road, Forest Hill, London
SE23 2ES
Lewisham Child & Family Therapy Centre, 78 Lewisham Park, Lewisham, London SE13 6QJ
0181 699 5881/0181 690 1086
IFT

WATSON, J.P.
Sexual and Marital Psychotherapist
UMDS Div. of Psychiatry, Guy's Hospital, London SE1 9RT
BASMT

WAY, Patsy
Systemic Psychotherapist
72 Alleyn Road, Dulwich, London
SE21 8AH
0181 670 5315
KCC

WHITE, Jeremy
Group Analyst
4a Spenser Road, Herne Hill, London
SE24 0NR
0171 733 0834
IGA

WILFORD, Gerti
Family Therapist
The Belgrave Dept. of Child & Family Psychiatry, King's College Hospital, Bessemer Road, London SE5
30 Spencer Road, East Moseley, Surrey
KT8 0SR
0181 224 0539/0181 979 3003
AFT

WILLIAMS, Chris
Gestalt Psychotherapist
2b Plough Lane, East Dulwich, London
SE22 8JL
Natural Therapy Centres, 106A Denmark Hill, Camberwell, London
SE5
0181 693 1129
GPTI

WILLIAMS, Diana
Transpersonal Psychotherapist
17 Chestnut Road, London SE27 9EZ
0181 670 1035
CTP

WILLIAMS, Pat
Integrative Psychotherapist
79 Ermine Road, Lewisham, London
SE13 7JJ
0181 690 1229
MC

WILLIAMS, Ruth M.
Cognitive Behavioural Psychotherapist
Department of Psychology, Institute of Psychiatry, De Crespigny Park, London
SE5 8AF
0171 919 3242
BABCP

WILSON, Mary
Analytical Psychologist-Jungian Analyst
46 Erlanger Road, New Cross, London
SE14 5TG
0171 639 1867
SAP

WINDERS, Suzanne
Psychoanalytic Psychotherapist
21B Holmdene Avenue, London
SE24 9LB
0171 274 7517
IPC

WOODLEY, Ermine
Psychoanalytic Psychotherapist
40 Siddons Road, Forest Hill, London
SE23 2JQ
0181 291 3185
IPSS

WOOSTER, Frances
Psychoanalytic Psychotherapist
28 Holly Grove, London SE15 5DF
0171 635 0448/0171 732 8517 (f)
GUILD

YAZAR, Jale
Psychoanalytic Psychotherapist
46 Milton Road, London SE24 0NP
0171 652 0056
NAFSI

LONDON SOUTH WEST

ABBASI, Shafika
Psychoanalytic Psychotherapist, Group Analyst
2 Tunley Road, London SW17 7QJ
0181 675 0235
IGA, BASMT

ADAMS-LANGLEY, Stephen
Integrative Psychotherapist
24 Fairmount Road, London SW2 2BL
0181 678 0473
RCSPC

AGUIRREGABIRIA, Ana
Psychodrama Psychotherapist
8d Peterborough Villas, Bagleys Lane, London SW6 2AT
0973 281657/0171 7368751 (f)
BPA

AKINBORO-COOPER, Bobbie
Child Psychotherapist
9 Hotham Road, London SW15 1QL
0181 788 1642
ACP

ALLAWI, Nadia
Psychoanalytic Psychotherapist
Woolborough House, 40 Roedean Crescent, Roehampton, London
SW15 5JU
0181 876 4182
IPSS

ALLSOP, Pamela
Transpersonal Psychotherapist
68 Redcliffe Square, London
SW10 9BN
0171 373 0891
CTP

AMBROSE, Tony
Gestalt Psychotherapist
46 Dorien Road, Raynes Park, London
SW20 8EJ
Paul Street, London W2
0181 542 5930
GCL

ANDREW, Elizabeth
Psychoanalytic Psychotherapist
3 Camp View, Wimbledon, London
SW19 4UL
0181 947 2732
IPC

ARCHER, Ruth
Psychoanalytic Psychotherapist
8 Roundacre, Inner Park Road, Wimbledon, London SW19 6DB
0181 788 5128
IPC

ATHANASIADIS, Loukas
Cognitive Behavioural Psychotherapist
Flat 10D, Austen House, St. George's Grove, Strathdon Drive, London
SW17 0PZ
01811 672 9911 x 42961
BABCP

AZU-OKEKE, Okeke
Group Analyst
118 Streatham Vale, London
SW16 5TB
0181 661 1611/0181 764 8894
IGA

BARNES, Tricia
Sexual and Marital Psychotherapist
7 Grange Park Place, Thurstan Road, Wimbledon, London SW20 0EE
BASMT

BERGER, Jocelyn
Integrative Psychotherapist
15 Sandgate Lane, London SW18 3JP
0181 874 0763
RCSPC

BIBBY, Keith
Hypno-Psychotherapist
49 Klea Avenue, Clapham Common, London SW4 9HG
0181 673 6311
NSHAP

BIRKETT, Diana
Psychoanalytic Psychotherapist
95 Elspeth Road, London SW11 1DP
0171 652 6749
CPP, FIP

BLAND, Roger
Integrative Psychotherapist
15 Coleherne Court, The Little Boltons, London SW5 0DL
0171 373 2014
RCSPC

BLOMFIELD, Wolf
Psychoanalytic Psychotherapist
123 Hambalt Road, London SW4 9EL
0181 673 5342
LCP, BAP

BOAKES, Janet
Group Analyst
Department of Psychotherapy, Clare House, St. George's Hospital, Tooting, London SW17 0QT
0181 725 3846/0171 737 1364 (f)
IGA

BOLL, Antonia
Analytical Psychologist-Jungian Analyst
51 Coniger Road, London SW6 3TB
0171 736 0226
AJA

BORGES, Sheila
Integrative Psychotherapist
71 Mantilla Road, London SW17 8DY
0181 767 6595
MC

BOWDERY, Sally
Humanistic Psychotherapist
132 Babington Road, London SW16 6AH
0181 769 5298/0181 769 2590 (f)
AHPP

BRIDGE, Jenny
Transactional Analysis Psychotherapist
569 Upper Richmond Road West, Richmond TW10 5DX
0181 878 2658
ITA, MET

BROOKES, Sasha
Psychoanalytic Marital Psychotherapist, Psychoanalytic Psychotherapist
44a Bramham Gardens, London SW5 0HQ
0171 370 4689
ARBS, TMSI

BRYAN, Agnes
Gestalt Psychotherapist
3 Claverdale Road, Tulse Hill, London SW2 2DJ
0181 674 1613
GCL

BUCKLEY, Marie-Noël (Billie)
Psychoanalytic Psychotherapist
6 Trevor Place, Knightsbridge, London SW7 1LA
0171 581 3987/0171 589 1763 (f)
IPC

BURNARD, John
Analytical Psychologist-Jungian Analyst
76 Ryecroft Road, London SW16 3EH
SAP

BUTLER, John
Hypno-Psychotherapist
37 Orbain Road, Fulham, London SW6 7JZ
0171 385 1166
NRHP

BUTLER SMITH, Catherine
Personal Construct Psychotherapist
30 Cleveland Gardens, London SW13 0AG
0181 878 3017
CPCP

CAMPBELL, Christine
Integrative Psychotherapist
33 Montpelier Walk, London SW7 1JG
0171 581 3374
RCSPC

CARDWELL, Amynta
Systemic Psychotherapist
Riverside Mental Health Trust, 5 Collingham Gardens, London SW5 0HR
0181 846 6644
KCC

CASEY, Jan
Transpersonal Psychotherapist
1 Vere House, 15 Cheyne Row, Chelsea, London SW3 5HR
0171 352 6964
CCPE

CHANCER, Anne
Psychoanalytic Psychotherapist
35 Temple Sheen Road, London SW14 7QF
0181 876 1523
GUILD

CHILTON, Maggie
Group Analyst
35 Brompton Square, London SW3 2AE
0171 584 1589
IGA

CLERY, Cairns
Family Therapist
50 Girdwood Road, Southfields, London SW18 5QS
0181 333 8400
AFT

CLIFTON, Elaine
Integrative Psychotherapist
Flat 3, 55 Onslow Square, London SW7 3LR
0171 581 0387/0171 373 6440 (f)
MET

COLERIDGE, Jane
Psychoanalytic Psychotherapist
85 Erpingham Road, London SW15
0181 785 9891
GUILD

COLES, Walter
Educational Therapist
18 Spencer Road, Wandsworth, London SW18 2SW
0171 738 2455/0171 738 0196 (f)
FAETT

COLLARD, Patrizia C
Cognitive Behavioural Psychotherapist
(Peking) Foreign & Commonweath Office, King Charles Street, London SW1A 2AH
British Embassy, 11 Guang Hua Lu, 100600 Beijing, China
86 10 6532 2293/86 10 6532 6121
BABCP

COLSON, Louise
Cognitive Behavioural Psychotherapist
The Priory Hospital, Priory Lane, Roehampton, London SW2 4XQ
0181 674 0305/0181 876 8261
BABCP

CONLON, Ann
Psychoanalytic Psychotherapist
68 Sandbourne Avenue, Merton Park, London SW19 3EN
0181 540 1400
LCP

CORONAS, Ita
Gestalt Psychotherapist, Humanistic Psychotherapist
37 Barkston Gardens, London SW5 OER
0171 373 3989 (t/f)
GCL, AHPP

CORRY, Marilyn
Psychoanalytic Psychotherapist
20 Bemish Road, Putney, London
SW15 1DG
0181 789 3668
LCP

COSTELLO, John
Analytical Psychologist-Jungian Analyst
122 Lupus Street, London SW1V 4AN
0171 834 1708 (t/f)
IGAP

COTTEN, Naomi
Psychoanalytic Psychotherapist
Flat 4, 14 The Chase, London
SW4 0NH
0171 720 7090
IPSS

COUMONT GRAUBART, Valerie
Integrative Psychotherapist
18 Laitwood Road, Balham, London
SW12 9QL
0181 265 5504
MC

COURTAULT, Susie
Psychoanalytic Psychotherapist
8 Clifford Avenue, London SW14 7BS
0181 876 3552
IPSS

CULLISS, Andrew
Psychoanalytic Psychotherapist
55 Trelawn Road, Brixton, London
SW2 1DH
0171 326 4773
IPSS

DARE-BRYAN, Arminal
Psychoanalytic Psychotherapist
15 Melrose Road, Southfields, London
SW18 1ND
0181 874 3138
IPC

DAVIS, Emerald
Attachment-based Psychoanalytic Psychotherapist
64 Lyndhurst Avenue, Norbury, London SW16 4UF
0181 764 6740
CAPP

DE MARQUIEGUI, Asun
Sexual and Marital Psychotherapist
Clapham Common Clinic, 1st Floor, 151-153 Clapham High Street, London
SW4 7SS
0171 627 8890
BASMT

DENMAN, Cara
Analytical Psychologist-Jungian Analyst
23 Lawrence Street, London SW3 5NF
0171 351 7336
IGAP

DENNIS, Suzanne
Integrative Psychosynthesis Psychotherapist
54 Baldry Gardens, London SW16 3DJ
0181 679 3572
RE.V

DIGHTON, Rosemary
Sexual and Marital Psychotherapist, Systemic Psychotherapist
Claremont House, 44 High Street, Wimbledon Village, London
SW19 5AU
0181 946 1097
BASMT, KCC

DOE, Anthony
Psychoanalytic Psychotherapist
Allen Hall, 28 Beaufort Street, London
SW3 5AA
0171 351 7634
AGIP

DONINGTON, Laura
Core Process Psychotherapist
39 Blenkarne Road, London
SW11 6HZ
0171 228 1107/0171 223 7020 (f)
AAPP

DRUMMOND, Lynne
Cognitive Behavioural Psychotherapist
Department of Mental Health Sciences, St George's Hospital Medical School, Cranmer Terrace, London SW17 0RE
Behavioural Cognitive Psychotherapy, Top floor, White Lodge, Springfield Hospital, Glenburnie Road SW17 7DJ
0181 725 5561/0181 682 6961
BABCP

EDELMANN, Robert J.
Cognitive Behavioural Psychotherapist
School of Psychology &Counselling, Roehampton Institute, Whitelands College, West Hill SW15 3SN
0181 392 3471
BABCP

EDGELL, Marjory
Hypno-Psychotherapist
23 Crescent Grove, London SW4 7AF
0171 622 4755
NRHP

EGLIN, Patricia
Integrative Psychotherapist
36 Turret Grove, London SW4 0ET
0171 978 1180
RCSPC

ELLIOT, Patricia
Psychosynthesis Psychotherapist
4 Denmark Avenue, London
SW19 4HF
0181 946 6059/0181 947 6059
AAPP

EVANS, Chris
Group Analyst
12 Kingsmeade Road, Tulse Hill, London SW2 3JB
IGA

FARMER, Eddie
Psychoanalytic Psychotherapist
122 Hambalt Road, Clapham Park, London SW4 9EJ
Rowleth Edge, Gunnerside, Richmond, North Yorkshire DL11 6JP
0181 673 2044/01748 886 500
IPC

FERGUSON, Joyce
Transpersonal Psychotherapist
407 Grenville House, Dolphin Square, London SW1V 3LP
0171 798 8073
CCPE

FLATT, Deborah
Transactional Analysis Psychotherapist
Bramwell, 95a Earlsfield Road, London
SW18 3DA
0181 870 2821
ITA, MET

FLEMING, Peter
Humanistic Psychotherapist
15 Killyon Road, London SW8 2XS
0171 720 4499
AHPP

FRASER, Hugh Ross
Transpersonal Psychotherapist
London SW2
0181 674 2235
CCPE

FREDMAN, Glenda
Systemic Psychotherapist
Psychology Department, South Ken. & Chelsea Mental Health, 1 Nightingale Place, London SW10 9NG
0181 846 6051
KCC

FULLER, Victoria G.
Analytical Psychologist-Jungian Analyst, Group Analyst
10 Onslow Gardens, London SW7 3AP
0171 584 7939
IGA

GANDY, Rus
Biodynamic Psychotherapist
5 Avenue Mansions, Battersea, London SW11 5SL
0171 223 4269
BTC

GARNER, Cheryl
Transpersonal Psychotherapist
11 Allestree Road, London SW6 6AD
0171 381 3484
CCPE

GATTI-DOYLE, Fiorella G.
Personal Construct Psychotherapist
Flat 2a, Sloane Avenue Mansions, Sloane Avenue, London SW3 3JF
0171 584 9589
CPCP, RCSPC

GLANVILLE, Tony
Gestalt Psychotherapist
66 Valleyfield Road, London SW16 2HU
0181 769 5536
GPTI

GODFREY-ISSACS, Godfrey
Analytical Psychotherapist
105 Christchurch Road, East Sheen, London SW14 7AT
0181 876 5223
LCP, FIP

GOLDEN, Sylvia
Integrative Psychotherapist
Christchurch North Brixton, 88 - 96 Brixton Road, London SW9 6BE
0181 587 0375/0171 735 7229
RCSPC

GORDON, Virginia
Systemic Psychotherapist
64 Prospect Quay, 98 Point Pleasant, London SW18 1PR
0181 516 3745
KCC

GREEN, Roberta
Group Analyst
41 Woodlawn Road, Fulham, London SW6 6BQ
0181 846 7987/0171 385 3408
IGA

GREENWOOD, John
Psychoanalytic Psychotherapist
98 White Hart Lane, London SW13 OQA
0181 286 3533
ARBS

GULLIVER, Pamela
Psychoanalytic Psychotherapist
6 Cardinal Place, Putney, London SW15 1NX
0181 785 7149
IPC

HARDY, Jo
Core Process Psychotherapist
39 Gleneldon Road, London SW16 2AX
0181 769 1074
AAPP

HARTNUP, Trevor
Child Psychotherapist, Psychoanalytic Psychotherapist
William Harvey Centre, 313-315 Cortis Road, London SW15 6XG
93 Avondale Road, London SW14 8PU
0181 788 0074
ACP, BAP

HAY BURNS, Jean
Transpersonal Psychotherapist
1 Woolneigh Street, London SW6 3AU
0171 736 2397
CCPE

HAYES, Michael
Psychosynthesis Psychotherapist
Digby Stuart College, Roehampton Institute London, Roehampton Lane, London SW15 5PH
0181 878 9863
AAPP

HEAVEY, Anne
Family Therapist
51A Nightingale Lane, London SW12 8ST
0181 675 3983
IFT

HEDGES, Fran
Systemic Psychotherapist
Roehampton Institute London, Grove House, Froebel College, Roehampton Lane, London SW15 5PJ
0181 392 3387(f)/0181 392 3632
KCC

HENNY, Lindy
Group Analytic Psychotherapist
Colne Denton, 106 Cheyne Road, London SW10 0DG
0171 352 3977
IPC

HENRIQUES, Marika
Psychoanalytic Psychotherapist, Humanistic Psychotherapist
54 Campbell Court, Gloucester Road, London SW7 4PD
0171 584 9793
GUILD, AHPP

HICKMAN, Anya
Hypno-Psychotherapist
80a East Hill, Wandsworth, London SW18 2HG
0976 943030
NSHAP

HIPPS, Hilary
Integrative Psychotherapist
21 Malbrook Road, London SW15 6UH
0181 785 6707(t/f)
MET

HITCHMAN, Nini
Psychosynthesis Psychotherapist
4 First Avenue, Mortlake, London SW14 8SR
0181 876 9056
AAPP

HOPPING, Geoff
Transactional Analysis Psychotherapist
Flat 8, 126 Streatham Hill, London SW2 4RS
0181 674 7890
ITA, MET

HOPWOOD, Ann
Analytical Psychologist-Jungian Analyst
127 Grandison Road, London SW11 6LT
0171 924 5171/0171 228 9130
SAP

HORNE, David C
Existential Psychotherapist
Flat 3, 10 Bernay's Grove, London SW9 8DF
0171 733 0944
RCSPC

HOWARD, Rina
Analytical Psychologist-Jungian Analyst
103 Hurlingham Road, London
SW6 3NL
0171 736 2924
BAP

HOWELL, David
Analytical Psychologist-Jungian Analyst
7 Malcolm Road, London SW19 4AS
SAP

HUNTER, Margaret
Child Psychotherapist
Brixton Child Guidance Clinic, 19
Brixton Water Lane, London
SW2 1NU
0171 274 5459/0171 737 4140 (f)
ACP

INGRAM, Sonia
Group Analyst
10 Pelham Place, London SW7 2NH
0171 581 5033
IGA

IRVING, Susan
Psychoanalytic Psychotherapist
33 Greyhound Lane, Streatham
Common, London SW16 5NP
Enid Balint Psychotherapy Centre,
Barnes Hospital, South Worple Way,
London SW14 8SU
0181 878 4981 x266/0181 769 7988
FIP

ISAACS, Joy
Psychoanalytic Psychotherapist
105 Christchurch Road, East Sheen,
London SW14 7AT
0181 876 5223
LCP, FIP

JACOB, Emily
Sexual and Marital Psychotherapist
16 Avenue Gardens, East Sheen,
London SW14 8BP
0181 878 5835
BASMT

JAMES, Jo
Integrative Arts Psychotherapist
67 Rosebank, Holy Park Road, Fulham
SW6 6LJ
0171 385 2029
IATE

JAMESON, Anne
Transpersonal Psychotherapist
London SW17
0171 682 2286
CCPE

JARVIS, Eileen
Systemic Psychotherapist
52 Frewin Road, Wandsworth
Common, London SW18 3LP
0181 870 0037
KCC

JOHNSTONE, Mog
Cognitive Analytic Therapist
13a Abbeville Road, London SW4 9LA
0181 673 8503
ACAT

JONES, David
Humanistic Psychotherapist
39 Blenkarne Road, London
SW11 6HZ
0171 223 7020/01237 441691
AHPP

KEANE, Pamela
Transpersonal Psychotherapist
234 Worple Road, West Wimbledon,
London SW20 8RH
0181 946 8522
CCPE

KEMMIS BETTY, Sally
Systemic Psychotherapist
30 Lillian Road, London SW13 9JG
0181 563 7909
KCC

KENNEDY, Michael
Lacanian Analyst
43 Hans Place, London SW1X 0JI
fax:0181 964 8794/0181 968 3769
CFAR

KERRY, Sue
Transpersonal Psychotherapist
Flat 2, 42 Streathbourne Road, London
SW17 8QX
0181 672 6573
CCPE

KIND, Gill
Analytical Psychologist-Jungian Analyst
12 Daisy Lane, London SW6 3DD
Soberton, Nr Wickham, Southampton
S032 3QD
IGAP

KIRBY, Babs
Humanistic Psychotherapist
194 Ferndale Road, London SW9 8AH
0171 733 2748
AHPP

KITSON, Nicholas
Psychoanalytic Psychotherapist
65 Church Road, Wimbledon, London
SW19 5DQ
0181 784 2708/0181 944 9951
LCP

KOLB, Peter John
Cognitive Behavioural Psychotherapist
Cottage Day Hospital, Springfield
Hospital, Glenburnie Road, Tooting,
London SW17 0QT
0181 672 9911 ext 42973
BABCP

KOLBUSZEWSKI, Marianne
Integrative Psychotherapist
187 Latchmere Road, Battersea,
London SW11 2JZ
0171 228 1560
MC

LANG, Peter
Systemic Psychotherapist
Kensington Consultation Centre, 2
Wyvil Court, Trenchold Street, London
SW8 2TG
0171 720 7302(f)/0171 720 7301
KCC

LAWRENCE, Margaret
Psychoanalytic Psychotherapist
14 Lancaster Gardens, Wimbledon,
London SW19
0181 789 0614
GUILD

LAYTON, Sandy
Child Psychotherapist
70A Leopold Road, London SW19 7JQ
0181 946 0865
ACP

LE BRUN, Christine
Integrative Psychotherapist
56 Haldon Road, London SW18 1QG
0181 874 5439
RCSPC

LEMA, Juan Carlos
Systemic Psychotherapist
Kensington Consultation Centre, 2
Wyvil Court, Trenchold Street, London
SW8 2TG
Flat 1A, 13 York Terrace East, London
NW1 4PT
0171 720 7301/0171 631 8325 (t/f)
KCC

LEON, Sara
Integrative Arts Psychotherapist,
Humanistic Psychotherapist
17 Josephine Avenue, London
SW3 2JX
0181 674 3074
IATE, AHPP

LEWIS, Richard
Integrative Psychotherapist
63 Franciscan Road, London
SW17 8EA
0181 672 5035
MC

LISTER, Mary
Analytical Psychologist-Jungian Analyst
138 Brundenell Road, London
SW17 8DF
0181 672 1554
BAP

LITTLE, Martin
Systemic Psychotherapist
Kensington Consultation Centre, 2
Wyvil Court, Trenchold Street, London
SW8 2TG
0171 720 7302(f)/0171 720 7301
KCC

LOEWENTHAL, Del
Psychoanalytic Psychotherapist
70 Kenilworth Avenue, London
SW19 7LR
Mater Project, School of Educational
Studies, University of Surrey, Guildford
GU2 5XH
01483 300800 x 3143/0181 947 7085
PA

LOWDEN, Barbara
Transpersonal Psychotherapist
London SW16
c/o CCPE, Beauchamp Lodge, 2
Warwick Crescent, London W2 6NE
0181 266 3006
CCPE

LYON, Josephine
Hypno-Psychotherapist
15 Brunswick Court, Regency Street,
London SW1P 4AE
0171 834 7418
NSHAP

MAGNER, Valerie
Integrative Psychotherapist
203 Crowborough Road, London
SW17 9QE
0181 672 8569
MET

MAGUIRE, Marie
Psychoanalytic Psychotherapist
6 Stockwell Park Road, London
SW9 0AJ
0171 820 1344
GUILD, WTC

MARCUS, Marietta
Analytical Psychologist-Jungian Analyst
16 Sunbury Avenue, East Sheen,
London SW14 8RA
0181 876 1040
LCP

MARSDEN, Patricia
Psychoanalytic Psychotherapist
48 Wandle Road, London SW17 7DW
0181 767 0563
IPC

MASTERS, Sue
Transpersonal Psychotherapist
Putney, London SW15
0181 788 0706
CCPE

MATHERS, Dale
Psychosynthesis Psychotherapist
63 Briarwood Road, Clapham, London
SW4 9PJ
0171 720 5681
AAPP

MCGUINNESS, Mark
Hypno-Psychotherapist
31 Granfield Street, London SW11 3JG
The Life Centre, 15 Edge Street,
London W8 7PN
0171 221 4602/0171 978 5397
NSHAP

MCMANUS, Gaynor
Systemic Psychotherapist
35 Sutherland Street, London
SW1V 4JU
0171 834 3113
KCC

MEADEN, Rosaleen
Psychoanalytic Psychotherapist
78 Ringford Road, London SW18 1RR
0181 355 9569/0181 870 0743
IPC

MERZ, Juliet
Cognitive Analytic Therapist
93 Clarence Road, Wimbledon,
London SW19 8QB
0181 542 2412
ACAT

MIKARDO, Julia
Child Psychotherapist
Wandsworth Town Child & Family
Clinic, 7 Ram Street, London
SW18 1TJ
0181 870 0161/0181 549 3815
ACP

MILBURN, Irene
Psychoanalytic Psychotherapist
33 Boscobel Place, London SW1W 9PE
0171 235 3533
GUILD

MILLAIS, Suzy
Transpersonal Psychotherapist
3 Cadogan Mansions, 15 Sloane Square,
London SW1V 8EH
0171 730 5527
CTP

MILLAR, Wilma
Integrative Psychotherapist, Body
Psychotherapist
52 Finborough Road, London SW10
0171 351 4830
CCBP

MILLIER, Sylvia
Psychoanalytic Psychotherapist
18 Mercier Road, London SW15 2AR
0181 788 9016
IPC

MITCHELL, Ruth
Sexual and Marital Psychotherapist
41 Nassau Road, London SW13 9QF
BASMT

MOHLALA, Morris
Systemic Psychotherapist
119 Edgeley Road, London SW4 6HD
0171 622 5494
KCC

MUNT, Stephen
Humanistic Psychotherapist
279 Sheen Lane, London SW14 8RN
0181 789 9257
AHPP

MUSGRAVE, Beatrice
Group Analytic Psychotherapist
Flat 7, 416 Wimbledon Park Road,
London SW19 6PW
0181 789 7208
IPC

NANCARROW, Kiya
Core Process Psychotherapist
50 Elmhurst Mansions, Edgeley Road, London SW4 6ET
0181 450 9514
AAPP

NAPPEZ, Sue
Transpersonal Psychotherapist
147 The High, Streatham High Road, London SW16 1HD
0181 769 5101
CCPE

NEAL, Lalage
Psychoanalytic Psychotherapist
2 Rossdale Road, Putney, London SW15 1AD
0181 780 3171
IPC

NEATE, Patricia
Systemic Psychotherapist
2 Daylesford Avenue, Putney, London SW15 5QR
0181 876 1902
KCC

NETZER-STEIN, Antje
Child Psychotherapist
40 Ryecroft Road, London SW16 3EQ
0181 670 2075/0181 766 0406
ACP

NOONAN, Mairead
Systemic Psychotherapist
Roehampton Institute, Counselling Service, Froebel College, Roehampton Lane, London SW15 5PJ
12 The Crossway, Mottingham, Eltham, London SE9 4JJ
0181 392 3636
KCC

NUTTALL, Serena
Cognitive Analytic Therapist
49 Felden Street, London SW6 5AE
0171 736 6740
ACAT

O'CALLAGHAN, Jean
Integrative Psychotherapist
c/o School of Psychology & Counselling, Roehampton Institute, London SW15
0181 392 3624
MET

O'NEILL, James
Psychoanalytic Psychotherapist
20 Elms Crescent, Clapham Common, London SW4 8RA
0171 622 0607/0171 498 5576 (f)
PA

OLIVER, Christine
Systemic Psychotherapist
3 Beverley Gardens, Barnes, London SW13 0LZ
0181 878 3601
KCC

PARIKH, P.N.
Family Therapist
218 Mitcham Lane, London SW16 6NT
0181 769 8708/0181 877 1561
AFT

PARKER, Mary
Humanistic and Integrative Psychotherapist
66 Brixton Water Lane, London SW2 1QB
0171 274 6531
AHPP

PARKIN, Gwendolyn
Integrative Psychotherapist
26 Clareville Street, London SW7 5AW
0171 447 3753/0171 370 1855
RCSPC

PARKINSON, Phil
Transpersonal Psychotherapist
Tooting Bec, London SW17
0181 767 7464
CCPE

PAVINCICH, Lesley
Psychoanalytic Psychotherapist
20 Rydal Road, London SW16 1QN
0181 677 5776
ARBS

PEACOCK, Anne
Hypno-Psychotherapist
83 St. George's Square Mews, Pimlico, London SW1V 3RZ
South Westminster Centre for Health, 2nd Floor,82 Vincent Square, Westminster, London SW1P 2PF
0171 976 5352
NSHAP

PENNICEARD, Sandy
Psychoanalytic Psychotherapist
8 Loxley Road, London SW18 3LJ
0181 874 1569
IPC

PICK, Rachel
Child Psychotherapist
Imperial College Health Service, Watt's Way, 14 Prince's Garden, London SW7 1NA
0181 584 6301/0171 359 2461
ACP

POLLITZER, Juliette
Transactional Analysis Psychotherapist
Flat 5, 64 Rutland Gate, London SW7 1PJ
0171 584 4951/0171 823 9451 (f)
ITA

PRICHARD, Lois
Transpersonal Psychotherapist
1 The Clockhouse, Windmill Road, Wimbledon SW19 5NG
CCPE

QUAINE, Mary
Group Analytic Psychotherapist
7 Harwood Terrace, Fulham, London SW6 2AF
0171 731 5974
IPC

QUINN, Asher
Transpersonal Psychotherapist
Putney, London
Little Venice, London
0181 874 6955
CCPE

RAESIDE, Dominic
Family Therapist
154 Elsenham Street, Southfields, London SW18 5NP
0181 8705375/0181 87125870
AFT

RAMAGE, Margaret
Sexual and Marital Psychotherapist
14 Tenham Avenue, London SW2 4XS
0181 674 6522
BASMT

RANI, R S
Cognitive Behavioural Psychotherapist
Behavioural/Cognitive Psychotherapy Unit, Cottage Day Hospital, Springfield Hospital, 61 Glenburnie Rd., London SW17 7DJ
0181 682 6548
BABCP

RAYMOND, Caroline
Hypno-Psychotherapist
4 Clare Court, Grosvenor Hill, Wimbledon Village, London SW19 4RZ
0181 947 0962 (t/f)
NRHP

REARDON, Paula
Integrative Psychotherapist
28 Seaton Close, Lynden Gate, Putney Heath, London SW15 3TJ
0181 332 8302/0181 788 7020
RCSPC

REID, Marguerite
Child Psychotherapist
Dept. of Child & Adolescent Mental Health, Chelsea & Westminster Hospital, Fulham Road, London SW10 9NH
0171 746 8617/0171 946 0647
ACP

REUVID, Jennie
Sexual and Marital Psychotherapist, Autogenic Psychotherapist
26 Birley Street, Battersea, London SW11 5XF
0171 223 9236
BASMT, BAFAT

REYES, Paulina
Child Psychotherapist
Wandsworth Town Child & Family Clinic, 7 Ram Street, London SW18 1TJ
0181 994 7529/0181 870 0161
ACP

ROSE, Wendy
Transpersonal Psychotherapist
101 Elsenham Street, London SW18 5NY
0181 870 2446/0181 870 8140 (f)
CCPE

SANDERS, Susie
Transpersonal Psychotherapist
11 Thurloe Square, London SW7 2TA
0171 584 5251
CCPE

SCHOFIELD, Lynn-Ella
Psychoanalytic Psychotherapist
105 Warwick Way, London SW1V 1QL
0171 821 0518
GUILD

SCHWARTZ, Chuck
Analytical Psychologist-Jungian Analyst
7c Carlton Drive, London SW15 2BZ
01822 860236/0181 789 0301
IGAP

SILVER-LEIGH, Vivienne
Transpersonal Psychotherapist
64B Princes Way, London SW19 6JF
0181 788 5291
CCPE

SILVERSTONE, Jennifer
Psychoanalytic Psychotherapist
58 Alderney Street, London SW1V 4EX
0171 932 0858/0171 834 7891
LCP

SMAIL, Rachid
Cognitive Behavioural Psychotherapist
40 Kingsley, Beaufort Street, London SW3 5BD
0171 351 6604
BABCP

SMALLWOOD, Imogen
Integrative Psychotherapist
98 Bonneville Gardens, London SW4 9LE
0181 675 6836
RCSPC

SMITH, Anne
Psychoanalytic Psychotherapist
39 Dornton Road, Balham, London SW12 1NB
0181 675 3098
GUILD

SMOLIRA, David
Hypno-Psychotherapist, Family Psychotherapist
9 Edge Hill, Wimbledon, London SW19 4LR
0181 947 4251/0181 944 6571
NSHAP, AFT

SMYLY, Penelope
Transpersonal Psychotherapist
13a Fieldhouse Road, London SW12 0HL
0181 673 6190
CCPE

SNOW, Randa
Psychoanalytic Psychotherapist
8 Gunter Grove, London SW10 0UJ
0171 349 9423/0171 351 7105
IPC

SOUTHAN, Rosemary
Psychoanalytic Psychotherapist
The Old Tile House, 71 Archway Street, London SW13 0AS
0181 876 2808
LCP

SPENCER, Janet
Analytical Psychologist-Jungian Analyst
7a Carlton Drive, Putney, London SW15 2BZ
0181 785 0390/0181 789 3727
IGAP

SPY, Terri
Humanistic and Integrative Psychotherapist
12 Derwent Road, London SW20 9NH
0181 330 4045
AHPP

STEELE, Marion
Integrative Psychotherapist
38 Heyford Avenue, London SW8 1EE
0171 735 2724
RCSPC

STEVENSON, Kate
Systemic Psychotherapist
Kensington Consultation Centre, 2 Wyvil Court, Trenchold Street, London SW8 2TG
Home Practice, Highgate, London N6 4TA
0171 720 7301
KCC

STOKES, Jean
Psychoanalytic Psychotherapist, Analytical Psychologist-Jungian Analyst
5 Sispara Gardens, Southfields, London SW18 1LG
0181 874 6631
IPC, AJA

STRACEY, Amarilla
Integrative Psychotherapist, Body Psychotherapist
22 Elms Crescent, London SW4 8RA
0171 720 4601
CCBP

STRUTHERS, Cassandra
Psychoanalytic Psychotherapist
31 Cambridge St., London SW1V 4PR
0171 976 6973
AGIP

TAJET-FOXELL, Britt
Cognitive Behavioural Psychotherapist
Eton House, 23 Sudbourne Road,
London SW2 5AE
0171 733 8348
BABCP

TANDY (PILBROW), Alannah
Psychosynthesis Psychotherapist
25 Lamont Road, London SW10 OHR
0171 352 9540
AAPP

TANGUAY, Daniel
Biodynamic Psychotherapist
Flat 1, Langley Mansions, Langley Lane,
London SW8 1TJ
0171 582 4287
BTC

TAUSSIG, Maggie
Integrative Psychotherapist
30 Bathgate Road, Wimbledon, London
SW19 5PJ
0181 879 7437
MET

TAYLOR, Jackie
Transpersonal Psychotherapist
36 Babington Road, Streatham, London
SW16 6AH
0181 677 9212
CCPE

TAYLOR, Jane
Sexual and Marital Psychotherapist
136 Sutherland Grove, London
SW18 5QN
0181 780 9890
BASMT

THOLSTRUP, Margaret
Integrative Psychotherapist
10 Parkmead, Roehampton, London
SW15 5BS
0181 789 0090 (t/f)
MET

THOMAS, Marcia
Gestalt Psychotherapist
25 Guildersfield Road, Streatham,
London SW16 5LS
0181 679 4338
GPTI

TUBY, Molly
Analytical Psychologist-Jungian Analyst
60 Stanhope Gardens, London
SW7 5RR
0171 373 0892
IGAP

TURNER, Annie
Systemic Psychotherapist
81 Pendle Road, London SW16 6RX
Institute of Family Therapy, 24 - 32
Stephenson Way, London NW1 2HY
0171 391 3950/0181 677 5026
IFT

WAINWRIGHT, Claire
Systemic Psychotherapist
65 Penwortham Road, Furzedown,
London SW16 6DF
KCC

WALLINE, Sandra
Analytical Psychologist-Jungian Analyst
26 Disraeli Road, London SW15 2DS
0181 785 9647
SAP

WALROND-SKINNER, Sue
Family Therapist
78 Stockwell Park Road, London
SW9 0DA
0171 733 8676
AFT

WALSH, Aine
Psychoanalytic Psychotherapist
56c Sarsfeld Road, Balham, London
SW12 8HN
0181 767 8997
IPC

WARBURTON, Geoff
Gestalt Psychotherapist
192 Balvernie Grove, London
SW18 5RW
0181 875 1096 (f)/0181 874 3303
GPTI

WATSON, Gordon
Psychoanalytic Psychotherapist
149 Faraday Road, London SW19 8PA
0181 540 7825
PA

WEBSTER, Anne
Psychoanalytic Psychotherapist
92 Rossiter Road, Balham, London
SW12 9RX
0181 675 1397
IPC

WEST, Virginia
Cognitive Analytic Therapist
37 Blenkarne Road, London
SW11 6HZ
0171 223 8502
ACAT

WHEELER, Maria
Systemic Psychotherapist
Kensington Consultation Clinic, 2
Wyvil Court, Trenchold Street, London
SW8 2TG
64 Gloucester Road, New Barnet,
Herts EN5 1NB
0181 440 8693/0171 720 7301
KCC

WHITE, H.
Psychodynamic Psychotherapist
8 Thirlmere Road, Streatham, London
SW16 1QW
0181 769 6535
WMIP

WHITTON, Eric
Humanistic Psychotherapist
31 Ovington Street, Chelsea, London
SW3 2JA
0171 584 8819
AHPP

WIDLAKE, Bernard C.
Psychodrama Psychotherapist
1 Redenham House, Tangley Grove,
Roehampton, London SW15 4DW
0181 876 0868
BPA

WIGHAM, Avril
Psychosynthesis Psychotherapist
21 Elms Road, London SW4 9ER
0171 622 9530/0171 498 6851 (f)
AAPP

WILKINSON, Heward
Integrative Psychotherapist
1 Quinton Street, London SW18 3QR
0181 947 5167
SPTI

WILKS, Frances
Integrative Psychotherapist
115 Alderney Street, London
SW1V 4HE
0171 477 8260/0171 834 9264
RCSPC

WILSON, Catherine
Psychoanalytic Psychotherapist
21 Trelawn Road, London SW2 1DH
0171 326 0084
BAP

WILSON, Norman
Sexual and Marital Psychotherapist
16 Lower Common South, Putney,
London SW15 1BP
BASMT

WILSON, Teresa
Systemic Psychotherapist
The Elm Therapists, 45a High Street, Wimbledon Village, London SW19 5AU
55 Cloudesdale Road, London SW17 8ET
0181 946 1097/0181 675 7848
KCC

WILTON, Angela
Cognitive Analytic Therapist
27F Bramham Gardens, London SW5 0JE
0171 370 4841 (f)/0171 373 7520
ACAT

WINGROVE-GIBBONS, Kenneth
Hypno-Psychotherapist
10 Greycoat Place, Victoria, London SW1P 1SB
0171 799 2388
NRHP

WOOD, Jane
Transactional Analysis Psychotherapist
27 Barker Walk, Mount Ephraim Road, Streatham, London SW16 1AT
ITA

WOODCOCK, Jeremy
Family Therapist
13 Barnwell Road, Brixton, London SW2 1PN
0171 274 6543
IFT

WOODWARD-SMITH, Nicholas
Family Psychotherapist
9 Lindesfarne Road, Wimbledon, London SW20 0NW
0181 947 3272
IFT

WRIGHT, James
Psychoanalytic Psychotherapist
50 Burnfoot Avenue, Fulham, London SW6 5EA
Three Chimneys, Crown Lane, Orford, Woodbridge, Suffolk IP12 2NB
0171 385 6279/01394 450497
IPC

WYNN-PARRY, Charlotte
Integrative Psychotherapist
19 Furzedown Drive, London SW17 9BL
0181 677 1677
MC

YOUNG, Sabine
Transpersonal Psychotherapist
284 Cowley Mansion, Mortlake High Street, London SW14 8SL
c/o CCPE, Beauchamp Lodge, 2 Warwick Crescent, London W2 6N0
0181 876 2439
CCPE

YOUNG, Sarah
Integrative Psychotherapist
21 Broomhouse Road, London SW6 3QU
0171 736 1343
RCSPC

LONDON WEST

ARBIA, G. Nicoletta
Transpersonal Psychotherapist
424A Edgware Road, London W2 1EG
0171 402 8853
CCPE

ARMSTRONG, Caroline
Biodynamic Psychotherapist
22 Bolton Road, London W4 3TB
0181 994 0951
BTC

ARNOLD, Lynn
Integrative Psychotherapist
296 Westbourne Park Road, London W11 1EH
0171 727 0688
MC

ARZOUMANIDES, Yiannis
Integrative Psychotherapist
218 Randolph Avenue, London W9 1PF
0171 328 8955
RCSPC

ASSEILY, Alexandra
NLP Psychotherapist
13 Addison Road, London W14 8DJ
0171 602 5647(f)/0171 602 1402
ANLP

BABARIK, Anthony
Integrative Psychotherapist
106 Sutherland Avenue, London W9 2QP
0171 700 1323/0171 286 8154
RCSPC

BAKER, Jan
Integrative Psychotherapist
30 Beaconsfield Road, Ealing, London W5 5JE
0181 840 3849
MC

BAMBER, James
Group Analyst, Analytical Psychologist-Jungian Analyst
115 Ladbroke Grove, Notting Hill, London W11 1PG
0171 727 6368
IGA, AJA

BARCLAY, Elizabeth
Transpersonal Psychotherapist
Flat 4, 43 Ladbroke Grove, London W11 3AR
0171 727 4613
CTP

BARHAM, Peter
Psychoanalytic Psychotherapist
23 Randolph Crescent, London W9 1DP
0171 289 4026
GUILD

BARRY, Suzy
Integrative Psychotherapist
Flat 4, 9 Elsham Road, London W14 8HA
0171 565 0843
RCSPC

BARTLETT, Beatrice
Psychoanalytic Psychotherapist
73c St. Charles' Square, London W10 6EJ
0181 969 0092 (t/f)
IPC

BASHARAN, Harika
Transpersonal Psychotherapist
9 Fletcher Road, Chiswick, London W4 5AT
0171 589 6414/0181 995 3836
CCPE

BAUM, Stefanie
Biodynamic Psychotherapist
c/o Eucke, 23 Whitehall Gardens, London W3 9RD
BTC

BEGUIN, Agnes
Psychoanalytic Psychotherapist
Flat 3, 88 Holland Park, London W11 3RZ
0171 727 9448
IPC

BENNETT, Rosanagh
Transpersonal Psychotherapist
c/o C.T.P., 7-11 Kensington High Street, London W8 5NP
0171 937 9190
CTP

BISHOP, Beata
Transpersonal Psychotherapist
27 Waldeck Road, Strand-on-the-Green, London W4 3NL
0181 994 8895
CTP

BLOOMFIELD, Irene
Psychoanalytic Psychotherapist
3 Marlborough, 38/40 Maida Vale, London W9 1RW
0171 286 8265
AGIP

BLUM, Miranda
Integrative Psychotherapist
104 Rannoch Road, London W6 9SW
RCSPC

BOENING, Joachim
Integrative Psychotherapist, Body Psychotherapist
1 Studley Grange Road, Hanwell, London W7 2LU
0181 579 2993
CCBP

BOENING, Michaela
Integrative Psychotherapist, Body Psychotherapist
1 Studley Grange Road, Hanwell, London W7 2LU
0181 579 2993
CCBP

BONADIE-ARNING, Sondra
Psychoanalytic Psychotherapist
38 Stamford Brook Road, London W6 0XL
0181 743 4023
NAFSI

BONNER, David Calvert
Hypno-Psychotherapist
26 Compton Crescent, Chiswick, London W4 3JA
Twickenham Health Care, 88 Heath Road, Twickenham, Middlesex TW1 4BW
0181 892 2356/0181 994 5520
NRHP

BOYESEN, Ebba
Biodynamic Psychotherapist
170 Goldhawk Road, London W12
BTC

BOYESEN, Gerda
Biodynamic Psychotherapist
170 Goldhawk Road, London W12
BTC

BOYESEN, Mona Lisa
Biodynamic Psychotherapist
170 Goldhawk Road, London W12
BTC

BRAIN, Sara
Transpersonal Psychotherapist, Analytical Psychotherapist
c/o CTP, 7 - 11 Kensington High Street, London W8 5NP
0171 937 9190
CTP

BROWNE, Margaret
Integrative Psychotherapist
28 West Lodge, London W3 9SF
0181 985 0861 x 2013/0181 896 1046
RCSPC

BROWNE, Maureen
Integrative Psychotherapist, Body Psychotherapist
16 Cavendish Avenue, Ealing, London W13 0JQ
0181 998 1168
CCBP

BUIRSKI, Diana
Transpersonal Psychotherapist
Basement Flat, 3 Essendine Road, London W9 2LS
0171 289 9368
CCPE

CALEB, Ruth
Integrative Psychotherapist
31 Emlyn Road, Stamford Brook, London W12 9TF
0181 354 0987/0181 231 2579
RCSPC

CANTELO, Frances
Transpersonal Psychotherapist
London W12
0181 749 5974
CCPE

CARDILE, Pietro
Transactional Analysis Psychotherapist
10e Cumberland Park, Acton, London W3 6SY
0181 993 0177
ITA

CASEMENT, Ann
Analytical Psychologist-Jungian Analyst
5 Kensington Park Gardens, London W11 3HB
0171 727 8218/0171 727 4788 (f)
AJA

CATOVSKY, Mina
Integrative Psychotherapist
68 Salisbury Road, Ealing, London W13 9TT
0181 567 1958
CCBP

CHATAWAY, Carola
Systemic Psychotherapist
66 Maida Vale, London W9 1PR
0171 624 4052
KCC

CHOUDREE, Sangamithra U.D.
Cognitive Analytic Therapist
3 Millwood Street, London W10 6EH
York Clinic, Thomas Guy House, Guys Hospital, 47 Weston Street, London SE1 3RR
0171 955 4823/0181 969 9527
ACAT

CLANCY, Catherine
Psychoanalytic Psychotherapist
48 Sutton Court Road, Chiswick, London W4 4NL
0181 747 9202 (t/f)
IPC

CLARE, John
Psychoanalytic Psychotherapist
15 Waldeck Road, Strand-on-the-Green, London W4 3NL
0181 747 3213
IPSS

CLARKSON, Petruska
Individual and Group Humanistic Psychotherapist, Transactional Analysis Psychotherapist
12 North Common Road, Ealing, London W5 2QB
0181 567 0388 (t/f)
MET, AHPP, ITA, UPA

COCHLIN, Marion
Analytical Psychologist-Jungian Analyst
41 Antrobus Road, London W4 5HY
0181 995 2560
BAP

COGILL, Stephen
Group Analyst
60 Ranelagh Road, London W5 5RP
0181 993 7892 x 22/0181 566 1771
IGA

CROCKATT, Gabrielle
Child Psychotherapist
Parkside Clinic, 63-65 Lancaster Road, London W11 1QG
0171 221 4656/0171 243 0276 (f)
ACP

CROOK, Didi
Biodynamic Psychotherapist
15 Powis Court, 29-39 Powis Square, London W11 1JQ
0171 221 4912
BTC

DAINTRY, Penelope
Gestalt Psychotherapist
83 Stile Hall Gardens, London W4 3BT
0181 995 4531 (t/f)
GPTI, MET

DALAL, Caroline
Systemic Psychotherapist
Riverside Mental Health Trust, 1 Wolverton Gardens, London W6 7DQ
0181 846 7806/0181 846 7817 (f)
KCC

DALTON, Peggy
Personal Construct Psychotherapist
20 Cleveland Avenue, Chiswick, London W4 1SN
0181 994 7959
CPCP

DALY, John
Transpersonal Psychotherapist
c/o CCPE, 2 Warwick Crescent, London W2 6NE
0171 266 3006
CCPE

DANKS, Alan
Psychoanalytic Psychotherapist
33 Park Road, Chiswick, London W4 3EY
0181 994 3131
IPC

DAVIDGE, Maggie
Gestalt Psychotherapist
36 Newburgh Road, Acton, London W3 6DQ
0181 993 0868 (t/f)
GCL

DAVIS, Joyce
Analytical Psychologist-Jungian Analyst
66 South Edwardes Square, London W8 6HL
0171 602 6348/0171 602 1015
IGAP

DAWKINS, Sue
Integrative Arts Psychotherapist
7 Ladbroke Square, London W11
0171 727 6259
IATE

DE LEON, Heather
Psychoanalytic Psychotherapist
11 Whitehall Gardens, London W4 3LT
0181 994 2930
PA

DE NORDWALL, Luci
Transpersonal Psychotherapist
West London
0181 994 1054
CCPE

DE SERDICI-PARKER, Simona
Transpersonal Psychotherapist
11 Brackley Road, London W4 2HW
0181 995 5320
CTP

DEAR, Judith
Analytical Psychotherapist
Flat 6a, Douglas House, 6 Maida Vale, London W2 1TG
0171 724 4036
LCP

DILLON WESTON, Marisa
Group Analyst
23 Rusthall Avenue, London W4 1BW
0181 994 6749
IGA

DINWOODIE, John
NLP Psychotherapist
68 Fielding Road, Chiswick London W4 1HL
0181 995 0384
ANLP

DONALDSON, Gillian
Integrative Psychotherapist
Flat 2, 7 Tring Avenue, London W5 3QA
0181 992 3177
MET

EICHELBERGER CLEESE, Alyce Faye
Child Psychotherapist
43 Holland Park Mews, London W11 3SP
0171 229 6344
ACP

EIDEN, Bernd
Integrative Psychotherapist, Body Psychotherapist
26 Eaton Rise, Ealing, London W13 2ER
0181 997 5219
CCBP, AHPP

ELLIOTT, Dena
Integrative Psychotherapist, Humanistic Psychotherapist
7 Grove Road, Acton W3 6AW
0181 993 0523
CCBP

ENCOMBE, Jock
Cognitive Analytic Therapist
14 Hartswood Road, London W12 9QN
0171 259 4100 (f)/0171 259 4021
ACAT

ERRINGTON, Meg
Psychoanalytic Psychotherapist
19 Hanover Court, Uxbridge Road, London W12 9EP
0181 740 1981
IPC

FELL, Angela
Integrative Psychotherapist
87 Rothschild Road, London W4 5NT
0181 994 6206
MC

FLOWER, Charles
Transpersonal Psychotherapist
c/o Centre for Counselling & Psychotherapy Educat., 2 Warwick Crescent, London W2 6NE
01580 201 495
CCPE

FORSSANDER, Jennifer
Transpersonal Psychotherapist
27 Bathurst Mews, London W2 2SB
0171 402 0290
CCPE

FRASER, Lynett
Psychoanalytic Psychotherapist
6 Hereford House, Links Road, London W3 0HX
0181 993 1380
LCP

FREEMAN, Linda
Analytical Psychologist-Jungian Analyst
23 Chilworth Mews, London W2 3RG
0171 402 2204
IGAP

FREEMAN, Martin
Psychoanalytic Psychotherapist
2 Clarendon Place, London W2 2NP
0171 262 3693
LCP, FIP

FRY, Caroline
Psychoanalytic Psychotherapist
56 Elers Road, London W13 9QD
5 Ranelagh Mews, Ranelagh Road, Ealing, London W5 5RN
0181 567 3071/0181 579 6582 (t/f)
GUILD

GEORGE, Evan
Family Psychotherapist
Brief Therapy Practice, 4d Shirland Mews, London W9 3DY
33 Kingsmead Road, London SW2 3HY
0181 671 2854/0181 968 0070
IFT

GIBSON, Melanie
Psychoanalytic Psychotherapist
99 Vicarage Court, Vicarage Gate, Kensington, London W8 4HQ
0171 937 6280
IPC

GILBERT, Maria
Integrative Psychotherapist, Transactional Analysis Psychotherapist
P.O. Box 2512, London W5 2QG
0973 432831/0181 998 9866
MET, ITA, GPTI

GLENN, Liza
Group Analyst
38 Chepstow Road, London W2 5BE
Group Analytic Practice, 88 Montagu Mansions, London W1H 1LF
0171 935 3103/3085/0171 229 6399
IGA

GOLDMAN, John
Sexual and Marital Psychotherapist
22 De Walden Street, London W1M 7PH
0171 486 5148
BASMT

GRACE, Carole
Existential Psychotherapist
170 Valetta Road, London W3 7TP
0181 743 8096
RCSPC

GRANT, Bob
Psychoanalytic Psychotherapist
72 Sinclair Road, London W14 0NJ
0171 603 0529
ARBS

GREEN, Charlotte
Cognitive Behavioural Psychotherapist
Psychology Department, St Charles Hospital, Exmoor Street, London W10 6DZ
0181 962 4332(t/f)
BABCP

GREENBERG, Maurice
Group Analyst
53 Rowan Road, London W6 7DT
0171 387 4411/0171 603 5425
IGA

GRIFFITHS, Pamela
Transpersonal Psychotherapist, Integrative Psychotherapist
10 Livingstone Mansions, Queens Club Gardens, London W14 9RW
0171 385 8937
CCPE

GURNANI, Prem D.
Cognitive Behavioural Psychotherapist
237 The Colannades, 34 Porchester Square, London W2 6AS
0171 402 7047
BABCP

HAMILTON, Nigel
Transpersonal Psychotherapist
Beauchamp Lodge, 2 Warwick Crescent, London W2 6NE
0171 266 3006
CCPE

HAMILTON, Susan
Transpersonal Psychotherapist
40 Finstock Road, London W10 6LU
0181 969 5715
CCPE

HARRINGTON, Finola
Cognitive Behavioural Psychotherapist
Flat 1, 104 Sutton Court Road, Chiswick, London W4 3EQ
BABCP

HARRIS, Michele
Biodynamic Psychotherapist
126 Rainville Court, Rainville Road, London W6 9HJ
0171 385 3570
BTC

HAUPTS, Brigitte
Transpersonal Psychotherapist
Flat 2, 64 Kensington Gardens Square, Bayswater, London W2 4DG
0171 221 9040 (f)/0171 221 2501
CCPE, ACAT

HAUSER, Susan
Biodynamic Psychotherapist
20 Goldsmith Road, London W3 6PX
0181 992 9586
BTC

HENDERSON, Andrew
Integrative Psychotherapist
178 Lancaster Road, London W11 1QU
0171 229 6790
MET

HEUER, Agnes Birgit
Analytical Psychologist-Jungian Analyst, Individual and Group Humanistic Psychotherapist
13 Mansell Road, London W3 7QH
0181 749 4388
BAP, AHPP

HEUER, Gottfried
Analytical Psychologist-Jungian Analyst, Individual and Group Humanistic Psychotherapist
13 Mansell Road, London W3 7QH
0181 749 4388
AJA

HINSHELWOOD, Robert
Psychoanalytic Psychotherapist
18 Artesian Road, London W2 5AR
0171 229 2855
LCP

HIRST, Diane Zervas
Analytical Psychologist-Jungian Analyst
19 Avondale Park Gardens, London W11 4PR
0171 792 1654/0171 603 0767
IGAP

HITCHINGS, Paul
Integrative Psychotherapist
132 Princes Avenue, Acton, London
W3 8LT
0181 992 3736 (t/f)
MET

HOBART, Angela
Psychoanalytic Psychotherapist
Flat 3, 25 Stanley Crescent, London
W11 2NA
0171 221 2935
NAFSI

HOLMES, Lynne
Body Psychotherapist, Holistic Psychotherapist
21 Woodfield Crescent, London
W5 1PD
0181 997 0942
CCBP

HORROCKS, Roger
Individual and Group Humanistic Psychotherapist
5 West Kensington Mansions, North End Road, London W14 9PE
0171 385 4091
AHPP

IVESON, Chris
Family Therapist
The Brief Therapy Practice, 4d Shirland Mews, London W9 3DY
77 Muswell Avenue, London N10 2EH
0181 883 5731/0181 968 0070
IFT

JARVIS, Cecilia
Psychosynthesis Psychotherapist
11 Walmer Gardens, Ealing, London
W13 9TS
0181 567 1331
AAPP

JOHNSON, Ellie Kavner
Systemic Psychotherapist
51a Faraday Road, London W10 5SF
0181 968 0510
IFT

JOYCE, Philip
Gestalt Psychotherapist
2 Richmond Road, Ealing, London
W5 5NS
0181 567 9217/0181 840 9443 (f)
GPTI, MET

KAFTON, Maggie
Transpersonal Psychotherapist
5A Ladbroke Gardens, London
W11 2PT
0171 221 8717
CCPE

KARAN, Alexandra
Psychoanalytic Psychotherapist
47 Lanark Road, London W9 1DE
0171 286 7090
GUILD

KEAL, Susan
Integrative Psychotherapist
68D Netherwood Road, London
W14 0BG
0171 603 1604
RCSPC

KEARNS, Anne
Gestalt Psychotherapist, Integrative Psychotherapist
83 Stile Hall Gardens, Chiswick, London W4 3BT
0181 995 4531 (t/f)
MET, GPTI

KEGERREIS, Susan
Child Psychotherapist
67 Addison Gardens, London
W14 0DT
0171 603 9609
ACP

KINDER, Diana
Group Analyst
23 Woodville Gardens, London
W5 2LL
0181 997 1207
IGA

KUJAWSKI, Pedro
Analytical Psychologist-Jungian Analyst
Flat 4, 57 Holland Park, London
W11 3RS
0171 229 3527
IGAP

LAMPLOUGH, Lyn
Transpersonal Psychotherapist
41 Craven Avenue, Ealing, London
W5 2SY
0181 579 9955
CCPE

LEE, Graham
Psychoanalytic Psychotherapist
21 Poplar Grove, London W6 7RF
0171 603 1021
AGIP

LEE, Jan
Psychoanalytic Psychotherapist
85 Speldhurst Road, London W4 1BY
0181 994 1430
GUILD

LEITMAN, Norman
Integrative Psychotherapist
37 Madeley Road, Ealing, London
W5 2LS
0181 998 9390/0181 810 4792 (f)
MET, RCSPC

LEVEQUE, Brigitte
Integrative Psychotherapist
7 Rivercourt Road, London W6 9LD
0181 748 9656
RCSPC

LEVY, Colette
Psychoanalytic Psychotherapist
Flat 3, Hamilton Court,149 Maida Vale, London W9 1QR
0171 289 5044
IPC

LITTLE, Ray
Transactional Analysis Psychotherapist
16 Hatfield Road, Chiswick, London
W4 1AF
0181 994 2905
ITA

LOCK, Josephine
Integrative Psychotherapist
74 Elgin Avenue, London W9 2HB
0171 286 4996
MC

LOUDEN, Penny
Systemic Psychotherapist
6, Albion House, 39 St. Peter's Square, London W6 9NN
0181 741 3568
KCC

LUBBOCK, Philippa
Gestalt Psychotherapist
15 Lena Gardens, London W6 7PY
95A Earlsfield Road, London
SW18 3DA
0171 602 2053 (t)/0171 602 2503 (f)
GPTI

LUCIANI, Dorothy
Child Psychotherapist
17 Wimpole Street, London
W1M 7AD
0171 436 1144
ACP

LUDE, Jochen
Integrative Psychotherapist, Body Psychotherapist
26 Eaton Rise, Ealing, London W5 2ER
0181 997 5219
CCBP, AHPP

MANOJLOVIC, Jelena
Systemic Psychotherapist
3 St Mary's Place, London W8 5UE
KCC

MASOLIVER, Chandra
Psychoanalytic Psychotherapist
Flat 15, Argyll Mansions, Hammersmith Road, London W14 8QG
0171 602 1525
ARBS

MATTHEWS, Carol
Psychoanalytic Psychotherapist
122 St. Albans Avenue, Chiswick, London W4 5JR
0181 987 8786
IPC, SIP

MCCREANOR, Teresa
Group Analytic Psychotherapist
65a Randolph Avenue, London W9 1DW
LCP, FIP

MCELDOWNEY, Dennis
Psychoanalytic Psychotherapist
39 Leythe Road, Acton, London W3 8AW
0181 993 1559
IPSS

MCNULTY, Claire
Analytical Psychotherapist
45 Hormead Road, London W9 3NQ
0181 960 5194
AJA

MEAD, Christine
Psychosynthesis Psychotherapist
41 Cromwell Grove, London W6 7RQ
0171 603 2490
AAPP

MELEAGROU-DIXON, Mando
Child Psychotherapist, Psychoanalytic Psychotherapist
The Garden Flat, 90 Cambridge Gardens, London W10 6HS
Flat 4, 137-39 Gloucester Terrace, London W2 6DX
0181 354 0747/0171 262 5373
ACP, WTC

MENDOZA, Steven
Psychoanalytic Psychotherapist
34 Thornfield Road, London W12 8JQ
0181 749 5027
LCP

MENEZES, Ray
Transpersonal Psychotherapist
c/o CCPE, 2 Warwick Crescent, London W2 6NE
0171 266 3006
CCPE

METAXA, Jennie
Psychoanalytic Psychotherapist
23 Randolph Crescent, London W9 1DP
0171 289 4026
NAFSI

MILLER, Juliet
Analytical Psychotherapist
60 Grove Park Terrace, Chiswick, London W4 3QE
0181 742 2322
AJA

MITCHELL, Louise
Sexual and Marital Psychotherapist
2 Littlewood Close, West Ealing, London W13
BASMT

MORANTE, Flavia
Psychoanalytic Psychotherapist
65 Victoria Road, London W8 5RH
0171 602 6647
IPSS

MORRIS, Clare
Personal Construct Psychotherapist
65 Braybrook Street, London W12 0AL
0181 749 9059
CPCP

MULDOON, Nuala
Integrative Psychotherapist
2 Denbigh Road, Ealing, London W13 8PX
0181 574 2444/0181 357 9737
RCSPC

MURPHY, Katherine
Integrative Psychotherapist
29 Stilehall Gardens, Chiswick, London W4 3BS
0181 747 1041
MET

MURRAY, John
NLP Psychotherapist
The Boadicea, Lower Mall, London W6 9DJ
0181 741 4407
ANLP

NADIRSHAW, Zenobia
Cognitive Behavioural Psychotherapist
Psychology Department, Riverside Mental Health Trust, 20 Kingsbridge Road, London W10 6PU
0181 746 5858/0181 746 5841 (f)
BABCP

NIEBOER, Sarah
Transpersonal Psychotherapist
8 Kinnoul Road, London W6 8NQ
0171 385 7123
CCPE

O'CONNOR, Nadia
Transpersonal Psychotherapist
c/o CCPE, Beauchamp Lodge, 2 Warwick Crescent, London W2 6NE
CCPE

OPIENSKI, Jacek
Gestalt Psychotherapist
13 Clovelly Road, Ealing, London W5 5HF
0181 579 9013
GPTI

OWEN, Mike
Family Therapist
11 Stowe Road, London W12 8BQ
01895 624070/0181 740 0603
AFT

PARKER, Gabrielle
Systemic Psychotherapist
34 Heathstan Road, White City, London W12 0RA
0181 746 0809
KCC

PHILLIPS, Adam
Child Psychotherapist, Psychoanalytic Psychotherapist
Flat 2, 99 Talbot Road, London W11 2AT
0171 221 9237
ACP, GUILD

PIMENTEL, Allan
Transpersonal Psychotherapist
c/o CCPE, Beauchamp Lodge, 2 Warwick Crescent, London W2 6NE
0171 266 3006
CCPE

PLOTEL, Angela
Hypno-Psychotherapist
168A Coningham Road, Shepherds Bush, London W12 8BY
0181 740 4674 (t/f)
NRHP

POOLE, Robert
Group Analytic Psychotherapist
59/61 Ladbroke Grove, London W11 3AT
0171 727 9551
LCP

POPE, Alan
Psychoanalytic Psychotherapist
38 Greenside Road, London W12 9JG
0181 749 2085/0181 723 1785
PA

PORTER, Christine
Child Psychotherapist
Flat 3, 42 Cleveland Square, London W2 6DA
0171 262 4289
ACP

PRENDERGAST, Teresa
Integrative Psychotherapist, Body Psychotherapist
Ground Floor Flat, 19 Essex Road, London W3 9JA
0181 993 1697
CCBP

PRIOR, Robin
Transpersonal Psychotherapist
c/o CCPE, 2 Warwick Crescent, London W2 6NE
CCPE

PRONER, Karen
Psychoanalytic Psychotherapist, Child Psychotherapist
83 Strand on the Green, London W4 3PU
0181 995 8319
ACP

RAMSDEN, Sandra
Child Psychotherapist
Department of Child Psychiatry, Middlesex Hospital, North House, Cleveland Street, London W1N 8AA
0171 380 9089/0181 624 8605
ACP

RANSLEY, Cynthia
Integrative Psychotherapist
3 Binden Road, London W12 9RJ
0181 740 7580/0181 740 7580 (f)
MET

RATNER, Harvey
Family Psychotherapist
Brief Therapy Practice, 4D Shirland Mews, London W9 3DY
14 Leicester Road, London N2 9EA
0181 968 0070/0181 444 3390
IFT

READ, Jane
Sexual and Marital Psychotherapist
16 Hatfield Road, Chiswick, London W4 1AF
BASMT

REDDY, William
Transpersonal Psychotherapist
56A Kingsdown Avenue, Ealing W13 9PT
CCPE

RICHARDSON, Ann
Transpersonal Psychotherapist
Chiswick, London W4 5EH
0181 994 5964
CCPE

ROBINSON, Sue
Psychoanalytic Psychotherapist
7 Richford Street, London W6 7HH
0181 740 1120/0181 746 1388 (f)
GUILD

ROGERS, Maggie
Psychoanalytic Psychotherapist
137 Fielding Road, Chiswick, London W4 1DA
0181 994 3580
IPSS

ROSS, Miroslava
Child Psychotherapist
Maisonette 1, 16 Bristol Gardens, Little Venice, London W9 2JG
0171 289 6759
ACP

ROUHIFAR, Zhila
Cognitive Behavioural Psychotherapist
LBH &F Social Services Dept, 145 Kings Street, London W6 9XY
0181 748 3020 x 5361/0181 429 9141
BABCP

SCHAIBLE, Monika
Integrative Psychotherapist, Body Psychotherapist
31 Berrymead Gardens, Acton, London W3 8AA
0181 752 0246
CCBP

SCHUFF, Heiner
Psychoanalytic Psychotherapist
119 Elgin Avenue, London W9 2NR
LCP

SCOTT, Janice
Gestalt Psychotherapist
2 Oak Cottages, Green Lane, Hanwell, London W7 2PE
0181 840 4886
GPTI, MET

SELL, Patrick
Integrative Psychotherapist, Body Psychotherapist
5 Shalimar Road, London W3 9JD
0956 192 121/0181 248 5631
CCBP

SHARMAN, Juliet
Psychoanalytic Psychotherapist
209 Hammersmith Grove, London W6 0NP
0181 749 0270
IPC

SHARPE, Meg
Group Analyst
The Group Analytic Practice, 88 Montagu Mansions, London W1H 1LF
0171 935 3103/3085/0171 794 0210
IGA

SHERIDAN, Dolores
Transpersonal Psychotherapist
53 Matlock Court, Kensington Park Road, London W11 3BS
0171 221 0331
CCPE

SHERWIN-WHITE, Sue
Child Psychotherapist
Child & Family Consultation Centre, 1 Wolverton Gardens, London W6
0181 846 7807/0181 453 1702
ACP

SHIELDS, Ellen Attracta
Integrative Psychotherapist
26 Fairlea Place, Woodfield Road, London W5 1SP
0181 810 4552
RCSPC

SHIPTON, Sunita
Biodynamic Psychotherapist
132 Kings Street, London W6 0QU
0181 748 2061
BTC

SHREEVES, Rosa
Humanistic and Integrative Psychotherapist, Integrative Arts Psychotherapist
24 Strand-on-the-Green, London W4 3PH
0181 995 5904
SPEC

SHULMAN, Graham
Child Psychotherapist
Parkside Clinic, 63-65 Lancaster Road, London W11 1QG
0171 221 4656/0181 453 1702
ACP

SICHEL, David
Integrative Psychotherapist
194 Sutton Court Road, Chiswick, London W4 3HR
0181 995 7175
MC

SILLS, Charlotte
Transactional Analysis Psychotherapist, Integrative Psychotherapist
Rectory Lawn, 2 Richmond Road, London W5 5NS
0181 567 9217/0181 840 9443 (f)
MET, ITA

SIM, Camilla
Integrative Psychotherapist
18a Dunraven Road, London W12 7QY
0181 743 3251
RCSPC

SIMPSON, Steve
Psychosynthesis Psychotherapist
13a Bridge Avenue, London W6 9JA
0181 741 1214/0181 741 2839
AAPP

SKINNER, Charmian
Psychoanalytic Psychotherapist
6 Ruston Mews, London W11 1RB
0171 792 2145
IPC

SMITH, Jonathan
Gestalt Psychotherapist
36 Newburgh Road, London W3 6DQ
0181 993 0868 (t/f)
GCL

SMITH, Patsy
Psychoanalytic Psychotherapist
4 Ealing Park Gardens, Ealing W5 4EU
0181 568 3811
CPP

SOBAT, Milica
Child Psychotherapist
Maisonette 2, 16 Bristol Gardens, Little Venice, London W9 2JG
0171 289 6759
ACP

SOMERS, Barbara
Transpersonal Psychotherapist
c/o CTP, 7-11 Kensington High Street, London W8 5NP
0171 938 1503 (f)/0171 937 9190
AAPP, CTP

SOUTHWELL, Clover
Biodynamic Psychotherapist
3 Bulstrode Street, London W1M 5FS
0171 935 5107
BTC

SPITZ, Shirley
Integrative Psychotherapist
Flat 4, 2 Hyde Park Gardens, London W2 2LT
0171 706 4930
SPTI

STANG, Pamela
Psychoanalytic Psychotherapist
3 Irving Mansions, Queens Club Gardens, London W14 9SL
0171 385 4476
IPC

STANLEY, Elizabeth
Sexual and Marital Psychotherapist
82 Harley Street, London W1N 1AE
BASMT

STRAKER, Gill
Integrative Psychotherapist
Sherwood Psychotherapy Training Institute, Thiskney House, 2 St.James Terrace, Nottingham NG1 6FW
0115 924 3994
SPTI

SYRETT, Karin
Analytical Psychologist-Jungian Analyst
27 Royal Crescent, London W11 4SN
0171 602 0864
AJA

SZYMANSKA, Kasia
Cognitive Behavioural Psychotherapist
83 Felix Road, Ealing, London W13 0NZ
0370 478880/07071 8803947
BABCP

TAYLOR, Sajada Katalin
Transpersonal Psychotherapist
c/o CCPE, Beauchamp Lodge, 2 Warwick Crescent, London W2 6NE
0171 266 3006
CCPE

THOMAS, Kerry
Psychoanalytic Psychotherapist
93 Bleinham Crescent, London W11 2EQ
0171 727 8572
FIP

THOMAS, Lennox
Psychoanalytic Psychotherapist
63 Church Path, Chiswick, London W4 5BH
0181 995 4362
NAFSI

THORPE, C
Psychoanalytic Psychotherapist
Flat 10, Old Court House, 24 Old Court Place, London W8 4DD
0171 937 3030
AGIP

TUGENDHAT, Julia
Systemic Psychotherapist
Basement Flat, 35 Westbourne Park Road, London W2 5QD
0171 221 9036
KCC

TYRRELL, Susannah
Transpersonal Psychotherapist
c/o CTP, 7 - 11 Kensington High Street, London W8 5NP
0171 937 9190
CTP

VAN DER WATEREN, Jan-Floris
Biodynamic Psychotherapist
52 Blenheim Crescent, London W11 1NY
0171 221 6221
BTC

WALSH, Eileen
NLP Psychotherapist
Flat 13, 9 Devonhurst Place, Heathfield Terrace, Chiswick W4 4JB
0181 987 9566(f)/0181 995 1934
ANLP

WARNER, Barbara
Family Therapist
41 Wallingford Avenue, London W10 6PZ
0181 968 5372
AFT

WATERMAN, Zak
Transpersonal Psychotherapist
16 Bradiston Road, London W9
0181 969 4077
CCPE

WEBSTER, Sarah Craven
Humanistic and Integrative Psychotherapist
18 Riverview Road, Chiswick, London W4 3QH
0181 994 5681
SPEC

WELLS, Lesley
Psychoanalytic Psychotherapist
1 Hart Grove, London W5 3NA
0181 992 4920
GUILD

WIGRAM, Penny
Psychoanalytic Psychotherapist
2 Clarendon Place, London W2 2NP
0171 723 8925/0171 262 3693
IPC, FIP

WILLIAMS, Claerwen
Integrative Psychotherapist
4 Wellesley Avenue, London W6 0UP
0181 743 7823
RCSPC

YAWETZ, Christine
Sexual and Marital Psychotherapist
2 Aubrey Road, Campden Hill, London W8 7JJ
0171 727 6121
BASMT

ZARBAFI, Ali
Psychoanalytic Psychotherapist
30 Magnolia Road, Strand-on-the-Green, Chiswick, London W4 3QW
0181 747 0408
IPSS

ZINOVIEFF, Nicholas
Existential Psychotherapist
74 Hazledene Road, London W4 3JB
RNES
0181 995 5265
RCSPC

MANCHESTER

APPLEBY, Joy
Gestalt Psychotherapist, Integrative Psychotherapist
3 The Beeches, West Didsbury, Manchester M20 2BG
0161 445 0766
GPTI

BACHA, Claire
Group Analyst, Psychoanalytic Psychotherapist
20 Kersal Road, Prestwich, Manchester M25 8SJ
0161 773 0409
IGA, NWIDP

BARNETT, Gillian
Psychoanalytic Psychotherapist
Uni. of Manchester and UMIST Counselling Service, Crawford House, Precinct Centre, Oxford Road, Manchester M13 9QS
0161 275 2859/0161 275 2281 (f)
NWIDP

BERMAN, Linda
Psychoanalytic Psychotherapist
Gaskell House, Swinton Grove, Manchester M13 0EU
0161 273 2762
NWIDP

BISHAY, Nagy R.
Cognitive Behavioural Psychotherapist
North Manchester General Hospital, Crumpsall, Manchester M8 6RL
The Roselands, 4 Middleton Road, Manchester M8 5DS
0161 653 4294/0161 720 2034
BABCP

BROOKHOUSE, Shaun
Hypno-Psychotherapist
Richmael House, 25 Edge Lane, Chorlton, Manchester M21 9JH
0161 882 0376(f)/0161 881 1677
CTS

BUCKLEY, Michael
Psychoanalytic Psychotherapist
Macartney House, Psychotherapy Service, Beech Mount, Rochdale Road, Manchester M9 1XS
1 Dobcross New Road, Dobcross, Saddleworth, Oldham OL3 5AY
0161 205 7555
NWIDP

BUROW, Birgit
NLP Psychotherapist
Flat 3, 114 Kingsbrook Road, Manchester M16 8Q
0161881 8779 (t/f)
ANLP

CHURCHER, John
Psychoanalytic Psychotherapist
Hampden House Psychotherapy Centre, 2 - 4 Palatine Road, Manchester M20 3JA
0161 445 4399/0161 445 2099
NWIDP

COOKE, Bob
Transactional Analysis Psychotherapist
The Manchester Institute for Psychotherapy, 454 Barlow Moor Road, Chorlton, Manchester M21 1BQ
0161 862 9456/0161 881 8225 (f)
ITA

COSTA, Jan
Psychodrama Psychotherapist
6 Bethel Avenue, Failsworth, Manchester M35 OAG
0161 684 8660
BPA

DAVENPORT, Sarah
Psychoanalytic Psychotherapist
Dept of Rehabilitation Mental Health Services of Salford, Bury New Road, Manchester M25 3BL
0161 772 3698(f)/0161 772 3607
NWIDP

DAVIS, Jim
Transactional Analysis Psychotherapist
7 Talbot Road, Ladybarn, Manchester M14 6TA
0161 225 2556
ITA

ELLIS, R.M.
Family Therapist
6 Sudbury Road, Chorlton, Manchester M21 8XN
0161 861 9979
AFT

EMINSON, Mary
Family Therapist
23 Egerton Park, Worsley, Manchester M28 2TR
01204 390 663
AFT

FEASEY, Don
Psychoanalytic Psychotherapist
16 Raynham Avenue, Didsbury, Manchester M20 6BW
0161 445 3612
WMIP

FISCHER, Michael
Group Analyst
Red House Psychotherapy, 78 Manchester Road, Swinton, Manchester M27 5FG
0161 794 0875
IGA

GOWRISUNKUR, Jaya
Psychoanalytic Psychotherapist
Gaskell House, Department of Psychotherapy, Swinton Grove, Manchester M13 0EU
0161 273 2762
NWIDP

GUTHRIE, Else
Psychoanalytic Psychotherapist
The Rawnsley Building, Department of Psychiatry, Manchester Royal Infirmary, Oxford Road, Manchester M13 9BX
0161 276 5383
NWIDP

HORNE, Alan
Psychoanalytic Psychotherapist
Gaskell House, Swinton Grove, Manchester M13 0EU
0161 273 2762/0161 273 4876 (f)
NWIDP

HYDE, Keith
Psychoanalytic Psychotherapist, Group Analyst
The Red House Psychotherapy Service, 78 Manchester Road, Swinton, Manchester M27 5FG
0161 794 0875/0161 727 8661(f)
IGA, NWIDP, NWIDP

JACKSON, Elizabeth
Gestalt Psychotherapist
Manchester Gestalt Centre, 7 Norman Road, Rusholme, Manchester M14 5LF
0161 257 2202
GPTI

JUKES, Rachel
Psychoanalytic Psychotherapist
The Red House, 78 Manchester Road, Swinton, Manchester M27 5FG
0161 794 0875
NWIDP

KABERRY, Susan
Psychoanalytic Psychotherapist
18a Atwood Road, Didsbury, Manchester M20 6TD
Macartney House, Psychotherapy Service, Beech Mount M9 1XS
0161 205 7555/0161 448 1475
NWIDP

KAY, Malcolm
Psychodrama Psychotherapist
45 Chadwick Road, Eccles, Manchester M30 0WU
0161 788 0490
BPA

KINCEY, John
Cognitive Behavioural Psychotherapist
Dept Clinicial & Health Psychology, Central Manchester Healthcare Trust, Gaskell House, Swinton Grove M13 0EU
0161 273 4825/0161 273 3271
BABCP

LENDRUM, Susan
Psychoanalytic Psychotherapist
Hampden House, 2-4 Palatine Road, Manchester M20 3JA
0161 445 2099
NWIDP

LEVER, Maria A.
Cognitive Behavioural Psychotherapist
Palliative Care Counselling Service, Ordsall Health Centre, Belfort Drive, Salford M5 3PP
0161 872 2004 x 161/01204 493914
BABCP

LINDSAY, Marion
Psychoanalytic Psychotherapist
The Red House Psychotherapy Service, 78 Manchester Road, Swinton, Manchester M27 5FG
0161 794 0875
LPDO

LITTLEJOHN, Sarah
Integrative Psychotherapist
5 Stephens Terrace, Didsbury, Manchester M20 6WB
0161 446 1311
MC

LOBEL, Sandra
Sexual and Marital Psychotherapist
84 Langham Court, Mersey Road, Didsbury, Manchester M20 3QA
0161 434 9804
BASMT

LOBEL, Sidney
Sexual and Marital Psychotherapist
84 Langham Court, Mersey Road, Didsbury, Manchester M20 3QA
0161 434 9804
BASMT

LUCAS, Carol
Transactional Analysis Psychotherapist
The Didsbury Therapy Centre, 42a Barlow Moor Road, Didsbury, Manchester M20 8GT
0161 443 1628/0161 434 1448
ITA

MARGISON, Frank
Psychoanalytic Psychotherapist
Gaskell House, Swinton Grove, Manchester M13 0EU
0161 273 2762/0161 273 4876 (f)
NWIDP

MARRIOTT, Alison
Family Therapist
Clinical Psychology, SCOPE, Carisbrooke, Wenlock Way, West Gorton, Manchester M12 5LF
0161 273 3818/0161 274 4173
AFT

MCDONNELL, Fokkina
NLP Psychotherapist
65 Norwood Road, Manchester M32 8PN
0161 865 3193 (t/f)
ANLP

MCGRATH, Graeme
Psychoanalytic Psychotherapist
Department of Psychotherapy, Gaskell House, Swinton Grove, Manchester M13 0EU
0161 273 2762/0161 273 4876 (f)
NWIDP

MEREDITH, Joan
Psychodynamic Psychotherapist
11 Shaftesbury Road, Manchester M8 0WL
0161 795 8365
HIP

MITCHELL, Lesley
Psychoanalytic Psychotherapist
Macartney House Psychotherapy Service, Beech Mount, Rochdale Road, Harpurhey, Manchester M9 1XS
0161 205 7555/0161 203 5731 (f)
NWIDP

NICHOLSON, Jane
Psychoanalytic Psychotherapist
Psychotherapy Unit, Gaskell House, Swinton Grove, Manchester M13 0EU
0161 273 2762
NWIDP

O'NEILL, Tom
Family Therapist
301 Brantingham Road, Chorlton cum Hardy, Manchester M21 0GU
AFT

PERRIOLLAT MUNRO, Elizabeth
Psychoanalytic Psychotherapist
43 Pine Grove, Eccles, Manchester M30 9JP
0161 281 8416
ARBS

PHILIPPSON, Peter
Gestalt Psychotherapist
Manchester Gestalt Centre, 7 Norman Road, Rusholme, Manchester M14 5LF
0161 257 2202 (t/f)
GPTI, MET

POOLE, Nick
NLP Psychotherapist
386 Kingsway, Burnage, Manchester M19 1PL
0161 432 8624
ANLP

POTTER, Steve
Psychoanalytic Psychotherapist
Uni. of Manchester & UMIST Counselling Service, Crawford House, Oxford Road, Manchester M13 9QS
0161 275 2854
LPDO

PRODGERS, Alan
Psychoanalytic Psychotherapist
The Red House Psychotherapy Service, 78 Manchester Road, Swinton, Manchester M27 5FG
0161 794 0875
NWIDP

RAWSTHORNE, Jean
Psychoanalytic Psychotherapist
The Red House Psychotherapy Service, 78 Manchester Road, Swinton, Manchester M27 5FG
0161 794 0875
NWIDP

RHODES, Adrian M.
Psychoanalytic Psychotherapist
58 Errwood Road, Burnage, Manchester M19 2QH
Chaplaincy, Manchester Royal Infirmary, Manchester M13 9TB
0161 276 4726/0161 224 1739
NWIDP

SAWYER, Albert
Hypno-Psychotherapist
5 Lyndene Avenue, Roe Green, Worsley, Manchester M28 2RJ
0161 727 8551/0161 799 5537
NSHAP

SHARPLES, Geraldine
Psychoanalytic Psychotherapist
85 Baines Avenue, Irlam, Manchester M44 6AS
0161 775 7498
LPDO

SIDDLE, Ronald
Cognitive Behavioural Psychotherapist
Dept. of Clinical Psychology, Withington Hospital, West Didsbury, Manchester M20 8LR
0161 445 9263(f)/0161 447 4846
BABCP

STEIN, Nathan Bernard
Personal Construct Psychotherapist
12 Ravensway, Prestwich, Manchester M25 0EU
0161 7952895
CPCP

SUTTON, Adrian
Psychoanalytic Psychotherapist
Child & Family Service, Winnicott Centre, 195 Hathersage Road, Manchester M13 0JE
0161 248 9494/0161 225 9338(f)
NWIDP

SYKES, Kathleen
Psychoanalytic Psychotherapist
Macartney House, Psychotherapy Unit, Beech Mount, Harpurhey M9 1XS
0161 203 5731(f)/0161 205 7555
NWIDP

TATHAM, Alan
Cognitive Behavioural Psychotherapist
Psychology Services, M.H.Services of Salford NHS Trust, Bury New Road, Prestwich M25 3BL
11 St John Street, Manchester M3 4DW
0161 834 4122/0161 772 3487
BABCP

TOWSE, Esme
Psychoanalytic Psychotherapist
Hampden House Psychotherapy Centre, 2-4 Palatine Road, Withington, Manchester M20 3JA
0161 445 2099/0161 445 4399 (f)
NWIDP

VERDUYN, Christine M.
Family Therapist, Cognitive Behavioural Psychotherapist
Dept. of Clinical Psychology, Royal Manchester Children's Hospit., Hospital Road, Pendlebury, Manchester M27 4HA
0161 727 2125
AFT, BABCP

WEBSTER, Jeni
Family Psychotherapist
Red House, Psychotherapy Service, 78 Manchester Road, Swinton Manchester M27 5FG
0161 794 0875
AFT

WELFORD, Enid
Transactional Analysis Psychotherapist
41 Derby Road, Fallowfield, Manchester M14 6UX
0161 225 0514
ITA

WHITMORE, Robert
Psychoanalytic Psychotherapist
15 Moorland Road, Didsbury, Manchester M20 6BB
0161 445 2941/0161 446 1223 (f)
NWIDP

WILKINS, Paul
Psychodrama Psychotherapist
Manchester Metropolitan University, Centre for Human Communication, 799 Wilmslow Road, Didsbury, Manchster M20 8RR
131 Nicolas Road Univers, Chorlton, Manchester M21 9LS
0161 860 4437/0161 247 2142
BPA

MERSEYSIDE

BERGEL, Edith
Psychoanalytic Psychotherapist
41 Menlove Gardens West, Liverpool L18 2ET
01539 740605
LPDO

BERRY, Margaret
Hypno-Psychotherapist
37 Orton Road, Liverpool L16 6AR
0151 280 1021
CTS

BIELICZ, Paul
Psychoanalytic Psychotherapist
33 Great George's Road, Waterloo, Liverpool L22 1RA
0151 920 8905
IPC, NWIDP

BOLTON, Adrian Mark Tom
Hypno-Psychotherapist
161a Manor Road, Wallasey, Merseyside L44 0EN
0151 638 6706
CTS

BRYSON, Sandra
Psychoanalytic Psychotherapist, Family Therapist
59 Vaughan Road, Wallasey, Merseyside L45 1LJ
0151 639 7830
AFT

BURGESS, Jo
Group Analyst
3 Bluesfield Street, Liverpool L8 1YT
0151 708 0719
IGA

CAMPBELL, Hedda A.
Cognitive Behavioural Psychotherapist
3 Poulton Hall Cottages, Poulton Road, Bebington, Wirral L63 9LN
0151 346 1354
BABCP

CAWLEY, Anthony
Hypno-Psychotherapist
44 Wellesley Road, Liverpool, Merseyside L8 3SU
0151 727 1485
NRHP

CROCKER, Allen
Family Therapist
Child Mental Health Services, The Elms, 50 Cowley Hill Lane, St. Helens, Merseyside WA10 2AW
01744 454368
AFT

DICKINSON, Paul
Psychoanalytic Psychotherapist
Liverpool Psychotherapy & Consultation Service, Mossley Hill Hospital, Park Avenue, Liverpool L18 8BU
0151 250 6128
LPDO

DOYLE, Elizabeth
Psychoanalytic Psychotherapist
18 Dunraven Road, Little Neston, South Wirral L64 9QU
0151 336 4692
LPDO

ESSEX, Delia
Psychoanalytic Psychotherapist
The Counselling Service, Liverpool University, 14 Oxford Street, Liverpool L7 7BL
0151 794 3304
LPDO

EVANS, John K.
Behavioural Psychotherapist
438 Longmoor Lane, Fazakerley, Liverpool L9 9BY
0151 474 2574
BABCP

FAIRHURST, Patricia
Hypno-Psychotherapist
55 Wyndham Avenue, Liverpool L14 0LA
0151 289 2942
CTS

FOSTER, Paul
Psychoanalytic Psychotherapist
University of Liverpool Counselling Services, 14 Oxford Street, Liverpool L7 7BL
0151 794 3304
LPDO

GABBAY, Mark
Psychoanalytic Psychotherapist
Department of Primary Care, University of Liverpool, Whelan Building Quarangle, Brownlow Hill, Liverpool L69 3GB
0151 794 5610
LPDO

GAUTHIER, J.B.
Family Therapist
Child Mental Health Services, The Wellcroft Centre, Wellcroft Road, Huyton, Merseyside L36 7TA
0151 489 6137/0151 480 2460
AFT

GOODSON, Christina
Hypno-Psychotherapist
29 Pilkington Road, Southport, Merseyside PR8 6PD
01704 537753
CTS

HAGAN, Patricia
Psychoanalytic Psychotherapist
District Psychology Service, University of Liverpool, Whelan Building Quarangle, Brownlow Hill,Liverpool L69 3BG
0151 794 5534
LPDO

HAMILTON, Sheila L.L.
Psychoanalytic Psychotherapist
Department of Clinical Psychology, Oakdale Unit, Fazakerley Hospital, Longmoor Lane, Liverpool L9 7AL
0151 529 3249
LPDO

HARDMAN, Anne
Hypno-Psychotherapist
22 Lawton Road, Rainhill, Merseyside L35 0PP
0151 426 1795
CTS

HARMSWORTH, Peter
Family Psychotherapist
Barnardos Family Therapy Service, Mornington Terrace, 29 Upper Duke Street, Liverpool L1 9DY
0151 709 0540
AFT

HAZLEHURST, Jean
Hypno-Psychotherapist
Grange Hall, Blackhorse Hill, West Kirby, Merseyside L48 7EF
0151 625 1809
NRHP

HELLIN, Kate
Psychoanalytic Psychotherapist
Ashworth Hospital, Parkbourn, Maghull, Liverpool L31 1HW
0151 471 2201
NWIDP

HENDRICKSE, Begum
Sexual and Marital Psychotherapist
25 Riverbank Road, Heswall, Merseyside L60 4SQ
BASMT

HIGGO, Robert J.
Psychoanalytic Psychotherapist
Park Lodge, Orphan Drive, Liverpool L6 7UN
0151 287 6917
LPDO

HOOPER, Molly
Cognitive Behavioural Psychotherapist
'Panache', Venables Close, Spital, Bebington, Wirral L63 9HS
0151 334 6619
BABCP

JAMESON MILNER, Jane
Gestalt Psychotherapist
15 Princes Park Mansions, Liverpool L8 3SA
0151 727 5501/0151 707 1311
GPTI

JONES, Caroline
Sexual and Marital Psychotherapist
4A Greenfields Avenue, Bromborough, Wirral L62 6DD
BASMT

JONES, Judith
Sexual and Marital Psychotherapist
Irby Farm, Thingwall Road, Irby, Wirral L61 3UA
BASMT

KEENAN, Paul Stephen
Cognitive Behavioural Psychotherapist
Dept of Psychiatry, Clatterbridge Hospital, Bebington, Wirral, Merseyside L63 4JY
0151 334 4000 x 4028/0151 327 5867
BABCP

KENNEDY, Des
Gestalt Psychotherapist
Shalom, 36 Hillside Road, West Kirby, Wirral L48 8BB
0151 625 9839
GPTI, MET

LYON, Martin
Child Psychotherapist
Child & Family Services, Royal Liverpool Childrens NHS Trust, Scarisbrook Ave., Litherland, Liverpool L21 6NJ
0151 928 5045/0151 928 4120 (f)
ACP

MARKS, Helen
Family Therapist
8 Salisbury Road, Liverpool L19 0PJ
0151 709 0540
FIC

MARTIN, Susan
Hypno-Psychotherapist
10 Moss Lane, Orrell Park, Liverpool L9 8AJ
0151 525 1043
CTS

MATTISON, Sheila
Psychoanalytic Psychotherapist
Wellcroft Centre, Wellcroft Road, Huyton, Liverpool L36 7RT
0151 489 6136
LPDO

MCALEER, Eileen
Integrative Psychotherapist
Flat 6, 80-82 Egerton Street, Wallasey, Merseyside L45 2LT
0151 637 0219
RCSPC

MCGRATH, Adrian
Hypno-Psychotherapist
82 St. Georges Road, Wallasey, Merseyside L46 6TX
0151 639 6660
CTS

MCNAB, Stuart
Psychoanalytic Psychotherapist
Bridge House Clinic, 73 Village Road, Higher Bebington, Wirral, Merseyside L63 8PS
0151 608 1991
LPDO

MCVEY, Damien
Hypno-Psychotherapist
12 Rodney Street, Liverpool L1 2TE
0151 722 1044
CTS

MERCER, Annie
Psychoanalytic Psychotherapist
Paediatric Liaison, Royal L'pool Children's NHS Trust, Alder Hey Children's Hosp., Eaton Rd., Liverpool L12 2AP
0151 228 4811 x 2586
LPDO

NELKI, Julia
Family Therapist
18 Kingsmead Road, North AFT, Oxton, Birkenhead L43 6TB
0151 653 3550/0151 652 7857
AFT

PITT, Christopher
Family Therapist
Flat 4, 8 Mannering Road L7 8TR
0151 728 8716
AFT

PROTHERO, Peggy
Psychoanalytic Psychotherapist
Vine House, 26 Parkgate Road, Neston, Wirral L64 9XE
0151 336 2423
LPDO

SCOTT, Michael
Cognitive Behavioural Psychotherapist
39 Hayles Green, Liverpool L25 4SG
0151 428 6846
BABCP

SMITH, Flo M.F.
Psychoanalytic Psychotherapist
Psychological Therapies Services, Saint Catherines Hospital, Church Road, Birkenhead, Wirral L42 0LQ
0151 604 7276/01928 722544
LPDO

SMITH, Ged
Family Therapist
29 Hillside Drive, Woolton, Liverpool L25 5NR
AFT

SMITH, Margaret
Psychoanalytic Psychotherapist
13 St. Anthony's Road, Blundellsands, Liverpool L23 8TN
0151 250 3235/0151 931 5194
LPDO, IGA

STEWART, June
Psychoanalytic Psychotherapist
c/o The Wellcroft Centre, Wellcroft Road, Huyton, Liverpool L36 7RT
0151 489 6136
LPDO

TAYLOR, Patsy
Psychoanalytic Psychotherapist
8 Victoria Mount, Birkenhead, Merseyside L43 5TH
0151 651 0558
LPDO

TRANTER, Paul
Family Therapist
Royal Liverpool Children's NHS Trust, Aldey Hey Hospital, Eaton Road, Liverpool L12
0151 252 5503
AFT

WETHERILL, Julie
Group Analyst
6 Waverley Grove, Prenton, Wirral L42 9PU
Halton Psychotherapy Family Unit, Thorn Road, Runcorn WA7 5HQ
01928 575073/0151 608 7442
IGA, WMIP

WOODS, Angie
Psychoanalytic Psychotherapist
Occupational Therapy/Physiotherapy Department, Whiston Hospital, Prescot, Merseyside L35 5DR
0151 430 1131
LPDO

WOODWARD, Raie
Psychoanalytic Psychotherapist
Psychology & Counselling Dept., St. Catherine's Hosp., Derby Rd., Birkenhead, Wirral L42 0LQ
0151 604 7276
LPDO

WYNN, Michelle
Cognitive Behavioural Psychotherapist
11 Rosslyn Drive, Moreton, Wirral, Merseyside L46 0SU
0151 678 4620
BABCP

MIDDLESEX

ARDEMAN, Jacqueline
Family Therapist
44 Stanmore Hill, Stanmore, Middlesex HA7 3BN
0181 954 1163
AFT

ASMALL, Ismail
Existential Psychotherapist
134 Priory Road, Hampton, Middlesex TW12 2PS
0181 941 1460/0181 749 8747
RCSPC

AUFFLICK, Julia
Systemic Psychotherapist
North Surrey Family Centre, Stanwell Road, Ashford, Middlesex TW15 3DU
26 Grove Close, Old Windsor, Berks. SL4 2LY
KCC

AVIGAD, Jocelyn
Systemic Psychotherapist
26 Rosecroft Walk, Pinner, Middlesex HA5 1LL
0181 429 0884
IFT

BANKS, Jan
Transactional Analysis Psychotherapist, Transactional Analysis Psychotherapist
116 Thornbury Road, Osterley, Isleworth, Middlesex TW7 4NH
0181 560 5989/0181 560 9071 (FAX)
ITA, MET

BOSTOCK, Elizabeth
Psychoanalytic Psychotherapist
1 Selborne Gardens, Greenford, Middlesex UB6 7PD
0181 998 2883
BAP, NAFSI

BRISTOW, John
Cognitive Analytic Therapist
261 St. Margaret's Road, Twickenham TW1 1NJ
0181 891 4443(f)/0181 891 4997
ACAT

BROWN, Lesley
Integrative Psychosynthesis Psychotherapist, Gestalt Psychotherapist
'Brightwater', Dunally Park, Shepperton, Middlesex TW17 8LJ
97 Brondesbury Road, Queens Park, London NW6 6RY
01932 220590
MET, GPTI, RE.V

BRUNT, Clare
Humanistic Psychotherapist
97 Warren Road, Whitton, Twickenham, Middlesex TW2 1DJ
0181 755 0353
AHPP

CARROLL, Helen
Integrative Psychosynthesis Psychotherapist
39 Rushout Avenue, Kenton, Harrow, Middlesex HA3 0AS
0181 427 6209
RE.V

CHALK, Caroline
Psychosynthesis Psychotherapist
Flat B, 4 Somerset Road, Teddington, Middlesex TW11 8RS
0181 977 8224
AAPP

CLAPP, Tony
Psychoanalytic Psychotherapist
10 Willow Road, Enfield, Middlesex EN1 3NE
0181 366 7338
LCP

CLARK, Nita
Analytical Psychologist-Jungian Analyst
16 Bellfield Avenue, Harrow Weald, Middlesex HA3 6SX
0181 421 1879
AJA

CLEAVELY, Evelyn
Psychoanalytic Marital Psychotherapist
8 Cox's Avenue, Grange Farm, Upper Halliford, Shepperton, Middlesex TW17 8TE
01932 789088 (t/f)
TMSI

COHEN, Pat
Attachment-based Psychoanalytic Psychotherapist
Noahs Ark, Spring Lake, Stanmore, Middlesex HA7 3BX
0181 954 9366
CAPP

COOPER, Cassie
Personal Construct Psychotherapist, Psychodynamic Psychotherapist
12 Coniston Court, High Street, Harrow on the Hill, Middlesex HA1 3LP
0181 423 9386
CPCP, AIP

COOPER, Suzanne
Holistic Psychotherapist, Body Psychotherapist
5 Lawrence Road, Pinner, Middlesex HA5 1LH
0181 866 1521
CCBP

COURTMAN, Anita
Psychosynthesis Psychotherapist
252 St. Margarets Road, Twickenham, Middlesex TW1 1PR
0181 893 2324
AAPP

CRICK, Verena
Child Psychotherapist
Barnet Child & Family Consultation Service, Edgware General Hospital, Edgware, Middlesex HA8 OAD
0181 905 6679/0171 431 1761
ACP

CUSSINS, Anne
Psychoanalytic Psychotherapist
55a Pope's Avenue, Strawberry Hill, Twickenham, Middlesex TW2 5TD
0181 898 1366
IPSS

DAY, Lesley
Integrative Psychotherapist
41 Ailsa Avenue, St. Margarets, Twickenham, Middlesex TW1 1NF
0181 892 2076
MET

DAY, Michael
Systemic Psychotherapist, Family Therapist
1 Burtons Road, Hampton Hill TW12 1DB
0181 977 7280
AFT

DAY, Sally
Psychoanalytic Psychotherapist
27 Trafalgar Road, Twickenham, Middlesex TW2 5EJ
0181 894 1609
IPC

DEAN, Paul
Individual and Group Humanistic Psychotherapist, Integrative Arts Psychotherapist
74 Lincoln Avenue, Twickenham, Middlesex TW2 6NP
0181 898 2522
MET, IATE

DEAN, Sally
Psychoanalytic Psychotherapist
74 Lincoln Avenue, Twickenham, Middlesex TW2 6NP
0181 898 2522
IPC

DREWNOWSKA, Alicja
Integrative Psychotherapist, Body Psychotherapist
72 Hindes Road, Harrow, Middlesex
0181 427 9516
CCBP

EISEN, Shelley
Sexual and Marital Psychotherapist
Kings Oak Hospital, Chase Farm (North Side), The Ridgeway, Enfield EN2 8SD
0181 364 5520
BASMT

FASHT, Ruth
Group Analyst
'Gayton', 23 Aylmer Drive, Stanmore, Middlesex HA7 3EJ
0181 954 4710
IGA

FITZGERALD-BUTLER, Albina
Hypno-Psychotherapist
'Ivy Cottage', Ealing Road, Northolt Village, Middx UB5 6AA
0181 841 4092
NRHP

GILLI, Liliana
Psychosynthesis Psychotherapist
16 Clovelly Close, Ickenham, Middlesex UB10 8PT
01895 677405
AAPP

GOLDSTEIN, Pam
Systemic Psychotherapist
18 Hazledene Drive, Pinner, Middlesex HA5 3NJ
0181 429 1640
KCC

GOLDWYN, Margaret
Psychoanalytic Psychotherapist
7 Cross Deep, Twickenham, Middlesex TW1 4QJ
LCP

GOLTEN, Carole
Transpersonal Psychotherapist
Stanmore, Middlesex
Edgware Road W2
0181 958 4708
CCPE

GORDON, Deidre
Core Process Psychotherapist
19 Sudbury Court Drive, Harrow, Middlesex HA1 3SZ
0181 904 6488
AAPP

GORMAN, Graham
Hypno-Psychotherapist
33 Westholme Gardens, Ruislip, Middx HA4 8QJ
01895 633753
NRHP

GORODENSKY, Arlene
Integrative Psychotherapist
9 Orchard Drive, Edgware, Middlesex HA8 7SE
0181 958 7021
RCSPC

GRAHAM, Marilyn
Gestalt Psychotherapist
29 Court Close, Twickenham, Middlesex TW2 5JH
0181 755 1029
GPTI

GREEN, June
Psychoanalytic Psychotherapist
'Redholme', 15 Ducks Hill Road, Northwood, Middx HA6 2NW
01923 824858
IPSS

HABERLIN, Jane
Psychoanalytic Psychotherapist
37 Chase Side, Enfield EN2 6NB
0961 355792/0181 366 0505
ARBS

HARARI, Michael
Analytical Psychologist-Jungian Analyst, Child Psychotherapist
15 Woodside Road, Northwood, Middlesex HA6 3QE
01923 825880 (t/f)
SAP, ACP

HARRINGTON, Rufus
Cognitive Behavioural Psychotherapist
The Shakespeare Suite, Ashford Hospital NHS Trust, Lakeside Mental Health Unit, West Middlesex, Isleworth TW7 6AF
Dept of Clinical Psychology, Hounslow & Spelthorne CMH NHS Trust, Lakeside MHU, West Middlesex Hospital TW7 6AF
01961 378329/01784 884111
BABCP

HEARST, Liesel
Group Analyst
78 Elm Park, Stanmore, Middlesex HA7 4BQ
0181 440 1451/0181 954 7999
IGA

HILL, Jennifer
NLP Psychotherapist
30 Wakehams Hill, Pinner, Middlesex HA5 3BQ
0181 601 3021/0181 866 6729
ANLP

HOBBS, Anita
Sexual and Marital Psychotherapist
89 Syon Park Gardens, Osterley, Middlesex TW7 5NF
0181 568 4967
BASMT

IKKOS, George
Group Analyst
Postgraduate Medical Centre, Egware Community Hospital, Burnt Oak Broadway, Edgware HA8 0AD
IGA

JOHNSON, Deirdre
Analytical Psychologist-Jungian Analyst
16 Barrow Point Avenue, Pinner, Middlesex HA5 3HF
AJA, 7 Eton Avenue, London NW3 3EL
0181 866 9006
AJA

KINGSNORTH, Wendy
Psychoanalytic Psychotherapist
91 First Avenue, Bush Hill Park, Enfield EN1 1BW
0181 363 3821
IPC

KULYK, Michael
Hypno-Psychotherapist
313 Martindale Road, Hounslow, Middlesex TW4 7HG
0181 570 3795
NRHP

LASCHINGER, Bernie
Attachment-based Psychoanalytic Psychotherapist
27 Chalkhill Road, Wembley Park, London HA9 9DS
0181 904 2176
CAPP

LAU, Bernard Wai Kai
Cognitive Behavioural Psychotherapist
18 Wakehams Hill, Pinner, Middlesex HA5 3BQ
BABCP

LAVENDER, Lesley
Transpersonal Psychotherapist
Flat 8, Watertower, 1 The Straight, Southall UB1 1QU
0181 893 6602
CCPE

LUCAS, Tina
Group Analyst
24 Montpelier Row, Twickenham, Middlesex TW1 2NQ
0181 892 6584
IGA

MARSDEN, Veronica
Gestalt Psychotherapist
59 Manor Lane, Sunbury on Thames TW16 5EB
Gestalt Consortium, 33 Croftdown Road, London NW5 1EL
01932 786147/0171 485 2316
GCL

MARTIN, Brandy
Transpersonal Psychotherapist
1 Amhurst Gardens, Isleworth, Middx TW7 6AN
CCPE

MATTAR, Gretta
Hypno-Psychotherapist
14 Chestnut Manor Close, Staines, Middlesex TW18 1AQ
01784 243409
NRHP

MEINRATH, Monica
Group Analyst
31 Bushey Park Gardens, Teddington, Middlesex TW11 0LQ
0181 977 2242
IGA

MENCKHOFF, Beckie
Analytical Psychologist-Jungian Analyst
22 The Chase, Eastcote, Pinner, Middlesex HA5 1SJ
0181 866 9093
BAP

MICHAUD-LENNOX, Suzanne
Psychoanalytic Psychotherapist
20 Heming Road, Edgware, London HA8 9AE
0181 952 2418
IPSS

MOORHOUSE, Anni
Systemic Psychotherapist
CFCS,, Windmill Lodge, Uxbridge Road, Southall UB1 3EU
21 Covent Gardens, London W5 4UT
0181 568 2900/0181 967 5485
IFT

MORRIS, Bridget
Transpersonal Psychotherapist
65 Francis Road, Harrow, Middlesex HA1 2RA
0181 861 1265
CCPE

MOSTAEDDI, Bahman
Child Psychotherapist
Children & Family Consultation Service, Windmill Lodge, Ealing Hospital, Uxbridge Road, Southall, Middlesex UB1 3EU
0181 967 5484
ACP

NEWNS, David
Transpersonal Psychotherapist
110 Waterloo Road, Uxbridge, Middlesex UB8 2QY
01895 467046
CCPE

NORSA, Giuliana
Child Psychotherapist
Enfield Child & Family Service, 8 Dryden Road, Bush Hill, Enfield EN1 2PP
0181 360 6771/0181 455 7290
ACP

PARTRIDGE, Karen
Systemic Psychotherapist
Maddison Centre, 140 Church Road, Teddington, Middlesex TW11 8QL
1 Woodside Road, Kingston upon Thames, Surrey KT2 5AT
KCC

PERRY, Christopher
Analytical Psychologist-Jungian Analyst
64 Sidney Road, St. Margarets, Twickenham TW1 1JR
0181 948 2412/0181 892 3126
BAP

PETKOVA, Petia
Family Therapist
The Windmill Lodge, West London Health Care NHS Trust, Uxbridge Road, Southall, Middlesex UB1 8PN
0181 967 5248/0181 967 5485/5190
AFT

PETRIE-KOKOTT, Julie
Integrative Psychotherapist, Body Psychotherapist
19 Clitherow Road, Brentford, Middlesex TW8 9JT
0181 568 0589
CCBP

PHILLIPS, Asha
Child Psychotherapist
11 Fallowfield, Stanmore, Middlesex HA7 3DF
0181 385 7831(f)/0181 954 4909
ACP

POKORNY, Barbara
Psychoanalytic Psychotherapist
28 Glendale Gardens, Wembley, Middx. HA9 8PS
0181 904 7878
LCP

POPLE, Sue
Group Analytic Psychotherapist
Enfield Counselling Service, St. Paul's Centre, 102A Church Street, Enfield EN2 6AR
0181 367 2333
IPC

RAWSON-JONES, Elizabeth
Hypno-Psychotherapist
96 Highland Road, Northwood Hills, Middlesex HA6 1JU
Psychotherapy Clinic, 18B North End Road, Golders Green, London NW11
01923 824755
NRHP

REES-ROBERTS, Diane
Psychoanalytic Psychotherapist
12 Cambridge Crescent, Teddington, Middlesex TW11 8DY
0181 287 7417/0181 977 7282
IPC

RIMMER, Janet
Psychosynthesis Psychotherapist
Northlands, 24 Parkfield Gardens, Harrow, Middlesex HA2 6JR
0181 863 1931
AAPP

ROBERTS, June
Psychoanalytic Psychotherapist
57 St. Margaret's Road, Twickenham TW1 2LL
0181 891 1205
IPSS

ROSS, Suzanne
Transpersonal Psychotherapist
15 Holmes Road, Twickenham, Middlesex TW1 4RF
0181 891 3234
CCPE

RUTHERFORD, Penny
Family Therapist
9 College Drive, Ruislip, Middlesex HA4 8SD
AFT

SEAMAN, Daphne
Sexual and Marital Psychotherapist
29 Manor Way, North Harrow, Middlesex HA2 6BZ
BASMT

SHORTALL, Thomas R.
Cognitive Behavioural Psychotherapist
309 Carr Road, Northolt, Middlesex UB5 4RW
0181 966 7000 x 299/0181 864 1482
BABCP

SHUTTLEWORTH, Judy
Child Psychotherapist
Enfield Child & Family Service, Avenue House, 8 Bycullah Avenue, Enfield EN2 8DW
0181 367 8844/0181 883 7908
ACP

SINGER, Iris
Attachment-based Psychoanalytic Psychotherapist
1 Fairfield Avenue, Edgware, Middlesex HA8 9AG
0181 952 3931
CAPP

SKLAN, Cheryl
Analytical Psychologist-Jungian Analyst
9 Dorset Drive, Edgware, Middlesex HA8 7NT
0181 952 9743/0181 381 1709
BAP

SLATER, Joan
Integrative Psychotherapist
17 Blenheim Close, Greenford, Middlesex UB6 8ET
0181 813 2235
RCSPC

STEARMAN, Frances
Psychoanalytic Psychotherapist
20 South Road, Twickenham, Middx. TW2 5NU
0181 977 1658
LCP

STOCKLEY, Rosalind
Integrative Psychotherapist
103 Copse Wood Way, Northwood, Middlesex HA6 2TU
01923 842351/01923 829190
RCSPC

STORRING, Susan
Child Psychotherapist
Barnet Child & Family Consultation Service, Child Guidance Centre, East Road, Burnt Oak, Edgware, Middlesex HA8 0BT
0181 445 5539/0181 359 3801
ACP

SUSSMAN, Susan
Transpersonal Psychotherapist
Ruislip, Middlesex
01895 622202
CCPE

SUTHERLAND, Robert I.
Hypno-Psychotherapist
69 Sherwood Avenue, Greenford, Middlesex UB6 OPQ
0181 864 8795
NRHP

SWIFT, Joanna
Psychoanalytic Psychotherapist
5 Beresford Avenue, Twickenham, Middlesex TW1 2PY
0181 892 4722
PA

SWINBURNE, Barbara C.
Cognitive Behavioural Psychotherapist
Thelma Golding Health Centre, Room 26, 92 Bath Road, Hounslow, Middlesex TW3 3EL
110 Thorton Road, Charshalton, Surrey SM5 1NQ
0181 565 2320/0181 641 6108
BABCP

TAYLOR, Jill
Biodynamic Psychotherapist
65 Mereway Road, Twickenham, Middlesex TW2 6RF
0181 898 2805
BTC

THOMAS, Carmel
Cognitive Behavioural Psychotherapist
152 Somervell Road, South Harrow, Middlesex HA2 8TS
01344 773111 x4661/0181 248 7422
BABCP

THORNDYCRAFT, Bill
Group Analytic Psychotherapist
90 Court Way, Twickenham, Middlesex TW2 7SW
St Thomas'Hospital Psychotherapy Dept, St Thomas' Hospital, London SE1
0171 928 9292/0181 892 4376
IPC

TRAYNOR, Barbara
Transactional Analysis Psychotherapist, Gestalt Psychotherapist
24 Bristow Road, Hounslow, Middlesex TW3 1UP
0181 572 0650/0181 570 9438 (f)
ITA, MET

VICKERS, Salley
Psychoanalytic Psychotherapist
Top Flat, 5 The Butts, Brentford, Middlesex TW8 8BJ
0181 560 6490
GUILD

WADLAND, Liz
Family Therapist
Wembley Vicarage, 3 Crawford Avenue, Wembley, London HA0 2HX
0181 902 0273
AFT

WARD, John
Psychoanalytic Psychotherapist
123 Amyand Park Road, Twickenham TW1 3HN
0181 744 2780
AGIP

WHINES, Jonathan
Gestalt Psychotherapist
86 Colne Road, Twickenham, Middlesex TW2 6QE
62 Unthank Road, Norwich NR2 2RN
0181 755 0992/01603 663186
GPTI, MET

WILKINS, David
Hypno-Psychotherapist
9 Burbidge Road, Shepperton, Middlesex TW17 0ED
Dorchester Clinic, Dorchester Road, North Cheam, Surrey
01932 254031(f)/01939 232401
NRHP

WISHART, Marian
Transpersonal Psychotherapist
197 Jersey Road, Osterley, Isleworth, Middlesex TW7 4QJ
0181 560 5363
CTP

WOLFE, Pamela
Psychosynthesis Psychotherapist
48 Fairacres, Ruislip, Middlesex HA4 8AW
01845 631 094
AAPP

NORFOLK

AQUARONE, Luc-Remy
Psychoanalytic Psychotherapist
11 Pottergate, Norwich NR2 1DS
0958 956871/01603 633115
LCP, FIP

BURTON, Simon
Systemic Psychotherapist
Bethel Child & Family Centre, Mary Chapman House, Hotblack Road, Norwich
17 Eade Street, Norwich
01603 667072/01603 421950
KCC

COULSON, Christopher
Individual and Group Humanistic Psychotherapist
63 Bury Street, Norwich, Norfolk NR2 2DL
31 Bucklesham Road, Kirton, Suffolk IP10 0PD
01394 448435/01603 611394
AHPP

DAYKIN, Amanda
Group Analyst
6 Elvenden Close, Norwich NR4 6AS
01603 458 620
IGA

DOCKING, Raymond F.
Systemic Psychotherapist
1 Kettlewell Lane, King's Lynn, Norfolk PE30 1PW
01553 767520
KCC

ENDER, Christine
Psychosynthesis Psychotherapist
8 Russell Terrace, Trowse, Norwich NR14 8TQ
01603 626 831
AAPP

HARBEN, Ursula
Systemic Psychotherapist
The Bethel Child and Family Centre, Hotblack Road, Norwich NR2 6HN
01603 630 681
KCC

HART, Sally
Humanistic Psychotherapist
26 Grant Street, Norwich NR2 4HA
01603 623795
AHPP

HENDERSON, Ned
Gestalt Psychotherapist
Sawmill Cottage, The Street, Aylmerton Norfolk NR11 8AA
01263 837 489
CCBP

HOARE, Elizabeth
Systemic Psychotherapist
St Nicholas Yard, DISS, Norfolk IP22
38 Abingdon Court, Abingdon Villas, London W8 6BT
0171 937 9249/01379 651762
KCC

HUGHES, Jacqui
Gestalt Psychotherapist
62 Unthank Road, Norwich NR2 2RN
01603 625090
GPTI, MET

IRVING, Nicholas
Transactional Analysis Psychotherapist
22 Lynn Road, Hillington, Kings Lynn, Norfolk PE31 6DD
Orientation Training Consultancy, Unit 1b Docking Rural Workshops, Sandy Lane, Docking PE31 8LT
ITA

KERKHAM, Patricia
Psychoanalytic Psychotherapist
Banklands, Clenchwarton, King's Lynn, Norfolk PE34 4DB
15 Tuesday Market Place, King's Lynn, Norfolk PE30 1JN
01553 762693(f)/01553 773854
IPSS

LITTLE, Jon
Integrative Psychotherapist
14 Central Close, Hethersett, Norwich NR9 3ER
01603 810946
RCSPC

MACGREGOR, Wynne
Integrative Psychotherapist
20 Neville Street, Norwich NR2 2PR
01603 461864
MET

MACKINNON, Sylvia
Hypno-Psychotherapist
4 Witton Close, Heacham, Kings Lynn, Norfolk PE31 7TD
29 Trent Road, Langley, Slough Berks. SL3 8AW
01485 572547
NSHAP

MCADAM, Elspeth
Systemic Psychotherapist
Bethel Child & Family Centre, Hotblack Road, Norwich NR2 6HN
01603 421 966
KCC

MUNDY, Jean
Biodynamic Psychotherapist
7 Castreward, Great Yarmouth,
Norfolk NR30 7AS
01493 850867
BTC

PITTMAN, Karen
Behavioural Psychotherapist
Admirality House, Northgate Hospital,
Northgate Street, Great Yarmouth,
Norfolk NR30 1BU
01493 337677
BABCP

POLDEN, Jane
Psychoanalytic Psychotherapist
16 Catton Grove Road, Norwich
NR3 3NN
01603 404363
AGIP

REYNOLDS, Francois
NLP Psychotherapist
8 Town Close Road, Norwich, Norfolk
NR2 2NB
01603 622542 (t/f)
ANLP

RICHARDSON, Susan
Hypno-Psychotherapist
25 Cypress Close, Taverham, Norwich,
Norfolk NR8 6QG
01603 861019 (t/f)
NRHP

SHETTY, Grish Chander
Psychoanalytic Psychotherapist
The Norvic Clinic, St Andrews
Business Park, Thorpe, Norwich
NR7 0HT
01603 421024
LPDO

WILKINSON, Mary
Systemic Psychotherapist
Yew Tree Cottage, Stocks Hill,
Bawburgh, Norwich NR9 3LL
01603 811456
KCC

WILMOT, David
Family Therapist
The White House, Brandon Creek,
Downham Market, Norfolk PE38 0PR
01353 676365
AFT

WOOD-BEVAN, Rosemary
Integrative Psychotherapist
St. Augustine's Psychotherapy Practice,
26 St. Augustine's Street, Norwich
NR3 3BZ
01603 633791
MC

NORTHAMPTONSHIRE

BEECH, Julie C.
Cognitive Psychotherapist
Psychology Department, 3 Spencer
Parade, Northampton
01604 250445
BABCP

CLARK, Alec
Family Therapist
280 Wellingborough Road, Rushden,
Northants NN10 9XP
01933 386354
AFT

FITZGERALD, Pen
Psychodrama Psychotherapist
91 Upper Thrift Street, Northampton
NN1 5HR
01604 28769
BPA

GARDNER, Damian
Cognitive Behavioural Psychotherapist
Dept. of Clinical Psychology, St Mary's
Hospital, London Road NN14 1JP
01536 493033
BABCP

ILOYD, Patricia
Psychoanalytic Psychotherapist
Fernvilla, Daventry Road, Newnham,
Northants NN11 3HF
01327 879524
IPSS

JANE, Susan
Psychodynamic Psychotherapist
103 Queens Park Parade,
Northampton NN2 6LR
01604 717763
ULDPS

LEAR, Terry
Group Analyst
140 St. George's Avenue,
Northampton NN2 6JF
01604 713616
IGA

LONG, Clive G.
Cognitive Behavioural Psychotherapist
St. Andrews Hospital, Billing Road,
Northampton NN1 5DG
01604 29696
BABCP

MACPHERSON, David
Hypno-Psychotherapist
The Rectory, Great Brighton,
Northampton NN7 4JB
CTS

MARSDEN-ALLEN, Peter
Family Therapist
33 Alfred Street, Rushden,
Northamptonshire NN10 9YS
01604 604608/01933 411476
AFT

MILNE, Pamela
Cognitive Behavioural Psychotherapist
St. Andrew's Hospital, Billing Road,
Northampton NN1 5DG
01604 29696 x6580
BABCP

O'NEILL, Helen M.
Cognitive Behavioural Psychotherapist
Occupational Therapy Dept, St.
Andrews Hospital, Northampton
NN1 5DG
01604 29696 x 533
BABCP

PHILLIPS, Marianne
Psychoanalytic Psychotherapist
Cattleshed Cottage, 1 Bakers Lane,
Shutlanger, Nr. Towcester, Northants
NN12 7RT
01604 863313
ARBS, FIP

PLOWMAN, Polly
Integrative Psychosynthesis
Psychotherapist
1 Faugere Close, Brackley, Northants
NN13 6LR
c/o Re.Vision, 97 Brondesbury Road,
London NW6 6RY
01280 705617
RE.V

REES, Myfanwy
Analytical Psychologist-Jungian Analyst
Ford Cottage, 1 High Street, Denford,
Northants NN14 4EQ
01832 733502
IGAP

ROBERTS, Julie
Group Analyst
4 Clumber Drive, Edgemont Grange, Northampton NN3 3NX
01604 412376
IGA

SPRINCE, Jenny
Child Psychotherapist
Thornby Hall, Peper Harrow Foundation, Northampton NN6 8SW
01604 740001/0171 241 2911
ACP

TOUGH, Harry
Group Analyst
106 Church Way, Weston Favell, Northampton NN3 3BQ
01604 28984
IGA

NORTHERN IRELAND

BENSON, Jarlath
Psychosynthesis Psychotherapist, Psychoanalytic Psychotherapist
The Belfast Counselling and Training Centre, Office 22, 40 Victoria Street, Belfast, Northern Ireland BT1 4QB
01232 242597
AAPP

BROWN, Avril
Sexual and Marital Psychotherapist
113 University Street, Belfast, Northern Ireland BT7 1HP
01232 312 942
BASMT

CAIRNS, Mary
Psychoanalytic Psychotherapist
171 Barnett's Road, Belfast, N. Ireland BT5 7BG
01232 489 422
ARBS

COULTER, Stephen
Family Therapist
20 Kingsway Park, Belfast BT5 7EU
AFT

CROMEY, Terry
Cognitive Behavioural Psychotherapist
'Brakken', 43 Sheridan Drive, Helen's Bay, Co. Down, N. Ireland BT19 1LB
01247 853473/01247 454276
BABCP

CUNNINGHAM, Gerry
Family Therapist
c/o Old Railway Station, Duke Street, Londonderry, Northern Ireland BT48
01504 343501
AFT

DAVIS, Patrick
Psychoanalytic Psychotherapist
28 Brookvale Avenue, Belfast BT14 6BW
01232 744676/01232 757615
WMIP

DAVREN, Moira
Family Therapist
1 Laurel Grove, Newry, Co. Down, Northern Ireland BT34 1TP
01762 392112/01762 361968 (f)
AFT

GILLESPIE, Kate
Cognitive Behavioural Psychotherapist
Cognitive Therapy Centre, Erne House, T & F Hospital, Omagh BT79 0NS
01662 245211
BABCP

GRANT, Mary
Transpersonal Psychotherapist
Lifespring, 111 Cliftonville Road, Belfast, Nothern Ireland BT14 6JQ
Natural Options, 85 Glasnevin Avenue, Dublin, Ireland
01232 753658/00 3531 862 2258
CTP

HANLEY, Ian G.
Cognitive Behavioural Psychotherapist
7 Lynnehurst Drive, Comber, Co. Down, Northern Ireland BT23 5LN
01247 873644
BABCP

HEALEY, Arlene
Family Therapist
35 Manse Road, Kircubbin, Co.Down, N. Ireland
01232 661825/12477 38749
AFT

JOHNSON, Duncan B.
Hypno-Psychotherapist
28 Drumill Road, Cullyhanna, Newry, Co. Down, N. Ireland BT35 0ND
01693 868715
NRHP

KELLY, Anne
Cognitive Behavioural Psychotherapist
92 - 94 Lisburn Road, Belfast BT9 6AG
0836 318636/01232 491759
BABCP

KENNY, Marie
Family Therapist
16 Broughton Gardens, Belfast BT6 0BB
01232 641268
AFT

LAWSON, Ruth
Cognitive Behavioural Psychotherapist
Redburn Clinic, 364 Old Holywood Road, Co. Down, Northern Ireland BT18 8QH
Martello House, 228 Bangor Road, Craidavad, Holywood Co.Down BT18 0JH
01232 425102/01232 421235
BABCP

MCGOWAN, Dominica
Gestalt Psychotherapist
30 North Parade, Belfast BT7 2GG
01232 326803/01232 237392 (f)
MET

MCGREEVY, Edith
Hypno-Psychotherapist
238 Townhill Road, Portglenone, Ballymena. Co Antrim, N.Ireland BT44 8HA
71 Rugby Avenue, Belfast BT11
01232 321603(f)/012665 71625
NSHAP

MCKEOWN, Patricia
Transpersonal Psychotherapist
2 Beechvale Court, Banbridge, Co. Down, N. Ireland BT32 3YR
018206 24806
CCPE

O'NEILL, Arthur
Family Therapist
Whitefield House, 2 The Hawthorns, Belfast, Northern Ireland BT10 0NR
01232 301611
AFT

QUINN, Paul
Cognitive Behavioural Psychotherapist
38 Garland Hill, Belfast, N. Ireland BT8 4YL
01232 797139
BABCP

NORTHUMBERLAND

JELLEMA, Anna
Cognitive Analytic Therapist
'Denethorpe', Stockton Road, Ryhope,
Sunderland SR2 0NE
0191 569 9427(f)/0191 569 9408
ACAT

NOTTINGHAMSHIRE

ADLINGTON, Jethro
NLP Psychotherapist
Hollydean House, 12 Nelson Road,
Daybrook, Nottingham NG5 6JE
0706 0706 666
ANLP

ANDERSON, Judith
Psychoanalytic Psychotherapist
(Jungian)
6 The Park, Newark, Nottingham
NG24 1SD
01636 701 997 (f)/01636 701996
WMIP

AVELINE, Mark
Psychoanalytic Psychotherapist
Nottingham Psychotherapy Unit
(NHS), St. Ann's House, 114
Thorneywood Mount, Nottingham
NG3 2PZ
0115 960 6888
AUTP

AVERY, Anna
Gestalt Psychotherapist
Clovers, Little Lane, Clarborough,
Retford, Nottingham DN22 9LR
01777 869913
SPTI

BASSETT, George
Gestalt Psychotherapist
c/o SPTI, 2 St. James Terrace,
Nottingham NG1 6FW
0115 924 3994
SPTI

BEECHCROFT, Diane
Transactional Analysis Psychotherapist
178 Harrington Drive, Lenton,
Nottingham NG7 1JH
01159 414378
ITA

BLORE, David C.
Cognitive Behavioural Psychotherapist
19 George Street, Sutton-in-Ashfield,
Nottinghamshire NG17 2HJ
01623 551570
BABCP

BROWNING, Peter
Gestalt Psychotherapist
30 Park Row, Nottingham NG1
0115 969 2442
SPTI

BRYANT, Pat
Gestalt Psychotherapist
c/o SPTI, Thiskney House, 2 St James
Terrace, Nottingham NG1 6FW
0115 924 3994
SPTI, MET

CARRETTE, Timothy
Gestalt Psychotherapist
274 Porchester Road, Nottingham
NG3 6GT
0115 985 8116
SPTI

CHERRY-SWAINE, Janine
Child Psychotherapist
Thorneywood Child & Adolescent
Unit, Porchester Road, Mapperley
NG3 6LF
0115 959479/0115 587888
ACP

COATS, Sonia
Sexual and Marital Psychotherapist
The Orchards, Church Lane,
Attenborough, Nottinghamshire
NG9 6AS
BASMT

COOPER, Penny
Sexual and Marital Psychotherapist
25 Cresta Gardens, Mapperley,
Nottingham NG3 5GD
BASMT

DALGARNO, Rebecca
Cognitive Behavioural Psychotherapist
Stonebridge Centre, Cardiff Street,
Carlton Road NG3 2FH
0115 985 9894(f)/0115 948 3268
BABCP

DAVIES, John
Cognitive Behavioural Psychotherapist
10 North Road, West Bridgford,
Nottingham NG2 7NH
0973 305578
BABCP

DUNN, Katie
Behavioural Psychotherapist
32A George Road, West Bridgford,
Nottingham NG2 7QG
0115 945 5990
BABCP

ERSKINE, Richard
Integrative Psychotherapist
c/o 2 St. James Terrace, Nottingham
NG1 6FW
0115 924 3994
SPTI

EVANS, Kenneth
Integrative Psychotherapist
31 Foxhill Road, Burton Joyce,
Nottingham NG14 5DB
0115 924 3994
SPTI

EVANS, Mairi M.
Transactional Analysis Psychotherapist
31 Foxhill Road, Burton Joyce,
Nottingham NG14 5DB
0115 931 4081
SPTI, ITA

FOOKES, Andrew
Gestalt Psychotherapist
2 St Jame's Terrace, Nottingham
NG1 6FW
0115 924 3994
SPTI, GPTI

GENT, Michael
Hypno-Psychotherapist
14 Sherwood Road, Rainworth,
Mansfield, Notts NG21 0LJ
01623 796251
NRHP

GRAHAM, Hilary E.
Hypno-Psychotherapist
25 George Road, West Bridgford,
Nottingham NG2 7PT
100 Derby Road, Long Eaton,
Nottinghamshire/Derbyshire
01159 455290
NRHP

GREENWAY, Ian
Gestalt Psychotherapist
100 Gertrude Road, West Bridgeford,
Nottingham NG2 5DB
0115 982 1834
MET, GPTI

HAYMAN, Penny
Integrative Psychotherapist
37 Chaworth Road, West Bridgford,
Notts NG2 7AE
0115 9825770
SPTI

HELPS, Davina
Sexual and Marital Psychotherapist
RELATE, 96 Mansfield Road,
Nottingham NG1 3HD
BASMT

HINDLE, Deborah
Child Psychotherapist
Thornywood Child & Adolescent
Psychiatry Unit, Porchester Road,
Mapperley, Nottingham NG3 6LF
01159 587888/01159 529479 (f)
ACP

HOWELL, Julia
Psychodrama Psychotherapist
7 Dean Road, Woodthorpe,
Nottingham NG5 4FG
00 617 3395 7226/00 617 3899 1077 (f)
BPA

HUTCHBY, Rosemary
Gestalt Psychotherapist
c/o The Sherwood Psychotherapy
Training Institute, Thiskney House, 2 St.
James Terrace, Nottingham NG1 6FW
0115 924 3994
SPTI

JACK, Bridget
Family Therapist
Curzon House, 14a Curzon Street,
Gotham, Notts NG11 0HQ
AFT

KEENAN, Paul
Transactional Analysis Psychotherapist
34 Adbolton Grove, Nottingham
NG2 5AR
0115 981 2778
ITA

KERRY, Helen
Gestalt Psychotherapist
3 Dagmar Grove, Alexandra Park,
Notts NG3 4JE
0115 962 1107
SPTI

LEE, Adrienne
Transactional Analysis Psychotherapist
2 Castle Grove, The Park, Nottingham
NG7 1DN
The Berne Institute, 29 Derby Road,
Kegworth, Nottingham DE74 2EN
01509 673649/01159 473296
ITA

LEE, Helen
Psychoanalytic Psychotherapist
Nottingham Psychotherapy
Dept.(NHS), St. Ann's House, 114
Thorneywood Mount, Nottingham
NG3 2PZ
0115 952 9452
STTDP

MAAS, Willem
Integrative Psychotherapist
17 Brancaster Close, Cinderhill,
Nottingham NG6 8SL
0115 9272940
SPTI

MANN, David
Gestalt Psychotherapist
274 Porchester Road, Mapperley,
Nottingham
0115 985 8116
SPTI

MORLEY, Ann
Psychoanalytic Psychotherapist
(Jungian)
36 Crosby Road, West Bridgford,
Nottinghamshire NG2 5GH
0115 914 0255 (f)/0115 914 0256
WMIP, ULDPS, FIP

MOULDING, Jacqueline
Integrative Psychotherapist
24 Cobwell Road, Retford, Notts
DN22 7BW
01777 702565
SPTI

NATHAN, (Jennifer) Ruth
Gestalt Psychotherapist, Integrative
Psychotherapist
4 Blackacre, Burton Joyce, Nottingham
NG14 5BS
0115 931 4275
GPTI, MET

O'REILLY, Thomas J
Psychoanalytic Psychotherapist
132 Edward Road, West Bridgeford,
Nottingham NG2 5GF
0115 974 9953
LPDO

PHILLIPS, Susan
Integrative Psychotherapist,
Transactional Analysis Psychotherapist
1 Orchard Close, Southwell,
Nottingham NG25 0DY
01636 813 794 (t/f)
MET, ITA

PIGOTT, Sheila
Gestalt Psychotherapist
St. Paul's House, Boundary Road, West
Bridgeford, Nottingham NG2 7DB
0115 923 3998
SPTI

RAPPARD, Marie Chalotte
Integrative Psychotherapist
17 Brancaster Close, Cinderhill,
Nottingham
0115 9272940
SPTI

REGEL, Stephen
Cognitive Behavioural Psychotherapist
Nottingham Natural Health Centre,
354 Mansfield Road, Nottingham
NG5 2EF
0115 960 8855
BABCP

RICHARDS, Paul
NLP Psychotherapist
Flat 2, 12a Alexandra Street, Sherwood
Rise, Nottingham NG5 1AY
0115 985 7372
ANLP

SALISBURY, Jonathan
Psychodrama Psychotherapist
21 Church Drive, Arnold, Nottingham
NG5 6JD
01159 200470
BPA

SENIOR, Maggie
Gestalt Psychotherapist
5 Second Avenue, Sherwood Rise,
Notts NG7 6JT
0115 9243994
SPTI

SHORT, Deborah
Gestalt Psychotherapist
20 Regent Street, Nottingham NG1
0115 924 3994
SPTI

SMITH, Cora
Integrative Psychotherapist
Sherwood Psychotherapy Training
Institute, Thiskney House, 2 St. James
Terrace, Nottingham NG1 6FW
0115 924 3994
SPTI

STAINES, Jill
Psychoanalytic Psychotherapist
Nottingham Psychotherapy Unit (NHS), St. Ann's House, 114 Thorneywood Mount, Nottingham NG3 2PZ
0115 952 9452
STTDP

STEPHENS, June
Gestalt Psychotherapist
22 The Paddocks, London Road, Newark, Nottingham NG24 1SS
01636 73456
SPTI

STERN, Erika
Integrative Psychotherapist
The Sherwood Psychotherapy Training Institute, Thiskney House, 2 St. James Terrace, Nottingham NG1 6FW
0115 924 3994
SPTI

STEWART, Ian
Transactional Analysis Psychotherapist
Old School House, Kingston on Soar, Nottingham NG11 ODE
The Berne Institute, Berne House, 29 Derby Road, Kegworth DE74 2EN
e.mail ian@theberne.u-net.com/01509 673569
ITA

SWAN PARENTE, Alison
Child Psychotherapist, Psychoanalytic Psychotherapist
Welbeck Abbey, Welbeck, Worksop, Notts S80 3LN
01909 500263/01909 531 054 (f)
ACP, WTC

THOMPSON, Jean Mary
Psychodrama Psychotherapist
21 Church Drive, Arnold, Nottingham NG5 6JD
0115 920 0470
BPA

TOMS, David A.
Psychodynamic Psychotherapist
2 Regent Street, Nottingham NG1 5BQ
0115 958 7098 (f)/0115 947 4755
WMIP

VAN WIJK, Jacqueline
Integrative Psychotherapist
17 Brancaster Close, Cinderhill, Nottingham NG6 8SL
0115 927 2940
SPTI

WARD, Keltie
Sexual and Marital Psychotherapist
64 Musters Road, West Bridgford, Nottingham NG2 7PR
BASMT

WATERSTONE, Carolyn
Gestalt Psychotherapist
10 Hampden Grove, Beeston, Nottingham NG9 1FG
0115 925 9083
SPTI

WATTERS, Catherine
Child Psychotherapist
Oakdene, 51 Anston Avenue, Worksop, Nottingham S81 7HU
01909 479327
ACP

WATTS, Jackie
Integrative Psychotherapist
Sherwood Psychotherapy Training Institute, Thiskney House, 2 St. James Terrace, Nottingham NG1 6FW
0115 924 3994
SPTI

WOOD, Chrissie Jones
Transactional Analysis Psychotherapist
The Oakwood Centre, 64 Henry Road, West Bridgford, Nottingham NG2 7ND
0115 982 5498
ITA

WOOD, Sally
Family Therapist
8 Curzon Street, Long Eaton, Nottingham NG10 4FT
01159 725621
AFT

WOOLFSON, Myra
Psychodynamic Psychotherapist
87 Sherwood Vale, Mapperley, Nottingham NG5 4EB
0115 960 3355
HIP

WYATT, Gill
Transactional Analysis Psychotherapist, Integrative Psychotherapist
Flat 2 68 Trent Boulevard, Nottingham NG2 5BD
0115 9140823 (t/f)
MET, ITA

YOUNG, Raymond
Psychoanalytic Psychotherapist
Nottingham Psychotherapy Unit (NHS), St. Ann's House, 114 Thorneywood Mount, Nottingham NG3 2PZ
0115 952 9452
STTDP

OXFORDSHIRE

ALLEN, Patricia M.
Transactional Analysis Psychotherapist
Grassington, 142 Gidley Way, Horspath, Oxford OX33 1TD
01865 872388
ITA

AMIES, Peter
Cognitive Psychotherapist
77 Victoria Road, Summertown, Oxford OX2 7QG
31 Wood Street, Swindon SN1 4AN
01865 556322/01793 491917
BABCP

BAGNALL, Steve
Family Therapist
Advent House, Manor Court, Kingham, Oxfordshire OX7 6YZ
Herbert Gray College, Little Church Street, Rugby, Warwickshire CV21 3AP
01788 563 823/01788 535 007 (f)
IFT

BLOCH, Linda
Group Analyst
33 Manor Road, South Hinskey, Oxford OX1 5AS
01865 730733
IGA

BLOW, Kirsten
Family Therapist
Oxford Family Inst., 2 Woodlands , Mill End, Kidlington, Oxon OX5 2ER
01865 842407
AFT

BLUM, Arna
Psychoanalytic Psychotherapist
Abbey Cottage, Sutton Courtenay, Abingdon, Oxford OX14 4AF
01235 848719
IPC

BLYTH, Fiona
Transactional Analysis Psychotherapist
Longbarn, 22 St. Georges Road, Wallingford, Oxon OX10 8HP
ITA

BRADLEY, Natalie
Psychoanalytic Psychotherapist
29 Boulter Street, St. Clements, Oxford OX4 1AX
CPP, FIP

BRANKIN, Maire
NLP Psychotherapist
19 Norham Road, Oxford OX2 6SF
01865 510340(f)/01865 310320
ANLP

BREWER, Madelyn
Psychoanalytic Psychotherapist
38 Rectory Road, St Clements, Oxford OX4 1BU
01865 430866/01865 725588
PA, FIP

BROWN, Robin Richard
Psychoanalytic Psychotherapist
23 Alexandra Road, Oxford OX2 0DD
3 Meadow Prospect, Wolvercote, Oxford OX2 8PP
01865 514806/01865 242400
SIP

CAMPBELL, Janet
Group Analyst
227 Kennington Road, Kennington, Oxford OX1 5PG
01865 735519/01865 730347
IGA

CAMPBELL, Margaret
Psychoanalytic Psychotherapist
Kiln House, Church Road, Sanford on Thames OX4 4XZ
01865 226518/01865 779556
CFAR

CARR, Jean
Analytical Psychologist-Jungian Analyst
12 Windsor Street, Headington, Oxford OX3 7AP
01865 750796
BAP, FIP

COREN, Alexander
Psychoanalytic Psychotherapist
86 Church Way, Iffley, Oxford OX4 4EF
01865 717974/01865 270300
BAP

CUNNINGHAM, Gordon
Group Analyst
19 St.Anne's Road, Headington, Oxford OX3 8NN
IGA

DANIEL, Gwyn
Family Therapist
8 Chalfont Road, Oxford OX2 6TH
Oxford Family Institute, 2 Woodlands, Mill End, Kidlington, Oxon OX5 2ER
01865 842407/01865 311518 (t/f)
IFT

DOUGLAS, Sue
Humanistic and Integrative Psychotherapist
Fawler Barn, Kingston Lisle, Nr. Wantage, Oxon OX12 9QJ
01367 820562
BCPC

DOWNES, Vanessa Susan
Cognitive Behavioural Psychotherapist
Cotswold House, Warneford Hospital, Headington, Oxford OX3 7JX
01865 226247
BABCP

ELWELL, Louise
Cognitive Analytic Therapist
57 Western Road, Grandpont, Oxford OX1 4LF
01865 724685
ACAT

GAGE, Michael
Sexual and Marital Psychotherapist
West Street Surgery, 12 West Street, Chipping Norton, Oxon
BASMT

GELL, Sally
Educational Therapist
98 Tower Hill, Witney, Oxon OX8 5ES
01993 705547
FAETT

GERHARDT, Sue
Psychoanalytic Psychotherapist
12 Kingston Road, Oxford OX2 6RB
01865 556592/01865 311772 (f)
AIP

GOSS, Thomas
Psychosynthesis Psychotherapist
Rose Cottage, Pound Lane, Stanton St. John, Oxon OX33 1HF
01865 351765
AAPP

GUY, Liana
Psychoanalytic Psychotherapist
33 Marlborough Road, Oxford OX1 4LW
96B Fortress Road, London NW5 2HJ
01865 251 812/0171 267 8936
GUILD

HANAWAY, Monica
Integrative Psychotherapist
79 Fairacres Road, Iffley Fields, Oxford OX4 1TQ
01865 450027/01865 436538
RCSPC

HARRIS, Gordon
Analytical Psychologist-Jungian Analyst
Hillside, 72 Honey Lane, Cholsey, Wallingford, Oxon OX10 9NJ
01491 651 271/01491 652 840 (f)
SIP

HAWORTH, Peter
Psychodrama Psychotherapist
8 Rahere Road, Cowley, Oxford OX4 3QC
St. Bartholomew's Medical Centre, Manzil Way, Cowley, Oxford OX4 1XL
01865 747604/01865 242334
BPA

HAYHURST, Sohani
Integrative Psychotherapist
1 Upper Fisher Row, Oxford OX1 2EZ
01865 727351
MC

HERBERT, Claudia
Cognitive Behavioural Psychotherapist
The Oxford Development Centre, 25 Templar Road, Oxford OX2 8LR
01865 428426/0802 831197
BABCP

HILL, Penny
Psychoanalytic Psychotherapist
17 Norreys Avenue, Oxford OX1 4ST
01865 722259
PA

HOBBS, Michael
Group Analyst
Warnesford Hospital, Warneford Lane, Headington, Oxford OX3 7JA
01865 226 331
IGA

HOCK, Gaby
Transpersonal Psychotherapist, Psychodynamic Psychotherapist
63 Warwick Street, Oxford OX4 1SZ
01865 247851
CTP

HODSON, Pauline
Psychoanalytic Marital Psychotherapist
14 Brookside, Headington, Oxford OX3 7PJ
01865 762991
TMSI

HOLMES, Anne
Group Analyst
59 Oxford Road, Old Marston, Oxford
OX3 0PH
IGA

HUNT, Susan
Sexual and Marital Psychotherapist
The Rainbow House, Wellsprings,
Brightwell-Cum-Sotwell, Wallingford
OX10 0RN
BASMT

HUTCHINSON, Peter
Psychodrama Psychotherapist
95 Sunningwell Road, Oxford OX1 4SY
01865 246194
BPA

JAMES, Anthony
Family Psychotherapist, Systemic
Psychotherapist
7 Queens Cottage, Toot Baldon,
Oxfordshire OX44 9NG
01865 226285/01865 343695
IFT

JAQUES, Penny
Psychoanalytic Psychotherapist
7 Stanley Road, Oxford OX4 1QY
01865 724141/01865 203225 (f)
BAP, FIP

JONES, David
Psychoanalytic Psychotherapist
23 Alexandra Road, New Botley,
Oxford OX2 0DD
01865 202904
LCP

KEATING, Jacqueline
Analytical Psychologist-Jungian Analyst
Abbots Piece, Church Lane, Islip
OX5 2TA
01865 375055(f)
IGAP

KüECHEMANN, Christine
Psychoanalytic Psychotherapist
3 Northmoor Road, Oxford
OX2 6UW
01865 515160
AGIP

LANDALE, Margaret
Integrative Psychotherapist, Body
Psychotherapist
Mill House, Mill Lane, Dyers Hill,
Charlbury, Oxon OX7 3QG
01608 810485
CCBP

LEVICK, Barbara
Psychoanalytic Psychotherapist
12 Frenchay Road, Oxford OX2 6TG
01865 552394 (F)/01865 512683
IPC

LINDLEY-JONES, Kirstin
Transpersonal Psychotherapist
15 Warwick Street, Oxford OX4 1SZ
01865 243351
CTP

LUTYENS, Marianna
Psychoanalytic Psychotherapist
99 Woodstock Road, Oxford
OX2 6HL
7 Fabyc House, Cumberland Road,
Kew Garden, Surrey TW9 3HH
01865 331104(t/f)
IPC

LUXMOORE, Nick
Psychodrama Psychotherapist
176 Divinity Road, Oxford OX4 1LR
The Flat, Old Police Station Buildings,
Church Green, Witney, Oxon
01865 245510/01993 702060
BPA

MACK SMITH, Catharine
Child Psychotherapist
23 Alexandra Road, Oxford OX2 0DD
01865 242400
ACP

MILLARD, Sheila
Group Analyst
78 Cumnor Hill, Oxford OX2 9HU
01865 862 224
IGA

MILLER, John
Analytical Psychologist-Jungian Analyst
19 Stanley Road, Cowley, Oxford
OX4 1QY
01865 725203
AJA

MILLS BURTON, M.
Psychoanalytic Psychotherapist
The Old Rectory, Childrey OX12 9UP
WMIP

MORRIS, Petrina
Analytical Psychologist-Jungian Analyst
7 Dovehouse Close, Oxford OX2 8BG
01845 557253
IGAP

MORRISON, Philippa
Existential Psychotherapist
Church Wing, The Old Rectory,
Church Street, Somerton, Bicester,
Oxfordshire OX6 4NB
0171 706 6936/01869 346770
RCSPC

NISSIM, Ruth
Family Therapist
Dores Cottage, 17 High Street,
Finstock, Oxon OX7 3DA
01604 859411 ext 262/01993 868147
AFT

O'BRIEN, Maja
Psychoanalytic Psychotherapist
28 Wytham Street, Oxford OX1 4TS
01865 728111
BAP

ORTON, Jane
Humanistic and Integrative
Psychotherapist
28 Bloxham Road, Banbury,
Oxfordshire OX16 9JN
BCPC

PORTER, Barbara
Transactional Analysis Psychotherapist
Silver Birches, Kingwood Common,
Henley-on-Thames, Oxon RG9 5LR
MET, ITA

POWELL, Andrew
Group Analyst, Psychoanalytic
Psychotherapist
Dept. of Psychotherapy, Warneford
Hospital, Warneford Lane, Headington,
Oxford OX3 7JX
Bramley Cottage, 2 Crown Lane,
Dorchester on Thames, Oxon
OX10 7L
01865 226337
IGA, BAP

RENDALL, Davina
Sexual and Marital Psychotherapist
5 Abberbury Avenue, Iffley Village,
Oxford OX4 4EU
BASMT

REYNAL, Carmen
Analytical Psychologist-Jungian Analyst
31 Warnborough Road, Oxford
OX2 6JA
Keyneton Hayes, Upper Slaughter,
Gloucestershire GL54 2JG
01865 511063/01451 821947
IGAP

RUGGIERI, Gloria
Integrative Psychotherapist
40 Cavendish Road, Summertown,
Oxford, Oxon OX2 7TW
01865 513363
RCSPC

RUSCOMBE-KING, Gillie
Psychodrama Psychotherapist
12 The Green, Cuddesdon, Oxford
OX44 9JZ
01865 873721
BPA

RYAN, Elizabeth
Sexual and Marital Psychotherapist
The Old Stores, Wellshead Lane,
Harwell, Oxon OX11 0HD
01235 674118
BASMT

SHADBOLT, Carole
Transactional Analysis Psychotherapist
11 Alexandra Square, Chipping
Norton, Oxon OX7 5HL
01608 645 862(f)/01608 644 748
ITA

SHEWAN, Doreen
Psychoanalytic Psychotherapist
19 Stanley Road, Oxford OX4 1QY
01865 725203
SIP

SLEEPER, Julia
Psychoanalytic Psychotherapist
42 Lonsdale Road, Oxford OX2 7EW
01865 311394
LCP

SMITH, Eva
Cognitive Analytic Therapist
9 Western Road, Oxford OX1 4LF
01865 724 351
ACAT

SOTH, Michael
Integrative Psychotherapist, Body
Psychotherapist
16 Riverside Road, Oxford OX2 OHU
01865 723613
CCBP

SPARKES, Frances
Personal Construct Psychotherapist
Finches, Hilltop Lane, Chinnor,
Oxfordshire OX9 4BH
01844 351411
CPCP

SPILIOS, Joanne
Analytical Psychologist-Jungian Analyst
15 Brasenose Driftway, Cowley, Oxon
OX4 2QX
99 Woodstock Road, Oxford
OX2 6HL
07020 921286/01865 777959
AJA

STANDISH, Elizabeth
Psychoanalytic Psychotherapist
30 East St.Helen's Street, Abingdon,
Oxon OX14 5EB
01235 528806
SIP

STAUNTON-SOTH, Theresa
Integrative Psychotherapist, Body
Psychotherapist
16 Riverside Road, Oxford OX2 0HU
01865 723613
CCBP

STEVENSON, Beaumont
Group Analyst
Chaplain's Office, Littlemore Hospital,
Littlemore, Oxford OX4 1SW
01765 620 253/01865 778 911
IGA

STEWARD, Jill
Psychoanalytic Psychotherapist
Kenricks, Hambleden, Henley-on-
Thames, Oxon RG9 6RP
01491 571 320/01491 413 942 (f)
IPC

STRICH, Sabina
Group Analyst
1 Folly Bridge Court, Thames Street,
Oxford OX1 1SW
01865 251741
IGA

TAYLOR, Susie
Psychodrama Psychotherapist
St. Brelades, 15 Swinbourn Road,
Littlemore, Oxford OX4 4PQ
01865 454932
BPA

THOMPSON, Patricia
Integrative Psychotherapist
'Beggars Roost', 28 Whittall Street,
Kings Sutton, Banbury, Oxon
OX17 3RD
01295 812232
RCSPC

THOMSON, Simon
Psychodrama Psychotherapist
41b Church Street, Ardington, Oxon
OX12 8QA
01235 821603
BPA

TUCKER, Joanna
Psychoanalytic Psychotherapist
42, Oakthorpe Road, Oxford OX2 7BE
01865 557 244
WMIP

WATSON, Andrea
Child Psychotherapist
12 Rectory Road, St. Clements, Oxford
OX4 1BW
01865 243491
ACP

WAYGOOD, Rob
Transpersonal Psychotherapist
59 Warwick Street, Oxford OX4 1SZ
9 Grove Road, Willesden Green,
London W1H 3PL
01865 247851
CTP

WILLIAMS, Gill
Psychodrama Psychotherapist
121 Southfield Road, Oxford
OX4 1NY
Isis Centre, Dartington House, Little
Clarendon Street, Oxford
01865 434638/01865 556648
BPA

WINTER, Wendy
Transpersonal Psychotherapist
St. Ethelwold's House, 30 East St. Helen
Street, Abingdon, Oxon OX14 5EB
CCPE

SCOTLAND – ABERDEEN

HOUGHTON, Judith E
Cognitive Behavioural Psychotherapist
Cathkin, Glenfarquhar Road,
Auchenblae, Laurencekirk AB3 1WU
0151 320222
BABCP

HOWIE, David D.
Hypno-Psychotherapist
9B Millburn Street, Aberdeen,
Grampian, AB11 6SS
01224 574190
NRHP

KOHLER, Christiane
Hypno-Psychotherapist
51 Cairngrassie Circle, Portlethen, Aberdeen, AB12 4TZ
01224 781747
NSHAP

MACPHERSON, Malcolm
Psychoanalytic Psychotherapist
15/17 Belmont Street, Aberdeen AB1 1JR
01224 620495/01569 730963
NAAP

MILNE, Frances
Analytical Psychologist-Jungian Analyst
24 North Sliver Street, Aberdeen AB1 1RL
4 Lennox Street, Edingburgh EH4 1QA
01224 620903/0131 332 8049
IGAP

ROBINSON, J.G.
Child Psychotherapist
South Leylodge Farmhouse, Leylodge, Kintore, Aberdeen AB5 0XY
01330 860333
ACP

SAWYER, Ken
Hypno-Psychotherapist
31 Cairngrassie Circle, Portlethen, Aberdeen AB1 4TZ
01224 781452
CTS

WRIGHT, W. Harry
Psychoanalytic Psychotherapist
Psychotherapy Day Unit, Upper Garden Villa, Royal Cornhill Hospital, Aberdeen AB25 2ZH
WMIP

SCOTLAND – AYRSHIRE

ELLWOOD, Jane
Psychoanalytic Psychotherapist, Child Psychotherapist
78 Main Street, Dunlop, Kilmarnock, Ayreshire KA3 4AG
Dept. of Child & Family Psychiatry, Royal Hospital for Sick Children, Yorkhill, Glasgow G3 8SJ
0141 201 0000/01560 485828
ACP

RICKARD, Ian
Cognitive Behavioural Psychotherapist
Beechbank, 7 Main Street, Staiton, Ayrshire KA19 7NF
01655 770677
BABCP

ROSS, Michael Killoran
Cognitive Behavioural Psychotherapist
c/o CCPS, Stradoon House, 50 Racecourse Road KA7 2UZ
c/o Bons Securs Hospital, 36 Mansionhouse Road, Langside, Glasgow G41 3DN
0141 632 9231/01292 285607
BABCP

SMITH, Alica
Hypno-Psychotherapist
17 Fotheringham Road, Ayr, Scotland KA8 0EY
01292 281793
NRHP

TOLLAN, John H
Hypno-Psychotherapist
3 Berriedale Road, Barassie Troon, Ayrshire KA10 6TS
CTS

WHITE, Craig A
Cognitive Behavioural Psychotherapist
CCPS, Strathdoon House, 50 Racecourse Road KA7 2UZ
Abbey Carrick Glen Hospital, Dalmellington Road KA6 6PG
01292 288882/01292 285607
BABCP

WIGHT, Zena J.
Cognitive Behavioural Psychotherapist
Clinical Psychology Services, Strathdoon House, 50 Racecourse Road, Ayr KA7 2UZ
01292 285607
BABCP

SCOTLAND – BORDERS

HUNT OVERZEE, Anne
Core Process Psychotherapist
Newburgh Cottage, Ettrick, Selkirk TD7 5HS
01750 622 36
AAPP

SCOTLAND – DUMFRIES

CAMPBELL, Colin B.G.
Hypno-Psychotherapist
Scaleridge Cottage, Waterbeck, Lockerbie DG11 3EU
01461 600288
NRHP

DAVIES, Debra
Core Process Psychotherapist
Diaryman's Cottage, Balgray, Lockerbie, Dumfriesshire DG11 2JT
01576 610375
AAPP

SCOTLAND – DUNDEE

ANTONSON, Kate
Family Therapist
12 Leomore Terrace, Gowrie Park, Dundee DD2 4UF
AFT

COYLE, Christina H.
Cognitive Behavioural Psychotherapist
65 Bruce Road, Downfield, Dundee DD3 8LW
01382 833780
BABCP

MALCOLM, Hanne
Hypno-Psychotherapist
29 Bell Street, Tayport, Fife DD6 9AP
01382 553596
NRHP

MORTON, Richard Victor
Cognitive Behavioural Psychotherapist
40 Carlogie Road, Carnoustie, Angus, Scotland DD7 6EY
01382 580441 ext 4965/01241 853002
BABCP

NESS, Bill
Family Therapist
St. Helens, 29 Mount Road, Montrose, Angus, Scotland DD10 8SP
01382 402002/01674 674659
AFT

SMART, Kate
Cognitive Behavioural Psychotherapist
Lour Road Surgery, 3 Lour Road, Forfar, Angus DD8 2AS
c/o Sue Hunt, Stress Management Services, Women's Health& Fam.Project, 1 Russel Place DD3 7RU
01382 810 230/01307 463 122
BABCP

STEWART, Henry B.
Cognitive Behavioural Psychotherapist
43 Provost Reid's Road, Montrose, Angus DD10 8DZ
01674 673823
BABCP

SWAN, John S.
Cognitive Behavioural Psychotherapist
Ardbeg, 55 Brechin Road, Kirriemuir, Angus DD8 4DE
01575 575427
BABCP

WILSON, Fiona
Cognitive Behavioural Psychotherapist
Clayholes, Balmachie Road, Carnoustie, Angus DD7 6LA
01241 855378
BABCP

SCOTLAND – EDINBURGH

ADAMSON, Fiona
Humanistic Psychotherapist
88 Morningside Drive, Edinburgh EH10 5NT
0131 446 9436
AHPP

ANGOLD, Monica
Sexual and Marital Psychotherapist
17 Morningside Park, Edinburgh EH10 5HD
0131 447 4342
BASMT

BECHHOFER, Jean B.
Behavioural Psychotherapist
51 Barnton Park View, Edinburgh EH4 6HH
0131 339 4083
BABCP

BOYLE, Pauline
Cognitive Behavioural Psychotherapist
Ballenden House, 28 - 32 Howden Street, Edinburgh EH11 1LJ
07775 503/0131 536 9490
BABCP

BRAID, Rosemary
Humanistic and Integrative Psychotherapist
8 Clarendon Crescent, Edinburgh, Scotland EH4 1DT
Channel Farm, Kinross, Scotland KY13 7HD
0131 332 1449/01592 84236
AHPP

CAMPBELL, Caroline
Hypno-Psychotherapist
7/2 Academy St. Leith, Edinburgh EH6 7EE
0131 555 3267
CTS

CHILD, Nick
Family Therapist
8 Lee Crescent, Portobello, Edinburgh EH15 1LW
01698 254551/0131 669 2184
AFT

CRAWFORD, George
Child Psychotherapist
4 Melgund Terrace, Edinburgh, Scotland EH7 4BU
0131 557 3039
ACP

FRASER, Bobbie
Sexual and Marital Psychotherapist
Sexual Problems Clinic, Western Gen. Hospital (NHS Trust), Crewe Road, Edinburgh EH4 2XU
BASMT

FREEMAN, Christopher
Cognitive Behavioural Psychotherapist
Department of Psychotherapy, Cullen Centre, Royal Edinburgh Hospital, Morningside Pk, Edinburgh EH10 5HF
14 Moray Place, Edinburgh EH1
0131 225 5320/0131 537 6599
BABCP

GRAY, Maggie
Cognitive Behavioural Psychotherapist
Cullen Centre, 29 Morningside Park, Edinburgh EH10 5HF
0131 537 6797
BABCP

HAMILTON, Eira
Sexual and Marital Psychotherapist
8 Duddingston Crescent, Edinburgh EH15 3AS
BASMT

HART, Mary A.M.
Hypno-Psychotherapist
3 Sciennes Road, Edinburgh EH9 1LE
0131 668 3051/0131 667 9708 (f)
NRHP

KENNEDY, Helen
Gestalt Psychotherapist
Edinburgh Gestalt Institute, 51 Lothian Road, Edinburgh EH9 1NR
0131 667 6257/0131 228 3841
GPTI

KJELLSTROM, Laila
Psychodrama Psychotherapist
16 Roseneath Place, Edinburgh EH9 1JB
0131 229 3310
BPA

KUNKLER, Jane
Cognitive Behavioural Psychotherapist
Department of Health Psychology, Astley Ainslie Hospital, 133 Grange Loan, Edinburgh EH9 2HL
0131 537 9000 x 49128/0131 667 3454
BABCP

MACNICOL, Annie
Cognitive Behavioural Psychotherapist
Dept. of Psychological Medicine, Royal Infirmary, Edinburgh EH3 9YW
0131 536 2875
BABCP

MCFARLANE, Alison M.
Cognitive Behavioural Psychotherapist
Cullen Centre, 29 Morningside Park, Edinburgh EH10 5HF
0131 537 6797
BABCP

MILTON, Harry
Hypno-Psychotherapist
14 House O'Hill Road, Edinburgh EH4 2AP
0131 332 6363
NRHP

MWELWA, Edward
Hypno-Psychotherapist
4 (2F2) Hermand Terrace, Edinburgh EH11 1QZ
0131 538 0189
CTS

NICOLSON, Elaine
Cognitive Behavioural Psychotherapist
Cullen Centre, Royal Edinburgh Hospital, 29 Morningside Park, Edinburgh EH10 5HF
0131 537 6797
BABCP

ROBINSON, Peter
Cognitive Behavioural Psychotherapist
The Young People's Unit, Royal Edinburgh Hospital, Tipperlinn Road, Edinburgh EH10 5HF
0131 537 6364
BABCP

SHORTER, Bani
Analytical Psychologist-Jungian Analyst
9 South East Circus Place, Edinburgh EH3 6TJ
0131 225 1297
IGAP

SIBLEY, Susan
Child Psychotherapist
17 Ferryfield, Edinburgh EH5 2PR
0131 551 2613
ACP

SMITH, Gerry
Transpersonal Psychotherapist
Tara Rokpa Edinburgh, 250 Ferry Road, Edinburgh EH3 5AN
Felton Cottage, Felton, West Linton, Borders EH46 7AA
01968 660786/0131 552 1431
CTP

STEVEN, David B.
Hypno-Psychotherapist
16 Granville Terrace, Edinburgh EH10 4PQ
0131 229 7823
NRHP

WILLIAMS, Guinevere
Gestalt Psychotherapist
4 East Brighton Crescent, Portobello, Edinburgh EH15 1LR
Edinburgh Gestalt Institute, Teamwork, 51 Lothian Road, Edinburgh EH1 2DJ
0131 657 3496
GPTI

SCOTLAND – FALKIRK

KENNEDY, Kay
Individual and Group Humanistic Psychotherapist
Dalmore, 15 High Station Road, Falkirk FK1 5LP
01324 621930
AHPP

WILSON, Tom C
Cognitive Behavioural Psychotherapist
Westbank Day Clinic, Westbridge Street, Falkirk, Stirlingshire FK1
01324 624111
BABCP

SCOTLAND – FIFE

AGNEW, Joyce
Personal Construct Psychotherapist
Citra, Cupar Road, Ceres, Fife, Scotland KY15 5LP
01334 828340
CPCP

MIDDLETON, Margaret
Hypno-Psychotherapist
Glenesk, 20 Lade Braes, St. Andrews, Fife KY16 9DA
01334 475270
CTS

PETRIE, Clare
Transpersonal Psychotherapist
Earlsneuk, Chapel Green, Earlsferry, Leven, Fife KY9 1AD
01333 330853
CCPE

SCOTLAND – GLASGOW

ANDREW, Alison
Family Therapist
10 Belhaven Terrace, Great Western Road, Glasgow G12
0141 531 6107/0141 531 6106
AFT

BATES, Helen
Family Therapist
12 Skaterigg Drive, Jordanhill, Glasgow G13 1SR
0141 201 9226
AFT

BEGG, E.C.M
Analytical Psychologist-Jungian Analyst
30 Westbourne Gardens, Glasgow G12 9PF
0141 334 8391/0141 334 9214 (f)
IGAP

BROWN, Teresa
Psychodrama Psychotherapist
Scottish Institute of Human Relations, 13 Park Terrace, Glasgow G3 6BY
The McDonald Partnership, 16 Fitzroy Place, Glasgow G3 7RW
0141 204 3455/0141 332 0011
BPA

CARRUTHERS, Barbara
Humanistic Psychotherapist
115 Dowanhill Street, Glasgow G12 9EQ
0141 357 3371
AHPP

CHRISTIE, Jim
Group Analyst
The Garnethill Centre Ltd., 28 Rose Street, Glasgow G3 6RE
0141 333 0730/0141 357 5676
IGA

COIA, Grace
Hypno-Psychotherapist
10 Carment Drive, Glasgow G41 3PP
0141 632 6663
NRHP

FRASER, Douglas A.
Psychoanalytic Psychotherapist
5 Hampden Terrace, Mount Florida, Glasgow G42 9XG
Preston Guild Com.NHS Trust, Dept of Psychotherapy, 1 Albert Road, Fulwood, Preston PR2 8PJ
01772 787197/0141 632 3800
WMIP

HAMILTON, Angela
Psychoanalytic Psychotherapist
The Garnethill Centre, 28 Rose Street, Glasgow G3 6RE
0141 333 0730
LPDO

HAMILTON, Wallace
Child Psychotherapist, Psychoanalytic Psychotherapist
17 Schaw Drive, Bearsden, Glasgow, Scotland G61 3AT
0141 942 1226
ACP

HOGG, Christine Retson
Hypno-Psychotherapist
26 Westbourne Crescent, Bearsden, Glasgow G61 4HD
31 Nasmyth Avenue, Beasden, Glasgow G61 4HD
0141 931 5957/0141 942 5286
NRHP

HUME, Anne J.A.
Cognitive Behavioural Psychotherapist
101 Parkville Drive, Burnside Park, Blantyre, Lanarkshire G72 0LF
01698 711405
BABCP

LINDSAY, Robert
Family Therapist
Dept. of Child and Family Psychotherapy, Knightswood Hospital, Knightswood Road, Glasgow G13 2XG
Glenoonah, Kippey, Stirling SK8 3EW
01786 870 414/0141 531 6107
AFT

MACDONALD, Ross
Hypno-Psychotherapist
Aros, 2 Campbell Drive, Dumbarton G82 3QH
01389 732104
NRHP

MACKINNON, Hetty
Autogenic Psychotherapist
An Airigh, 20 Borden Road, Glasgow
G13 1QX
0141 954 2007(f)/0141 959 3230
BAFAT

MCMASTER, Catherine
Cognitive Psychotherapist
SCOTACS, 201A Bath Street, Glasgow
G2 4HZ
0141 226 4373
BABCP

MOLLESON, John Ivitsky
Cognitive Behavioural Psychotherapist
Scottish Training & Counselling Serv.,
201A Bath Street, Glasgow G2 4HZ
0131 667 4408/0141 226 4373
BABCP

MOODIE, Alastair
Transactional Analysis Psychotherapist
5 Buckingham Terrace, Glasgow,
Scotland G12 8EB
0141 357 6790
ITA

RUSSELL, Wilson
Group Analyst
The Garnethill Centre, 28 Rose Street,
Glasgow G3 6RE
0141 333 0730/0131 447 6038
IGA

SCANLAN, Celia
Psychodrama Psychotherapist
Heather Cottage, The Clachan,
Rosneath, Argyll Bute G84 0RF
0161 445 4399/0161 445 2099
BPA

SHEARER, Anne
Hypno-Psychotherapist
The Phoenix Centre, 201 St. James
Road, Glasgow G4 0NT
c/o Beechgrove, Broughton, By Biggar,
Lanarkshire
01899 830288/0141 553 2353
NRHP

TURNER, Martin S.
Cognitive Behavioural Psychotherapist
Larkfield Centre, Garngaber Avenue,
Lenzie, Glasgow G66 3UG
0141 776 7100
BABCP

SCOTLAND – HIGHLAND

EDMONDSTONE, Yvonne G.
Cognitive Behavioural Psychotherapist
Craig Dunain Hospital, Inverness
IV3 6JU
01463 234001
BABCP

SCOTLAND – LOTHIAN

BIENKOWSKI, Geraldine
Cognitive Behavioural Psychotherapist
Psychology Department, St John's
Hospital, Howden, Livingston, Scotland
EH54 6PP
01506 419666 x 4570
BABCP

BROWN, Thomas M.
Cognitive Behavioural Psychotherapist
St Johns Hospital at Howden,
Livingston, West Lothian EH54 699
01506 419666
BABCP

FOLKER, Sheena
Family Therapist
4 kirkhill Court, Broxburn, West
Lothian EH52 6ES
01506 856943
AFT

HERRMANN, Joan
Child Psychotherapist
The Old Hall, Ormiston, East Lothian,
Scotland EH35 5NJ
0131 556 0924/01875 340536
ACP

MCDONALD, Christina
Transpersonal Psychotherapist
39 West Crescent, East Saltoun, East
Lothian EH34 5EF
01875 341316(f)/01875 341191
CTP

TENNANT, Duncan
Family Therapist
Outpatients 5, St John's Hospital,
Howden Road, West Livingstone,West
Lot EH54 6PP
01506 419666
AFT

SCOTLAND – MORAY

SHERIFFS, Alison
Psychosynthesis Psychotherapist
Sluie Lodge, Dunphail, Forres, Moray,
Scotland IV36 0QG
01309 611 263
AAPP

YOUNG, Courtenay
Humanistic Psychotherapist
The Park, Findhorn, Forres, Moray,
Scotland IV36 OTZ
01309 690251/01309 690974 (f)
AHPP, KI

SCOTLAND – PERTH

DOLAN, Lesley Catherine
Cognitive Behavioural Psychotherapist
Murray Royal Hospital, Perth, Scotland
PH2 7BH
01738 621 151
BABCP

YATES, Kath
Psychodynamic Psychotherapist,
Integrative Psychotherapist
Blairs Farm, Trinity Gask, Madderty,
Auchterarder, Perthshire PH3 1LL
01764 683385
WMIP

SCOTLAND – STIRLING

TURNER, Senga
Transpersonal Psychotherapist
7 Allan Park, Stirling FK8 2QG
01786 465211
CTP

YOUNG, Katherine
Cognitive Behavioural Psychotherapist
20 Kellie Place, Alloa,
Clackmannanshire, Scotland
FK10 2DW
01786 434000 x 7841/01259 314623
BABCP

SHEFFIELD

ALLEN, Penny
Integrative Psychotherapist
415 Fulwood Road, Sheffield S10 3GF
0114 230 5702
SPTI

BARKER, Lily
Psychodynamic Psychotherapist
14 Southbourne Road, Sheffield
S10 2QN
0114 266 2565
HIP

BEARD, Hilary
Psychodynamic Psychotherapist
177 Rustlings Road, Sheffield S11 7AD
0114 268 5884
HIP

BLACKBURN, John
Rational Emotive Behaviour Therapist
Specialist Psychotherapy Services, St. Georges, Winter Street, Sheffield
S3 7ND
0114 271 6901
BABCP

BLACKER, Polly
Psychodynamic Psychotherapist
32 Havelock Street, Sheffield S10 2FP
0114 272 1814
HIP

BOYSAN, Zehra
Analytical Psychotherapist
2 Moorbank Close, Sheffield S10 5TP
0114 230 1050
HIP

BRENNAN, Joady
Personal Construct Psychotherapist
Centre for Psychotherapeutic Studies, University of Sheffield, 16 Claremont Crescent, Sheffield S10 2TA
0114 276 8555 x 4970
CPCP

COLVER, Stephen
Psychoanalytic Psychotherapist
16 Alms Hill Road, Parkhead, Sheffield
S11 9RS
0114 2620364
GUILD

COOPER, Faye
Sexual and Marital Psychotherapist
Whiteley Wood Clinic, Woofinden Road, Sheffield S10 3TL
BASMT

COOPER, Fiona
Psychosynthesis Psychotherapist
2 Edgehill Road, Sheffield S7 1SP
0114 255 1202
AAPP

DAINES, Brian
Psychodynamic Psychotherapist, Sexual and Marital Psychotherapist
Ferndale, 61 Fern Road, Sheffield
S6 5AX
176 Crooksmoor Road, Sheffield
S6 3FS
0114 233 5641/0114 268 2883 (f)
BASMT, YAPP, HIP

DALE, Carole
Psychodrama Psychotherapist
99 Meersbrook Park Road, Sheffield
S8 9FP
0114 258 8088
BPA

DONOVAN, Maxine
Psychodynamic Psychotherapist
c/o Victim Support Sheffield, 69 Division Street, Sheffield S1 4GE
20 Birkendale View, Sheffield S6 3NN
0114 273 1817
HIP

DRUCQUER, Helen
Analytical Psychotherapist, Psychodynamic Psychotherapist
84 Southgrove Road, Sheffield
S10 2NQ
0114 268 5240
HIP

EDWARDS, David
Psychodynamic Psychotherapist
University of Sheffield, Counselling Services, Mushroom Lane S10 2TS
93 Fraser Road, Woodseats, Sheffield
S8 0JU
0114 222 4134/0114 274 9117
HIP

ELLIS, Lynda
Psychoanalytic Psychotherapist
16 East Grove Road, Sheffield
S10 2NN
0114 266 9616
HIP

EMBLETON-TUDOR, Louise
Integrative Psychotherapist
Temenos, 13a Penrhyn Road, Hunter's Bar, Sheffield S11 8UL
0114 266 3931
MC

FITZGERALD, Geariod
Psychoanalytic Psychotherapist
Community Health Sheffield, Brunswick House, 299 Glossop Road, Sheffield S10 2HL
0114 271 6890
HIP

GARLOVSKY, Rita
Psychoanalytic Psychotherapist
41 Oakhill Road, Sheffield S7 1SJ
0114 258 7190
GUILD, HIP

GUDJONSSON, Ingolf
Psychoanalytic Psychotherapist
69 Nether Edge Road, Sheffield
S7 1RW
0113 243 3144
HIP, YAPP

GUITON, Anita
Psychodynamic Psychotherapist
Share Psychotherapy Agency, 176 Crookesmoor Road, Sheffield S6 3FS
John Oram & Associates Psychotherapy Centre, 13 Rustlings Road, Sheffield
S11 7AA
0114 266 3910/0114 268 2883
HIP

HADDOCK, Ray
Group Analyst, Analytical Psychotherapist
108 Totley Brook Road, Dore, Sheffield
S17 3QU
01742 716890/01742 716893 (f)
IGA

HALLAM-JONES, R.A.
Sexual and Marital Psychotherapist
123 Ecclesall Road, Ecclesall, Sheffield
S11 9PJ
BASMT

HART, Carolyn
Child Psychotherapist
Shirle Hill Hospital, 6A Cherry Tree Road, Sheffield S11 9AA
0114 268 4480/0114 271 6860
ACP

HUNT, Patricia A.
Psychodynamic Psychotherapist
Share Psychotherapy Agency, 176 Crookesmoor Road, Sheffield S6 3FS
0114 268 2883
HIP

HUWS, Rhodri
Sexual and Marital Psychotherapist
117 Walkley Street, Sheffield S6 2WT
01633 263388
BASMT

KENDALL, Tim
Psychoanalytic Psychotherapist,
Psychodynamic Psychotherapist
Centre for Psychotherapeutic Studies,
University of Sheffield, 16 Claremont
Crescent, Sheffield S10 2TA
0114 222 2991
HIP, UPA

LIDMILA, Alan
Psychoanalytic Psychotherapist
5 Cliffe House, 10 Whitworth Road,
Ranmoor, Sheffield S10 3HD
University of Sheffield, Centre for
Psychotherapeutic Stud, 16 Claremont
Crescent, Sheffield S10 2TA
0114 222 2981/0114 230 9163
YAPP, HIP

LOFTUS, Patrick A.
Psychodynamic Psychotherapist
114 Industry Street, Walkley, Sheffield
S6 2WX
0114 233 6570
HIP

LOXLEY, David
Psychodynamic Psychotherapist
193 Crimicar Lane, Sheffield S10 4EH
0114 230 5602
HIP

MACASKILL, Norman D.
Cognitive Behavioural Psychotherapist
52 Linden Avenue, Sheffield S8 0GA
Southfield House, 40 Clarendon Road,
Leeds LS2 9PJ
0114 281 7561
BABCP

MACDONALD, Helen F.
Behavioural Psychotherapist
Specialist Psychotherapy Service,
Brunswick House, 299 Glossop Road,
Sheffield S10 2HL
0114 271 6890
BABCP

MACNEILL, Enid
Psychodynamic Psychotherapist,
Psychodrama Psychotherapist
21 Knaresborough Road, Sheffield
S7 2LA
0114 236 4349
BPA, HIP

MAITLIS, Marion
Psychodynamic Psychotherapist,
Psychoanalytic Psychotherapist
13 Park Avenue, Sheffield S10 3EY
0114 266 0888
HIP

MARSHALL, Myra
Psychoanalytic Psychotherapist
11 Rutland Park, Broomhill, Sheffield
S10 2PB
HIP

MCAULEY, John
Analytical Psychotherapist
Share Psychotherapy Agency, 176
Crookesmoor Road, Sheffield S6 3FS
HIP

METTAM, Lisa
Cognitive Behavioural Psychotherapist
Specialist Psychotherapy Services,
Brunswick House, 299 Glossop Road,
Sheffield S10 2HL
0114 234 2332/0114 271 6890
BABCP

MOHAMED, Carol
Psychoanalytic Psychotherapist
136 Crookesmoor Road, Sheffield,
South Yorkshire S6 3FS
WTC

MONACH, Jane
Psychodynamic Psychotherapist
Cocked Hat Cottage, 100 Bolehill Lane,
Crookes, Sheffield S10 1SD
0114 266 7395
HIP

MOORE, Margaret C
Sexual and Marital Psychotherapist
Goatscliff Farm, Stoke Grindleford,
Hope Valley S30 2HW
01433 631259/01433 630420
BASMT

ORAM, John E.D.
Psychodynamic Psychotherapist
12 Montgomery Road, Sheffield
S7 1LQ
John Oram & Associates Psychotherapy
Centre, 13 Rustlings Road, Sheffield
S11 7AA
0114 221 4982/0114 266 3910
HIP

PARRY, Glenys
Cognitive Analytic Therapist
Director of Research & Development,
Comm. Health Sheffield NHS Tru,
Fulwood House, Old Fulwood Rd.,
Sheffield S10 3TH
University of Sheffield, School of Health
&Related Research, Regent Court,
Regent Street, Sheffield S1 4DA
0114 271 6377
ACAT

PERRETT, Angie
Sexual and Marital Psychotherapist
53 Endowood Road, Sheffield S7 2LY
BASMT

PETHEN, Susan
Psychodynamic Psychotherapist
62 Brincliffe Edge Road, Sheffield
S11 9BW
0114 255 1576
HIP

PICKVANCE, Deborah
Psychodynamic Psychotherapist
108 Carr Road, Sheffield S6 2WZ
HIP

PORTEOUS, Louise
Psychodynamic Psychotherapist
151 Chelsea Road, Sheffield S11 9BQ
Sheffield Natural Health Centre, 289
Abbeydale Road, Sheffield S7
0114 258 1644
HIP

RAYNER, Beryl Ann
Psychoanalytic Psychotherapist,
Psychodynamic Psychotherapist
5 Sherwood Chase, Totley Brook Road,
Sheffield S17 3QT
0114 236 2825
HIP

REJAIE, Carol
Psychoanalytic Psychotherapist
12 Lawson Road, Broomhill, Sheffield
S10 5BW
0114 268 6965
UPA

RICKETTS, Thomas N.
Cognitive Behavioural Psychotherapist
299 Glossop Road, Sheffield S10 2HL
0114 271 6890
BABCP

ROBINSON, Felicity
Psychodynamic Psychotherapist
12 Brincliffe Edge Road, Sheffield
S11 9BW
0114 255 2989
HIP

ROSEMARY, Margaret
Gestalt Psychotherapist
3 Strathtay Road, Greystones, Sheffield
S11 7GU
0114 266 0229 (t/f)
GPTI, MET

ROSENFELD, Angela
Group Analyst
78 Carr Road, Walkley, Sheffield
S6 2RW
01742 752157/01742 330523
IGA

SHIPTON, Geraldine
Psychoanalytic Psychotherapist
7 Psalter Lane, Sheffield S11 8YL
Centre for Psychotherapeutic Studies, University of Sheffield,, 16 Claremont Crescent, Sheffield S10 2TA
0114 222 2980/0114 255 4326
HIP

SMITH, Val
Group Analyst
Flat 2, Hopton House, 27 Collegiate Crescent, Sheffield S10 2BJ
01742 660677/0114 268 6429
IGA

TANTAM, Digby
Psychodynamic Psychotherapist, Group Analyst
Centre for Psychotherapeutic Studies, 16 Claremont Crescent, Sheffield S10 2TA
0114 222 2000/2979/0114 275 0026(f)
IGA, NWIDP, UPA

THOMSON, Pat
Psychodynamic Psychotherapist
35 Slayleigh Avenue, Sheffield S10 3RA
0114 230 7471
HIP

TODD, Margaret C
Psychodynamic Psychotherapist
16 Prospect Road, Coal Aston, Dronfield, Sheffield S18 6EA
01246 415 175
HIP

TUDOR, Keith
Transactional Analysis Psychotherapist
13A Penrhyn Road, Hunter's Bar, Sheffield S11 8UL
0114 266 3931
MET, ITA

VAN DEURZEN, Emmy
Existential Psychotherapist
Warden's House, 33 Shore Lane, Sheffield S10 3AY
0114 268 4025
RCSPC, UPA

WILLOWES, Jean
Psychodynamic Psychotherapist
79 Highton Street, Walkley, Sheffield
S6 3TQ
0114 285 3752
HIP

WILSON, Llynwen
Sexual and Marital Psychotherapist
25 Meadow Bank Avenue, Sheffield
S7 1PB
BASMT

WYLIE, Kevan R.
Sexual and Marital Psychotherapist
Whiteley Wood Clinic, Woofinden Road, Sheffield S10 3TL
BASMT

SHROPSHIRE

ARNOLD, Sue
Psychosynthesis Psychotherapist
Willow Cottage, Tallarn Green, Nr. Malpas, Cheshire SY14 7LJ
01948 770 697
AAPP

BLACK, Teresa J.
Psychoanalytic Psychotherapist
Upper House, Buildwas Road, Ironbridge, Salop TF8 7DW
NWIDP

BLISS, Sonia
Psychoanalytic Psychotherapist
31 Port Hill Gardens, Shrewsbury, Shropshire SY3 8SB
01743 232745
WMIP

FOULKES, Michael
Systemic Psychotherapist
14 Greenfields Drive, Bridgenorth, Shropshire WV16 9JR
01782 575723/01782 837736 (f)
FIC

FOX, Margaret
Family Therapist
The Child and Family Service, Bourne House, Radbrook Centre, Radbrook Road, Shrewsbury SY3 9BL
01743 272569/01743 233196
AFT

GOODWILLIE, Gill
Systemic Psychotherapist
'Invergarry', 15 North Hermitage, Belle Vue, Shrewsbury SY3 7JW
01743 249 194
KCC

GRIFFITHS, Tina C
Cognitive Analytic Therapist
102 Luth Hill Road, Bayston Hill, Shropshire SY3 0AT
ACAT

HOAG, Linda M.
Psychoanalytic Psychotherapist (Jungian)
Rose Cottage, Wrockwardine, Nr. Wellington, Telford TF6 5DG
01952 244803
WMIP, GUILD

MATTHEWS, Sharon
Cognitive Behavioural Psychotherapist
Oak Ward, Shelton Hospital, Shropshire Mental Health NHS Trust, Bicton Heath, Shrewsbury SY3 8DN
01743 261276
BABCP

MORGAN, Elizabeth
Sexual and Marital Psychotherapist
70 Kingston Drive, London Road, Shrewsbury, Shropshire SY2 6SJ
01743 354007
BASMT

NUTHALL, Alexander R.
Cognitive Behavioural Psychotherapist
The Mount, 1 Haygate Road, Wellington, Telford, Shropshire
TF1 1QX
01952 641580
BABCP

PURNELL, Chris
Attachment-based Psychoanalytic Psychotherapist
Fern Cottage, 5 St Luke's Road, Doseley, Telford, Shropshire TF4 3BE
01952 503523
CAPP

RATOFF, Tammy
Psychoanalytic Psychotherapist
1 Greyfriars, Bridgenorth, Shropshire
WV16 4JX
01746 768675(t/f)
LCP

SPENCER, Margaret
Psychoanalytic Psychotherapist
44 Underdale Road, Shrewsbury, Shropshire SY2 5DT
01743 232103
WMIP

THORLEY, Helen
Psychoanalytic Psychotherapist
Black Firs, Birks Drive, Ashley Heath, Near Market Drayton, Shropshire TF9 4PQ
01630 672636
LPDO

WARD, Dawn
Hypno-Psychotherapist
61 Stanton Road, Ludlow, Shropshire SY8 2PF
01584 876113
NSHAP

SOMERSET

ALEXANDER, Paul T.
Cognitive Behavioural Psychotherapist
Psychology Department, Taunton & Somerset Hospital, Musgrove Park, Taunton TA1 5DA
01823 333444
BABCP

BODDAERT, Michael
Transpersonal Psychotherapist
'Earlwood', 22 Hexton Road, Glastonbury, Somerset BA6 8HL
01458 830063
CTP

BROUGHTON, Vivian
Gestalt Psychotherapist
Fox Cottage, 49 Witham Friary, Near Frome, Somerset BA11 5HF
The Swan Clinic, Vicarage Street, Warminster, Wiltshire BA12 8JE
01985 217158/01749 850661
GPTI, MET

BURBACH, Frank
Cognitive Behavioural Psychotherapist
Psychology Department, Rosebank, Priory Parks, Wells Somerset BA5 1TH
01749 670445
BABCP

COX, Miranda
Core Process Psychotherapist
Cobblestones, Fore Street, Milverston, Taunton, Somerset TA4 1JX
01823 400152
AAPP

GOTTLIEB, Sue
Psychoanalytic Psychotherapist
Babbs Farm, Westhill Lane, Watchfield, Highbridge, Somerset TA9 4RF
01278 793244
LCP, SIP

GOTTO, Jane
Humanistic and Integrative Psychotherapist
The Terrace, Therapy and Natural Health Centre, 35 Staplegrove Road, Taunton, Somerset TA1 1DU
01823 338968
SPEC

GREGORY, Kirby
Cognitive Analytic Therapist
2 Exeter Close, Burnham on Sea, Somerset TA8 1JF
01278 795406
ACAT

HASKAYNE, Amanda
Integrative Psychotherapist
10 Bluebell Road, Trinity Fields, Weston-Super-Mare BS22 9QJ
01934 513021
RCSPC

HOLDAWAY, Elizabeth
Sexual and Marital Psychotherapist
Godney House, Godney, Nr. Wells, Somerset BA5 1RX
BASMT

HOPKINS, Jill
Psychoanalytic Psychotherapist
Badger's Hay, Lodes Lane, Kingston St. Mary, Taunton TA2 8HU
01823 451656
GUILD, SIP

HOWE, Patricia
Psychosynthesis Psychotherapist
27 Roman Way, Glastonbury, Somerset BA6 8AB
01458 833864
AAPP

LOCKIE, Gisela
Integrative Psychotherapist, Body Psychotherapist
16 Fowler Street, Taunton, Somerset TA2 6JB
01823 323240
CCBP

MITCHELL, John
Gestalt Psychotherapist
Fox Cottage, Witham Friary, Nr. Frome, Somerset BA11 5HF
The Swan Clinic, Vicarage Street, Warminster, Wiltshire BA12 8JE
01985 217158/01749 850661
GPTI, MET

NOWLAN, Kate
Psychoanalytic Psychotherapist
3 West End, Frome, Somerset BA11 3AD
01373 464919
IPC

PARFITT, Will
Psychosynthesis Psychotherapist
27 Roman Way, Glastonbury, Somerset BA6 8AB
01458 833864
AAPP

PERSSON, Rose
Group Analytic Psychotherapist
Ham Manor, Ham Lane, Shepton Mallet, Somerset BA4 5JR
01225 873245/01749 342141
IPC

PROCTER, Harry
Personal Construct Psychotherapist, Family Therapist
Petrel House, Broadway Park, Bridgwater, Somerset TA6 5YA
01278 446909
CPCP, AFT

PROCTOR, Ann
Transpersonal Psychotherapist
Coombe Quarry, Keinton Mandeville, Nr Somerton TA11 6DQ
Coombe Quarry, Keinton Mandeville, Nr Somerton, Somerset TA11 6DQ
01458 223215
CTP

PULLIN, Andrew
Group Analyst
85 Weymouth Road, Frome, Somerset BA11 1HJ
Bath Practice for Group Analysis, 1 Frome Road, Beckington, Near Bath BA3 6TD
01373 472170
IGA

QUARRY, Andrew
Cognitive Behavioural Psychotherapist
Beech Court, Southgate Park, Taunton Road, Bridgwater, Somerset TA6 3LS
01278 444737
BABCP

REIMERS, Sigurd
Family Therapist
179 Cheddon Road, Taunton, Somerset TA2 7AH
01823 272043
FIC

ROBINSON, Louise
Humanistic and Integrative Psychotherapist
38 Belvedere Road, Taunton, Somerset TA1 1HD
01823 353009
MC

SANDERS, Jane
Core Process Psychotherapist
93 Roman Way, Glastonbury, Somerset
01458 833382/01458 833378
AAPP

SCOTT, Judy
Integrative Psychotherapist
The Old School House, Church Street, Croscombe, Near Wells BA5 3QS
01749 343069
MET

SCOVELL, Michael
Psychoanalytic Psychotherapist
63 Summerland Avenue, Minehead, Somerset TA24 5BW
01643 706675
SIP

STEVENS, Yvonne
Cognitive Analytic Therapist
The Carthouse, Crossways Farm, Heath House, Wedmore BS28 4UG
01934 713557(f)/01934 713693
ACAT

TAIT, Adrian
Psychoanalytic Psychotherapist
Flat 3, 62 Trull Road, Taunton, Somerset TA1 4QL
01823 321588
GUILD

THOMAS, Madeleine
Cognitive Behavioural Psychotherapist
Ashford Lodge, Cannington, Bridgwater, Somerset TA5 2NL
01823 432136/01278 671595
BABCP

WEDDERKOPP, Abigail
Psychoanalytic Psychotherapist
St Michael's, 3 Upper High Street, Tauton, Somerset TA1 3PX
01823 353409/01823 327917
SIP

WELLS, Roger
Psychoanalytic Psychotherapist
Prioryfield House, 20 Canon Street, Taunton, Somerset TA1 1SW
Argyle House, New Buildings Lane, Gandy Street, Exeter EX4 3LS
01823 323363/01392 494466
GUILD

WILLIAMS, Nigel
Humanistic and Integrative Psychotherapist
38 Belvedere Road, Taunton, Somerset TA1 1HD
01823 353009
MC

WINDLE, Ruth
Psychoanalytic Psychotherapist, Analytical Psychologist-Jungian Analyst
25 Vallis Way, Frome, Somerset BA11 3BH
Studio E, 49 The Avenue, London NW61
0181 459 5442/01373 467 661
IPC, AJA

YOUNG, Raymond
Transpersonal Psychotherapist
25 Chamberlain Street, Wells, Somerset BA5 2PQ
CCPE

ZEAL, Paul
Psychoanalytic Psychotherapist
12 Elm Grove, Taunton, Somerset TA1 1EG
01823 323099/01823 323860 (f)
PA, SIP

STAFFORDSHIRE

ADAMS, Megan
Hypno-Psychotherapist
Hawthorn Cottage, Church Farm, Church Road, Dosthill, Tamworth, Staffs B77 1PU
01827 281233
NSHAP

ANEES, Nabil
Psychoanalytic Psychotherapist
3 Cooke Close, Penkridge, Stafford ST19 5SL
31 Compton Road, Gemini House, Wolverhampton
WMIP

BREEZE, Graham
Integrative Psychotherapist
87 Basford Bridge Lane, Cheddleton, Nr. Leek, Staffordshire ST13 7EQ
01538 361193
NSAP

BROUGH, Sue
Psychoanalytic Psychotherapist, Integrative Psychotherapist
38 Gable Croft, Lichfield, Staffordshire WS14 9RY
01543 301050
WMIP

CHALLIS, Suzy
Psychoanalytic Psychotherapist
Department of Clinical Psychology, City General Hospital, Newcastle Road, Stoke-on-Trent ST4 6QG
01782 552073
LPDO

CLEGG, Alison
Sexual and Marital Psychotherapist
The Dower House, Bonehill, Tamworth, Staffordshire B78 3HX
BASMT

CORKER, Enid
Psychoanalytic Psychotherapist
55 The Avenue, Hartshill, Stoke-on-Trent ST4 6BT
01782 662655
AGIP

COX, Margaret
Psychoanalytic Psychotherapist
18, The Charters, Lichfield WS13 7LX
01543 263916
WMIP

CRISP, Jennifer
Psychodynamic Psychotherapist
Richmond Complex, Richmond Terrace, Shelton, Stoke on Trent ST1 4ND
WMIP

DUNN, Elizabeth
Psychodynamic Psychotherapist
The Mount, Longton Road, Barlaston, Stoke on Trent ST12 9AA
01782 372424
ULDPS

GHENT, Rita
Integrative Psychotherapist
7 Tolkien Way, Hartshill Road, Hartshill, Stoke on Trent, Staffordshire
01782 849474
NSAP

GOODMAN, Mary
Family Therapist
Greenlow Bank, Butterton, Nr. Leek, Staffordshire ST13 7TD
01538 304340
AFT

GRAY, Pete
Family Therapist
33 Church Lane, Oulton, Nr. Stone, Staffs ST15 8UB
AFT

GREGORY, Kayt
Integrative Psychotherapist
28 Lichfield Drive, Great Haywood, Stafford ST18 0SX
01889 882435
NSAP

GRIFFITH, E Anne
Psychoanalytic Psychotherapist
59 Stockwood Road, Seabridge, Newcastle, Staffs ST5 3LQ
01782 611972
UPA

HALLARD, Sharon
Group Analyst
3 Bodkin House, Stanley Street, Leek ST13 5HG
IGA

HORROCKS, Pam
Psychodynamic Psychotherapist
36 Station Road, Alsager, Stoke on Trent ST7 2PP
01270 877284
ULDPS

MOLONEY, Paul
Cognitive Behavioural Psychotherapist
29 Main Street, Alrewas, Burton on Trent, Staffordshire DE13 7AA
Sutton CMHT, Patrick House, 5 Maney Corner, Birmingham Road, Sutton Coldfield B7 1QL
0121 685 6685/01283 791754
BABCP

MOYES, Theresa
Cognitive Behavioural Psychotherapist
The Chartley Centre, The Foundation NHS Trust, Corporation Street, Stafford ST16 3AG
01785 57888 x 5656
BABCP

NEWELL, Adrian
Cognitive Psychotherapist
Clinical Psychology Service, Foundation NHS Trust, Corporation Street, Stafford ST16 3AG
01785 57888 x 5429/0121 354 1392
BABCP

OSBORN, James
Family Therapist
Child & Fam.Consultation Centre, 161 Eccleshall Road, Stafford ST16 1PD
01785 222708
FIC

REAGAN, Catherine
Integrative Psychotherapist
18 Hartington Street, Wolstanton, Newcastle-under-Lyme, Staffordshire ST5 8DR
01782 866973
NSAP

WHEELEY, Shirley
Psychoanalytic Psychotherapist (Jungian)
70 Fecknam Way, Lichfield, Staffs WS13 6AN
01543 264801
WMIP, GUILD

WILES, Margaret
Integrative Psychotherapist
18 Cornwall Avenue, Clayton, Newcastle under Lyme, Staffordshire ST5 3DJ
01782 614222
NSAP

SUFFOLK

ALLEN, Tessa
Psychoanalytic Psychotherapist
63 Victoria Road, Woodbridge, Suffolk IP12 1EL
01394 388654
NWIDP

BUCKLER, Jackie
Sexual and Marital Psychotherapist
Pilgrims, Powney Street, Milden, Lavenham IP7 7AL
BASMT

CRAIB, Ian
Group Analytic Psychotherapist
Mill House, Kitchen Hill, Bulmer Road, Sudbury, Suffolk CO10 7EZ
01787 310210
LCP

CULLUM, Sylvia
Sexual and Marital Psychotherapist
Briar Hill, Aldringham, Leiston, Suffolk IP16 4QL
01728 452442
BASMT

FAULL, Keith
Family Therapist
46 Oxford Road, Ipswich, Suffolk IP4 1NL
01473 211700
AFT

FRANCES, Jane
Humanistic Psychotherapist
1 The Row, Long Thurlow, Great Ashfield, Bury St. Edmunds, Suffolk IP31 3JH
01359 259654
AHPP

GRAHAM, Hilary
Family Therapist
29 Benhall Green, Benhall, Saxmundham, Suffolk IP17 1HL
01728 602563
AFT

HUGHES, Linda
Humanistic Psychotherapist
Fox Hall, The Croft, Bures, Suffolk CO8 5JB
01787 228402(f)/01787 227195
AHPP

KEITH, Charlotte
Hypno-Psychotherapist
The Old School House, Westleton Saxmundham, Suffolk IP17 3AD
01728 648650
NSHAP

MCCABE, Ruth
Group Analyst
Threeways,, Coles Hill, Wenhaston, Halesworth Suffolk IP19 9DS
01502 478 295
IGA

MCCORMICK, Elizabeth Wilde
Cognitive Analytic Therapist, Transpersonal Psychotherapist
East Friars, Dunwich, Nr. Saxmundham, Suffolk IP17 3DW
19 Chester Mews, London SW1
01728 648672/0171 2358276/01728 648771 (f)
CTP, ACAT

MOHAN, Terence
NLP Psychotherapist
20 Nelson Road, Bury St. Edmunds, Suffolk IP33 3AG
01284 701505
ANLP

RANSOME, Helen
Psychoanalytic Psychotherapist
31 Crown Street, Bury St. Edmunds, Suffolk IP33 1QU
01284 769205
GUILD

READER, Frances
Sexual and Marital Psychotherapist
The Old Rectory, 100 Seckford Street, Woodbridge, Suffolk IP12 4LZ
BASMT

VAIZEY, Philippa
Integrative Psychotherapist
Dragon Tye, Church Street, Belchamp St.Paul, Sudbury, Suffolk CO10 7DJ
01787 278704
CTP

WHITTAKER, Ruth
Sexual and Marital Psychotherapist
Low Farm, Westleton, Saxmundham, Suffolk IP17 3BT
BASMT

WOOD-BEVAN, Martyn
Group Analytic Psychotherapist
Ipswich Psychotherapy & Counselling Centre, 10 St. Margaret's Green, Ipswich, Suffolk IP4 2BS
St. Augustine's Psychotherapy Practice, 26 St. Augustine's Street, Norwich, Norfolk NR3 2BZ
01473 216559/01603 633791
IPC

WRIGHT, Kenneth
Psychoanalytic Marital Psychotherapist
Slaney House, Magdalen Road, Hadleigh, Suffolk IP7 5AD
The Oak Hospital, Milend, Colchester, Essex CO4 5XR
01473 828976/01206 263004 (f)
TMSI

SURREY

AIRD, Eileen
Psychoanalytic Psychotherapist
32 Westfield Road, Surbiton, Surrey KT6 4EL
0181 390 5705
NAAP

ASTOR, Bronwen
Psychoanalytic Psychotherapist
Tuesley Manor, Godalming, Surrey GU7 1UD
01483 417281/01483 420415 (f)
AGIP, GCP, FIP

ATKINS, Lorna
Family Therapist
25 Mayflower Drive, Yately, Surrey, GU46 7RR
01252 876931
AFT

BAKER, Moke
Psychoanalytic Psychotherapist
59 Hillside Road, Ashtead, Surrey KT21 1RZ
01372 275885/01372 278412 (f)
IPC

BAYLEY, Eva
Psychosynthesis Psychotherapist
125 Addison Road, Guildford, Surrey GU1 3QE
01483 31552
AAPP

BEER, Margaret
Psychoanalytic Psychotherapist
7 Fabyc House, Cumberland Road, Kew Gardens, Surrey TW9 3HH
0181 940 7353
IPC

BENJAMIN, Joan E
Psychoanalytic Psychotherapist
The Roses, Farnham Lane, Surrey GU27 1HA
01428 644605
AGIP

BENNETT, Margaret
Family Therapist
285 Kings Road, Kingston, Surrey KT2 5JJ
Child Adolescent & Family Centre, Elm House, 84 Ewell Road, Surbiton
0181 390 8151/0181 546 9785
IFT

BLACKBURNE, Vivien
Psychoanalytic Psychotherapist
36 Cambrian Road, Richmond, Surrey TW10 6JQ
0181 332 9834
LCP

BLACKWOOD, Renate
Psychoanalytic Psychotherapist
7 Esher Park Avenue, Esher, Surrey KT10 9NP
01372 462852
LCP, GCP, IPC

BLAIR, George
Integrative Psychotherapist
Flat 6, 6 Uxbridge Road, Kingston upon Thames KT1 2LL
0181 974 6127
CCBP

BOA, Cherry
Cognitive Analytic Therapist
3 Holmesdale Road, Kew Gardens, Richmond, Surrey TW9 3JZ
0181 940 1501
ACAT

BOA, Quint
Integrative Psychotherapist
300 Kings Road, Kingston, Surrey KT2 5JL
0181 546 5190
RCSPC

BOLTON, Jan
Systemic Psychotherapist
Child & Family Consultation Service, 11 Church Road, Frimley, Camberley GU16 5AD
The Barn, 26 High Street, Odiham, Hants RG29 1LG
01483 782900
KCC

BOWER, Margaret
Family Therapist
5 Old Compton Lane, Farnham, Surrey GU9 8BS
01252 722556
AFT

BRASSINGTON, Pauline
Sexual and Marital Psychotherapist
Maldon Lodge, Crawley Ridge, Camberley, Surrey GU15 2AD
01276 27571
BASMT

BROADBENT, Sara
Psychoanalytic Psychotherapist
4 Dynevor Road, Richmond, Surrey TW10 6PF
0181 332 0181 (f)/0181 940 2228
IPSS

BROWN, Gillian A.
Family Psychotherapist
29 Mountside, Guildford, Surrey
GU2 5JD
01483 504360
AFT

BROWNE, Val
Psychoanalytic Psychotherapist
22 Ruskin Avenue, Kew, Richmond,
Surrey TW9 4DJ
0181 878 9803
IPC

BUCHANAN, Sarah-Jill
Autogenic Psychotherapist
Lanercost, Lynx Hill, East Horsley,
Surrey KT24 5AX
01483 284497
BAFAT

BUKOVICS-HEILLER, Birgit
Transactional Analysis Psychotherapist,
Integrative Psychotherapist
More House, 13 Warwicks Bench,
Guildford, Surrey GU1 3SZ
34 Sheen Road, Richmond, Surrey
TW9 1AW
01483 574 304 (t/f)
MET, ITA

BURKEMAN, Fiona
Sexual and Marital Psychotherapist
Hurston House, Stoke Road, Kingston,
Surrey KT2 7NX
0181 949 6714
BASMT

BURNS-LUNDGREN, Eva
Cognitive Analytic Therapist
Kingston University Student Services,
Health & Counselling Section, Penrhyn
Road, Kingston upon Thames KT1 2EE
0181 547 7178(f)/0181 547 7204
ACAT

BUSH, Malcolm
Sexual and Marital Psychotherapist
35 Crossways, South Croydon, Surrey
CR2 8JQ
BASMT

CARR, Brede
Psychoanalytic Psychotherapist
9 Chepstow Rise, Croydon, Surrey
CR0 5LX
0181 667 0970
IPC

CARROLL, Helen
Humanistic Psychotherapist
25A St. Barnabas Road, Sutton, Surrey
SM1 4NP
0181 643 1439
AHPP

CHANDLER, Diana
Psychosynthesis Psychotherapist
9 Basil Gardens, Shirley Oaks Village,
Croydon CR0 8XD
0181 656 9209
AAPP

CHANNON, Michael
Psychoanalytic Psychotherapist
Flat 2 Fabyc House, Cumberland Road,
Kew, Richmond, Surrey TW9 3HH
0181 940 1092
IPC

CHIMERA, Kathleen
Family Psychotherapist, Systemic
Psychotherapist
39 Church Walk, Leatherhead, Surrey
KT22 8HH
0411 731138/01372 376 577
IFT

CHINOY, Freni
Child Psychotherapist
Sutton Child & Family Clinic, Robin
Hood Lane Health Centre, Camden
Road, Sutton, Surrey SM1 2SH
0181 770 6781/0181 288 1207 (f)
ACP

CHURCH, John
Cognitive Behavioural Psychotherapist
The Counselling Concern, 66 Avenue
Road, Belmont, Sutton, Surrey SM2 6JB
Balham Health Centre, 120 Bedford
Hill, Balham, London SW12
0181 715 4547/0958 651 322
BABCP

CLARK, Margaret
Psychoanalytic Psychotherapist
11 The Broadway, Manor Lane, Sutton,
Surrey SM1 4BU
26 Woodcote Avenue, Wallington,
Surrey SM6 0QY
0181 661 0007
IPC

CLAXTON, Brenda
Integrative Psychotherapist
8 High Beech, South Croydon
CR2 7QB
0181 686 1694
MC

COHN, Hans W.
Existential Psychotherapist
7 Fabyc House, Cumberland Road,
Kew, Surrey TW9 3HH
0181 940 3748
RCSPC

COLDICOTT, Tim
Family Therapist
The White Cottage, Hamlash Lane,
Frensham, Surrey GU10 3AU
01252 792 609
AFT

COOMBES, Clare
Primal Psychotherapist
64 Montacute Road, Morden, Surrey
SM4 6RL
0181 640 7665
LAPP

COOPER, Jane
Gestalt Psychotherapist
67 Southdown Road, Hersham,
Walton-on-Thames, Surrey KT12 4PJ
01932 246 407
SPTI

COPSEY, Nigel
Humanistic Psychotherapist
30 Devon Road, Merstham, Surrey
RH1 3EU
01737 789824/01737 642522
AHPP

DAVENPORT, Hilary
Psychodrama Psychotherapist
4 Bradstone Brook Cottages, New
Road, Chilworth GU4 8LS
01483 504882
BPA

DAVIES, Ann
Psychoanalytic Psychotherapist
The Old Dog Kennel, Hill House,
Woodside Road, Chiddingfold, Surrey
GU8 4RF
01428 683102
AGIP, GCP

DAWSON, Neil
Family Psychotherapist
10 Grena Gardens, Richmond, Surrey
TW9 1XP
0171 704 9620 (f)/0171 704 6112
IFT

DAY, Laurie
Integrative Psychotherapist
34 St. Stephens Avenue, Ashtead,
Surrey KT21 1PL
01372 272670
MET

DE BERKER, Patricia
Psychoanalytic Psychotherapist
Ferndown Cottage, 3 Hillier Road,
Guildford, Surrey GU1 2JG
01483 504554
LCP, GCP, FIP

DE BERKER, Paul
Psychoanalytic Psychotherapist
Ferndown Cottage, 3 Hillier Road,
Guildford, Surrey GU1 2JG
01483 504554
LCP, GCP, BAP

DE WITT, Jacqueline
Systemic Psychotherapist
8 Highclere Road, New Malden, Surrey
KT3 3HJ
KCC

DHILLON, Harbrinder
Integrative Psychotherapist
Corner Cottage, Guildford Road,
Ottershaw, Surrey KT16 9RU
01932 874902 (t/f)
MET

DODSWORTH, Evelyn
Sexual and Marital Psychotherapist
8 Croham Close, South Croydon,
Surrey CR2 0DA
BASMT

DOOLEY, Pat
Psychoanalytic Psychotherapist
43 Guildford Road, Croydon, Surrey
CR0 2HL
7 Woburn Close, Frimley, Camberley,
Surrey GU16 5NU
0181 683 1041/01276 506301
IPC

DOWLING, Deirdre
Child Psychotherapist
Cassel Hospital, Ham Common,
Richmond, Surrey TW10 7JF
0181 390 4548/0181 940 8181
ACP

DUBINSKY, Alexandre
Child Psychotherapist
Richmond Child & Family Consultation
Centre, Windham Road Clinic,
Windham Road, Richmond TW9 2HP
0181 940 4775/0171 794 5047
ACP

DUCKHAM, Jennifer
Psychoanalytic Psychotherapist
(Jungian)
7 Upper Park Road, Kingston-upon-
Thames, Surrey KT2 5LB
0181 546 4173
IGA

DUNCAN, Sally
Sexual and Marital Psychotherapist
1 George Denyer Close, Pathfields,
Haslemere, Surrey GU27 2BH
BASMT

DURBAN, Ann
Transpersonal Psychotherapist
Omega, Shaftesbury Road, Bisley,
Surrey GU24 9ER
01483 799277
CCPE

DYKES, Andrea
Analytical Psychologist-Jungian Analyst
Fox Glade, Bunch Lane, Haslemere,
Surrey GU27 1ET
01428 652363
AJA

EDELEANU, Andrea K
Cognitive Behavioural Psychotherapist
Dept. Comm. Health Psychology,
Buryfields Clinic, Lawn Road,
Guildford, Surrey GU2 5AZ
01483 783344/01483 783399 (f)
BABCP

EVANS, Ray
Personal Construct Psychotherapist
6 Fabyc House, 8 -14 Cumberland
Road, Kew, Richmond, Surrey
TW9 3HH
0181 940 1597
CPCP

EVANS, Tricia
Sexual and Marital Psychotherapist
38 Blackborough Road, Reigate, Surrey
RH2 7BX
01737 240952
BASMT

FAWKES, Liz
Cognitive Analytic Therapist
Bethany, Snowdenham Lane, Bramley,
Guildford GU5 ODB
c/o Psychological Therapies Service,
Dept of Psychiatry,, Royal South Hants
Hospital, Southampton
01438 894021/01703 634288 ext 2527
ACAT

FELIX, Susan
Sexual and Marital Psychotherapist
Tilewood, Seale Lane, Seale, Farnham,
Surrey GU10 1LE
01252 782509
BASMT

FIELD, Kate
Psychoanalytic Psychotherapist
31 Havelock Road, Croydon, Surrey
CR0 6QQ
0181 656 3666/0181 654 1566
GUILD

FRANCIS, Anne M.
Psychoanalytic Psychotherapist
1 Orchard Close, Epsom Road,
Guildford, Surrey GU1 2PR
01483 567688
AGIP, GCP, FIP

FREEMAN, Pat
Family Therapist
5 Shaftesbury Road, Richmond upon
Thames, Surrey TW9 2LD
0181 948 7197
AFT

FURST, Lena
Psychoanalytic Psychotherapist
313 Ewell Road, Surbiton, Surrey
KT6 7BX
Bournewood NHS Trust, ACU,
Holloway Hill, Chertsey, Surrey
KT16 0AE
01932 872010/0181 390 7800
BAP

GARDNER, Philippa
Cognitive Analytic Therapist
12 Mayfield Road, Weybridge, Surrey
KT13 8XD
01932 827374
ACAT

GLAISTER, Brian
Cognitive Behavioural Psychotherapist
135 Foxley Lane, Purley, Surrey
CR8 3HR
0181 660 7465
BABCP

GOTTESMAN, Ewa
Group Analyst
'Foxbreak, 28 Courts Mount Road, Haslemere, Surrey GU27 2PP
01428 642483
IGA

GOWER, Myrna
Family Therapist
Cranford, 14 The Crest, Surbiton, Surrey KT5 8JZ
0181 390 6002/0181 399 2012
AFT

GRAYSON, Juliet
NLP Psychotherapist
268 Canbury Park Road, Kingston, Surrey KT2 6LG
0181 974 5573
ANLP

GRIMSHAW, Francoise
Personal Construct Psychotherapist
Alternatives, 8 Cosdach Avenue, Wallington, Surrey SM6 9RA
0181 288 2796
CPCP

HART, Azina
Systemic Psychotherapist
55 Aveley Lane, Farnham, Surrey GU9 8PS
0973 695 884/01252 710 427
KCC

HASHEMI, Beth
Psychoanalytic Psychotherapist
7 Nightingale Road, Guildford, Surrey GU1 1ER
01483 563135/01483 579458 (f)
IPC, GCP, FIP

HASLER-WINTER, Susan
Group Analyst
Coniston, 25 Bodley Road, New Malden, Surrey KT3 5QD
IGA

HEATLEY, John
Group Analyst
4 Pine Cottages, 174 Forest Road, Liss, Surrey GU3 7BX
IGA

HEAVENS, Anita
Psychoanalytic Psychotherapist
60 Melfort Road, Thornton Heath, Surrey CR7 7RL
0181 684 3579
AGIP

HEDINGER-FARRELL, Korinna
Body Psychotherapist, Integrative Psychotherapist
36 Woodbines Avenue, Kingston, Surrey KT1 2AY
0181 255 3468
CCBP

HELM, Caroline
Child Psychotherapist
40 Park Road, Hampton Wick, Surrey KT1 4AS
0181 541 4615 (f)/0181 977 2950
ACP

HENLEY, June
Family Therapist
Walwood House, Park Road, Banstead, Surrey SM7 3ER
01737 352626
IFT

HEWETT, Rachael
Transactional Analysis Psychotherapist
13 Cambrian Road, Richmond, Surrey TW10 6JQ
ITA, MET

HOLVE, Harriet
Psychoanalytic Psychotherapist
11 Littleworth Common Road, Esher, Surrey KT10 9UE
GCP

HOPWOOD, Jean
Analytical Psychotherapist
Waverley, Somerswey, Shalford, Guildford GU4 8EQ
01483 568669
GCP

HOPWOOD, Michael
Analytical Psychotherapist
Waverley, Somerswey, Shalford, Guildford GU4 8EQ
4 Junction Place, Praed Street, London W2 1RG
0171 723 3584/01483 568669
GCP

HOUGHTON, Christine
Integrative Psychotherapist
3 Locke King Road, Weybridge Road, Surrey KT13 0SY
01932 844478
MET, GPTI

HOWELL, Sylvia
Transpersonal Psychotherapist
South West London and Surrey
0181 748 3722
CCPE

HUDSON, Marjorie
Psychoanalytic Psychotherapist
19 Downsview Gardens, Dorking, Surrey RH4 2DX
01306 888919/01306 888281 (f)
IPC, GUILD

HUSSAIN, Fakhir
Integrative Psychotherapist
7, Kingswood Court, Marchmont Road, Richmond, Surrey TW10 6EU
0181 948 4551
MC

HYDE, Dennis
Integrative Psychotherapist
32 Amis Avenue, New Haw, Addlestone, Surrey KT15 3ET
01932 345526
MC

INGHAM, Nida
Autogenic Psychotherapist, Transpersonal Psychotherapist
Heath Cottage, Pitch Hill, Ewhurst, Nr. Cranleigh, Surrey GU6 7NP
Neal's Yard Therapy Rooms, 2 Neal's Yard, London WC2H 9DP
0171 379 7662/01483 277333
CCPE, BAFAT

JEFFERIES, J.I.
Psychodrama Psychotherapist
15 Audley Road, Richmond, Surrey TW10 6EY
0181 948 5595
BPA

JESSON, Alison
Transactional Analysis Psychotherapist
85 Fairfield Drive, Dorking, Surrey RH4 1JG
MET, ITA

JONATHAN, Arthur
Existential Psychotherapist
'The Jays', 27 Aultone Way, Sutton, Surrey SM1 3LD
0171 487 7406/0181 641 1601
RCSPC

JONES, Alan
Humanistic Psychotherapist
3 Bushey Road, Sutton, Surrey SM1 1QR
0181 641 1792
AHPP

JONES, Peggy
Psychoanalytic Psychotherapist
52 The Vineyard, Richmond, Surrey
TW10 6AT
0181 948 1083
IPC, SAP

KEITH, Joyce
Sexual and Marital Psychotherapist
The Links House, The Warren,
Ashstead, Surrey KT21 2SN
01372 275703
BASMT

LAFON, Robert
Family Therapist
36 Hardman Road, Kingston upon
Thames, Surrey KT2 6RH
Ashwood Centre, Stonemason Court,
Cemetery Pales, Brookwood Woking
GU24 0BL
0181 549 1922/01483 487979
IFT

LAKE, Moira
Gestalt Psychotherapist
11 St. John's Road, Kingston-on-
Thames, Surrey KT1 4AN
0181 943 5507
GPTI

LAUCHLAN, Sheila
Systemic Psychotherapist
3 Weston Avenue, Thames Ditton,
Surrey KT7 0NB
0181 398 8572
KCC

LAW, Susan
Integrative Psychotherapist, Body
Psychotherapist
Flat 6, 6 Uxbridge Road, Kingston -
upon-Thames KT1 2LL
0181 974 6127
CCBP

LAWSON, Christine
Psychoanalytic Psychotherapist
19 The Vineyard, Richmond, Surrey
TW10 6AQ
PA

LIEBERMAN, Stuart
Family Therapist
The Lynbrook Priory Hospital,
Chobham Road, Knaphill, Woking,
Surrey GU21 2QF
Ridgewood Centre, Old Bisley Road,
Frimley, Camberley GU16 5QE
01276 678298/01483 489211
AFT

LINGARD, Shirley Ruth
Systemic Psychotherapist
Rosemead,Churt, Nr. Farnham, Surrey
GU10 2NX
KCC

LLOWELLYN, Martha
Biodynamic Psychotherapist
103 Richmond Hall Court, Richmond,
Surrey TW10 6BG
0181 940 4726
BTC

LOOMS, Suzanne
NLP Psychotherapist
18 Southcote Road, Croydon
CR2 OEQ
0181 651 5898(t/f)
ANLP

LOVETT-DARBY, Linda
Transpersonal Psychotherapist
Rua, 66 Reigate Road, Ewell, Surrey
KT17 3DT
0181 786 7664
CCPE

LUND, Leslie Ann
Integrative Psychotherapist
'Suncroft', 3 Norrels Ride, East
Horsley, Surrey KT24 5EH
01483 281435/01483 285905
RCSPC

LYNCH, Valerie
Psychoanalytic Psychotherapist
2 Church Court, Foxenden Road,
Guildford, Surrey GU1 4DY
GCP, LCP

MACKENNA, Christopher
Analytical Psychologist-Jungian Analyst,
Psychoanalytic Psychotherapist
Hascombe Rectory, Godalming, Surrey
GU8 4JA
01483 208362
GCP

MANICOM, Hilary
Systemic Psychotherapist
Kingsdown, 112 Orchard Road,
Sanderstead, Surrey CR2 9LQ
0181 651 5611
KCC

MAPLE, Norma Anderson
Cognitive Analytic Therapist, Group
Analyst
25 Burlington Avenue, Kew, Richmond,
Surrey TW9 4DF
0181 878 5244/0181 876 3977
ACAT, IGA

MARSHALL, Janet
Autogenic Psychotherapist
12 Churchfields Avenue, Weybridge,
Surrey KT13 9YA
01932 821721
BAFAT

MARSHALL, Jill
Hypno-Psychotherapist
6 Perryfield Way, Richmond, Surrey
TW10 7SP
The Putney Natural Therapy Clinic, 11
Montserrat Road, Putney, London
SW15
0181 789 2548/0181 948 1573
NRHP

MARSHALL, Levana
Group Analyst
4 Queen's Rise, Richmond, Surrey
TW10 6HL
0181 878 0723/0181 876 3268
IGA

MARSHALL, Vivien
Psychoanalytic Psychotherapist
29 Dale Road, Purley, Surrey CR8 2ED
0181 668 2148
IPC

MARTIN, Gloria
Systemic Psychotherapist
Clinical Psychology Department, 84
Ewell Road, Kingston upon Thames,
Surrey KT6 6EX
0181 390 8445
KCC

MAXWELL, Brian
Group Analyst
98 Leatherhead Road, Chessington,
Surrey KT9 2HY
0181 397 3971
IGA

MAYNERD, Cynthia
Family Psychotherapist, Family
Therapist
15 Smoke Lane, Reigate, Surrey
RH2 7HJ
Stepping Stones, Cotswold House,
Sutton Hospital, Sutton SM2 5NF
01737 242051
AFT

MCCARRY, Nicola
Systemic Psychotherapist
180 Acre Road, Kingston upon
Thames, Surrey KT2 6EU
0181 549 7186/0181 255 0376(f)
KCC

MELLER, Carolyn
Sexual and Marital Psychotherapist
52 Park Hill Road, Wallington, Surrey
SM6 0SB
0181 669 0805
BASMT

MILLS, Nigel
Cognitive Behavioural Psychotherapist
Department of Psychology, Horsham
Hospital, Hurst Road, Horsham
RH1 2DR
01323 811469
BABCP

MILTON, Martin
Integrative Psychotherapist
Dept. of Psychology, University of
Surrey, Guildford, Surrey GU2 5XH
0171 289 5201/01483 259176
RCSPC

MITCHELL, Diana
Existential Psychotherapist
32 Cambridge Road, Walton-on-
Thames, Surrey KT12 2DP
01932 225599/0958 3724
RCSPC

MORICE, Michael
Child Psychotherapist
Child and Family Consultation Service,
Richmond Royal Hospital, Kew Foot
Road, Richmond, Surrey TW10 6EF
0181 940 4199/0181 355 1984
ACP

MORRISON, Lesley
Psychoanalytic Psychotherapist
The Cottage, 27 Burghley Avenue,
New Malden Surrey KT3 4SW
0181 949 5628/0181 949 2663 (f)
IPC

MOUNTJOY, Lesleen
Hypno-Psychotherapist
16 Middle Bourne Lane, Lower Bourne,
Farnham, Surrey GU10 3NE
01252 725574
NRHP

MUDARIKIRI, Maxwell
Systemic Psychotherapist
52 Mann Close, Croydon, Surrey
CR0 1TQ
0181 667 9221
KCC

MYCROFT-MILES, June
Sexual and Marital Psychotherapist
The Flint House, Church Road,
Caterham, Surrey CR3 5RA
01883 348497
BASMT

NATH, Krish
Cognitive Behavioural Psychotherapist
72 Chaffers Mead, Ashtead, Surrey
KT21 1NH
01372 278831/0831 425712
BABCP

NICHOLS, Hamish
Integrative Psychotherapist
Flat 2, Berrylands Lodge, No 2, The
Avenue, Surbiton KT5 8JQ
0181 390 1924
MET

O'BRIEN, Pat
Family Psychotherapist
'Corner Cottage', Abinger Lane,
Abinger Common, Dorking, Surrey
RH5 6JH
Child Family Consultation Services,
Buryfields Clinic, 61 Buryfields,
Guilford GU2 5AZ
0181 725 5055/01306 730818
IFT

O'DELL, Tricia
Psychoanalytic Psychotherapist
Lichfield, 161 New Haw Road,
Addlestone, Weybridge, Surrey
KT15 2DP
01932 851897/01932 850661(f)
IPC, GCP, FIP

O'DWYER, Annegret
Integrative Psychotherapist
9 Westbury Avenue, Claygate, Surrey
KT10 0DW
01372 465039
MET

O'NEILL, Christopher J.
Hypno-Psychotherapist
14 Chapelfields, Charterhouse Road,
Godalming, Surrey GU7 2BS
Brooke Hall, Charterhouse,
Godalming, Surrey GU7 2DX
01483 291671/01483 414437
NSHAP

OLDMAN, David
Psychoanalytic Marital Psychotherapist
5 Buckland Court, Bletchworth, Surrey
RH3 7EA
The Counselling Partnership, 5 Albert
Mansions, Luxborough Street, London
W1M 3LN
0171 487 3766/01737 844079
TMSI, GCP

OSBORNE, Lynda
Gestalt Psychotherapist
Crossways, 8 Lancaster Avenue,
Farnham, Surrey GU9 8JY
01252 724403/01252 711439 (f)
GPTI, MET

OWTRAM, Peter
Psychoanalytic Psychotherapist
14 Busbridge Lane, Godalming, Surrey
GU7 1PU
01483 417443 (t/f)
GCP

PEARMAN, Cathy
Psychosynthesis Psychotherapist
'Tzaneen', Blackhorse Road, Woking,
Surrey GU22 ORE
01483 232030
AAPP, CTP

PEARSE, Joanna
Family Therapist
105 Burlington Road, Thorton Heath,
Surrey CR7 8PJ
0181 653 1281
AFT

PEET, Sandra
Transpersonal Psychotherapist
Chestnuts, 31 Firfield Road,
Addlestone, Surrey KT15 1QU
01932 853667
CTP

PEOVER, Brenda
Psychoanalytic Psychotherapist
Melrose Villa, Jocelyn Road, Richmond,
Surrey TW9 2TJ
0181 940 5574
LCP

PERERA, Ajit
Cognitive Behavioural Psychotherapist
Sandy Ridge, 2 Park Lane East, Reigate,
Surrey RH2 8HN
0958 935050/01737 222246
BABCP

PETHICK, Belinda
Psychoanalytic Psychotherapist
71 Kew Green, Richmond, Surrey
TW9 3AH
0181 940 2426
LCP

PHILLIPS, Mary
Sexual and Marital Psychotherapist
The Tudors, 20a Fernhill Lane, Upper Hale, Farnham GU9 0JJ
01252 723522
BASMT

PLATT, Monique
Integrative Psychotherapist
1 South Lodge, Ham Common, Richmond, Surrey TW10 7JL
0181 940 8890
RCSPC

POULOPOULOS, Katerina
Integrative Psychotherapist
22 Hare Hill Close, Pyrford, Surrey
GU22 8UH
01932 341107
RCSPC

PRATT, Sheila
Psychoanalytic Psychotherapist
44 East Meads, Onslow Village, Guildford, Surrey GU2 5SP
01483 572 093
GUILD, WMIP, GCP

PRESTON, Kay
Group Analytic Psychotherapist, Attachment-based Psychoanalytic Psychotherapist
4 Ringley Park Road, Reigate, Surrey
RH2 7BJ
01737 243 177
IPC, CAPP

RABE, Marie-Louise
Psychoanalytic Psychotherapist
23 Addiscombe Court Road, Croydon
CR0 6TT
0181 656 7954
ARBS

REID, Rosamund
Psychoanalytic Psychotherapist
The Cottage, Ivy Lane, Woking, Surrey
GU22 7BY
GCP

REYNOLDS, Hilary
Psychoanalytic Psychotherapist
11 The Waldrons, Oxted, Surrey
RH8 9DY
Flat 5, 130 Fellows Road, London
NW3 3JH
01883 712783/0171 483 4649
IPC

RIDLEY, Jane
Sexual and Marital Psychotherapist
77 Church Road, Richmond, Surrey
TW10 6LX
0181 940 7678
BASMT

SAGE, Nigel A.
Cognitive Behavioural Psychotherapist
W.Surrey & N.Hants Psychology, 2 Barossa Road, Camberley, Surrey
GU15 4JE
01276 66772
BABCP

SAGOE, Pauline
Transpersonal Psychotherapist
Surbiton, Surrey
0181 399 9973
CCPE

SANDBANK, Audrey
Family Therapist
30 Beech Road, Reigate, Surrey
RH2 9NA
01737 221347
AFT

SAROFF, Rahel
Integrative Psychotherapist
'Westside', 142 Nutfield Road, Merstham, Surrey RH1 3HG
01737 646068
RCSPC

SCOTT-CHINNERY, Jean
Cognitive Behavioural Psychotherapist
173 Southway, Guildford, Surrey
GU2 6DJ
Surrey Hampshire Borders NHS Trust, South House, Cranleigh, Surrey
01483 502787/0973 338310
BABCP

SEVITT, Michael
Group Analyst
7 Upper Park Road, Kingston-upon-Thames, Surrey KT2 5LB
01372 729 136/0181 546 4173
IGA

SHEPPARD FIDLER, Angela
Family Therapist, Systemic Psychotherapist
3 Sunnybank, Epsom, Surrey KT18 7DY
01372 727200
AFT

SNOWDEN, Patricia
Sexual and Marital Psychotherapist
15 Hookfield, Epsom, Surrey KT19 8JQ
01372 725874
BASMT

STARTE, Gordon
Analytical Psychologist-Jungian Analyst
Northwood, Seale Lane, Puttenham, Nr. Guildford, Surrey GU3 1AX
01483 811271/01483 810542 (f)
AJA

STEWART, Lisa
Cognitive Behavioural Psychotherapist
Practise 2, York House Medical Centre, Heathside Road, Woking, Surrey
GU22 7XL
01483 766736
BABCP

SUTTON, Bobbie
Psychoanalytic Psychotherapist
17 Sheen Park, Richmond, Surrey
TW9 1UN
0181 940 7628
IPC

TARSH, Helen
Psychoanalytic Marital Psychotherapist
Wentworth House, The Green, Richmond upon Thames, Surrey
TW9 1PB
0181 332 0597/0181 948 1913
TMSI

THORNTON, Suzanne
Integrative Psychotherapist
Ivy Cottage, Clockhouse Lane East, Egham, Surrey TW20 8PF
01784 433480
RCSPC

TOMS, Moira
Family Therapist
Bramblewood, Guildford Road, Cranleigh, Surrey GU6 8PR
01483 274183
AFT

UPTON, Jay
Psychoanalytic Psychotherapist
2 Eversfield Road, Kew, Richmond, Surrey TW9 2AP
0181 940 9263
GUILD

VALLINS, Yvonne
Psychoanalytic Psychotherapist
21 Hardwicke Road, Reigate, Surrey RH2 9HJ
01737 247 608
GUILD

VEASEY, Helen
Psychoanalytic Psychotherapist
8 Hilgay Close, Guildford, Surrey GU1 2EN
Student Counselling Service, University of Surrey, Guildford GU2 5XH
01483 259051/01483 38077
GUILD

VOLLANS, Audrey
Gestalt Psychotherapist
36 Gumbrells Close, Fairlands, Guildford, Surrey GU3 3NG
01483 234861
GPTI

WALKER, Mary J.
Child Psychotherapist, Psychoanalytic Psychotherapist
Merton Child Guidance Service, Cricket Green Polyclinic, Mitcham, Surrey CR4 4LQ
79 Blegborough Road, London SW16 6DL
0171 919 2384/5/0181 770 8828
ACP, BAP

WALLACE, Norma
Integrative Psychotherapist
100 Grosvenor Road, Langley Vale, Epsom Downs, Surrey KT18 6JB
01372 274779/01372 800510 (f)
MET

WALTON, Michael
Integrative Psychotherapist
18 Fern Close, Frimley, Camberley GU16 5UV
01276 27151
RCSPC

WHITAKER, Christine
Transpersonal Psychotherapist
Home Farmhouse, The Street, Puttenham, Guildford, Surrey GU3 1AR
01483 810632
CCPE

WHITELEY, J. Stuart
Group Analyst
Wheelwright's Cottage, Wheeler's Lane, Brockham, Surrey RH3 7LA
01737 843446/01737 843634 (f)
IGA

WILKINS, Max
Humanistic Psychotherapist
Manor Cottage, 1 Ivydene, West Molesey KT8 2HG
0181 672 5253/0181 941 6404
CCBP

WILLIAMS, Heather
Psychosynthesis Psychotherapist
76 Deerings Road, Reigate, Surrey RH2 0PN
01737 240638
AAPP

WILLIAMS, Jill
Integrative Psychotherapist
91 Sandy Lane South, Wallington, Surrey SM6 9RF
0181 669 0038
RCSPC

WILLIS, Sally
Group Analyst
50D Maple Road, Surbiton, Surrey KT6 4AE
0181 876 3216(f)/0181 399 3334
IGA

WILMOT, Vivienne
Psychoanalytic Psychotherapist
'Ithaca', 62 Petworth Road, Haslemere, Surrey GU27 3AU
GCP

WILSON, James
Psychoanalytic Psychotherapist
115 Longdown Lane South, Epsom, Surrey KT17 4JL
01372 204195/01372 745089
LCP

WOOD, Margarita
Child Psychotherapist
13 Uxbridge Road, Kingston-upon-Thames, Surrey KT1 2LH
0181 546 4668/0181 547 3419 (f)
ACP

WOOLMER, Tim
Group Analyst
79 North Road, Richmond, Surrey TW9 4HQ
0171 937 6956/0181 878 1259
IGA

WYSE, Hymie
Integrative Psychotherapist
47 Ashcombe Road, Carshalton, Surrey SM5 3ET
0181 647 8568
MC

YALLOP, Melanie
Psychoanalytic Psychotherapist
11 Mount Pleasant, Weybridge, Surrey KT13 8EP
01932 855 873(f)/01932 844688
IPC, GCP, FIP

SUSSEX EAST

ALEXANDER, Gail
Analytical Psychotherapist
47 Rugby Place, Kemptown, Brighton BN2 5JB
01273 600307
FIP

ANDERSON, Tony
Psychoanalytic Psychotherapist
4 Elmstead Road, Bexhill on Sea, Sussex TN40 5NJ
01424 734027
CSPK

ARCARI, Stephen
Group Analyst
37 Ruskin Road, Hove, East Sussex BN3 5HA
01273 731458/01273 778383 x 162
IGA

ARTHUR, Andrew R.
Psychoanalytic Psychotherapist
Flat 3,2 Upper Lake, Battle, East Sussex TN33 0AN
01424 774846
WMIP

BARNETT, Mary
Psychoanalytic Psychotherapist
33 Southdown Avenue, Brighton, East Sussex BN1 6EH
District Psychotherapy Service, South Downs Health NHS Trust, 9/11 Rutland Gardens, Hove BN3 5PA
01273 778383/01273 506258
GUILD

BEAZLEY-RICHARDS, Joanna
Transactional Analysis Psychotherapist, Integrative Psychotherapist
2 Quarry View, Whitehill Road, Crowborough, East Sussex TN6 1JT
01892 655195
ITA, MET

BLOWERS, Colin M.
Cognitive Behavioural Psychotherapist
Glenside, Wincombe Road, Brighton, East Sussex BN1 5AR
The Priory Hospital, Priory Lane, Roehampton, London SW15 5JJ
01273 504980/0181 876 8261
BABCP

BOTT, David
Systemic Psychotherapist
Preston House, 200 High Street, Lewes, East Sussex BN7 2NS
01273 471341
AFT

BOWMAN, Elizabeth
Hypno-Psychotherapist
Ridgeway, High Hurstwood, nr. Uckfield, East Sussex TN22 4BF
No.5 Calle.Consuelo, Jimena de la Frontera.Cadiz, Spain
01825 732273
NSHAP

BRADBURY, Sue
Psychodrama Psychotherapist
18 Hanover Crescent, Brighton BN2 2SB
01273 672411
BPA

BRENNAN, Clare
Psychoanalytic Psychotherapist, Group Analytic Psychotherapist
The Merchant House, English Passage, Cliffe High Street, Lewes, East Sussex BN7 2AP
01273 479157
LCP, WTC

BROSSKAMP, Cornelia
Biodynamic Psychotherapist
94 Graham Avenue, Brighton BN1 8HD
01273 385228
BTC

BUFFERY, Elli
Systemic Psychotherapist
1 Clover Lea, Grange Road, Hastings, East Sussex TN34 2RZ
01424 751 184
KCC

BURTON, Michael
Psychoanalytic Psychotherapist
Brackley, 11A Harrington Road, Brighton, Sussex BN1 9RE
Counselling & Psychotherapy, Health Centre Building, University of Sussex, Brighton
01273 678156/01273 502923
GUILD

BUTTON, Rachel
Transpersonal Psychotherapist
Old End Cottage, Priory Road, Forest Row, Sussex RH18 5HS
01342 822871
CCPE

CASARES, Jonathan
Transpersonal Psychotherapist
34 Lower Market Street, Hove, East Sussex BN2 2NX
CCPE

CHILTON, Barbara
Hypno-Psychotherapist
4 Ashburnham Road, Eastbourne, East Sussex BN21 2HU
01323 638558
NRHP

CLAIRMONTE, Tosin
Group Analyst
Hillview, 1 Hope Villas, Highcross, Rotherfield, East Sussex TN6 3QD
0189 285 2997
IGA

COLE, Barbara
Humanistic Psychotherapist
4 Offham Terrace, Lewes, East Sussex BN7 2QP
01273 473113
AHPP

COX, Christine
Hypno-Psychotherapist
8 Combermere Road, St. Leonards on Sea, East Sussex TN38 0RR
01424 424797
NRHP

CROSBY, Simon
Personal Construct Psychotherapist
Hindleap Corner, Priory Road, Forest Row, East Sussex RH18 5JF
4 Sandringham Court, Dufour's Place, London W1
01342 824545
CPCP

CRUTHERS, Helan
Integrative Arts Psychotherapist
24 Buckingham Street, Brighton BN1 3LT
01273 779 176
IATE

DARGERT, Guy
Humanistic Psychotherapist
175 Preston Drove, Brighton, East Sussex BN1 6FN
01273 557503
AHPP

DE LUCHI, Martin
Gestalt Psychotherapist
25 Meeching Road, Newhaven, East Sussex BN9 9RL
01273 512770
GCL

DESMOND, Hanora
Transpersonal Psychotherapist
30 The Esplanade, Seaford, East Sussex BN25 1JJ
31 Ashleigh Court, Morpeth Terrace, London SW1P 1EN
0171 630 0515/01323 490 721
CCPE

DIXON-NUTTALL, Rosemary
Group Analytic Psychotherapist
1 Coronation Cottages, Western Road, Jarvis Brook, Crowborough, East Sussex TN6 3EX
01892 663192
IPC, AGIP

DRIJVER, Caroline
Cognitive Behavioural Psychotherapist
37 Princes Terrace, Brighton, E Sussex BN2 5JS
Behavioural Psychotherapy Dept, Hove Polyclinic, Hove BN2 7HY
01273 240018/01273 690770
BABCP

DUNCAN-GRANT, Alec John
Cognitive Behavioural Psychotherapist
c/o Robert Dodd Building, 49 Darley Road, Eastbourne BN20 7UR
01273 643857/01273 643665
BABCP

EASTHAM, Peter
Cognitive Behavioural Psychotherapist
School Hill Medical Practice, School Hill House, School Hill, High St., Lewes BN7 2LU
01273 480888
BABCP

EISENBARTH, Heiner
Biodynamic Psychotherapist
94 Graham Avenue, Brighton
BN1 8HD
01273 385228
BTC

ELDRIDGE, Melanie
Psychodrama Psychotherapist
7 Hartington Terrace, Brighton, East Sussex BN2 3LT
01273 608987
BPA

FELLOWS, Ron
Family Therapist
Lavender Cottage, 90 Turkey Road, Bexhill on Sea, East Sussex TN39 5HE
01424 213200
AFT

FIELD, Rosalind
Integrative Psychotherapist
Flat 2, 9 Lewes Crescent, Brighton
BN2 1FH
01273 677721
MC

FOX, Jessica
Psychoanalytic Psychotherapist
Flat 2, Adelaide Court, 15 Adelaide Crescent, Hove, E. Sussex BN3 2JF
01273 732177
LCP

GALLAGHER, Eogain
Psychoanalytic Psychotherapist
8 Tivoli Crescent, Brighton BN1 5ND
01273 887332
LCP

GODDARD, Lynne
Transactional Analysis Psychotherapist
137 Montgomery Street, Hove, East Sussex BN3 5FP
01273 202721
ITA

GORDON, Inger
Systemic Psychotherapist
31 Castlefields, Hartfield, East Sussex
TN7 4JA
01892 770651
KCC

GRACIA, Olga
Psychosynthesis Psychotherapist
Derwent, Burwash Road, Broad Oak, Nr Heathfield TN21 8ST
01435 863 494/01825 766 888
AAPP

GREEN, Joe
Family Therapist, Systemic Psychotherapist
114 Havelock Road, Brighton
BN1 6GQ
St. Stephens House, 45A Borough Street, Brighton BN1 3BG
01273 327 221/01273 502 674
IFT

GREEN, Prudence
Psychoanalytic Psychotherapist
22 St Swithun's Terrce, Lewes, E Sussex
BN7 1UJ
01273 471 422
PA

GRIFFITHS, Anne
Psychoanalytic Psychotherapist
Bedford Cottage, 36 Prince Edward's Road, Lewes, E. Sussex BN7 1BE
01273 478365
GUILD

HALL, Jill
Gestalt Psychotherapist
22 Collier Road, Hastings TN34 3JR
01424 431154 (t/f)
GCL

HALPIN, Jill
Psychoanalytic Psychotherapist
Stonerunner Cottage, Rye Harbour, East Sussex TN31 7TT
01797 224351
GUILD

HARDCASTLE, Mark
Cognitive Behavioural Psychotherapist
The Eastbourne Clinic, 21 Grange Road, Eastbourne BN21 4HE
Millwood, Ukfield Hospital, Framfield Road, Ukfield East Sussex TN22 5AW
0976 8860278/01323 430831
BABCP

HARVEY, Andrew
Cognitive Behavioural Psychotherapist
Seaford Day Hospital, Sutton Road, Seaford, East Sussex BN25 1SS
26 Sycamore Drive, Hailsham, East Sussex BN27 3TT
01323 490989
BABCP

HAXBY, Kit
Psychoanalytic Psychotherapist
28 Withdean Road, Brighton, Sussex
BN1 5BL
01273 554027
LCP

HOLLAND, Sue
Psychosynthesis Psychotherapist
12 Shawcross House, 235-7 Preston Road, Brighton BN1 6SW
01273 563098
AAPP

HOLMES, Paul
Psychodrama Psychotherapist
23 Western Street, Brighton BN1 2PG
87 Carleton Road, London N7 0EZ
01273 776640/0171 700 5778
BPA

HUETING, Margaret
NLP Psychotherapist
31 Elm Grove, Hampden Park, Eastbourne, East Sussex BN22 9NN
01323 511150/01323 520372 (f)
ANLP

IRONSIDE, Lesley
Psychoanalytic Psychotherapist, Child Psychotherapist
35 Clermont Terrace, Brighton, East Sussex BN1 6SJ
01273 709660
ACP

JONES, Helen
Biodynamic Psychotherapist
52 Newmarket Road, Brighton, Sussex
BN2 3QF
01273 621347
BTC

JONES, Ros
Transpersonal Psychotherapist
Flat 1, Clermont Court, Clermont Road, Brighton BN1 6SS
01273 540875
CCPE

JOSEPH, Jerome Devakumar
Cognitive Psychotherapist
Gilgal, 17 Nyetimber Hill, Brighton, East Sussex BN2 4L
01273 706084(f)/01273 604404
BABCP

LAMBOR, Florangel
Psychoanalytic Psychotherapist
82 Hythe Road, Brighton, Sussex
BN1 6JS
01273 334421
CPP

LEEBURN, Jennifer
Psychoanalytic Psychotherapist
12 Priory Crescent, Lewes, East Sussex
BN7 1HP
01273 46444
FIP

LEWIN, Melanie
Transactional Analysis Psychotherapist
24 Kedale Road, Seaford, East Sussex
BN25 2BX
2 Railway Cottages, Railway Hill,
Barham, Nr. Canterbury CT4 6PZ
01227 831757/01323 892720
ITA

LIDSTER, Wendy
Sexual and Marital Psychotherapist
19 Shirley Drive, Hove, East Sussex
BN3 6NQ
01273 330262
BASMT

LITTLE, Marie
Psychoanalytic Psychotherapist
29 Kings Drive, Eastbourne, East
Sussex BN21 2NX
01323 649656
IPSS

LLOYD, Elizabeth
Psychoanalytic Psychotherapist
12 Preston Park Avenue, Brighton
BN1 6HJ
01273 555017
GUILD

LOVE, Mollie
Psychoanalytic Psychotherapist, Group
Analytic Psychotherapist
Larkswood, 162 Warren Road,
Woodingdean, Brighton BN2 6DD
01273 607529
LCP, AGIP

MACKENZIE, Nancy
Group Analyst
18 Wolston Bury Road, Hove, Sussex
BN3 6EJ
01273 678156/01273 736740
IGA

MARSHALL, Susan
Integrative Psychotherapist
Moat Mill Farm, Newick Lane, Mayfield,
East Sussex TN20 6RF
01435 873483
RCSPC

MAXWELL, Hugh
Psychodrama Psychotherapist
Westwood Day Hospital, Westwood
House, 7 Holmesdale Gdns, Hastings
TN34 1LY
BPA

MCLEOD, Paula
Biodynamic Psychotherapist
68 Stanley Road, Brighton, East Sussex
BN1 4NH
01273 383429
BTC

MICHAELSON, Sue
Transpersonal Psychotherapist
34 St Mary's Terrace, Hastings, East
Sussex TN34 3LR
01424 429858
CTP

MILLS, Jeremy George
Cognitive Behavioural Psychotherapist
Flat 1, 12 Denton Road, Eastbourne,
East Sussex BN20 7SU
01323 419172/0976 716540
BABCP

MORGAN-JONES, Richard
Psychoanalytic Psychotherapist
25 Lewes Road, Eastbourne, East
Sussex BN21 2BY
01323 647531
LCP

MOTHERSOLE, Geoff
Integrative Psychotherapist
6 Albert Road, Brighton, East Sussex
BN1 3RL
01273 738677
MET

NICHOLSON, Christine
Psychoanalytic Psychotherapist
42 Temple Street, Brighton BN1 3BH
01273 202178
LCP, FIP

O'BRIEN, John
Integrative Psychotherapist
Foxes, Berwick, East Sussex BN26 6TB
01323 871081/0171 290 2627
RCSPC

PALMER, Dorothy
Sexual and Marital Psychotherapist
Cobbler's Cottage, High Street,
Burwash, East Sussex BH23 2AE
BASMT

PARKINSON, Jane
Attachment-based Psychoanalytic
Psychotherapist
61b Beaconsfield Villas, Brighton, East
Sussex BN1 6HB
01293 739281
CAPP

REEVES, Alan
Transpersonal Psychotherapist
83 Shaftesbury Road, Brighton
BN1 4NG
01273 695390
CCPE

RICHARDS, Michael
Psychoanalytic Psychotherapist
65 Southover High Street, Lewes, East
Sussex BN7 1JA
01273 478244
IPC

RICHARDSON, Madeleine J.
Sexual and Marital Psychotherapist
74 Malden Road, Brighton BN1 5BE
01273 504385
BASMT

RIGNALL, John
Psychoanalytic Psychotherapist
4 Temple Gardens, Brighton BN1 3AE
01273 204314
IPC

ROBINSON, Judy
Psychoanalytic Psychotherapist
St Laurence House, Park Street,
Falmer, Brighton BN1 9PG
01273 606928
GUILD

ROLAND, Saskia
Integrative Psychotherapist
Tillingham, Peasmarsh, Nr. Rye, East
Sussex TN31 6XG
01797 230 796
RCSPC

SALAMANDER, Jas Ananda
Transpersonal Psychotherapist
24 Lancaster Road, Brighton, Sussex
BN1 5DG
01273 382289
CCPE

SANDERS, Peter
Transactional Analysis Psychotherapist
'Midsummer House' 66 St. Helen's Park
Road, Hastings, East Sussex TN34 2JJ
01424 420615
ITA

SAVAGE, Patrick
Family Therapist
37 Princes Terrace, Brighton BN2 5JS
AFT

SAVINS, Charlotte
Integrative Arts Psychotherapist
11 Hanover Street, Brighton BN2 2ST
01273 691166
IATE

SECRETT, David
Family Therapist
37 Princes Terrace, Brighton BN2 5JS
AFT

SIDHU, Frankie
Psychosynthesis Psychotherapist
4 Gerard Street, Brighton, Sussex
BN1 4NW
01273 603896/01273 887303
AAPP

SOUTAR, Sarah
Psychoanalytic Psychotherapist
Star Breweries Workshops and
Studios, Castleditch Lane, Lewes
BN7 1YJ
01273 486782
AGIP

SPEARMAN, Penny
Psychoanalytic Psychotherapist
244 Harbour Way, Shoreham-By-Sea,
West Sussex BN43 5HZ
01273 463033
LCP

SPRINGFORD, Kate
Psychoanalytic Psychotherapist
21 St.Anne's Crescent, Lewes, East
Sussex BN7 1SB
01273 473125
GUILD

SWIFT, Sue
Transactional Analysis Psychotherapist
Pimlico Cottage, Mark Cross, East
Sussex TN6 3PF
01892 783207/01892 783349 (f)
ITA

TOMLINSON, Moya
Sexual and Marital Psychotherapist
53 Southover High Street, Lewes, East
Sussex BN7 1JA
BASMT

TREDGOLD, Clare
Psychoanalytic Psychotherapist
13 Florence Road, Brighton, Sussex
BN1 6DL
01273 502112
LCP

VALLELY, Patricia M.
Transpersonal Psychotherapist
41 The Cliff, Brighton, East Sussex
BN2 5RF
c/o CCPE, Beauchamp Lodge, 2
Warwick Crescent, London W2 6NE
0171 266 3006/01273 691 162
CCPE

VAN HALM, Corrie
Transactional Analysis Psychotherapist
St. John's Lodge, Burgh Hill,
Etchingham, East Sussex TN19 7PE
01580 860 780
ITA

WHITE, Anne
Systemic Psychotherapist
33 Ridgeway, Hurst Green, Etchingham,
East Sussex TN19 7PJ
01580 860355
KCC

WHITE, Jennifer
Gestalt Psychotherapist
46 Shaftesbury Road, Brighton
BN1 4NF
01273 689580
GCL

WHITE, Lela Ljiljana
Psychoanalytic Psychotherapist
37 Surrenden Road, Brighton, Sussex
BN1 6PQ
01273 554543
IPC

WRATTEN, Stephen
Family Therapist
2 St. Leonard's Lodge, Maze Hill, St
Leonard's on Sea, East Sussex
TN38 0HW
01424 720495
AFT

SUSSEX WEST

ADDENBROOKE, Mary
Analytical Psychologist-Jungian Analyst
The Vicarage, Colgate, Horsham, West
Sussex RH12 4SZ
01293 851826/01293 851362
GUILD

ALDRIDGE, Janet
Integrative Psychotherapist
64 Stocks Lane, East Wittering, West
Sussex PO20 8NJ
01243 816042/01243 670924
RCSPC

ANSTICE, Christine
Sexual and Marital Psychotherapist
10 Selham Close, Ifield, Crawley, West
Sussex RH11 0GH
01293 535654
BASMT

AYRES, Kathleen
Hypno-Psychotherapist
Oakwood House, 6 Marshall Avenue,
Bognor Regis, West Sussex PO21 2TJ
01243 822263
NRHP

BARDELLE, Rosemary
Biodynamic Psychotherapist
1 Copper Hall Close, Rustington, West
Sussex BN16 3RZ
01903 850050
BTC

BODDINGTON, Daphne
Sexual and Marital Psychotherapist
28 Heathfield Park, Midhurst, West
Sussex GU29 9HN
BASMT

COLEMAN, Eva
Integrative Psychotherapist
Lattenbells, Farm Lane, Ditching,
Hassocks, West Sussex BN6 8UR
01273 622886/01273 844142
RCSPC

DAVIDSON, John
Cognitive Behavioural Psychotherapist
Greenwoods, Selsey Road, Sidlesham,
Chichester, W. Sussex PO20 7LR
Cuckfield Surgery, Glebe Road,
Cuckfield, West Sussex RH17 5BQ
01444 416778/01243 641436
BABCP

DAVIS, Paul E.
Cognitive Behavioural Psychotherapist
The Summit, 22 Sudley Road, Bognor
Regis, West Sussex PO21 1ER
01243 869234
BABCP

DUFFY, Kathleen
Integrative Psychotherapist
8 Malthouse Road, Crawley, West Sussex RH10 6BG
01293 531443
RCSPC

ESPOSITO, Claude
Family Psychotherapist
Smiles Cottage, 47 High Street, Ardingly, West Sussex RH17 6TB
Croydon Assessment and Therapeutic Services, Kingsdown, 112 Orchard Road, Sanderstead, Surrey CR2 9LQ
0181 651 5611/01444 892 497
IFT

EVANS, Richard
Gestalt Psychotherapist
Brook House, Quay Meadow, Bosham, West Sussex PO18 8LY
01243 573475/01243 574796 (f)
GPTI

FIELD, John C.
Cognitive Analytic Therapist
64 Wickham Hill, Hurstpierpoint, West Sussex BN6 9NP
01273 534716/01273 843012
ACAT

FILBY, Erica
Family Therapist
The Archdeaconry, Itchingfield, Horsham, West Sussex RH13 7NX
Child & Family Consultation Service, Langley House, Church Lane, Oxted RH8 9LH
01883 734003/01403 791153 (f)
AFT

HAGENBACH, Kitty
Transpersonal Psychotherapist
Nenthorne West, Hammerwood Road, Ashurst Wood, West Sussex RH19 3RU
also at St. Johns Wood NW8
01342 823461
CCPE

HARLING, Biljana
Transactional Analysis Psychotherapist
21 Kingsham Avenue, Chichester, West Sussex PO19 2AW
6 Swaines Lane, Highgate, London N6 6QU
0956 654 597/01243 532033
ITA, MET

HERDMAN, Linda
Cognitive Behavioural Psychotherapist
Bedale Mental Health, 1 Glencathara Road, Bognor Regis, West Sussex PO21 2SF
01243 841041
BABCP

HILLMAN, Christine
Psychosynthesis Psychotherapist
2 The Old Convent, East Grinstead, West Sussex RH19 3RS
01343 315097
AAPP

MARTIN, Linda
Gestalt Psychotherapist
14 Garden House Lane, East Grinstead, W Sussex RH19 4JT
01342 312974
GCL

MILLER, Bob
Attachment-based Psychoanalytic Psychotherapist
68 Clarence Road, Horsham, West Sussex RH13 5SS
01403 255387
CAPP

ORBACH, Ann
Psychoanalytic Psychotherapist
19 New Park Road, Chichester, W. Sussex PO19 1XH
01243 783667
GUILD

QUINN, Susan
Transpersonal Psychotherapist
The Psychology Service for Sexual Health, 16 Liverpool Gardens, Worthing BN11 1RY
CTP

REAVLEY, William
Cognitive Behavioural Psychotherapist
79 Whyke Road, Chichester, West Sussex PO19 2HU
01243 531455/01243 787970
BABCP

REILLY, Nicole
Transpersonal Psychotherapist
28 St. George's Road, Worthing, West Sussex BN11 2DR
01903 203533
CCPE

SCOTT, Liz
Sexual and Marital Psychotherapist
30 Haywards Road, Haywards Heath, West Sussex RH16 4JB
BASMT

THOMAS, Jennifer
Sexual and Marital Psychotherapist
11 East Bank, Selsey, Chichester, West Sussex PO20 0SP
BASMT

THORPE, Ivan
Integrative Psychotherapist
20 Hailsham Road, Worthing, West Sussex BN11 5PA
01903 606440/01903 249075
RCSPC

WALKER, Jim
Psychoanalytic Psychotherapist
Westlake, Broad Street, Cuckfield, West Sussex RH17 5LL
01444 440204
IPSS

WEST, Marcus
Analytical Psychologist-Jungian Analyst
Highbank 45, Cross Lane Findon, West Sussex BN14 0UB
01903 874140/01903 877039
FIP

WOODMAN-SMITH, Gillian
Psychoanalytic Psychotherapist, Child Psychotherapist
31 Whyke Road, Chichester, W Sussex PO19 2HW
62 Albert Street, London NW1 7NR
01243 782513/0171 388 5987
ACP, BAP

TYNE & WEAR

BATCHELOR, Henrietta
Sexual and Marital Psychotherapist
East Moorhouses, Matfen, Northumberland NE20 0RG
01661 886362
BASMT

BIANCARDI, Jenny
Psychodrama Psychotherapist
94 St. Georges Terrace, Jesmond, Newcastle Upon Tyne NE2 2DL
0191 281 6243
BPA

BIRCH, Jim
Family Therapist
Kiln Riggs, High Brunton, Wall, Hexham, Northumberland NE46 4ET
01434 681018
AFT

BLACK, Patricia Anne
Psychoanalytic Psychotherapist
Seatsides Farmhouse, Once Brewed, Northumberland NE47 7HE
NAAP

BLACKBURN, Ivy-Marie
Cognitive Behavioural Psychotherapist
Newcastle Cognitive Therapy Centre, Collingwood Clinic, St Nicholas Hospital, Gosforth, Newcastle NE3 3XT
0191 213 0151
BABCP

BRAZIER, David
Psychodrama Psychotherapist
Quannon House, 53 Grosvenor Place, Jesmond, Newcastle Upon Tyne NE2 2RD
0191 281 5592
BPA

CHARLTON, Anne
Group Analyst
Leehall, Wark on Tyne, Hexham, Northumberland NE48 3PT
IGA

CROMARTY, Paul
Cognitive Behavioural Psychotherapist
Cognitive & Behavioural Therapies Centre, Collingwood Clinics, Gosforth, Newcastle upon Tyne NE3 3XT
0191 223 2601
BABCP

DOBSON, Mary
Psychoanalytic Psychotherapist
10 Meadway, Forest Hall, Newcastle upon Tyne NE12 9RB
0191 266 6501
NAAP

GILLETT, Timothy P.
Cognitive Behavioural Psychotherapist
Sir Martin Roth Young Peoples Unit, Newcastle General Hospital, Westgate Road, Newcastle upon Tyne NE4 6BE
0191 219 5023/0191 219 5022 (f)
BABCP

GILLMAN, Maureen
Family Therapist
3 The Oval, Benton, Newcastle NE12 9PP
AFT

HODGSON, Susan
Family Therapist
University of Northumbria at Newcastle, Manor House, Coach Lane Campus, Newcastle NE7 7XA
0191 227 3266/0191 227 3270
AFT

JANSEN, Diana
Psychoanalytic Psychotherapist
The Cottage, Dalton, Newcastle upon Tyne NE18 5AA
01661 886200
NAAP, CPP

JOHN, Carolyn H.
Cognitive Behavioural Psychotherapist
11 Tankerville Terrace, Jesmond, Newcastle upon Tyne NE2 3AH
0191 281 0411
BABCP

JOHNSON, Frank
Psychoanalytic Psychotherapist
Fordwich House, Hepscott, Nr. Morpeth, Northumberland NE61 6LN
01607 515 219
NAAP

KAT, Bernard J B
Cognitive Behavioural Psychotherapist
Psynapse, 11 Tankerville Terrace, Jesmond, Newcastle upon Tyne NE2 3AH
Dept of Clinical Psychology, County Hospital, Durham DH1 4ST
BABCP

KENDAL, Jo Reed
Psychoanalytic Psychotherapist
Southern Wood, 2 Ridgeway Fenham, Newcastle upon Tyne NE4 9UL
0191 275 0612
NAAP

LAMBERT, Louise
Psychodrama Psychotherapist
Myrtle Cottage, Westmorland Avenue, Willington Quay, Walls, Tyne & Wear NE28 6SN
BPA

LUND, Charles
Psychoanalytic Psychotherapist
Claremont House, Off Framlington Place, Newcastle NE2 4AA
0191 232 5131
NAAP

MAHMOOD, Janet
Psychoanalytic Psychotherapist, Analytical Psychologist
11 Roseworth Avenue, Gosforth, Newcastle upon Tyne NE3 1NB
0191 285 7463
NAAP

MARSHALL, Patricia
Psychoanalytic Psychotherapist
45 Northfield Road, Gosforth Newscastle upon Tyne NE3 3UN
0191 2851093
NAAP

MCGREGOR-HEPBURN, Jan
Psychoanalytic Psychotherapist
Post Office Cottage, Station Bank, Mickley, Stocksfield, Northumberland NE43 7BX
01661 842727
LCP

MITCHISON, Sally
Group Analyst
46 West Lane, Forest Hall, Newcastle NE12 0BE
0191 565 6256 x 44387/0191 268 3168
IGA

MOORE, Gordon
Cognitive Behavioural Psychotherapist
Dept Psychological Therapies & Research, St Georges Hospital, Morpeth, Northumberland NE61 2NE
01670 516230(f)/01670 512121
BABCP

MORGAN, Shirley P.
Psychoanalytic Psychotherapist
High Rawgreen Cottage, Steel, Hexham, Northumberland NE47 OHL
NAAP

MORGAN, William
Cognitive Psychotherapist
Department of Social Policy, 5th Floor Claremont Bridge Building, University of Newcastle, Newcastle NE1 7RU
0191 222 7540
BABCP

NEDEN, Jeanette
Family Therapist
9 Hagg Bank Cottages, Wylam,
Northumberland NE41 8JT
01661 853 478
AFT

PHOENIX, Ashleigh
Psychoanalytic Psychotherapist
Dryden Road Hospital, Dryden Road,
Gateshead
0191 478 2388
NAAP

PROCTOR, Susan
Psychoanalytic Psychotherapist
St Georges Hospital, Morpeth,
Northumberland NE61 2NU
NAAP

REED, Alex
Systemic Psychotherapist
29 Hallstile Bank, Hexham,
Northumberland NE46 3PQ
01434 601928
AFT

ROBINSON, Rosalyn
Group Analyst
4 Stobhill Villas, Morpeth,
Northumberland NE61 2S
0191 227 5142/01670 511 445
IGA

SCOTT, Jan
Cognitive Behavioural Psychotherapist
University Dept. Psychiatry, Royal
Victoria Infirmary, Newcastle Upon
Tyne NE1 4LP
0191 227 5073
BABCP

SHRUBSOLE, Lindsay
Psychoanalytic Psychotherapist
David Grieve House, Headlam Street,
Byker NE6 2DX
0191 224 1251(F)/0191 224 2717
NAAP

STAFFORD, Amanda
Psychoanalytic Psychotherapist
Favell, Dipe Lane, East Boldon, Tyne &
Wear NE36 0PQ
0191 536 9503
NAAP

STANDART, Sally
Cognitive Psychotherapist
Newcastle Cognitive Therapy Centre,
Collingwood Clinic, St. Nicholas
Hospital, Gosforth, Newcastle
NE3 3XT
0191 223 2509
BABCP

TRIPPETT, Marie
Cognitive Psychotherapist
Psychology Department, Lobley Hill
Clinic, Lobley Hill Road, Gateshead,
Tyne & Wear NE11 0AL
0191 443 6860
BABCP

TURKINGTON, Douglas
Cognitive Psychotherapist
Leazes Wing Dept of Psychiatry,
Richardson Road, Newcastle-upon-
Tyne NE3 3XT
Lindisfarne Suite, Newcastle Nuffield
Hospital, Osborne Road, Jesmond
NE2 1JP
0191 281 4606/0191 232 5131
BABCP

WATSON, Dorothy
Hypno-Psychotherapist
6 Prestwick Terrace, Ponteland,
Newcastle upon Tyne NE20 9BZ
01661 820372
CTS

WALES – NORTH

BOARDMAN, Ian
Group Analyst
Garden House, Park Street, Denbigh,
Clwyd
0174 581 2871/0174 581 5332
IGA

BUTLER, Linda
Cognitive Behavioural Psychotherapist
Child and Family Service, 31 Grosvenor
Road, Wrexham, Clywd LL11 1BS
01978 350050
BABCP

DAVIES, Mike
Family Therapist
Bryn Ffwd, 17 Rock Terrace, Old
Ynysbwl, Pontypridd Mid Glamorgan
0114 7919339
AFT

FEARNS, Keith
Cognitive Behavioural Psychotherapist
Llys Deinol, Garth Road, Bangor,
Gwynedd LL57 2SE
BABCP

HUGHES, Lynette
Psychoanalytic Marital Psychotherapist,
Psychoanalytic Psychotherapist
Cartrefle, 149 Mwrog Street, Ruthin,
Denbighshire LL15 1LE
Winnicott Centre, 195-7 Hathersage
Road, Manchester M13 0JE
0161 248 9494/01824 702656
TMSI, NWIDP

HURD, Joan
Psychoanalytic Psychotherapist
Cwm Hardd, Nantyr, nr. Llangollen,
Clywd LL20 7DD
18 St John's Chambers, Ashwell Street,
Leiceister LE1 6JJ
01691 718450/0116 254 5451
PA

JENKINS, Sheila
Cognitive Behavioural Psychotherapist
Arfon Mental Health Centre, 26
College Road, Bangor, Gwynedd
LL57 4AN
01248 370137
BABCP

LANGLEY, Allen
Hypno-Psychotherapist
Bryn Hyfryd, Lon Sant Ffraid, Trearddur
Bay, Holyhead, Anglesey LL65 2UD
Osteopathic & Natural Therapy
Centre, 51 High Street, Menai Bridge,
Anglesey
01248 716297/01407 861258
NRHP

MARDULA, Jody
Transactional Analysis Psychotherapist
'Calon Y Mynydd', 30 Seiriol Road,
Penmaenmawr, Conwy LL34 6HB
ITA

MAY, Adam
Hypno-Psychotherapist
Cefn Cana, Llanddaniel Fab, Gaerwen,
Ynys Mon LL60 6EF
01248 421015
NRHP, BABCP

NIESSER, Arthur
Analytical Psychologist-Jungian Analyst
Fron Olau, Mersey Street Y Gest
Porthmadog, Gwynedd LL49 9UF
01766 514828(f)/01766 513041
AJA

OSBORN, Madeline Frances
Psychoanalytic Psychotherapist
Hergest Unit, Ysbyty Gwyneed, Bangor, Gwynedd LL57
01248 450266
NWIDP

PRUSSIA, Celia M.
Psychoanalytic Psychotherapist
Hoseley Bank Cottage, Park Lane, Rossett, Wrexham LL12 0BL
01978 852208/01978 853352
LPDO

STEVENS, Jean
Hypno-Psychotherapist
Holmlea, 48 Clwyd Park, Kinmel Bay, Rhyl, Clwyd LL18 5HH
01745 342544
NRHP

UDEN, Christine
Transactional Analysis Psychotherapist
Ty Gwyn, Pentrellyncymmer, Cerrigydrudion, Corwen, North Wales LL21 9TU
01490 420639
ITA

WHEELER, Anne
Psychoanalytic Psychotherapist
1 Church View, High Street, Gresford, Wrexham LL12 8RD
01978 854673
LPDO

WALES – SOUTH

ALDRIDGE, Barrie
Integrative Psychotherapist
12 Great House Meadow, Llantwit Major, Vale of Glamorgan, South Wales CF61 1SU
01443 482896/01446 790073
RCSPC

APPLETON, Richard
Family Therapist
47 Cilddewi Park, Johnstown, Carmarthen, Dyfed SA31 3HP
01267 237136
AFT

BELLIS, Stella
Analytical Psychologist-Jungian Analyst, Child Psychotherapist
Llwyn Aderyn, Brechfa, Carnarthen, Wales SA32 7BL
01267 202 479
ACP, BAP

BISGOOD, Bill
Transactional Analysis Psychotherapist
6 Ebens Lane, Cardigan, Ceredigion SA43 1HN
01239 613996
ITA

BRAZIER, Anna
Family Therapist
Centre for Training in Clinical Psychology, Whitchurch Hopital, Whitchurch, Cardiff CF4 7XB
01222 521120
AFT

BRETT, John
Systemic Psychotherapist
11 Church Park, Mumbles, Swansea SA3 4DE
01792 362155
FIC

CHATHAM, Jon
Family Therapist
Preswylfa Child and Family Centre, Clive Road, Canton, Cardiff CF5 1GN
01222 344489
AFT

CLEVELY, Sarah
Transactional Analysis Psychotherapist
'Ashera', Swansea, West Glamorgan
10 Bartholomew Terrace, Exeter, Devon EX4 3BW
01392 432952/01792 461413
ITA, MET

COX, Brenda
Family Therapist
The Family Institute, 105 Cathedral Road, Cardiff CF1 9PH
01222 226532/01222 236532 (f)
FIC

CURREN, Maureen
Psychoanalytic Psychotherapist
Penarth, Cregrina, Nr. Llandrindod Wells, Powys LD1 5SF
01982 570212
WMIP

DAVID, Johanna
Analytical Psychologist-Jungian Analyst
The Callow, Welsh Newton, Monmouth, Gwent NP5 3RL
01600 716634/01600 713286(f)
IGAP

DAVIES, Mairlis
Family Therapist
Preswylfa Child & Family Centre, Clive Road, Canton, Cardiff CF5 1GN
01222 344489
AFT

DAVIES, Rosina
Integrative Psychotherapist
98 Dulais Road, Seven Sisters, Neath, West Glamorgan SA10 9ES
01792 703312/01639 700429
RCSPC

DONNAI, Andrew
Integrative Psychotherapist
1 Glenhurst Villas, Trefechan, Aberystwyth, Ceredigion SY23 1BD
01970 612673
NSAP

DRYDEN, Jan
Humanistic and Integrative Psychotherapist
22 Talbot Street, Cardiff CF1 9BW
01222 238076
SPEC

FARIS, Jeff
Systemic Psychotherapist
105 Cathedral Road, Cardiff CF1 9PH
01222 226 532/01222 236 278 (f)
FIC

FISHER, Clare
Cognitive Analytic Therapist
Psychology OPT, St Tydfil's Hospital, Merther Tydfil CF47 0SJ
01685 383048 (f)/01685 723244 ext 4268
ACAT

GAGG, Susan M.
Systemic Psychotherapist
13 Gardde, Llwynhendy, Llanelli, Dyfed SA14 9NH
01554 771885
FIC

GAUNT, Pamela
Transpersonal Psychotherapist
Bach Y Gwyddel, Cwmpengraig, Felindre, Llandysul SA44 5HX
01559 371427
CCPE

GIBBIN, Jane
Sexual and Marital Psychotherapist
Mapsland, Laugharne, Carmarthen SA33 4QP
01994 427319
BASMT

GORDON CLARK, Thalia
Core Process Psychotherapist
4 Danyrallt, Llaneglwys, Builth Wells, Powys LD2 3BV
01982 560656
AAPP

GRAF, Fern
Family Therapist
Preswylfa Child and Family Centre, Clive Road, Canton, Cardiff CF5 1GN
01222 344489
AFT

GREGG, Annzella
Transpersonal Psychotherapist
Swansea
01792 281070
CCPE

HARDY, William
Systemic Psychotherapist
45 Esplanade Avenue, Porthcawl, Bridgend CF36 3YS
01656 786964
FIC

HARRIS, Anthony
Core Process Psychotherapist
'Harmony', 17 Prince's Avenue, Caerphilly County Borough, South Wales CF83 1HR
01222 451952/01222 881632
AAPP

HARRIS, Paul David Gwyn
Cognitive Behavioural Psychotherapist
109/ 109A Bolgoed Road, Swansea, West Glamorgan SA4 1JP
Psychology Department, Cefn Coed Hospital, Swansea SA2 0GH
01792 561155 x 6588/01792 884 952
BABCP

HAZELL, Jeremy
Psychoanalytic Psychotherapist
9 Fairleigh Road, Pontcanna, Cardiff CF1 9JT
01222 345832
SIP, BAP

HILL, Jenny
Psychoanalytic Psychotherapist
Harpton Gardens, New Radnor, Presteigne,Powys LD8 2RE
Phoenix House, Widemarsh Street, Hereford HR4 9EV
01432 264947/01554 350698
SIP

HILLMAN, Jan
Sexual and Marital Psychotherapist
The Gwent Counselling Centre, 25 St. Mary Street, Monmouth, Gwent NP5 3BD
01600 715717
BASMT

HOWES, Kathleen Mary
Cognitive Behavioural Psychotherapist
Y Bwthyn, Battle, Brecon, Powys, Wales LD3 9RN
c/o Llandaff Chiropractice Clinic, 116 Station Road, Llandaff North, Cardiff CF4 2FH
01874 623638
BABCP

HUGHES, Geraldine
Gestalt Psychotherapist
72 Roath Court Road, Roath, Cardiff CF2 3SD
01222 454001
GPTI

JONES, Elsa
Systemic Psychotherapist
The Natural Health Clinic, 98 Cathedral Road, Cardiff CF1 9LP
01873 810840 (f)/01222 222221
IFT

JONES, Susan
Systemic Psychotherapist
2 Caerty Clywd, Llantwit Major, South Glamorgan CF61 2SQ
01446 792369
FIC

KIRWIN, Mark
Psychosynthesis Psychotherapist
Old Church Cottage, Birches Road, Penallt, Monmouth NP5 4AW
01291 627417/01600 712857
AAPP

KOSTORIS, Laura
Integrative Psychotherapist
Erw yr Danty, Talybont-on-Usk, Brecon, Powys LD3 7YN
01874 676498
RCSPC

LISTER, Ian
Family Therapist
Fox Hollow, Croesyceiliog, Carmarthen SA32 8DS
01267 237327
AFT

LOWE, Julie
Existential Psychotherapist
32 Victoria Park Road East, Canton, Cardiff, Wales CF5 1EH
01222 340376
RCSPC

MACKENZIE, Ian D.
Psychoanalytic Psychotherapist
Penarth, Cregrina, Nr. Llandrindod Wells, Powys LD1 5SF
01982 570 212
WMIP

MYLAN, Trish
Systemic Psychotherapist
Ty Caehir, Peterston-Super-Ely, Cardiff CF5 6LH
01222 578918
FIC

PARSONS, Barbara
Family Therapist
Preswylfa Child & Family Centre, Clive Road, Canton, Cardiff CF5 1GN
01222 344489
AFT

PEACE, Susan
Hypno-Psychotherapist
The Peace Clinic, Cwm Meillion, Llangammarch Wells, Powys LD4 4EN
01591 620339
NRHP

PLOWMAN, John
Hypno-Psychotherapist
22 Goldcroft Common, Caerleon, Newport, Gwent NP6 1NG
01633 420095
NRHP

REGAN, Columba
Child Psychotherapist
Penalt, 91 Gower Road, Sketty, Swansea SA2 9BH
01792 201362
ACP

RIVETT, Mark
Family Therapist
3 Pitman Street, Pontcanna, Cardiff CF1 9DJ
AFT

ROUTLEDGE, Derek
Family Therapist
Preswylfa Child and Family Service, Clive Road, Canton, Cardiff CF5 1GN
01222 344489
AFT

ROWLANDS, Helen
Integrative Psychotherapist
32 Kingsland Crescent, Barry, Vale of Glamorgan CF63 4JQ
01446 740517
MET

SELIGMAN, Philippa
Systemic Psychotherapist
22 West Orchard Crescent, Llandaff, Cardiff CF5 1AR
01222 578215/01222 561491
AFT

STREET, Eddy
Systemic Psychotherapist
Llandough Special C. Centre, Llandough Hospital NHS Trust, Penarth, South Glamorgan CF64 2XX
01222 711711 x 5593
FIC

TELDERS, Martina
Psychoanalytic Psychotherapist
25 Pontcanna Street, Cardiff, S Wales CF1 9HQ
01222 371391
SIP

THOMAS, Jenny
Transactional Analysis Psychotherapist
'The Highlands', Old Llantrisant Road, Tonyrefail, Mid Glamorgan CF39 8YU
01443 676579
ITA

TOMSETT, Jean
Family Therapist
16 Stockland Street, Caerphilly, Mid Glamorgan CF83 1GD
01222 613333/01222 610894
AFT

WILSON, Jim
Family Therapist
105 Cathedral Road, Cardiff CF1 9PH
01222 236532/01222 236278 (f)
FIC

WARWICKSHIRE

ABBERLEY, Colette Theresa
Psychodynamic Psychotherapist
5 Highcroft Crescent, Avonside, Milverton, Leamington Spa, Warwickshire CV32 6BZ
01926 336066
WMIP

ALEXANDER, Erica
Family Therapist
5 Lloyd Close, Hampton Magna, Warwick CV35 8SH
01926 493018
FIC

BARRETT, James
Psychoanalytic Psychotherapist (Jungian)
45 Clarendon Avenue, Leamington Spa, Warwickshire CV32 4SQ
01926 316178/01926 452871 (f)
WMIP

BURNS, Paula
Psychoanalytic Psychotherapist
30 Langton Road, Rugby, Warwickshire CV21 3UA
01788 536446
IPSS

CHAPMAN, Jane
Rational Emotive Behaviour Therapist
107 Claremont Road, Rugby, Warks. CV21 3LU
01788 569372
BABCP

EDWARDS, Jennifer
Psychoanalytic Psychotherapist
2 Cozens Close, Bedworth, Warwickshire CV12 8TS
01203 641799/01203 643606
LPDO

ENSER, Nigel
Family Therapist
Department for Children and Young People and Family, 83 Radford Road, Leamington Spa CV31 1JQ
01926 490507
AFT

HILL, Brenda
Sexual and Marital Psychotherapist
93 High Street, Bidford-on-Avon, Warwickshire B50 4BD
01789 773016
BASMT

HOLMES, Dorothy
Psychoanalytic Psychotherapist (Jungian)
1 Quarry Lane, Nuneaton, Warwickshire CV11 6QB
WMIP

LACEY, Irene
Family Therapist
16 Keytes Lane, Barford, Warwick CV35 8EP
01926 624543
AFT

MCNAUGHT, Janet
Sexual and Marital Psychotherapist
Professional Counselling Services, The Cloisters, Lower Leam Street, Leamington Spa, Warwicks CV31 1DJ
01926 882521
BASMT

MYERS, Marion
Analytical Psychologist-Jungian Analyst
44 St. Mary's Road, Leamington Spa, Warks. CV31 1JP
WMIP

NICHOLAS, P. John
Psychoanalytic Psychotherapist (Jungian)
41 Portland Street, Leamington Spa CV32 5EY
01926 452891
WMIP

OWEN, William Meredith
Psychoanalytic Psychotherapist
Boscobel, Hatton Rock, Stratford - upon -Avon CV37 0NU
The Courtyard Flat, 6 Hollymount, London NW3 6SG
0171 794 4764
WMIP

PAYMAN, Barbara
Transactional Analysis Psychotherapist
40 Moseley Road, Kenilworth, Warwickshire CV8 2AQ
Creative Health Centre, 39A Regent Street, Leamington Spa CV32 5EE
01926 316500/01926 859924
ITA

SAMSON, Anne
Psychoanalytic Psychotherapist
19 St. Marys Crescent, Leamington Spa CV31 1JL
WMIP

SMITH, Robert
NLP Psychotherapist
5 Hall Close, Kilsby, nr. Rugby, Warwickshire CV23 8XZ
01788 822141 (t/f)
ANLP

WATSON, Roy
Psychodrama Psychotherapist
31 Dalehouse Lane, Kenilworth, Warwickshire CV8 2HW
01926 856574
BPA

WREN, Pauline
Hypno-Psychotherapist
13 Hillmorton Road, Rugby, Warwickshire CV22 5DF
01788 560793
NRHP

WEST MIDLANDS

BALDWIN, Sally
Psychoanalytic Psychotherapist
15 Carthusian Road, Coventry CV3 6HA
01203 844061/01203 502830
LCP

BEEDIE, Margaret.A.
Analytical Psychologist-Jungian Analyst
Queen Elizabeth Psychiatric Hospital, Vincent Drive, Edgbaston, Birmingham B15 2QZ
0121 475 7805
WMIP

BEER, Charmian
Sexual and Marital Psychotherapist
11a Salisbury Road, Moseley, Birmingham B13 8JS
0121 449 4343
BASMT

BIRLEY, Paul
Hypno-Psychotherapist
15 Lee Road, Hollywood, Birmingham B47 5NY
01564 822967
CTS

BIRTLE, Janice
Psychoanalytic Psychotherapist
Uffculme Psychotherapy Service, Devon House, Mindelsohn Way, Edgbaston, Birmingham B15 2QR
0121 678 5848(f)/0121 678 5800
WMIP

BLAKEY, Angela
Psychoanalytic Psychotherapist, Psychotherapist (Family & Relationship)
170 Hole Lane, Northfield, Birmingham B31 2DD
0121 475 3948
WMIP

BOND, Anne R.
Psychodynamic Psychotherapist
Uffculme Clinic, Queensbridge Road, Moseley, Birmingham B13 8QD
0121 442 4545
WMIP

BRAY, Jillyan
Psychodynamic Psychotherapist
26 Maney Hill Road, Sutton Coldfield, West Midlands B72 1JL
0121 354 2403
WMIP

BURKE, Robina
Psychoanalytic Psychotherapist
39 Beaumont Road, Bournville, Birmingham B30 2EA
0121 628 5124
WMIP

BURNHAM, John
Systemic Psychotherapist
Parkview Clinic, Moseley, Birmingham B13 8QE
KCC, 2 Wyvil Court, Trenchold Street, London SW8 2TG
0121 243 2000/0171 720 7301
KCC

BYRNE, Dorothy
Analytical Psychologist-Jungian Analyst
539 Warwick Road, Solihull B91 1AW
0121 704 0403
SAP

CALVERT, Jane
Psychoanalytic Psychotherapist
48 Hartopp Road, Four Oaks, Sutton Coldfield, Birmingham B74 2QR
0121 323 4233
WMIP

CARLISH, Sonia
Psychoanalytic Psychotherapist
8 Moor Green Lane, Moseley, Birmingham B13 8ND
0121 449 0544
WMIP

CARPENTER, David
NLP Psychotherapist
136 Lichfield Road, Walsall Wood, Walsall WS9 9PD
01543 820092
ANLP

COLE, Martin
Sexual and Marital Psychotherapist
40 School Road, Moseley, Birmingham B13 9SN
0121 449 0892
BASMT

COOPER, Grahame F.
Psychoanalytic Psychotherapist, Sexual and Marital Psychotherapist
6 Clarence Road, Moseley, Birmingham B13 9SX
0121 449 2308
BASMT, WMIP

CROWLEY, Valerie
Cognitive Analytic Therapist
48 Grosvenor Road, Solihull, West Midlands B91 3PU
Psychology Department, Brooklands, Coleshill Road, Marston Green, W.Midlands
0121 779 6981 ext208/0121 705 7906
ACAT

CUMMINS, Peter
Personal Construct Psychotherapist
Psychology Department, Adams Ward, Gulson Hospital, Gulson Road, Coventry CV1 2HR
01203 844 061
CPCP

DAYAL, Mahendra Singh
Psychoanalytic Psychotherapist, Psychotherapist (Family & Relationship)
17 Mead Rise, Edgbaston, Birmingham B15 3SD
0121 455 7986
WMIP

DOGGART, Elizabeth Anne
Cognitive Behavioural Psychotherapist
97 Wood Lane, Harborne, Birmingham B17 9AY
0850 990711/0121 427 7292
BABCP

FELTON, Maureen
Transactional Analysis Psychotherapist
The Unicorn, 14 Lower Hall Lane, Walsall WS1 1SL
34 Church Road, Hynch Cottage, Dordon, Tamworth B78 1RW
01922 616293/01827 897733
ITA

FOKIAS, Dene
Cognitive Behavioural Psychotherapist
18 Hazelbank, Kings Norton, Birmingham B38 8BT
0121 459 6364
BABCP

FRENCH, Anne
Hypno-Psychotherapist
57 Midland Road, Cotteridge,
Birmingham B30 2ES
0121 458 5069
NSHAP

GEORGE, Elizabeth
Child Psychotherapist
Beech House, Hewell Lane, Barnt
Green, Worcester B45 8NZ
0121 445 1338
ACP

GILLIVER, Cath
Psychodynamic Psychotherapist
Uffculme Clinic, Queensbridge Road,
Birmingham B13 8QD
WMIP

GLADWELL, Stephen
Psychodynamic Psychotherapist
Uffculme Clinic, Queensbridge Road,
Moseley, Birmingham B13 8QD
Derel House, Middelsohm Way,
Edgbaston, Birmingham B152 QR
0121 678 5848/0121 678 5800 (f)
WMIP

GOODYEAR, Patricia
Psychoanalytic Psychotherapist
139 Knightlow Road, Harborne,
Birmingham B17 8PY
0121 429 2364
WMIP

HANDY, S.
Cognitive Behavioural Psychotherapist
Birmingham Children's Hospital,
Steelhouse Lane, Birmingham B4 6NH
0121 333 9180
BABCP

HARRIS, Gerald A.
Hypno-Psychotherapist
78 Park View Road, Streetly, Sutton
Coldfield, West Midlands B74 4PS
0121 353 3131
NRHP

HARRIS, Nina
Child Psychotherapist
Oaklands Centre, Selly Oak Hospital,
Raddlebarn Road, Birmingham B29 6JB
0121 627 8231/0121 427 9546
ACP

HARVEY, Tricia A.
Psychoanalytic Psychotherapist, Child
Psychotherapist
6 Clarence Road, Moseley, Birmingham
B13 9SX
0121 449 2308
WMIP, ACP

HOWELL, Judy
Hypno-Psychotherapist
41 Badger Bank Road, Four Oates,
Sutton Coldfield
0121 308 7566
CTS

ILES, David
Hypno-Psychotherapist
flat 3, Bishops Court, 1 Birchtree
Drive, Kittsgreen, Birmingham
B33 0AF
0121 785 0772
CTS

INGHAM, Rosie
Integrative Arts Psychotherapist
35 Holmfield Road, Coventry
CV2 4DD
01203 454503
IATE

JOHNSON, Judy
Psychoanalytic Psychotherapist
173 Beaumont Road, Bournville,
Birmingham B30 1NT
0121 486 1057
WMIP

KINGSLEY, Laurence
Psychoanalytic Psychotherapist
131a Alcester Road, Birmingham
B13 8JP
WMIP

KUTTNER, Enno
Family Therapist
Child &Fam.Service, Pennfields Health
Centre, Upper Zoar Street,
Penfold,Wolverhampton WV3 OJH
AFT

LIEBLING, Angela J.
Psychoanalytic Psychotherapist
6 Cherry Hill Avenue, Barnt Green,
Birmingham B45 8LA
0121 445 3939
WMIP

LINN, Iris
Hypno-Psychotherapist
32 Clive Road, Pattingham, Nr.
Wolverhampton, West Midlands
WV6 7BY
01902 701023
NRHP

LLOYD, Helen
Psychoanalytic Psychotherapist
65 Blakedown Road, Halesowen, West
Midlands B63 4NG
0121 501 3194 (t/f)
WMIP

LOWERY, Ian
Psychoanalytic Psychotherapist
Flat 8, 1 Melton Drive, Edgbaston,
Birmingham B15 2NB
WMIP

MACE, Chris
Group Analyst
School of Post Grad. Medical
Education, University of Warwick,
Coventry CV4 7AL
01203 523523
IGA

MALE, David F.
Psychoanalytic Psychotherapist
81 Belle Vue, Wordsley, Nr.
Stourbridge, W. Midlands DY8 5DB
WMIP

MATÉ, Helen
Psychoanalytic Psychotherapist
177 Pineapple Road, Kings Norton,
Birmingham B30 2SY
WMIP

MCDONALD, James
Psychoanalytic Psychotherapist
20 Greenfields Road, Wombourne,
Staffs WV5 0HP
01902 893512
WMIP

MORBEY, Patricia Joyce
Hypno-Psychotherapist
12 Heycroft, Gibbet Hill, Coventry,
West Midlands CV4 7HE
01203 418202 (t/f)
NRHP

MORGAN, Linda
Hypno-Psychotherapist
15 Chandler Avenue,
Kinver.Stourbridge, West Midlands
DY7 6AG
Worcester Street Surgery, Worcester
Street, Stourbridge, W. Midlands
01384 370713
NSHAP

O'CONNOR, Anna
Psychoanalytic Psychotherapist
160 Uplands Road, Handsworth,
Birmingham B21 8BS
0121 515 2798
WMIP

OWEN, Ian
Integrative Psychotherapist
The Psychology Division, Wulfruna
Street, Wolverhampton WV1 1SB
01902 322 321/01902 333 887
RCSPC

PARAVA, Anna
Gestalt Psychotherapist
10 Elmdon Road, Selly Park,
Birmingham B29 7LF
0121 472 2769
GPTI

PHELPS, Gwyneth
Transactional Analysis Psychotherapist
77 Rowley Street, Walsall, West
Midlands WS1 2AZ
01922 635638/01922 721805 (f)
ITA

RENTOUL, Robert W.
Psychoanalytic Psychotherapist
Lane End, Love Lane, Stockwell End,
Wolverhampton WV6 9PJ
01902 758504 (t/f)
WMIP

REYNOLDS, Michael John
Analytical Psychotherapist
16 Bantock Court, Broad Lane,
Bradmore, Wolverhampton WV3 9DA
WMIP

ROBINSON, Jenny
Transactional Analysis Psychotherapist
32 Grove Avenue, Moseley,
Birmingham B13 9RY
0121 449 2204
ITA

ROPER HALL, Alison
Family Therapist
South Birmingham Psychology Service,
208 Monyhull Road, Kings Norton,
Birmingham B30 3QJ
0121 486 2498/0121 433 4488
AFT

ROSE, Sylvia
Transactional Analysis Psychotherapist
'Amida', 58 Oxford Road, Moseley,
Birmingham B13 9ES
0121 449 2822
ITA

ROY, Geraldine
Psychoanalytic Psychotherapist
174 Walmley Road, Sutton Coldfield
B76 2PY
0121 351 1651
WMIP

SPEED, Bebe
Psychodynamic Psychotherapist, Family
Therapist
c/o WMIP, Rm 123/124, First Floor,
Gazette Buildings, 68 Corporation
Street B4 6TS
0121 449 8503 (t/f)
WMIP, FIC

STOKES, Jenny
Psychoanalytic Psychotherapist
51 Greenhill Road, Moseley,
Birmingham B13 9SU
0121 449 1247
WMIP, GUILD

TAYLOR, Vivienne
Analytical Psychotherapist
146 Malt House Lane, Earlswood,
Solihull, West Midlands B94 5SD
WMIP

TILNEY, Anthony
Transactional Analysis Psychotherapist
63 Victoria Road, Sutton Coldfield,
West Midlands B72 1SN
0121 354 4042/0121 686 7659(f)
ITA

TOOLE, Stuart
Cognitive Behavioural Psychotherapist
24 Herondale Crescent, Stourbridge,
West Midlands DY8 3LH
01384 481965(f)/01384 481942
BABCP

TOWNEND, Michael
Cognitive Behavioural Psychotherapist
Solihull Health Care, 20 Union Road,
Solihull, West Midlands B91 3EF
0121 711 7171 x 2222
BABCP

TRUCKLE, Brian
Child Psychotherapist, Psychoanalytic
Psychotherapist
96 Park Hill, Birmingham B13 8DS
Oaklands Centre, Raddlebarn Road,
Selly Oak, Birmingham B29 6JB
0121 627 8684/0121 627 8681
ACP, WMIP

TRUCKLE, Shirley
Child Psychotherapist, Psychoanalytic
Psychotherapist
96 Park Hill, Birmingham B13 8DS
Oaklands Centre, Raddlebarn Road,
Selly Oak, Birmingham B29 6JB
0121 627 8231/0121 449 9552
ACP, WMIP

VALLANCE, Fiona
Psychodynamic Psychotherapist
Heron Brook House, Bakers Lane,
Knowle, West Midlands B93 8PW
01564 776214/01564 779504 (f)
WMIP

VAN MARLE, Susanna J
Psychoanalytic Psychotherapist
18 St. Mary's Road, Birmingham
B17 0HA
Uffculme Clinic, Puffnsdridge Road, nr.
Kings Health
0121 442 4545
WMIP

VILLIA-GOSLING, Athina
Psychoanalytic Psychotherapist
(Jungian)
1075 Bristol Road, Selly Oak,
Birmingham B29 6LX
0121 472 6587
WMIP

WAY, Jean
Psychoanalytic Psychotherapist
4 Carisbrooke Road, Edgbaston,
Birmingham B17 8NW
WMIP

WHEELER, Sue
Psychoanalytic Psychotherapist
17 Cambridge Road, Moseley,
Birmingham B13 9UE
0121 444 3201
WMIP

WINKLEY, Linda
Child Psychotherapist, Psychoanalytic Psychotherapist
Oaklands Centre, Selly Oak Hospital, Raddlebarn Road, Birmingham B20 2PA
0121 627 8231/0121 627 8684 (f)
ACP, WMIP

WOOD, Sue
Sexual and Marital Psychotherapist
34 Wollescote Road, Pedmore, Stourbridge, West Midlands DY9 7JJ
01384 372987
BASMT

WOODWARD, Joan
Psychoanalytic Psychotherapist
61 Selly Wick Drive, Selly Park, Birmingham B29 7JQ
0121 472 3055
WMIP, CAPP

WILTSHIRE

BANKS, Ron
NLP Psychotherapist
Littlebrook House, The Brownings, Box, Corsham, Wiltshire SN13 8HP
01225 742898/01225 742898(f)
ANLP

BARKER, Elizabeth
Biodynamic Psychotherapist
8 Brunkards Lane, Pewsey, Wilts SN9 5AP
01672 564 232
BTC

BROWN, Elizabeth Ann
Group Analytic Psychotherapist
Flat 30, Anthony Road, Wroughton Swindon, Wiltshire SN4 9HN
01793 813918
IPC

COLEMAN, Jane
Psychoanalytic Psychotherapist
'Cotswold', 99 High Street, Marshfield, Chippenham, Wiltshire SN14 8LT
01225 891478
IPSS

DAVIS, Brenda
Cognitive Behavioural Psychotherapist
Child & Adolescent Clinical Psyc., Child & Family Therapy Service, Trowbridge Fam.Health Centre, The Halve, Trowbridge BA14 8SA
01225 775769/01225 766161
BABCP

DE SOUZA, Janice
Cognitive Psychotherapist
31 Wood Street, Swindon, Wiltshire SN1 4AN
01793 491917
BABCP

EL-KHAYAT, Redwan
Cognitive Behavioural Psychotherapist
The Old Manor Hospital, Wilton Road, Salisbury, Wiltshire SP2 7EP
01722 336262
BABCP

ELTON WILSON, Jennifer
Integrative Psychotherapist
The Bakehouse, Thickwood, Colerne, Nr. Chippenham, Wilts SN14 8BN
01272 736818/01225 743081
MET

ENGLISH, Wendy
Psychoanalytic Psychotherapist
87 Greencroft Street, Salisbury, Wiltshire SP1 1JF
01722 321323
LCP

FOX, Fiona
Psychodynamic Psychotherapist
Swallow Cottage, Wylye Road, Hanging, Langford SP3 4NN
WMIP

GREEN, Michael
Psychoanalytic Psychotherapist
'Cotswold', 99 High Street, Marshfield, Chippenham, Wiltshire SN14 8LT
01225 891478
IPSS

HANCOCK, Patricia
Psychoanalytic Psychotherapist
1 Hockett's Close, Lyneham, Chippenham, Wilts SN15 4QX
01285 861239/01249 890254
SIP

HILLING, Richard
Cognitive Behavioural Psychotherapist
Stress Management & Post Truama Counselling Serv., Bentley Centre, Stratton Road, Swindon, Wiltshire SN1 2SH
01793 616333
BABCP

LASCELLE, Hasan
Psychodrama Psychotherapist
Flat 2, 66A Hythe Road, Old Town, Swindon, Wilts SN1 3NX
01793 422231
BPA

LEACH, Kathy
Transactional Analysis Psychotherapist
'Townsend', Ogbourne St. Andrew, Marlborough, Wiltshire SN8 1SE
01672 841528/01672 841254
ITA, MET

MACGREGOR, Alan
Cognitive Behavioural Psychotherapist
Ease Management Centre, 7 Newport Street, Old Town Swindon SN1 3DZ
01793 435544(f)/01793 433422
BABCP

MELLETT, Jane
Humanistic and Integrative Psychotherapist
16 Tutton Hill, Colerne, Chippenham, Wilts SN14 8DN
01225 742163
BCPC, AHPP

MIDDLETON-SMITH, Virginia
Systemic Psychotherapist
1 Queensberry Road, Salisbury, Wiltshire SP1 3PH
01722 327602
KCC

MILLAR, Peter
Analytical Psychologist-Jungian Analyst
36 Cotswold Community, Ashton Keynes, nr. Swindon, Wiltshire SN6 6QU
01285 861239/01285 862431
AJA

MUNDY, Pamela
Transactional Analysis Psychotherapist
Tannery House, 8 High Street, Downton, Wiltshire SP5 3PJ
01725 513426(f)/01725 513800
ITA

O'BRIEN, Kirsty M G
Cognitive Psychotherapist
Farmer Memorial Unit, Savernake Hospital, London Road, Marlborough SN8 3HL
01793 425428
BABCP

POCOCK, David
Family Psychotherapist
Child and Family Consultation Service, Marlborough House, Princess Margaret Hospital, Okus Road, Swindon SN1 4JU
01793 428800
AFT

POCOCK, Olga
Analytical Psychotherapist
32 Elizabeth Court, Cranebridge Road, Salisbury, Wiltshire SP2 7UX
01722 320093
SIP

PREGNALL, Sheila
Psychodrama Psychotherapist
70 Kent Road, Swindon, Wilts SN1 3NG
01793 541899
BPA

REES, Ian
Core Process Psychotherapist
60 Bristol Street, Malmesbury, Wiltshire SN16 0AX
01666 823471
AAPP

RHEINSCHMIEDT, Otto
Group Analyst
Ficino Cottage, 78 Farleigh Road, Wingfield, Bradford on Avon, Wilts BA14 9LG
01225 763531
IGA

RIMMER, Lynn
Psychoanalytic Psychotherapist
69 St. Mark's Road, Salisbury, Wilts
01722 332936/01722 330661
GUILD

ROBB, Melissa
Family Therapist
79 Gloucester Road, Malmesbury, Wiltshire SN16 0AJ
01666 822945
AFT, FIC

SHARPE, John
Group Analyst
Clare Cottage, 23 West Dean, Nr. Salisbury SP5 1JB
01794 340028
IGA

THAM, Anna
Core Process Psychotherapist, Autogenic Psychotherapist
Turleigh Farm, Turleigh, Nr. Bath, Wiltshire BA15 2HH
01225 868221
AAPP, BAFAT

VOELCKER, Cara
Humanistic and Integrative Psychotherapist
Avils Farm, Lower Stanton, Quinton, Chippenham, Wilts SN14 6DA
01249 720202
BCPC

WESTMAN, Stephen
Cognitive Behavioural Psychotherapist
Kingshill House, Kingshill Road, Swindon SN1 4LG
01793 491917
BABCP

WHITWELL, John
Group Analytic Psychotherapist
The Old Farmhouse, Cotswold Community, Ashton Keynes, Nr. Swindon, Wilts SN6 6QU
01285 861694
LCP

WILLIAMS-CONLEY, Debbie
Cognitive Behavioural Psychotherapist
31 Wood Street, Old Town, Swindon SN1 4AN
01793 491917
BABCP

WORCESTERSHIRE

CAMPBELL, Duine
Psychoanalytic Psychotherapist (Jungian)
Home Farm, High Park, Droitwich, Worcestershire WR9 0AG
01905 771588
WMIP

DENHAM, Juliet
Gestalt Psychotherapist
Orchard House, Prescott, Nr Cleobury Mortimer, Worc. DY14 8RR
10 Elmdon Road, Selly Park, Birmingham B29 7LF
01746 718 231
GPTI

DENHAM-VAUGHAN, Sally
Gestalt Psychotherapist, Integrative Psychotherapist
The Summer House, 127 Columbia Drive, Lower Wick, Worcester WR2 4XX
01905 763333 x 33103
GPTI

GILLIGAN, Toni
Gestalt Psychotherapist
22 Tileford Cottages, Long Lane, Throckmorton, Nr. Pershore, Worcs WR10 2LA
01386 561528
GCL

GROOM, Nigel
Psychoanalytic Psychotherapist
The Gap, Saleway, Nr. Droitwich Spa, Worcestershire WR9 7JY
01905 391212(f)/01905 391470
IPC, WMIP

LAW, Gordon
Transactional Analysis Psychotherapist
5 Bawdsey Avenue, Malvern, Worcester WR14 2EW
01684 566268 (t/f)
ITA

MORGAN, Jo
Hypno-Psychotherapist
Apt.4 Birchwood, Imperial Road, Worcs. WR14 3AW
01684 891128
NSHAP

NEWBY, Rita
Psychoanalytic Psychotherapist
78 Victoria Avenue, Worcester WR5 1ED
01905 763552
CPP

REDDIE, Mary
Psychoanalytic Psychotherapist
The Landscape, 41 East Road, Bromsgrove, Worcs. B60 2NW
WMIP

THOMPSON, Hilary
Psychosynthesis Psychotherapist
40D St. Johns, Worcester WR2 5AJ
01905 422 420
AAPP

VICKERS, Kate
Psychosynthesis Psychotherapist
The Worcester Counselling & Psychother. Foundation, 40D St Johns, Worcester WR2 5AJ
01905 422 420
AAPP

YORKSHIRE NORTH

BLACKLEY, Joanne
Psychoanalytic Psychotherapist, Psychodynamic Psychotherapist
Hazelwood, Appleton-le-Moors, York YO6 6TE
01751 417 577
LCP, YAPP

BRAY, Malcolm
NLP Psychotherapist
7 George Street, Carleton, Nr Skipton, North Yorks
01756 791110
ANLP

BULMER, Liz
Transactional Analysis Psychotherapist
7a Belgrave Crescent, Harrogate, North Yorkshire HG2 8HZ
ITA

BURDETT, C.W.
Cognitive Behavioural Psychotherapist
37 Broomfield Avenue, Northallerton, North Yorkshire DL7 8RH
01609 771 528/01325 743 566
BABCP

DAVIDOFF, Leslie
Psychoanalytic Psychotherapist
18 Broadway West, Fulford, York YO1 4JJ
6 Beverley Garden, Dodsworth Avenue, York YO3 7HH
01904 424 198/01904 621866
IPSS

DAVIDOFF, Suzanne
Hypno-Psychotherapist
Broadway West, Fulford, York YO1 4JJ
01904 621866
NRHP

DUNCAN, Ursula
Transactional Analysis Psychotherapist, Integrative Psychotherapist
18 Mayfield Grove, Harrogate, North Yorkshire HG1 5HB
01423 569640
SCPC, ITA

FARQUHARSON, Graeme
Group Analyst
Oaklands, 4 Aislabie Close, Clotherholme Road, Ripon, North Yorks HG4 2DD
0114 222 2979
IGA

GALLOWAY, Betsy
Transactional Analysis Psychotherapist, Integrative Psychotherapist
10 Gray Street, Scarcroft Green, York, YO23 1BN
01904 647893
SCPC, ITA

GREENING, Sarah
Transactional Analysis Psychotherapist, Integrative Psychotherapist
5 South Parade, Northallerton, North Yorkshire DL7 8SE
01609 776680
SCPC, ITA

HANDLEY, Rima
Psychosynthesis Psychotherapist
34 St. James Green, Thirsk, North Yorkshire YO7 1AG
0191 490 0274/01845 552719
AAPP

HEARD, Dorothy
Psychodynamic Psychotherapist
19 The Green, Richmond, North Yorkshire DL10 4RG
01748 823262
YAPP

HESTER, Bridget
Psychoanalytic Psychotherapist
The Old Rectory, Crayke, York YO6 4TA
01347 821593
YAPP, LPDO

JONES, Helen
Personal Construct Psychotherapist
2 Heslington Court, School Lane, York YO1 5EX
Director, CLD, Dept of Health Studies, Innovation, Centre, York Science Park, Heslington YO1 5DG
01904 435138/435139/01904 438 757(t/f)
CPCP

JONES, Marlene
Family Therapist
18 Guards Court, Burniston Road, Scarborough YO12 6QR
01723 371823 (t/f)
IFT

KENNARD, David
Group Analyst, Psychodynamic Psychotherapist
24 St Oswalds Road, Fulford, York YO1 4PF
01904 412551/01904 633415
IGA, YAPP

KENNETT, Christine
Gestalt Psychotherapist, Integrative Psychotherapist
38 Millfield Road, York YO2 1NQ
01904 638623
SPTI, GPTI

LAKE, Brian
Psychodynamic Psychotherapist
19 The Green, Richmond, North Yorkshire DL10 4RG
01748 23262
YAPP

LAWRENCE, Yvonne
Transactional Analysis Psychotherapist, Integrative Psychotherapist
Shannon House, 13 York Terrace, Whitby, North Yorkshire YO12 1QF
01947 603496
SCPC, ITA

MARTIN, Gill
Psychodynamic Psychotherapist
34 The Old Village, Huntington, York YO3 9RB
The Tuke Centre, 28 Green Dykes Lane, York YO1 3HH
01904 750285/01904 430370
YAPP

MCCLUSKEY, Una
Psychodynamic Psychotherapist, Family Therapist
Dept. of Social Policy & Social Work, University of York, Heslington, York YO1 5DD
The Yews, Waplington Hall, Allerthorpe, York YO4 4RS
01904 433492/01759 302104
YAPP, AFT

MILLER, Liza Bingley
Family Therapist
10 St. Oswald's Road, Fulford, York YO1 4PF
01904 633417
AFT

PAYNE, Graham
Psychoanalytic Psychotherapist
Dept. of Mental Health, Friarage Hospital, Northallerton DL6 1JG
01609 779911
NAAP

PROUDLEY, Helen
Sexual and Marital Psychotherapist
Doxford House, 73 Front Street, Sowerby, Thirsk, N.Yorks YO7 1JP
Darlington Memorial Hospital, Hollyhurst Road, Darlington, Co. Durham DL3 6HX
BASMT

REILLY, Stephen
Psychodynamic Psychotherapist
Bootham Park Hospital, York YO3 7BY
01904 610777/01904 453794 (f)
YAPP

RICHARDSON, Caroline
Sexual and Marital Psychotherapist
The Oakdale Centre, 49 Valley Drive, Harrogate HG2 0JH
01423 503080
BASMT

TYSON, Robert
Gestalt Psychotherapist
Forge House, 65 High Street, Snainton, Scarborough, North Yorkshire YO13 9AL
01723 859265
GPTI

WILKINSON, Kate
Gestalt Psychotherapist, Integrative Psychotherapist
25 Mayville Avenue, Scarborough, Yorks YO12
01723 376246
SPTI

WILLIAMS, Richard
Family Therapist
18A Rectory View, Lockington, Driffield, E. Yorks YO25 9SG
01482 640122/01430 810446
FIC

WOJCIECHOWSKA, Ewa
Group Analyst
'Oaklands', 4 Aislabie Close, Clotherholme Road, Ripon, North Yorkshire HG4 2DD
01904 430 370/01765 604982
IGA

YORKSHIRE SOUTH

BRADY, Alec
Cognitive Behavioural Psychotherapist
25 Hunshelf Park, Stocksbridge, Sheffield, S Yorkshire S36 2BT
Dept of Clinical Psychology, Stepping Hill Hospital, Stockport, Cheshire
0114 288 3276
BABCP

CARIAPA, Illana
Cognitive Behavioural Psychotherapist
Dept of Child & Family Psychiatry, Chatham House, Doncaster Gate, Rotherham S65 1DJ
01709 824808/9
BABCP

CAULFIELD, J. Heather
Psychodynamic Psychotherapist
35 Barrie Grove, Hellaby, Rotherham S66 8HG
01709 543336
HIP

DE CARTERET, John
Psychodynamic Psychotherapist
Child Adolescent & Family Therapy Service, Edmund Street Clinic, Edmund Street, Chesterfield
Springwoods, Thornhill, Bamford, Hope Valley S33 0BR
01433 651865/01246 451252
HIP

DONOHOE, Gillian
Cognitive Behavioural Psychotherapist
Department of Behavioural Psychotherapy, Doncaster Royal Infirmary, Armthorpe Road, Doncaster DN2 5LT
01302 366666 x 3214
BABCP

LEA, Mary
Behavioural Psychotherapist
Mental Health Unit, Rotherham Dist. General Hospital, Moorgate, Rotherham S60 2UD
01709 820000 x 6032
BABCP

SMITH, Eileen F.
Psychodynamic Psychotherapist
First Floor Flat, Hooton Pagnell Hall, Hooton Pagnell, Doncaster DN5 7BW
01977 642481
HIP

TOWNSEND, Pat
Cognitive Behavioural Psychotherapist
16 Marina Rise, Darfield, Barnsley, South Yorks S73 9PT
01226 340024/01977 606331
BABCP

TWEED, Mary
Transactional Analysis Psychotherapist
Flat 2, 54 Bennetthorpe, Doncaster, South Yorkshire DN2 6AD
148 Sir Hiltons Road, Birmingham, West Heath B31 3NW
0121 477 2420/01302 761915
ITA

WRIGHT, Christine M.J.
Cognitive Behavioural Psychotherapist
Dept. of Behavioural Psychotherapy, Doncaster Royal Infirmary, Armthorpe Road, Doncaster DN4 7DT
01302 366666 x 3214
BABCP

YORKSHIRE WEST

AGASS, Dick
Psychodynamic Psychotherapist
5c Chapel Lane, Bingley, West Yorkshire BD16 2NG
01274 510217/01274 561991
HIP

ANDERSON, Larry
Family Therapist
8 Selbourne Villas, St. Mary's Road, Bradford, West Yorkshire BD9 4NN
01274 493308
AFT

ASHTON, John
Psychodynamic Psychotherapist
16 Woodland Park Road, Leeds LS6 2AZ
HIP, YAPP, YAPP

BAILEY, Susanna
Psychoanalytic Psychotherapist
'Highgate', off Street Lane, Leeds LS8 1DF
0113 266 3649
YAPP

BONNER, Kate
Psychodynamic Psychotherapist
17 Launds, Rochdale Road, Golcar, Huddersfield HD7 4NN
01484 654508
YAPP

BOSTOCK, Christine
Psychodynamic Psychotherapist
Hawthorn House, Regent Street, Leeds
LS7 4PE
0113 269 7194
HIP, YAPP

BOSTON, Paula
Family Psychotherapist, Systemic Psychotherapist
Psychology Department, University of Leeds, Leeds LS2 9JT
68 Parish Ghyll Drive, Ilkley, West Yorkshire LS29 9PR
01943 601162/0113 233 6641
IFT

CANN, Lesley
Psychodynamic Psychotherapist
Lynfield Mount Hospital, (Bradford CMHT), Heights Lane, Bradford
BD9 6DP
01274 363233
YAPP

CONLON, Isobel
Psychoanalytic Psychotherapist, Analytical Psychotherapist
15 Ash Grove, Headingley, Leeds
LS6 1AX
0113 245 5725
NWIDP, YAPP

COTTRELL, David
Family Therapist
Academic Unit of Child & Adolescent Mental Health, 12A Clarendon Road, Leeds LS2 9NN
0113295 1761/0113 295 1760
AFT

COURTNEY, Mary
Psychodynamic Psychotherapist
St. James's University Hospital, Beckett Street, Leeds LS9 7TJ
0113 206 5078
YAPP

DOUGLAS, Angela
Psychodynamic Psychotherapist
5A Westgate, Otley, West Yorkshire
LS21 3AT
01943 468443
YAPP

EADIE, Yvonne
Cognitive Analytic Therapist
4 Alberta Avenue, Leeds LS7 4LX
0113 294 0141/0114 271 6894
ACAT

GARTLAND, Michael
Psychodynamic Psychotherapist
Fall Hall, Waterside, Marsden, Huddersfield HD7 6BU
01484 845851
HIP

GAUNTLETT, Tim
Psychoanalytic Psychotherapist
'Waske Hall', 50 Skircoat Green, Halifax HX3 0SA
01422 341391
IPSS

GILLJAM, Annika
Psychoanalytic Psychotherapist
24 Eaton Road, Ilkley, West Yorkshire
LS29 9PU
01943 602449
GUILD, YAPP

GLOVER, Jean
Sexual and Marital Psychotherapist
The Rectory, Church Side, Methley, Leeds LS26 9BJ
01977 515278
BASMT

GODSIL, Susan
Analytical Psychotherapist
1A Oakwood Lane, Leeds LS8 2PZ
0113 265 7169
YAPP

HAMILTON, Jane
Psychoanalytic Psychotherapist
Avenue Cottage, Harewood Avenue, East Keswick, Leeds LS17 9HL
01937 572291
WMIP

HAMLYN, Sarah
Integrative Psychotherapist
305a Harrogate Road, Leeds LS17 6PA
SCPC

HANKS, Helga
Family Therapist, Analytical Psychotherapist
Dept. of Clinical & Health Psychology, Ashley Wing, St. James's University Hospita, Leeds, Yorkshire LS9 7TF
Leeds Family Therapy & Research Centre, University of Leeds, Leeds
LS2 9JT
0113 206 4079(f)/0113 206 5897
YAPP

HARROW, Anne
Analytical Psychotherapist, Group Analyst
3 Woodbine Terrace, Headingley, Leeds
LS6 4AF
0113 278 6142
YAPP, IGA

HEENAN, Colleen
Analytical Psychotherapist
11 Milford Place, Bradford BD9 4RU
01274 493125/01274 774055 (f)
YAPP

HELBERT, Jan
Group Analyst
34 Leylands Terrace, Heaton, Bradford, W Yorks BD9 5QR
01274 544 259
IGA

JACKSON, Sherin
Personal Construct Psychotherapist
Highdale Cottage, 217 Barnsley Road, Denby Dale, W. Yorks HD8 8TS
01484 864824
CPCP

JONES, Maggy
Family Therapist
Bay House Cottage, 118 Main Street, Coronley, Nr. Keighley, W. Yorks
BD20 8NR
010535 690055
AFT

KAY, Margaret
Group Analyst
20 Kingswood Gardens, Leeds LS8 2BT
01977 605500/01532 666147
IGA

LANCELOT, Maggie
Psychodynamic Psychotherapist
5c Chapel Lane, Bingley, West Yorks
BD16 2NG
01274 510217/01274 778163
NWIDP, YAPP

LEWIS, Sheila
Psychoanalytic Psychotherapist
17 Princess Road, Ilkley, West Yorkshire LS29 9NP
01943 601948
GUILD

LUDOLF, Monica
Hypno-Psychotherapist
4 Riviera Gardens, Chapel Allerton, Leeds, Yorkshire LS7 3DW
0113 262 2355
NRHP

MANTON, Rosie
Psychosynthesis Psychotherapist
Lower Small Shaw Farm, Pecket Well, Hebden Bridge, W. Yorks HX7 8RF
01422 843 501
AAPP

MARSHALL, Pauline
Integrative Psychotherapist
5 Daisy Road, Brighouse, West York HD6 35Y
01484 710210
SPTI

MARTIN, Carol
Psychodynamic Psychotherapist
Dept. of Psychiatry and Behaviourial Sciences, University of Leeds, 15 Hyde Terrac, Leeds LS2 9JT
0113 233 2736
YAPP

MORRIS, Jane
Psychoanalytic Psychotherapist
4 Lower Chiserley, Old Town, Hebden Bridge, West Yorkshire HX7 8RZ
Department of Psychotherapy, Moor Lane Centre, Burley in Wharfdale, West Yorkshire
NWIDP

NOLAN, Philip
NLP Psychotherapist
67 Kaye Lane, Almondbury, Huddersfield, West Yorkshire HD5 8XT
01484 432847/0585 721318
ANLP

OAKLEY, Ian H.
Analytical Psychotherapist
Glen Royd, Birchcliffe Road, Hebden Bridge, West Yorkshire HX7 8DB
LPDO, YAPP

PAGE, Annabel
Analytical Psychotherapist
18 Crossbeck Road, Ilkley, W. Yorks LS29 9JN
01943 601184
YAPP

PARKER, John
Psychoanalytic Psychotherapist
18 Eaton Road, Ilkley, West Yorkshire LS29 9PU
01943 603837
LPDO

PATTINSON, Philip
Cognitive Behavioural Psychotherapist
Psychology Services, Northowram Hospital, Northowram, Halifax, West Yorkshire HX3 7SW
01422 201101 x 334
BABCP

PHILLIPS, Thomas Lambton
Cognitive Behavioural Psychotherapist
90 Redwood Drive, Bradley Manor, Huddersfield, West Yorkshire HD2 1PW
dept Behavioural Psychotherapy, 6A Greenhead Road, Huddersfield, West Yorkshire HD1 4ED
01484 455150/0973 470474
BABCP

RICHARDS, David
Cognitive Behavioural Psychotherapist
PTSD Clinic, c/o Roundhay Wing, St James University Hospital, Beckett Street LS9 7TF
Wingfield House, 22 Street Lane, Leeds LS8 2ET
0113 217 6785(t/f)/0113 206 5597
BABCP

ROSE, Sally
Psychoanalytic Psychotherapist, Psychodynamic Psychotherapist
4 Victoria Road, Kirkstall, Leeds LS5 3JB
0113 274 5147
ARBS, YAPP, FIP

ROWAN, Chris
Integrative Arts Psychotherapist
60 Victoria Road, Leeds LS6 1DL
0113 274 3065
IATE

ROWE, Carolyn
Psychodynamic Psychotherapist
Low Meadow, Hall Drive, Bramhope, Leeds LS16 9JF
0113 284 2567
HIP

ROWE, Celly
Analytical Psychotherapist
Dept. of Psychotherapy, Southfield House, 40 Clarendon Road, Leeds LS2 9PJ
0113 243 9000/0113 243 3348 (f)
YAPP

SIDEY, Brian
Psychoanalytic Psychotherapist
38 Wellington Crescent, Shipley, W. Yorks BD18 3PH
01274 599327/01274 784888
YAPP

SMALLEY, John
Analytical Psychologist-Jungian Analyst
270 Park Lane, Keighley, West Yorkshire BD21 4RL
5A Westgate, Otley, W Yorks
01535 665362
IGAP

SPENCELEY, Dave
Transactional Analysis Psychotherapist
27 Clare Road, Halifax, West Yorkshire HX1 2JP
01422 366356
ITA

STEWART, Kate
Family Therapist
8 Selbourne Villas, St. Mary's Road, Bradford BD9 4NN
01274 493308
AFT

STOKELD, Alasdair
Psychoanalytic Psychotherapist, Psychodynamic Psychotherapist
4 Victoria Road, Kirkstall, Leeds LS5 3JB
0113 274 5147
ARBS, YAPP, FIP

STRATTON, Peter M
Systemic Psychotherapist
Leeds Family Therapy and Research Centre, Department of Psychology, University of Leeds, Leeds LS2 9JT
0113 233 5728
KCC

SYME, Gabrielle
Analytical Psychotherapist
Mount Farm House, Town Street, Rawdon, Leeds LS19 6QJ
0113 250 5700 (t/f)
YAPP

TANNA, Nick
Group Analyst, Psychodynamic Psychotherapist
99 Netherton Lane, Netherton, W Yorkshire WF4 4HG
IGA, YAPP, NWIDP

TAYLOR, James
Integrative Psychotherapist
4 Beechwood Street, Leeds LS4 2LX
0113 226 8481
NSAP

TREPKA, Chris
Cognitive Psychotherapist
Ashgrove CMHC, 48 Ashgrove, Bradford, West Yorkshire BD7 1BL
The Yorkshire Clinic, Bradford Road, Bingley, West Yorkshire BD16 1TW
01274 560311/01274 391671
BABCP

VACIAGO SMITH, Marta
Child Psychotherapist, Psychoanalytic Psychotherapist
21 Milnthorpe Drive, Wakefield WF2 7HU
Dept of Child & Family Psychiatry, St.James University Hospital, Leeds LS9
0113 2433144 x 4292/01924 255629
ACP

VINCENT, Jane
Psychodynamic Psychotherapist
16 Pasture Terrace, Leeds LS7 4QR
Academic Unit of Child & Adolescent Mental Health, 12a Clarendon Road, Leeds LS2 9NN
0113 295 1771/0113 228 9885
HIP

WALFORD, Jane
Transactional Analysis Psychotherapist
2a Weetwood Lane, Far Headingley, Leeds LS16 5LS
01132 789953
ITA

WALFORD, Robin
Transactional Analysis Psychotherapist
2a Weetwood Lane, Far Headingley, Leeds LS16 5LS
01132 789953
ITA

WATTIS, Libby
Psychodynamic Psychotherapist, Psychoanalytic Psychotherapist
11 Cherry Rise, Leeds LS14 2HJ
WMIP, YAPP, LPDO

WEBB, Joan
Psychoanalytic Psychotherapist, Psychodynamic Psychotherapist
23 Henconner Lane, Chapel Allerton, Leeds LS7 3NX
01132 623766
LPDO, YAPP

WELCH, Lawrence
Cognitive Analytic Therapist
Psychology & Psychotherapy Service, Malham House, 25 Hyde Terrace, Leeds LS2 9LN
4 Alberta Avenue, Leeds LS7 4LX
0113 294 0141/0113 392 2640
ACAT

WELSH, Catherine
Psychodynamic Psychotherapist
54 Ridge End Villas, Leeds LS6 2DA
0113 225 6930 (f)
YAPP

WILLIAMS, Christopher John
Cognitive Psychotherapist
Malham House, 25 Hyde Terrace, Leeds LS2 9LN
0113 292 6716
BABCP

OVERSEAS

AUSTRALIA

CADE, Brian
Family Therapist
PO Box 386, Eastwood, New South Wales, Australia 2122
612 9876 6068/012 612 9868 2606
AFT

CEBON, Ann
Child Psychotherapist
8 Coombs Avenue, Kew, Victoria 3101, Australia
0061 398 533 114
ACP

CLARK, Giles
Analytical Psychologist-Jungian Analyst
1 Russell Street, Woollahra, Sydney, NSW 2025, Australia
02 9386 0648
IGAP

DUNK, Sarah
Psychoanalytic Psychotherapist
The Laurels'62 Diadem Street, Lesmore NSW 2480, Australia
02 66 22 33 51
LCP

DURLACH, Stefan
Integrative Psychotherapist
20 High Street, Glenbrook, NSW 2773, Australia
02 9716 7199/0247 393 210
RCSPC

FULLERTON, Peter B.
Psychoanalytic Marital Psychotherapist
42 Alandale Road, Eaglemont, Victoria 3084, Australia
61 3 9455 2791 (t/f)/pgfull@preston.-starway.net.au
TMSI, SAP

HENRY, Rachel M.
Child Psychotherapist
4 Wigram Road, Austinmer, NSW 2515, Australia
ACP

KENWOOD, Pat
Child Psychotherapist
51 Cole Street, Brighton, Victoria 3186, Australia
00 61 359 62306
ACP

KINBACHER, William
Transpersonal Psychotherapist
PO Box 4661, Cairns 4870, N. Queensland, Australia
CCPE

KONDOS, Sandra
Integrative Psychotherapist
20 High Street, Glenbrook, NSW 2773, Australia
0247 393 210
RCSPC

LEIGH, Elana
Integrative Psychotherapist
158 Wellington Street, Bondi 2026, Sydney, Australia
93 00 9907/93 00 9801 (f)
MET

MORRISSEY, Shirley
Cognitive Behavioural Psychotherapist
Dept. of Psychology and Sociology, James Cook University, PO Box 6811, Cairns 4870, Australia
00 61 70 939331/00 61 70 421183
BABCP

OGILVIE, Renata
Existential Psychotherapist
P O Box 314, Blackheath, NSW 2785, Australia
0247 875514
RCSPC

SCHMIDT-NEVEN, Ruth
Child Psychotherapist
Centre for Child & Family Development, 721A Riversdale Road, Camberwell, Victoria 3124, Australia
00 618 300422/00 618 57777 (f)
ACP

STRASSER, Alison
Integrative Psychotherapist
251 Underwood Street, Paddington, NSW 2021, Australia
010 612 9327 169/02 9363 5663
RCSPC

TAYLOR, Rosemary E.B.
Transactional Analysis Psychotherapist
Oxford House, 48 Oxford Terrace, Unley, Adelaide 5061, Australia
08 8271 7555/08 8373 4421 (f)
ITA

THOMPSON, Christine
Integrative Psychotherapist
16 Breen Terrace, Ferny Creek, Victoria 3786, Australia
03 9755 3048
RCSPC

VINEY, Linda
Personal Construct Psychotherapist
Department of Psychology, PO Box 1144, Wollongong University, NSW 2550, Australia
CPCP

BELGIUM

ROEX, Danielle
Psychosynthesis Psychotherapist, Gestalt Psychotherapist
Meersstraat 95, B-9000 Gent, Belgium
00 32 9221 0901/00 32 9221 4103 (f)
AAPP

BRAZIL

DE SOUZA, Joney
Psychoanalytic Psychotherapist
Alamada Santos, 927 - ap.52, Sao Paulo, Brazil
00-55-11-283 3815
IPSS

SAMSON, Andre
Biodynamic Psychotherapist
Rua Joao Batista Leme, Da Silva 53, 05449 - 030 Sao Paolo, Brazil
00 55 11 3021 4122
BTC

CANADA

BATE, Dolores
Gestalt Psychotherapist
1747 Gordon Avenue, West Vancouver, B.C., Canada V7V 1V4
604 922 5793/604 925 2012 (f)
GPTI

FISH, Deborah M.
Hypno-Psychotherapist
3437 W. 2nd Avenue, Vancouver, B.C., Canada V6R 1J3
604 737 7563
NRHP

ROSEMAN, Renee
Analytical Psychologist-Jungian Analyst
104 - 430 River Avenue, Winnipag, Manitoba, Canada R3L 0C6
01 204 474 0428
BAP

PHATERPEKAR, Hem
Psychoanalytic Psychotherapist
116-8434 120th Street, Surrey, British Columbia, V3W 7S2, Canada
604 543 4449
LPDO

DENMARK

VEJE, Margit
Psychoanalytic Psychotherapist
Skt. Pauls Gade 8b St., DK-8000, Arhus C., Denmark
00 45 86 128530
ARBS

FINLAND

RUISMAKI, Marjo
Systemic Psychotherapist
Ala-Malmintori 2,3krs, 00700, Helsinki, Finland
00358 9 310 58242/00358 9 310 58251 (f)
KCC

FRANCE

FOGUEL, Brenda
Group Analyst
21 rue Beranger, 75003 Paris, France
0033 1 42 77 04 30
IGA

GAVIN, Verity
Integrative Psychotherapist
Le Bastidon, Hameau de St Pierre, St Martin de Castillon 84750, France
04 90 75 10 65/04 90 75 25 71
RCSPC

GERMANY

CANOBBIO, Victoria
Primal Psychotherapist
Berlinerstrass 73, 14467 Potsdam, Germany
0049 33 12704035
LAPP

PERVOLTZ, Rainer
Integrative Psychotherapist, Body Psychotherapist
Oberan 49, 79102 - Freiburg, Germany
07668 94532
CCBP

POLLACK, Angela
Primal Psychotherapist
Neustadter Str.15, Bad Gogging, 93333, Germany
LAPP

GREECE

LAYIOU-LIGNOS, Effie
Child Psychotherapist
54 Aimonos Street, Colonos, 10442, Athens, Greece
00 301 514 8123
ACP

MOUTZOUKIS, Chris
Cognitive Behavioural Psychotherapist
63 Egmatia Street, 546 31, Thessalonikis, Greece
00 30 392 27081/00 30 31 288 380
BABCP

SAZATZOGLOU-HITZOS, M.
Child Psychotherapist
P. Levanti 8, Panorama, Salonica, Greece
00301 343741/031 344 644 (f)
ACP

SIMOS, Gregoris
Cognitive Behavioural Psychotherapist
69 Vas.Olgas Street, 546 42 Thessalonki, Greece
0030 31 268 841/0030 31 838 755
BABCP

HONG KONG

O'BRIAN, Charles
Family Psychotherapist
Dept. of Applied Social Sciences, City University of Hong Kong, 83 Tai Chee Avenue, Kowloon, Hong Kong
2788 8994/2788 8960 (f)
IFT

PRYDE, Nia
Sexual and Marital Psychotherapist
14A Block 1, Tam Towers, 25 Sha Wan Drive, Victoria Road, Hong Kong
BASMT

SHUEN, Dorcas
Psychoanalytic Psychotherapist, Group Analytic Psychotherapist
42, RN 8, Fairview Park, Yuen Long, N.T., Hong Kong
248 20308
LCP

TURNER, Vivien
Cognitive Analytic Therapist
0531, Tower 4, Hong Kong Park Preview, 88 Tai Tam Reservoir Road, Tai Tam, Hong Kong S.A.R
00 85 2 2813 1405
00 85 2 2813 1489(f)
ACAT

INDIA

BHARUCHA, Aiveen
Child Psychotherapist
125 Wodehouse Road, Colaba, Bombay 400005, India
009122 2151 260
ACP

BHARUCHA, Manek
Child Psychotherapist
125 Wodehouse Road, Colaba, Bombay 400005, India
00 91 22 215 1257
ACP

IRELAND

BANNON, Maureen
Transpersonal Psychotherapist
Ceathru Ban, RavensDale, Dundalk, Ireland
00353 4271901
CCPE

BRANAGAN, Noelle
Psychodrama Psychotherapist
Freeport, Bearna, Galway, Eire
01232 781165/01232 649557
BPA

BUTCHER, Gerard
Cognitive Behavioural Psychotherapist
St. John of God Hospital, Stillorgan, Co. Dublin, Ireland
69 Lower Baggott Street, Dublin 2, Ireland
353 1 288 1781
BABCP

CAIRD, Elizabeth J.
Hypno-Psychotherapist
22 Cherrymount Park, Dublin 7, Irish Republic
0956 159356/00 3531 838 9767
NSHAP

CONROY, Kay
Psychosynthesis Psychotherapist
White House, Templeogue, Dublin 6, Ireland
00 3531 280 0626/00 353 1 906615
AAPP

CULLEN, Anne M.
Cognitive Behavioural Psychotherapist
St. Mary's Hospital, Westport Road, Castlebar, Co. Mayo, Ireland
00 353 94 21 333
BABCP

DUBERRY, Mark
Integrative Psychosynthesis Psychotherapist
6 Woodlands Avenue, Stillorgan, Co. Dublin, Ireland
003531 2887216
RE.V

FLYNN, Stephen
Psychodrama Psychotherapist
Carrig Na Floinn, Lavally, Mallow, Co. Cork, Eire
010 353 22 21937
BPA

GROVER, Mary V.E.
Psychoanalytic Psychotherapist
Ardralla, Church Cross, Skibbereen, County Cork, Ireland
00 353 28 38373
LCP

HARRISON, Caroline
Sexual and Marital Psychotherapist
RCSI Dept. of OB/GYN, Rotunda Hospital, Dublin 1, Ireland
31531 8727599
BASMT

HOWARD, Sister Columba
Transactional Analysis Psychotherapist
1 Summerhill Heights, Wexford, Ireland
053 42396
ITA

HOWLETT, Brian
Sexual and Marital Psychotherapist
1B Belfield Court, Donnybrook, Dublin 4, Ireland
BASMT

MAC LIAM, Fionnula
Cognitive Behavioural Psychotherapist
4 Wynnefield Road, Rathmines Dublin 6, Ireland
Area 2 Psychiatric Services, Baggot St Hosp Outpatientt Dept, Baggot Street, Dublin
00 353 1 497 3498
BABCP

MASTERSON, Ingrid
Psychoanalytic Psychotherapist
'Alberta', Ardtona Avenue, Lower Churchtown Road, Dublin 14, Ireland
IPSS, FIP

MAUGER, Benig
Psychoanalytic Psychotherapist
69 Cowper Road, Rathmines, Dublin 6, Ireland
01 4970501/01 4978171 (f)
AGIP

MCCARRICK, Tom
Group Analyst
3 Greenlands, Rosses Point, Sligo, Ireland
IGA

MCCARTHY, Rita
Analytical Psychologist-Jungian Analyst
39 Balally Terrace, Dundrum, Dublin 16, Ireland
295 6002
AJA

MCFADDEN, Hugh E.
Cognitive Behavioural Psychotherapist
'Sancta Maria', Gortlee, Letterkenny, Co. Donegal, Ireland
St. Conal's Hospital, Dept. of Psychological Therapy, Letterkenny, Co.Donegal, Ireland
74 21022 x 3275/00 353 74 21919
BABCP

MCGOLDRICK, Mary
Cognitive Behavioural Psychotherapist
St. Patrick's Hospital, James's Street, Dublin 8, Ireland
00 3531 677 5423
BABCP

MCGROARY-MEEHAN, Maureen
Sexual and Marital Psychotherapist, Behavioural Psychotherapist
Donegal Community Services, East End House, Clar Road, Donegal Town, Ireland
00 353 72 41351/00 353 73 21933
BASMT, BABCP

MURPHY, Ger
Integrative Psychotherapist
Institute of Creative Counselling and Psychoth., 82 Upper Georges Street, Dun Laoghaire, Co Dublin
00 35 31 280 2523
MC

MURRAY, Catherine
Psychodrama Psychotherapist
Newtown House, Doneraile, Co.Cork, Eire
00 353 222 4117
BPA

MURRAY, Gus
Integrative Psychotherapist
2 Violet Ville, College Road, Cork, Ireland
00 353 21 273268 (t/f)
MET

O'CONNOR, Aine
Primal Psychotherapist
The Garden Studio, 15 Morehampton Road, Donnybrook, Dublin 4, Ireland
00 3531 668 3123
LAPP

O'CONOR, Mary
Sexual and Marital Psychotherapist
The Albany Clinic, Clifton Court, Lower Fitzwilliam Street, Dublin 2, Ireland
661 2222
BASMT

O'NEILL, Julia
Biodynamic Psychotherapist
Kilbeacanty, Gort, Co. Galway, Eire
00353 91 631194
BTC

O'SULLIVAN, Bernadette
Personal Construct Psychotherapist
VICO Consultation Centre, 2 Dungar Terrace, Dun Laogharie, Co. Dublin, Ireland
00 3531 284 3336
CPCP

OTTO, Joachim
Biodynamic Psychotherapist
56 Dun-na-mara, Renmore, Galway City, Ireland
BTC

REYNOLDS, Malcolm
Psychosynthesis Psychotherapist
21 Ardagh Park, Blackrock, Co. Dublin, Ireland
00 353 1288 77 37
AAPP

ROCHE, Sile
Systemic Psychotherapist
Stanhope Centre, Lr.Grangegorman, Dublin 7, Eire
KCC

RYAN, Mairead
Behavioural Psychotherapist
The Albany Clinic, Clifton Court, Lower Fitzwilliam Street, Dublin 2, Ireland
00 353 1 475 8602/00 353 1 661 4828
BABCP

SCOTT-MCCARTHY, Brian
Psychoanalytic Psychotherapist
Pigges Eye, South Schull, Schull, Co.Cork, Ireland
66 Lower O'Connell Street, Kinsale, Co.Cork, Ireland
353 21 77 26 22/353 28 28 429
AGIP

SCOTT-MCCARTHY, Miranda
Integrative Psychotherapist, Body Psychotherapist
Neifin, Knockroe, Ballydehob, Co. Cork, Ireland
353 2837561
CCBP

STEVENS, Jill
Sexual and Marital Psychotherapist
11 Tivoli Terrace North, Don Laoghaire, Co. Dublin, Ireland
BASMT

SULLIVAN, Gerry
Lacanian Analyst
14 The Belfry, Inchicore Road, Dublin 8, Ireland
0181 968 3769/00 353 1 4544304
CFAR

WARD, Shirley
Humanistic Psychotherapist
Curtlestown, Enniskerry, Co. Wicklow, Ireland
013531 2862428
AHPP

YOUNG, Anne
Transpersonal Psychotherapist
'Chertsey', 27 Rostrevor Road, Rathgar, Dublin 6, Ireland
003531 497 0331
CTP

ISRAEL

COHEN, Vivienne
Group Analyst
18 Smuts Street, Jerusalem 93108, Israel
9 Heathcroft, Hampstead Way, London NW11 7HH
00 972 2561 1262/0181 455 4781
IGA

DANA, Mira
Psychoanalytic Psychotherapist
22 Shimshon Street, Haifa 34615, Israel
00 9724 256130
WTC

HEITZLER, Morit
Body Psychotherapist, Integrative Psychotherapist
11/9 Giboret-Israel Street, Kfar-Sava, Israel
009729 765 1030
CCBP

MAZLIACH, Yaron
Child Psychotherapist
PO Box 42, Kefar-Monsh 42875, Israel
09 648213
ACP

ITALY

CORLANDO, Annalisa
Family Therapist
Via Giacinto Collegus No. 57, 110138
Torino, Italy
0039 11945 2139/0039 11433 5706
AFT

KENNY, Vincent
Personal Construct Psychotherapist
Via Benedetto Croce 68, Scale A:12,
Roma 001 42, Italy
Vico Consultation Centre, 2 Dungar
Terrace, Dun Laoire, Dublin, Ireland
00 39 6 592 3985/00353 1284 3336
CPCP

MOLINO, Anthony
Psychoanalytic Psychotherapist
Corso Garidbaldi, 107, Vasto (CH)
66054, Italy
0039 873 60386
AGIP

PIONTELLI, Alessandra
Child Psychotherapist
Largo Richini 1, 20100 Milan, Italy
00 392 583 07193
ACP

MALTA

VELLA, John
Integrative Psychotherapist
12 Tomb Street, Victoria, Gozo, Malta
00356 556850
RCSPC

NETHERLANDS

CARTON, Roy
Integrative Psychotherapist
Cremerstraat 370, 3532 br Utrecht,
Holland, Netherlands
0302 966785
SPTI

KALDERWAAY, Karina
Psychosynthesis Psychotherapist
Ouderkerkdijk 204, 1096 cr
Amsterdam, Netherlands
00 3120 692 9589
AAPP

SANDERS, Harmen
Integrative Psychotherapist
Moddermanlaan 5, 9721 GK
Groningen, Holland
050 5925800
SPTI

SCHOPMAN, Els (Elisabeth)
Psychodrama Psychotherapist
Menadostr. 49 B, 1095 TH Amsterdam,
Netherlands
00 31 (0) 20 668 0040
BPA

TJEPKEMA, Froukje
Psychoanalytic Psychotherapist
Johan De Wittstraat 7 bis, 3581 XX
Utrecht, The Netherlands
0031 30 233 3715/0031 30 231 3469
IPC

VAN BEEK, Ingrid
Psychosynthesis Psychotherapist
Kooikershof 7, 5256 KD Heusden,
Netherlands
0031 20 676 5171/00 31 41 62 3178
AAPP

VAN ROSSUM, Diederik
Psychosynthesis Psychotherapist
c/o Emmastraat 26, 1075 HV
Amsterdam, Netherlands
31 20 676 5171
AAPP

NEW ZEALAND

BULL, Graham E
Lacanian Analyst
Unit 2, 1 Chesley Place, Bucklands
Beach, Auckland, New Zealand
20 Golf Road, Manor Park, Lower Hutt,
New Zealand
09 533 1923
CFAR, NAFSI

FARRELL, Bill
Psychoanalytic Psychotherapist
P O Box 6097, Titirangi, Auckland
1007, New Zealand
LPDO

HUBBARD, Peter
Psychosynthesis Psychotherapist
Institute of Psychosynthesis, 7 Farnol
Street, Auckland 4, New Zealand
00 649625 9559
AAPP

NORRIS, Lynne
Cognitive Behavioural Psychotherapist
43 Moore Street, Howick, Auckland,
New Zealand
00649 535 6700/00649 535 6624
BABCP

PALMER, Helen
Psychosynthesis Psychotherapist
Institute of Psychosynthesis, 7 Farnol
Street, Auckland 4, New Zealand
00 649 625 9559
AAPP

PETERS, Anthony
Personal Construct Psychotherapist
117 Waitoki Road, Kautapakapa,
Auckland, New Zealand
CPCP

RYBURN, Murray
Systemic Psychotherapist
213 Centaurus Road, Christchurch
8002, New Zealand
KCC

VAN BILSEN, Henck P.J.G.
Cognitive Behavioural Psychotherapist
43 Moore Street, Howick, Auckland
1004, New Zealand
006496 258602
BABCP

NORWAY

BALMBRA, Steven
Family Therapist
Bodinveien 56, 8010 Bodo, Norway
47 75 58 11 90
AFT

PATRICIA, Thelma
Psychoanalytic Psychotherapist,
Humanistic Psychotherapist
Flaskecrokken, Flaskebekk, 1450
Nesoddtangen, Norway
46 66 913075
IPSS

PERU

MONTALBETTI, M.L.
Child Psychotherapist
Santander 147, Miraflores, Lima 18,
Peru
51 1 254 3491/51 1 254 0133 (f)
ACP

RUSSIA

SIZIKOVA, Tanya
Transactional Analysis Psychotherapist,
Integrative Psychotherapist
189620 Pushkin - 9 -, St Petersburg,
Prinvokzalnaua Square, House 2, Flat
75, Russia
0017 812 5520100
SCPC

SOUTH AFRICA

LOWN, Francois
Integrative Psychotherapist
PO Box 973, Cresta 2118, Republic of South Africa
012 420 2329
SPTI

MILLER, Sheila
Child Psychotherapist
PO Box 1399, Houghton 2041, South Africa
00 2711 646 9786/00 2711 486 3366 (f)
ACP

ROSENBAUM, Linda Ann
Integrative Psychotherapist
PO Box 650229, Benmore 2010, Gauteng, South Africa
0115 924 3994
SPTI

SALTERS, Diane
Transactional Analysis Psychotherapist
15 Disa Road, Murdock Valley North, Simons Town 7975, Republic of South Africa
021 786 1910
ITA

SINGAPORE

LIM, Leslie E.C.
Cognitive Behavioural Psychotherapist
Institute of Mental Health, 10 Buangkok Green, Singapore 539747, Republic of Singapore
00 65 385 0411
BABCP

SLOVENIA

PETERNEL, Franc
Group Analyst
Slovenceva 109, 61113 Ljubljana, Slovenia
010 061 302 899/010 38 061 344521
IGA

SPAIN

CAMPOS, Hanne
Group Analyst
Pasea San Gervasio 30, 008022 Barcelona, Spain
010 34 3 2475639
IGA

CAMPOS, Juan
Psychoanalytic Psychotherapist
Transito De Los Gramaticos 3, 15703 Santiago, Spain
IPSS

DRURY, Gitta
Gestalt Psychotherapist
Casa Media Luna, 03790 Orba, Alicante, Spain
96 558 3884
SPTI

IBANEZ, Julian
Psychoanalytic Psychotherapist
Alameda de Urquijo 94, lero Dech, 48013 Bilbao, Spain
00 344 4277340
ARBS, NAFSI

OROMI, Irene
Educational Therapist
Mallorca 239, 08008 Barcelona, Spain
03 3493 5897067 (t/f)
FAETT

TURNER, Carole
Transactional Analysis Psychotherapist
La Galera de Las Palmeras 119, 03590 Altea, Alicante, Spain
00 3496 584 6043 (f)/00 3496 584 6191
MET, ITA

SWEDEN

BRADSHAW-TAUVON, Kate
Psychodrama Psychotherapist
Sveavagen 52 2tr, S 111 34 Stockholm, Sweden
0046 8 411 0420/0046 8 201183 (f)
BPA

FRISCHER, Livia
Integrative Psychosynthesis Psychotherapist
Antelopgatan 7, 412 38 Molndal, Sweden
0046 31 205602
RE.V

HAGELTHORN, Christina
Psychodrama Psychotherapist
Foreningsgatan 7, 411 27 Goteborg, Sweden
0046 31 711 8732
BPA

SANDLER, Topsy
Systemic Psychotherapist
Skogalundsklippan 6 NB, 131 39 Nacka, Sweden
08 716 1692
KCC

SWITZERLAND

DONGES, Sascha
Psychosynthesis Psychotherapist
Institute fur Psychosynthese, Schneidergasse 7, CH-4051 Basel, Switzerland
00 4161 262 11 44/00 4161 262 11 45
AAPP

HERING-JOSEFOWITZ, Pauline
Child Psychotherapist
12 Chemin Des Eglantieres, 1208 Geneva, Switzerland
00 41 22 349 1230/00 41 22 349 1233 (f)
ACP

ITTEN, Theodor
Psychoanalytic Psychotherapist
Psychologe BPS, Psychotherapeut SPV, Bahnhofstre.15, CH-9000 St. Gallen
33 Shaftesbury Road, London N19 4QW
0171 877 2550 (f)/0171 223 5443
PA

OHNESORG, Johanna
Biodynamic Psychotherapist
Bachlerstrasse 62, Zurich, CH-8046, Switzerland
0041 1 371 7647
BTC

STEINMANN, Christina
Psychosynthesis Psychotherapist
Dorfstrasse 57, 8037 Zurich, Switzerland
00 411 271 2239
AAPP

TURKEY

SUNGUR, Mehmet
Cognitive Behavioural Psychotherapist
Medical School of Ankara University, Dept. of Psychiatry, Cebeci-Ankara, Turkey
Yuksel Sitesi, A Blok,No 12, Balgat, Ankara, Turkey
00 90 312 2851007/00 90 312 3192160 x 6697
BABCP

USA

BENOR, Ruth
Autogenic Psychotherapist
5 Birchwood Drive, Medford, NJ08055, USA
001 609 714 1885
BAFAT

BROWN, Rachel
Group Analyst
5090 Midland Terrace, Midland, Georgia 31820, USA
IGA

BUTLER, Todd
Gestalt Psychotherapist
620 Albion Street, San Diego, Ca.92106, USA
Todd.Butler@msn.com/001 619 523 6007
GPTI, MET

CARLSON, Cynthia
Child Psychotherapist
2516E. Newton Avenue, Milwaukee WI 53211, USA
ACP

EICHENBAUM, Luise
Psychoanalytic Psychotherapist
WTC, 562 West End Avenue, 1A, New York 10024, USA
WTC

EPTING, Franz
Personal Construct Psychotherapist
9310 NW 10th Pl., Gainesville, Florida, FL 32606, USA
CPCP

HAMILTON, Victoria
Child Psychotherapist
990 Hanley Avenue, Los Angeles, California 90049, USA
001310 471 1897/001310 472 0459 (f)
ACP

HERMON, Deborah
Child Psychotherapist
7120 Via Marbella, Boca, Raton, Florida, 33433
00561 4173400 (f)/00561 4173300
ACP

IRONSIDE, Karin Margaret
Integrative Psychotherapist
5138 Timbergate Street, San Antonio, Texas, 78250
0973 618792
RCSPC

LISMAN-PIECZANSKI, N.M.
Child Psychotherapist
4417 36th Street, N.W., Washington D.C., 20008, USA
001202 363 1909 (t/f)
ACP

LYNN, Rita
Group Analyst
622 North Linden Drive, Beverly Hills, California 90210, U.S.A.
310 285 0503
IGA

RILEY, Charlotte
Child Psychotherapist
270 26th St. Ste. 205, Santa Monica, California 90402, USA
310 395 2485/00 131 10 396 8329
ACP

RYAN, Angella M.J.
Psychodynamic Psychotherapist
868 Kiefer Trails Drive, Ballwin, St. Louis, Missouri, MO 63021, USA
+ (314) 527 3170
WMIP

SIDOLI, Mara
Child Psychotherapist
4307 Massachusetts Avenue NW, Washington DC 20016, USA
001 202 362 1886/001 202 966 0821 (f)
ACP

SORENSON, Pamela
Child Psychotherapist
2725 Hunt Country Lane, Charlottesville, Virginia 22901-8989, USA
010 1180 49795669/010 1804 9715540 (f)
ACP

WEST INDIES

HOPE-PRICE, Gloria
Group Analyst
Green Acre, 44 Sunset Ridge, St. James, Barbados, West Indies
010 1 809 432 6425
IGA

RATTRAY, Noemie
Psychoanalytic Psychotherapist
Full & By, 45 Spice Hill Road, Warwick, WK03, Bermuda
441 238 2980
LCP

ALPHABETICAL LISTING

C

D

E

F

G

H

I

J

K

L

M

S

W

Y

Z

ORGANISATION MEMBERSHIP LISTS

AAPP - Association for Accredited Psychospiritual Psychotherapists

Anjali, Yon
Anker, Ofra
Arnold, Sue
Attridge, Brian
Badenoch, Marion
Bayley, Eva
Beecher-Moore, Naona
Benson, Jarlath
Beresford, Marie
Blomfield, Valerie
Brankin, Irene
Burlington, Maggie
Campbell, Margaret
Carroll, Penny
Chalk, Caroline
Chandler, Diana
Clough, Andrea
Clover, Gillian
Clyne, Rachel
Connolly, Christopher
Conroy, Kay
Cooper, Fiona
Courtman, Anita
Cox, Miranda
Croft, Janet
Cutler, Jane
Davies, Debra
Diepeveen, Johanna Maria
Donges, Sascha
Donington, Laura
Douglas, Dana
Duffell, Nick
Dymond, Christina
Einzig, Hetty
Elliot, Patricia
Ender, Beckett
Ender, Christine
Ender, Dorry
England, David
Evans, Joan
Evans, Roger
Feldberg, Marilyn
Ferris, Mary
Finch, Auberon
Firman, Judith
Flower, Steven
Fox, Loretta
Friedman, Debbie
Gilbert, Sharon
Gilli, Liliana
Gordon, Deidre
Gordon Clark, Thalia
Goss, Thomas
Gracia, Olga
Greaves, Thomas
Greenfield, Frances
Gresty, Julie
Grigg, Roz
Hallen, Gervaise
Hamblin, David
Hancock, Pauline
Handley, Rima
Hanna, Dorothy
Hardy, Jo
Harris, Anthony
Harrison, Jane
Hayes, Michael
Hedley, Karen
Hedley, Nick
Hendry, Devam
Hillman, Christine
Hitchman, Nini
Holland, Sue
Hope, Francis
Howe, Patricia
Hubbard, Peter
Hunt, Maggie
Hunt Overzee, Anne
Huson, Richard
Jarvis, Cecilia
Jensen, Greta
Kalderwaay, Karina
Kalisch, David
Kernoff, Marilyn
Kerridge, Petra
Kevlin, Kunderke
Kirkland, Margot
Kirwin, Mark
Koeppelmann, Marianna
Labworth, Yig
Lemon, Marcia
Linnell, Maxine
Lövendal-Sörensen, Helena
Lown, Judy
Lyons, Kathleen
MacGregor, Catherine
Maloney, Sean
Manton, Rosie
Marcus, Deena
Mathers, Dale
McBurnie, Dolores
McGuinness, Maureen
McOstrich, June
Mead, Christine
Miles, Fiona
Millar, Gerry
Nancarrow, Kiya
Newson, Mary
Nightingale, Eileen
North, Joanna
Nye, Georgiana
Oliver, Jenny
Oliver, Rosamund
Padgett, Louise
Palmer, Helen
Parfitt, Will
Pearman, Cathy
Peart, Mary
Philbin, Mairead
Pickstock, Keith
Rand, Judith Ann
Rees, Ian
Reynolds, Malcolm
Rhind, Sue
Ridley, Wendy
Rimmer, Janet
Roex, Danielle
Rotas, Joanna
Sanders, Jane
Schaffer, Tom
Schild, Maureen
Sheriffs, Alison
Shingler, Christopher
Sidhu, Frankie
Sieroda, Helen
Sills, Franklyn
Sills, Maura
Silvester, Keith
Simpson, Steve
Somers, Barbara
Specterman, Liz
Spurgeon, Richard
Squires, Brenda
Stacey, Linda
Steinmann, Christina
Steverson, Jill
Sutherland, Elisabeth
Tandy (Pilbrow), Alannah
Tempest, Jeanette
Tham, Anna
Thomas, Alyss
Thompson, Hilary
Totman, Maria
Toubkins, Rita
van Beek, Ingrid
van Rossum, Diederik
Vickers, Kate
Ward, Barbara
Watson, Gay
Webber, Wendy
Welsh, Anne
Whitmore, Diana
Wigham, Avril
Williams, Heather
Willow, Angela
Wilson, Jancis
Wolfe, Pamela
Wooder, Bernard
Wynant, Vivienne

ACAT - Association of Cognitive Analytic Therapists

Ansari, Shakir
Beard, Hilary
Boa, Cherry
Bristow, John
Brooks, Beverly
Burns-Lundgren, Eva
Choudree, Sangamithra U.D.
Cowmeadow, Pauline
Crowley, Valerie
Curran, Annalee
Davies, Dilys
Denman, Francesca
Dunn, Mark
Eadie, Yvonne
Elwell, Louise
Encombe, Jock
Ennis, Sally-Anne
Fawkes, Liz
Field, John C.
Fisher, Clare
Fosbury, Jacqueline
Gardner, Philippa
Gray, Sally
Gregory, Kirby
Griffiths, Tina C.
Harvey, Linda Mary
Jellema, Anna
Johnstone, Mog
Knight, Michael
Kuhn, Sue
Leighton, Tim
Lettington, Lisa
Maple, Norma Anderson
Marlowe, Martin
Mead, Janet
Melton, Jane
Merz, Juliet
Nuttall, Serena
Palgrave, Lesley
Parry, Glenys
Pollard, Cynthia
Reidy, Rachel
Sackett, Kate
Smith, Eva
Stevens, Yvonne
Tanner, Claire
Turner, Vivien
Twist, Graham
Warin, Judy
Welch, Lawrence
West, Virginia
Wilton, Angela

ACP - Association of Child Psychotherapists

Akinboro-Cooper, Bobbie
Alvarez, Anne
Amez, Susana
Anderson, Janet
Armbruster, P.K.
Arnold, Katherine
Balogh Henghes, Tessa
Bandler Bellman, Debbie
Baradon, Tessa
Barrows, Paul
Barter, Ruth
Bartlett, Francesca
Bellis, Stella
Bender, Helen
Benjamin, Haydene
Bharucha, Aiveen
Bharucha, Manek
Blandy, Evanthe
Boston, Mary
Bradley, Catrin
Bradley, Jonathan
Briggs, Andrew
Britten, Stewart
Buckingham, Linda
Buckland, Richard
Bunster, Jane
Campbell, Donald
Cant, Diana
Carlson, Cynthia
Cebon, Ann
Champion, Lynn
Cherry-Swaine, Janine
Chinoy, Freni
Cohen, Maggie
Cohen, Pauline
Cohn, Nancy
Colloms, Anita
Copley, Beta
Coulson, Susan
Cousins, Jan
Crawford, George
Crick, Verena
Crockatt, Gabrielle
Davids, Jennifer
Daws, Dilys
Dawson, Linda
Domb, Yair
Dowling, Deirdre
Dubinsky, Alexandre
Dubinsky, Helene
Duffy, Rosemary
Duguid, Kathleen
Eccles, Barbara
Edgcumbe, Rose
Edwards, Judith
Eichelberger Cleese, Alyce Faye
Elkan, Judith
Elliott, Victoria
Ellwood, Jane
Emanuel, Louise
Emanuel, Ricky
Essenhigh, Caroline
Evans, Peter L.
Feldman, Wendy
Fleming, Robert W.K.
Gavshon, Audrey
George, Elizabeth
Golden, Ellen
Goodchild, Margaret
Grainger, Eve
Green, Viviane
Grunberg, Sheena
Guest, Nicola
Gurion, Michal
Hadary, Gideon
Halton, William
Hamilton, Victoria
Hamilton, Wallace
Harris, Nina
Hart, Carolyn
Hartnup, Trevor
Heath, Christine
Helm, Caroline
Henderson, John
Henry, Rachel M.
Hering-Josefowitz, Pauline
Hermon, Deborah
Herrmann, Joan
Hilder, Alison
Hindle, Deborah
Hodges, Jill
Holland, Louise
Horne, Ann
Hughes, Carol
Hunter, Margaret
Hurry, Anne
Hurst, Margaret
Ironside, Lesley
Jacobs, Joe
Jarvis, Charlotte
Kegerreis, Susan
Kenrick, Jennifer
Kenwood, Pat
Kerbekian, Rosalie
Kohon, Valli
Lanyado, Monica
Laport-Steuerman, M.
Layiou-Lignos, Effie
Layton, Sandy
Leite Da Costa, Mariza
Lillitos, Aleathea G.
Lisman-Pieczanski, N.M.
Loose, Judith Green
Loret de Mola, Maria
Loxterkamp, Lorne
Luciani, Dorothy
Lyon, Martin
Mack Smith, Catharine
Magagna, Jeanne
Maltby, Jane
Martin, Christine
Martin, Stephen
Mazliach, Yaron
McCann, Anita
McCartney, Meryl
McCutcheon, Moira
McKenzie-Smith, Savi
Meleagrou-Dixon, Mando
Mendelsohn, Annette
Mikardo, Julia
Millar, David
Miller, Lisa
Miller, Sheila
Model, Elizabeth
Mondadori, Roberta
Montalbetti, M.L.
Morice, Michael
Mostaeddi, Bahman
Nagle, Robin
Netzer-Stein, Antje
Ngah, Zah
Norsa, Giuliana
Oclander Goldie, Silvia
Oliver-Bellasis, Elizabeth
Orford, Eileen
Parker, Niki
Parsons, Marianne
Passey, Miranda
Penwarden, Mary M.
Phillips, Adam
Phillips, Asha
Philps, Janet
Pick, Rachel
Piontelli, Alessandra
Porter, Christine
Pozzi, Maria E.
Preston, Janet
Proner, Karen
Radford, Patricia
Ramsden, Sandra
Regan, Columba
Reid, Marguerite
Reid, Susan
Renton, Mirjana
Reyes, Paulina
Rhode, Maria
Ricketts, Susan
Riley, Charlotte
Robinson, J.G.
Ross, Miroslava
Rotenberg, Claudio
Roth, Priscilla
Rusbridger, Richard
Rustin, Margaret
Ryz, Patsy
Sadowski, Joseph
Sazatzoglou-Hitzos, M.
Schaffer-Fielding, Wendy
Schmidt-Neven, Ruth
Schnurmann, Anneliese
Segal, Barbara
Seglow, Ruth M.
Sherwin-White, Sue
Shulman, Graham
Shuttleworth, Alan
Shuttleworth, Judy
Sibley, Susan
Sidoli, Mara
Sinason, Valerie
Sobat, Milica
Sones, Joanne
Sones, Michael
Sorenson, Pamela
Sprince, Jenny
Spyropoulos, Nick
Steele, Miriam
Stern, Michele
Sternberg, Janine
Stiasny, Jennifer
Stone, Sandra
Storring, Susan
Swan Parente, Alison
Syz, Ann
Testa, Rita
Townley, Judy Rifkin
Trevatt, David
Truckle, Brian
Truckle, Shirley
Truscott, Frances
Urwin, Catherine
Usiskin, Judith
Vaciago Smith, Marta
Van Heeswyk, Paul
Vas Dias, Susan
Vastardis, Gethsimani
Waddell, Margot
Walker, Mary J.
Warwick, Kate
Watson, Andrea
Watters, Catherine
Weir, Felicity
Widdicombe, Anastasia
Williams, Gianna
Wilson, Gillian
Wilson, Jilian
Wilson, Peter
Winkley, Linda
Wittenberg, Isca
Wood, Margarita
Woodcock, Therese M-Y.
Woodman-Smith, Gillian
Woods, John
Woodward, Nicola
Zaphiriou Woods, Marie

AFT - Association for Family Therapy

Alabaster, Nigel
Allan, Brenda
Alnuaimi, Christine
Altschuler, Jenny
Anderson, Larry
Andrew, Alison
Antonson, Kate
Appleton, Richard
Ardeman, Jacqueline
Atkins, Lorna
Averbeck, Marcus
Balmbra, Steven
Barnes, Hugh
Bates, Helen
Bazeley-White, Diana
Bennun, Ian
Birch, Jim
Blow, Kirsten
Booth, Nick
Bott, David
Bowen, Barry
Bower, Margaret
Brazier, Anna

Brough, Julie
Brown, Gillian A.
Bruggen, Joan
Bryson, Sandra
Burgess, Alison
Burroughes, Christopher
Burrows, Joanna
Burton, Jean
Cade, Brian
Challender, David
Chatham, Jon
Child, Nick
Clark, Alec
Clements, Sue
Clery, Cairns
Cohen, Barbara
Colahan, Mireille
Coldicott, Tim
Cooper, Jan
Corlando, Annalisa
Cottrell, David
Coulter, Stephen
Cox, Keith
Crocker, Allen
Cubie, Paul
Cunningham, Gerry
Curti-Gialdino, Francesca
Daniels, Kate
Daum, Minna
Davies, Mairlis
Davies, Mike
Davren, Moira
Day, Michael
Delve, Stuart
Doolan, Moira
Ellis, R.M.
Eminson, Mary
Enser, Nigel
Essex, Suzanne
Faull, Keith
Fellows, Ron
Filby, Erica
Folker, Sheena
Fox, Hugh
Fox, Margaret
Freeman, Pat
Fry, Richard P.W.
Fyvel, Susan
Gaskell, Christine
Gauthier, J.B.
Geraghty, Wendy
Gillman, Maureen
Goodman, Mary
Gower, Myrna
Graf, Fern
Graham, Hilary
Gray, Elizabeth
Gray, Pete
Hale, John
Harmsworth, Peter
Hayward, Mark
Healey, Arlene
Heath, C.A.
Hendra, Theresa
Hewitt, Amanda
Hills, John
Hodd, Amanda
Hodgson, Susan
Honig, Peter
Hudson, Peter
Jack, Bridget
Jamieson, Eileen
Jones, Maggy
Kemps, Charmaine
Kenny, Marie
Kilgour, Joyce
King, Michael
Klein, Wendy
Krause, Inga-Britt
Kuttner, Enno
Lacey, Irene
Lazarus, Myrna
Lee, Denis
Lieberman, Stuart
Lindsay, Robert
Lister, Ian
Macdonald, Alasdair
Manning, Tony
Markham, Angela
Markovic, Olivera
Marriott, Alison
Marsden-Allen, Peter
Maynerd, Cynthia
McNab, Sue
Mendelssohn, Penny
Miller, Liza Bingley
Mouratoglou, Vassilis
Neden, Jeanette
Neill, Denis E.
Nelki, Julia
Ness, Bill
Nissim, Ruth
O'Neill, Arthur
O'Neill, Tom
O'Reilly, Paul
Owen, Mike
Parikh, P.N.
Parsons, Barbara
Pearse, Joanna
Petkova, Petia
Pitt, Christopher
Pocock, David
Raeside, Dominic
Reay, Ruth
Reed, Alex
Rivett, Mark
Robb, Melissa
Roberts, Phil
Roddick, Mary
Roff, Hermione
Roper Hall, Alison
Routledge, Derek
Rutherford, Penny
Sandbank, Audrey
Savage, Patrick
Sawyer, Alice
Schneider, Caroline
Secrett, David
Seligman, Philippa
Seymour, Charlotte
Sheppard Fidler, Angela
Simmons, Gloria
Simon, Dave
Sims, Lyn
Smith, Donna
Smith, Ged
Stein, Yvonne
Stewart, Kate
Stratford, Jacqueline
Taylor, Crispin
Tennant, Duncan
Toms, Moira
Tomsett, Jean
Tranter, Paul
Urry, Amy
Verduyn, Christine M.
Vetere, Arlene
Vine, Mike
Wadland, Liz
Wagstaff, Susan
Walker, George
Walker, Steven
Walrond-Skinner, Sue
Walsh, Stuart
Warner, Barbara
Webster, Jeni
Weeramanthri, Tara
Weider, Bilha
Western, Simon
Whatley, Ann
White, Jan
Wilford, Gerti
Wilmot, David
Wood, Sally
Wratten, Stephen
Zimmerman, Frankie

AGIP - Association for Group and Individual Psychotherapy

Anderson, Elizabeth
Ariel, Seema
Astor, Bronwen
Benjamin, Joan E.
Bloomfield, Irene
Brown, Sara
Caruana, Charles Victor
Claxton, Patricia
Codd, Anne Marie
Cooper, Howard
Corker, Enid
Corneck, Susan
Cox, Philip
Cross, John
Cryer, Valerie
Cunningham, Diane
Darling, Liv
Davies, Ann
Dobbs, Wendy
Doe, Anthony
Ellis, Sian
Figlio, Karl
Flannery, Jean
Francis, Anne M.
Frazer, Diane
Freeman, Catherine
Gardiner, Margaret
Good, Liz
Griffith, John
Haine, Stephen
Hamilton, Dorothy
Hamilton, Kim
Heavens, Anita
Humphries, Harold
Inlander, Antonia
Kaplan, Myron
Kenny, Angela
Küechemann, Christine
Langdon, Monica
Lee, Graham
Leggatt, Claire
Leggatt, Jenny
Lethbridge, Sue
Lewis, Jo-Ann
Longley, Joan
Mauger, Benig
McKenzie-Smith, Bryce
Mead, Betty
Miller, John Andrew
Miller, Lynda
Molino, Anthony
Neiva, Judith
Nesbit, Judith
O'Callaghan, Diane
O'Keeffe, Tim
Phillips, Laurie
Pokorny, Michael
Polden, Jane
Pompe, Marie
Price, Annie
Rogers, Anne
Rozenberg, Rosette
Scott-McCarthy, Brian
Seradi, Adriana
Siney, Sky
Soutar, Sarah
Spalding, John
Stanwood, Frederick
Stephens, Lyn
Stolte, Eva
Struthers, Cassandra
Taylor, Harvey
Thorpe, C
Trustam, Gillian
Ward, John
Wellings, Nigel
Wells, Lindsay
Wieland, Christina
Wildash, Sheila
Wilson, Maureen
Wotton, Annette

AHPP - Association of Humanistic Psychology Practitioners

Adamson, Fiona
Boadella, David
Bowdery, Sally
Braid, Rosemary
Brunt, Clare
Burnet-Smith, Tamara
Carroll, Helen

Carruthers, Barbara
Cole, Barbara
Collis, Whiz
Cooper, Rebecca
Copsey, Nigel
Coulson, Christopher
Dargert, Guy
Davis, Wendy
Dell, Judith
Fleming, Peter
Frances, Jane
Gale, Derek
Golz, Angelika
Graham, Judy
Hart, Sally
Haslam, Deidre
Horrocks, Roger
Hughes, Linda
Jelfs, Martin
Jones, Alan
Jones, Dave
Jones, David
Kennedy, Kay
Kirby, Alan
Kirby, Babs
Leder, Catherine
Lester, Hilary
March-Smith, Rosie
Mitchell, Richard
Morris, Elizabeth
Munt, Stephen
Noack, Miké
Parker, Mary
Payne, Helen
Pimentel, Edna
Reynolds, Alun
Rowan, John
Ryley, Brigitte
Schembri, Veronica
Scott, Tricia
Speyer, Josefine
Spy, Terri
Stewart, Lindsey
Sullivan, Anita
Twelvetrees, Heidy
Ward, Shirley
Waterston, John
Westland, Gill
Whitton, Eric
Woolliscroft, Jenny
Woolliscroft, Jessica
Young, Courtenay

AIP - The Association of Independent Psychotherapists

Crace, Gay
Dorey, Mary
Everest, Pauline
Gerhardt, Sue
Henderson, David
Perry, Ann
Sherman, Arthur
Shivakumar, H.
Shooter, Lesley
Taylor, Alan

AJA - Association of Jungian Analysts

Adler, Hella
Baring, Anne
Bell, Frances
Bierschenk, John H.
Boll, Antonia
ByGott, Catherine
Casement, Ann
Cashford, Jules
Clark, Nita
Davide, Adele
Doorley, Damien
Duckworth, Moira
Duddington, Alexander
Dykes, Andrea
Finlay, Rosalind
Freeman, David
French, Eileen
Heuer, Gottfried
Johnson, Deirdre
Maitra, Begum
McCarthy, Rita
McLean, Julienne
McNulty, Claire
Millar, Peter
Miller, John
Miller, Juliet
Mulhern, Alan
Newson, John
Niesser, Arthur
Noack, Amelie
Palmer Barnes, Fiona
Robinson, Martin
Royston, Robin
Silverman, Carl M.
Spilios, Joanne
Starte, Gordon
Stone, Martin
Stuart, Gillian
Syrett, Karin
Williams, Chris
Williams, Susan

ANLP - Association for Neuro-Linguistic Programming

Adlington, Jethro
Asseily, Alexandra
Banks, Ron
Beckett, Dale
Blake, Nancy
Brankin, Maire
Bray, Malcolm
Bray, Stephen
Brion, Marion
Brock, Sue
Burow, Birgit
Burtt, Isobel Lucy
Carpenter, David
Chamlee-Cole, Laurena
Christmann, Cornelia
Coleby, Gillian
Crisp, Dave
Daniels, Frank
Deahl, Kieron
Dinwoodie, John
Eaton, John
Eldon, Martin
Elliott, John
Grayson, Juliet
Hanchen, Thomasz
Hill, Jennifer
Hueting, Margaret
Johnson, Michael
Kilgour, Mimi
La Tourelle, Maggie
Lawley, James
Leakey, Peter
Lennox, Graham
Levine, Hanelle G.
Lewis, Philip J.
Llewellyn, Alice
Looms, Suzanne
Lowe, Judith
Macdonald, Laurie
McDonnell, Fokkina
Mills, Judith
Mohan, Terence
Moore, Terry
Murray, John
Nolan, Philip
Pain, Jean
Poole, Nick
Pope, Sian
Reynolds, Francois
Richards, Paul
Rowland, Gail
Russell, Julian
Scott Hayward, Anna
Sherlock, Teresa
Silmon, Mary
Smith, Robert
Strang, Susi
Szary, Gerard
Thompson, Joan
Tidy, Deirdre
Tompkins, Penny
Vine, Francis
Walsh, Eileen
Worth, Piers

ARBS - Arbours Association

Austin, Neil
Berke, Joseph
Berry, Sally
Brookes, Sasha
Buckley, Nicky
Burch, Nigel
Cairns, Mary
Cameron, Anna
Cameron, Roderick
Campbell-Thomson, Christina
Cave, Prue
Dianin, Gianni
Dyehouse, Pat
Ehlers, Hella
Eiles, Clive
Elliott, Lois
Fagan, Margaret
Fawkes, Caroline
Forti, Laura
Goodes, Deborah
Grant, Bob
Grant, Iona
Green, Margaret
Greenwood, John
Haberlin, Jane
Hacker, Roger
Hall, Kirsty
Ibanez, Julian
Kelly, Bridget
Kelly, Michael
Kleanthous, Dina
Kleinot, Pamela
Lanczi, Katalin
Lunardon, Francesco
Masoliver, Chandra
Mazaraki, Angeliki
McAndrew, Brigitte
Montero, Isabel
Navarro, Trinidad
Nielsen-Cernkovich, Rudy
O'Cleary, Susan
Pavincich, Lesley
Pearce, George
Perriollat Munro, Elizabeth
Phillips, Marianne
Pierides, Stella
Powell, Angela
Rabe, Marie-Louise
Ravensdale, Verity
Réguis, Marie-Christine
Rose, Sally
Rund, Malcolm
Ryan, Tom
Sabbadini, Andrea
Saltiel, Adam
Schaedel, Maggie
Schatzman, Morton
Schonfield, Tamar
Seu, Irene Bruna
Smith, Peter
Solemani, Hannah
Stokeld, Alasdair
Turner, Diana
Valentine, Marguerite
Veje, Margit
Wach, Karin Marie
Waterfield, Hilary
Whittle, Lorna
Whittle, Sonia

AUTP - Association of University Teachers of Psychiatry

Aveline, Mark
Pedder, Jonathan

BABCP - British Association for Behavioural & Cognitive Psychotherapies

Alderton, Chris
Alexander, Paul T.
Allinson, Mary A.
Altman, Michelle
Amies, Peter
Anderson, Christine
Ash, Jonathan
Athanasiadis, Loukas
Bactawar, Charles D.
Bassam, Bruce
Beach, Jan D.
Bechhofer, Jean B.
Beech, Julie C.
Bell, Lydia J.
Bennett, Gerald A.
Benson, Pauline
Bhunnoo, Z.
Bienkowski, Geraldine
Bishay, Nagy R.
Black, Nicholas J.
Blackburn, Ivy-Marie
Blackburn, John
Bland, John
Blore, David C.
Blowers, Colin M.
Boyle, Pauline
Brady, Alec
Bright, Jenifer A
Broadbent, Keith
Brosan, Lee
Brown, Thomas M.
Burbach, Frank
Burdett, C.W.
Butcher, Gerard
Butler, Linda
Cameron, Michael John
Campbell, Hedda A.
Cariapa, Illana
Chalkley, A.J.
Chapman, Jane
Childs-Clarke, Adrian
Chin, John C.L.
Church, John
Churchill-Moss, Duncan
Clancy, J. Patricia
Clarke, Isabel
Clarke, Stephen Lawrence
Clarke, Susan Elizabeth
Coles, Peter J.
Collard, Patrizia C.
Colson, Louise
Conroy, Jennifer J.
Cooper, Heather
Copley, Brian
Coyle, Christina H.
Cromarty, Paul
Cromey, Terry
Cullen, Anne M.
Curwen, Bernadette
Dabor, Thelma
Dalgarno, Rebecca
Daly, Kevin
Davidson, John
Davies, John
Davies, Stephen
Davis, Brenda
Davis, Paul E.
De Souza, Janice
Deale, Alicia
Deeble, Elizabeth A.
Denford, Lindsey D.
Dilks, Sarah L.E.
Doggart, Elizabeth Anne
Dolan, Lesley Catherine
Donohoe, Gillian
Downes, Vanessa Susan
Draper, Pim
Drijver, Caroline
Drummond, Lynne
Dryden, Windy
Duncan-Grant, Alec John
Dunn, Katie
Dyer, Ian P.
Eastham, Peter
Edeleanu, Andrea K.
Edelmann, Robert J.
Edmondstone, Yvonne G.
El-Khayat, Redwan
Elliott, Peter
Elliott, Sandra A.
Evans, John K.
Farley, Nancy M.
Fearns, Keith
Fernandez, Nigel R.
Fernandez, Valentina
Fincham, Felicity
Fisher, Linda
Flanagan, June
Fokias, Dene
Forsyth, Angus
Fortune, Rosalind
Fowler, Barry
Foxen, Tom
Freeman, Christopher
Gardner, Damian
Gauci, Kate
Gilboy, Carol A.
Gillespie, Kate
Gillett, Timothy P.
Gimblett, Jeanne
Glaister, Brian
Gordon, P. Kenneth
Gournay, Kevin
Gray, Maggie
Green, Charlotte
Greenfield, Terence
Gulcz, Magdalena
Gurnani, Prem D.
Hacker Hughes, Jamie G.H.
Hallam, Richard S
Handy, S.
Hanley, Ian G.
Hannigan, David J.
Hardcastle, Mark
Harrington, Finola
Harrington, Rufus
Harris, Paul David Gwyn
Harvey, Andrew
Haveman, Jolien
Hendry, Evelyn R.
Herbert, Claudia
Herdman, Linda
Hiestand, Rene
Hilling, Richard
Holyoak, Patricia
Hooper, Molly
Houghton, Judith E.
Howes, Kathleen Mary
Hume, Anne J.A.
Humphreys, A-L.
Huszcza, Anna K.
Issa, Soraya
Jakes, Simon
Jenkins, Dinah
Jenkins, Sheila
Jezard-Clark, P.H.
Jiah, Hildah
John, Carolyn H.
Jones, Janet D.
Jones, Rhiannon Marie
Joseph, Jerome Devakumar
Kat, Bernard J.B.
Keenan, Paul Stephen
Kelly, Anne
Kelly, Philip
Kemp, Paul David
Kennedy, Fiona
Kincey, John
Kolb, Peter John
Kunkler, Jane
Lau, Bernard Wai Kai
Lawson, Ruth
Lea, Mary
Lever, Maria A.
Lewis, Ken
Lillie, Francis
Lim, Leslie E.C.
Liness, Sheena
Lister, Patricia Anne
Long, Clive G.
Long, Jennifer
Lovell, Karina
Lucas, Rosemarie
Mac Liam, Fionnula
Macaskill, Norman D.
Macdonald, Helen F.
MacGregor, Alan
Macnicol, Annie
Malkin, Julius
Margolis, Susanne
Marklow, Christine
Mathews, Trevor J.
Matthews, Helen P.
Matthews, Sharon
McCarron, Gerard
McClure, John
McCoy, Sean
McFadden, Hugh E.
McFarlane, Alison M.
McGoldrick, Mary
McKay, Molly
McLoughlin, Brendan Nicholas
McMahon, Gladeana
McMaster, Catherine
Meldrum, Ron
Mettam, Lisa
Mills, Jeremy George
Mills, Nigel
Milne, Pamela
Molleson, John Ivitsky
Moloney, Paul
Moore, Gordon
Moorey, Stirling
Morgan, William
Morris, David
Morris, Peter A.
Morrissey, Shirley
Morton, Richard Victor
Moutzoukis, Chris
Moyes, Theresa
Nadirshaw, Zenobia
Nancarrow, Christine
Nath, Krish
Neenan, Michael
Newell, Adrian
Nicolson, Elaine
Norris, Lynne
Noyes, Elizabeth
Nuthall, Alexander R.
O'Brien, Kirsty M.G.
O'Carroll, Madeline
O'Carroll, Pierce J.
O'Neill, Helen M.
Palanisamy, Shan
Palmer, Lisa Elaine
Palmer, Stephen
Parker, Jonathan
Parrack, Norma
Pattinson, Philip
Peckitt, R.G.
Perera, Ajit
Phillips, Thomas Lambton
Pittman, Karen
Platts, June Elizabeth
Pollitt, Mo
Procter, Sue
Quarry, Andrew
Quinn, Paul
Rani, R.S.
Reading, Clive
Reavley, William
Regel, Stephen
Rice, Paul
Richards, David
Rickard, Ian
Ricketts, Thomas N.
Ridgeway, Nicola Louise
Robinson, Ferga
Robinson, Peter
Rogers, Lesley A.
Rose, Stuart
Ross, Michael Killoran
Ross, Susan M.
Rouhifar, Zhila
Ruddell, Peter
Ryan, Mairead
Sage, Nigel A.
Sawyer, Noel F.
Schreiber-Kounine, Christa

Scott, Jan
Scott, Michael
Scott-Chinnery, Jean
Serfaty, Marc A.
Serieys, Nicholas Michael
Shaw, Elizabeth
Shawe-Taylor, Metka
Sheldon, Brian
Shepherd, Eric
Sherriff, Deanne
Shortall, Thomas R.
Siddle, Ronald
Simos, Gregoris
Singh, Satwant
Smail, Rachid
Smart, Kate
Smith, R.L.
Smith, Trevor E.L.
Sookdeb, S.
Spratt, Graham S.
Stallard, Paul
Standart, Sally
Stewart, Henry B.
Stewart, Lisa
Strickland, Lynda
Sungur, Mehmet
Swan, John S.
Swinburne, Barbara C.
Szymanska, Kasia
Tajet-Foxell, Britt
Tatham, Alan
Taylor, Jon
Taylor, Tracey
Thomas, Carmel
Thomas, Madeleine
Thomas, Nigel
Thornton, Andy S.
Todd, Gillian
Toole, Stuart
Townend, Michael
Townsend, Pat
Trepka, Chris
Trippett, Marie
Trosh, Joanna
Tse, Claude
Tubbs, I.A.
Turkington, Douglas
Turner, Martin S.
van Bilsen, Henck P.J.G.
Venki, Malathi
Walker, Anne
Walsh, Belinda
Wang, Michael
Wardley, Jean
Watts, Mary
Westman, Stephen
White, Craig A.
Wight, Zena J.
Wilde, Verina
Williams, Christopher John
Williams, Ruth M.
Williams, Steve
Williams-Conley, Debbie
Willis, James
Wills, Frank
Wilson, Fiona
Wilson, Mary
Wilson, Tom C.
Wiltshire, Gill
Withers, Jacqueline
Woodcraft, Paul
Wright, Christine M.J.
Wynn, Michelle
Yapp, Robin
Young, Katherine

BAFATT - British Association for Autogenic Training and Therapy

Benor, Ruth
Bird, Jane
Bonnefin, Valerie
Buchanan, Sarah-Jill
Davidson, Brian
Free-Pearce, Carolyn
Greene, Alice
Gross, Grete
Kanji, Nasim
MacKinnon, Hetty
Marshall, Janet
Pinch, Christine

BAP - British Association of Psychotherapists

Blackie, Suzanne
Bostock, Elizabeth
Carr, Jean
Chapman, Sandy
Cochlin, Marion
Coren, Alexander
de Hoogh-Rowntree, Patricia
El-Hadi, Ali
Furst, Lena
Gross, Stephen
Harris, Dianne
Heuer, Agnes Birgit
Hewitt, Philip J.
Howard, Rina
Hutchison, Eric
Jaques, Penny
Kenny, Miranda
Lister, Mary
Menckhoff, Beckie
Morley, Elspeth
Morley, Robert
O'Brien, Maja
Perry, Christopher
Rentoul, Lynette
Roseman, Renee
Sklan, Cheryl
Sladden, Anna
Vernon, Paul
Vincent, Christopher
Watt, Ferelyth
Wilson, Catherine
Yeldham, Denise

BASMT - British Association for Sexual and Marital Therapy

Adler, Eve
Alexander, Sandra
Angold, Monica
Anstice, Christine
Ball, Derek
Barnes, Tricia
Batchelor, Henrietta
Beer, Charmian
Beighton, Chris
Berger, Iris
Berry, Mary
Blum, Anita
Boddington, Daphne
Bollinger, Charmian
Borghgraef, Guy
Brassington, Pauline
Brindle, Elisabeth
Brown, Avril
Buckler, Jackie
Burkeman, Fiona
Bush, Malcolm
Butcher, Josie
Carter, Paula
Clegg, Alison
Clements-Jewery, Sue
Clifton, S.
Coats, Sonia
Cole, Martin
Collins, Jane
Collis, Jeffrey
Cooper, Faye
Cooper, Grahame F.
Cooper, Penny
Crowe, Michael
Cullum, Sylvia
d'Ardenne, Patricia
Daines, Brian
De Groot, Marianne
de Marquiegui, Asun
Dighton, Rosemary
Dodsworth, Evelyn
Doogan, Kevin
Duncan, Sally
Dyer, Paula
Eisen, Shelley
Eisler, Zizana
Emeleus, Frances
Evans, G.E.
Evans, Tricia
Farquharson, Kay
Felix, Susan
Fraser, Bobbie
Gage, Michael
Galloway, Jan
Gann, Sandra
Gibbin, Jane
Glover, Jean
Goldman, John
Gregory, Peter
Griffin, Mary
Guilfoyle, John F.
Gurr, Rosalie
Hallam-Jones, R.A.
Hamilton, Eira
Harrison, Caroline
Harrison, Susan
Headon, Christopher
Helps, Davina
Hendrickse, Begum
Hill, Brenda
Hillman, Jan
Hobbs, Anita
Holdaway, Elizabeth
Hollingworth, Amanda
Hooper, Anne
Horton, Barbara
Howlett, Brian
Huish, Margot
Hunt, Susan
Huws, Rhodri
Jackson, Paul
Jacob, Emily
Jones, Caroline
Jones, Judith
Keith, Joyce
Keshet-Orr, Judi
Lang, Christine
Lawrence, E.
Leygraf, Bernd
Lidster, Wendy
Limbardet, Jean-Pierre
Lloyd, Patricia
Lobel, Sandra
Lobel, Sidney
Logue, Nancy
Loudon, Julia
Low, James
Malone, Sue
Marks-Pinfold, Shirley
Martin, Angela
May, Kath
McGroary-Meehan, Maureen
McNaught, Janet
Meller, Carolyn
Mitchell, Louise
Mitchell, Ruth
Moore, Jill
Moore, Margaret C.
Morgan, Elizabeth
Mulvey, Josephine
Mycroft-Miles, June
Nelson, Denise
Nelson, Maureen
O'Conor, Mary
Openshaw, Sally
Pacey, Susan
Pallenberg, Sue
Palmer, Dorothy
Perrett, Angie
Perry, Janet
Phillips, Mary
Plant, Barbara
Plen, Rene
Proudley, Helen
Pryde, Nia
Ramage, Margaret
Rayson, Joan
Read, Jane

Reader, Frances
Rendall, Davina
Reuvid, Jennie
Richards, Maureen
Richardson, Caroline
Richardson, Gillian
Richardson, Madeleine J.
Ridley, Jane
Rix, Sandra
Roy, Jane
Ryan, Elizabeth
Sandelson, Jennifer
Scott, Liz
Seaman, Daphne
Seigal, Anthony
Serpell, Vivienne
Shelley, Trevor
Sinclair, Ilse
Snowden, Patricia
Sparks, Rebecca
Stanley, Elizabeth
Stevens, Jill
Symes, Jan
Taylor, Jane
Thoburn, Marjorie
Thomas, Jennifer
Tomlinson, Moya
Tully, Daphne
Tunwell, Ann
von Bühler, José
Vora, Valerie
Wallace-Smith, Nigel
Wallis, V.A.
Ward, Keltie
Warwick, Heather
Watson, J.P.
Webster, Lynne
Wheeley, Eleanor
Whittaker, Ruth
Wilson, Llynwen
Wilson, Norman
Wood, Sue
Wylie, Kevan R.
Yawetz, Christine

BCPC - Bath Centre for Psychotherapy and Counselling

Adams, Sue
Barrett, Julie Patricia Ann
Crispin, Jean
Dewey, George
Douglas, Sue
Elman, Anthony
Feilden, Tish
Graham, Margaret
Hackett, Jenny
Hall, Kelvin
Hastings, Jon
Hastings, Kim
Hawkins, Peter
Hoare, Ian
Kessel, Inge
Lacy-Smith, Jo
Luthy, Barbara
Maslen, Gill
McGowan, Fran
Mellett, Jane
Milton, Thelma
Naydler, Nick
Newbery, Christopher
Orton, Jane
Pirani, Alix
Purkiss, Jane
Ryde, Judy
Sawers, Martin
Selby, Anne
Slattery, David
Thomas, Penny
Tracy, Colin
Valentine, Christine
Voelcker, Cara
Wheway, John Kirti

BPA - British Psychodrama Association

Aguirregabiria, Ana
Alexander-Graham, Cassy
Bannister, Anne
Barton, Alan
Biancardi, Jenny
Bould, Jane
Bradbury, Sue
Bradshaw-Tauvon, Kate
Branagan, Noelle
Brandwood, Pat
Brazier, David
Brown, Teresa
Casson, John
Chesner, Anna
Costa, Jan
Cramer, William
Dale, Carole
Daniels, Mo
Davenport, Hilary
Eldridge, Melanie
Farmer, Christopher
FitzGerald, Pen
Flynn, Stephen
Hagelthorn, Christina
Haworth, Peter
Hodges, Barbara
Holmes, Paul
Howell, Julia
Hutchinson, Peter
Jefferies, J.I.
Karp, Marcia
Kay, Malcolm
Kirk, Kate
Kjellstrom, Laila
Lambert, Louise
Langley, Dorothy
Lascelle, Hasan
Levens, Mary
Littledale, Nadine
Lousada, Olivia
Luxmoore, Nick
MacNeill, Enid
Maxwell, Hugh
Moggridge, Cass
Murray, Catherine
Potkonjak, Dusan
Pregnall, Sheila
Quin, Barbara
Ruscombe-King, Gillie
Salisbury, Jonathan
Scanlan, Celia
Schopman, Els (Elisabeth)
Simmons, Alison
Sprague, Ken
Taylor, Susie
Thompson, Jean Mary
Thomson, Simon
Tregear, Barbara
Turkie, Janine
Watson, Roy
Wheadon, Sylvia
White, Eve
Widlake, Bernard C.
Wilkins, Paul
Williams, Gill
Wooding, Sandra
Wright, Maureen

BTC - The Gerda Boyesen Centre

Armstrong, Caroline
Bardelle, Rosemary
Barker, Elizabeth
Baum, Stefanie
Boyesen, Ebba
Boyesen, Gerda
Boyesen, Mona Lisa
Brosskamp, Cornelia
Byford, Sally
Byring, Carola
Cleminson, Richard
Crook, Didi
Danthois, Didier
Davis, Valerie
Deniflee, Ursula
Eisenbarth, Heiner
Falkowska, Merlyn
Gagnere, Maryline
Gandy, Rus
Gilbert, Gillie
Harris, Michele
Hauser, Susan
Heinitz, Karin
Jones, Helen
Korte, Achim
Lederman, Tsafi
Liebling, Lauren
Llowellyn, Martha
McLeod, Paula
Mundy, Jean
O'Neill, Julia
Ohnesorg, Johanna
Otto, Joachim
Pawson, Chris
Pawson, Sheila
Quoilin-Lebrun, Michelle
Salles, Miriam
Samson, Andre
Scott, Brigitte
Shipton, Sunita
Southwell, Clover
Sutherland, Janet
Tanguay, Daniel
Taylor, Jill
Van der Wateren, Jan-Floris
van Heel, Carlien
Webb, Deborah

CAPP - Centre for Attachment-Based Psychoanalytic Psychotherapy

Adams, Janet
Barker, Gina
Bucknall, Valerie
Callaway, Hazel
Charter, Anne
Clifford, Victoria
Cohen, Pat
Davis, Emerald
Erskine, Judith
Henry, John
Hertzmann, Leezah
Holland, Stevie
Hosking, John
Hughes, Hatty
Hurst, Hannah
Jolliffe, John
Laschinger, Bernie
McMillan, Penny
Michael, Jess
Miller, Bob
Miller, Penny
Odgers, Andrew
Parkinson, Jane
Pollard, James
Purnell, Chris
Raicar, Maeja
Richardson, Sue
Rubie, Val
Schoenfeld, Hilde
Schwartz, Joe
Singer, Iris
Southgate, John
White, Kate
Wright, Laurie Jo

CCBP - Chiron Centre for Body Psychotherapy

Ablack, Joanne
Albrighton, Sylvia
Asheri, Shoshi
Blair, George
Boening, Joachim
Boening, Michaela
Browne, Maureen
Catovsky, Mina
Cooper, Suzanne
Coxwell-White, Jenny
Drewnowska, Alicja
Eiden, Bernd

Elliott, Dena
Hedinger-Farrell, Korinna
Heitzler, Morit
Henderson, Ned
Hills, Janet
Holland, Ray
Holmes, Lynne
Kelly, Gillian
Landale, Margaret
Law, Susan
Lockie, Gisela
Lude, Jochen
Millar, Wilma
O'Hara, Karen
Pervoltz, Rainer
Petrie-Kokott, Julie
Prall, Werner
Prendergast, Teresa
Schaible, Monika
Scott-McCarthy, Miranda
Sell, Patrick
Soth, Michael
Staunton-Soth, Theresa
Stevenson, Bruce
Stracey, Amarilla
Tristram, Sue
Tune, David
Weaver, Ziva
Wilkins, Max

CCPE - Centre for Counselling & Psychotherapy Education

Aldred, Sue
Alferoff, Tamara
Arbia, G. Nicoletta
Attias, Sandra
Bannon, Maureen
Basharan, Harika
Bilder, Tessa
Bond, Lesley
Brittain, Charlie
Buirski, Diana
Burrows, Brian
Button, Rachel
Cain, Dennis
Cantelo, Frances
Carlson, Theresa
Casares, Jonathan
Casey, Jan
Charley, Geoff
Daly, John
Dawson, Peter
de Nordwall, Luci
Desmond, Hanora
Donald, Philippa
Durban, Ann
Emery, Pamela
Emm, Susan
Fagan, Anthony F.
Fentiman, John
Ferguson, Joyce
Fitzgerald-Klein, Marianne
Flower, Charles
Forssander, Jennifer
Fox, Annie
Franks, Julia
Fraser, Daphne
Fraser, Hugh Ross
Garner, Cheryl
Gaunt, Pamela
Golten, Carole
Gregg, Annzella
Griffiths, Pamela
Griffiths, Thelma
Gruber, Angela
Hagenbach, Kitty
Hall, Linda
Hamilton, Nigel
Hamilton, Susan
Hanna, Gilli
Harper, Anita
Harris, Jonathan
Haskins, Nicola
Haupts, Brigitte
Hay Burns, Jean
Howell, Carolyn
Howell, Sylvia
Ingham, Nida
Jacobs, Paula
Jacques, Roma
Jameson, Anne
Jones, Ros
Kafton, Maggie
Keane, Agnes
Keane, Pamela
Kerry, Sue
Kinbacher, William
Kingsley, Mary
Lamplough, Lyn
Lavender, Lesley
Lovett-Darby, Linda
Lowden, Barbara
Martin, Brandy
Mason, Letizia
Masters, Sue
McDermott, Paul
McKeown, Patricia
Menezes, Ray
Meredith, Judith
Meza, Ann L.
Morris, Bridget
Murphy, Alan
Nappez, Sue
Newns, David
Nieboer, Sarah
O'Connor, Nadia
Parkinson, Phil
Patchett, Angela
Petrie, Bill
Petrie, Clare
Pimentel, Allan
Prichard, Lois
Prior, Robin
Quinn, Asher
Reddy, William
Reeves, Alan
Reilly, Nicole
Richardson, Ann
Richardson, Sacha
Richter, Nicola
Rose, Wendy
Ross, Suzanne
Sagoe, Pauline
Salamander, Jas Ananda
Sanders, Susie
Schimmelschmidt, Michael
Shaban, Dervishe
Sheridan, Dolores
Silver-Leigh, Vivienne
Singleton, Kryin
Smith, Richard
Smyly, Penelope
Stimpson, Quentin
Stobezki, Yael
Sussman, Susan
Taylor, Jackie
Taylor, Sajada Katalin
Thiel, Geoffrey
Vallely, Patricia M.
Ward, Hilary
Ward, Sharron
Waterman, Zak
Wheeler, Meredith
Whitaker, Christine
Winter, Wendy
Young, Diana
Young, Raymond
Young, Sabine
Yusef, Dori Fatima

CFAR - Centre for Freudian Analysis and Research

Benvenuto, Bice
Bull, Graham E.
Burgoyne, Bernard
Campbell, Margaret
Conolly, J.M.P.
Dachy, Vincent
Darcy, Gillian
du Ry, Marc
Farquhar, Kate
Gessert, Astrid
Hill, Philip
Hodgkiss, Andrew
Kennedy, Michael
Leader, Darian
Machado, Danuza
Pepeli, Hara
Reid, Liz
Rowan, Alan
Sullivan, Gerry
Watson, Lindsay

CPCP - Centre for Personal Construct Psychology

Agnew, Joyce
Botterill, Willie
Brennan, Damian
Brennan, Joady
Bury, Dennis R.
Butler Smith, Catherine
Button, Eric
Cooper, Cassie
Crosby, Simon
Cross, Malcolm C.
Cummins, Peter
Dalton, Peggy
Dupuy, Alan
Epting, Franz
Evans, Ray
Fogelberg, Don
Fransella, Fay
Gatti-Doyle, Fiorella G.
Goold, Peter
Grimshaw, Francoise
Harvey, Paul
Jackson, Sherin
Jones, Helen
Kenny, Vincent
Morris, Brenda
Morris, Clare
Murphy, Derry
O'Sullivan, Bernadette
Overs, Nicola
Peters, Anthony
Procter, Harry
Rawat, Shenaz
Rossotti, Nicole
Rowe, Dorothy
Selby, Gina
Smith, Alison
Sparkes, Frances
Stein, Nathan Bernard
Taylor, Helen
Thomson, Alan
Thorman, Chris
Viney, Linda
Winter, David

CPP - Centre for Psychoanalytical Psychotherapy

Birkett, Diana
Boulton, John
Bradley, Natalie
Graves, Jane
Hadary, Orna
Lambor, Florangel
Lippitt, Gwenda
Newby, Rita
Polledri, Patricia
Reddish, Elisabeth
Romm-Bartfeld, Goldie
Smith, Patsy
Tan, Richard

CSP - Cambridge Society for Psychotherapy

Arriens, Pamela
Briant, Steve
Briggs, Margarete
Corrigall, Jenny

Dasgupta, Carol
Davies, Judy
Evans, Michael
Gentry, Valerie
Gordon, Leila
Greaves, Sarah
Klug, Liebe
Lew, Clara
Paramour, Annabelle
Parkinson, Dorn
Randall, Rosemary
Robinson, Carole
Seymour Clark, Vivienne
Smith, Gillian
Wilde, Deborah

CSPK - Centre for the Study of Psychotherapy (University of Kent)

Anderson, Tony
Bunker, Carol
Bunker, Nigel
Cairns, Mary
Carey, Jean
Cartwright, Alan
Cartwright, Kate
Darnley, Hazel
Hiron, Ruth
Leiper, Rob
Reading, Bill
Reilly, Anne
Riding, Ann
Riding, Nick
Roberts, Jane
Shaw, Maureen
Thomason, June

CTP - Centre for Transpersonal Psychology

Allen, Dorothy
Allsop, Pamela
Anthony, Monica
Barclay, Elizabeth
Bennett, Rosanagh
Birch, Cathy
Bishop, Beata
Boddaert, Michael
Brain, Sara
de Serdici-Parker, Simona
Fieldhouse, Pauline
Fowles, Anne
Grant, Mary
Guest, Hazel
Haywood, Carol
Hock, Gaby
Holden, Maxine
Lindley-Jones, Kirstin
Marshall, Hazel
McCormick, Elizabeth Wilde
McDonald, Christina
McGouran, Gill
Merriot, Peter
Michaelson, Sue
Millais, Suzy
Muschamp, Maureen
Peet, Sandra
Peters, Maggie
Pool, Nicky
Preece, Rob
Proctor, Ann
Quinn, Susan
Saabor, Geraldine
Salmon, Cindy
Smith, Gerry
Swallow, Joan
Swallow, Reynold
Turner, Senga
Tyrrell, Susannah
Vaizey, Philippa
Vibert, Eva
Vick, Philippa
Waygood, Rob
White, Ruth
Williams, Diana
Wishart, Marian
Young, Anne

CTS - Centre Training School of Hypnotherapy and Psychotherapy

Berry, Margaret
Birley, Paul
Bolton, Adrian Mark Tom
Bonnebaight, Andre
Brookhouse, Shaun
Campbell, Caroline
Curtis, Marjorie
Cutner, Adrienne
Doyle, Alan
Fairhurst, Patricia
Gonsalkorale, Wendy
Goodson, Christina
Hardman, Anne
Howell, Judy
Iles, David
Isaac, Toni-Lee
MacPherson, David
Martin, Susan
McGrath, Adrian
McVey, Damien
Middleton, Margaret
Moon, Barbara
Mwelwa, Edward
Renwick, Fran
Sawyer, Ken
Stableford, Joyce
Stokes, Fergus
Taylor, Elizabeth
Tollan, John H.
Washington, Sue
Watson, Dorothy

FAETT - Forum for the Advancement of Educational Therapy & Therapeutic Teaching

Axson, Barbara Astrid
Burridge, Ellora Polly
Chappell, Claire
Clifford-Poston, Andrea
Coles, Walter
Daniel, Catherine
Dover, Jennifer
Geddes, Heather
Gell, Sally
Greenwood, Angela
Hannon, Sr. Mary Letizia
Haussman, Rochelle
High, Helen
Holloway, Sheila
Jennings, Lyn C.
Kee, Cynthia
Lyndon, Barbara
Marsden, Lee
Morton, Gillian
Oromi, Irene
Salmon, Gillian
Selby, Marilyn
Taube, Idonea
Tillett, Penny

FIC - The Family Institute, Cardiff

Alexander, Erica
Benbow, Susan
Brett, John
Cartwright, Tony
Cox, Brenda
Crossling, Paddy
Faris, Jeff
Foulkes, Michael
Gagg, Susan M.
Hardy, William
Howell, Hilary
Jones, Susan
Marks, Helen
Marshall, Cherrith A.
Matthews, Shane
Mylan, Trish
Osborn, James
Ostler, Dorothy
Pieczora, Marek
Reimers, Sigurd
Robinson, Gary
Roys, Clare
Sayers, Jacqui
Street, Eddy
Williams, Richard
Wilson, Jim

FIP - The Forum for Independent Psychotherapists

Alexander, Gail
Alexander, Gina M.V.
Bamber, Nicola
Christopher, Elphis
Fanning, Alexandra
Ford, Susan
Godsil, Geraldine
Gottesman, Robert
Haddington, Janet
Hall, Guy
Irving, Susan
Leeburn, Jennifer
Mellows, David
Mellows, Hilary
Power, Kevin
Richardson, Elizabeth
Sinclair, Fiona
Thomas, Kerry
West, Marcus
Wetherell, Jean
Zinkin, Hindle

GCL - The Gestalt Centre, London

Allport, Maggie
Ambrose, Tony
Becker, Amely
Bryan, Agnes
Coronas, Ita
Crombie, Clare
Davidge, Maggie
de Luchi, Martin
Ellis, Michael
Gilligan, Toni
Hall, Jill
Hancock, Maureen
Houston, Gaie
John-Wilson, Deb'bora
Leary-Joyce, John
Leary-Tanner, Judith
Marsden, Veronica
Martin, Linda
Morgan, Barbara
Puddy, Jane Kahan
Rose, Alivia
Sherno, Peggy
Siederer, Carol
Smith, Jonathan
Styles, Heather
Veale, Maurice
White, Jennifer
White, Nuala

GCP - Guildford Centre for Psychotherapy

Hatswell, Valerie
Holve, Harriet
Hopwood, Jean
Hopwood, Michael
Lynch, Valerie
MacKenna, Christopher
Owtram, Peter
Reid, Rosamund
Seymour, E. John
Wilmot, Vivienne

GPTI - Gestalt Psychotherapy Training Institute

Appleby, Joy
Ashcroft, Dinah
Bar-Yoseph, Talia Levine
Bate, Dolores
Bentley, Ros
Bodgener, Sue
Broughton, Vivian
Butler, Todd
Daintry, Penelope
Dawson, Jenny
Denham, Juliet
Denham-Vaughan, Sally
Edwards, Dagmar
Evans, Richard
Fish, Sue
Fitton, Freda
Glanville, Tony
Goodfellow, Joanna
Graham, Marilyn
Gregory, Judith
Harris, Neil
Hemming, Judith
Higgins, Judith
Hughes, Geraldine
Hughes, Jacqui
Jackson, Elizabeth
Jacques, Glenys
Jameson Milner, Jane
Joyce, Philip
Kelly, Caro
Kennedy, Des
Kennedy, Helen
Kwei, Daniel
Lake, Moira
Leiper, Elizabeth
Levitsky, Patricia D.
Lubbock, Philippa
MacKenzie, Liz
Mackewn, Jennifer
Makin, Anne
Mitchell, John
Mukuma, Diana
Nathan, (Jennifer) Ruth
Opienski, Jacek
Orlans, Vanja
Osborne, Lynda
Parava, Anna
Parlett, Malcolm
Parmley, Alison
Philippson, Peter
Retallick, Malcolm
Rosemary, Margaret
Scott, Janice
Skeet, Maggie
Thomas, Marcia
Thomas, Mark
Turton, Mike
Tyson, Robert
Vollans, Audrey
Warburton, Geoff
Weller, Celia
Whines, Jonathan
Williams, Chris
Williams, Guinevere

GUILD - Guild of Psychotherapists

Adams, Tessa
Addenbrooke, Mary
Amiel, Olivia
Armstrong-Perlman, Eleanore
Arnold, Rosemary
Atkins, Coral
Atkinson, Paul
Ayres, Anthony
Bacon, Roger
Bar, Vivien
Barham, Peter
Barnett, Mary
Barrett, Jean
Barwell, Peter
Battersby, Audrey
Beaumont, Mia
Berry, Peter
Bhatt, Vibha
Bickerton, Tricia
Bosanquet, Camilla
Briant, Michael
Buckroyd, Julia
Burton, Michael
Campbell, Elizabeth
Chancer, Anne
Chandler, Philip
China, Jacques
Clackson, Suzanne
Clare, Louise
Clendon, David
Cohen, Sylvia
Coleridge, Jane
Collins, Natalie
Colver, Stephen
Coombs, Suzanne
Cooper, Sara
Couzyn, Jeni
Cronin, Jeremiah
Daniel, Barbara
Draney, Sue
Dunn, Jenny
Dutton, Andrew
Easter, Judith
Egert, Susan
Eisen, Susan
Farhi, Nina
Farrell, Margaret
Ficarra, Berthe
Field, Kate
Fry, Caroline
Gal, Oshrat
Garlovsky, Rita
Gilljam, Annika
Goldblatt, Phyllis
Good, Simon
Goodrich, Diana
Gosling, Pat
Gow, Marion
Grant, Rosamund
Gray, Anne
Gray, Kati
Griffiths, Anne
Grocott, Annie
Guy, Liana
Hall, David
Halpin, Jill
Harvard-Watts, Olivia
Henriques, Marika
Hopkins, Jill
Hort, Daphne
Howard, Angela
Hughes, Ann
Jones, Margaret
Joyce, Angela
Kane, Ros
Karan, Alexandra
Kerr, Anna
Kerridge, Jack
Krzowski, Sue
Lawrence, Margaret
Lee, Jan
Lewis, Sheila
Lloyd, Elizabeth
Maguire, Marie
Marsh, Jennifer
Milburn, Irene
Miller, Michael
Moore, Rosemary
Morgan, Sian
Morris, Monique
Morris, Shosh
Nabarro, Elizabeth
Naylor-Smith, Alan
Nicholson, Elizabeth
Noble, Jane
O'Connor, Noreen
Oakley, Haya
Orbach, Ann
Payne, John
Pearmain, Rosalind
Percy, David
Porter, Ruth
Pratt, Sheila
Price, Susan
Ransome, Helen
Rea, Judith
Richards, Christopher
Richards, Janet
Richards, Val
Rickett, Marion
Rimmer, Lynn
Robertson, Zuleika
Robinson, Hazel
Robinson, Judy
Robinson, Sue
Rumney, Boris
Schofield, Lynn-Ella
Scott, Glenys
Sinclair, Alison
Smith, Anne
Springford, Kate
Spurling, Lawrence
Tait, Adrian
Taussig, Hanna
Upton, Jay
Vallins, Yvonne
Veasey, Helen
Vickers, Salley
Voikhanskaya, Marina
Watkins, Judy
Wells, Lesley
Wells, Roger
Westcott, Rosemary
White, Jean
Wilce, Gillian
Wilson, Michael
Wooster, Frances
Worrall, Chrysoula

HIP - The Hallam Institute of Psychotherapy

Agass, Dick
Ashton, John
Barker, Lily
Beard, Hilary
Bennison, Judy
Berry, Juliet
Blacker, Polly
Bolsover, G.N.
Bostock, Christine
Boysan, Zehra
Caulfield, J. Heather
De Carteret, John
Donovan, Maxine
Drucquer, Helen
Edwards, David
Ellis, Lynda
FitzGerald, Geariod
Gartland, Michael
Gudjonsson, Ingolf
Guiton, Anita
Hopkins, Vera M.
Hunt, Patricia A.
Kendall, Tim
Littlewood, Ann
Loftus, Patrick A.
Loxley, David
Maitlis, Marion
Marshall, Myra
McAuley, John
Meredith, Joan
Monach, Jane
Oram, John E.D.
Pethen, Susan
Pickvance, Deborah
Porteous, Louise
Rayner, Beryl Ann
Robinson, Felicity
Rowe, Carolyn
Shipton, Geraldine
Smith, Eileen F.
Sudbury, John
Thomas, Sandra V.M.
Thomson, Pat
Todd, Margaret C
Vincent, Jane
Vipan, Sheila
Ward, Ruth

Willowes, Jean
Woolfson, Myra

IATE - Institute for Arts in Therapy and Education

Blench, Graeme
Cruthers, Helan
Dawkins, Sue
Ingham, Rosie
James, Jo
Leon, Sara
Plunkett, Eileen
Raphael, Francesca
Rowan, Chris
Savins, Charlotte
Sunderland, Margot
Waterfield, Julia
Wilson, Veronica

IFT - Institute of Family Therapy

Adcock, Margaret
Aggett, Percy
Anthias, Louise
Attwood, Peter
Avigad, Jocelyn
Bagnall, Steve
Barratt, Sara
Bennett, Margaret
Bentovim, Arnon
Bianco, Vicky
Blackburn, Paul
Bor, Robert
Boston, Paula
Bousfield, Anne
Burck, Charlotte
Burns, Elizabeth
Butt, Diana
Byng-Hall, Sue
Campbell, David
Chimera, Kathleen
Cooklin, Alan
Cornish, Ursula
Dale, Barbara
Daniel, Gwyn
Dawson, Neil
Dodge, Elizabeth
Dowling, Emilia
Draper, Ros
Dutton, Jane
Egert, Stella
Eisler, Ivan
Erskine, Ruth
Esposito, Claude
Farzim, Pari
Gee, Irene
George, Evan
Green, Joe
Gross, Vivien
Harrson, Gillian
Heavey, Anne
Henley, June
Herington, Steve
Hildebrand, Judy
Hooper, Christine M.
Humphreys, David
Inglebright, Shanti
Iveson, Chris
Iveson, Diana
Jacobs, Brian
James, Anthony
James, Christopher
Jenkins, Hugh
Johnson, Ellie Kavner
Jones, Elsa
Jones, Marlene
Lafon, Robert
Lask, Judith
Lau, Annie
Lewington, Paul
Lindsey, Caroline
Mandin, Philippe
Mason, Barry
Mayer, Robert
McCann, Damian
McCann, Linda
McGrath, Rita
McHugh, Brenda
Messent, Philip
Miller, Riva
Moorhouse, Anni
Morris, Allan
O'Brian, Charles
O'Brien, Pat
Paulson, Diana
Pettle, Sharon
Pike, Margery
Ratner, Harvey
Robinson, Margaret
Sheehan, Nuala
Smith, Gerrilyn
Stedman, Maire Aine
Stevens, Ann
Stogdon, Mark
Topliss, Nick
Tufnell, Guinevere
Turner, Annie
Van Schoor, Linda
Van-Loo, Douglas
Virtanen, Helena
Waters, Kathleen
Wieselberg, Huguette
Woodcock, Jeremy
Woodward-Smith, Nicholas

IGA - Institute of Group Analysis

Abbasi, Shafika
Anderson, Linda
Antao, Ivor
Arcari, Stephen
Arnott, Biddy
Azu-Okeke, Okeke
Bacha, Claire
Bamber, James
Barratt, Gillian
Behr, Harold
Berman, Paul
Berry, Eileen
Bhat, Radha
Birchmore, Terry
Bloch, Linda
Boakes, Janet
Boardman, Ian
Boronat, Dascha
Boswood, Bryan
Brown, Rachel
Burgess, Jo
Campbell, Janet
Campos, Hanne
Canete, Maria
Canty, Josephine
Charlton, Anne
Chatfield, Anne
Chilton, Maggie
Christie, Jim
Clairmonte, Tosin
Cogill, Stephen
Cohen, Vivienne
Cooper, Robin
Corbett, Martyn
Cunningham, Gordon
Dalal, Farhad
Daykin, Amanda
de Mare, Patrick
Denton, Marika
Dillon Weston, Marisa
Duckham, Jennifer
Eagles, Marjorie
Einhorn, Sue
Elliott, Barbara
Ernst, Sheila
Evans, Chris
Ezquerro-Adan, Arturo
Fagbadegun, Rufus
Farquharson, Graeme
Fasht, Ruth
Feeney, Michael
Festenstein, Geraldine
Fischer, Michael
Foguel, Brenda
Fuller, Victoria G.
Glenn, Liza
Gold, Bonnie
Gorman, Susan
Gottesman, Ewa
Green, Roberta
Greenberg, Maurice
Haddock, Ray
Hallard, Sharon
Hamrogue, Tom
Hasler-Winter, Susan
Hearst, Liesel
Heatley, John
Heimann, Michael
Helbert, Jan
Hobbs, Michael
Holden, Sarah
Holmes, Anne
Hook, Beatrice
Hook, John
Hope-Price, Gloria
Hopper, Earl
Hudson, Inge
Hughes, Patrick
Hutchinson, Sylvia
Hyde, Keith
Ikkos, George
Ingram, Sonia
James, Jessica
Jenkins, Anne
Kay, Margaret
Kennard, David
Kinder, Diana
Knowles, Jane
Lear, Terry
Lee, John
Lilley, Davina
Lilley, Diana
Lintott, Bill
Love, Derek
Lucas, Tina
Lynn, Rita
Lyon, Heather
MacAlister, Eileen
Mace, Chris
MacKenzie, Nancy
Maratos, Jason
Mark, Peter
Marshall, Levana
Maxwell, Brian
Mayer-Johnson, Jessica
McCabe, Ruth
McCarrick, Tom
McGrath, Patrick
Meinrath, Monica
Millard, Sheila
Mitchison, Sally
Morgan, Anne
Nathan, Gill
O'Leary, Carmen
Ormay, Tom
Panchkowry, Marion
Parker, Michael
Patalan, Anna-Maria
Pennycook-Greaves, Wil
Peternel, Franc
Powell, Andrew
Pullin, Andrew
Rance, Christopher
Read, Tim
Reik, Herta
Rheinschmiedt, Otto
Roberts, Jeff
Roberts, Julie
Robinson, Mardi
Robinson, Rosalyn
Rogers, Cynthia
Rosenfeld, Angela
Russell, Wilson
Sarra, Nicholas
Schlapobersky, John
Schneider, Evelyne
Scott, Michael
Sepping, Paul
Sevitt, Michael
Sharpe, John
Sharpe, Meg
Skynner, Robin

Smith, Val
Sproul-Bolton, Robin
Stevenson, Beaumont
Strich, Sabina
Sutton-Smith, Deirdre
Tait, Mike
Tanna, Nick
Tantam, Digby
Thompson, Joy
Tough, Harry
Vella, Norman
Vincent, David
Walker, David
Westcott, Bernard
Wetherill, Julie
White, Jeremy
Whiteley, J. Stuart
Wilke, Gerhard
Williams, Jane
Willis, Sally
Wojciechowska, Ewa
Woolmer, Tim

IGAP - The Independent Group of Analytical Psychologists

Anderton, Michael
Begg, E.C.M
Burritt, William
Campbell Nye, Aileen
Clark, Giles
Costello, John
David, Johanna
David, Julian
Davis, Joyce
Denman, Cara
Edwards, Michael P.
Freeman, Linda
Gordon, Elizabeth
Harwood, Matthew
Hiller, Ruth
Hirst, Diane Zervas
Jackson, Eve
Keating, Jacqueline
Kind, Gill
Kujawski, Pedro
Maguire, Anne
Milne, Frances
Morris, Petrina
Papadopoulos, Renos
Rees, Myfanwy
Reynal, Carmen
Schwartz, Chuck
Shearer, Ann
Shorter, Bani
Smalley, John
Spencer, Janet
Tatham, Peter
Tuby, Molly
Weinrich, Hildegard
Whan, Michael

IPC - Institute of Psychotherapy and Counselling

Albrecht, Gisela
Allan, Kay
Allison, Virginia
Andrew, Elizabeth
Archer, Ruth
Arundell, Jane
Baker, Moke
Bannister, Gill
Bartlett, Beatrice
Baynes, Gay
Beard, Dorrie
Beer, Margaret
Beguin, Agnes
Bielicz, Paul
Bingham, Jane
Blum, Arna
Botha, Marie
Brown, Elizabeth Ann
Browne, Val
Buckley, Marie-Noël (Billie)
Carr, Brede
Cathie, Sean
Cazalet, Deborah
Channon, Michael
Chapman, Maureen
Clancy, Catherine
Clark, Christine
Clark, Margaret
Clifford, Jennifer
Combes, Ann
Cooper, Ian
Costello, Marie
Crawford, Stephen
Crowley, Julia
Czubinska, Grazyna
Danks, Alan
Dare-Bryan, Arminal
Dawson, Joyce
Day, Sally
de Jong, Corrie
Dean, Sally
Dixon-Nuttall, Rosemary
Dooley, Pat
Driver, Christine
Errington, Meg
Farmer, Eddie
Fenton, Christopher
Freeman, Sue
Gibson, Melanie
Goodrich, Anne
Greally, Brid
Green, Brian
Groom, Nigel
Gulliver, Pamela
Hamilton-Duckett, Paule
Harding, Celia
Hartman, Wendy
Hashemi, Beth
Henny, Lindy
Hoang, Astrid
Holden, John
Hudson, Marjorie
Hudson, Rachel
Hughes, Jennifer
Jones, Janet
Jones, Merryn
Jones, Peggy
Kell, Midge
Kidd, Lee
Kingsnorth, Wendy
Knowles, Valerie
Lallah, Regine
Lamprell, Michael
Leeming, Gareth
Leon, Barbara D.
Levick, Barbara
Levy, Colette
Linden, Roger
Lodrick, Michael
Lutyens, Marianna
Mander, Gertrud
Marsden, Patricia
Marshall, Vivien
Marx, Philippa
Matthews, Carol
Maunder, Brian Lawrence
McDouall, Veronica
McKeon, Mary
McLoughlin, Brendan
Meaden, Rosaleen
Millier, Sylvia
Monticelli, Wendy
Morrison, Lesley
Moses, Susan
Murdin, Lesley
Musgrave, Beatrice
Neal, Lalage
Nowlan, Kate
O'Dell, Tricia
Parker, Rosie
Parkinson, Judy
Parks, Val
Pawsey, Jack
Penniceard, Sandy
Persson, Rose
Peters, Linda
Pople, Sue
Porter, David
Preston, Kay
Quaine, Mary
Rees-Roberts, Diane
Reynolds, Hilary
Richards, Michael
Rignall, John
Roberts, Pauline
Rosseter, Bill
Russell, Gillean
Saville, Sue
Sharman, Juliet
Sharp, Belinda
Skinner, Charmian
Snow, Randa
Somerville, Gwynnedd
Stang, Pamela
Steward, Jill
Stewart, John A.
Steyn, Angela
Stokes, Jean
Stone, Miriam
Sutton, Bobbie
Taylor-Thomas, Caroline
Thorndycraft, Bill
Tjepkema, Froukje
Tompkins, Susan
Trayling, Laurie
Walsh, Aine
Webster, Anne
White, Lela Ljiljana
Wigram, Penny
Williams, Sherly
Winders, Suzanne
Windle, Ruth
Wood, Rob
Wood-Bevan, Martyn
Wright, James
Yallop, Melanie
Yariv, Gaila
Yates, Tony

IPS - Institute of Psychosynthesis

Conroy, Beth

IPSS - Institute of Psychotherapy and Social Studies

Allawi, Nadia
Bennett, Lesley
Bensimon, Marlene
Bishop, Patricia
Black, Sandra
Blackwell, Frances
Brave-Smith, Anna
Broadbent, Sara
Buckley, Judy
Burns, Alex
Burns, Paula
Byrne, Deidre
Cameron, Katherine
Campos, Juan
Chandwani, Lilian
Chessell, Karen
China, Giselle
Clare, John
Coleman, Jane
Cotten, Naomi
Coulter, Theresa
Courtault, Susie
Culliss, Andrew
Cussins, Anne
Daniels, Susan
Davidoff, Leslie
de Souza, Joney
Dogmetchi, Geri
Dowber, Hilary
Duckworth, Rosemary
Feldberg, Tom
Ferid, Heidi
Fiasche, Mara
Franklyn, Frank
Gauntlett, Tim
Gladstone, Guy

Gordon, Paul
Goslett, Kate
Green, June
Green, Michael
Grey, David
Hawkes, Bernadette
Horwood, Tone
Howard, Heather
Joffe, Riva
Kerkham, Patricia
Law, Heather
Lehrer, Pam
Letts, Muriel
Little, Marie
Lloyd, Patricia
Lovel, Mary
Manglani, Dona
Marshall, Antoinette
Masterson, Ingrid
McEldowney, Dennis
McGee, Colin
Michaud-Lennox, Suzanne
Morante, Flavia
Mycroft, Jessica
Norburn, Veronica
Oakley, Madeleine
Patricia, Thelma
Rabin, Norman
Rapp, Hilde
Roberts, June
Rogers, Maggie
Rose, Kevin
Sünkel, Sue
Shetland, Llrich
Smith, Carol
Smith, Jonathan
Spyer, Natalie
Steiner, Monika
Stopher, Andy
Stovell, Joy
Sucher, Ingerborg
Utting, Julia
Walker, Jim
Whitby, Susan
Wise, Penny
Woodley, Ermine
Young, Robert M.
Zarbafi, Ali

ITA - Institute of Transactional Analysis

Agar, James
Allen, Patricia M.
Arredondo, Beverly
Banks, Jan
Beazley-Richards, Joanna
Beechcroft, Diane
Bisgood, Bill
Blyth, Fiona
Boyd, Suzanne
Brereton, June
Bridge, Jenny
Brunt, Mervyn
Bulmer, Liz
Cardile, Pietro
Clevely, Sarah
Cooke, Bob
Cox, Mary
Cunningham, Valerie
David, Ann
Davis, Jim
Dennis, Stephen
Etherington, Mary
Felton, Maureen
Flatt, Deborah
French, Jean
Gildebrand, Katarina
Goddard, Lynne
Gowling, David
Green, Eliott
Hannah, Francesca
Harley, Ki
Harling, Biljana
Heath, John
Henshaw, Judith
Hewett, Rachael
Hewson, Julie Ann
Hirst, Hazel
Hobbes, Robin
Hopping, Geoff
Horton, Annie
Hostick, Kathie
Howard, Sister Columba
Irving, Nicholas
Keenan, Paul
Klein, Mavis
Lapworth, Phil
Law, Gordon
Leach, Kathy
Lee, Adrienne
Lewin, Melanie
Lister-Ford, Christine
Little, Ray
Lucas, Carol
Mardula, Jody
McNamara, Jennifer
McQuillin, Jane
Midgley, David
Monk-Steel, John
Moodie, Alastair
Morrish, Susan
Mountain, Anita
Mundy, Pamela
Oates, Stephanie
Pamphlett, Nicholas
Parkinson, Jillian
Parr, John
Payman, Barbara
Phelps, Gwyneth
Pollitzer, Juliette
Reddy, Michael
Ring, Brendan
Robinson, Jenny
Rose, Sylvia
Salters, Diane
Sanders, Peter
Shadbolt, Carole
Shearman, Christine
Sless, Deborah
Spenceley, Dave
Stevenson, Alice
Stewart, Ian
Stuart, Lilly H.
Swift, Sue
Taylor, Rosemary E.B.
Thomas, Jenny
Tilney, Anthony
Traynor, Barbara
Tweed, Mary
Uden, Christine
Van Halm, Corrie
Walford, Jane
Walford, Robin
Ward, Shona
Warner, Kerri
Waters, Anne
Welford, Enid
Wells, Martin
Whitley, Liz
Wood, Chrissie Jones
Wood, Jane

KCC - Kensington Consultation Centre

Abeles, Margi
Anderson, Eleanor
Anson, Carol
Aufflick, Julia
Bailey-Smith, Yvonne A.
Bentley, Patrick Joseph
Bevan, Judith Lesley
Blacker, Sandra R.
Bolton, Jan
Bownas, Jo
Buffery, Elli
Burnham, John
Burton, Simon
Cardwell, Amynta
Carr, Samantha
Charvet, Anne
Chataway, Carola
Cutteridge, Simon
D'Aguilar, Yvonne
Dalal, Caroline
De Witt, Jacqueline
Docking, Raymond F.
Egan, Jude
Ekdawi, Isabelle
Fausset, Ann
Fredman, Glenda
Goldstein, Pam
Goodwillie, Gill
Gordon, Inger
Gordon, Virginia
Gorney, Carry
Griffiths, Sheila
Haddon, Jarmaine
Hannah, Chris
Hannah, Clare
Harben, Ursula
Hart, Azina
Harvey, Pam
Hedges, Fran
Heismann, Elisabeth
Hickman, Sue
Hoare, Elizabeth
Howard, Trevor
Hudson, Pauline
Jackson, Jo
Jarvis, Eileen
Jones, Amanda
Kavanagh, Sister Catherine
Kemmis Betty, Sally
King, Madeleine
Lang, Peter
Lang, Susan
Lauchlan, Sheila
Lema, Juan Carlos
Levitt, Olga
Lingard, Shirley Ruth
Little, Martin
Louden, Penny
Makatini, Zethu
Manicom, Hilary
Manojlovic, Jelena
Markovic, Desa
Martin, Gloria
McAdam, Elspeth
McCafferty, Stewart
McCarry, Nicola
McEvoy, Patricia E.
McKay, Barbara
McManus, Gaynor
McNair, Ann G.
Middleton-Smith, Virginia
Milani, Belinda
Mohlala, Morris
Mudarikiri, Maxwell
Neate, Patricia
Noonan, Mairead
O'Connor, Michael
Ohene, Margaret D.
Oliver, Christine
Parker, Gabrielle
Partridge, Karen
Penalosa-Clarke, Adriana
Pidgeon, Patricia
Priest, Caroline
Quinn, John J.
Rae, Frances
Roberts, Alison
Roberts, Sylvia M.
Roche, Sile
Ruismaki, Marjo
Ryburn, Murray
Sandler, Topsy
Schreiber, Kaye
Short, Pat
Simon, Gail
Smart, Tanya
Smith, Margaret E.
Stacey-Ong, Lesley
Stevenson, Kate
Stone, Barry L.
Stratton, Peter M.
Taylor, Mary
Teng, Christina
Togher, Margaret
Tugendhat, Julia
Van Der Eijk, Mike
Vincent, Christopher
Wainwright, Claire

Walby, Jane
Way, Patsy
Webb, Ann
Wheeler, Maria
White, Anne
Whitfield, Gwyn
Wigglesworth, Julia K.
Wilkinson, Mary
Wilson, Teresa

LAPP - The London Association of Primal Psychotherapists

Canobbio, Victoria
Coombes, Clare
Cowan-Jenssen, Susan
Jenssen, Einar D.
Kostic, Jasna
Lafargue, Martine
Messner, Heather Lee
Messner, Hans Jorg
Nodelman, Marsha
O'Connor, Aine
Pollack, Angela

LCP - London Centre for Psychotherapy

Abram, Jan
Andry, Robert
Appleby, Sonia
Aquarone, Luc-Remy
Asmus, Elke
Baldwin, Sally
Barnett, Ruth
Bishop, Bernardine
Blackburne, Vivien
Blackley, Joanne
Blackwood, Renate
Blomfield, Wolf
Brennan, Clare
Carey, Faye
Carolan, Nicholas
Charalambous, Praxoulla
Clapp, Tony
Clark, Margaret
Cockburn, Andrew
Cohen, David
Colledge, Lorraine
Conlon, Ann
Conyers, Marie
Corry, Marilyn
Craddock, Jenny
Craib, Ian
Daniell, Dorothy
de Berker, Patricia
de Berker, Paul
Dear, Judith
Deering, Christine
Dickinson, Adrian
Dunk, Sarah
Elder, Penny
English, Wendy
Erskine, Archibald
Everington, Madeleine
Field, Nathan
Fitzsimmons, Janet
Foster, Angela
Fox, Jessica
Fraser, Lynett
Freeman, Martin
Froshaug, Ann
Gallagher, Eogain
Gell, Eva
George, Pamela
Gerrard, Jackie
Gledhill, Maureen
Godfrey-Issacs, Godfrey
Goldwyn, Margaret
Gordon, Sheila
Gottlieb, Sue
Grover, Mary V.E.
Haine, Ann
Hanley, Marie
Harris, Tirril
Haxby, Kit
Hinshelwood, Robert
Holender, Gisele
Isaacs, Joy
Isaacs Hemmings, Gillian
Jobbins, Bryan
Johnson-Smith, Camilla
Jones, David
Jones, Edgar
Kadish, Faigie
Khaleelee, Olya
Kilich-Walpole, Suna
Kitson, Nicholas
Kitto, Jane
Klein, Josephine
Levitsky, Jackie
Likierman, Meira
Lipkin, Marion
Love, Mollie
Mann, David
Marcus, Marietta
Marks, Gaby
Marrone, Mario
Marshallsay, Carol
McConnach, Judith
McConville, Lily
McCreanor, Teresa
McGregor-Hepburn, Jan
Mears, Sylvia
Mendoza, Steven
Mittwoch, Adele
Morgan-Jones, Richard
Mosse, Lucy
Nathan, Jack
Nicholson, Christine
Norrington, Susan
O'Connell, Victoria
Peover, Brenda
Pethick, Belinda
Pinto, Eliano
Piper, Robin
Pitchon, Eduardo
Pokorny, Barbara
Pollard, Elena
Poole, Robert
Quinn, Eilish
Ratoff, Tammy
Rattray, Noemie
Read, Celia
Reynolds, Michelle
Roeber, Johanna
Roith, Estelle
Rosen, Maria
Samuels, Carole
Saunders, Sally
Scarlett, Jean
Schuff, Heiner
Shuen, Dorcas
Silverstone, Jennifer
Simmons, Monty
Sleeper, Julia
Smith, Judith
Southan, Rosemary
Sovin, Edna
Spearman, Penny
Stadlen, Anthony
Stafford, Barbara
Stanton, Martin
Stearman, Frances
Stewart, Angus
Szabo, Heather
Taylor, Mary
Thistlethwaite, Harriet
Thompson, Paul
Toibin, Eileen
Tredgold, Clare
Tytel, Laurie
Vellacott, Julia
Wantman, Linda
Whitwell, John
Wilson, James
Woolf, Ralph

LPDO - Liverpool Psychotherapy Diploma Organisation (University of Liverpool)

Applegarth, Janet
Baynes, Monica
Bergel, Edith
Callaghan, Joan
Challis, Suzy
Clarke, Elaine
Collins, Gloria
Cooper, Graham
Dickinson, Paul
Dorndorf, Rhoda
Doyle, Elizabeth
Edwards, Jennifer
Essex, Delia
Farrell, Bill
Ferguson, Mary
Foster, Paul
Gabbay, Mark
Geldeard, Bryan W.J.
Glynn, Julie
Green, Barbara A.
Hagan, Patricia
Hamilton, Angela
Hamilton, Sheila L.L.
Haworth, Ann
Higgo, Robert J.
Kiemle, Gundi
Kirkland-Handley, Nick V.
Lamb, Kirsten
Lindsay, Marion
Maguire, Claire
Mattison, Sheila
McIntee, Jeannie
McNab, Stuart
Mercer, Annie
Nevin, Jaqui
O'Reilly, Thomas J.
Oakley, Ian H.
Parker, John
Phaterpekar, Hem
Pollet, Sheena
Potter, Steve
Prothero, Peggy
Prussia, Celia M.
Ross, Julie
Sexton, Janette G.
Sharples, Geraldine
Shetty, Grish Chander
Simpson, Kevin J.
Smith, Flo M.F.
Smith, Margaret
Stewart, June
Taylor, Patsy
Thorley, Helen
Wallace, Daphne
Webb, Joan
Wells, Peter G.
Wheeler, Anne
Wilkin, Peter
Woods, Angie
Woodward, Raie

MC - Minster Centre

Abrahams, Elisabeth
Alder, Helena
Alder, Roger
Arnold, Lynn
Baker, Jan
Bathai, Parizad
Borges, Sheila
Bowman, Heather
Claxton, Brenda
Conwell, Jim
Cook, Jane
Coumont Graubart, Valerie
Coussens, Kay
Davis, Helen
Dunn, Nicola
Dyson, Margaret
Embleton-Tudor, Louise
Fell, Angela
Field, Rosalind
Flinspach, Elisabeth
Geen, Sheryle
Gibson, Walter
Gomez, Lavinia
Gottschalk, Margaret S.
Granowski, Margaret
Gravelle, John

Harrison-Mayor, Susan
Hayhurst, Sohani
Henderson Dalal, Pauline
Holloway, Max
Holtrop, Anna
Hussain, Fakhir
Hyde, Dennis
Jefferies, Alison
Johnson, Pat
Jordan, Ruth
Kolbuszewski, Marianne
Lang, Richard
Lester, Clare
Lewis, Richard
Littlejohn, Sarah
Lock, Josephine
Moore, Julie
Morgan, Ruth
Morrison, Barbara
Murphy, Ger
Music, Graham
Newbigin, Alison
O'Callaghan, Lesley
O'Gorman, Mary Pat
Pixner, Stefanie
Platt, Sue
Preisinger, Kristiane
Presant, Fern
Renoux, Martine
Robinson, Louise
Roth, Ruth
Schiemann, Margot
Scovell, Janet
Shapiro, Adella
Sichel, David
Simmonds, Tina
Slade, John
Smith, Gill
Soloway, Clare
Steel, Sandra
Sutters, Amabel
Virgo, Leslie
Wanless, Peter
Williams, Nigel
Williams, Pat
Wiseman, Anna
Wood-Bevan, Rosemary
Wynn-Parry, Charlotte
Wyse, Hymie
Young, Margot

MET - Metanoia Institute

Borsig, Su
Brown, Lesley
Bukovics-Heiller, Birgit
Clarkson, Petruska
Clifton, Elaine
Critchley, Bill
Davies, Peggy
Day, Laurie
Day, Lesley
Dean, Paul
Dhillon, Harbrinder
Donaldson, Gillian
Elton Wilson, Jennifer
Fry, Julie
Gibson, Jenny
Gilbert, Maria
Greenway, Ian
Hargaden, Helena
Henderson, Andrew
Hipps, Hilary
Hitchings, Paul
Houghton, Christine
Isaksson-Hurst, Gun I.E.
Jeffries, Rosie
Jesson, Alison
Jones, Sue
Kearns, Anne
Kowszun, Grazyna
Leigh, Elana
Leitman, Norman
Macgregor, Wynne
Magner, Valerie
McGowan, Dominica
McKeown, Andy
Mothersole, Geoff
Murphy, Katherine
Murray, Gus
Nichols, Hamish
O'Callaghan, Jean
O'Dwyer, Annegret
Perring, Michael
Phillips, Susan
Porter, Barbara
Ransley, Cynthia
Renwick, John
Rimmer, Annie
Rowlands, Helen
Scott, Judy
Sills, Charlotte
Smith, Juliet
Summers, Graeme
Taussig, Maggie
Tholstrup, Margaret
Tudor, Keith
Turner, Carole
Valentine, Victoria
Wallace, Norma
Watters, Tamara
Wyatt, Gill

NAAP - Northern Association for Analytical Psychotherapy

Aird, Eileen
Black, Patricia Anne
Cooper, Margaret
Dobson, Mary
Firth, Sue
Gilbert, Barbara
Heller, Mary B.
Hurren, Karolyn
Jansen, Diana
Johnson, Frank
Kendal, Jo Reed
Longford, Joan
Lund, Charles
MacPherson, Malcolm
Mahmood, Janet
Marshall, Patricia
Miles, Carolyn
Morgan, Shirley P.
Morris, Ann
Payne, Graham
Phoenix, Ashleigh
Proctor, Susan
Shrubsole, Lindsay
Stafford, Amanda
Stanbury, Christine
Tod, Ian
Watson, Pauline

NAFSI - NAFSIYAT

Al Jarrah, Nadina
Alleyne, Aileen
Andrews, Gill
Bartels-Ellis, Phillida
Bonadie-Arning, Sondra
Brauner, Rita
Cassidy, Anita
Dupont-Joshua, Aisha
Ferguson, Geoff
Güngör, Dilek
Hobart, Angela
Hussain-Shackle, Shakrukh
Kaur-Love, Jasminder
Landesmann, Sonya
McKenzie-Mavinga, Isha
Metaxa, Jennie
Mordecai, Aslan
Mordecai, Kay
Nippoda, Yuko
Nkumanda, Rachel
Richards, Diana M.
Ross, Ronald J.
Thomas, Lennox
Yazar, Jale

NRHP - The National Register of Hypnotherapists and Psychotherapists

Ashworth, Freda
Ayres, Kathleen
Blake, Adrian
Bonner, David Calvert
Butler, John
Campbell, Colin B.G.
Campbell-Beattie, John
Cawley, Anthony
Challis, Raymond T.
Chilton, Barbara
Coia, Grace
Cox, Christine
Davidoff, Suzanne
Dearsley, Sandra
Diyaljee, Angeli
Edgell, Marjory
Faruki, Shirley
Fish, Deborah M.
Fitzgerald-Butler, Albina
Gausden, Christopher
Gent, Michael
Gilkes, Pauline
Glasspool, Patricia
Golding, Pauline
Gorman, Graham
Graham, Hilary E.
Grew, Lesley
Harris, Gerald A.
Hart, Mary A.M.
Hazlehurst, Jean
Hormasji, Faridoon
Howie, David D.
Johnson, Duncan B.
Johnstone, Janice
King, Christine
Kulyk, Michael
Langley, Allen
Linn, Iris
Luce, Peter James
Ludolf, Monica
MacDonald, Ross
Mahon, David
Malcolm, Hanne
Mallardo, Renee
Marshall, Jill
Mattar, Gretta
May, Adam
McGregor, Tony
Milton, Harry
Morbey, Patricia Joyce
Mountjoy, Lesleen
Peace, Susan
Penn, Joyce
Peters, Sheila
Plotel, Angela
Plowman, John
Rawson-Jones, Elizabeth
Raymond, Caroline
Redgrave, Kenneth
Retson Hogg, Christine
Richardson, Susan
Sarkic, Julia
Savage, Peter J.D.
Sever, Michael
Shearer, Anne
Smith, Alica
Smith, Susan Diane
Steel, Patricia
Steven, David B.
Stevens, Jean
Stevenson, Krystyna
Sutherland, Robert I.
Timmann, S.
Toyne, Joy K.
Trewhella, John
Wesson, Peter M.J.
Wilkins, David
Williams, Ann
Wingrove-Gibbons, Kenneth
Wren, Pauline

NSAP - North Staffs. Association for Psychotherapy

Barry, Anne
Breeze, Graham
Donnai, Andrew
Ghent, Rita
Gregory, Kayt
Hassall, Alan
Pantall, Marlis
Reagan, Catherine
Taylor, James
Whittam, Enid
Wiles, Margaret

NSHAP - National School of Hypnosis and Psychotherapy

Adams, Ghislaine
Adams, Megan
Al Rubaie, Talal
Bibby, Keith
Black, Judith
Black, Margaret
Bowman, Elizabeth
Boyden, Christina
Braterman, Eleanor
Burgess, Shanti
Busolini, Don
Butcher, Barbara
Caird, Elizabeth J.
Carder, Misha
Clegg, Ian
Cole, Shanti
Coutts, Linda
Dale, Anne M.
Duck, Dorothy M.
Duncan, Fraser
French, Anne
Gawler-Wright, Pamela
Gould, Geraldine
Green-Thompson, Cyril
Haynes, Eric
Hickman, Anya
Holm, Kirsti E.
Howtone, Christina
Jones, Pamela
Kalitowski, Matthew
Kanakam, Jonathan
Keedy-Lilley, Ray
Keith, Charlotte
Kendrick, Margaret
Kohler, Christiane
Luckcock, Ronald Cosmo
Lyon, Josephine
Mackinnon, Sylvia
McGreevy, Edith
McGuinness, Mark
Morgan, Jo
Morgan, Linda
O'Brien, Ann
O'Neill, Christopher J.
Peacock, Anne
Porter, Jim
Sawyer, Albert
Smolira, David
Tomlinson, Andy
Ward, Dawn

NWIDP - North West Institute for Dynamic Psychotherapy

Allen, Tessa
Arkwright, Lynda
Barnett, Gillian
Berman, Linda
Bird, John
Black, Teresa J.
Brown, Philip
Buckley, Michael
Churcher, John
Conlon, Isobel
Cornell, Maria
Davenport, Sarah
Gowrisunkur, Jaya
Guthrie, Else
Hellin, Kate
Horne, Alan
Hunt, Patricia
Judkins, Malcolm
Jukes, Rachel
Kaberry, Susan
Lancelot, Maggie
Lendrum, Susan
Liddle, Helen
Lunt, Aidan
Margison, Frank
McAllister, Susan
McGrath, Graeme
Mitchell, Lesley
Morris, Jane
Nicholson, Jane
Osborn, Madeline Frances
Prodgers, Alan
Rawsthorne, Jean
Rhodes, Adrian M.
Sheldon, Helen
Smith, Janet M.
Sutton, Adrian
Sykes, Kathleen
Towse, Esme
Whitmore, Robert

PA - Philadelphia Association

Azgad, Racheli
Brewer, Madelyn
Caviston, Paul
Clapham, Miles
Cooper, Hilary
Davenport, Marie-Laure
Davies, Alison
de Leon, Heather
Duhig, Mary
Ellis, Mary Lynne
Fielder, Michael
Friedman, Joe
Gans, Steve
Ghiaci, Golshad
Gill, Douglas
Gordon, John Fredrick
Green, Prudence
Guild, Liz
Gurney, Paul
Hardy, Liz
Hill, Penny
Hurd, Joan
Itten, Theodor
King, Lucy
Kreeger, Angela
Lawson, Christine
Loewenthal, Del
Nevins, Peter
O'Neill, James
Pope, Alan
Redler, Leon
Ryan, Joanna
Swift, Joanna
Touton-Victor, Patricia
Watson, Gordon
Zeal, Paul

RCSPC - Regent's College School of Psychotherapy and Counselling

Adams, Martin
Adams-Langley, Stephen
Adey, John
Aldridge, Barrie
Aldridge, Janet
Arzoumanides, Yiannis
Ashwin, Mary
Asmall, Ismail
Aston, John
Austin, Lesley
Babarik, Anthony
Baker, Adrienne
Barry, Suzy
Berger, Jocelyn
Bland, Roger
Blum, Miranda
Boa, Quint
Browne, Margaret
Budgell, Rosemary
Caleb, Ruth
Cameron, Angela
Campbell, Christine
Campher, Rosemary
Carsley, Carol
Cleminson, Dorel
Cohn, Hans W.
Coleman, Eva
Collins, Leila
Cooper, Jillian
Corbett, Gemma
Crouch, Carol
Daniels, Deborah
David, Anna
Davies, Rosina
Du Plock, Simon
Duffy, Kathleen
Durlach, Stefan
Eglin, Patricia
Eisenhauer, Gary
Eleftheriadou, Zack
Epstein, Frances
Farrell, Em
Fox, Almuth-Maria
Gallagher, Teresa
Gardner, Peter
Gavin, Verity
George, Dorothy
Golden, Sylvia
Gorodensky, Arlene
Grace, Carole
Gunton, Gaye
Hanaway, Monica
Harding, Michael
Harlap, Nahum
Harman, Josephine
Haskayne, Amanda
Hay, Jennifer
Hazelton, Sally
Holmes, Carol
Horne, David C.
Ironside, Karin Margaret
Isaacson, Zelda
Jacobson, Rosemary
Jonathan, Arthur
Julien, Michael
Kahr, Brett
Karban, Barbara
Keal, Susan
Kerr, Libby
Kondos, Sandra
Kostoris, Laura
Kristal, Barbie
Lawlor, Virginia Katherine
Le Brun, Christine
Lemma, Alessandra
Leveque, Brigitte
Lever, Maureen
Lewis, Jacqueline
Little, Jon
Lowe, Julie
Luca-Stolkin, Maria
Lund, Leslie Ann
Malkin, Marion
Manifold, Claire
Mansall, Cordelia
Marshall, Susan
Massara, Catharine
McAleer, Eileen
McKenna, Clare
Milton, Martin
Mitchell, Diana
Moja-Strasser, Lucia
Morgan-Williams, Sue
Morrison, Philippa
Muldoon, Nuala
Murphy, Susan
Myers, Piers
Nelson, Margaret
Ngone, Mary
O'Brien, John
O'Sullivan, Renee
Oaten, Gae

Ogilvie, Renata
Oldfield, Nina
Owen, Ian
Owens-Ward, Lyn
Pae, Linda L.S.
Parissis, Maria
Parkin, Gwendolyn
Parr, Meriel A.
Platt, Monique
Popple, Gillian
Poulopoulos, Katerina
Purpura, Davide
Rabin, Judith
Radlett, Marty
Reardon, Paula
Roland, Saskia
Romisch-Clay, Liza
Royle, Anthony
Ruggieri, Gloria
Sabayinda, Michael
Sachs, Adah
Saroff, Rahel
Shields, Ellen Attracta
Sim, Camilla
Singer, Daniela
Slater, Joan
Smallwood, Imogen
Spendelow, Lyndsay
Spinelli, Ernesto
Steele, Marion
Stehle, Peter
Stockley, Rosalind
Strasser, Alison
Strasser, Freddie
Sullivan, E. Mary
Swynnerton, Richard
Thompson, Christine
Thompson, Patricia
Thornton, Suzanne
Thorpe, Ivan
Ticktin, Steven
van Deurzen, Emmy
Vella, John
Walker, Jillian
Walton, Michael
Warburton, Kitty
Warren, Yvonne
Weisensel, Karin
Weixel-Dixon, Karen
Wilks, Frances
Williams, Claerwen
Williams, Jill
Wilson, Carol
Wilson, Shula
Wolf, Darren
Worrell, Michael
Young, Sarah
Zinovieff, Nicholas

RE.V - Re.Vision

Adams, Eve
Carroll, Helen
Crawford, Joan
Dennis, Suzanne
Duberry, Mark
Findlay, David Alistair
Fisher, Anstice
Frischer, Livia
Hutchinson, Gary
Plowman, Polly
Robertson, Chris
Robertson, Ewa
Ryall, Sue
Woodroffe, Roe

SAP - Society of Analytical Psychology

Ballance, Gillian
Blows, Derek
Brieger, Johanna
Bruce, Ann
Burnard, John
Byrne, Dorothy
Carvalho, Richard
Colman, Warren
Crowther, Catherine
Diggle, Sedwell
Harari, Michael
Haynes, Jane
Herst, Edward
Hopwood, Ann
Howell, David
Lepper, Georgia
Martin, Edward
Newton, Kathleen
Peterson, Corinna
Redfearn, Joseph
Ross, Fiona
Rushton, Malcolm
Samuels, Andrew
Thomson, Jean
Walline, Sandra
Williamson, Ian
Wilson, Mary

SCPC - Stockton Centre for Psychotherapy and Counselling

Andrews, Carol
Duncan, Ursula
Galloway, Betsy
Greening, Sarah
Hamlyn, Sarah
Homer, Marjorie
Johnson, Janette
Lawrence, Yvonne
Sizikova, Tanya
Thacker, Rose

SIP - Severnside Institute for Psychotherapy

Ash, Robert
Batten, Cecilia
Box, Sally
Brown, Ray
Brown, Robin Gordon
Brown, Robin Richard
Collens, Louise
Cottman, Barbara
Davies, Miranda
Davies, Sheila
Dresser, Iain
Forryan, Barbara
Frye, Helen
Gardner, Fiona
Gracie, Jane
Green, Sylvia
Hahn, Herbert
Hancock, Patricia
Harris, Gordon
Hawdon, Sheila
Hazell, Jeremy
Hill, Jenny
Holmes, Jeremy
James, Glenys
Jones, Nicole
McNamara, Barbara
Mitcheson Brown, Muriel
Morris, Stephen
Newman, Alexander
Patterson, Linda
Pehrsson-Tatham, Lena
Pocock, Olga
Rowe, Jill
Scovell, Michael
Seigal, Elizabeth
Shewan, Doreen
Sproston, Suzanne
Standish, Elizabeth
Stones, Christine
Telders, Martina
Turner, Philip
Tute, Iris
Wedderkopp, Abigail
Wilson, Alexandra

SPEC - Spectrum

Allsop, Paul
Bennett, Ross
Bradley, Rex
Brennan, Stan
Carruthers, Dianna
Cooper, Terry
Dahle, Josephine
Doust, Gill
Dryden, Jan
Fletcher, Joan
Gabriel, Jill
Gotto, Jane
Greaves, Margaret
Hargreaves, Judy
Hollings, Avril
McKenzie, Maggie
McNeil, Delcia
Methuen, Oriel
Naish, Julia
Neal, Charles
Paterson, Stuart
Patterson, Anna
Rose-Smith, Gillian
Roth, Jenner
Russell, Marion
Salter, Gill
Shreeves, Rosa
Stone, Anthony
Webster, Sarah Craven
Williams, Kate
Willmott, Susan
Witt, John

SPTI - The Sherwood Psychotherapy Training Institute

Allen, Penny
Avery, Anna
Bassett, George
Browning, Peter
Bryant, Pat
Carrette, Timothy
Carton, Roy
Catersby, Cynthia
Cooper, Jane
Davies, Rae
Derrick, Stephen
Drury, Gitta
Erskine, Richard
Evans, Kenneth
Evans, Mairi M.
Fitzgerald, Patricia
Fookes, Andrew
Green, Marion
Hayman, Penny
Hutchby, Rosemary
Jordan, Karen
Kennett, Christine
Kerry, Helen
Loiseau, Kate
Lown, Francois
Maas, Willem
Mann, David
Marshall, Pauline
Maudling, Caroline
Moulding, Jacqueline
Paris, Jan
Pigott, Sheila
Rappard, Marie Chalotte
Rosenbaum, Linda Ann
Sanders, Harmen
Scott Combes, Jacqueline
Senior, Maggie
Shaw, Robert
Shmukler, Diana
Short, Deborah
Smith, Cora
Spitz, Shirley
Stephens, June
Stern, Erika
Straker, Gill
Stratton-Woodward, Sally
Tilley, Alison
van Wijk, Jacqueline
Waterstone, Carolyn
Watts, Jackie
Whitworth, Patricia
Wilkinson, Heward
Wilkinson, Kate

STTDP - South Trent Training in Dynamic Psychotherapy

Bailey, James
Bradley, Marie
Curry, Naomi
Denness, Brian
Fisk, Geoff
Headworth, Jean
Jones, Richard
Lee, Helen
Marshall, Pam
Ratigan, Bernard
Schröder, Thomas
Smith, David
Staines, Jill
Watson, Clare
Whyte, Chris
Young, Raymond

TMSI - Tavistock Marital Studies Institute

Abse, Susanna
Binnington, Linda
Bollinghaus, Elaine
Buss-Twachtmann, Christel
Cleavely, Evelyn
Clulow, Christopher
Cudmore, Lynne
Daniell, Diana
Daniels, Orpa
Dearnley, Barbara K.
Fullerton, Peter B.
Hodson, Pauline
Hughes, Lynette
Koppelman, Liora
Millington, Malcolm
Morgan, Mary
Oldman, David
Olney, Felicia
Pengelly, Paul
Rosenthall, Joanna
Seligman, Eva
Tarsh, Helen
Wright, Kenneth
Yass, Marion

ULDPS - University of Leicester Diploma in Psychodynamic Studies

Dent, Peter
Dunn, Elizabeth
East, Patricia
Horrocks, Pam
Hurwood, Judith
Jacobs, Michael
Jane, Susan
Janickyj, John
Jarrett, Betty
Jewson, Sue
King, Gail
Peglar, Graham
Strang, Jenny
Walker, Moira

UPA - Universities Psychotherapy Association

Clarkson, Petruska
Dixon, Linda
Griffith, E. Anne
Kendall, Tim
Rejaie, Carol
Riding, Nick
Smith, David L.
Strasser, Freddie
Tantam, Digby
van Deurzen, Emmy
Waller, Diane

WMIP - West Midlands Institute of Psychotherapy

Abberley, Colette Theresa
Anderson, Judith
Anees, Nabil
Arthur, Andrew R.
Barden, Nicola
Barker, John F.
Barrett, James
Beedie, Margaret A.
Birtle, Janice
Blakey, Angela
Bliss, Sonia
Bond, Anne R.
Bray, Jillyan
Brough, Sue
Burke, Robina
Burton, Mary V.
Calvert, Jane
Campbell, Duine
Carlish, Sonia
Champs, Thomas
Cox, Margaret
Crisp, Jennifer
Curren, Maureen
Davis, Patrick
Dayal, Mahendra Singh
Elliott, Lea K.
Ellis, June
Feasey, Don
Fox, Fiona
Fraser, Douglas A.
Gilliver, Cath
Gladwell, Stephen
Goodyear, Patricia
Hamilton, Jane
Harvey, Tricia A.
Hoag, Linda M.
Holmes, Dorothy
James, Pat
Johnson, Judy
Kenny, Peter
Kingsley, Laurence
Liebling, Angela J.
Lloyd, Helen
Lowery, Ian
Mackenzie, Ian D.
Madden, Felicity W.
Male, David F.
Maté, Helen
McCormick, Helen
McDonald, James
McFarland, Alf
Mills Burton, M.
Morley, Ann
Myers, Marion
Nicholas, P. John
O'Connor, Anna
Owen, William Meredith
Reddie, Mary
Rentoul, Robert W.
Reynolds, Michael John
Roy, Geraldine
Ryan, Angella M.J.
Samson, Anne
Schaverien, Joy
Shrimpton, David
Skailes, Claire
Speed, Bebe
Spencer, Margaret
Stokes, Jenny
Taylor, Vivienne
Toms, David A.
Tucker, Joanna
Vallance, Fiona
Van Marle, Susanna J.
Villia-Gosling, Athina
Wattis, Libby
Way, Jean
Wheeler, Sue
Wheeley, Shirley
White, H.
Woodward, Joan
Wright, W. Harry
Yates, Kath

WTC - The Women's Therapy Centre

Dana, Mira
Eichenbaum, Luise
Land, Patricia
Mohamed, Carol
Orbach, Susie
Ritchie, Sheila
Smith, Ruthie

YAPP - Yorkshire Association for Psychodynamic Psychotherapy

Aylard, Paul
Bailey, Susanna
Bonner, Kate
Cann, Lesley
Courtney, Mary
Douglas, Angela
Godsil, Susan
Hanks, Helga
Harrow, Anne
Heard, Dorothy
Heenan, Colleen
Hester, Bridget
Lake, Brian
Lidmila, Alan
Martin, Carol
Martin, Gill
McCluskey, Una
Page, Annabel
Reilly, Stephen
Rowe, Celly
Sidey, Brian
Syme, Gabrielle
Welsh, Catherine

PRACTITIONERS ABLE TO WORK IN LANGUAGES OTHER THAN ENGLISH

Afrikaans

Botha, Marie
Kent

Clarkson, Petruska
London West

Davids, Jennifer
London North West

Fowler, Barry
Lancashire

Law, Gordon
Worcestershire

Lown, Francois
Overseas – South Africa

Nkumanda, Rachel
London South East

Salters, Diane
Overseas – South Africa

Sanders, Harmen
Overseas – Netherlands

Vallance, Fiona
West Midlands

Akan

Ohene, Margaret D.
London North

Arabic

Al Rubaie, Talal
London North

Allawi, Nadia
London South West

Bishay, Nagy R.
Manchester

El-Khayat, Redwan
Wiltshire

El-Hadi, Ali
Essex

Issa, Soraya
Kent

Azarbija

Rouhifar, Zhila
London West

Balineese

Hobart, Angela R.
London West

Cantonese

Lau, Annie
Essex

Teng, Christina
Essex

Chinese

Chin, John C.L.
London North

Lau, Bernard Wai Kai
Middlesex

Tse, Claude
Kent

Croatian

Nielsen-Cernkovich, Rudy B.
London Central

Danish

Blow, Kirsten
Oxfordshire

Krause, Inga-Britt
Bedfordshire

Patricia, Thelma
Overseas – Norway

Veje, Margit
Overseas – Denmark

Dutch

Burbach, Frank
Somerset

Burck, Charlotte
London North West

Bukovics-Heiller, Birgit
Surrey

Carton, Roy
Overseas – Netherlands

Clarkson, Petruska
London West

de Jong, Corrie
Hampshire

Draper, Pim
County Durham

du Ry, Marc
London Central

Hiestand, Rene
Kent

Holve, Harriet C.J.
Surrey

Lockie, Gisela
Somerset

Maas, Willem
Nottinghamshire

McDonnell, Fokkina
Manchester

Mitchell, Diana
Surrey

Rappard, Marie Charlotte
Nottinghamshire

Schopman, Els
Overseas – Netherlands

Tjepkema, Froujke
Overseas – Netherlands

van Bilsen, Henck P.J.G.
Overseas – New Zealand

Van der Wateren, Jan-Floris
London West

van Deurzen, Emmy
Sheffield

van Halm, Corrie
Sussex East

van Wijk, Jacqueline
Nottinghamshire

Farsi

Bathai, Parizad
London North West

Farzim, Pari
London North West

Ghiaci, Golshad
London North West

Hussain, Fakhir
Surrey

Rouhifar, Zhila
London West

Zarbafi, Ali
London West

Finnish

Byring, Carola
London North

Gordon, Leila
Cambridgeshire

Lettington, Liisa
Kent

Ruismaki, Marjo
Overseas – Finland

French

Adams, Ghislaine
Buckinghamshire

Alexander, Erica
Warwickshire

Aquarone, Luc-Remy
Norfolk

Asseily, Alexandra
London West

Ayres, Kathleen
Sussex West

Banks, Ron
Wiltshire

Barrows, Paul
Avon

Begg, E.C.M.
Scotland – Glasgow

Bensimon, Marlene
London North

Bentovim, Arnon
London Central

Bibby, Keith
London South West

Birkett, Diana
London South West

Black, Teresa
Leicestershire

Blackburn, P.
Humberside

Bousfield, Annie
Kent

Bowman, Elizabeth
Sussex East

Boyesen, Ebba
London West

Boyesen, Gerda
London West

Browne, Maureen
London West

Buckley, Marie-Noel
London South West

Burck, Charlotte
London North West

Cannobbio, Victoria
Overseas – Germany

Carr, Brede
Surrey

Chalkley, A.J.
Avon

Champion, Lynn
Essex

China, Giselle
London North West

China, Jacques
London North

Christman, Cornelia
London North West

Clare, Louise
Bedfordshire

Coia, Grace
Scotland – Glasgow

Colahan, Mireille
London North West

Cole, Shanti
Cumbria

Conolly, J. M. P.
London North

Courtault, Susie
London South West

Coxwell-White, Jenny
Berkshire

Craddock, Jenny
London North West

Crossling, Paddy
Lancashire

Dachy, Vincent
London Central

Danthois, Didier
London North

Davenport, Marie-Laure
London North

Davis, Joyce H
London West

de Berker, A. Patricia
Surrey

Domb, Yair
London North

Dorey, Mary
Hertfordshire

Draper, Ros
Hampshire

Duck, Dorothy
Kent

du Ry, Marc
London Central

Elliott, Dena
London West

Farhi, Nina
London North West

Ferid, Heidi
London North West

Ficarra, Berthe
London North West

Forti, Laura
London North

Freeman, Catherine
London North

Gagnere, Maryline
Cambridgeshire

Gale, Derek
Essex

Gauthier, J.
Merseyside

Gavin, Verity J.
Overseas – France

Godsil, Susan
Yorkshire West

Gorodensky, Arlene
Middlesex

Gowrisunkur, Jaya
Manchester

Graham, Judith
London North

Green, Charlotte
London West

Grimshaw, Francoise
Surrey

Hall, Guy
London North

Hamilton-Duckett, Paule
London North

Hanna, Gilli
London North West

Hartnup, Trevor
London South West

Henny, Lindy
London South West

Hering-Josefowitz, Pauline
Overseas – Switzerland

Hoang, Astrid
London East

Hobart, Angela R.
London West

Hodges, Jill
London Central

Holmes, Jeremy
Devon

Houston, Gaie
London North West

Hussain, Fakhir
Surrey

Jackson, Eve
London North

Jenkins, Hugh
London South East

Jones, Nicole
Devon

Judd, Dorothy
London North West

Julien, Michael
Essex

Kelly, Anne
Northern Ireland

Kerr, Anna
London South East

Kirk, Kate
Cheshire

Kohon, Valli
London North West

Kolbuszewski, Marianne
London South West

Korte, Achim
London Central

Lafargue, Martine
London North

Lallah, Regine
London North

Lemma, Alessandra
London North

Lendrum, Susan
Manchester

Leveque, Brigitte
London West

Liddle, Helen
Lancashire

Loiseau, Kate
County Durham

Lousada, Olivia
London North

MacDonald, Helen F.
Sheffield

MacKewn, Jennifer
Avon

Maguire, Anne
Lancashire

Maitlis, Marion
Sheffield

Mandin, Philippe
London North West

Marshall, Antoinette
London North

Marshall, Myra
Sheffield

Masoliver, Chandra
London West

Massara, Catharina
Hampshire

McAndrew, Brigitte
Hampshire

McEldowney, Dennis
London West

Messner, Hans Jorg
London North

Millais, Suzy
London South West

Miller, John Andrew
London North West

Mills-Burton, M. F.
Oxfordshire

Milne, Frances
Scotland – Edinburgh

Moja-Strasser, Lucia
London North West

Morgan, Barbara
Hertfordshire

Morris, Monique
London North West

Morrish, Susan Lesley
Kent

Mostaeddi, Bahman
Middlesex

Nabarro, Elizabeth
London North West

Neal, Lalage
London South West

Nesbit, Judith
London East

Nichols, Hamish
Surrey

O'Cleary, Susan
London North West

O'Connor, Aine
Overseas – Ireland

O'Dwyer, Annegret
Surrey

Pain, Jean
Cambridgeshire

Passey, Miranda
Isle of Wight

Pepeli, Hara
London North

Perriollat Munro, Elizabeth
Manchester

Pirani, Alix
Avon

Pitt, Chris
Merseyside

Pocock, Olga
Wiltshire

Pollitzer, Juliette
London South West

Porter, Barbara
Oxfordshire

Proner, Barry D.
London West

Purkiss, Jane
Avon

Quoilin-Lebrun, Michelle
Berkshire

Reddy, Michael
Buckinghamshire

Reguis, Marie-Christine
London North

Reid, Liz
London North

Reilly, Nicole
Sussex West

Renoux, Martine
London North

Reynal, Carmen
Gloucestershire

Rhode, Maria
London North West

Richards, Val
London North

Robertson, Zuleika
Devon

Robinson, Felicity
Sheffield

Roddick, Mary
Devon

Rosemary, Margaret
Sheffield

Rozenberg, Rosette
London North

Scarlett, Jean
London North West

Shipton, Geraldine
Sheffield

Sills, Charlotte
London West

Sinclair, Alison
Cambridgeshire

Sinclair, Fiona
Cambridgeshire

Smith, Gillian
Cambridgeshire

Smith, Judith
London North West

Sookdeb, S.
London North West

Soutar, Sarah
Sussex East

Springford, Kate
Sussex East

Stanton, Martin
London South East

Stern, Erika
Nottinghamshire

Stewart, Ian
Nottinghamshire

Struthers, Cassandra
London South West

Tanguay, Daniel
London South West

Taussig, Hanna
Cambridgeshire

Touton-Victor, Patricia
Cambridgeshire

Tuby, Molly
London South West

Upton, Jay
Surrey

van Deurzen, Emmy
Sheffield

van Schoor, Linda
London North

Ward, Dawn
Shropshire

Watson, Lindsay
London North West

Watters, Tamara
Kent

Whatley, Ann
Essex

White, H.
London South West

Whittle, Lorna
Cambridgeshire

Wieselberg, Huguette
London North

Wigram, Penny
London West

Wren, Pauline
Warwickshire

Wyse, Hymie
Surrey

Gaelic

Caird, Elizabeth
Overseas – Ireland

German

Albrecht, Gisela
London North

Albrighton, Sylvia
London North West

Al Rubaie, Talal
London North

Averbeck, Marcus
Kent

Ayres, Kathleen
Sussex West

Baum, Stefanie
Overseas – Germany

Brauner, Rita
London North

Becker, Amely
London North West

Begg, E.C.M.
Scotland – Glasgow

Bishop, Beata
London West

Bloomfield, Irene
London West

Boening, Joachim
London West

Boening, Michaela
London West

Boyesen, Ebba
London West

Boyesen, Gerda
London West

Boyesen, Mona Lisa
London West

Briggs, Margarete
Essex

Brosskamp, Cornelia
Sussex East

Bukovics-Heiller, Birgit
Surrey

Burnet-Smith, Tamara
Berkshire

Canobbio, Victoria
Overseas – Germany

Chesner, Anna
London East

China, Giselle
London North West

Cohn, Hans W.
Surrey

Collard, Patrizia C.
London South West

Coombes, Clare
Surrey

Coronas, Ita
London South West

Coxwell-White, Jenny
Berkshire

Crick, Verena
Middlesex

Daniels, Mo
Hampshire

David, Anna
London East

Deniflee, Ursula
London South East

Draper, Ros
Hampshire

Drury, Gitta
Overseas – Spain

Durlach, Stefan
Overseas – Australia

Eiden, Bernd
London West

Eisenbarth, Heiner
Sussex East

Ehlers, Hella
London Central

Ferid, Heidi
London North West

Flinspach, Elisabeth
London North

Fox, Almuth-Maria
Essex

Gessert, Astrid
Dorset

Godsil, Susan
Yorkshire West

Hanks, Helga
Yorkshire West

Harris, Gordon
Oxfordshire

Haupts, Brigitte
London West

Hauser, Susan
London West

Hedinger-Farrell, Korinna
Surrey

Heinitz, Karin
Kent

Heismann, Elisabeth
London North

Herbert, Claudia
Oxfordshire

Hiller, Ruth
London North

Hoang, Astrid
London East

Hobart, Angela R.
London West

Hock, Gaby
Oxfordshire

Hudson, Inge
London North

Hussain, Fakhir
Surrey

Jones, Nicole
Devon

Karan, Alexandra
London West

Karban, Barbara
London North West

Kessel, Inge
London North

Kohler, Christiane
Scotland – Aberdeen

Korte, Achim
London Central

Kuttner, Enno
West Midlands

Landale, Margaret
Oxfordshire

Landesmann, Sonya
London North

Lendrum, Susan
Manchester

Leygraf, Bernd
London North

Liddle, Helen
Lancashire

Louden, Penny
London West

Lude, Jochen
London West

Lutyens, Marianne
Oxfordshire

MacLiam, Fionnula
Overseas – Ireland

Mander, Gertrud
London North West

Mansall, Cordelia
Nottinghamshire

Messner, Hans Jorg
London North

Milne, Frances
Scotland – Edinburgh

Nesbit, Judith
London East

Netzer-Stein, Antje
London South West

Nicholson, Jane
Manchester

Noack, Mike
Devon

O'Dwyer, Annegret
Surrey

Ogilvie, Renate
Overseas – Australia

Ohnesorg, Johanna
Overseas – Switzerland

Parker, Niki
Kent

Pervoltz, Rainer
Overseas – Germany

Pollack, Angela
Overseas – Germany

Prall, Werner
London North West

Preisinger, Kristiane
London North West

Rabe, Marie-Louise
Surrey

Reid, Liz
London North

Reynal, Carmen
Gloucestershire

Richards, Val
London North

Richter, Nicola
Hertfordshire

Schaible, Monika
London West

Schiemann, Margot
London North West

Schoenfeld, Hilde
London North West

Schreiber-Kounine, Christa
Avon

Shearman, Christine
London East

Smith, Jonathan
London

Soth, Michael
Oxfordshire

Speyer, Josefine
London North West

Stehle, Peter
London North West

Steiner, Monika Celebi
Buckinghamshire

Stern, Erika
Nottinghamshire

Stewart, Ian
Nottinghamshire

Stolte, Eva
Hampshire

Stuart, Lilly H.
London South East

Sucher, Ingerborg
Essex

Sünkel, Sue
London North

Taussig, Hanna
Cambridgeshire

Tute, Iris
Avon

Twelvetrees, Heidy
Kent

van Bilsen, Henck P.J.G.
Overseas – New Zealand

Wach, Karin-Marie
London South East

Ward, Ruth
Lincolnshire

Weinrich, Hildegard
London North West

Weisensel, Karin
London North West

Wieland, Christina
London North

Wittenberg, Isca
London North West

Wyse, Hymie
Surrey

Yallop, Melanie
Surrey

Greek

Andreo, Chriso
London North

Arzoumanides, Yiannis
London West

Cameron, Anna
London North

Charalambos, Praxoulla
London North

Eleftheriadou, Zack
London North

Jackson, Eve
London North

Layiou-Lignos, Effie
Overseas – Greece

Luca-Stolkin, Maria
London North

Luckcock, Ronald Cosmo
London North

Mazaraki, Angeliki
London East

Meleagrou, Mando
London West

Metaxa, Jennie
London West

Morris, Elizabeth
Gloucestershire

Mouratoglou, Vassilis
London North West

Moutzoukis, Chris
Overseas – Greece

Papadopoulos, Renos K.
London East

Pepeli, Hara
London North

Simos, Gregoris
Overseas – Greece

Spyropoulos, Nick
Hertfordshire

Vastardis, Gethsimani
London North

Villia-Gosling, Athina T.
West Midlands

Wieland, Christina
London North

Worrall, Chrysoula
London North

Gujurati

Hormasji, Faridoon
Essex

Nadirshaw, Zenobia
London West

Parikh, P.N.
London South West

Hebrew

Altman, Michelle M.
London Central

Asheri, Shoshi
London North

Azgad, Racheli
London North

Baradon, Tessa
London North

Berke, Joseph H.
London North

Dana, Mira
Overseas – Israel

Dresner, Ora
London North West

Frischer, Livia
Overseas – Sweden

Gal, Oshrat
London North West

Gurion, Michal
London North

Hadary, Gideon
London North

Harlap, Nahum
London North West

Heitzler, Morit
Overseas – Israel

Oakley, Haya
London North West

Rabin, Judith
London North West

Rozenberg, Rosette
London North

Schonfield, Tamar
London North

Selwyn, Ruth
London North West

Singer, Iris
Middlesex

Spyer, Natalie
London North West

Steiner, Monika Celebi
Buckinghamshire

Taussig, Hanna
Cambridgeshire

Weaver, Ziva
London North

Weider, Bilha
London North West

Heldakiew

Teng, Christina
Essex

Hindi

Cariapa, Illana
Yorkshire South

Dayal, Mahendra Singh
West Midlands

O'Brian, Charles
Overseas – Hong Kong

Parikh, P.N.
London South West

Sookdeb, S.
London North West

Hungarian

Bishop, Beata
London West

Lanczi, Katalin
Kent

Moja-Strasser, Lucia
London North West

Vibert, Eva
London Central

Icelandic

Gudjonsson, Ingolf
Yorkshire South

Kjartanzdottir, Saeunn
Overseas – Iceland

Israeli

Lederman, Tsafi
London North

Italian

Arbia, G. Nicoletta
London West

Benvenuto, Bice
London South East

Buckley, Marie-Noel
London South West

Canobbio, Victoria
Overseas – Germany

Cardile, Pietro
London West

Coia, Grace
Scotland – Glasgow

Corlanda, Annalisa
Overseas – Italy

Coronas, Ita
London South West

Curti-Gialdino, Francesca
London North

Davies, Judy
Cambridgeshire

Dianin, Gianni
London North

Doe, Anthony
London South West

du Ry, Marc
London Central

Forti, Laura
London North

Gatti-Doyle, Fiorella
London South West

Hirst, Diane F. Zervas
London West

Jacques, Glenys
London East

Kenny, Vincent
Overseas – Italy

Lemma, Alessandra
London North

Lunardon, Francesco
London North West

Maitlis, Marion
Sheffield

Masoliver, Chandra
London West

Mellows, David
London North

Mendelsohn, Annette
London North West

Messner, Hans Jorg
London North

Molino, Anthony
Overseas – Italy

Mondadori, Roberta
London North West

Morante, Flavia
London West

Morrish, Susan Lesley
Kent

O'Dwyer, Annegret
Surrey

Panetta-Crean, Simona
London North

Pavincich, Lesley
London South West

Pozzi, Maria E
Hertfordshire

Ruggieri, Gloria
Oxfordshire

Sabbadini, Andrea
London North

Seu, Irene Bruna
London North West

Sidoli, Mara
Overseas – USA

Smith, Judith
London North West

Spinelli, Ernesto
London South East

Toole, Stuart
West Midlands

Usiskin, Judith
London North

Smith, Marta Vaciago
Yorkshire West

Wilson, Teresa
London South West

Wyse, Hymie
Surrey

Japanese

Nippoda, Yuko
London North

Kannada

Shivakumar, H.
London North West

Kikuyu

Ngone, Mary
Hertfordshire

Luganda

Sabayinda, Michael
Essex

Malay

Ngah, Zah
London North

Singh, Satwant
London North

Maltese

Caruana, Charles Victor
London South East

Vella, John
Overseas – Malta

Mandarin

Lau, Annie
Essex

Ndebele

Mudarikiri, Maxwell
Surrey

Norwegian

Balmbra, Steven
Overseas – Norway

Boyesen, Ebba
London West

Boyesen, Gerda
London West

Boyesen, Mona Lisa
London West

Bukovics-Heiller, Birgit
Surrey

Holm, Kirsti E.
London North West

Jenssen, Einar D.
London North

Patricia, Thelma
Overseas – Norway

Tajet-Foxell, Britt
London South West

Persian

Collins, Leila
Hertfordshire

Polish

Czubinska, Grazyna
London South East

Drewnowska, Alicja
Middlesex

Gulcz, Magdalena
London North West

Hanchen, Tomasz
London South East

Kolbuszewski, Marianne
London South West

Kowszun, Grazyna
London South East

Stevenson, Krystyna
London North

Szymanska, Kasia
London West

Portuguese

Bacha, Claire
Manchester

de Souza, Joney
London West

Elliott, Léa K
Gloucestershire

Kujawski, Pedro
London West

Leite Daa Costa, Mariza
Essex

Machado, Danuza
London North West

Morante, Flavia
London West

Pimentel, Edna
London North

Rotenberg, Claudio
London North

Salles, Miriam
London North

Samson, André
Overseas – Brazil

Sell, Patrick
London West

Punjabi

Dayal, Mahendra Singh
West Midlands

Dhillon, Harbrinder
Surrey

Kaur-Love, Jasminder
Hertfordshire

Krause, Inga-Britt
Bedfordshire

Romanian

Moja-Strasser, Lucia
London North West

Russian

Lowery, I.M.
West Midlands

Pocock, Olga
Wiltshire

Sizikova, Tanya
Cleveland

Voikhanskaya, Marina
Cambridgeshire

Serbo-Croat

Harling, Biljana
Sussex West

Kostic, Jasna
London North

Manojlovic, Jelena
London West

Markovic, Desa
London Central

Markovic, Olivera
Lancashire

Papadopoulos, Renos K.
London East

Renton, Mirjana
London North West

Shona

Mudarikiri, Maxwell
Surrey

Slovenian

Nielsen-Cernkovich, Rudy B.
London Central

Shawe-Taylor, Metka
London North

Spanish

Aguirregabiria, Ana
London South West

Amez, Susan
Hampshire

Arrendondo, Beverly
Middlesex

Bacha, Claire
Manchester

Batten, Cecilia
Gloucestershire

Begg, E.C.M.
Scotland – Glasgow

Bowman, Elizabeth
Sussex East

Catovsky, Mina
London West

Coronas, Ita
London South West

de Souza, Joney
London West

Dianin, Gianni
London North

Drury, Gitta
Overseas – Spain

Feldberg, Tom
London North West

Fiasche, Mara
London North West

Graham, Judith
London North

Green, Eliott
Kent

Ibanez, Julian
Overseas – Spain

Lema, Juan Carlos
London North West

Lew, Clare
Cambridgeshire

Llewellyn, Martha
Surrey

Loret de Mola, Maria
London North

Lunardon, Francesco
London North West

Maitlis, Marion
Sheffield

Masoliver, Chandra
London West

Millais, Suzy
London South West

Montalbetti, M.L.
Overseas – Peru

Montero, Isabel
London North

Oclander Goldie, Sylvia
London North West

Pain, Jean
Cambridgeshire

Penalosa-Clarke, Adriana
London North

Rae, Frances
Kent

Reddy, Michael
Buckinghamshire

Reynal, Carmen
Gloucestershire

Robinson, Ferga
London South East

Sinclair, Alison
Cambridgeshire

Smith, Judith
London North West

Testa, Rita
London North West

Turner, Carole
Overseas – Spain

Valentine, Victoria
London North

Wheeler, Maria
London South West

Swahili

Ngone, Mary
Hertfordshire

Sabayinda, Michael
Essex

Swedish

Bradshaw-Tauvon, Kate
Overseas – Sweden

Burns-Lundgren, Eva
Surrey

Frischer, Livia
Overseas – Sweden

Furst, Lena
Surrey

Gildebrand, Katarina
London North

Gilljam, Annika
Yorkshire West

Hagelthorn, Christina
Overseas – Sweden

Harley, Ki
London North

Isaksson Hurst, Gun
London North West

Kjellstrom, Laila
Scotland – Edinburgh

Lindley-Jones, Kerstin
Oxfordshire

Massara, Catharina
Hampshire

Patricia, Thelma
Overseas – Norway

Perera, Ajit
Surrey

Ruismaki, Marjo
Overseas – Finland

Sandler, Topsy
Overseas – Sweden

Seymour, Charlotte
London North

Sullivan, Anita
London North West

Tajet-Foxell, Britt
London South West

Tham, Anna
Wiltshire

Swiss German

Twelvetrees, Heidy
Kent

Tamil

Venki, Malathi
Dorset

Turkish

Boysan, Zehra
Sheffield

Gungor, Dilek
London North

Sungur, Mehmet Z.
Overseas – Turkey

Yazar, Jale
London South East

Urdu

Dayal, Mahendra Singh
West Midlands

Guernina, Zouida
Humberside

Hormasji, Faridoon
Essex

Hussain, Fakhir
Surrey

O'Brian, Charles
Overseas – Hong Kong

Parikh, P.N.
London South West

Welsh

Bisgood, Bill
Wales – South

Davies, Dilys R.
Leicestershire

Davies, Mairlis
Wales – South

Davies, Rosina
Wales – South

Ellis, Sian
Essex

Howes, Kathleen Mary
Wales – South

Hughes, Lynette
Manchester

Kendrick, Margaret
Essex

Morgan, Sian
Cambridgeshire

Thomas, Jenny
Wales – South

Yiddish

Rozenberg, Rosette
London North

Zimbabwean

Jiah, Hildah
London South East

ORGANISATION CONTACT ADDRESSES AND TELEPHONE NUMBERS

1 Analytical Psychology Section

Association of Jungian Analysts
Flat 3
7 Eton Avenue
London NW3 3EL
Tel: 0171 794 8711

Independent Group of Analytical Psychologists
PO Box 1175
London W3 6DS
Tel: 0181 993 3996

Society of Analytical Psychology
1 Daleham Gardens
London NW3 5BY
Tel: 0171 435 7696

2 Behavioural and Cognitive Psychotherapy Section

British Association for Behavioural and Cognitive Psychotherapies
PO Box 9
Acrington
Lancashire BB5 2GD
Tel: 01254 875277

3 Experiential Constructivist Therapies Section

Association for Neuro-Linguistic Programming
PO Box 78
Stourbridge
West Midlands DY8 4ZJ
Tel: 01384 443935

Centre for Personal Construct Psychology
Vigilant House
120 Wilton Road
London SW1V 1JZ
Tel: 0800 731 6859

4 Family, Couple, Sexual, and Systemic Therapy Section

The Association for Family Therapy and Systemic Practice in the UK
Administrator: Chris Frederick
12 Mabledon Close
Heald Green
Cheadle
Cheshire SK8 3DB
Tel: 0161 493 9012

British Association of Sexual and Marital Therapy
PO Box 13686
London SW20 9ZH
Tel: 0181 543 2707

The Family Institute, Cardiff
105 Cathedral Road
Cardiff CF1 9PH
Tel: 01222 226532

Institute of Family Therapy
24-32 Stephenson Way
London NW1 2HX
Tel: 0171 391 9150

Kensington Consultation Centre
2 Wyvil Court
Trenchold Street
London SW8 2TG
Tel: 0171 720 7301

5 Humanistic and Integrative Psychotherapy Section

Association of Accredited Psychospiritual Psychotherapists
65a Watford Way
London NW4 3AQ
Tel: 0181 202 4525

Association of Cognitive Analytic Therapists
Munro Clinic
Guy's Hospital
London SE1 9RT
Tel: 0171 955 2906

Association of Humanistic Psychology Practitioners
BCM AHPP
London WC1N 3XX
Tel: 0345 660326

Bath Centre for Psychotherapy and Counselling
1 Walcot Terrace
London Road
Bath BA1 6AB
Tel: 01225 466635

British Psychodrama Association
Heather Cottage
Rosneath
Helensburgh
Argyll Bute G84 0RF
Tel: 01436 831838

Centre for Counselling & Psychotherapy Education
Beauchamp Lodge
2 Warwick Crescent
London W2 6NE
Tel: 0171 266 3006

Centre for Transpersonal Psychology
86a Marylebone High Street
London W1M 3DE
Tel: 0171 935 7350

Chiron Centre for Body Psychotherapy
26 Eaton Rise
London W5 2ER
Tel: 0181 997 5219

The Gerda Boyesen Centre
170 Goldhawk Road
London W12 8ER
Tel: 0181 743 2437

The Gestalt Centre, London
64 Warwick Road
St Albans
Herts AL1 4DL
Tel: 01727 864806

Gestalt Psychotherapy Training Institute
2 Bedford Street
London Road
Bath BA1 6AF
Tel: 01225 482135

The Institute of Psychosynthesis
65a Watford Way
Hendon
London NW4 3AQ
Tel: 0181 202 4525

Institute of Transactional Analysis
66 Paines Lane
Pinner
Middlesex HA5 3BL
Tel: 0181 866 4288

The Institute for Arts in Therapy and Education
The Windsor Centre
Windsor Street
London N1 8QL
Tel: 0171 704 2534

Karuna
Natsworthy Manor
Widecombe in the Moor
Newton Abbot
Devon TQ13 7TR
Tel: 01647 221457

London Association of Primal Psychotherapists
West Hill House
6 Swains Lane
London N6 6QU
Tel: 0171 267 9616

The Metanoia Institute
13 North Common Road
London W5 2QB
Tel: 0181 579 2505

The Minster Centre
Unit 1/2 Drakes Court Yard
291 Kilburn High Road
London NW6 7JR
Tel: 0171 372 4940

North Staffs. Association for Psychotherapy
2 Gower Street
Newcastle under Lyme
Staffordshire ST5 1JQ
Tel: 01782 719705

Psychosynthesis and Education Trust
92/94 Tooley Street
London SE1 2TH
Tel: 0171 403 2100

Regent's College School of Psychotherapy and Counselling
Regent's College
Inner Circle
London NW1 4NS
Tel: 0171 487 7406

Re.Vision
97 Brondesbury Road
London NW6 6RY
Tel: 0181 357 8881

The Sherwood Psychotherapy Training Institute
Thiskney House
2 St James Terrace
Nottingham NG1 6FW
Tel: 0115 9243994

Spectrum
7 Endymion Road
London N4 1EE
Tel: 0181 341 2277/0181 340 0426

Stockton Centre for Psychotherapy and Counselling
77 Acklam Road
Thornaby on Tees
Cleveland TS17 7BD
Tel: 01642 649004

6 Hypno-Psychotherapy Section

British Association for Autogenic Training and Therapy
c/o Royal London Homeopathic Hospital
Great Ormond Street
London WC1M 3HR

Centre Training School for Hypnotherapy and Psychotherapy
145 Chapel Lane
Longton
Preston PR4 5NA
Tel: 01772 617663

The National College of Hypnosis and Psychotherapy
12 Cross Street
Nelson
Lancs BB9 7EN
Tel: 01282 699378

The National Register of Hypnotherapists and Psychotherapists
12 Cross Street
Nelson
Lancs BB9 7EN
Tel: 01282 699378

National School of Hypnosis and Psychotherapy
28 Finsbury Park Road
London N4 2JX
Tel: 0171 354 9938(general)/0171 359 6991(training)

7 Psychoanalytic and Psychodynamic Psychotherapy Section

Arbours Association
6 Church Lane
London N8 7BU
Tel: 0181 340 7646

Association for Group and Individual Psychotherapy
1 Fairbridge Road
London N19 3EW
Tel: 0171 272 7013

The Association of Independent Psychotherapists
PO Box 1194
London N6 5PW
Tel: 0171 700 1911

British Association of Psychotherapists
37 Mapesbury Road
London NW2 4HJ
Tel: 0181 452 9823

Cambridge Society for Psychotherapy
1 Dean Drive
Cambridge CB1 4SW
Enquiries by mail only

Centre for Attachment Based Psychoanalytic Psychotherapy
12a Nassington Road
London NW3 5JY
Tel: 0171 794 4306

Centre for Freudian Analysis and Research
60 Ivydale Road
London SE15 3BS
Tel: 0171 639 8289

Centre for Psychoanalytical Psychotherapy
538 Finchley Road
London NW11 8DD
Tel: 0181 922 8551

Centre for the Study of Psychotherapy
Kent Research and Development Centre
University of Kent
Canterbury CT2 7PD
Tel: 01227 764000 x3691

Forum for Independent Psychotherapists
167 Sumatra Road
London NW6 1PN

Guild of Psychotherapists
149 Faraday Road
London SW19 8PA
Tel: 0181 540 4454

Guildford Centre for Psychotherapy
PO Box 63
Guildford
Surrey GU1 2UZ
Tel: 01483 560607

Hallam Institute of Psychotherapy
PO Box 1098
Sheffield S19 6YQ
Tel: 0114 2768555 x4971

Institute of Group Analysis
1 Daleham Gardens
London NW3 5BY
Tel: 0171 431 2693

Institute of Psychotherapy and Counselling (WPF)
607 The Chandlery
50 Westminster Bridge Road
London SE1 7QY
Tel: 0171 721 7660

Institute of Psychotherapy and Social Studies
West Hill House
6 Swains Lane
London N6 6QU
Tel: 0171 284 4762

Liverpool Psychotherapy Diploma Organisation
Department of Clinical Psychology
Whelan Building
PO Box 147
Liverpool L69 3BX
Tel: 0151 794 5529

London Centre for Psychotherapy
32 Leighton Road
London NW5 2QE
Tel: 0171 482 2002/0171 482 2282

NAFSIYAT
278 Seven Sisters Road
London N4 2HY
Tel: 0171 263 4130

Northern Association for Analytical Psychotherapy
Consulting Room
Post Office Cottage
Mickley
Stocksfield
Northumberland NE43
Tel: 01661 842727

North West Institute for Dynamic Psychotherapy
c/o Dr Graeme McGrath
Gaskell House Psychotherapy Service
Swinton Grove
Manchester M13 0EU
Tel: 0161 273 2762

Philadelphia Association
4 Marty's Yard
17 Hampstead High Street
London NW3 1PX
Tel: 0171 794 2652

Severnside Institute for Psychotherapy
Administration Secreteary:
Vivien Hagen
11 Orchard Street
Bristol BS1 5EH
Tel: 01275 333266

South Trent Training in Dynamic Psychotherapy
c/o The Department of Psychology,
1 St Ann's Road, Lincoln LN2 5RA
Tel: 01522 512000

Tavistock Marital Studies Institute
Tavistock Centre
120 Belsize Lane
London NW3 5BA
Tel: 0171 435 7111

University of Leicester Diploma in Psychodynamic Studies
Dept of Adult Education
Vaughan College
St Nicholas Circle
Leicester LE1 4LB
Tel: 0116 251 7368

West Midlands Institute of Psychotherapy
Rooms 123/124, First Floor
Gazette Building
168 Corporation Street
Birmingham B4 6TF
Tel: 0121 248 4450

Westminster Pastoral Foundation
23 Kensington Square
London W8 5HN
Tel: 0171 937 6956

Women's Therapy Centre
6-9 Manor Gardens
London N7 6LA
Tel: 0171 263 6200

Yorkshire Association for Psychodynamic Psychotherapy
5a Westgate
Otley
West Yorkshire LS21 3AT
Tel: 01943 851110

8 Psychoanalytically-based Therapy with Children

Association of Child Psychotherapists
120 West Heath Road
London NW3 7TU
Tel: 0181 458 1609

Forum for the Advancement of Educational Therapy and Therapeutic Teaching
13 Highbury Terrace
London N5 1UP
Tel: 0171 226 8103

Institutional Members

Association of University Teachers of Psychiatry
41 St Michael's Hill
Bristol
BS2 8DZ
Tel: 0117 930 3165

Tavistock Clinic
120 Belsize Lane
London NW3 5BA
Tel: 0171 435 7111

Universities Psychotherapy Association (UPA)
Centre for Psychotherapeutic Studies
16 Claremont Crescent
Sheffield S10 2TA
Tel: 0114 222 2989

Special Members

British Psychological Society
St Andrews House
48 Princess Road East
Leicester LE1 7DR
Tel: 0116 254 9568

Royal College of Psychiatrists
17 Belgrave Square
London SW1X 8PG
Tel: 0171 235 2351

Friends of the Council

British Association for Counselling
1 Regent's Place
Rugby
Coventry
CV21 2PJ
Tel: 01788 578328